PROFESSIONAL
SHAREPOINT® 2013 DEVELOPME

Professional SharePoint® 2013 Development

Published by
John Wiley & Sons, Inc.
10475 Crosspoint Boulevard
Indianapolis, IN 46256
www.wiley.com

Published simultaneously in Canada

ISBN: 978-1-118-49582-7
ISBN: 978-1-118-49578-0 (ebk)
ISBN: 978-1-118-65496-5 (ebk)
ISBN: 978-1-118-65501-6 (ebk)

Manufactured in the United States of America

10 9 8 7 6 5 4 3 2

For general information on our other products and services please contact our Customer Care Department within the United States at (877) 762-2974, outside the United States at (317) 572-3993 or fax (317) 572-4002.

Wiley publishes in a variety of print and electronic formats and by print-on-demand. Some material included with standard print versions of this book may not be included in e-books or in print-on-demand. If this book refers to media such as a CD or DVD that is not included in the version you purchased, you may download this material at http://booksupport.wiley.com. For more information about Wiley products, visit www.wiley.com.

Library of Congress Control Number: 2012954766

PROFESSIONAL

SharePoint® 2013 Development

Reza Alirezaei
Brendon Schwartz
Matt Ranlett
Scot Hillier
Brian Wilson
Jeff Fried
Paul Swider

WILEY

John Wiley & Sons, Inc.

To Natalia, you always put a smile on my face. I am so thankful to have you in my life.

—REZA ALIREZAEI

To Heidi, without you this would not have been possible.

—BRENDON SCHWARTZ

To Kim, whose love and support have encouraged and inspired me to always reach for more.

—MATT RANLETT

To Hayley, Katherine, and Charlie; thank you for your support and understanding, especially after many weekends of writing. I love you with all my heart!

—BRIAN WILSON

To my lovely and patient wife Eve

—JEFF FRIED

CREDITS

ACQUISITIONS EDITOR
Mary James

PROJECT EDITOR
Kelly Talbot

TECHNICAL EDITORS
Andy Au
Mehrdad Mehroo
Siavash Fathi

PRODUCTION EDITOR
Christine Mugnolo

COPY EDITOR
San Dee Philips

EDITORIAL MANAGER
Mary Beth Wakefield

FREELANCER EDITORIAL MANAGER
Rosemarie Graham

ASSOCIATE DIRECTOR OF MARKETING
David Mayhew

MARKETING MANAGER
Ashley Zurcher

BUSINESS MANAGER
Amy Knies

PRODUCTION MANAGER
Tim Tate

VICE PRESIDENT AND EXECUTIVE GROUP PUBLISHER
Richard Swadley

VICE PRESIDENT AND EXECUTIVE PUBLISHER
Neil Edde

ASSOCIATE PUBLISHER
Jim Minatel

PROJECT COORDINATOR, COVER
Katie Crocker

PROOFREADERS
Jennifer Bennett, Word One New York
Josh Chase, Word One New York
Jeff Holt, Word One New York
Scott Klemp, Word One New York
James Saturnio, Word One New York

INDEXER
Johnna VanHoose Dinse

COVER DESIGNER
Elizabeth Brooks

COVER IMAGE
© mbbirdy / iStockphoto

ABOUT THE AUTHORS

REZA ALIREZAEI is the founder and president of Development Horizon, a Microsoft Gold Partner based in Toronto. Reza has been a Microsoft Most Valuable Professional (MVP) for SharePoint since 2006. In addition to consulting, Reza has a decade of experience in training and speaking for corporations and the SharePoint community. He has authored several SharePoint books, papers, and online articles. Reza blogs at `http://blogs.devhorizon.com/reza` and can be reached at `reza@devhorizon.com`.

BRENDON SCHWARTZ is a SharePoint expert with over 10 years of SharePoint experience, starting in the early days of the product. Known as an expert on collaboration, social computing, enterprise content management, business process management, and application development, Brendon has presented at conferences and built innovative product solutions. He has managed projects for many clients, including Fortune 500 companies such as AT&T, Coca-Cola, AutoTrader.com, and The Home Depot. While leading a team for one of the first Microsoft-hosted solutions for Coca-Cola Enterprises, he helped shape the future of Office 365. Brendon has proudly received the Microsoft MVP award for both ASP.NET and SharePoint. An avid writer on SharePoint, he has authored numerous articles and books including *Professional SharePoint 2007 Development* and *Social Computing with Microsoft SharePoint 2007*. Brendon enjoys spending time with his wife, son, and new daughter.

MATT RANLETT is a SharePoint Server MVP and works as a solution architect and consulting practice lead with Slalom Consulting. When he's not organizing or presenting at user group-related events, Matt writes and edits white papers, magazine articles, and books on SharePoint.

SCOT HILLIER is an independent consultant and Microsoft SharePoint Most Valuable Professional focused on creating solutions for Information Workers with SharePoint, Office, and related technologies. He is the author/coauthor of 18 books on Microsoft technologies including *Inside SharePoint 2013* and *App Development in SharePoint 2013*. Scot splits his time between consulting on SharePoint projects, speaking at SharePoint events like the Microsoft SharePoint Conference, and delivering training for SharePoint developers through Critical Path Training. Scot is a former U. S. Navy submarine officer and graduate of the Virginia Military Institute. Scot can be reached at `scot@scothillier.net`.

BRIAN WILSON is a SharePoint solution and information architect and director of WiredLight, a SharePoint solutions business. With 15 years of experience (including four years as a Senior Consultant in the SharePoint and Information Worker team in Microsoft Consulting Services), Brian works with some of Microsoft's largest customers architecting and developing solutions for enterprise environments using SharePoint technologies. Since the first version of SharePoint, he has been involved in a variety of leading-edge SharePoint projects for clients in the USA, Europe, Asia, and South Africa across many industries. Brian provides innovative design and development expertise through WiredLight, which focuses on providing consultancy, products, and solutions for SharePoint. When he gets the time, he enjoys skiing, scuba diving, and watching a great game of rugby. For more information about Brian, see `http://www.wiredlight.net/` or his LinkedIn profile at `http://uk.linkedin.com/in/bkvwilson`.

JEFF FRIED is the CTO at BA Insight, focused on the development of search-based applications with SharePoint. Jeff is a frequent speaker and writer in the industry, holds 15 patents, has authored more than 50 technical papers, and has led the creation of pioneering offerings in next generation search engines, networks, and contact centers

PAUL SWIDER is an international speaker, trainer, and freelance consultant. In addition, he is the founder of the Charleston SharePoint Users Group and an accomplished entrepreneur straight from a barrier island near Charleston, SC where Paul also chases the tides and winds as an avid boater and sailor. Paul is involved in many community and philanthropic efforts including a founding member of Sharing the Point, an international effort which offers free SharePoint training opportunities in emerging markets. Seventeen years of software consulting experience combined with many Microsoft certifications and speaking credentials has made Paul an authority in the SharePoint community. As an MCT, Paul has trained and consulted thousands of SharePoint administrators, developers, and architects.

ABOUT THE TECHNICAL EDITORS

ANDY AU is the team lead at the consulting firm Development Horizon, a Microsoft Gold Certified Partner for SharePoint based in Toronto, Canada. Andy has over eight years of experience in which six years were spent working with SharePoint 2003, 2007, and 2010. Andy has been entrusted with the leadership and development of many solutions in his career, and he holds Microsoft Certified Technology Specialist (MCTS), Microsoft Certified IT Professional (MCITP), and Microsoft Certified Professional Developer (MCPD) certificates. In his free time, Andy enjoys watching sports and spending time relaxing with family and friends.

MEHRDAD MEHRJOO has dedicated the last seven years of his career to working with SharePoint. Mehrdad has become so well known as the guy who can make almost any software work and integrate with SharePoint. He is currently working in Development Horizon as a senior SharePoint consultant where he leads the foundation and infrastructure design and development practice. He is a recognized Microsoft Certified Technology Specialist (MCTS), Microsoft Certified IT Professional (MCITP), and Microsoft Certified Professional Developer (MCPD). Mehrdad enjoys spending time with his wife and son.

SIAVASH FATHI is a senior SharePoint consultant in Development Horizon. Siavash is passionate about SharePoint apps and is focused on client-side and remote programming. Besides SharePoint, Siavash likes to do research in robotics and artificial intelligence (AI) and has published several papers in those fields. Siavash holds Microsoft Certified Technology Specialist (MCTS), Microsoft Certified IT Professional (MCITP), Microsoft Certified Professional Developer (MCPD), and Certified ScrumMaster (CSM) certificates.

ACKNOWLEDGMENTS

WRITING A BOOK IS NEVER AN EASY TASK. It takes a lot of people who don't get their name on the front of the book but who put in a tremendous amount of work. Thanks to my wife Heidi, who makes this all possible. Your sacrifices and willingness to take care of the family on your own never stop amazing me. Although our kids are too young to know that Daddy going to work all day on Saturdays and Sundays is not normal, I am very grateful for how wonderful our children are. No person is complete without a good support system, and I would like to thank everyone I have worked with who has pushed me to become better. First, thanks to all of our team members at Wrox for making this possible — Mary, Kelly, and all of the editors, you all rock! I'd like to thank my friend Aaron Richards for his innovative thinking and endless pursuit of solutions and InfoPath. Thanks also to my technical support system that I reach out to, such as Andrew Connell, Douglas McDowell, Robert Bogue, and Doug Ware. Doug Ware never lets me down when I have tough questions and need a blog post to explain something. Thanks to all of the SharePoint MVPs for being great friends and the best MVP community there is. And thanks for the years of encouragement from my good friends Matt Ranlett, Jeremy Howard, Jerry Pattenaude, and Chris Haldeman. A big thanks to the SharePoint team and their willingness to always provide an answer. Finally, I want to thank some of the people who have had an impact in helping me grow, learn, and keep on track, including my parents, Doug Turnure, Aaron Cutlip, Dan Attis, and countless others.

—BRENDON SCHWARTZ

FIRST AND FOREMOST I NEED TO THANK my family for putting up with the endless hours researching, writing, and editing book content. I also need to thank the talented team of editors and reviewers at Wrox who worked tirelessly to make this book a reality.

—MATT RANLETT

A BIG THANK YOU TO BILL BAER and Vesa Juvonen for your contribution to various chapters in this book. Your advice, expertise and contribution helped the writing team produce a high-quality SharePoint 2013 book. Thank you! To the SharePoint and Office product teams, and to all of you in the SharePoint Community: To standing on the shoulders of giants…!

—BRIAN WILSON

THANKS TO MY WIFE AND FAMILY for their support, to my SharePoint friends for their inspiration, and to the editors of this book for their hard work and consistent pushing.

—JEFF FRIED

CONTENTS

INTRODUCTION

IF YOU ALREADY HAVE SOME exposure to the SharePoint platform and its complementary technologies, you probably know that SharePoint is a versatile platform for building solutions that address a wide range of business needs. The growing importance and use of SharePoint in general has played an important role in the investment Microsoft has made in this platform over the years. Today, the latest version of this great product is SharePoint 2013!

There are many new features and improvements made to the core platform in SharePoint 2013. However, what is the most exciting addition is the new app model that enables developers to build apps and deploy them in isolation with few or no dependencies on any other software on the platform where it is installed and with no custom code that runs on the SharePoint servers.

In SharePoint 2013, the emphasis is more on the cloud programming and standard web technologies such as JavaScript and HTML. In that respect, it is fair to say that the majority of other changes made to the SharePoint 2013 platform are made to support this new app development model.

WHO THIS BOOK IS FOR

This book is for anyone interested in developing applications on top of SharePoint 2013 or SharePoint Online in Office 365. Although some knowledge is assumed about SharePoint, the examples are comprehensive and easy to follow if you have previous knowledge of web development and development tools.

WHAT THIS BOOK COVERS

SharePoint 2013, just like its predecessors, is a big product and this book is a big, diverse book. So, before you dive into the book, here's a little about what each chapter entails and what you can expect after you have read the chapter.

This book starts off with giving you an architectural overview in SharePoint and then covers the new features that matter to developers in Chapters 1 and 2. Chapters 3 and 4 walk you through the tooling experience in SharePoint 2013, as well as some important information about Application Life Cycle Management (ALM) in SharePoint 2013.

Due to the importance of the app model in SharePoint 2013, Chapters 4 through 7 are dedicated to app development and the cloud.

Chapters 8 through 15 walk you through some of the important areas in SharePoint 2013, many of which received considerable updates. This section also includes Chapter 11, "Using InfoPath with SharePoint 2013." Because there is some uncertainty about the future of InfoPath in the SharePoint stack and there are customers with existing investments, that chapter will hopefully shed some light to help developers make better decisions as they move forward.

Chapters 16 through 19 are focused on Business Intelligence (BI) and SharePoint. BI in SharePoint 2013 provides better capabilities in analysis, reporting, dashboarding, and visualizations compared to SharePoint 2010. This is made available through better BI tools and tighter integration between SharePoint, Microsoft Office applications, and SQL Server 2012.

HOW THIS BOOK IS STRUCTURED

This book is structured to build logically on the skills you learn as you progress through it. After the initial introduction and base platform chapters, the book moves into the advanced part of the platform. Each chapter builds on knowledge acquired from earlier in the book, so you should read through the chapters in succession or at least read the introductory and platform chapters before reading later chapters in the book.

WHAT YOU NEED TO USE THIS BOOK

To get the most of this book, and because this is a book for developers, you need a development environment. There are two ways to do this:

➤ Build your own development machine. The best resource for building a full-fledged development machine is documented at MSDN at `http://msdn.microsoft.com/en-us/library/ee554869.aspx`.

➤ Use an Office 365 developer site. This shortens your setup time and gets you started in less than five minutes. In this setup all you need is to sign up for a developer site at `http://msdn.microsoft.com/en-us/library/fp179924.aspx`.

If you choose to use an Office 365 developer site, please note that you can also deploy Napa, which is an Office 365 exclusive development tool, to your developer site. This allows you to build SharePoint-hosted apps without installing Visual Studio 2012 and Office Developer Tools for Visual Studio 2012 on your development computer.

Last, but certainly not least, Microsoft has released many code samples for SharePoint 2013 covering almost every area of SharePoint development. You can find these code samples at `http://msdn.microsoft.com/en-us/library/jj901637.aspx`.

CONVENTIONS

To help you get the most from the text and keep track of what's happening, we've used a number of conventions throughout the book.

> **WARNING** *Boxes like this one hold important, not-to-be forgotten information that is directly relevant to the surrounding text.*

> **NOTE** *Notes, tips, hints, tricks, and asides to the current discussion are offset like this.*

As for styles in the text:

➤ New terms and important words are *italicized* when introduced.

➤ Keyboard strokes are shown like this: Ctrl+A.

➤ Filenames, URLs, and code within the text looks like this: `persistence.properties`.

➤ Code is presented in two different ways:

```
We use a monofont type with no highlighting for most code examples.
```

```
We use bold to emphasize code that is particularly important in the present context
or to show changes from a previous code snippet.
```

SOURCE CODE

As you work through the examples in this book, you may choose either to type in all the code manually or to use the source code files that accompany the book. All the source code used in this book is available for download at `www.wrox.com`. When at the site, simply locate the book's title (use the Search box or one of the title lists) and click the Download Code link on the book's detail page to obtain all the source code for the book.

> **NOTE** *Because many books have similar titles, you may find it easiest to search by ISBN; this book's ISBN is 978-1-118-49582-7.*

After you download the code, just decompress it with your favorite compression tool. Alternatively, you can go to the main Wrox code download page at `www.wrox.com/dynamic/books/download.aspx` to see the code available for this book and all other Wrox books.

ERRATA

Every effort is made to ensure that there are no errors in the text or in the code. However, no one is perfect, and mistakes do occur. If you find an error in one of our books, like a spelling mistake or faulty piece of code, your feedback is welcome. By sending in errata, you may save other readers hours of frustration and at the same time you will be helping us provide even higher quality information.

To find the errata page for this book, go to www.wrox.com and locate the title using the Search box or one of the title lists. Then, on the book's detail page, click the Book Errata link. On this page, you can view all errata that has been submitted for this book and posted by Wrox editors. A complete book list, including links to each book's errata, is also available at www.wrox.com/misc-pages/booklist.shtml.

If you don't spot "your" error on the Book Errata page, go to www.wrox.com/contact/techsupport.shtml and complete the form there to send us the error you have found. After the information is checked, a message is posted to the book's errata page, and the problem is fixed in subsequent editions of the book.

P2P.WROX.COM

For author and peer discussion, join the P2P forums at p2p.wrox.com. The forums are a web-based system for you to post messages relating to Wrox books and related technologies, and interact with other readers and technology users. The forums offer a subscription feature to e-mail you topics of interest of your choosing when new posts are made to the forums. Wrox authors, editors, other industry experts, and your fellow readers are present on these forums.

At p2p.wrox.com you can find a number of different forums that can help you not only as you read this book, but also as you develop your own applications. To join the forums, follow these steps:

1. Go to p2p.wrox.com and click the Register link.

2. Read the terms of use and click Agree.

3. Complete the required information to join, as well as any optional information you want to provide, and click Submit.

4. You will receive an e-mail with information describing how to verify your account and complete the joining process.

> **NOTE** *You can read messages in the forums without joining P2P, but to post your own messages, you must join.*

After you join, you can post new messages and respond to messages other users post. You can read messages at any time on the web. If you would like to have new messages from a particular forum e-mailed to you, click the Subscribe to This Forum icon by the forum name in the forum listing.

For more information about how to use the Wrox P2P, be sure to read the P2P FAQs for answers to questions about how the forum software works, as well as many common questions specific to P2P and Wrox books. To read the FAQs, click the FAQ link on any P2P page.

1

Architectural Overview of SharePoint 2013

WHAT'S IN THIS CHAPTER?

- ➤ Understanding on-premise server farm architecture
- ➤ Deploying, configuring, and publishing applications with the service application architecture
- ➤ Discovering the improved scalability and redundancy of the search architecture
- ➤ Exploring the SQL Server database architecture
- ➤ Understanding the cloud-hosted architectures

Microsoft SharePoint Server 2013 introduces a lot of new functionality that you need to understand to write better applications on the SharePoint 2013 platform. Developing new functionality relies on a sound logical and physical architecture. Therefore, you must have a good appreciation and understanding of your SharePoint farm architecture to take advantage of and develop long-lasting SharePoint solutions.

This chapter provides a succinct overview of the common on-premise server farm architectures available for SharePoint 2013. You take a detailed look at service applications and dive into the evolved SharePoint 2013 search architecture. Then, you look at the improvements and updates related to the SQL database tier. Lastly, you take a look at the cloud-hosted farm architectures.

The content presented in this chapter targets architects, lead developers, and developers developing solutions tailored to their SharePoint 2013 farm topologies, but the chapter is also useful for anyone working with the product. Although all topics covered in this chapter are important, this chapter has been designed to enable you to jump to the sections you are interested in.

WHAT'S NEW FROM AN ARCHITECTURAL PERSPECTIVE?

From an architectural perspective there are a number of enhancements to the SharePoint 2013 topology. These additions and improvements continue to evolve the SharePoint platform capabilities to better handle the ever-increasing workload placed on the SharePoint platform. The key updates include:

➤ *SQL improvements and shredded storage* — A number of improvements have been made at the database layer to reduce the impact of scenarios that might invoke full table scans, improve usage of advanced indexing features in SQL Server 2008 R2 and SQL Server 2012, and incorporate a new feature called shredded storage that changes the way SharePoint stores and updates files in SQL. Files are now shredded, and only the changed pieces are updated at the database layer. This reduces the impact caused by document updates.

➤ *Distributed cache service* — A new cache service, based on Windows Server AppFabric Distributed Caching, has been implemented in SharePoint 2013. By default it is enabled on all web front ends and application servers. It improves performance by caching information such as social data authentication tokens.

➤ *Unified search architecture* — SharePoint 2013 unifies the search offerings available in SharePoint 2010. SharePoint 2013 search provides numerous improvements to content crawling, content processing, analytics processing, indexing, query processing, and search administration components.

➤ *Integrated Request Management* (RM) — Request Management provides SharePoint more knowledge and control over incoming requests. This includes throttling and routing requests to appropriate web front ends, prioritization and filtering of requests, and load balancing based on weighting schemes.

➤ *New service applications* — New service applications include the App Management Service to support and manage apps in SharePoint 2013, the Machine Translation Service that supports automated language translation of files, and the Work Management Service that provides task aggregation functionality.

➤ *Office Web Applications is now a separate product* — Office Web Applications have been split into a dedicated product to provide a uniform application for viewing and editing files, including files not necessarily in SharePoint. The Office Web Apps Server supports the Web application Open Platform Interface (WOPI) that SharePoint implements to support office files hosted in SharePoint.

➤ *Web analytics platform* — The web analytics platform replaces the web analytics service application that was in SharePoint 2010. It has been completely redesigned and integrated into the search service application of SharePoint 2013.

➤ *Windows Azure Workflow* — Windows Azure Workflows are now supported for on-premise and hosted deployments in SharePoint 2013.

ON-PREMISE SERVER FARM ARCHITECTURE

Server farms represent the topology that delivers SharePoint services to end users. A *server farm* is a collection of server machines acting together to host SharePoint services and workloads.

SharePoint 2013 provides a high degree of flexibility for planning your topology. The core principle behind implementing a server farm is the ability to scale the environment as required to support additional workloads, scenarios, and load placed on the farm by your organization.

Farms can range in size from a single SharePoint server to highly scaled-out architectures hosting server roles on dedicated sets of physical servers. Figure 1-1 shows a typical medium SharePoint server farm, as published in the *TechNet* article "Topologies for SharePoint Server 2013: Model" (http://go.microsoft.com/fwlink/p/?LinkId=259119).

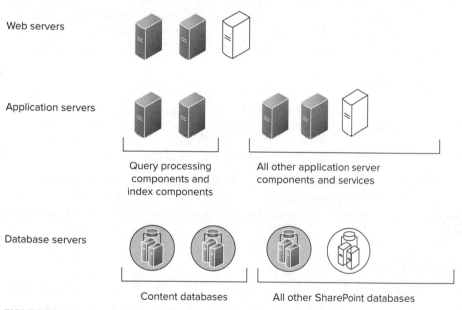

FIGURE 1-1

Each tier in a topology represents the purpose of the server machines hosted within it, or the services dedicated to those server machines. The core components of a server farm can be categorized into the following three tiers (refer to Figure 1-1):

➤ *Web servers* — Web servers are servers that respond to user requests and render the SharePoint web pages. All web servers in a farm are mirrors of each other and are load balanced.

➤ *Application servers* — Application servers are used to describe any server that runs back-end application services (for example, servers that host search crawl and query components). Multiple redundant application servers can be load balanced.

➤ *Database servers* — The database tier hosts nearly all the data of your farm in SQL databases. This includes configuration databases, service application related databases, and content databases. All databases can be assigned to one database server or spread across multiple servers.

SharePoint 2013 can be deployed in a number of topology configurations. The basic topologies include small, medium, and large — otherwise known as single-tier, two-tier, and three-tier deployments — that define the placement and purpose of individual server machines in your server farm's topology.

Web Server Tier

The web server tier is composed of web servers or other servers that receive and respond to HTTP requests. Web servers host SharePoint web applications in Internet Information Services (IIS). They can support additional services such as the search query component sending requests to database servers in the database server tier, or communicating with application servers in the application server tier to consume services hosted on those servers. Servers in the web server tier are exposed directly to end users and should be secured behind a firewall or within a perimeter network.

Application Server Tier

The application server tier is an optional tier composed of servers that are dedicated to the hosting of service applications associated with SharePoint 2013. Examples of servers in the application server tier include dedicated server machines that host the search service, administration, and query components, in addition to services such as PerformancePoint or Excel Services.

The application server tier is most commonly associated with large server farm environments, in which dedicated compute resources are required to support high search query volumes, large indexes, or to isolate service applications to free up resources on the web server tier to support high concurrency rates.

Database Server Tier

The database server tier is composed of servers hosting SQL Server. Database servers in the database tier respond to requests initiated by web and application servers, and update the underlying databases that support SharePoint 2013. The database server tier can be scaled both up (to improve performance) and out (to improve performance and provide additional server farm resiliency).

Small or Single-Tier Topology

A small or single-tier topology commonly consists of a single server deployment in which all components required to instantiate a SharePoint environment are installed on one machine including the database server. Figure 1-2 shows an example of a single-tier topology, which is designed to support development or small businesses where scale and redundancy are not concerns.

All roles on one server, including SQL Server

FIGURE 1-2

A single-tier topology does not provide any level of redundancy. Therefore, it requires an aggressive backup-and-restore strategy to be implemented because this is the extent of data protection that can be provided in this deployment topology. Because all components are installed on a single server, single-tier topologies are the least flexible and do not support seamless scale.

Medium or Two-Tier Topology

A medium or two-tier topology consists of two or more servers that support separation of SharePoint and SQL Server components. This includes one or more web servers installed with SharePoint 2013, and one or more database servers installed with SQL Server. Medium or two-tier topologies benefit from their flexibility in that they can seamlessly scale to meet the changing business needs or the demands of the organization.

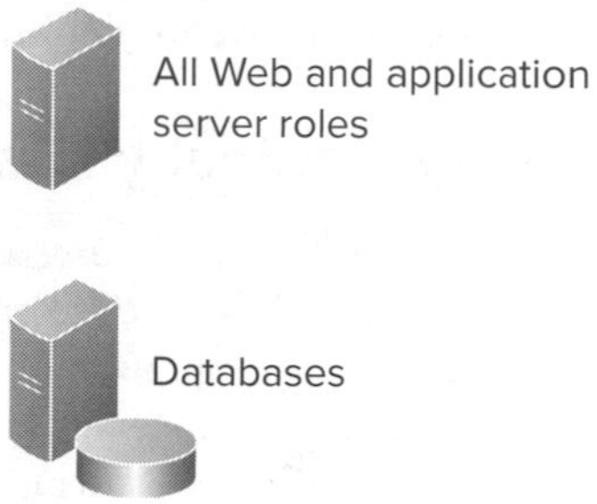

All Web and application server roles

Databases

FIGURE 1-3

Figure 1-3 shows a minimal two-tier topology composed of one web server running SharePoint Server 2013 in the web tier and one database server running SQL Server 2008 R2 SP1 or SQL Server 2012 in the database server tier.

Figure 1-4 shows a scaled, two-tier topology that includes two load-balanced web servers running SharePoint Server 2013 in the web server tier and two database servers running SQL Server 2008 R2 SP1 or SQL Server 2012 in the database server tier that can be clustered or mirrored to provide high availability and redundancy.

The two-tier topology provides the most flexible deployment type and is recommended for organizations of all sizes as a base topology. This topology can be expanded or contracted through the addition or removal of server machines. As such, it is one of the most common deployments of a server

Web servers

All databases

FIGURE 1-4

farm, providing a flexible and scalable solution. A two-tier server farm enables an organization to seamlessly implement hardware or software load balancing such as Windows NT Load Balancing Service (WLBS) to distribute incoming HTTP requests evenly between web servers. This provides a means to handle an increase in demand as the number of requests submitted to it rise (for example, as the result of a merger or acquisition).

A two-tier server farm can also seamlessly scale at the database server tier through the introduction of additional database servers in a mirrored or clustered configuration. This provides additional resiliency and distribution of load within a server farm environment.

Large or Three-Tier Topology

A large or three-tier topology is designed for large organizations that require performance, scale, and adherence to strict business-continuity management objectives.

Figure 1-5 shows a three-tier topology that consists of two or more web servers installed with SharePoint 2013, one or more application servers installed with SharePoint 2013, and two or more database servers installed with SQL Server.

Web servers

The physical topology selected for SharePoint 2013 can drive the layout of the service application topology. In many cases, it may be easier to map the service-application topology to a physical topology to help ensure that sufficient resources exist to support the overall deployment.

Application servers running all service application roles

Geographically Distributed Topology

All databases

FIGURE 1-5

Geographically dispersed deployments refer to distributing SharePoint resources to support regional or global users. For example, an organization may have its headquarters in Seattle, Washington. However, many users may be distributed globally to support various corporate functions, or to respond to opportunities in specific geographic locations.

In this scenario, it can be costly to deploy a dedicated instance of SharePoint 2013 to support small pockets of users. Therefore, the organization may opt to introduce WAN optimization devices, whether symmetric or asymmetric, to accommodate latency or leverage technologies such as BranchCache in Windows Server 2008 R2 or Windows Server 2012.

In scenarios in which the geographically dispersed user base is substantial enough to justify the cost of a localized, dedicated SharePoint 2013 deployment, an organization can opt to federate or publish service applications from the centralized server farm to the distributed regional server farms. This provides a unified experience to the remote user base. You could optionally isolate these server farms to support regulatory compliance related to those specific geographic locations.

SERVICE APPLICATION ARCHITECTURE

This section focuses on helping you understand services in SharePoint 2013. The objective is to make you familiar with the service application architecture in SharePoint 2013, and how this architecture is used in the platform to offer new and improved functionality.

Service Application Model

SharePoint 2013 uses the service application model first introduced in SharePoint 2010. Starting with SharePoint 2010 and continued in SharePoint 2013, SharePoint Foundation 2013 provides the infrastructure for hosting service applications. Figure 1-6 shows the service application model in SharePoint 2010 and 2013.

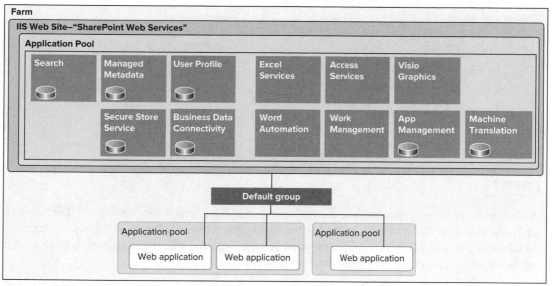

FIGURE 1-6

The idea with the service application model in SharePoint 2013 is simple. If you don't need a particular service application, you don't deploy it to your farm — period! In addition, you can deploy multiple instances of the services. Actually, you can create as many instances of a given service application as you like.

The second layer of granular configuration with the service model comes at the web application level. In SharePoint 2013, web applications can be configured with the service applications they want to consume, and in which combination.

After you have an instance of a service application deployed to your farm, it can be shared across multiple web applications in the same farm, or even across different farms. Regardless of the sharing model, you can always modify the association between a web application and service applications at a later time.

Service applications can be deployed to different application pools to support process isolation. You can pick and choose which service applications should be within the same process, or within separate processes.

> **NOTE** *One possible reason to think about process isolation from performance or security perspectives is when sharing service data across multiple applications.*

Figure 1-7 shows how various services are distributed in two application pools.

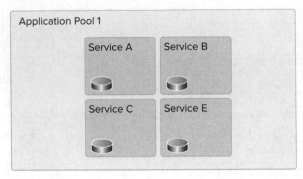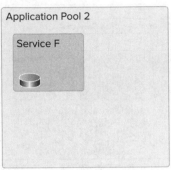

FIGURE 1-7

Although in most implementations, the performance of your farm is best optimized if services exist in one application pool; in some scenarios the highest physical isolation of services is required. The SharePoint 2013 service application model enables you to create separate instances of service applications and place them in different application pools.

Service applications provide a better scalability model. You can select which servers host and run a particular service application service using the Services on Server page in Central Administration.

SharePoint 2013 provides a basic load balancer that uses a round-robin algorithm to send requests to service applications. When a web application requests an endpoint for an associated service application (through a *proxy*), the out-of-the-box load balancer returns the first available endpoint. Certain services (such as Excel Calculation Services) provide their own software load-balancing feature to ensure that no instance of a given service is overloaded at any time.

SharePoint 2013 supports cross-farm service applications. In other words, any farm can both publish and consume service applications from other farms. Each farm can consume services from more than one parent farm. This enables web applications in your SharePoint 2013 farm to use both local and remote service applications.

Available Service Applications

As an architect or developer, you must know what service applications your licensed edition of SharePoint provides. Table 1-1 provides an overview of all the service applications that ship out-of-the-box with different editions of SharePoint 2013, excluding service applications provided by other Microsoft products such Project Server, PowerPivot service, and so on.

TABLE 1-1: Service Applications Available by SharePoint 2013 Editions

SERVICE APPLICATIONS	STORAGE TYPE	SHAREPOINT FOUNDATION	SHAREPOINT STANDARD	SHAREPOINT ENTERPRISE
Access Services	App DBs			✓
Access Services 2010	Content DBs			✓
App Management Service	DB	✓	✓	✓

Service	Storage			
Business Data Connectivity Service	DB	✓	✓	✓
Excel Services	Cache			✓
Machine Translation Services	DB		✓	✓
Managed Metadata Service	DB		✓	✓
PerformancePoint	Cache			✓
PowerPoint Automation			✓	✓
Search Service	DB		✓	✓
Secure Store Service	DB		✓	✓
State Service	DB		✓	✓
Usage and Health Data Collection	DB	✓	✓	✓
User Profile	DB		✓	✓
Visio Graphics Service	Blog Cache			✓
Word Automation Services	DB	✓	✓	✓
Work Management Service			✓	✓
Subscription Settings Service	DB	✓	✓	✓

NOTE *Office Web Application Services is now a separate product and no longer provided as a service application. Web analytics service application is now managed as a key component of the search service application.*

Following are descriptions of each service application:

➤ *Access Services* — This service application enables you to create, view, edit, and interact using either the access 2013 office client or in the browser.

➤ *Access Services 2010* — This service application enables continued maintenance of SharePoint 2010 Access service applications by using Access 2010 and 2013 Office clients. It does not enable users to create new applications.

➤ *App Management Service* — The App Management Service enables you to install apps from the internal App Catalog or the public SharePoint store.

➤ *Business Data Connectivity Service* — The Business Connectivity Service (BCS) enables you to upload data (BDC) models that define interfaces of other enterprise line-of-business (LOB) systems and enables connectivity to those systems.

➤ *Excel Services* — This service application enables viewing and interacting with Excel files from within the browser.

➤ *Machine Translation Services* — This service provides automatic machine translation of files and sites.

➤ *Managed Metadata Service* — This service application enables you to manage taxonomy hierarchies, keywords, and social tagging features of SharePoint 2013. This service application also handles content-type publishing across site collections.

➤ *PerformancePoint* — This service application supports configuration and monitoring of PerformancePoint as a business intelligence (BI) product integrated with the Enterprise edition of SharePoint 2013.

➤ *PowerPoint Automation Service* — This service application enables server-side presentation conversions to and from a variety of file formats.

➤ *Search Service* — As its name implies, this service application (which comes with its own topology management configuration) is used to index content and serves search queries performed by users or custom code.

➤ *Secure Store Service* — This is a credential mapping service to access other enterprise-level service applications or back-end enterprise systems.

➤ *State Service* — The State Service provides temporary storage of any data that deals with a user session.

➤ *Usage and Health Data Collection* — This service application provides storage usage and health information at the farm level, and provides various reporting functionality on such data.

➤ *User Profile* — This user profile service application is one of the core service applications in SharePoint 2013. This service application supports features such as My Sites, My links, Colleague tracker, profile pages, personal tags and notes, and other social features.

➤ *Visio Graphics Service* — This service application enables viewing, interacting, and refreshing of Visio diagrams within a browser.

➤ *Word Automation Services* — This service application enables you to view and edit Word documents in a web browser. It can also be used for document conversions.

➤ *Work Management Service* — This Work Management Service enables key user-related information to be aggregated to a central location. The service supports a provider model to enable other systems to leverage this service.

➤ *Subscription Setting Service* — This is the key enabling component of the Multitenancy features provided by the SharePoint 2013 platform.

Now that you are familiar with service applications in different editions of SharePoint, consider the life cycle of a service application.

Service Application Life Cycle

A typical life cycle for a service application consists of several stages. When you plan your service application, consider each stage of this cycle. For example, you should understand when you should use the Configuration Wizard to provision your service applications or use Windows PowerShell, and when you should create a custom proxy group for your service applications.

Figure 1-8 shows the stages in a life cycle for a service application.

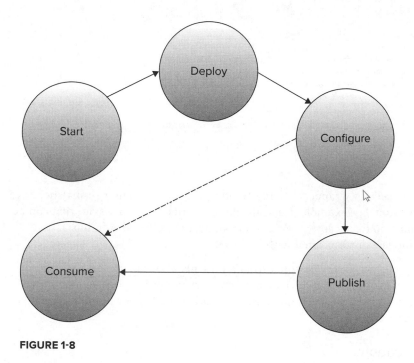

FIGURE 1-8

Starting Services

Although service applications are different from services, they still confuse many people working with SharePoint 2013.

If you browse to the Services on Server page in SharePoint Central Administration, that page lists all services that can be started and stopped on specific servers of the farm, as shown in Figure 1-9.

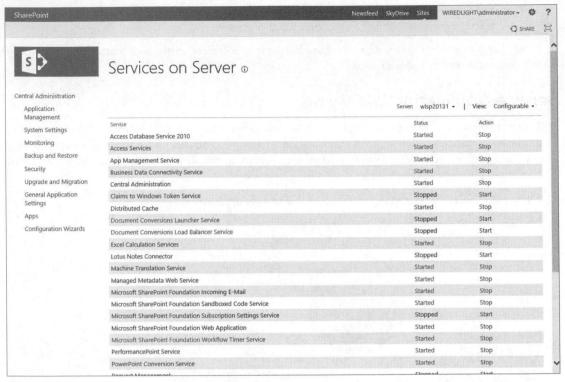

FIGURE 1-9

These services are mostly SharePoint wrappers around Windows services and may or may not have an associated service application. For example, Central Administration is just a service that can be started on a server of the farm to turn it into a server that can host the Central Administration site — there is no service application associated with it.

As mentioned earlier in this chapter, a service application represents a specific instance of a given service that can be configured and shared in a particular way. Service applications are composed of Windows services, timer jobs, caching, SQL databases, and other stuff. They are just a broader concept than Windows services.

Deploying Service Applications

You can deploy service applications within a farm by using the following methods:

➤ Selecting the service applications in the Initial Configuration Wizard of your farm

➤ Adding new service applications or new instances of the existing service application in the Central Administration site

➤ Using Windows PowerShell

Table 1-2 describes the Windows PowerShell commands that you can use to manage service applications.

TABLE 1-2: Service Application Windows PowerShell Commands

COMMAND	DESCRIPTION
Install-SPService	Installs the services in the farm. It runs once per farm.
Get-SPServiceInstance Start-SPServiceInstance Stop-SPServiceInstance	Operations related to managing the services instance for a specific server or the entire farm.
Get-SPServiceApplication Publish-SPServiceApplication Remove-SPServiceApplication Set-SPServiceApplication Unpublish-SPServiceApplication	Operations related to managing service applications deployed to a farm (such as sharing the specified local service application outside the farm).
Get-SPServiceApplicationProxy Remove-SPServiceApplicationProxy Add-SPServiceApplicationProxy GroupMember	Operations related to managing service application proxies.
Get-SPServiceApplicationPool New-SPServiceApplicationPool Remove-SPServiceApplicationPool Set-SPServiceApplicationPool	Operations related to managing the logical architecture of service applications.

Regardless of your deployment approach, service applications can be isolated. To do so, during the provisioning process, you can either specify to use an existing application pool, or create a new application pool and have the service application run in its own worker process.

Configuring Service Applications

After the service applications are configured at the farm level, they can all be managed in the Central Administration site. When you click Manage Service Applications, you are taken to the Service Applications page, as shown in Figure 1-10.

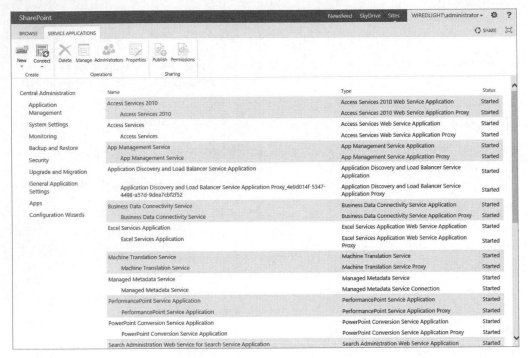

FIGURE 1-10

In the Service Applications page, you should note three things:

➤ All deployed service applications are listed.

➤ All service application connections (proxies) are listed.

➤ You can add new service applications by clicking the New button on the Ribbon.

When service applications are provisioned, if you open up the Internet Information Services (IIS) manager, you can see that there is a web application called SharePoint Web Services, and underneath that web application are a bunch of virtual directories. Each of those virtual directories is seen by a globally unique identifier (GUID), or its identifier for the service application, as shown in Figure 1-11.

At a service database level, most of the service applications use their own set of databases.

FIGURE 1-11

> **NOTE** *An important point to remember is that a service application may have one or more databases. For example, the User Profile service application has profile, synchronization, and social tagging databases. Another example is the Search service application with crawl, link, analytics, and administration databases. The number of databases can quickly add up and be difficult to manage if you do not properly plan capacity.*

One issue with configuring service applications using the Configuration Wizard is that the associated virtual directory databases can end up having a lot of GUIDs. For example, the name for one of the User Profile databases could be `User Profile Service Application_ProfileDB _899fd696a54a4cbe965dc8b30560dd07`.

Though this might be acceptable in some cases, generally, a more intuitive naming convention makes a more sense. One way to resolve this issue is to use the Manage Service Applications page in the Central Administration site to add service applications individually and then specify meaningful database names. The other alternative approach is to use Windows PowerShell to provision your service applications.

The following code snippet shows how you can provision a State Service service application using Windows PowerShell. Note how the SQL Server database and server name are specified in the code.

```
New-SPStateServiceDatabase -Name "StateServiceDatabase" -DatabaseServer
    "dhsqlsrv" | New-SPStateServiceApplication -Name "State Service Application"
    | New-SPStateServiceApplicationProxy -Name " State Service Application Proxy"
    -DefaultProxyGroup > $null
```

As mentioned previously, you can create and deploy your own service application. In that case, you can override the previous Windows PowerShell commands and add your own parameters.

Configuring Service Application Proxies

If you deploy your service applications using either the Configuration Wizard or via Central Administration, service-application proxies are automatically created for you. If you use Windows PowerShell, then you must also manually create the proxy that goes along with that service application.

So, what's the service application proxy, anyway?

Essentially, the *service application proxy* is a virtual link that connects web applications to a particular service application. So, when you create your web application, you can specify your association to a service-application proxy, and it's the proxy that actually manages the communication back and forth.

In addition to linking web applications to service applications, some proxies also include settings that can be modified independently from the service applications. For example, the proxy for the Managed Metadata Service application indicates whether the associated service application is the default storage location for the corporate taxonomy store (such as keywords and column-specific term sets), as shown in Figure 1-12.

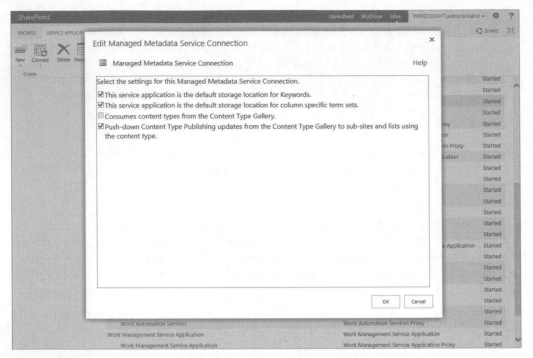

FIGURE 1-12

> **NOTE** *If there are multiple instances of the Managed Metadata Service application, (and, hence, multiple proxies), one of the instances must be specified as the primary, which hosts the corporate taxonomy store. All other instances are then secondary, providing additional data to the primary data. As an exception, the web parts that work with Managed Metadata Service applications work with data from all instances.*

Configuring Proxy Groups

As its name implies, a service application proxy group is a grouping for service application proxies that are selected for a Web application. A single service application proxy can be included in multiple proxy groups, or a proxy group may choose not to include a service application proxy based on the requirements of the target Web applications.

When you set up your farm, a default proxy group is created that includes all service application proxies. During the creation of a Web application, you have your choice to select the default proxy group or create a custom proxy group. Figure 1-13 shows the list of service applications configured in the default proxy group.

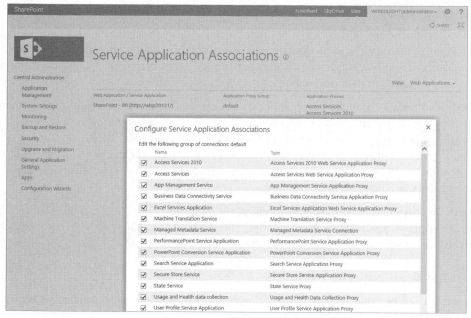

FIGURE 1-13

> **NOTE** *A custom service application proxy group created for one web application cannot be associated with other web applications.*

From Windows PowerShell you can run the `Get-SPServiceApplicationProxy` cmdlet, as shown in Figure 1-14, and that lists the service application proxy IDs. You can then use `Remove-SPServiceApplicationProxy` (which takes the ID as a parameter) and `Add-SPServiceApplicationProxyGroupMember` to remove a service application proxy, or to add a member to the service application proxy group.

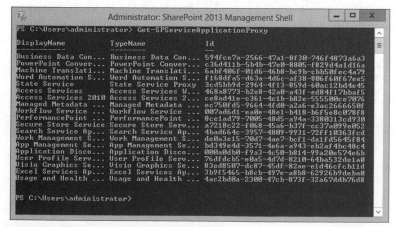

FIGURE 1-14

Consuming Service Applications

By default, all web applications in the local farm are associated with the default proxy group. This means that consuming the services in the local farm is not something that you must worry about, and it's automatically set up for you. If you decide to create a custom proxy group, you must decide how you want a specific web application to consume service applications.

To change the default proxy group for a web application, you must select Application Management in the Central Administration site, and click Configure Service Application Associations. In the Service Application Association page, you can see the default text under the Application Proxy Group heading. If you click it, you go to a page where you can manage the members of that default proxy group. In addition, if there were any custom proxy groups for each web application, they would be listed in the same page.

Again, it's worth mentioning that some connections might include settings that can be modified. For example, if a web application is connected to multiple instances of the Managed Metadata Service, you must indicate which service application hosts the corporate taxonomy.

Publishing Service Applications

A service application can be consumed with one or more web applications within the local farm, or it can be consumed by web applications in a remote farm.

Before going into more detail, consider some terminology to ensure that you have a clear understanding:

➤ *Publishing a service application* — This means making a service application available for consumption across farms.

➤ *Cross-farm service application* — This is a service application made available to be consumed by remote farms.

At a high level, three things must happen to deploy service applications across farms:

1. You must ensure that the farm that hosts the service application and the farm that needs to consume the service application have exchanged certificates to trust each other.

2. You must publish the service application. To publish a service application, you must go to the Manage Service Applications page in Central Administration, and, from the Ribbon, click the Publish button. This takes you to the Publish Service Application page, where you specify a few settings, as shown in Figure 1-15.

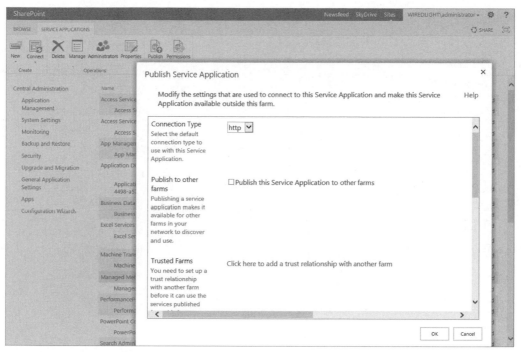

FIGURE 1-15

> **NOTE** *One thing that must be highlighted is the Published URL available in the Publish Service Application dialog. This is the URL that used in the remote farm to locate the service application.*

3. To consume a published service, go to the Manage Service Applications page in the remote farm, and click the Connect button on the Ribbon. Next, choose which type of service you are connecting to, which, in turn, prompts you to enter the URL of the published service, as shown in Figure 1-16. Assuming that the trust has been already set up and properly working, just a service application proxy on the local farm is created to connect to the service application on the remote farm. When the proxy is there, any web application in the local farm can consume the service application from the remote farm.

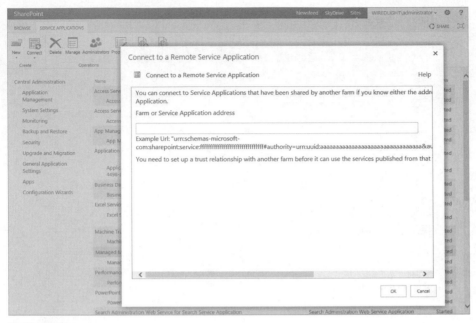

FIGURE 1-16

Not all service applications can be shared between farms. For example, BCS is a cross-farm service application, whereas other service applications are not designed to be shared between farms. Some cross-farm service applications are not recommended for use in wide area network (WAN) environments. Simply put, those cross-farm service applications that use Windows Communication Foundation (WCF) endpoints are the ones that use ASMX web service.

Table 1-3 lists current recommendations for deploying service applications across farms or over a WAN.

TABLE 1-3: Recommendations for Deploying Service Applications

SERVICE APPLICATIONS	CROSS-FARM	WAN-FRIENDLY
Access Services	No	N/A
Access Services 2010	No	N/A
App Management Service	No	N/A
Business Data Connectivity Service	Yes	With limitations
Excel Services	No	N/A
Machine Translation Services	Yes	Yes
Managed Metadata Service	Yes	Yes

PerformancePoint	No	N/A
PowerPoint Automation	No	N/A
Search	Yes	Yes
Secure Store Service	Yes	No
State Service	No	N/A
Usage and Health Data Collection	No	N/A
User Profile	Yes	No
Visio Graphics Service	No	N/A
Word Automation Services	No	N/A
Work Management Service	No	N/A
Subscription Settings Service	No	N/A

MULTITENANCY HOSTING ARCHITECTURE

Multitenancy is the ability to host unique deployments for multiple tenants on the same SharePoint 2013 server farm by isolating the data, operational services, and management of a tenant from other tenants using the same farm.

The traditional (and most accurate) definition of *Multitenancy* is a single instance of software that services multiple organizations or clients, virtually partitioning its data and configuration, which enables clients to work within a customized application instance. The features and capabilities delivered by SharePoint Server 2013 contribute to supporting true multitenant architectures that are useful not only to hosting providers, but also equally to the enterprise.

When carefully planned and applied within the enterprise, Multitenancy is one of many solutions that contribute to reduced cost, complexity, and overall management.

In SharePoint 2013, multitenancy requires configuring the server farm, and its service applications, to support multiple tenants. To achieve Multitenancy–based architectures requires a combination of the following key capabilities:

- ➤ Site subscriptions
- ➤ Service application partitioning
- ➤ Tenant administration
- ➤ Feature packs

Now look at each of these in more detail.

Site Subscriptions

Site subscriptions are the core of the hosting feature set in SharePoint 2013. Site collections are grouped together by their subscription ID, which forms the basis of the tenant. The subscription ID is used to map features, settings, and service partitions to tenants. In other words, site subscriptions can be loosely described as a collection of sites that subscribe to a set of service partitions, settings, and individual features. Site subscriptions are also known as *tenants*.

You can approach site subscriptions as a loose association of content. In the object model, site subscriptions are represented through `Microsoft.SharePoint.SPSiteSubscription`.

The limitations and constraints of this are as follows:

➤ Site collections grouped within a site subscription cannot span farms.

➤ Site subscriptions with site collections that span web applications cannot be managed through the Tenant Administration template. (More information about this is described in the section "Tenant Administration.")

➤ Multiple site subscriptions are supported within a single web application and content database.

➤ Services can be partitioned and served to specific tenants to enable granular data isolation.

➤ Tenants can consume non-partitioned services.

Service Application Partitioning

Data, usage, and operational isolation are provided through new service application capabilities. The capability to partition many of the SharePoint 2013 service applications enables individual and unique tenants to consume the service application, while maintaining logical separation from other tenants also consuming from the partitioned service application.

To create a new partitioned service application in SharePoint Server 2013, an administrator must follow these steps:

1. Create a partitioned Service Application using the `-partitionmode` flag.

2. Create a partitioned Service Application proxy using the `-partitionmode` flag.

Figure 1-17 shows the relationships between these concepts in a hosting model.

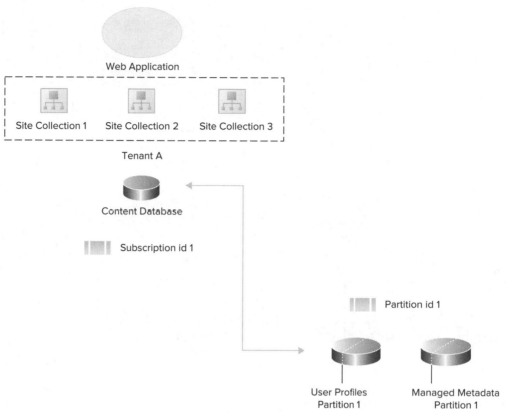

FIGURE 1-17

SharePoint 2013 uses the Subscription ID for the site subscription to map to the Partition ID, which represents the subset of data exposed to the tenant.

Figure 1-18 shows a practical implementation of Multitenancy in SharePoint 2013. This implementation has one web application with two tenants, each owning a few site collections within the same web application. The web application consumes service applications that are multitenant-aware, and service data for each tenant is partitioned in the back-end database (that is, data isolation). Although both tenants use the same service application, they have no visibility to the other tenant's data because the service data is partitioned.

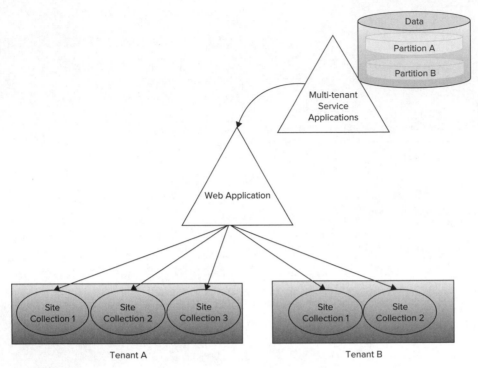

FIGURE 1-18

Two things about the Figure 1-18 are highlighted here:

First, not all service applications can be partitioned. That's because some services do not need to store tenant data, so they can be shared across multiple tenants without risk of exposing tenant-specific data. Table 1-4 lists the service applications that don't include the capability to be partitioned. Second, a service application that cannot be partitioned is not a multi-tenant aware service application.

Service Applications can be configured to partition data that resides in a single database.

TABLE 1-4: Service Applications That Cannot Be Partitioned

SERVICE APPLICATIONS	MULTITENANT-AWARE
Access Services	No
Access Services 2010	No
App Management Service	No
Business Data Connectivity Service	Yes
Excel Services	No
Machine Translation Services	Yes
Managed Metadata Service	Yes

PerformancePoint	No
PowerPoint Automation	No
Search	Yes
Secure Store Service	Yes
State Service	No
Usage and Health Data Collection	No
User Profile	Yes
Visio Graphics Service	No
Word Automation Services	Yes
Work Management Service	No
Subscription Settings Service	Yes

If you decide to keep all your tenants in one web application using different site collections, several new or improved site collection features are at your disposal:

➤ Additional support is provided for vanity domains using host header site collections (that is, multiple root-level site collections within a web application).

➤ Host header site collections support managed paths. (For example, site collections `http://foo.com` and `http://foo.com/sites/foo` for tenant A, and `http://bar.com` and `http://bar.com/sites/bar` for tenant B can coexist in the same web application.)

➤ Additional wildcard is now available for managed host header paths in SharePoint 2013.

➤ Load balancer Single Sockets Layer (SSL) termination support is included.

➤ The Windows PowerShell cmdlet `New-SPSite` accepts a parameter that enables you to target a site collection to reside in a specific content database.

➤ Pluggable custom code (Site Creation Provider) enables you to enforce database organization across all your tenants. This is basically to ensure that if a tenant creates a new site collection, that site collection ends up in the database you want, not just following the out-of-the-box, round-robin algorithm.

➤ Sandboxed solutions enable each tenant to deploy custom code to their own site collections.

Although partitioned service applications and new features of site collections in SharePoint 2013 play an important role in the overall multi-tenant architecture, in reality, many features enable Multitenancy in SharePoint 2013. Following are some of these features:

➤ Microsoft SharePoint Foundation Subscription Settings Service adds multitenant functionality for service applications (available in all editions of SharePoint).

➤ Feature sets are groups of product features allowed by farm administrators for tenants to activate and use.

➤ Site subscriptions are a logical group of site collections that can share settings, features, and service data. Each site subscription has a subscription ID that is used to map features, services, and sites to tenants, as well as partitioning their service data.

➤ Centralized and delegated administration allows the delegation of certain Central Administration tasks to tenant administrators using their own administration user interface, while the main Central Administration site is used to administer the entire SharePoint installation.

Tenant Administration

The management of site subscriptions occurs through a new administration site template, Tenant Administration, which is used to manage many aspects of the site collections that consume services from their assigned subscription. Multiple tenants are supported within a single server farm environment, which enables IT administrators to centrally manage the deployment of both features and capabilities. In addition, the IT administrator can delegate specific administrative control of site collections contained within a tenant, to the respective owner or business administrator.

For example, in a hosting scenario, the organization hosting the server farm environment manages farm-level settings and configurations. The consumer (or tenant) can manage the site collections, and, specifically, delegated features and capabilities (such as services). Figure 1-19 shows the Tenant Administration user interface.

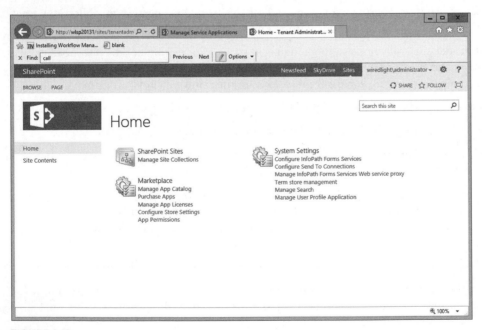

FIGURE 1-19

To create a new site subscription object in SharePoint Server 2013, an administrator must create an SPSiteSubscription object and then create and add an SPSite object to SPSiteSubscription.

To create a new SPSiteSubscription object, follow these steps:

1. Open the Microsoft SharePoint 2013 Management Shell by clicking Start ⇨ All Programs ⇨ Microsoft SharePoint 2013 ⇨ Microsoft SharePoint 2013 Management Shell.

2. Within the Management Shell, at the command prompt, enter the following Windows PowerShell commands:

```
$subscription=New-SPSiteSubscription

$site=New-SPSite -Url http://AdventureWorks.com/sites
  /TenantAdministration -Template TenantAdmin#0
  -OwnerEmail someone@example.com
  -OwnerAlias Domain\Username
  -SiteSubscription $subscription
Set-SPSiteAdministration -Identity http://AdventureWorks.com/sites
  /TenantAdministration
  -AdministrationSiteType TenantAdministration
```

Feature Packs

Feature packs are a method that enables the developer to group a collection of individual features (site- or web-scoped) into a larger overall package. Feature packs provide functionality or capabilities to individual site subscriptions in a multitenant model, enabling or preventing access to certain functionality or solutions on a tenant-by-tenant basis.

SEARCH ARCHITECTURE

SharePoint Server 2013 search architecture has been greatly improved with a new set of components to improve scalability and redundancy provided by the SharePoint server farm.

As you can see in Figure 1-20, the search architecture of SharePoint Server 2013 is now spread across four primary areas: crawl and content processing, analytics, index and query processing components, and search administration.

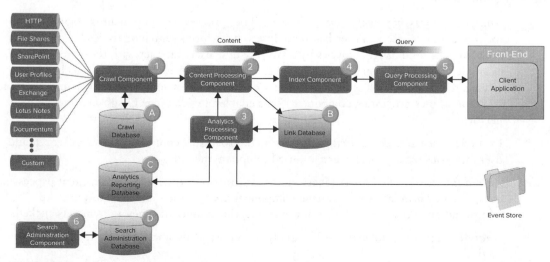

FIGURE 1-20

Now let's have a look at each of these areas in more detail.

Crawl and Content Processing Components

In SharePoint Server 2013, the crawl and content processing architecture is responsible for crawling content from support content sources, delivering crawled items and their meta data to the content processing component, and processing the content. These break down into the following components

➤ *Crawl component* — The crawl component crawls configured content sources using the associated connectors and protocol handlers for the target content source. The actual content and associated meta data is then passed to the content processing component.

➤ *Crawl database* — The crawl database is used by the crawl component to store information about crawled items and to track information and history of crawls that have taken place.

➤ *Content processing component* — The content processing component receives items, processes and parses items using format handlers and iFilters, and transforms items into artifacts that can be added to the search index. This includes mapping extracted properties to properties defined using the search administration component.

➤ *Link database* — The Link database stores information relating to links and URLs found during the content processing process.

SharePoint Server 2013 crawl and content processing search architecture is flexible in that it enables you to scale out the crawl and content processing operations by seamlessly adding additional crawl component instances to your search topology.

Analytics Processing Component

In SharePoint Server 2013, the analytics processing component is now directly integrated into the search architecture and is no longer an individual service application. These break down into the following components

➤ *Analytics processing component* — The analytics processing component is responsible for processing search and user-based analytics. It performs search analytics by analyzing crawled items and usage analytics by analyzing how users interact with those items. For example, user interaction information is retrieved from the event store that has been aggregated from usage files on each of the web front ends in your server farm, and analyzed by the analytics processing component. This enables a wide range of sub-analyses to be performed.

➤ *Content processing component* — The content processing component receives search and user analytics results that in turn are used to update the index.

➤ *Link database* — The Link database stores information extracted by the content processing component. The analytics processing component updates the Link database to store additional analytical information, for example, the number of times an item was clicked.

➤ *Analytics reporting database* — The analytics reporting database stores the result of usage analysis.

SharePoint Server 2013 analytics processing search architecture is flexible in that it enables you to scale out analytics processing operations by seamlessly adding additional analytics component instances to your search topology. This enables analytics processing to complete faster.

Index and Query Processing

In SharePoint Server 2013, the indexing and query processing architecture is responsible for writing processed items received from the content processing component, handling queries and returning result sets for the query processing component, and moving indexed content based on changes to the search topology.

As shown in Figure 1-21, SharePoint Server 2013 search maintains an index of all processed content (including analytical information). The indexing component can scale using the following features:

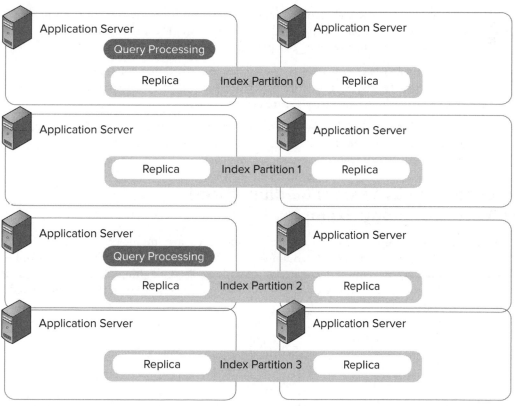

FIGURE 1-21

➤ *Indexing partition* — Index partition is a logical portion of the entire search index. Index partitions enable horizontal scaling in that it enables you spread your entire index over multiple servers in your server farm.

➤ *Index components* — An individual index partition can be supported by one or more index components. These index components host a copy or replica of the index partition. A primary index component is responsible for updating the index partition, whereas passive index components are used for fault tolerance and increased query throughput. This, in essence, supports vertical scaling of your search topology.

➤ *Query processing component* — The query processing component is responsible for receiving queries from web front ends, analyzing and processing the query, and submitting the processed query to the index component.

Search Administration Component

In SharePoint Server 2013, the search administration component is responsible for running the system processes based on the configuration and search topology. The search administration component breaks down into the following components:

➤ *Search administration component* — The search administration component executes the system processes required for search, performs changes to the search topology, and coordinates activities of the various search components in your search topology.

➤ *Search administration database* — The search administration database stores search configuration information. This includes topology, crawl rules, query rules, managed property mappings, content sources, and crawl schedules.

Multi-Purpose (with Search) Medium-Sized Search Farm Topology Example

Figure 1-22 shows an example of a medium-sized search server farm topology. There are a few things to consider here. First, the term "medium-sized" refers to the number of items that can be handled by the search subsystems of the SharePoint topology. Second, although the farm shows the web tier and application tier, for this section ignore those and focus purely on the search-related aspects of this topology.

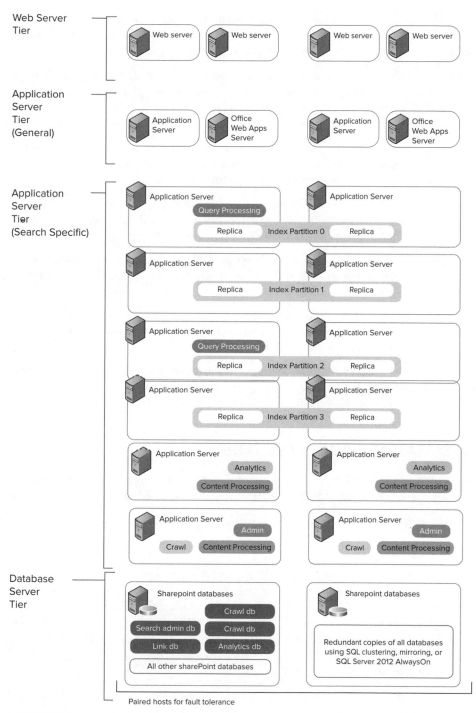

Web Server Tier

Application Server Tier (General)

Application Server Tier (Search Specific)

Database Server Tier

FIGURE 1-22

Third, this medium-sized search farm topology, based on the TechNet recommendation at `http://www.microsoft.com/en-us/download/details.aspx?id=30383`, can support approximately 40 million items in the index. Take a look at the key elements relating to this search topology:

➤ *Search databases* — Microsoft recommends fault tolerance at the database tier to keep your environment up in the case of a database tier failure. Although only one SQL cluster is recommended, keep in mind that the closer you get to 40 million items in the index, the more you should be thinking of moving search-related databases to a dedicated SQL cluster.

➤ *Admin and crawl components* — The admin and crawl components have been placed on two application servers. This provides fault tolerance to the administration components and increases capacity of the crawl operations over multiple servers.

➤ *Content processing components* — Items received from crawl operations are processed on four application servers. This contributes to decreasing the overall crawl time taken and thereby increases the search result freshness.

➤ *Analytics components* — The analytics component has been placed on two application servers. This provides fault tolerance in the event of failure of an application server hosting the analytics component.

➤ *Indexing components* — The global search index has been split into four partitions, and each partition resides on two application servers. This provides both fault tolerance and improves query latency and query throughput.

➤ *Query processing* — The query processing components have been placed on two application servers. This provides fault tolerance to the query processing components and increases the capacity to process queries received from the web server tier.

SQL SERVER DATABASE ARCHITECTURE

SharePoint Server 2013 relies heavily on well-planned and performant database tier. As a result, the Microsoft product group has invested heavily to improve the performance and manageability of the databases used by the SharePoint server farm.

Database Topologies

Determining the appropriate topology for your database server is an important step to ensure adequate overall SharePoint 2013 platform performance. As you begin to plan your hardware, you should understand that SharePoint 2013 is a 64-bit–only application and requires the 64-bit version of Windows and SQL Server products. Either SQL Server 2008 R2 Service Pack 1 or SQL Server 2012 are supported on Windows Server 2008 R2 Service Pack 1 or Windows Server 2012.

Single-Server Deployment

A *single-server deployment* configuration is recommended under the following circumstances:

> ➤ For small-to-moderate user volumes, and when the number of concurrent sessions is easily handled by the processing capability of the database server

> ➤ For developers who must develop custom solutions that integrate with SharePoint 2013

> ➤ When evaluating SharePoint 2013

The single-server deployment configuration is the easiest to install and maintain. The default SQL Server installation options result in this deployment topology. During the evaluation, if you find that this deployment configuration meets the needs of your organization, you should continue with this deployment configuration, knowing that you can upgrade hardware or add additional server instances later when demand increases. Figure 1-23 shows an example of a single-server deployment configuration.

All roles on one server, including SQL Server

FIGURE 1-23

If you use a design based on a single SQL Server instance, you should consider the use of SQL Server connection aliases to allow seamless migration to a new database server topology (such as Failover Clustering or Database Mirroring).

Through the use of a *connection alias*, you can keep the application configuration the same. However, you must instruct the underlying operating system to look somewhere else for the database.

You can create an alias using one of two utilities:

> ➤ SQL Server Configuration Manager

> ➤ SQL Server Client Network Utility

> **NOTE** *To learn more about configuring aliases, see* http://msdn.microsoft
> .com/en-us/library/ms188635.aspx.

Standard Server Deployment

In a *standard server deployment*, two database servers serve SharePoint databases in either a Failover Clustering or Database Mirroring design. Figure 1-24 shows an example of a standard server deployment configuration.

The standard deployment configuration is recommended for moderate user volumes where demand for processing is evenly spaced throughout the day, and the number of concurrent sessions is easily handled by the processing capability of the servers.

In addition to greater resiliency, the standard deployment scenario can offer improved performance over the single-server deployment. For example, in a Database Mirroring design, the load can be distributed across the principal and mirroring

Web servers

Application servers running all service application roles

All databases

FIGURE 1-24

server, therefore mitigating common strains to include processing resources such as CPU time, memory, and disk access when they are hosted on the same computer. Some SharePoint operations are resource-intensive, so running these on separate servers can reduce the competition for processing resources. In addition, the footprint of a SharePoint database might be small at first, but disk space requirements and I/O subsystem utilization can grow significantly at run time.

When you are deciding whether to choose a single-server deployment or a standard server deployment, consider the following points based on your hardware configuration:

➤ Processing resources

➤ Memory resources

➤ Disk space availability

➤ I/O capacity

➤ Redundancy

If you find that this deployment configuration meets the needs of your organization, you should continue with this deployment configuration, knowing that you can upgrade hardware or add additional server instances later if demand increases.

Web servers

Scale-Out Server Deployment

In a *scale-out server* deployment, multiple SQL Servers in a Failover Clustering or Database Mirroring configuration support SharePoint databases. Topologies include Active, Active, Passive (AAp) Failover Clustering topologies, or two distinct Database Mirroring pairs. Figure 1-25 shows an example of a scale-out server deployment configuration.

Application servers running all service application roles

A scale-out deployment enables workload distribution in high-volume environments. In a scale-out deployment, each back-end database server in the deployment is referred to as a *node*.

All databases

FIGURE 1-25

A scale-out server deployment configuration is recommended for the following circumstances:

➤ For high-volume user loads, in which activity is measured in concurrent users, or in the complexity of operations that take a long time to process or render (such as high-capacity search scenarios)

➤ For high-availability scenarios, in which it is important that the SharePoint environment does not encounter unplanned downtime or become unavailable

➤ When you want to improve the performance of scheduled operations or service applications

By hosting your SharePoint databases on an instance that is part of a failover cluster, you can enhance the fault tolerance of your environment. Failover clustering is also possible for standard deployments, but typically there is less need for failover clustering when the environment is not configured for high-availability scenarios (such as environments with scale-out deployments).

You must determine and document carefully your availability needs, and test the solution to ensure that it provides the expected availability. Table 1-5 lists supported and non-supported high-availability configurations.

TABLE 1-5: Supported and Nonsupport High-Availability Configurations

CONFIGURATION	SUPPORTABILITY STATEMENT
Failover Clustering	Supported
Log Shipping	Supported
Database Mirroring	Supported
Transactional Replication	Not Supported
Merge Replication	Not Supported
Snapshot Replication	Not Supported

SharePoint 2013 Databases

If you're new to SharePoint 2013, you may be astounded to see the number of databases used by SharePoint 2013. Don't be alarmed; this is by design and is vital to the performance your SharePoint server farm. Table 1-6 provides an overview of the databases in SharePoint 2013.

TABLE 1-6: SharePoint 2013 Core and Related Databases

CATEGORY	DATABASE NAME	NUMBER	DESCRIPTION
App Management	App License	Single	Stores the App licenses and permissions downloaded from the global marketplace.
Business Data Connectivity		Single	Stores External Content types and Related objects.
Core Databases	Configuration Database	Single	Contains data about all SharePoint databases, all Internet Information Services (IIS) websites or Web applications, trusted solutions, Web Part Packages, site templates, and Web application and farm settings specific to SharePoint 2013 Preview, such as default quota and blocked file types.

continues

TABLE 1-6 *(continued)*

CATEGORY	DATABASE NAME	NUMBER	DESCRIPTION
	Central Administration Content	Single	Content database for the Central Administration site.
	Content Databases	Multiple	Stores all site content, including site documents or files in document libraries, list data, web part properties, audit logs, sandboxed solutions, and usernames and rights. All the data for a specific site resides in one content database. Content databases can contain more than one site collection. Also stores data for Office Web Applications, if in use.
Machine Translation Services		Single	Stores information about pending and completed batch document translations with file extensions that are enabled.
Managed Metadata Service		Single	Stores managed meta data and syndicated content types.
PerformancePoint		Single	Stores temporary objects and persisted user comments and settings.
PowerPivot		Single	Stores data refresh schedules and PowerPivot usage data copied from the central usage data collection database. PowerPivot for SharePoint 2013 requires SQL Server 2012 Analysis Services, Business Intelligence, or Enterprise Edition.
Project Server		Single	Stores all the data for a single Project Web App (PWA), along with the following: All Project and Portfolio Management (PPM) data Time tracking and Timesheet data Aggregated SharePoint project site data
Search	Search Administration	Single	Hosts the Search application configuration and access control list (ACL) for the crawl component.

	Link	Single	Stores the information extracted by the content processing component and the click-through information.
	Analytics	Multiple	Stores the results for usage analysis reports and extracts information from the Link database when needed.
	Crawl	Multiple	Stores the state of the crawled data and the crawl history.
Secure Store	Secure Store		Stores and maps credentials such as account names and passwords.
Subscription Settings Service		Single	Stores features and settings information for hosted customers. This database is not created by default but must be created by using Windows PowerShell or SQL Server.
State Service		Multiple	Stores temporary state information for InfoPath Forms Services, Exchange, the chart web part, and Visio Services.
SQL Server	Master	Single	Records all system-level information for a SQL Server instance, including logins, configurations, and other databases.
	Model	Single	Used as the template for all databases created In an instance.
	MSDB	Single	Records operators, and used by SQL Server Agent to schedule alerts and jobs.
	TempDB	Single	Holds all temporary tables and temporary stored procedures and fills any other temporary storage needs. The tempdb database is re-created every time the SQL Server instance is started.
Usage and Health	Usage and Health Database		Stores health monitoring and usage data temporarily, and also used for reporting and diagnostics. The Usage database is the only SharePoint database that can be queried directly and have schema modified by either Microsoft or third-party applications.

continues

TABLE 1-6 *(continued)*

CATEGORY	DATABASE NAME	NUMBER	DESCRIPTION
User Profiles	Profile		Stores and manages users and their social information.
	Synchronization		Stores configuration and staging data for use when profile data is synchronized with directory services such as Active Directory.
	Social Tagging		Stores social tags and notes created by users along with their respective URLs.
Word Conversion			Stores information about pending and completed document conversions.
Word Automation			Stores information about pending and completed document conversions.

SharePoint 2013 uses a variety of databases (refer to Table 1-6). The databases in your environment depend on a combination of the SKU and service applications you deploy. With proper database planning, you can meet current and future needs related to scale and performance. Make sure you understand what each database purpose is, as well as its characteristics, to provide seamless scalability and performance required by your database server tier.

CLOUD-HOSTED ARCHITECTURES

SharePoint Online is available in two unique offerings (Standard and Dedicated) tailored to an individual organization's size, requirements, and objectives — each provided at a per-user monthly fee. The SharePoint Online offerings can be differentiated at a high level based on capabilities, flexibility, and pricing.

SharePoint Online provides a rich feature set and collection of capabilities to both serve as an organization's primary collaborative platform, to augment an organization's existing on-premise deployment to support lightweight extranet or external sharing scenarios, or to enable collaboration outside of an organization's firewall.

SharePoint Online delivers SharePoint 2013 as a cloud service through Microsoft data centers across the globe, enabling people to share ideas and expertise, build custom sites and solutions, and quickly locate information to respond to changing business needs — without the need to deploy SharePoint in their own data centers. In addition to the services and solutions provided by SharePoint, SharePoint Online provides high availability, comprehensive security, and simplified management, so organizations can be confident in choosing it for a collaboration platform.

SharePoint Online is designed to support some of the most complex user distribution patterns, whether users are centrally located or geographically dispersed. Without the need to purchase and deploy servers, organizations can quickly deploy SharePoint to remote offices, or support growth as the result of acquisitions. This flexibility enables users to quickly benefit from SharePoint with minimal cost and delay.

Security Features

SharePoint Online provides business-class reliability and flexibility through a set of features that ensure a secure collaborative environment. SharePoint Online provides the following set of common features:

➤ *Secure access* — SharePoint Online is provided through 128-bit Secure Sockets Layer (SSL) or Transport Layer Security (TLS) encryption.

➤ *Intrusion* — SharePoint Online is continuously monitored for unusual or suspicious activity.

➤ *Audit* — Microsoft regularly assesses the SharePoint Online infrastructure to ensure compliance policies and antivirus signatures are available. Configuration settings and security updates include the following:

   ➤ Achieved ISO 27001 certification

   ➤ Completed Statement on Audit Status (SAS) 70 Type I and II audits

   ➤ Added controls that assist customers in complying with Health Insurance Portability and Accountability Act (HIPAA) and Family Educational Rights and Privacy Act (FERPA)

   ➤ Achieved the European Union (EU) Safe Harbor seal

Identity Features

SharePoint Online provides multiple methods for the management and consumption of identity — whether a small-to-medium business without an existing identity infrastructure or a larger organization using Active Directory Domain Services (ADDS).

Organizations with an existing identity infrastructure such as ADDS can implement a Single Sign-On (SSO) approach to authentication by configuring Active Directory Federation Services (ADFS) to federate with the Microsoft Online Services Federation gateway. Users whose identities are derived from the federated domain can use their existing credentials to automatically authenticate to the service.

Microsoft Online Services provides the Directory Synchronization Tool to facilitate directory synchronization. The Directory Synchronization Tool provides one-way directory synchronization of all user accounts and mail-enabled contacts and groups from your local ADDS directory service to Microsoft Online Services. The Directory Synchronization Tool should be installed on a server joined to the ADDS Forest to be synchronized and capable of reaching all domain controllers for each domain in your forest.

Administration Model

Microsoft Online Services provides a delegated and granular administration model through role-based access. User accounts can be assigned either global or password administrator rights that provide either full access to all settings of the service, or the capability to read company and user information, reset user passwords, and manage support requests.

The administration of SharePoint Online occurs through a web portal where the SharePoint Online administrator creates and manages site collections, as shown in Figure 1-26.

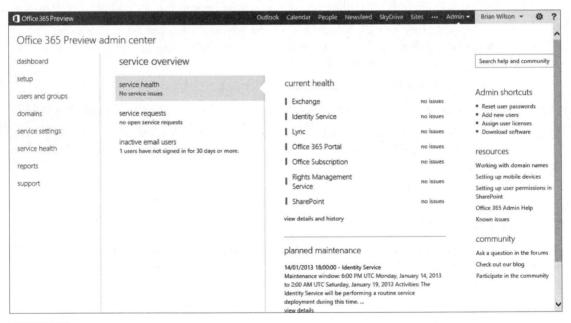

FIGURE 1-26

The SharePoint Online administrative web portal is independent from the overall Microsoft Online Services administration portal. As shown in Figure 1-27, the SharePoint Online administrative web portal enables an administrator to manage site collections, configure Send To connections, configure InfoPath Forms Services and a web service proxy, manage user profiles, and manage the Term Store used by the service's site collections.

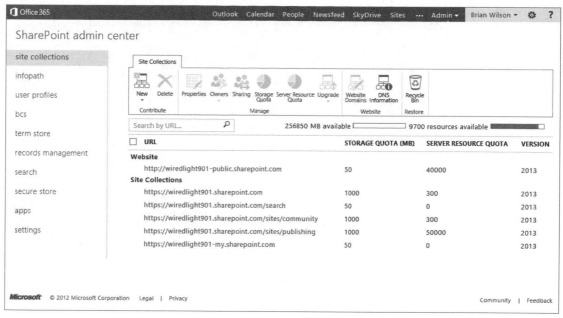

FIGURE 1-27

SUMMARY

This chapter provides a broad view of the architecture in SharePoint 2013. It provides a good overview to help developers and architects understand where your customizations and add-ons "live." Throughout the rest of the book, you learn more details about these new features and learn how to program against these features to build robust and capable SharePoint 2013 applications.

2

What's New in SharePoint 2013

INTRODUCTION TO SHAREPOINT 2013

The year 2012 was definitely a revolution in Microsoft history. If you look at the list of Microsoft deliverables in this year, the list is incredible. Beside all the enhanced and new features targeting end users, development in SharePoint 2013 is different than in previous versions. In SharePoint 2013, the emphasis is more on standard web technologies such as JavaScript and HTML, client-side programming, and remote calls. To accomplish this, SharePoint 2013 offers developers various options for extending the out-of-the-box capabilities of the product and building business solutions with no or minimal use of server-side code.

Each of the new features and development options in SharePoint 2013 depends on many factors that a developer needs to know up front. That's what you should take away after reading this chapter.

DEPLOYMENT SCENARIOS

In SharePoint 2013, the physical location of the SharePoint server farm plays an important role in the development pattern you should follow and the options available to you. As the developer the first question you should ask yourself is which deployment scenario you are building your custom solutions for. SharePoint 2013 offers four different types of deployment scenarios: on-premise, Office 365, hosted, and hybrid deployment.

On-Premise Deployment

In this deployment scenario, SharePoint sits behind the corporate firewall and is maintained by your IT department. Just like previous versions of SharePoint, this scenario offers you a lot of flexibility for development options and the tools you use.

Office 365 Deployment

In this deployment scenario, your SharePoint farm is kept in Office 365 and managed by Microsoft. You can use all the development options and tools available in on-premise deployment (scenario 1), except for running server-side code in apps. Apps are a new mechanism for packaging and deploying your code in SharePoint 2013 and are discussed throughout this chapter.

> **NOTE** *You can use Office 365 and SharePoint Online (SPO) as interchangeable terms in this chapter. In reality, Office 365 is an umbrella term that refers to a bundle of cloud-based products such as SharePoint Online, Office Web Apps, Exchange Online, Lync Online, and Office Suites. You can apply for a free developer tenancy for Office 365. For more information, see the product documentation at* `http://msdn.microsoft.com/en-us/library/ fp179924(v=office.15).aspx.`

Hosted Deployment

Similar to an Office 365 deployment scenario, in hosted deployments your SharePoint server farm is installed and hosted by third-party providers, which may or may not be Microsoft. For example, you can deploy your fully virtualized SharePoint farm to CloudShare, Amazon EC2, or on Windows Azure virtual machines owned by Microsoft. Depending on the vendor hosting your SharePoint farm, your mileage may vary, and your development pattern and options could differ. Some third-party hosting providers offer your own dedicated cloud without sharing it with anyone else, which gives you more options.

Hybrid Deployment

This is the only deployment scenario that spans across your corporate firewall and the cloud. In this scenario, part of the installation is managed internally by corporate IT, and some applications are deployed to another SharePoint farm in the cloud in Office 365 or a third-party hosting provider.

PACKAGING SCENARIOS

Where and how SharePoint is installed and deployed dictates your options in how you can package and deploy your custom code. There are three deployment options: full-trust farm solutions, partial-trust farm solutions, and apps.

Full-Trust Farm Solution

Farm solutions were introduced in SharePoint 2007, and they are only available in on-premise deployments in SharePoint 2013 and some dedicated cloud-based deployments. These types of solutions can contain customizations used across an entire farm. Custom code in full-trust solutions is deployed to the SharePoint web application's \BIN directory or global assembly cache (GAC). Code can be secured using .NET's Code Access Security (CAS) but typically is run in full trust. These types of solutions are added to the farm in SharePoint by an IT pro with console access and deployed by someone with farm administrator rights.

Partial-Trust Sandboxed Solution

This option, introduced in SharePoint 2010, is available in all types of deployment scenarios. Sandboxed solutions are available to all sites across an entire site collection where they were deployed. These types of solutions can be uploaded and deployed by site collection administrators. Sandboxed solutions impose quite a few restrictions on the developer, which are covered in more detail throughout this chapter.

Apps for SharePoint

There is a new way of packaging and deploying your code in SharePoint 2013. This approach is heavily dependent on the notion of isolation and small widgets called apps. If you own a smartphone, you are already familiar with the notion of apps. Apps are built and deployed to target specific business needs, and they are transactional in nature. Apps for SharePoint are different than those built for smartphones because they do not live in SharePoint, and the actual execution doesn't happen in SharePoint. Apps execute in the browser client or on a remote web server; they're granted permission into SharePoint sites via OAuth and communicate over the newly improved SharePoint 2013 CSOM APIs.

Apps, OAuth, and new improvements in CSOM will be covered in more detail shortly. Keep reading!

THE PROGRAMMING MODEL

SharePoint 2013 ships with one fundamental difference in its programming model. In the new programming model, the emphasis is more on cloud computing, standard web technologies such as JavaScript and HTML, and remote access. All new changes are aligned with the company's overall strategy of "Everything has to be available in the cloud."

Before you dive too much into the new changes, first go back a few years in time to refresh your memory about the evolution of customization and coding in SharePoint.

The Evolution of SharePoint Programming

At a high level, Figure 2-1 shows the programming models in SharePoint 2007 and 2010.

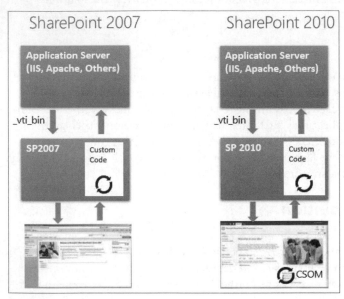

FIGURE 2-1

In SharePoint 2007, your custom code either ran server side in SharePoint or hosted in your own service layer (IIS, Apache, others) working with some areas of the SharePoint object model remotely via built-in web services located in the _vti_bin folder (%COMMONPROGRAMFILES%\Microsoft Shared\web server extensions\12\ISAPI). SharePoint 2007 had a limited client-side object model, which was implemented in the Core.js JavaScript file (which was OWS.js in Windows SharePoint Services 2003). The JavaScript file was referenced from most SharePoint pages and contained limited logic necessary to handle various events on the client without having to modify the out-of-the-box Core.js file. For example, Core.js provided a hook through which additional menu items could be shown in the context menu (ECB), as demonstrated in the following code snippet:

```
function AddDocLibMenuItems(m, ctx)
{
    if (typeof(Custom_AddDocLibMenuItems) != "undefined")
    {
        if (Custom_AddDocLibMenuItems(m, ctx)) return;
    }
    ... // build the rest of OOTB ECB menu items
}
```

By using SharePoint Designer (or Microsoft Office FrontPage in Windows SharePoint Services 2003), developers injected their implementation of Custom_AddDocLibMenuItems function into a SharePoint page, or they could use the Content Editor Web Part (CEWP) to inject the custom JavaScript function into web part pages. Either way, Core.js was calling its function in run time. The problem with this extensibility model was that it was limited and not flexible. For example, if for any reason Core.js is not loaded, your custom function won't work either.

In SharePoint 2010, the Client Side Object Model (CSOM) was substantially improved to address the challenges with client-side programming in the earlier versions of SharePoint. SharePoint 2010 CSOM fundamentally was a Windows Communication Foundation (WCF) service called `Client.svc` and shipped with three different proxies to enable Silverlight, JavaScript, and .NET managed clients (C# or VB.NET) to call into the product remotely. The following code snippet shows how a developer can use the supported proxy for JavaScript (`sp.js`) to execute an asynchronous query against CSOM in SharePoint 2010:

```
            ExecuteOrDelayUntilScriptLoaded(GetTitle, "sp.js");
// Code omitted for brevity
function GetTitle() {
    //Retrieve current client context
    context = SP.ClientContext.get_current();

    //Load the site
    site = context.get_web();
    context.load(site);

    //Execute asynchronously with callbacks for successful or failed calls
    context.executeQueryAsync(onQuerySucceeded, onQueryFailed);
}
```

Challenges with CSOM in SharePoint 2010

Developers had two major issues using CSOM in SharePoint 2010.

First, direct calls to `Client.svc` were not supported, and all the calls had to go through the supported entry points (for example, `sp.js`). Proxies were only available for .NET managed, Silverlight, and JavaScript clients, so platforms or devices that didn't understand either of these technologies could not call SharePoint remotely.

Second, CSOM covered only APIs in the `Microsoft.SharePoint.dll` and limited workloads in the product. To overcome this limitation, developers had no option but to rely on `ListData.svc`, jQuery against built-in ASMX Web Services, or server-side code to get better coverage of the product's object model.

Developers preferred to use CSOM from managed code (for example, C# and VB.NET) more than from JavaScript. That's because they could program against strongly typed objects and experience compile-time type IntelliSense and easier debugging. JavaScript development against CSOM was not easy. The code was harder to write and debug because the calls had to be asynchronous with no compile-time type checking and IntelliSense.

The next section discusses why you should think twice before writing server-side code in SharePoint 2013.

Challenges with Server-Side Code

Microsoft has several reasons to push client-side programming and remote access in SharePoint 2013. The most candid reason is that the root cause of most SharePoint performance and security issues has been the server-side code included in farm or sandboxed solutions. Now play the role of devil's advocate for a second. If you were a software company building a platform for others to host their products in it, and potentially make money, how would you feel if someone writes a web part that brings your baby to its knees? How would you feel if someone says your product is slow, but in reality it's someone else's code or misconfiguration that has made you look bad?

Another problem with the SharePoint server-side object model is that it's difficult to learn and it lacks cross-technology interoperability with other non-Microsoft technologies. In many cases, SharePoint had problems catching up with the newer Microsoft technologies, too. How many times as a developer have you suffered from the SharePoint object model being tightly coupled with a specific version of the .NET Framework or Windows Workflow Foundation? How many times did you wish that your PHP buddy could give you a hand in your SharePoint projects?

The new programming model in SharePoint 2013 introduces a much quicker ramp-up time for developers who may not know SharePoint APIs and enables those developers who use other technologies to be productive. Now, you can build solutions that are a lot more technology-agnostic and loosely coupled from the product. This means you can choose your preferred scripting language (PHP, JavaScript, LAMP, and so on) or any version of ASP.NET (ASP.NET Web Forms, MVC, and Web Pages), build apps for SharePoint, and use remote calls to accomplish various tasks that were previously only possible through the server-side object model.

In addition to perception and tactical challenges, server-side solutions often had lots to deploy and required direct access to the server. This is fine in on-premise deployment scenarios, but it is not an option in the cloud unless you have your own private server. You could get around this limitation by using sandboxed solutions, but sandboxed solutions had their own issues. First, there are limited sets of operations you can do in the sandboxed because only a subset of the server-side SharePoint APIs is available in sandboxed solutions. Sandboxed solutions can't execute for longer than 30 seconds, and they cannot exceed a certain amount of resource usage per day. In addition, server-side code cannot make calls/requests to externally hosted web services. However, developers can use client-side based solutions (using JavaScript or Silverlight) to call external services and even make cross-domain calls using techniques such as HTTP post messages.

Another common developer challenge pre-SharePoint 2013 was solution upgrading. WSP versioning, feature upgrading, assembly versioning, and redirections, you name it, were all there, but it is fair to say that it was not easy to manage the life cycle of complex solutions and their features in enterprise-scale projects where developers had to upgrade the solutions over time to meet the ever-changing business requirements. So, unless the developer put a lot of forethought into it, upgrading and uninstalling solutions was not a great story in the earlier versions of SharePoint. SharePoint 2013 changes that with a robust infrastructure to support the upgrade and uninstallation of apps, and to ensure that if an app upgrade fails, it is rolled back, so the hosting SharePoint website isn't left in an undesirable state without any burden on the side of the developer.

Now that you understand the challenges, it's time to discuss the improvements.

The New Programming Model

If you have been reading this chapter from the beginning, you may wonder what makes the new programming model so special and different in SharePoint 2013 compared to its predecessors. Couldn't you write client-side code and use standard web technologies in previous versions of the product?

Figure 2-2 shows the new programming model.

In SharePoint 2013 the server-side code runs off the SharePoint server farm via declarative hooks such as apps, declarative workflow, and remote events, which then communicate back to SharePoint using CSOM or REST. In other words, in the new programming model, the emphasis is on client-side code and remote access. Depending on your deployment scenarios (which were discussed earlier in this chapter), you can still use sandboxed and farm solutions to push server-side code to SharePoint 2013; however, Microsoft recommends that developers follow the new app model as the preferred way of building their custom applications for SharePoint 2013. The message is, "don't make any new sandboxed solutions" and "build new farm solutions only if you absolutely have to" (and, of course, if your deployment scenario allows you to deploy farm solutions).

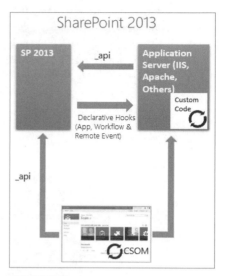

FIGURE 2-2

In SharePoint 2013, `_vti_bin/client.svc` is now aliased with `_api`, which makes it easier to reach out to the service endpoint. Microsoft also made the `client.svc` and made it a full-blown OData-compliant service.

> **NOTE** *OData is the leading industry protocol for performing CRUD (Create, Read, Update, and Delete) operations against data. CRUD operations map to standard HTTP verbs like Get, Put, Update, Delete, and Merge. OData payloads are based on popular standards such as Atom (for reading web resources) and AtomPub (for creating and updating resources). OData is available for many non-Microsoft platforms such as iOS and Android and is used in well-known data sources such as Netflix. For more information, see* `http://www.odata.org`.

If you have been working with SharePoint long enough, you probably remember that in SharePoint 2003 you could use Windows SharePoint Services Remote Procedure Call (RPC) protocol to make HTTP GET requests (only HTTP GET) to the `OWSSVR.dll` ISAPI extension. For example, if you type in the following URL, it exports the schema of a list specified by the GUID and renders it in CAML format:

```
http://Tailspintoys/sites/marketing/_vti_bin/owssvr.dll?Cmd=ExportList&List=
e6a9bb54-da25-102b-9a03-2db401e887ec
```

URLs play an important role in SharePoint. Microsoft has been attempting to make it easier for users to get to SharePoint data for a long time; some of those attempts are still there in the new version (for example, Export to Excel in a list). However, due to restrictions in the design patterns and infamous protocols used in such patterns, the attempts have not been successful. The basic promise behind OData (as the protocol and enabler) and REST (as the design pattern) is to make SharePoint data accessible to just about any other platform and any type of device via URL and standard HTTP verbs.

> **NOTE** `ListData.svc` *is still there in SharePoint 2013 to ensure SharePoint 2010 code against CSOM can migrate to SharePoint 2013 without any major problems. It's there for backwards compatibility. The message, however, is that you should use* `client.svc` *moving forward.*

Figure 2-3 shows an architectural diagram representing the remote API changes in SharePoint 2013 discussed in this section.

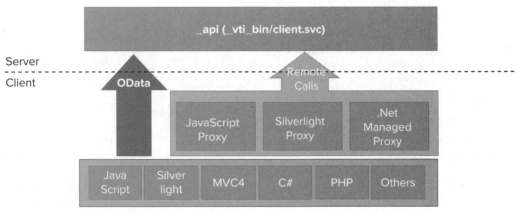

FIGURE 2-3

To use the new client-side OData service in SharePoint 2013, you construct a RESTful HTTP request against `client.svc`, which maps to an HTTP verb and corresponds to the CSOM API you want to use. In response, you get an Atom XML (default type) or JavaScript Object Notation (JSON) that can be easily converted to a nested object. The following example demonstrates how you can use REST to query the Contacts list and retrieve an item where the ID equals 1:

```
http://Tailspintoys.com/_api/web/lists/getByTitle('Contacts')/
getItemByStringId('1')
```

The following code snippet demonstrates an example of how you can use JavaScript and REST to delete an item from the Contacts list. First, you build a REST URL by concatenating the `id` parameter passed to the JavaScript function with `_spPageContextInfo.webServerRelativeUrl` that's available to you when you use CSOM in JavaScript. Then, you send a request to the SharePoint web server using the jQuery `$.ajax` function using the HTTP DELETE verb. Finally, you register the callback handlers for success and error operations, and the call is executed asynchronously.

```
removeItem = function (id) {
    $.ajax(
        {
            url: _spPageContextInfo.webServerRelativeUrl +
                "/_api/web/lists/getByTitle('Contacts')/
                getItemByStringId('" +
```

```
                            id + "')",
                    type: "DELETE",
                    headers: {
                        "accept": "application/json",
                        "X-RequestDigest": $("#__REQUESTDIGEST").val(),
                        "IF-MATCH": "*"
                    },
                    success: function (data) {
                        readAll();
                    },
                    error: function (err) {
                        alert(JSON.stringify(err));
                    }
                }
            );
        }
```

Note in the code snippet how the request headers for the HTTP request were created. The code queries the value of the form digest control on the page with the standard name of __REQUESTDIGEST and adds the value to the X-RequestDigest header. This is important to ensure the HTTP requests that modify the content database can pass the form digest, which is SharePoint's inherent security check.

Microsoft also extended CSOM to user profiles, workflow, and search, to name a few, and many other workloads that were only available through server-side APIs in SharePoint 2010. But, that's not all. Microsoft further improved CSOM, so they can support bulk or synchronized operations without causing a significant burden on server performance when SharePoint is used in a production environment with a large user base.

That's enough abstract talking about apps without discussing what they actually are. In the following section you will enter a new world of extensibility in SharePoint 2013 with apps.

THE APP MODEL

The new app model enables you to build applications that act like they are part of SharePoint, but they are not. As mentioned previously, apps run 100 percent outside of the SharePoint server within the context of the client browser (via client-side scripts, REST, and CSOM) or in remote servers hosted in the cloud or your own infrastructure.

When considering apps, you are dealing with two domains: Office 2013 and SharePoint 2013. You can build apps for both products; however, the focus of this chapter, and the rest of this book, is on the apps for SharePoint. There are three types of apps you can build for SharePoint 2013: SharePoint-hosted apps, provider-hosted apps, and Azure auto-hosted apps.

SharePoint-Hosted Apps

SharePoint-hosted apps are available in all deployment scenarios. These types of apps are deployed to SharePoint, and their business logic executes within the client browser. These types of apps cannot interact with other apps because they run in isolation.

Provider-Hosted Apps

Provider-hosted apps are available in all deployment scenarios. These types of apps are deployed to SharePoint, and the bulk of their business logic executes as server-side code external to SharePoint, such as on another web server in the corporate network or in the cloud.

> **NOTE** *Provider-hosted apps require a separate server, in addition to the servers already participating in your farm. You need to consider this in your hardware and software planning exercises in the early stages of your projects.*

A provider-hosted app (also sometimes referred to as a developer-hosted app or self-hosted app) cannot interact with other apps.

Azure Auto-Hosted Apps

Azure auto-hosted apps are available only in the Office 365 deployment scenario. These types of apps are similar to the provider-hosted apps except the external components, which consist of a Windows Azure website and optionally an Azure SQL database, are invisibly provisioned by Office 365. An Azure auto-hosted app cannot interact with other apps. Figure 2-4 shows an end-to-end platform support and tooling experience (Visual Studio, SharePoint Designer, Access, or Napa) across Office 365 and Windows Azure to enable an Azure auto-hosted app model.

FIGURE 2-4

> **NOTE** *The term* cloud-hosted apps *refers to provider-hosted apps and Azure auto-hosted Apps throughout this chapter.*

As a developer or Office 365 customer, you do not need to set up anything to integrate Windows Azure with Office 365. You don't even need to have a Windows Azure account. The integration is already there and provided automatically when you sign up for tenancy in Office 365. When an end user decides to install an Azure auto-hosted app, Office 365 automatically deploys and provisions a copy of the app as a Windows Azure website, and Office 365 can then manage it on behalf of the end user who installed it. This new type of app provides a compelling way to create and distribute your apps in an auto-provisioning way.

Apps or Solutions — Which Way to Go?

The answer to this simple question can become surprisingly difficult. When developers start coding a solution, they have no idea how big the solution may grow over time. There are several factors that impact the way solutions evolve, such as requirement changes, timeline pressures, and budget cuts. To overcome this up-front uncertainty, you always must make assumptions and build and deliver your solutions based off those assumptions. Remember, shipping is a feature. After your product is shipped, you can always monitor the usage pattern and user adoption, and come back and iteratively improve your solutions. To make assumptions you need to ask yourself questions and compare the answers to find your preferred options.

Apps provide the highest level of isolation in three levels: process, users, and content levels. Apps also provide the most flexibility for standard web technologies and infrastructure choices because they will not run on the same machines that SharePoint 2013 is installed on.

When deciding between SharePoint apps and SharePoint solutions, there are several factors that can help you decide whether you should develop an app or a solution:

➤ *Server-side object model* — A server-side object model is not allowed in apps. Use the restricted server-side code of sandboxed solutions or the unrestricted server-side code of farm solutions.

➤ *Access to external resources* — Apps can be granted permission, when installed, to content outside the hosting SharePoint website scope (SPWeb); for example, the entire site collection. It's obvious that all types of apps can access web services and other sources that are not hosted in SharePoint if they have access to them.

➤ *Target user* — This one is easy; for example, if you build an extension that allows farm administrators or web application administrators to do some maintenance or cleanup work, it's probably not a good idea to do it in an app. Farm solutions would not be a good candidate for a SharePoint app.

➤ *Complexity* — There are still tasks you can do using either apps or solutions, and the level of complexity is the same or a bit more complex if you do the tasks in apps. For example, you can deploy custom field controls, site columns, content types, or branding artifacts using apps or sandboxed solutions. It's probably more difficult to do these tasks in apps. If you ever get stuck in such scenarios, lean toward apps because you know they are the future that SharePoint and many other products are moving toward.

➤ *Dependency* — If you build a custom extension tightly coupled with another custom extension and it requires the dependent extension to be present prior to the installation, building it as an app is probably not a good idea. Again, apps are isolated and self-contained containers that should easily install, upgrade, and uninstall. Similarly, you should not use an app to install resources that other apps or solutions depend on because this would either block the clean uninstallation of the app or break the other extension when the app is uninstalled.

➤ *Scope* — SharePoint-hosted apps should not be full applications, such as case management or payroll. A SharePoint-hosted app should do only a few closely related tasks that surround only a few primary resources. Unlike previous versions where you used to build mega business solutions to target various use cases, your SharePoint-hosted apps are isolated, transactional in nature, and built to satisfy specific business needs. If you need full applications, either use SharePoint solutions or use cloud-hosted apps.

Table 2-1 summarizes the decision factors that you should consider when deciding between SharePoint solutions (farm or sandboxed) and apps.

TABLE 2-1: SharePoint Solutions and Apps Head-to-Head

DECISION FACTOR	FARM SOLUTIONS	SANDBOXED SOLUTIONS	APPS
Use client-side SharePoint API	✓	✓	✓
Use server-side SharePoint API	✓	Limited	X
Use remote services	X	Limited	✓
App authentication (OAuth2)	X	X	✓
On-premise deployment-friendly	✓	✓	✓
Hosted deployment-friendly	X	✓	✓
Distribution via the marketplace	X	X	✓
Install/upgrade/uninstall-friendly	X	X	✓

Table 2-2 summarizes the decision factors that you should consider when deciding between types of apps.

TABLE 2-2: Apps for SharePoint

SHAREPOINT-HOSTED APPS	CLOUD-HOSTED APPS
Good for smaller use cases targeting specific business needs	Good for small or big use cases
Some web technologies (HTML, JavaScript, jQuery, and so on)	Full power of web; choose your preferred technology
Automatically hosted	May require your own infrastructure
Inherent Multitenancy support and isolation	May require your own logic for handling tenancy and isolation
Inherent semantic for install/upgrade/upgrade	May require your own logic for install/upgrade/upgrade

If you put together everything you've learned so far, it should look like Figure 2-5. Packaging options in hosted or hybrid deployments depend on the hosting provider or how SharePoint is deployed and therefore are not included in Figure 2-5.

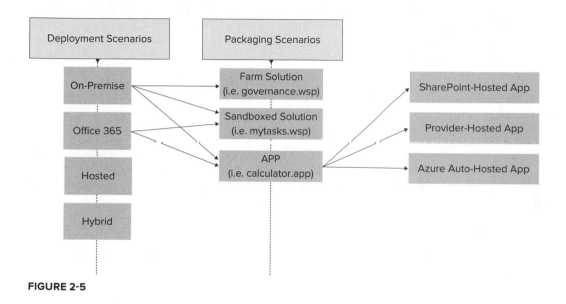

FIGURE 2-5

The App Security Model

Unless you have turned on anonymous access for a SharePoint site, every incoming request that lands in SharePoint must identify itself, which is the process known as *authentication*. The authentication is essential because if SharePoint doesn't know who you are, it doesn't know to authorize your access level to its resources.

> **NOTE** *SharePoint has never been in the authentication and identity management business, which is still the case in SharePoint 2013. As a relying party (RP), SharePoint relies on directory services such as Active Directory or identity providers (IdPs) such as Google and Facebook, and services such as IIS, Azure Access Control Service (ACS), and Active Directory Federation Services (ADFS) to externalize its authentication business. SharePoint also understands identity standards and specifications such as SAML, WS-Trust, and WS-Federation.*

Due to the changes in its programming model, the SharePoint 2013 authorization pipeline must deal with two different types of identities: user identity and app identity. The latter is new in SharePoint 2013.

To understand the need for app identity in SharePoint 2013, here's an example: Think about a scenario in which you want a remote app to access some product pictures in your site and tweet them to a Twitter feed owned by the Marketing Department. Obviously, the Twitter app needs to log in to SharePoint first before it can access and tweet those pictures. One way to do this is to give the app a set of credentials (username and password) so that it can sign in as you or someone else and complete its work. This is not a good option for a number of obvious reasons. First, everything in SharePoint is tied to a user identity, and the SharePoint authorization pipeline must distinguish the Twitter app and its actions from you and your actions — that's just how SharePoint works. Second, the Twitter app can do anything you can do such as deleting content or posting a comment to the CEO's blog on behalf of you. You don't want that either. Furthermore, what if you decided not to use the Twitter app anymore? What happens to your credentials? What if you use many apps like the Twitter app? How do you manage the credentials for many apps?

SharePoint tracks user identities using SharePoint security groups and *Access Control List (ACL)* entries stored in the content databases. For authenticating and authorizing app identities, however, SharePoint takes a different route.

First, consider authentication. An app is a first-class principal in SharePoint 2013; therefore, it needs its own identity. App identity is provided to SharePoint by *Azure Access Control Service (ACS)* via a widely adopted Internet security protocol called *OAuth*. OAuth 2.0 is the next release of OAuth that requires HTTPS.

The new architecture enables SharePoint 2013 users to approve an app to act on their behalf without sharing their credentials. To enable this, a number of different types of security tokens are issued, and there are back-and-forth communications between user, SharePoint, ACS, and the app itself, all done to ensure an app can transparently authenticate to SharePoint.

> **NOTE** *An OAuth security token service such as ACS does not issue sign-in tokens. Sign-in tokens are issued by an identity provider (IdP), and that's why ACS is and will remain just an app identity provider to SharePoint.*

When SharePoint 2013 receives an incoming request, the process starts with examining the request to see if it contains a sign-in token representing a user identity. If the user identity is found, SharePoint assumes that the request was initiated by an authenticated user and not an app. SharePoint then inspects the target URL of the incoming request to see whether it references a standard SharePoint site or a subsite associated with an app. (It's called *AppWeb*.) If the incoming request targets a standard site, SharePoint 2013 follows its typical authorization process identically to how things worked in SharePoint 2010. If the incoming request targets an AppWeb, however, SharePoint 2013 initializes the context with both a user identity and an app identity.

When an incoming request does not contain a sign-in token, SharePoint 2013 knows that it was not a user who initiated the request. In this scenario, SharePoint looks for an OAuth token to identify the remote app (provider-hosted). When SharePoint 2013 finds this security token, it sets up the context with the app identity and optionally the user identity.

Now, consider authorization.

After a provider-hosted app authenticates to SharePoint and the right context is created, SharePoint determines what actions the app is authorized to perform in the calling context. It's worth mentioning that SharePoint 2013 does not leverage ACS or OAuth protocol in any way to track or pass app permissions. Instead, SharePoint relies on its own internal content databases to track authorization just as it does with user permissions.

Each app has a manifest.xml file where the developer can define a list of resources that the app needs access to using the AppPermissionRequests element. The following code snippet shows an example of this element used in a provider-hosted app:

```
<AppPermissionRequests AllowAppOnlyPolicy="true">
  <AppPermissionRequest Scope="http://sharepoint/content/sitecollection"
  Right="Read"/>
  <AppPermissionRequest Scope="http://sharepoint/content/sitecollection/web/list"
  Right="Write">
    <Property Name="BaseTemplateId" Value="101"/>
  </AppPermissionRequest>
  <AppPermissionRequest Scope="http://sharepoint/userprofilestore/feed"
  Right="Post"/>
  <AppPermissionRequest Scope="http://exchange/calendars" Right="Schedule"/>

</AppPermissionRequests>
```

Note the highlighted line in the code snippet. The app permission requests enable the app-only policy, which means that only the app, and not the current user, requires the needed permissions. If an app-only policy is not used, both the app and the current user require the necessary permissions to complete a task such as accessing the entire site collection or writing to a list. The result would be a context that contains both the app and the user identities.

An important aspect of an app-only policy is that it can elevate the permissions of the app so that it can do more than the current user. It also makes it possible for an app to call back to SharePoint and access the *app web* (the SharePoint website associated with the app) and *parent web* (for example, a SharePoint website that is hosting the app) when there is no current user. When an app with AppPermissionRequest entries is installed by a user, the user must grant permissions to those placed in the manifest.xml file and requested by the app at the time of installation.

As mentioned previously, when creating a provider-hosted app that needs to communicate back to SharePoint, there are several types of security tokens needed for back-and-forth communications such as a context token and an OAuth token. Thankfully, Visual Studio automatically adds a helper class named TokenHelper.cs to help you access and work with the security tokens.

ACS cannot be used in on-premise deployments without involving an Office 365 tenancy. That means there is no OAuth token either. Apps need to use a different security token created using the *Server-to-Server (S2S)* configuration. For more information, see the product documentation at MSDN http://msdn.microsoft.com/en-us/library/fp179901(v=office.15).aspx.

Just because apps run in their own domain (to prevent cross-site scripting attacks) and they are written using JavaScript, it doesn't mean they are secure. As a developer, you are still on the hook to think about the security breaches and sensitive information disclosure caused by how you have designed your apps. Here are some examples of SharePoint security considerations:

➤   SharePoint-hosted apps are not authorized at a specific list or web level. In other words, if a SharePoint-hosted app is authorized to write to one list, it can also write to another list.

➤   When a user grants permission to a provider-hosted app. Granting permission is a one-time only process, so if the app's logic and its code behind change later, SharePoint won't detect this.

➤   When the app uses its OAuth token to perform some tasks, another app on the same page can use this token to perform actions on behalf of the app identity, the user identity, or both. It's also possible for a hacker to hijack the OAuth token in an unsecure communication channel (HTTP).

As you can see, there are many security considerations in app development you need to be aware of. To make apps secure and to protect sensitive information, you need to design with security in mind and to use HTTPS to secure the communication channel.

REMOTE EVENTS

With SharePoint becoming the main collaboration hub in many organizations, two-way integration with external systems (meaning external to SharePoint) has become a popular requirement over the past couple years.

Tight integration with Business Intelligence technologies such as Reporting Services, PerformancePoint, and Excel, and workloads such as Search and Business Connectivity Services have been used for surfacing external data inside SharePoint. Reversibly, SharePoint web services and CSOM have offered a set of options for surfacing SharePoint data in external systems, although in limited ways. SharePoint, however, has not provided a robust notification infrastructure for informing external systems of SharePoint events or getting notified when changes are made in the underlying data in the external systems.

Consider this scenario: The Tailspin Toys management team has issued a new mandate that the sales force in the field must provide the quickest response possible to sales leads created in its CRM system. In the past, its salespeople had to go to CRM to see the sales leads. However, with a proper notification system in place, the salespeople can be notified via SharePoint via e-mail that a sales lead has been received. The contact information for a sales lead is attached so that, when in the field, the sales representative can call the customer immediately and provide that personal touch that the senior manager wants them to have.

In the earlier versions of SharePoint, it was not easy to build an efficient solution to implement a scenario like the one for Tailspin Toys, except through some complex, full-trust farm solutions that used several custom event receivers and web service calls into CRM. One way to do this was to use pluggable workflow services in SharePoint 2010 to create custom workflow activities to implement remote event receivers. Figure 2-6 shows how pluggable workflow services can be utilized in SharePoint 2010 using `callExternalExternalMethodActivitiy1` and `hanldeExternalEventActivity1` activities. For more information on pluggable workflow services, see Chapter 13 of *Professional SharePoint 2010 Development*.

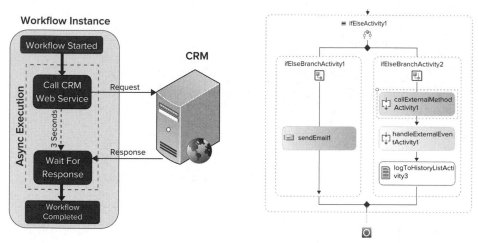

FIGURE 2-6

Given that full-trust farm solutions are not allowed in Office 365 and hosted deployments, and pluggable workflow services were poorly documented and not well received by developers, Microsoft had to come up with inherent semantics and the supporting infrastructure to enable remote events in SharePoint 2013.

To address challenges associated with cross-platform notifications, Microsoft has introduced three new options: Reporting Services data alerts, events in external lists, and remote event receivers. Now quickly review each option.

Reporting Services 2012 Data Alerts

Introduced in SQL Server 2012 and only available in SharePoint integrated mode, this new feature of Reporting Services enables you to set up alerts in reports that use stored credentials in their data source. When the underlying data in the report is changed, some recipients are notified. Because in data alerts you can specify recipient e-mail addresses (see Figure 2-7), a recipient can be an e-mail enabled document library where you have already registered an event receiver of type `SPEmailReceiver` to listen to incoming e-mails and then parse and take actions based on the information included in the From, To, Subject, Body, and Sent properties of the e-mail.

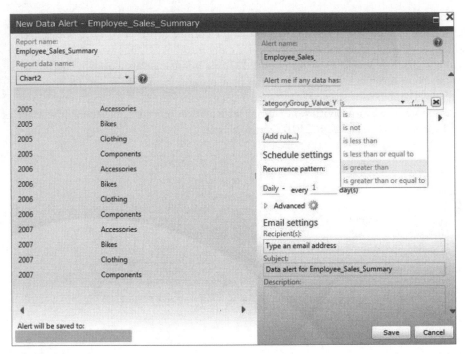

FIGURE 2-7

Events in External Lists

External lists in Business Connectivity Services in SharePoint 2013 support events. Two new stereotypes (Subscribe and Unsubscribe) have been added to the BCS object model to support notifications in external lists. `ItemAdded`, `ItemUpdated`, and `ItemDeleted` events are supported for setting up subscriptions. External lists will be covered in Chapters 13 and 14.

Remote Event Receivers

New in SharePoint 2013, developers can register remote event receivers with SharePoint similar to the way that local event receivers are registered in SharePoint 2010. The only major difference is that the developer provides a web service URL rather than an assembly and class name in that web service that needs to be called when registering the event receiver. When the event in question occurs, SharePoint sends the event properties to the web service, and it expects information about the result of the event receiver in response.

> **NOTE** *Think of remote event receivers in SharePoint 2013 as a provider-hosted app. Instead of a remote app, you get a web service, and instead of the* `default` `.aspx`*, you get a service (*`*.svc`*) that you need to call back to SharePoint. The same core remote communication technologies such as CSOM, REST, and OAuth apply.*

The following code snippet shows the Element XML of a remote event receiver specified for a list deployed as part of a SharePoint-hosted App. Note how in the URL and Type elements the web service URL and type of event is specified:

```xml
<?xml version="1.0" encoding="utf-8"?>
<Elements xmlns="http://schemas.microsoft.com/sharepoint/">
  <Receivers ListTemplateId="10000">
    <Receiver>
      <Name>AnnouncementsReceiverItemAdded</Name>
      <Type>ItemAdded</Type>
      <SequenceNumber>10000</SequenceNumber>
      <Url> http://tailspintoys.com/AnnouncementsReceiver.svc</Url>
    </Receiver>
  </Receivers>
</Elements>
```

The web service is just a public class that implements the `IRemoteEventService` interface and `ProcessEvent` for -ing events (that is, `ItemAdding`) before an event happens and `ProcessOneWayEvent` for –ed events (that is, `ItemAdded`) after an event happens:

```csharp
public class AnnouncementsReceiver : IRemoteEventService
{
    public SPRemoteEventResult ProcessEvent(RemoteEventProperties properties)
    {
        SPRemoteEventResult result = new SPRemoteEventResult();

        switch (properties.EventType)
        {
            case RemoteEventType.ItemAdding:
                //Code to handle ItemAdding
                break;

            case RemoteEventType.ItemDeleting:
                //Code Omitted for brevity
    break;
        }

        return result;
    }

    public void ProcessOneWayEvent(RemoteEventProperties properties)
    {
        if (properties.EventType == RemoteEventType.ItemAdded)
        {
            //Code Omitted for brevity
        }

    }
}
```

The Security Model in Remote Events

When it comes to remote events and the ability of systems to work and notify each other, a major concern is always security. Figure 2-8 shows how different players of a remote event scenario work together in SharePoint 2013.

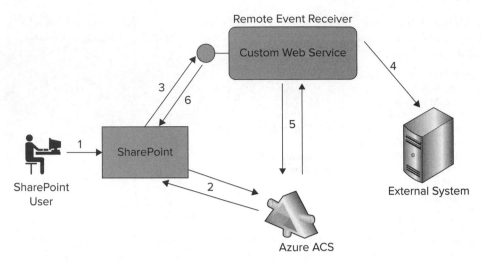

FIGURE 2-8

Here are the basic steps as shown in Figure 2-8:

1. The user causes an event in SharePoint to fire (for example, ItemDeleting).

2. SharePoint calls ACS to obtain a security token representing the current user identity.

3. SharePoint calls the registered event receiver (the web service) and passes the security token to the web service. The web service authorizes the call by validating the token.

4. The web service may perform any operation in the external system such as updating Line of Business (LOB) data.

5. The web service requests a security token from ACS to call back into SharePoint.

6. The web service uses the security token to authenticate and call back to SharePoint to perform a task.

The following code snippet shows how a web service in the remote event receiver can obtain a context token from ACS and build a SharePoint context and the remote client context to perform a task in SharePoint:

```
HttpRequestMessageProperty requestPro =
(HttpRequestMessageProperty)OperationContext.
Current.IncomingMessageProperties[HttpRequestMessageProperty.Name];
string ctxTokenString = requestPro.Headers["X-SP-AccessToken"];
SharePointctxToken ctxToken = TokenHelper.ReadAndValidatectxToken(ctxTokenString,
requestPro.Headers[HttpRequestHeader.Host]);
Uri spUrl = new Uri(properties.ItemEventProperties.WebUrl);
string accessToken = TokenHelper.GetAccessToken(ctxToken,
spUrl.Authority).AccessToken;
ClientContext clientContext =
TokenHelper.GetClientContextWithAccessToken(spUrl.ToString(), accessToken))
```

You can use the `TokenHelper` class to create the security token and authenticate to SharePoint just like provider-hosted apps covered earlier in this chapter.

In Office 365 deployments, the security token for the web service to be able to call into SharePoint can be created using OAuth, and ACS needs to be involved. For on-premise deployments, this security token should be created using an S2S configuration. For more information, see the product documentation at `http://msdn.microsoft.com/en-us/library/fp179901(v=office.15).aspx`.

The next section will cover the new changes in workflow.

WORKFLOWS

You have been learning about the tight integration between Office 365 and Windows Azure-based services such as ACS since the beginning of this chapter. So far, you have learned about this integration in the context of apps and remote events.

Using the same behind-the-scenes plumbing, you can now easily author and upload a declarative workflow to Office 365, and the workflow runs in the Windows Azure Workflow execution host completely outside of the SharePoint server farm. The workflow running in Windows Azure can then communicate back to SharePoint via the same core remote access technologies you saw in cloud-based apps such as CSOM, REST, and OAuth.

Following the same approach in this chapter, take a look at the challenges with workflows in the earlier versions of SharePoint.

Challenges with Workflows in SharePoint 2010

If you remember, workflow was first introduced to the platform in SharePoint 2007 via Workflow Foundation 3.0. From an architectural perspective, workflows weren't much different in SharePoint 2010 because the platform leveraged Workflow Foundation based on the .NET Framework 3.5 SP1.

Think of workflow in SharePoint 2010 in four primary scenarios:

➤ *Scenario 1* — A power user builds a declarative workflow in SharePoint Designer 2010 and deploys it to SharePoint 2010. Declarative workflows contain no custom code and are strictly serial in nature (no support for state machine workflows).

➤ *Scenario 2* — A power user builds a declarative workflow in SharePoint Designer 2010 and engages a developer to extend the workflow programmatically in Visual Studio 2010. This could be because of one of the following limitations in SharePoint Designer Workflows:

    ➤ Implementation of custom business logic

    ➤ Calling of SharePoint APIs

    ➤ Calling of external systems (web services, feeds, and databases)

➤ *Scenario 3* — A developer builds custom activities in Visual Studio 2010 and wraps them in actions for use in SharePoint Designer 2010. Those actions can then be used by power users who own the workflow business logic to be used in their declarative workflows.

➤ *Scenario 4* — A developer builds a programmatic workflow in Visual Studio 2010 and packages it for deployment. In this scenario, all development is done in Visual Studio 2010.

Although the preceding scenarios cover most customer needs and fulfills their requirements, the workflow technology had some limitations. Now look at them:

➤ *Scalability* — Unlike many workloads that followed the SharePoint 2010 service application model for better scalability and tenancy support, workflow was not a true service in SharePoint 2010. As a result, customers can have only one workflow execution host per SharePoint 2010 farm, shared between all web applications and tenants.

➤ *Stability and performance* — SharePoint 2010 workflows are frequently hydrated and dehydrated between different tiers of the farm. An unhappy workflow or too many running instances can considerably impact the farm performance and its availability.

➤ *High-privileged context* — Workflows execute under the security context of the site's application pool as a super user. This is not preferable in many use cases in which the security context of the user who initiated the workflow is needed. For example, Created By and Modified By fields on a workflow payload are always shown as a System Account. For more information on workflow security context, see the TechNet article at `http://technet .microsoft.com/library/dd365119.aspx`.

➤ *On-premise deployments* — Because workflows run as a super user in SharePoint 2010, sandboxed solutions cannot be used to host a programmatic workflow. Your only option in sandboxed solutions is to deploy a workflow action that later can be used in SharePoint Designer 2010.

➤ *Flexibility* — SharePoint 2010 is tightly coupled with a specific version of .NET Framework and Windows Workflow Foundation, so workflow developers cannot harness the latest workflow technologies from Microsoft. Again, that's an expected result when you tightly couple a product to a specific version of a given technology.

Workflow Architecture in SharePoint 2013

SharePoint 2013 takes a different approach to workflow than its predecessor. In SharePoint 2013, workflow (the technology) is now treated as a true service. This means SharePoint workflows no longer run in SharePoint servers; instead, the execution is handled by Windows Azure Workflow on a separate server.

> **NOTE** *Interestingly enough, Microsoft refers to the infrastructure executing the SharePoint 2013 workflows as a Windows Azure Workflow farm.*

Windows Workflow Foundation 4.0 and .NET Framework 4.5 are the base to empower this new architecture. They both have been substantially redesigned from earlier versions. Figure 2-9 illustrates the workflow platform technology stack in SharePoint 2013.

The focus in SharePoint 2013 workflows is to build workflows declaratively. This is different from SharePoint 2010 where power users use SharePoint Designer to build declarative workflows and developers use Visual Studio to build programmatic workflows.

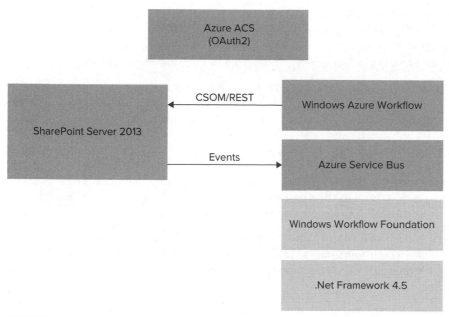

FIGURE 2-9

All out-of-the-box SharePoint 2013 workflows are now declarative, and the new workflows you build either by using SharePoint Designer 2013 or Visual Studio 2013 will also be declarative.

By making all SharePoint 2013 workflows declarative, you can use sandboxed solutions to deploy your workflow in its entirety. This is different than SharePoint 2010 where you could deploy workflow actions only using sandboxed solutions.

Microsoft recommends that you build new workflows using the SharePoint 2013 workflow model and push the custom code to web services. Building a programmatic workflow all from scratch is still possible, but for two reasons it may not be a preferable option:

➤   Given the new features in the platform, you don't need to build programmatic workflows. These new features are covered shortly.

➤   SharePoint can't host a programmatic workflow, and it has to be deployed to Windows Azure Workflow as a non-SharePoint 2013 workflow. The developer is then on the hook to implement the communication channel between the workflow and SharePoint 2013.

> **NOTE** *Think of Windows Azure Workflow as an Azure auto-hosted app offering a "service" to host and execute your SharePoint 2013 workflows. SharePoint instructs this app to execute a workflow, and the app executes the workflow and sends the result back. Both products communicate with each other using a messaging infrastructure that sits between and allows them to exchange messages. The messaging infrastructure is Windows Azure Service Bus.*

From a backward-compatibility and legacy standpoint, existing SharePoint 2010 workflows can migrate to SharePoint 2013 without any problems. In addition, SharePoint 2013 workflows can call SharePoint 2010 workflows. This is a welcome feature because it allows customers to carry on with their investments in SharePoint 2010 workflows to SharePoint 2013.

Another interesting aspect of the new architecture is that *Windows Azure Workflow* and *Service Bus* are available in on-premise and in Office 365 deployments. You can use this to build your own workflow development environment. The next section covers the steps to do this.

Building Your Workflow Development Environment

Introduced as a separate download, the *Windows Azure Workflow* product enables customers to set up and configure a workflow farm in their on-premise deployments. You can benefit from this and build your workflow development environment the same way.

One thing to keep in mind is that you can't install SharePoint 2013 and Windows Azure Workflow on a domain controller without some hacks. Therefore, at a minimum you need a separate server to serve as a domain controller and one server that hosts both SharePoint 2013 and Windows Azure Workflow and Service Bus.

At a high level, here are the required steps to build your workflow development environment:

1. Create a workflow service account (for example, `Tailspintoys\wrkflowSvc`).

2. Add the service account `securityadmin` and `dbcreator` server roles in SQL Server. It's also part of the local administrators group.

3. Enable TCP/IP in SQL Server, which is required by Windows Azure Service Bus.

4. Log on to your SharePoint server using the workflow service account you created in step 1. This is an important step to ensure the installation wizard runs under the security context of the workflow service account.

5. Download and install *Microsoft Web Platform Installer* from `http://www.microsoft .com/web/downloads/platform.aspx`. Use this program to download and install Windows Azure Workflow and Service Bus. You need to search for Workflow 1.0 Beta.

6. Still logged on to the machine as the workflow service account, run the installation and choose Create a New Farm ⇨ Using Default Settings (Recommended), as shown in Figure 2-10.

    a. Select Allow Workflow Management over HTTP on this Computer; otherwise, you must set up HTTPS, which is overkill for development purposes.

    b. When specifying the workflow service account, use a fully qualified UPN format (`wrkflowSvc@Tailspintoys.com`), not the default value shown in the wizard (`wrkflowSvc@Tailspintoys`) or NetBios name (`tp\wrkflowSvc`).

    c. In the Certificate Generation Key and Confirm Certificate Generation Key, enter **pass@word1** or another passphrase of your choice.

WINDOWS AZURE WORKFLOW CONFIGURATION WIZARD
Welcome
This wizard helps you configure a Workflow farm. Wizard will also configure the Service Bus farm required by the Workflow farm.
Create a New Farm
Using Default Settings (Recommended)
Choose this option to create a new Workflow farm using default settings. The same default settings will also be used to create Service Bus farm required by the Workflow farm. The computer on which you run this wizard will be added to both Workflow farm and Service Bus farm.
With Custom Settings
Choose this option to create a Workflow farm with custom configuration settings. The Service Bus farm required by Workflow farm will also be configured as part of this operation. The computer on which you run this wizard will be added to both Workflow farm and Service Bus farm.
Join an Existing Farm
Choose this option to add this computer to existing Workflow farm and Service Bus farm.

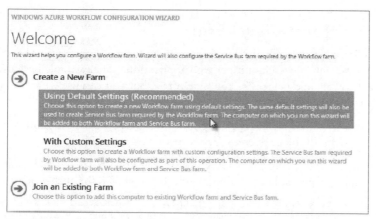

FIGURE 2-10

If everything goes smoothly, you should see a summary page like the one shown in Figure 2-11.

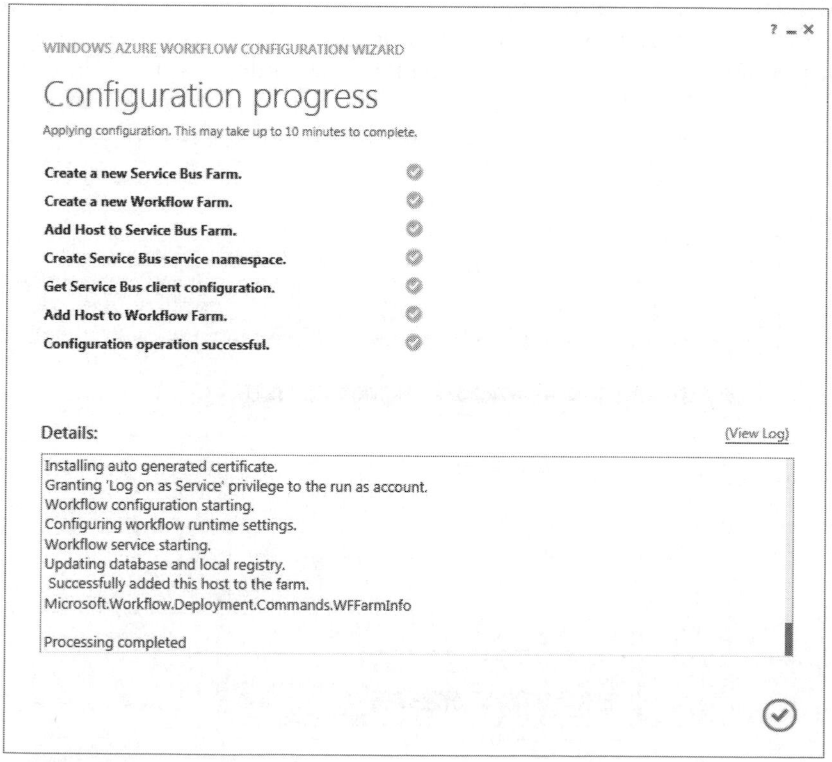

WINDOWS AZURE WORKFLOW CONFIGURATION WIZARD
Configuration progress
Applying configuration. This may take up to 10 minutes to complete.
Create a new Service Bus Farm.
Create a new Workflow Farm.
Add Host to Service Bus Farm.
Create Service Bus service namespace.
Get Service Bus client configuration.
Add Host to Workflow Farm.
Configuration operation successful.
Details:
(View Log)
Installing auto generated certificate.
Granting 'Log on as Service' privilege to the run as account.
Workflow configuration starting.
Configuring workflow runtime settings.
Workflow service starting.
Updating database and local registry.
Successfully added this host to the farm.
Microsoft.Workflow.Deployment.Commands.WFFarmInfo
Processing completed

FIGURE 2-11

7. Log off and log back in using the farm account.

8. Pair your SharePoint farm with the workflow farm by executing the following PowerShell script. In this script the parameters are important:

   a. `-SPSite` specifies the endpoint for the workflow farm to communicate to SharePoint. There can be only one endpoint per web application. (The example here uses `http://Tailspintoys.com/sites/workflow`, but you can use whatever value is appropriate for your specific needs.)

   b. `-WorkflowHostUri` specifies the endpoint for SharePoint to communicate to the workflow farm. (Replace `mydevserv` with your own values.)

   c. `-AllowOAuthHttp` specifies HTTP is allowed for OAuth calls, which is fine for development purposes, but you don't want to use HTTP for authentication.

   ```
   Register-SPWorkflowService -SPSite "http://Tailspintoys.com/sites/workflow" -
   WorkflowHostUri "http://mydevserv:12291" -AllowOAuthHttp
   ```

9. Configure Active Directory Synchronization in User Profile Service Application. Windows Azure Workflow looks up the `UserPrincipalName` (UPN) attribute of the user from the User Profile Service Application to validate and ensure the user has enough rights to start a workflow.

At this point Windows Azure Workflow and Service Bus have been successfully installed, and the SharePoint 2013 farm and workflow farm have been successfully paired. Now, you should crack open SharePoint Designer to create a new SharePoint 2013 workflow, as shown in Figure 2-12.

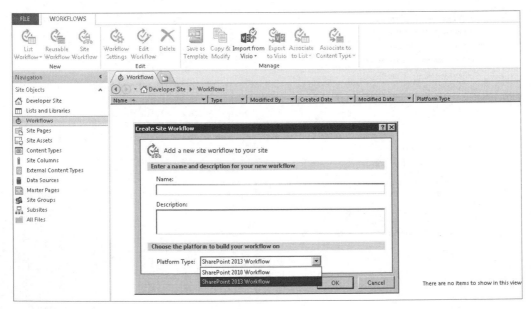

FIGURE 2-12

SharePoint Designer 2013 Workflows

SharePoint Designer 2013 offers two authoring and customization experiences for developers and power users:

➤ *Text-based designer* — This is the improved version of the designer canvas. For example, you select multiple objects in the workflow design canvas and copy and paste them within the same workflow or across workflows. Interestingly enough, this was the #1 requested feature by SharePoint Designer customers.

➤ *Visual designer* — This is a new design canvas available when Visio 2013 is installed alongside SharePoint Designer 2013.

You can switch between the designers by clicking on the Views button on the Ribbon. Figure 2-13 shows the new visual designer.

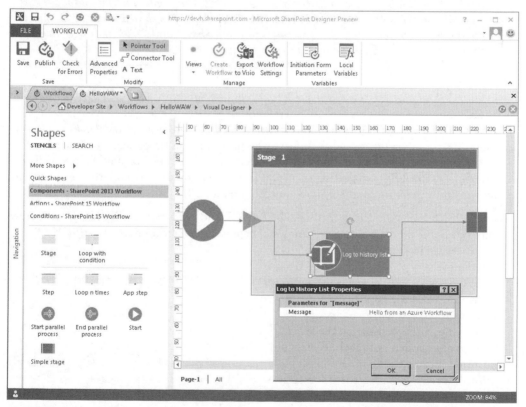

FIGURE 2-13

In Figure 2-13, note the Visio shapes in the left pane. Also, note how you can modify the properties of workflow actions (for example, Log to History List) directly within the visual designer. You can set all the properties by selecting the shape and then clicking the action tag that appears on the left-bottom corner of the shape. If you click Properties on the action tag, the property grid for conditions and actions appears in the visual designer just as they do in the text-based designer.

Aside from the design canvas improvements, SharePoint Designer 2013 now supports new top-level containers and actions. Here are a few important ones:

➤ *Loops* — A new top-level container; as its name implies, a loop is a container that groups together actions, conditions, and steps that you want to process repeatedly. The iteration logic in a loop can be fixed (*n* times) or dynamic (based on a condition or expression).

➤ *Stages* — As discussed earlier, declarative workflows have been notoriously serial in nature in the previous versions of SharePoint. They have a starting point and endpoint, everything runs sequentially, and everything processes forward. In SharePoint Designer 2013, a new top-level container called *stage* lets you group together actions, conditions, or steps to have them executed in the listed order. After the control reaches to the end of the stage (the gate), it transitions via a Go To action to any other stage in the workflow.

> **NOTE** *You can insert a condition in the* Go To *transition gate and move the control from one stage to another until the logic concludes that the workflow has completed. That means declarative workflows in SharePoint 2013 no longer need to be sequential and can be used to model state machine workflows as well.*

➤ *Calling SharePoint 2010 list and site workflows* — SharePoint Designer 2013 enables SharePoint 2013 workflows to call SharePoint 2010 list and site workflows. There are two new coordination actions called *Start a List Workflow* and *Start a Site Workflow* to support this. This is important for the customers who have existing investments in SharePoint 2010 workflows and want to migrate to SharePoint 2013 while keeping their workflow investments until fully migrating them at a later time. You can also use this technique to call on workflow activities not integrated into SharePoint 2013.

➤ *Call HTTP Web Service* — Calling SOAP, WCF and OData-compliant services is now supported within declarative workflows. There is a new action named *Call HTTP Web Service* to support this. The calls to the remote services are originated from where the workflow runs (Windows Azure Workflow) and the returned data is stored in workflow variables, which can be accessed by other actions in the workflow. The recommended approach to embedding custom logic and code in SharePoint 2013 workflows is to create a custom web service and use the new Call HTTP Web Service action to consume the service.

Figure 2-14 illustrates the new Stage concept in a SharePoint Designer 2013 workflow and how you can conditionally transition (jump) from *Wait for Approval* stage to *Approved* or *Rejected* stages.

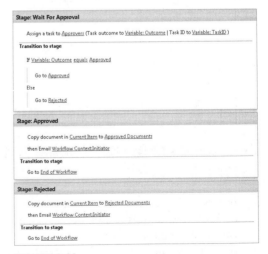

FIGURE 2-14

Another compelling use of SharePoint 2013 workflows is in apps, which is covered in the next section.

Using Workflows in Apps

The new workflow model in SharePoint 2013 enables an interesting type of development scenario. You can now use workflows as the middle-tier host for business logic in apps.

Similar to the pluggable workflow service discussed earlier, this technique is useful for protecting the intellectual property (IP) of your business logic in an app or for handling long-running business logic that the developer wants to offload from the app. For example, if your app needs to integrate with CRM sales leads, the business logic can be encapsulated in a workflow and executed in the Windows Azure Workflow execution host.

> **NOTE** *You need to use Visual Studio 2012 to build apps with workflow. SharePoint Designer 2013 doesn't have support for workflows in apps.*

Apps can initiate and interact with declarative workflows using a new workflow JavaScript Object Model (JSOM). JSOM enables an app to deploy workflow definitions to both an App Web and a Parent Web.

ENTERPRISE CONTENT MANAGEMENT

Enterprise Content Management (ECM) was first introduced to the platform in SharePoint 2007 by adding two site templates (Records Center and Document Center) and capabilities such as check-in, check-out, versioning, information management policies, holds, and many other features tied to SharePoint content.

SharePoint 2010 expanded on these capabilities by wrapping the base ECM capabilities to Features. SharePoint 2010 also introduced many other core and compliance capabilities to ECM, such as in-place records management, the document ID service, the document set, and the content organizer.

In SharePoint 2013, although Microsoft has introduced several new ECM features and enhancements such as eDiscovery and site mailboxes, there are two areas that matter the most to developers: site policies and managed meta data.

Now look at site policies.

Site Policies

Information management policy is a set of rules that define certain behaviors or restrictions on the content kept in SharePoint. For example, auditing sensitive information is a common requirement for many departments such as HR. Questions like, "Who has changed the permissions of the HR site in the past 10 days?" or "Did someone move the content in the Payroll document library to another site?" are among many other auditing questions that may arise during the life cycle of a SharePoint site.

In SharePoint 2010, you could create only policies attached to content types or at the site collection level. SharePoint 2013 has a new set of policies. If you browse to Site Settings ⇨ Site Collection Administration, there is a new link called Site Policies, which enables you to control the life cycle of a site.

Figure 2-15 illustrates some of the options available in a site policy.

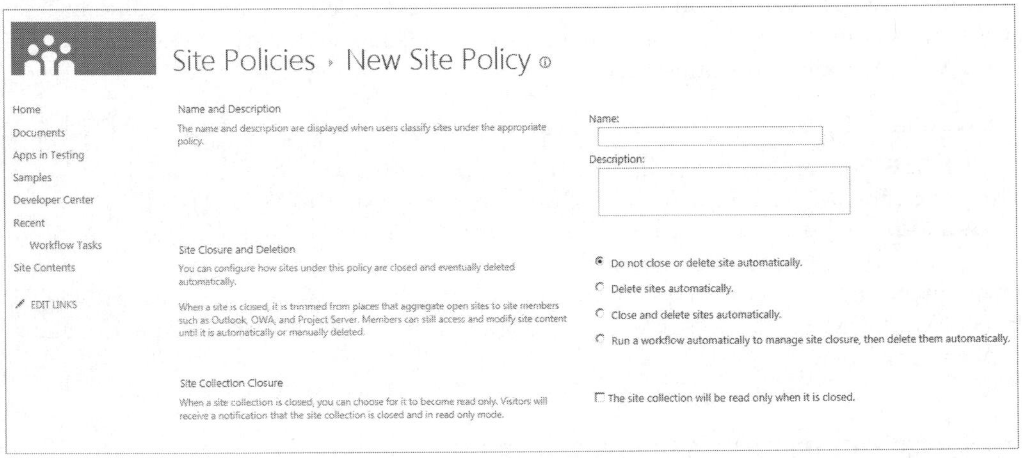

FIGURE 2-15

As shown in Figure 2-15, you can choose how a site should expire and what should happen when it expires. For example, a site can be deleted automatically seven months after it was created, and a workflow executes to handle some custom business logic before deletion. Conveniently, if the site collection in which you define the policy is a content type hub, you can push your policies down to all subscribed site collections.

> **NOTE** *When combined with self-service site creation, site policies offer a powerful mechanism for site life-cycle management in SharePoint 2013. Users can select a site policy when requesting a site, and the site policy will be automatically enforced based on its logic.*

After a site policy is defined at the site collection level, the site owner can browse to the Site Closure and Deletion page on a subsite's settings page, and select the site policy. This can also be done programmatically through improved CSOM interfaces in SharePoint 2013.

The next section discusses managed meta-data improvements in SharePoint 2013.

Managed Meta Data

Managed meta data plays a more prominent role in SharePoint 2013 than in SharePoint 2010. However, from an architectural standpoint, the core capabilities are the same.

To use managed meta data in your site, you still need a managed meta-data service (MMS) application and a tool called Term Store. The tool enables you to work with one instance of the managed meta-data service application at a time. Terms are categorized in groups (top-level container) and then in term sets within each group. The term hierarchy is stored in MMS application databases along with syndicated content types. If social tags are enabled, the MMS application also uses a social tag database created by a user profile service application.

Just like SharePoint 2010, SharePoint 2013 managed meta-data groups can be local or global. A global group is the one that can be used by any site collection connected to the same instance of the MMS application. A local group is one that although stored in the MMS application database is only available to a specific site collection. What is different in SharePoint 2013 is the ability to make a local group available to other site collections (in read-only mode) by specifying the URL of the consumer site collection.

Figure 2-16 shows cross-site collection term access in the improved term store tool in SharePoint 2013.

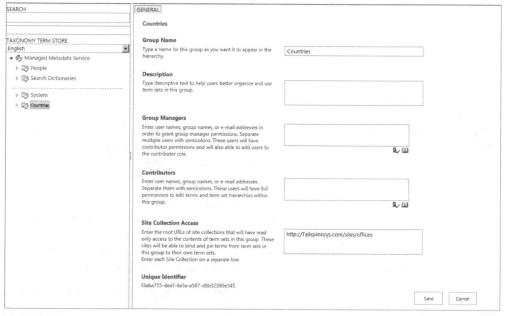

FIGURE 2-16

In SharePoint 2010, users could reuse terms in the term hierarchy. After these terms were reused, they could be updated and deleted in both the source and the referenced term sets. Updating on any ends would have been applied to the entire term hierarchy, but deleting was slightly different. Deleting a reused term from the source was not deleting the term from the referenced term sets. So, reused terms were supposed to be pointers, but in reality they were not pointers — kind of confusing.

Reusing terms is still there in SharePoint 2013 and functions exactly as in SharePoint 2010. SharePoint 2013 introduced a new operation for terms: *term pinning*. A pinned term is just like a reused term except it is read-only and cannot be modified (updated or deleted) in the referenced term sets. In addition, if you delete a pinned term from the source, it will be deleted from all the referenced term sets. Now, you have the real pointers.

> **NOTE** *Cross-site collection terms are based on pinned terms, not reused terms.*

Another major improvement is custom properties for terms. In SharePoint 2010, terms had property bags that could be accessed only via taxonomy server-side APIs. SharePoint 2013 now includes the ability to work with custom properties in terms and term sets through the browser, and CSOM APIs are added for remote clients. Custom properties are either shared or local. Those available in all reused and pinned instances of the term are called *shared custom properties*. Local properties are only accessible for the term within the source term set.

Great news for bilingual customers and businesses is the ability to add working languages in an MMS application *without* having to install the language packs, as shown in Figure 2-17.

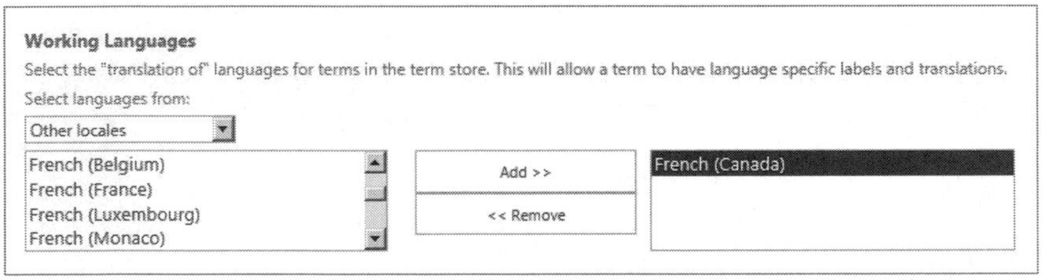

Working Languages
Select the "translation of" languages for terms in the term store. This will allow a term to have language specific labels and translations.
Select languages from:

Other locales

French (Belgium)
French (France)   Add >>   French (Canada)
French (Luxembourg)
French (Monaco)   << Remove

FIGURE 2-17

This is definitely a welcome change for those customers who want to have their taxonomy in multiple languages, but their content is primarily authored and consumed in English. This also is handy for developers who don't like to install and manage multiple language packs just to work with multilingual taxonomies.

After new working languages are added to the MMS application, a new tab becomes available for each term set that enables you to choose three options for term translation. The options are Machine Translate, which is powered by a new machine translation service application in SharePoint 2013; Create Translation Package to export the term sets into a XLIFF package for professional translation; or Upload Translation, which basically imports the translation package back to the MMS application.

You briefly looked at new features in ECM; the next workload to explore is Web Content Management.

WEB CONTENT MANAGEMENT

In SharePoint 2013, Microsoft paid special attention to the Web Content Management (WCM) workload. With the new search and managed meta-data improvements in the product, SharePoint 2013 takes two different approaches toward publishing content: structural and dynamic publishing models.

Now consider each model in more detail.

The Structural Publishing Model

This is how publishing sites work in SharePoint 2010. Content authors create content pages individually and make them available in publishing sites. For example, if you need to create a detail page for a product called *foo*, you browse to the products site at `http://www.tailspintoys.com/products` and you create a publishing page based on a predefined template (Page Layout) to showcase foo as a product. After the page is checked in and published, it serves as a detail page, and visitors can see that page by typing the following URL in their browsers: `http://www.tailspintoys.com/products/pages/foo.aspx`.

This approach is useful for the content that needs to live in SharePoint and is static in nature. After authoring content pages, you need to somehow roll them up onto another page, often referred to as the roll-up page. You can use a Content by Query Web Part (CBQ) or other custom aggregation techniques to show your products in a master/detail manner.

In a structural model, publishing content can be moved and localized to variation sites using content deployment. Alternatively, you can use content deployment to move the content across your authoring and publishing farms and across the network boundary between your intranet sites, extranet sites, and Internet sites.

The Dynamic Publishing Model

New in SharePoint 2013, roll-up and detail pages can be automatically generated from the indexed content. For example, your product catalogue, which in most organizations is kept in non-SharePoint external systems, can be indexed by search and automatically be included in SharePoint 2013 publishing sites.

Using the new managed meta data feature, the product pages can be accessed using much cleaner and more SEO-friendly URLs such as `http://www.tailspintoys.com/foo.aspx`.

In dynamic publishing, content can then be made available to other sites using a new feature in SharePoint 2013 called *cross-site publishing*. Now look at how the dynamic publishing model works under the hood.

Taxonomy-Driven Navigation

Navigation infrastructure in SharePoint 2013 leverages taxonomy to generate SEO-friendly URLs and paths to publishing pages. If you look at the navigation settings in a publishing site, you should see that there are two ways you can design your site navigation: structural and managed.

Structural navigation is what exists in SharePoint 2010. Managed navigation is new and is driven by site taxonomy. This is an important concept because now you can abstract site navigation from how your business operates without changing the underlying structure of your sites. This also enables site owners to easily reorganize the navigation by modifying the term sets.

Figure 2-18 shows the new managed navigation option in the Navigation Settings of a publishing site in SharePoint 2013.

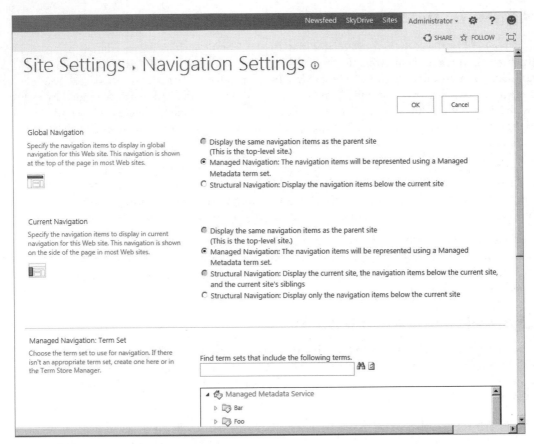

FIGURE 2-18

It's not just the navigation that can be based off taxonomy. The next section discusses taxonomy-driven pages in SharePoint 2013 WCM.

Term-Driven Publishing Pages

When a publishing page is created in SharePoint 2013 using either structural or dynamic models, SharePoint automatically adds a new term to the Site Navigation term set that points to the new page. In addition, SharePoint automatically generates a home page for that term just like social tag profiles.

The term's home page is simply a Page Layout (.aspx) that displays the content of the page. As always, developers and designers have the opportunity to customize this template to meet specific rendition requirements.

Through a new tab in the term store called *Intended Use*, term sets can opt in to participate in taxonomy-driven navigation and then further be customized. Selecting this option enables the Navigation and Term-Driven Pages tabs, which enables you to customize features such as friendly URLs, SEO options, target page settings, and many others.

Cross-Site Publishing

If you have been programming for SharePoint even for a short period of time, you probably know that getting out of a site collection boundary and aggregating content across multiple site collections is not an easy task. There are several patterns and techniques to enable cross-site collection aggregation, but they all require extra development effort and each one comes with its own limitations.

SharePoint 2013 enables developers to make content in lists and document libraries available for consumption on other site collections. The idea is simple and involves a few high-level steps:

1. Create a list (or document library) with site columns and content types.

> **NOTE** *Only site columns automatically have managed properties and appear in the search index without any extra configuration efforts. If you use list columns, you must create managed properties and map them to the crawled properties of the list columns. Remember, cross-site publishing heavily depends on indexed content.*

2. Designate the list as a *Catalog*. There is a new setting to do this in the list setting page. This makes the content in the list available to other site collections through the MMS applications. A catalog has a minimum of one *Primary Key* (a maximum of five) that uniquely identifies an item in the list. A catalog also has one column designated as *Catalog Navigation*. Consuming site collections use this column to display it in their own navigation hierarchy. The Catalog Navigation column is a Managed Metadata field and is bound to a term set, referred to as a *tagging term set*.

3. Share the catalog's tagging term set with other consuming site collections using the same technique discussed earlier in the "Enterprise Content Management" section

4. Run a full crawl, and ensure columns participating in the catalog (that is, Catalog Navigation) are automatically queryable through managed properties on the consuming site collections.

5. In the consuming site collections, set the navigation to Managed Navigation. See the "Taxonomy-Driven Navigation" section for more information.

6. Connect the consuming site collections, and connect to the catalog by browsing to Site Settings ⇨ Manage Catalog Connections.

Figure 2-19 shows an example of product catalog implementation in a consuming site collection.

When you click on an item on the roll-up page, the page is created dynamically and directly from the search index. There is no timer job involved in this process.

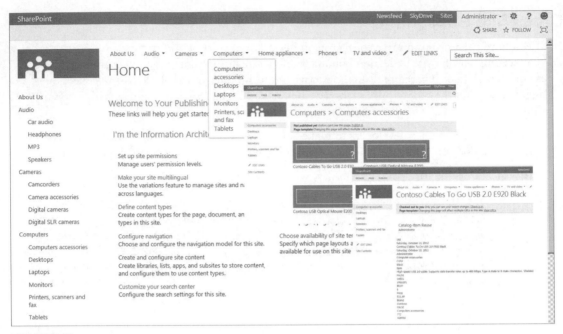

FIGURE 2-19

The notation of the catalog is so important in SharePoint 2013 that Microsoft decided to ship an out-of-the-box template called *Product Catalog*. This template already has a designated list as a catalog named Products. The idea is to give you a starting point to hit the ground running toward building your own corporate product catalog system.

> **NOTE** *When you combine new features introduced in ECM, WCM, and search together, hopefully you can see a lot of potential to implement interesting development scenarios such as cross-site collection navigation, publishing, and deployment.*

Before moving on to the next section, there are two important things that need to be highlighted: First, the new cross-site publishing feature in WCM is not meant to replace traditional content deployment. There are still many scenarios where you should prefer content deployment over cross-site publishing. For more information, see the product documentation at `http://msdn.microsoft.com/en-us/library/jj163225(v=office.15).aspx`.

Second, structural and dynamic publishing and the techniques used in each model are not mutually exclusive. They can co-exist or be mixed together to enable complex publishing requirements. For example, you can combine cross-site publishing with a variation to enable authoring multilingual sites from a common authoring site collection.

Hostname Site Collections

SharePoint 2007 supported extending a web application to multiple zones and giving each zone a unique hostname (host header). Because SharePoint has a limit in the number of web applications hosted in a single farm, SharePoint 2010 introduced Host Name Site Collections (HNSC) to address this scalability issue. The problem was that HNSCs in SharePoint 2010 had to be in the Default zone and couldn't use alternative access mapping. In addition, there was only one hostname per site collection.

SharePoint 2013 took HNSC to the next level by supporting an unlimited number of hostnames per site collection and by mapping each hostname to a zone at the web application level. You still need to extend the web application, and there is a limit of five zones per web application: Default, Intranet, Internet, Extranet, and Custom. The difference, however, is how SharePoint 2013 enables hostnames to be in different zones.

> **NOTE** *Software boundaries and limits have changed in SharePoint 2013. For more information, see the product documentation at* http://technet.micro soft.com/en-us/library/cc262787(v=office.15).

The following code snippet creates an HNSC with the URL http://www.bar.com in a web application with the URL http://foo. This web application has two zones: Default and Internet.

The code then adds additional URLs to the new HNSC; http://foo.bar.com to the Default zone and https://foo.bar.com to the Internet zone of the web application.

```
#Create a new HNSC
New-SPSite "http://www.bar.com" -HostHeaderWebApplication "http://foo" -Name "Bar
Portal" -Description "Bar Portal" -OwnerAlias "Tailspintoys\administrator"
-language 1033 -Template "STS#0"

# Get a reference to the new HNSC
$site = Get-SPSite 'http://www.bar.com'

# Add an alternative URL and map to Default zone
Set-SPSiteURL -Identity $site -Url http://foo.bar.com -Zone 0

# Add an alternative URL and map to Internet zone
Set-SPSiteURL -Identity $site -Url https://foo.bar.com -Zone 2
```

You can specify which zone to use (0 = Default zone and 2 = Internet zone) when creating the alternative names. If you list all zones created for the new HSNC using the following code, you can see what's shown in Figure 2-20:

```
Get-SPSiteUrl -Identity http://www.bar.com
```

FIGURE 2-20

If the Internet zone of the web application supports anonymous access, so does the alternative URL used in HNSC.

Multilingual Features

If you live in a multilingual country such as Canada, you probably know how important it is to enable users to vary the presentation of their content in another language. If you read this chapter from the beginning, you have already seen some of the multilingual support in SharePoint 2013 in cross-site publishing and managed meta data, but there is more.

Variation has been always the primary feature in SharePoint to satisfy multilingual requirements. Variation works based on the following four principles to replicate content from a source to a variation label (destination):

➤ URLs

➤ Language redirection

➤ Translation

➤ Content deployment

Variation is still constrained to one site collection; however, it is a faster and much more reliable process in SharePoint 2013. You get smaller export packages, and there is a replication list that allows for easy start and stop of the replication content. That means the content deployment is no longer a monstrous all-or-nothing process; instead, you can select to replicate the entire list or one or more variation labels at once.

Similar to terms in managed meta data, variations in SharePoint 2013 support the ability to send site content to the Machine Translation Service application. Alternatively, you can export or import site content for translation by a third party in the industry standard XLIFF format. When exporting content you can include the entire variation label, one page, or just a document. In case you need to develop your own custom translation solutions, the Machine Translation Service object model is similar to the Word Automation Services object model, and is available in server-side as well as CSOM and REST.

> **NOTE** *When the Machine Translation Service application receives a translation request, it forwards the request to a Bing translation service in the cloud. Communicate this with your clients up front.*

By using Host-Named Site Collections (HNSC) and friendly URLs in term-driven publishing pages, a multilingual resource can be mapped to a URL that's much easier to understand for search engines and end users. For example, a publishing page called *foo* in a French site can be mapped to `http://bar.fr/foo` instead of `http://www.bar.com/fr-fr/Pages/foo.aspx`.

Another big change in Variation involves SEO optimization. Page meta data emits the page locale for search engines. In addition, SharePoint now uses HTTP 301 code instead of HTTP 302 for homepage redirection, which is preferable for search engines.

The Content by Search Web Part

The Content by Query (CBQ) Web Part has always been a powerful tool in publishing sites to fulfill content aggregation and rollup requirements. Because publishing sites now heavily rely on search to function, there is this new web part called the *Content by Search (CBS) Web Part*.

As its name implies, CBS enables users to aggregate content directly from the search index. If you look in the cross-publishing section earlier in this chapter, CBS was used in roll-up pages in the product catalog example.

Unlike CBQ, CBS is not constrained to one site collection. It's based on search, so it must to go beyond the site collection boundary. For the same reason, the query results in CBS may not be up to date. Aside from lag time, CBS renders only major versions and cannot query content from site collections marked to be excluded from the search. The simplest way to prove CBS queries are directly served from the index is to reset the index and see how results are instantaneously gone. You don't want to prove this in production.

A query in CBS can be configured to aggregate content based on values on the page or within the URL. Before the results are rendered, you have the option to style them.

> **NOTE** *CBS returns the results in raw XML format. Results can be styled using snippets of HTML and JavaScript instead of XSLT. These snippets are referred to as display templates in SharePoint 2013 and are stored in the Master Page gallery.*

Using display templates, it's much easier to customize CBS results than CBQ because you work with pure HTML and JavaScript. Display templates are also used in search-related web parts, which are covered later in this chapter.

Design Manager

With the advent of SharePoint 2013, Design View in SharePoint Designer is officially removed from the product. Whether this was the best decision and whether it makes sense to carry the word "Designer" as part of the product name are both beyond the scope of this book; however, what's obvious is that there should be an easier option for power users to customize SharePoint.

Microsoft recommends customers use SharePoint to customize the product. To help do so, Microsoft has introduced another tool called *Design Manager*, which helps customers customize SharePoint sites in a wizard-like approach.

Developers work with a designer or a design agency to brand SharePoint. First, the developer receives the non-SharePoint branding assets (HTML, CSS, images, and so on) from the design agency. The design agency can create these files using any web design tool such as Dreamweaver or Microsoft Expression. The developer uploads the received files to SharePoint. Then, with a behind-the-scenes automatic process, SharePoint-specific assets (*.master & *.aspx) are generated. This process repeats until the branding task is complete. Then the developer exports the branding assets and creates a package (*.wsp) to deploy the custom brand to the production farm.

Figure 2-21 shows new Design Manager that replaces SharePoint Designer to customize SharePoint.

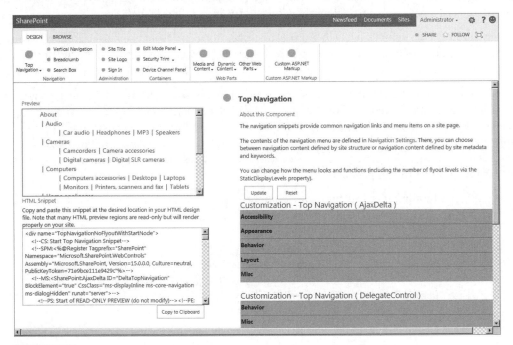

FIGURE 2-21

Design Manager provides a snippet gallery, so SharePoint controls can be quickly added to the design (refer to Figure 2-21). The Ribbon on the top helps you find and add other SharePoint components. When a new control is added, only HTML representation of the control is generated, so the design agency can see how the control looks in SharePoint, even if its toolsets don't understand SharePoint. When it sends the branding assets back, SharePoint ignores the HTML representations and renders ASP.NET and SharePoint controls.

Design Manager is not perfect, but then again, this is the first iteration of the tool.

Mobile Support

SharePoint 2010 had support for mobile devices, but it was rather limited and difficult to customize. New to SharePoint 2013 are device channels. A *device channel* can be targeted at specific mobile devices and associated with a master page allowing for specific custom branding implementations for each targeted device. In addition, site designers can decide which sections of the Page Layouts should be included in a channel. This makes it easy to manage the user experience on mobile devices.

You can configure device channels by browsing to Site Settings ⇨ Look and Feel ⇨ Device Channels. This setting is only available in publishing sites.

Image Rendition

SharePoint 2013 enables site owners to optimize the user experience by creating different rendition formats for media files used in their sites. This new feature is called *image rendition* but can be used for both images and videos.

When image rendition is properly configured, SharePoint dynamically transforms an image to the settings specified in its rendition and then it caches it on the web front end to serve future requests. Because dynamic transformation to the appropriate rendition setting is a costly operation, SharePoint 2013 relies on disk-based BLOB caching to improve performance.

> **NOTE** *Image rendition does not work until the disk-based Binary Large Object (BLOB) cache is enabled for a web application. Disk-based BLOB caching is disabled by default. For information about turning it on, see the product documentation at* `http://msdn.microsoft.com/en-us/library/aa604896.aspx`.

The process starts with site owners defining the right renditions by browsing to Site Settings ⇨ Look and Feel ⇨ Image Renditions on their sites. Simply, an image rendition has three elements: name, height, and width.

After image renditions are defined, content authors can upload an image, and then click the image hover panel to see the different renditions in effect or click the Click to Change link to further crop the image to ensure the important details in the image are still focused after being resized by a specific rendition. At this point, image rendition for the uploaded image is complete.

The next step would be for the content authors to pick the wanted image rendition when adding a media file to a page. Figure 2-22 demonstrates how a content owner is about to pick a rendition for the uploaded image optimized for viewing on Windows Phone 7.

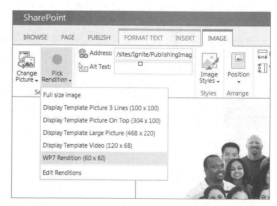

FIGURE 2-22

Images with renditions can be referenced by any combination of rendition ID, width, or height. Here are two examples:

```
<img src="/sites/tp/PublishingImages/ppl.jpg?RenditionID=2"/>
<img src="/sites/tp/PublishingImages/ppl.jpg?Width=60"/>
```

When used with device channels, image renditions can provide a great user experience on mobile devices. Image rendition also helps reduce the bandwidth consumption on mobile devices for remote users with bandwidth-constrained connections.

App-Driven Publishing Sites

The majority of public-facing websites on the Internet are built using a SharePoint publishing template. As you saw in this chapter, there are many new capabilities and improvements in WCM for building powerful public-facing websites. In addition to those improvements, the new SharePoint apps can be leveraged within public-facing sites to extend the user experience. For example, a provider-hosted app can be used to inject a shopping card application to the site, or a SharePoint-hosted app can be used to render a stock ticker on the homepage of the site.

In summary, apps can be used to take some of the functionality commonly developed for public-facing sites away from the site and put it in the context of some companion apps that ship on the side or in future iterations of the site.

SEARCH

Search in SharePoint knows no boundaries. It can surface physically living content in a SharePoint farm or external content outside of the farm.

With the advent of the service application model in SharePoint 2010, search became a first-class service that could scale beyond just one farm. You could publish a search service application from Farm A and consume it in Farm B. Search in SharePoint 2010 came in two flavors: enterprise search and FAST search. In enterprise search you had SharePoint Foundation search, SharePoint Server search, and Search server. FAST search, sold as a separate SKU, was added to the product when Microsoft acquired FAST. Each of the search products in SharePoint 2010 had their own focus (and cost) and demonstrated unique strengths and limitations.

With the current wave of Office 2013 products, Microsoft decided to unify search under one product and to extend it so that it can support the new programming model and architectural changes made to the platform. With the new unified product came many changes, which are highlighted next.

Search Schema

Search schema is a new name for search meta-data properties. Links to search schema, where you make meta-data property mapping, are now available in both site settings and site collection settings. That said, site owners no longer must be given access to or go to the search service application to work with meta-data properties.

Search Navigation

In SharePoint 2010, the only way to let users quickly jump between different search experiences was to create new scopes and new results pages, and bind them together. That way, new scopes would show up in the scope drop down in the top navigation, enabling users to perform a vertical search.

In SharePoint 2013, you can configure search navigation per site by browsing to Site Settings ⇨ Search Settings. This enables you to create different search experiences for users and includes them directly in the search box without using an additional scope drop down.

Figure 2-23 shows the new search navigation on the Search Settings page.

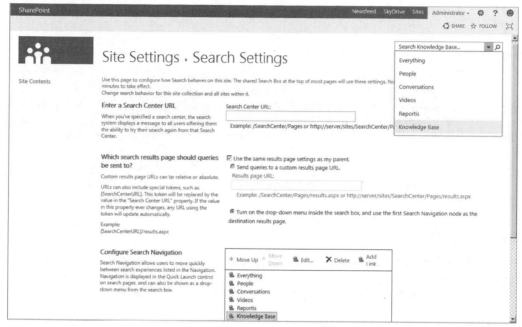

FIGURE 2-23

Search settings performed at the site level can be overridden at the site collection level by going to the Search Settings under the Site Collection Administration group. For example, you can configure all sites in a given site collection to use a search center and totally ignore the search navigation settings at the site levels.

Result Sources

Result source is the new name for scopes and federated locations in SharePoint 2010 with three major changes.

First, result sources can be accessed from the search service application and in Search Settings at each site.

Second, FAST is no longer an information source protocol; instead there are two new protocols: Exchange and Remote SharePoint. Select Exchange protocol for results from Exchange and Remote SharePoint for results from a search service application hosted in a separate farm.

Third, you can specify a filter that will be applied to your queries using new Query Transformation settings. This replaces Search Scope Rules in SharePoint 2010 and is handy when performing vertical search against something specific such as a Customers list or broad list such as a Sales statistics database. There is also a nice query builder that enables you to build your query transformations using a designer and sort and see the returned results in real time.

For example, using query transformation you can restrict the queries to information with a specific value for a managed property. The query transformation {searchTerms} author="Andy Au" returns only documents that have the user's search terms (contained in the {searchTerms} token), and authored by "Andy Au". You can also prefix the queries. The query transformation Hockey{searchTerms} always adds the prefix Hockey and concatenates (AND) it with the user's search terms.

> **NOTE** *The term* scope *is no longer used in SharePoint 2013 search and has been removed from the search UI. The concept, however, still exists. To perform a vertical search, you use a combination of search navigation and result sources to accomplish the same thing.*

The inclusion of result sources in SharePoint 2013 search provides a powerful mechanism to perform vertical searches against various information sources across your organization, such as sales data or knowledge-base articles.

Display Templates

As mentioned previously, SharePoint 2013 takes a different approach than SharePoint 2010 to customize the search results. Now, search-related web parts (that is, Search Result Web Part) heavily rely on display templates to control the appearance and behavior of results served from the index.

> **NOTE** *Search results in SharePoint 2013 are still in the raw XML format that you need to parse and extract. However, search results can be styled using display templates instead of XSLT.*

Display templates are snippets of HTML and JavaScript. There are many preconfigured display templates that ship with the product, but you can also create your own. Similar to customizing other templates in SharePoint, just copy an existing one that's similar to what you want, and start from there. To do so, you can use any HTML editor you want.

Display templates can be found in Master Page Gallery ⇨ Display Templates ⇨ Search. As you can see, there are other types of display templates in the Master Page gallery used in other workloads such as WCM.

Result Types

Result types tie everything together. You use a result type to bind a result source or a type of search result to a display template that the search engine should use to render the search result.

Just like display templates, there are many out-of-the-box result types, and you can create your own. Each result type must have one or more conditions to compare search results against and an action that specifies what display template to use for the search result. For example, a custom result type named Knowledge Base specifies that if a search result is served from the result source *KbRs*, then use the display template `KbDispTemplate.aspx` to render the results.

Result types along with many other search configurations can be configured at the site collection level and at the site level.

Query Rules

A query rule is the last stop to modify and enhance the search experience before the core results are shown to the end user. A query rule has one or more conditions that must be met to make the rule fire. You can also define a query rule that fires for any search (which in turn means there is no rule).

A query rule is where you decide if you want to do one or more of the following:

1. Add promoted or sponsored links above the core results.

2. Rank a block of additional results (known as the *result block*) above the core results. This makes the result block always show on the top of the core results.

3. Rank a result block within the core results. This result block may not show in the first page if it is not highly relevant.

4. Change the ranked results, such as changing their ordering. For example, you can sort the ranked result so that PDF documents show up higher on the search result page.

5. Route a result block to a CBS Web Part instead of being shown in the Search Results Web Part.

6. Make the query rule expire after a certain date.

Figure 2-24 illustrates a query rule that has been configured against the local SharePoint result source (used in Everything vertical) and is triggered when the user's search term contains the word SharePoint.

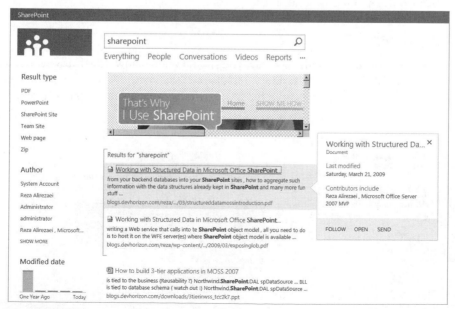

FIGURE 2-24

After the rule triggers, it adds a promoted link (`http://sharepoint.microsoft.com/iusesharepoint/landing.aspx`) as a banner (it could also be a link) and then renders a result block that contains results from another result source pointing to an external website (`http://blogs.devhorizon.com/reza`). The rule puts everything above the core ranked results.

Conceptually, some of the things you can do by using query rules are similar to search keywords and best bets in SharePoint 2010. However, query rules are more powerful and highly dynamic, conditional, and customizable.

Continuous Crawl

SharePoint search plows through content using either full or incremental crawls. Full crawl focuses on almost everything about the content, whereas incremental crawls focus on picking up the changes in content or pushing the updated ACLs down to the affected items within the index. Because SharePoint 2013 relies heavily on search in some of the workloads such as WCM and Social, Microsoft introduced a new type of crawl: *continuous crawl.*

To provide maximum freshness, continuous crawls focus on smaller changes and use the change logs to pick up those changes faster and in more efficient ways. Continuous crawls overlap each other, which means one continuous crawl doesn't hold up the other one in picking up the changes.

> **NOTE** *Continuous crawl plays an important role to ensure maximum freshness of search results. Stale content was a major push back to leverage search in content query and aggregation scenarios in the earlier versions of SharePoint.*

Two important tips about continuous crawls: First, they are only available for SharePoint content sources, where the choice is between continuous or incremental. Second, continuous crawl can't be paused or stopped. Your only option is to disable it.

Putting It All Together

If you put together everything you have learned so far, you should realize how drastically search has been changed in SharePoint 2013. Figure 2-25 shows a high-level architectural overview of the new architecture side by side with the enterprise search in SharePoint 2010. You can see the difference.

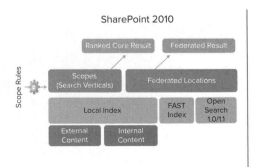
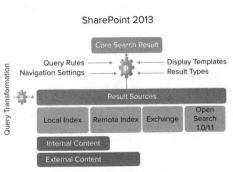

FIGURE 2-25

To recap everything, here are the high-level steps you need to take to perform a vertical search in SharePoint 2013:

1. *Result page* — Create a result page using (Welcome Page) Search Results Page Layout (that is, knowledgebase.aspx). This page shows the results of a vertical search such as Knowledge Base.

2. *Search Navigation* — Add a link to the result page in the Search Navigation settings.

3. *Result source* — Create a result source with a query transformation to filter the results to something narrow such as a Knowledge Base site or database.

4. *Search result web part binding* — Edit the search result web part on the result page you created in step 1, and bind it to the result source.

5. *Display template* — Create a display template that controls how the result should be shown in the result page you created in step 1.

6. *Result type* — Create a result type to bind the result source to the display template.

7. *Query rule* — Optionally, create a query rule to render promoted links and a results block served from the result source you created in step 3 in other search verticals such as Everything.

Query Languages

For developers, search has been always a great way to access content across site collections when the content freshness was not a deal breaker. In SharePoint 2013, continuous crawl resolves this issue to an extent. Another new change for developers is the query language they would use.

Let's start with the bad news for many of you who know and love T-SQL style queries. SQL Query Language (SQL) using the `FullTextSqlQuery` class is no longer supported in SharePoint 2013. Start changing your SQL queries today if you plan to migrate to SharePoint 2013.

FAST Query Language (FQL) is still available, but developers are advised to use Keyword Query Language (KQL) and syntax to build their queries against a search engine. KQL has received some enhancements and is used almost everywhere you need to build a search query, such as those in query transformation and query rules. Table 2-3 includes a few examples of KQL queries:

TABLE 2-3: KQL Queries

KQL QUERY	EXECUTION RESULT
Hockey	Returns items containing Hockey or hockey
Hockey Soccer	Returns items containing hockey AND soccer
Hockey OR Soccer	Returns items containing hockey OR soccer
Hockey*	Returns items like "Hockey" and "Hockey Jersey"

continues

TABLE 2-3 *(continued)*

KQL QUERY	EXECUTION RESULT
"Hockey Jersey"	Returns items with exact phrase "Hockey Jersey"
Firstname:A	Returns all people whose first name starts with "A"
Title:Hockey IsDocument:1	Returns all documents with "Hockey" in the title
Author:Andy IsDocument:1	Returns all documents authored by "Andy"
Hockey FileExtension:pdf	Returns PDF documents containing "Hockey"
contentClass:STS_ListItem_Events	Returns all events from all calendars
contentClass:STS_ListItem_Tasks	Returns all task items

Exporting and Importing Search Settings

If you have configured search or developed SharePoint applications that use search as the data access mechanism, you probably know that migrating your search configurations and settings across DEV, QA, and PROD environments was not an easy task. To target deployment scenarios, you had to write PowerShell scripts and XML configuration files to ensure your settings were applied consistently across your server farms.

In SharePoint 2013, you can export search settings or import them at the site level. This process handles query rules, result sources, and managed properties that you have created for a site, but you need to move the branding artifacts such as search master pages, display templates, and web parts. Any customization to the search result pages won't be handled by the new search export and import feature.

You can export or important your search settings by browsing to Site Settings ➪ Search ➪ Configuration Export or Configuration Import.

Search-Driven Solutions

Because of the new improvements in search, you can build custom solutions that execute search queries using CSOM and REST. For example, the following REST query returns all the results containing the term "hockey":

```
http://server/sites/sc/_api/search/query?querytext='hockey'
```

The following REST query returns all the results containing the term "hockey" sorted by last modified date and time, and in an ascending rank order:

```
http://server/site/_api/search/query?querytext='hockey'&sortlist='LastModifiedTime:
descending,Rank:ascending'
```

The code snippet shown here demonstrates how to perform the same REST search call using CSOM within your apps:

```
ClientContext ctx = new ClientContext("http://Tailspintoys.com/sites/sc");
var query = new KeywordQuery(ctx, ctx.Site);
query.QueryText = "hockey";
query.ResultTypes = ResultType.RelevantResults;
query.Id = Guid.NewGuid();
var queries = new KeywordQuery[1];
queries[0] = query;
SearchExecutor searchExecutor = new SearchExecutor(ctx);
var rcc = searchExecutor.ExecuteQueries(queries);
ctx.ExecuteQuery();
```

No matter what approach you take to execute a KQL query in your apps or workflow, the results are always in the raw XML that you need to parse and extract what you want. You don't get JSON objects in search queries.

BCS

Business Connectivity Services (BCS) makes it easy to integrate SharePoint with external systems. To do so, BCS maps external systems capabilities to standardized interfaces to define how to interact with them. At the core, there are four concepts in BCS that you must understand:

➤ *External system* — Any supported source of data that BCS can access using out-of-the-box or custom connectors. Examples of external systems are a web service, a database, a Line of Business (LOB) system, Web 2.0 service, or even a .NET object that contains data.

➤ *External content type (ECT)* — An external content type defines the schema and data access capabilities of an external system and its behavior. External content types are often referred to as the building blocks of BCS.

> **NOTE** *Conceptually, you can think of an external content type as a business entity. An entity is an abstraction of something real such as a customer, sales order, and so on. An entity is an entity whether used in BCS, C# class, Entity Framework, or database schema. Each entity has a name, meta data, associations, and stereotyped operations — such as create, read, update, and delete — that enables access to external data. Each entity can have multiple instances such as rows in a database table, SharePoint list items, or instances of an object.*

➤ *BDC model (BDCM)* — The XML representation of one or more external content types along with resources, such as localized strings, meta data, permissions, and connectivity information. With a BDC model, developers do not need to learn the nuances of each external system.

➤ *External list* — External lists enable users to present LOB data as if they are native SharePoint lists. In external lists the data does not actually reside within SharePoint; instead it is pulled directly from the backend external system each time the list is accessed.

Thankfully, BCS core concepts have not changed in SharePoint 2013. However, there are a few enhancements. Now review the changes.

OData Connector

SharePoint 2013 ships with an OData connector for BCS. This enables developers to consume data from OData-compliant services in their BCS solutions. In the Windows Azure marketplace, Microsoft exposes many free or paid OData data sources that you can consume in your BCS solutions. For example, you can consume the free Northwind OData source at `http://services .odata.org/Northwind/Northwind.svc/`. The following code snippet shows a portion of a BDCM built around the Northwind OData source:

```
<LobSystem Name="ODataNWModel" Type="OData">
  <Properties>
    <Property Name="ODataServiceMetadataUrl" Type="System.String">
      http://services.odata.org/Northwind/Northwind.svc/$metadata</Property>
    <Property Name="ODataMetadataAuthenticationMode"
    Type="System.String">PassThrough</Property>
    <Property Name="ODataServicesVersion" Type="System.String">2.0</Property>
  </Properties>
  <LobSystemInstances>
    <LobSystemInstance Name="http://services.odata.org/Northwind/Northwind.svc">
      <Properties>
        <Property Name="ODataServiceUrl" Type="System.String">
         http://services.odata.org/Northwind/Northwind.svc
        </Property>
        <Property Name="ODataServiceAuthenticationMode"
        Type="System.String">PassThrough</Property>
        <Property Name="ODataFormat"
        Type="System.String">application/atom+xml</Property>
      </Properties>
    </LobSystemInstance>
  </LobSystemInstances>

  <!-- Code Omitted for brevity -->

</LobSystem>
```

As discussed earlier, SharePoint list data is already exposed as an OData source. When you put everything together, it's fair to say SharePoint can be a producer and a consumer of OData sources.

BCS Powered Apps

One of the issues with ECTs in SharePoint 2010 was that they had to be configured at the farm level and required farm administrators to be involved. With the new programming model introduced in SharePoint 2013 and the emphasis on cloud computing and granular isolation, this is not possible anymore.

In SharePoint 2013, developers can include ECTs in their apps and access external data from any external system such as Netflix or Windows Azure directly from their apps without involving the tenant administrator.

> **NOTE** *Only Visual Studio 2012 has the support to generate BDCM from an OData source. There is currently no support for this in SharePoint Designer 2013.*

The following code snippet demonstrates how an external list can be defined in an app:

```
<ListInstance Url="$Resources:core,lists_Folder;/BCSEmpoweredList"
Description=" A BCS Empowered External List"
OnQuickLaunch="TRUE" Title="BCS-ECT" Id="BCSEmpoweredList">
    <DataSource>
      <Property Value="" Name="LobSystemInstance"/>
      <Property Value="" Name="EntityNamespace"/>
      <Property Value="" Name="Entity"/>
      <Property Value="" Name="SpecificFinder"/>
      <Property Name="MetadataCatalogFileName"
                       Value="BDCMetadata.bdcm" />
    </DataSource>
</ListInstance>
```

As you can see the code snippet has a few elements, each representing a property for the external list. For example, the `Entity` property should contain the name of the business entity that this external list points to in the backend system.

CSOM and REST Interface

Just like other workloads discussed so far, BCS has a new JavaScript object model to support remote calls.

For example, the following REST query returns all customers from an external list called Customers. This list is deployed by an app:

```
http://server/sites/sc/_api/lists/getbytitle('Customers')/items
```

The following code snippet shows how to make the same REST call, but uses JavaScript against CSOM and then binds the results to a grid:

```
BCSEmpoweredList.Grid.prototype = {
      init: function () {
          $.ajax({
              url: this.surlWeb + "_api/lists/getbytitle('Customers')/
              items?$select=BdcIdentity,CustomerID,ContactName",
              headers: {
                  "accept": "application/json",
                  "X-RequestDigest": $("#__REQUESTDIGEST").val()
              },
              success: this.showItems
          });
      }
```

The following code snippet shows how to use a BCS object model in C# code against CSOM:

```
var ctx = new SP.ClientContext();
var web = ctx.get_web();
entity = web.getAppBdcCatalog().getEntity(entityNameSpace, entityName);
ctx.load(entity);
lobSystem = entity.getLobSystem();
ctx.load(lobSystem);
lobSystemInstances = lobSystem.getLobSystemInstances();
ctx.load(lobSystemInstances);
ctx.executeQueryAsync(success, failure);
```

The code starts with establishing the context and referencing the business entity. Once the entity is referenced, the content is loaded and two event handlers are registered for call backs. In the success event handler, you will write code to deal with the returned result.

SUMMARY

If you have made it this far, congratulations!

In this chapter you were introduced to many new features and enhancements that accompany SharePoint 2013 and the changes to the SharePoint programming model. All these new features were introduced to help you understand what is needed at a high level for a SharePoint developer to build applications in SharePoint 2013. You saw how many times you can use the same CSOM and REST code pattern and just change the endpoints to target different workloads in the product. That's how you can code in SharePoint 2013.

You will find more detailed coverage of each workload discussed in this chapter throughout the book. Keep reading!

3

Developer Tools for SharePoint 2013

WHAT'S IN THIS CHAPTER?

➤ Understanding the different tools available to SharePoint developers

➤ Exploring what's new in SharePoint Designer 2013

➤ Using the new SharePoint tools in Visual Studio

SharePoint has become one of the most developed-on platforms over the last decade, and Microsoft has invested in the developer experience with every release of SharePoint. SharePoint 2013 continues to improve the tools available for developers such as Visual Studio and SharePoint Designer while making tremendous strides with the addition of apps, Office 365, and Microsoft Office development. The addition of apps in SharePoint 2013 is a drastic change along with using familiar programming web standards such as HTML, CSS, JavaScript, OData, REST, and OAuth. The developer tools have included this support as well with full support for development against the cloud platforms. If you have used SharePoint 2010, you will see that many of the same project files are available, but there are new additions to the array of items you can now use.

The development tools are more integrated with the platform; debugging is easier in complex scenarios such as the web and more; and new tooling containing designers and templates was added so that you can easily work on SharePoint and transition to another web-based framework. This chapter takes a deeper look at each of these tools so that you can understand what they can do for development with SharePoint.

CUSTOMIZATION OPTIONS WITH SHAREPOINT

SharePoint is full of options for customization and development. These changes can be made from many different tools by many different users. Although every developer doesn't need to know each tool in depth, it helps to know what each tool's capabilities are and what the strengths are of each tool. Table 3-1 shows an overview of the different types of users and the tools they use to customize their SharePoint experience.

TABLE 3-1: Tools for Customization

USER	PRIMARY TOOL
End user	SharePoint Sites
Power user/Designers	Microsoft SharePoint Designer 2013
Developer	Visual Studio 2012

The largest group of users is end users. They understand how to use the user interface to build an application for a specific need. End users primarily make out of the box (OOB) changes directly in the SharePoint site that the user has access to. Although many developers don't initially think of these changes as development, SharePoint has grown over the years to include end users that fully understand how to make small modifications to HTML, CSS, JavaScript, and customizable web parts that allow them to build dynamic applications.

Check out the user community at `https://www.nothingbutsharepoint.com/sites/eusp/`.

Many of the changes focus on changing the look and feel of the site, input entry, and information management with deep knowledge of the problem domain the user works on. For many end users SharePoint development is not their primary job, but a requirement to have functional and optimal applications for the solutions they solve.

The next group of users is the power users. They need more capabilities than the user interface provides them, and the tool of choice is Microsoft SharePoint Designer. As the name implies, the tool has its roots as an HTML editor for designing web pages. The tool is a must-have for many power users, especially with improved capabilities added in SharePoint Designer 2010 that included additional workflow capabilities, packaging integration, BCS integration, and richer HTML capabilities. The SharePoint Designer team understands the importance of both the end user and developers, especially for Application Lifecycle Management (ALM). Developers using SharePoint Designer can deploy solutions directly to their production sites if they build only a single site, or they can save the changes locally. The changes stored locally can be reopened in Visual Studio for further customization and stored in source control when they are completed.

The final group of users is developers, and the tool for coded or packaged solutions is Visual Studio 2012. Visual Studio 2012 gives a familiar interface for developers of .NET languages such as ASP. NET that requires less learning time to quickly start building apps. One of the major challenges facing new developers has always been learning the SharePoint API Framework and understanding how to modify the XML that defines SharePoint. The enhancements in Visual Studio 2012 have created an improved experience and added new tools to give developers a user interface for many common changes in the XML.

OOB DEVELOPER EXPERIENCE

The user interface for SharePoint has become one of the most used development platforms. This is due to the number of users of SharePoint and the different ways users can change the application directly through the user interface. Many end users can create powerful applications and experiences with a few clicks. In addition to building the applications directly on the site, you can use the UI to quickly create mock-up lists and sites that can be reused in SharePoint designer and Visual Studio. This adds a great capability for developers looking for a rapid application development (RAD) platform for proof-of-concept code or expediting development. Each option has been improved with SharePoint 2013 for creating full-featured business applications.

The Get Started with Your Site web part provides users with a quick set of actions to start customizing their sites. They can change the look and feel, title, and logos, and share the site with others. Not every site must have the getting started web part, but you can allow site owners to add and remove it easily through the user interface. When the users no longer need the web part, they can click the Remove This link and start using the Settings menu for any future changes.

One of the quick actions is to add the new Project Summary web part. This new Project Summary web part can be quickly added to the page using the Working on a Deadline? link on the Get Started with Your Site web part. Click the link and you are prompted to add two apps: the Tasks (with a Timeline) and Calendar (as shown in Figure 3-1).

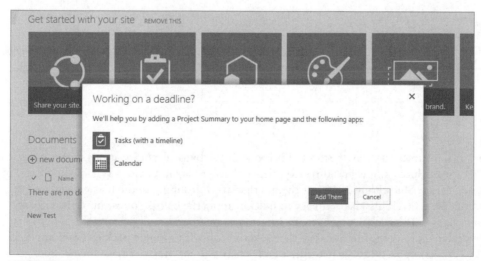

FIGURE 3-1

You can add other applications to the site to further customize the look or provide added functionality, such as a Site Mailbox. From the quick actions, click Add Lists, Libraries and Other apps to bring up the Add apps menu. The new SharePoint store enables you to select from a number of prebuilt applications without coding them. When you select the SharePoint store, you can access full prebuilt apps or apps that enhance your site.

Understanding the User Interface for Customization

Customization of sites is one of the main actions that a developer needs to perform, whether that modifies the look and feel or just uses web parts and apps on the page. There have been major changes to the user interface look and feel, but the page customization experience remains familiar. This means that the major changes to the page with editing using the SharePoint Ribbon have not changed. Don't forget to click the Page tab if the Ribbon does not automatically appear. The Ribbon is still there; it just might not be needed at the moment. There are still contextual tabs based on the actions you perform and the web part that you select. There is a subtle difference with how the Ribbon displays to the user. Instead of requiring page real estate to always be reserved, the Ribbon now drops down onto the page and then can be hidden to display the content under the Ribbon as shown in Figure 3-2 (hidden Ribbon) and Figure 3-3 (displayed Ribbon).

FIGURE 3-2

FIGURE 3-3

Branding the site continues to evolve because this is one of the biggest modifications performed. SharePoint 2013 introduces a new branding experience that builds on previous versions of SharePoint called *composed looks*. SharePoint 2010 has themes that are a grouping of the files needed to change the colors on a site. This makes it easy to quickly apply the colors you want to the CSS on the SharePoint pages without changing the CSS location or making any changes to the page. This did not allow designers to completely change the look and feel with a single package, as composed looks provide. Each composed look is made up of a Display Name, Master Page, Theme, Background Image, and Font Scheme. Also, a new Try It Out link has been added to make it easier to view the site before applying any changes. As you can see from Figure 3-4, you can change the entire look and feel of the site with a single click.

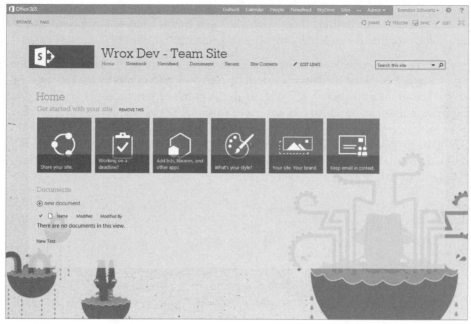

FIGURE 3-4

SharePoint 2010 made great changes to the way users edited pages using wiki page editing and adding the ability to place web parts anywhere on the page. The ability to create and design your layouts remains part of the rich user experience. Major changes have been added in SharePoint 2013 to the Web Content Management (WCM) and Publishing pages that can be reviewed in Chapter 10, "Web Content Management."

Microsoft has created a more intuitive user interface by adding common language terminology and adding inline editing for some common navigation. The use of the Pencil icon, along with the text "Edit", can be seen in any location that allows users to edit. For navigation you can now click the Edit Links icon to manage the top navigation links or the quick launch links.

Anyone new to SharePoint finds that the page editing still provides the familiar Microsoft Word experience using the wiki pages that enable you to add all types of rich content, from text to images. The experience is more fluid than previous versions with new features such as Paste Clean and a pre-view of applying styles before you select them. Users were always asking what the styles looked like to know which one to apply to the content. The Change with Preview feature enables users to know what the pages, styles, and fonts are before they make the content changes. Also the Styles menu is now similar to the Microsoft Word Style menu layout with the name and a preview of what the style looks like. Users now see the full set of styles on the Ribbon without needing to try each one or have a style guide printed out and next to each computer.

One feature that users have wanted is to add code to the page without the page manipulating it when it is saved. Two new options enable this change: the Embed Code option and the Video and Audio embedding option. With the exponential growth of many cloud services, users need a way to add embedded video from such sites as YouTube and Vimeo (in addition to adding custom scripts to sites such as Facebook, LinkedIn, and Twitter). These cloud services enable users to build customized sites by using generated code that users can add by copying and pasting.

Getting your web parts onto the page and customizing them has not changed from SharePoint 2010. The Web Part menu appears on the Ribbon for inserting your web parts onto the page. You can select your web parts and insert them into the page as in the previous version. In SharePoint 2013 there are also app parts that can be added to your pages to enrich the content. These app parts are added to the page in the same way that traditional web parts are added to the page through the Parts viewer. To make it easier to find all of the parts, the layout of the Web Part menu has categories: the web parts available in that category, a description of the web part, and the location of where to add to the web part, as shown in Figure 3-5.

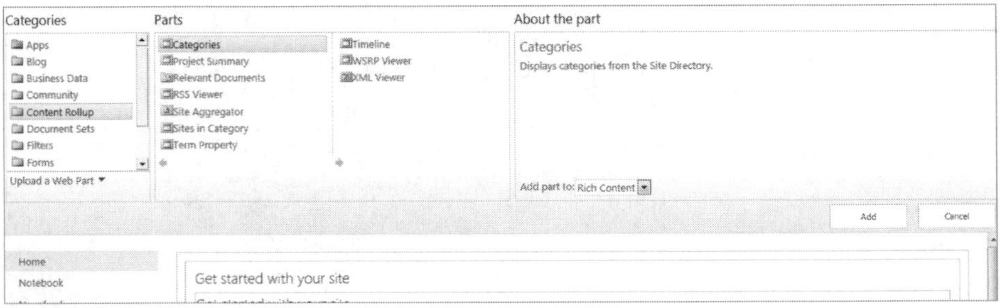

FIGURE 3-5

The Modify Web Part settings have not changed from previous versions of SharePoint. They continue to appear on the right-side tool pane, enabling you to customize the properties for the web part, change its appearance, or modify its layout.

One of the nice things about SharePoint development is that you get a number of out of the box (OOB) web parts to speed your development so that you do not need to write everything from scratch. Although the following isn't an exhaustive list of all the web parts in SharePoint, it includes a number of key, new web parts that you should be aware of: Timeline, Project Summary, and Community Changes.

Microsoft focused on the needs of users to keep all their tasks organized. One area that was needed was to keep tasks visible and updated. The quickest way to add the Project Summary web part to the page is to use the quick actions from the Get Started web part as previously mentioned. After the web part has been added to the page, you can allow end users to update the timeline or manage the task list providing the data to the web part. You can see that the Project Summary web part provides an overview of the upcoming tasks and a timeline of the current tasks. Now you can manage all your tasks, create a project site, and allow users to have a full view of the timeline, all within the user interface, as shown in Figure 3-6.

The Timeline web part provides the timeline without the Summary or Quick Edit links. This allows the user that is managing the site to use the web part that fits their needs, whether that is managing the tasks or simply viewing them. The Timeline web part provides the ability to move the layout of the tasks. Users can still quickly interact with the tasks on the timeline by clicking the task, which brings up a dialog with common editing options such as opening the full item or removing the task from the timeline.

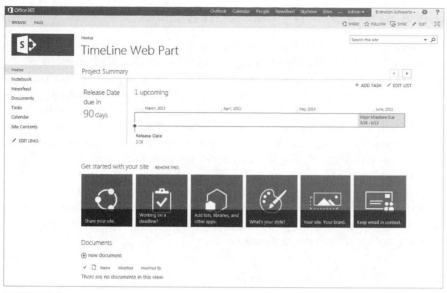

FIGURE 3-6

Microsoft has created a new set of web parts based on the new Community features. The new web parts are About This Community, Join, My Membership, Tools, and What's Happening. These web parts can be added to a site that has the Community features enabled, shown in Figure 3-7. The community site already has the web parts on the page, but you can also add them or move them on the communities you create. You can see they are all grouped into the Community category to easily find and add them.

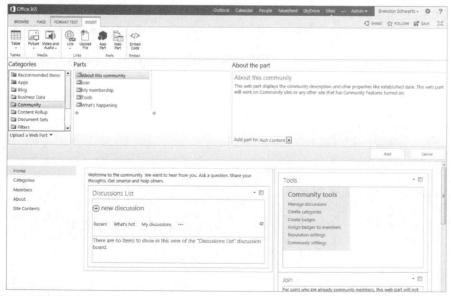

FIGURE 3-7

UNDERSTANDING SHAREPOINT DESIGNER 2013

SharePoint Designer (SPD) can be a powerful tool for developers and power users offering the ability to upgrade solutions to Visual Studio and the ability to export work directly from your site. SharePoint Designer 2013 has become the tool of choice for power users, especially with the additional workflow and BCS additions it received in SharePoint 2010. The design community now has other options for HTML editors, but none of them are as integrated to SharePoint as SharePoint Design. Even with the addition of SharePoint Design Manager in the SharePoint user interface, SharePoint Designer has improvements and will continue to be a useful tool for power users. One of the key goals for page layout and design by the SharePoint team was to make it easier to modify the key aspects. This means there will be alternatives to SharePoint Designer, but tight integration for designers and power users will still be SharePoint Designer for their tool of choice. For users building workflows, SharePoint Designer will be the primary tool of choice. When choosing the tool you will use for development, keep in mind that every tool has its purpose, and if you use the right tool for the job, it will make your SharePoint development easier.

New Features in SharePoint Designer

Because this is a professional development book, you will not see deep coverage of SPD here, but you still should know the primary features and enhancements in SharePoint 2013 beyond the user interface that is provided. These include features such as integration with Business Connectivity Services, Visio Integration, and enhancements to workflow.

Improved Workflow Experience

SharePoint Designer has become the one-stop shop for building, packaging, and installing workflows to SharePoint sites. This section covers the improvements within SharePoint Designer around workflow. For more information on building workflows for SharePoint, see Chapter 15.

Two types of workflow platforms are available in SharePoint Designer: the SharePoint 2010 workflows and now the SharePoint 2013 workflows. The workflow enhancements in SharePoint Design

2010 and the SharePoint 2010 workflow framework still work in SharePoint Designer 2013, but there is now the ability to create SharePoint 2013 workflows with the same level of support in the product. This enables users to maintain work already done with previous versions of SharePoint and the workflows that already are in place today, while creating new workflows that are maintainable and upgradeable in the future. Any time you select to create a new workflow, you will be prompted for the workflow platform type, as shown in Figure 3-8.

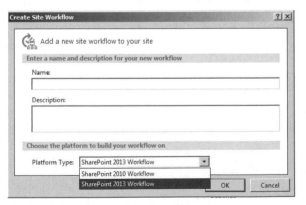

FIGURE 3-8

The new SharePoint 2013 workflow platform type is built using Windows Azure Workflow services. This requires that the SharePoint site that you connect SharePoint Designer with must have Windows Azure Workflow services installed prior to creating SharePoint 2013 workflows. The reason you need to have the new workflow service installed is because the underlying actions in SharePoint Designer must be able to communicate to the service for details on how the action will work. If you use Microsoft Office 365, you have integrated Windows Azure Workflow without needing to install any additional software, but you need to install the service locally if you use the On Premise installation.

New shapes and control of workflow is provided with the Windows Azure Workflows. These new shapes available in SharePoint Designer are Stages, Loops, and Steps. These new shapes enable branching and looping logic that was provided by the new SharePoint 2013 workflows. No longer is it required to use Visual Studio Workflow Designer for support of looping. The new shapes can be added to the designer surface within SharePoint Designer by either dragging and dropping them or using the workflow Ribbon bar to add them in the selected location. When using SharePoint Designer to build your workflows, the required elements of the new shapes are added for you when they are placed on the design surfaces.

The Visual Designer view in SharePoint Designer extends the ability of business users and developers to work on workflows with Visio 2013 and SharePoint Designer. The layout of the Visual Designer provides the same rich representation as Visio with a graphical design surface and sets of shapes for use on the designer surface. To get the built-in functionality of Visual Designer, you must have Visio 2013 installed on the same machine as SharePoint Designer. You can see how quickly a workflow can be started by using this Workflow Visual Designer, as shown in Figure 3-9.

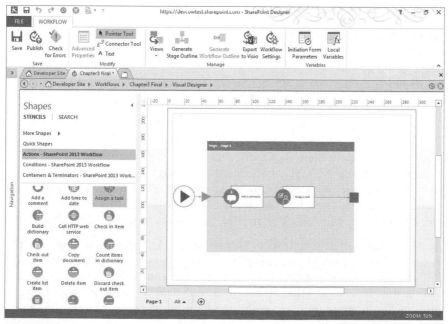

FIGURE 3-9

In addition to using the Visual Designer you can still switch the view back to the Text Based Designer that many users are accustomed to using with previous versions of SharePoint Designer. The changes that are made in the text-based designer are translated into the visual designer as well as the other way, too. If you need a high-level view of the stages, you now switch to the Stages view. The option still exists if you want to export to Visio and allow your business users to modify the workflow in a tool they commonly use.

Performing the same task multiple times in the workflow was difficult, especially if you wanted to quickly reuse some of the conditions or actions that had already been configured. The new Copy and Paste feature can help when designing large workflows that have some repeating information. Workflow designers can now use the same shortcut keys for copy and paste or the Ribbon bar to select a single action or an entire stage with all the contained actions. There are few limitations to this new feature such as no ability to use CTNL+Z to undo the last command. The copy and paste functionality is not like Excel or Word, and you cannot use control to select multiple objects or drag and drop items on the workflow. You can use this Copy and Paste feature in either the SharePoint 2013 Workflow type or the SharePoint 2010 Workflow type.

To make it easier to pass data around a workflow, the Dictionary type variable has been introduced into SharePoint 2013 Workflows. A Dictionary type has a collection of Name/Value pairs, and the value has a type. You can now create complex types that are stored in memory for use within the workflow. There are a number of actions that use the Dictionary type such as Build Dictionary, Count Items in a Dictionary, and Get an Item from a Dictionary, as well as actions such as Call HTTP Web Service. Some of the new actions create the dictionary object, whereas others use it to define the action.

New Workflow Actions

With the addition of Windows Azure Workflow, SharePoint Designer has added a number of new workflow actions that resolve a lot of the difficulties in the previous release. *Workflows* are composed of conditions and actions. *Actions* perform the functions you want, and you can customize workflows by writing custom actions. The new actions are designed for integration with SharePoint 2010 workflows and implement a similar custom action that was available on CodePlex for SharePoint 2010 workflows.

A new action that enables designers to call REST services and OData web services is called the Call Web Service Action. This action is designed to make an HTTP web service call and return the data in the JSON format. This action could be used to call any website that exposes web-based APIs, in addition to frameworks such as ASP.NET Web API endpoints. The importance of directly calling these services using the basic authentication supported in the RequestHeader is that you can now connect to data with dynamic structures. This action is available when you select the SharePoint 2013 workflows and can be added to the design surface using the new Shapes or the Actions drop down.

The Start Workflow Action has been added to allow SharePoint 2013 workflows to start SharePoint 2010 workflows' direction from the workflow. This provides an easy way to use the new workflow platform, but still use the investments that have been made in built and tested works using the SharePoint 2010 version. Just like all the other actions, you can add it directly from the Shapes or workflow Actions menu. When configured, your existing workflows are ready to use again without any modifications until you are ready to modify them.

Navigating the User Interface

SharePoint Designer provides a consistent user interface with the common Ribbon UI to help discover the tasks you can perform in SPD against your SharePoint sites. The navigation of SPD uses grouping of logical SharePoint artifacts for users to quickly navigate to the actions needed. This interface makes navigation and discovery of your SharePoint site and information architecture easier. Figure 3-10 shows SharePoint Designer in action.

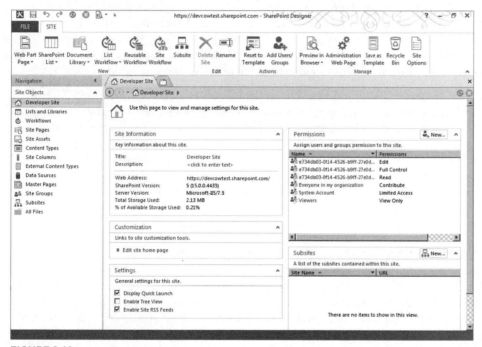

FIGURE 3-10

SharePoint Designer is tightly integrated to the SharePoint sites you are editing, and you must be connected to a SharePoint site to use the features of SharePoint Designer. After you connect to a site, the details display along with the permissions and settings. Connecting to a site is required for the information that is displayed and to allow for the direct changes to be made to the site. SharePoint Designer does not store the data locally but always makes the changes directly to the site after the Save and/or Publish buttons are pressed.

The navigation for SharePoint Designer 2013 has remained the same as the previous version with the site objects grouped in the navigation pane, which makes it easy to find what you are looking for. The site objects are grouped into common actions by the following categories: Site Information, Lists and Libraries, Workflows, Site Pages, Site Assets, Content Types, Site Columns, External Content Types, Data Sources, Master Pages, Site Groups, Subsites, and All Files. From the Navigation menu you can begin changing the content of the site as needed. Select the site objects you would like to change, and the Summary menu shows a list of all the items on that site. For example, if you select Site Page, you see a list of all the site pages with actions on the Ribbon to make modifications.

The Ribbon was introduced in SharePoint Designer 2010 and is used to perform actions in SharePoint Designer just like in Microsoft Office products. The Ribbon user interface makes it easier for you to work with site objects by showing contextual tabs based on the selected objects that you click. The Ribbon interface makes it simple to manage your site with all the options available in a single interface and grouped together.

Workflow developers new to SharePoint Designer can find the full and rich capabilities wanted for any development, testing, and quick changes. New workflows that can be created for a site are based on the list, reusable, or site workflow. In addition to the new features added, you still have the capabilities around the existing actions and conditions. Management of the workflows can be done directly in SharePoint Designer as well as publishing the new workflows created.

Having the ability to create, design, and work with Business Connectivity Services (BCS) in SharePoint 2013 allows users to quickly manage their external content types. Using SharePoint Designer you can view your external content types and make new ones. The external content types can connect to databases, .NET types, or web services, and you can have SharePoint Designer autogenerate the methods needed to perform your create, read, update, and delete (CRUD) changes, and finder/query operations against the back ends. Finally, you can create the external lists associated with your external content type in SharePoint Designer. You learn more about the BCS in Chapter 13, so jump ahead if this topic interests you.

UNDERSTANDING VISUAL STUDIO 2012 TOOLS

SharePoint development with Visual Studio has become the primary developer tool familiar to most custom developers. Visual Studio 2010 made SharePoint development tools a first-class citizen inside of Visual Studio, and the improvements build on this progress. Visual Studio 2012 ships with a number of new templates and tools that make SharePoint development easier. The SharePoint and Microsoft Office development experience has been bridged and provides many enhancements.

In addition to the Visual Studio changes and enhancements, the SharePoint and Office teams focused improvements on some of the critical areas of need. The primary areas of focus were on the common tasks performed such as working with lists, debugging, and testing. You can see many new Visual Studio Templates as well for quickly building new apps and Office components. There are new Visual Designers, which provide the comfortable interaction similar to other data used in Visual Studio. Office 365 has become a popular tool for many organizations to leverage SharePoint 2013. To enable customizations on the Office 365 platform, Visual Studio now also enables Publishing SharePoint Solutions to the servers remotely, directly within Visual Studio.

With the introduction of apps both for SharePoint and Office as a recommended option for building enhancements in SharePoint, Visual Studio has added support for the four stages of developing apps. These stages are start, design, develop, and publish. Visual Studio provides the tools to accomplish both the develop and publish stages of building your app. All the hosting models for app development are supported as well as the ability to debug your apps when they are built. No matter which type of integration or SharePoint UX extensions you select, the development experience within Visual Studio remains the same.

SharePoint 2013 focuses more on web development than ever before. The client-side frameworks, REST-based endpoints, and standards-based code now enable developers to create powerful applications without major changes to many components. Visual Studio improves the experience for developers with added IntelliSense for JavaScript. This can be one of the most difficult and time-consuming development tasks because the language does not show errors with a compilation like compiled code. To assist developers with this issue, Visual Studio now supports debugging the JavaScript.

> **NOTE** *The SharePoint 2010 templates for Visual Studio will be installed by default with Visual Studio 2012. These project templates would still work for non-deprecated features, but you should use the SharePoint 2013 templates for any new development.*

Finally, there have been improvements to building components such as Web Parts Project Item templates. To make it easier to create Silverlight components, there is now a Silverlight Web Part template. You can use this template to add your own Silverlight application or create one with Visual Studio. This might be useful if you know that Silverlight is supported in an environment such as an intranet and allows for another way to present data and information. The Sandboxed Visual Web Part is also a part of Visual Studio templates provided to developers. The SharePoint Project templates have been updated and streamlined to allow for a clean development experience. This process included moving some project templates to the project items list to allow for fewer items to select from when creating a Visual Studio project.

Before diving into the project types that Visual Studio supports for SharePoint, spend some time doing a quick walk around Visual Studio and the capabilities it provides for SharePoint regardless of the project type you select. These features include the templates for SharePoint 2013, the ability to import Web Solutions Packages (WSPs) in the Visual Studio environment, SharePoint Server Explorer node integration, exploring the Project Explorer, and finally the changes to the Package Designer that make it possible to build and deploy both SharePoint apps and SharePoint WSP packages.

Starting a New SharePoint 2013 Project

To start building solutions for SharePoint 2013 with Visual Studio 2012 you need to install the Microsoft Office Developer Tools for Visual Studio 2012. This set of tools installs all the project templates needed for apps, Microsoft Office, and SharePoint development. The developer tools are delivered using the Web Platform Installer (WebPI) and fully configure the system during the installation. The tools install on Visual Studio Ultimate, Premium, or Professional, which must be installed prior to installing the tools. The default target platform for the developer tools is x86-bit platforms, and you must install the required x64-bit assemblies separately for systems built targeting x64-bit hardware.

> **NOTE** *The page* `http://msdn.microsoft.com/en-us/office/apps/fp123627` *has a list of apps you can build and what you should download, as well as a link to the WebPI package needed for SharePoint 2013.*

After the tools are installed, you can create a SharePoint 2013 project by using the New Project menu, as shown in Figure 3-11. Depending on the language of choice, you can select either C# or Visual Basic, and then select Office/SharePoint to see all the project templates for the three categories: apps, Office, and SharePoint.

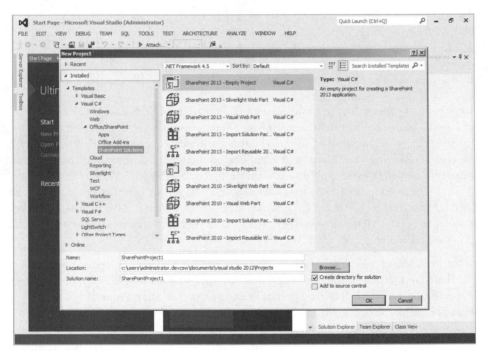

FIGURE 3-11

Visual Studio Integrated List and Content Type Support

One of the most common tasks associated with Visual Studio was creating lists and content types. This could be difficult at times because it required modifying XML files. There have been major improvements with the new editors that are provided and project items. To help assist in building out a content type, Visual Studio provides a project template item to create a custom list schema for use as a reusable column definition. Visual Studio also provides the new Content Type Editor that provides a visual interface for the name, type, and required fields of the XML, which generate the Elements.xml behind the scenes. This editor capability can be seen in the enhanced list editing experience. The List Editor provides the ability to change the list, views, and properties.

SharePoint Connections in Server Explorer

The Visual Studio Server Explorer provides a powerful way to visually represent different components of your server infrastructure, such as browsing through your data connections, services, event logs, and performance counters. When developing against SharePoint, you may want to browse your SharePoint site to understand what content types, fields, workflows, lists, and libraries are on your site. With the SharePoint Connections in the Server Explorer, you can see all this information inside of Visual Studio with a tree view of the site as well as browse the properties of these items. The SharePoint Connections in Server Explorer are read-only and cannot be used to modify the properties. Server Explorer saves you the time required to view the structure, look at properties, and open them quickly in a web browser. Figure 3-12 shows the SharePoint Connections within the Server Explorer.

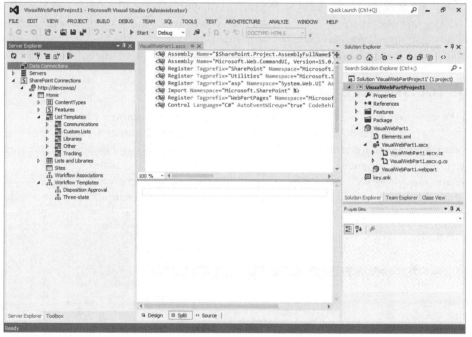

FIGURE 3-12

Solution Explorer Integration

As part of the Visual Studio experience, the SharePoint tools for Visual Studio integrate with the Solution Explorer so that you can see the files that make up your solution. By default, when you select your project type, Visual Studio creates all the projects and files needed for your solutions, such as the feature XML file, the package XML file, and a key to sign your features, so you can deploy it. In addition, Visual Studio logically lays out your solution so that you can quickly add new features or other projects to it.

Mapped Folders

Starting with SharePoint 2010, Visual Studio introduced the concept of Mapped Folders. Mapped Folders provides a quick solution to get files into the SharePoint Root or SharePoint Hive (`%Program Files%\Common Files\Microsoft Shared\web server extensions\15`). This was extremely difficult to do prior to the integration with Visual Studio due to how deep the files are buried in the filesystem. You could use different techniques, such as creating Windows Explorer shortcuts, to get to the different folders quickly, but that doesn't help you inside of Visual Studio projects, where you want to plan an image or add an artifact to the Layouts folder.

The Mapped Folders provide a way within the Visual Studio project to map to a designated SharePoint folder such as the Layouts folder in the SharePoint root. To add a Mapped Folder, you simply right-click your project in the Solution Explorer, and under the Add menu, you see three commands: SharePoint Images Mapped Folder, SharePoint Layouts Mapped Folder, and SharePoint Mapped Folder. The last one displays a user interface for you to select the folder you want to map to. By using these capabilities, you can drag and drop items into your Mapped Folders, and Visual Studio will deploy your artifacts to the right location in SharePoint.

Applications for SharePoint

The new SharePoint app model brings along with it new experiences for developing for SharePoint. The primary difference is more reliance on web-based technologies such as JavaScript. Luckily with Visual Studio there have been enhancements to the JavaScript IntelliSense features to make it a more fluid development experience. There are new Visual Studio templates for supporting the app model, as well as a Project Layout and Packaging framework. All apps for SharePoint can be developed within Visual Studio, but you need a developer site to run and debug the apps, as shown in Figure 3-13.

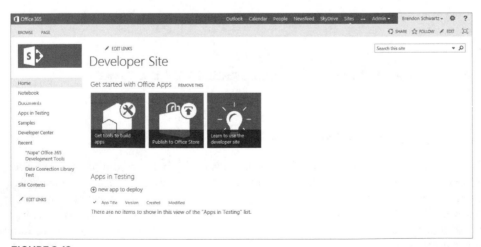

FIGURE 3-13

SharePoint Solutions Project and Item Type Templates

The new Project Type templates needed for supporting apps is straightforward, with only a single project type needed for the SharePoint apps that you will build (see Table 3-2). After you create the project, you can build any of the specific app designs based on what the functionality of your app needs (see Table 3-3).

TABLE 3-2: App Project Type Templates

NAME	DESCRIPTION
App for SharePoint 2013	The project type enables developers to create apps built for SharePoint and include the ability to choose the hosting type and UX experience.
App for Office 2013	The project type is used to create apps inside of Office 2013 to provide additional content and functionality.

TABLE 3-3: App Item Type Templates

NAME	DESCRIPTION
List	This template now provides the ability to create a list with a custom set of fields or create a new list from an existing list.
Remote Event Receiver	This template enables you to create a remote event receiver to handle SharePoint events using a remote service.
Content Type	This template provides a wizard for creating a content type item with a reusable collection of fields.
Workflow	This template provides a wizard that enables you to create SharePoint 2013 workflows that can be based on a list or site in Visual Studio.
Empty Element	This template creates an elements.xml file that enables you to define SharePoint artifacts using XML. The most common usage would be defining a field in your SharePoint project.
Site Column	This template creates the elements.xml file and default field attributes for the custom site columns that can be used in the fields or content types.
Module	This template creates a simple module file with a sample text file showing how to deploy files.
Client Web Part (Host Web)	This template creates the elements.xml needed to host an app for SharePoint inside of a web part called a Client Web Part.
UI Custom Action (Host Web)	This template creates the elements.xml needed to create a SharePoint custom action that links to an app for SharePoint as the resulting URL action.

continues

TABLE 3-3 *(continued)*

NAME	DESCRIPTION
Task Pane App	This template provides a wizard for creating an app for Office 2013 with the Task Pane option selected and the available Office applications selectable.
Content App	This template creates an app for Office 2013 for building out content that appears in the body of the Office documents.

Files and Project Layout

The new SharePoint App template in Visual Studio creates the solution with the project, project items, and files needed to get started. The basic code with all the required properties are set up with the wizard. The files created will be based on the type of hosting model you select for the apps for SharePoint.

The cloud-hosted apps with either the Auto-Hosted or Provider-Hosted apps have the same folder and files structure. The difference between the two is how Visual Studio handles packaging, deploying, and debugging the apps based on where they are hosted. The projects contain an App Project and a Web Application Project. The App Project contains the app-specific files, whereas the Web Application Project contains the files needed to host the app. The following files are required for the app projects:

➤ *AppIcon.png* — This image is the one used to display on the homepage.

➤ *AppManifest.xml* — This file contains the app elements just like the elements and feature .xml files in SharePoint Solutions.

The Web Application Project contains a specific file called the TokenHelper file that enables your app to make secure access calls into SharePoint resources. This is accomplished by using the access tokens defined per application and stored within the app. For more details on building apps, read Chapter 6 for deep-dive details. The other files are all standard web files with the app framework built into them, such as the ClientID and ClientSecret values stored in the Web.config file.

The SharePoint-hosted apps provide a slightly different layout because the packaging for a SharePoint Solution is needed in addition to the app components. Also, these projects are hosted within SharePoint and do not need a separate web application because SharePoint is a web application. If you are familiar with traditional SharePoint Solutions, you can quickly see that this solution is similar to those in SharePoint 2010 and that the project layout is similar with Features, Packages, and HTML folders. Because this is still an app, you still need the AppManifest.xml file that will be created for you from the Project template.

Depending on the type of project you are working with, either the App Project or the Web Application Project, you can set the required project properties from the Properties window, and you can use the built-in designers for any support tool such as the AppManifest.xml Editor, Feature Editor, and SharePoint Packaging Editor. Figure 3-14 shows the Autohosted app with the App properties and AppManifest.xml Editor opened.

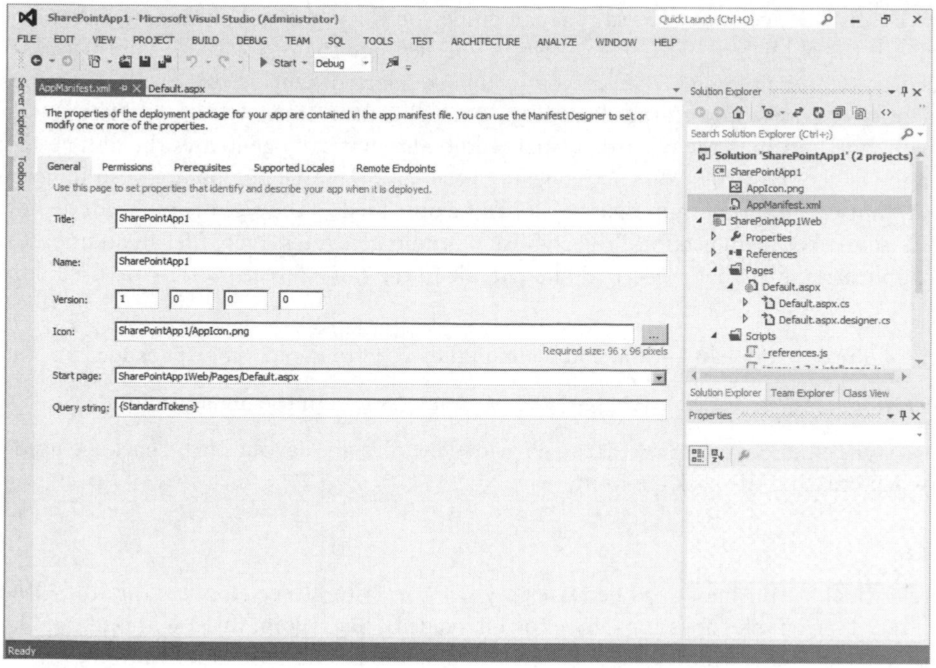

FIGURE 3-14

Packaging

A new packaging framework is used specifically for apps based on the Open Packaging Conventions (OPC). This new packaging format is what enables apps to be hosted outside of SharePoint and even integrated into Microsoft Office. Each app for SharePoint package has the extension of .app. The file that drives all the supporting app files is the AppManifest.xml file, which contains the properties and links to other files. This file is required in an app to allow it to be packaged correctly. In addition to the required app files, there could also be other packages for SharePoint (WSP), Resource files (RESX), Data Tier Application Packages (DACPACs), and Web Deploy Packages.

> **NOTE** *The .app packaging format, which is based on the Microsoft Office format, is essentially .zip files. To view the contents of an app, just rename the file extension to .zip, and you can view it in Windows Explorer.*

To complete the packaging, you need to decide where you will publish your app to for other users to consume. There are two places that you can publish your packages to:

➤ *The public Office Store* — This enables other users to view and download your app.

➤ *An internal organization app catalog* — This option enables you to create internal organization apps for users of your internal deployment.

There is a new Publish Office apps Wizard that can guide you through final packaging of your app for SharePoint for publishing. This wizard walks you through the process and asks different questions based on the type of app for SharePoint you have selected. During this process you must provide the identity of your app with the client ID and the client secret that was found in the web.config. After you work through the wizard, Visual Studio automatically generates the files needed to publish your app. To see these files you can navigate to the <app>\bin\Debug\app.publish folder in your project. All apps contain the .app file, which can be uploaded to the right catalog for deployment. If there is also a Web Application Project, Visual Studio generates a few files in addition to the required web application files that are stored in a .zip file in the same directory that are used during Web Deploy:

➤ *ProjectName*.deploy.cmd — The batch commands used to deploy your package.

➤ *ProjectName*.SetParameters.xml — The parameters used in the deploy.cmd file.

➤ *ProjectName*.SourceManifest.xml — Provides the files and layout of the package used only when creating the package itself.

Apps for Office

These apps are critical for business apps because they work in both Office Applications and Office Web Applications. This enables apps for Office to run inside of SharePoint 2013 without any changes. These apps are built with the same concept of portability and use standard web technologies such as HTML, CSS, REST, JavaScript, and more. Currently, the supported Office Web Applications that are supported are Excel and Outlook; although the Rich Office Application also supports Word and Project. Other Office Applications will be supported in the future as well as enhancements to current applications. These apps are displayed using the IE9 add-in, so all HTML 5 is supported just like the browser.

SharePoint Solutions (Classic Solution)

SharePoint Solutions, which are now referred to as Classic Solutions, are recommended only for administration automation and tasks. To create these solutions you must install SharePoint on a Windows Server machine and develop locally with Visual Studio.

Feature Designer

Building SharePoint Solutions as Classic Solutions will still require using the Feature Designer to manage your solutions features and package. A feature can have multiple items in it, such as a Delegate Control or Event Receiver. In addition, features can be dependent on the activation of other features. For example, Feature A may require that Feature B be activated. Features are also scoped to different levels in SharePoint at the Farm, Site, Web, and Web Application level. The Feature Designer enables you to configure your features with all this functionality. Figure 3-15 shows the Feature Designer.

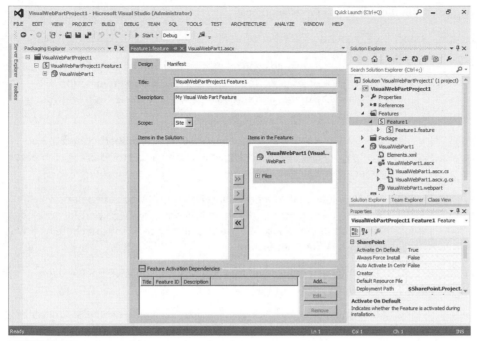

FIGURE 3-15

In addition to working with the graphical designer, you can also work with the XML that Visual Studio creates for your feature. You have two choices in working with the XML. First, you can add custom XML to the auto-generated XML that Visual Studio creates. Second, you can edit all the XML, even the auto-generated parts. If you get your edits wrong, it could stop you from working with your feature in Visual Studio. Editing all the XML is recommended only for advanced users who cannot meet their needs by inserting new XML into the Visual Studio auto-generated XML.

SharePoint Solutions Project and Item Type Templates

The project types for Visual Studio 2012 are based on a combination of SharePoint 2010 and SharePoint 2013 project templates. There are some overlapping items for each version, but all project templates are listed together under the Office/SharePoint ⇨ SharePoint Solutions category. Table 3-4 lists the different project type templates, and Table 3-5 lists the item type templates that you can use. Many of the project types have been moved to item types to make it easier to find what type you are looking for.

TABLE 3-4: SharePoint Solutions Project Type Templates

NAME	DESCRIPTION
SharePoint 2013 Project	This templates enables you to start with an empty project that has all the necessary elements for you to get started, such as folders for references, features, and solutions, and a key to strong-name your assembly.
SharePoint 2013 Silverlight Web Part	This template provides the files need to create a SharePoint 2013 package that hosts a Silverlight application and also provides the web part project with which to associate the Silverlight application.
SharePoint 2013 Visual Web Part	This template creates a new SharePoint 2013 Visual web part, which enables you to drag and drop controls onto your web part for your user interface rather than writing the user interface in code. It contains a Web Part and a User Control item.
Import SharePoint 2013 Solution Package	This template enables you to import an existing WSP package for SharePoint 2013.
Import Reusable SharePoint 2013 Workflow	This template enables you to import an existing reusable SharePoint 2013 Workflow that you create in SharePoint Designer 2013, which you can then customize and deploy from Visual Studio. The import is one way, and after it is modified in Visual Studio, you cannot go back to SharePoint Designer.
SharePoint 2010 Project	This templates enables you to start with an empty project that has all the necessary elements for you to get started, such as folders for references, features, and solutions, and a key to strong-name your assembly.
SharePoint 2010 Silverlight Web Part	This template provides the files needed to create a SharePoint 2010 package that hosts a Silverlight application and also provides the Web Part project with which to associate the Silverlight application.
SharePoint 2010 Visual Web Part	This template creates a new SharePoint 2010 Visual web part, which enables you to drag and drop controls onto your web part for your user interface rather than writing the user interface in code. It contains a Web Part and a User Control item.
Import SharePoint 2010 Solution Package	This template enables you to import an existing WSP package for SharePoint 2010.
Import Reusable SharePoint 2010 Workflow	This template enables you to import an existing reusable SharePoint 2010 Workflow that you create in SharePoint Designer 2010, which you can then customize and deploy from Visual Studio. The import is one way, and after it is modified in Visual Studio, you cannot go back to SharePoint Designer.

TABLE 3-5: SharePoint Solutions Item Type Templates

NAME	DESCRIPTION
Silverlight Web Part	This template adds the required Silverlight project and asks how you would like to associate the web part in the project by either creating a new Silverlight Web Part or associating it later.
Visual Web Part	This template adds a new Visual Web Part to the current solution.
Web Part	This template enables you to create a web part for your SharePoint environment.
List	This template now provides the ability to create a list with a custom set of fields or create a new list from an existing list.
Event Receiver	This template provides a wizard that enables you to select the type of event receiver to create, the event source it is created with, and the events you would like to implement.
Content Type	This template provides a wizard to create a content type item with a reusable collection of fields.
Workflow	This template provides a wizard that enables you to create SharePoint 2013 workflows that can be based on a list or site in Visual Studio.
Workflow Custom Activity	This template creates a custom activity that can be reused in Visual Studio or in SharePoint Designer.
Sequential Workflow (Farm Solution Only)	This template provides the ability to create the SharePoint 2010 sequential workflows.
State Machine Workflow (Farm Solution Only)	This template provides the ability to create the SharePoint 2010 state machine workflows.
Business Data Connectivity Model	Use this template to create a resource file for your BCS model. A resource file enables you to localize the names in your model and apply permissions to objects.
Empty Element	This template creates an elements.xml file that enables you to define SharePoint artifacts using XML. The most common usage would be defining a field in your SharePoint project.
Application Page (Farm Solution Only)	Use this template to create an application page, which is just an ASP.NET page hosted in SharePoint.
Site Column	This template creates the elements.xml file and default field attributes for the custom site columns that can be used in the fields or content types.

continues

TABLE 3-5 *(continued)*

NAME	DESCRIPTION
Module	This template creates a simple module file with a sample text file showing how to deploy files.
Site Definition (Farm Solution Only)	This template enables you to create the SharePoint 2010 site definition files that can be deployed at a farm level.
User Control (Farm Solution Only)	You can create a user control that you can use in an application page or web part with this template. You can design the control using the graphical designers in Visual Studio by dragging and dropping your controls onto the design surface.

Importing Packages

The concept of importing and exporting SharePoint packages has been around in the user interface since SharePoint 2007. Since then the product team has improved the capabilities and standardized on the packages that are created. The capabilities are now found in SharePoint, Visio, SharePoint Designer, and Visual Studio. This means that the combination of those tools enables you to develop your solutions quickly and use the tool that is right for the step in development. Visual Studio provides the largest set of capabilities for completing the packages and fine-tuning changes. To import SharePoint packages known as Web Solution Packages (WSP) there are two options: either a generic WSP package or a Reusable workflow. Both of the packages have a Visual Studio Project template with wizards to help guide you through importing the packages. If you are unfamiliar with WSPs, you should learn more about the internals of how they work because they provide valuable features that enable you to install and ship your SharePoint Solutions to multiple environments.

Importing WSPs

When doing SharePoint development, you must perform your work inside of the user interface or SharePoint Designer. After you complete designing your solution, you must export items or even the entire sites to move the information around and modify it. With Visual Studio you can import the WSP solution, which contains the exported site or items that you have exported to move into your Visual Studio solution. Visual Studio imports your lists, fields, content types, and other artifacts, so you can start working on them quickly in Visual Studio. WSPs are still the recommended packaging format for all SharePoint Solutions that are not apps.

Reusable Workflows

Similar to the project template for importing a generic site WSP, you can also import a reusable workflow that you created using SharePoint Designer. The reusable workflows created in SharePoint are declarative workflows that consist of XML statements to define the workflow instead of code. The reusable workflow template enables you to create your workflow in SharePoint Designer and then import it into Visual Studio to convert it to a code workflow that can be reused on your SharePoint sites.

Package Designer and Explorer

After you create your features, you need to package them together and deploy them to your server. This is where the Package Designer and the Explorer come into play. If you have used SharePoint previously, you know that SharePoint supports a format called a Web Solution Package (WSP), which is just a CAB file that contains your solution files and a manifest or XML file that tells SharePoint what to do with your solution when deployed. You could write all the XML yourself and compile your CAB file, but Visual Studio makes this much easier. Figure 3-16 shows the Package Designer.

The Package Designer gives you the ability to do the following:

➤ Add multiple items to the solution using a graphical interface

➤ Control whether the web server resets

➤ Add assemblies to your package

➤ Write package rules that enable you to validate your package programmatically before deploying it to the server

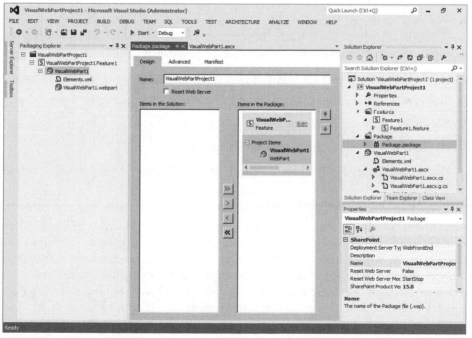

FIGURE 3-16

SETTING UP YOUR DEVELOPMENT ENVIRONMENT

There are many options for SharePoint development with the changes to SharePoint and Office 2013. With all these changes, understanding what you are trying to develop and the components needed to be set up is critical. The two most common development environments are the Office 365 solutions or the On Premises solutions. The new app model makes it easier to create development environments and has fewer dependencies than previous versions of SharePoint. This change also brings back a restriction that all classic development for SharePoint Solutions must be done on a server OS. In addition to setting up a local development environment, Microsoft has provided a full set of development tools for apps that are hosted on the web for quick development.

Applications for SharePoint and Office 365 Development Environment

The steps to create an environment to develop apps are simple in SharePoint 2013. Microsoft has recommended that app developers sign up for an Office 365 Developer Site to help with development and debugging. These sites are already configured with the required app isolation and OAuth that would be required to set up in a local SharePoint deployment. Also you get the full deployment experience from Visual Studio, and you can deploy only to the Developer Site. As discussed earlier all you need to do is install Visual Studio on any support operating system for Visual Studio that includes Windows 7. After Visual Studio is installed, you install the Office Developer Tools for Visual Studio, which includes the following necessary developer components:

➤ Office Developer Tools for Visual Studio 2012 — Preview

➤ SharePoint Client Components (containing the client assemblies)

➤ Windows Identity Foundation (WIF) SDK

➤ Workflow Tools SDK and Workflow Client SDK

➤ Windows Identity Foundation SDK and Windows Identity Foundation Extensions

Napa Office 365 Development Tools

The Napa Office 365 Development Tools are a set of tools provided with Office 365 that enable apps developers to start quickly without installing any tools locally. To develop apps you can use the full code editor with syntax highlighting that is provided in the browser. To get this tool you must sign up for an Office 365 account and create a developer site that enables you access the tools. If at any time you want to continue to edit your solution in Visual Studio, there is a button to open your project in Visual Studio. This is a straightforward way to create your apps, as shown in Figure 3-17.

When you have an Office 365 account, you can access the editor directly from the URL `https://www.napacloudapp.com/`.

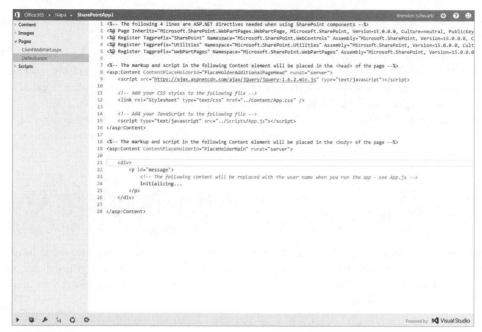

FIGURE 3-17

Local Development Environment

The local SharePoint development environment maps to the traditional SharePoint environment that current developers of SharePoint are accustomed to. This environment requires that you install SharePoint 2013 locally on a Windows Server 2008 x64-bit server to begin development. The major change is that you cannot perform the installation of SharePoint 2013 on a Windows 7 operating system and therefore cannot do classic SharePoint development on these system configurations.

System Requirements

The system requirements for a machine required for local development are not as large as a production environment, but you should be aware of a couple key requirements when setting up your development workstation. Because SharePoint 2013 has only x64-bit installations, your development machine also needs to be an x64-bit machine. The current recommendation is that the machine has at least 6 GB of RAM to install and run SharePoint 2013. This is less than the single server instance of the production hardware, and you should optimize the development environment when working with less memory.

Virtual or Physical?

This local development environment can be installed either on virtual or physical hardware depending on what systems are available and your budget. Installing SharePoint virtually or physically on your machine is usually a tough decision. Many times, the answer depends on the operating system you want to run on your guest OS and also whether you want to trade off performance for flexibility. Now step through each issue in a little more detail.

For the host OS, if you don't mind using Windows Server 2008 as your primary operating system, you will have many options for installing SharePoint (whether that's physical or virtual) because Windows Server 2008 supports Hyper-V. When you know the hardware and software, you can decide whether you want a physical or virtual environment. The advantages of Hyper-V for a developer are that you can have an isolated development environment that can be copied or moved to another location.

> **NOTE** *To install a local development environment using Hyper-V, your hardware must support Hyper-V.*

If you want to run on a desktop operating system such as Windows 7, your choices are more limited because these desktop operating systems don't support Hyper-V. This means that if you want to virtualize, you need to use another product such as VMWare or Virtual Box because Virtual PC and Virtual Server don't support x64-bit.

When you have the right virtualization technology for your host OS, the question becomes whether to virtualize. Virtualization provides a lot of nice features, such as portability, ability to roll back changes, different environments on a single host OS, and so forth. With all these positives to virtualization, there is also a negative with the cost of performance. Of course, this performance cost has decreased over the years with improvements to software and hardware changes. The reason for the performance impact is that you need to give the guest OS and SharePoint a few GBs of memory, and you definitely need a fast hard drive, preferably 7200 RPM and above. If you have the necessary hardware and you're developing solutions, the first choice should be virtualization. One last option that developers have started to look at is the dual-boot system with the Windows 7 dual-boot capabilities. This is sometimes not an option for larger organizations due to adding machines to a domain ad hoc but can be a quick way to evaluate a machine or use the full hardware.

> **NOTE** *Many scripts and deployment guides will be released as the product releases. For a full guide, check out the SharePoint Server 2013 Preview Virtual Machine Setup Guide (v0.5) in the free members section at* `http://www` `.criticalpathtraining.com/`.

SQL Server Version

SharePoint 2013 supports SQL Server 2008 R2 and SQL Server 2012. If you select the stand-alone option when installing the product, SharePoint installs SQL Server 2008 RS Express with SP1. Although this option installs the product quickly, you might run into issues with development if you try to access the database through Visual Studio. A good alternative would be if you have an MSDN subscription, you should use the SQL Server Developer Edition for a full set of features that you can develop with.

TROUBLESHOOTING WITH DEBUGGING

Development is the first part to create an application, but when there are issues with the code, having an easy way to debug the code and determine the issues is critical. Visual Studio and SharePoint provide the tools needed to do this during the development of the code as well as after the code has been deployed to a production site. The major changes for this release are around debugging SharePoint apps and the authentication needed to debug code running on remote servers. The Developer Dashboard has been given a makeover and now provides integrated debugging with logging output.

F5 Debugging

The standard for debugging in Visual Studio is called *F5 Debugging* after the shortcut key to start the debugger and attach the code to the running process. Visual Studio added F5 Debugging to the previous version of SharePoint for the classic SharePoint Solutions, and now that same feature can be used with SharePoint apps.

SharePoint Applications

Debugging apps for SharePoint requires a few more authentication handshakes than the classic SharePoint Solutions due to the architecture. Luckily Microsoft has made pressing F5 just as simple as it is for the classic SharePoint Solutions. By default, Visual Studio uses IIS Express as the localhost for debugging sessions. The IIS Express application is a portable version of IIS that does not need to be installed prior to running it. If there is interaction with the remote app and host web, you may be promoted to grant permissions prior to debugging. To debug the app for SharePoint, you need to be connected to SharePoint Developer Site and allow the application to be trusted if needed. If you are not, you will see an error like the one shown in Figure 3-18.

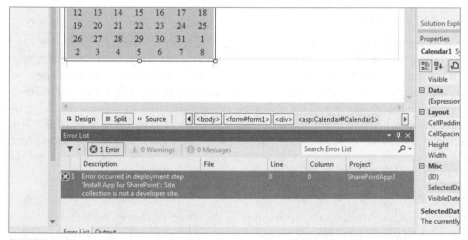

FIGURE 3-18

Following are the steps performed by Visual Studio when you press F5:

1. It builds the Web Application Project if needed.

2. It changes the URLs in the AppManifest.xml and other project files.

3. It packages only the SharePoint-specific artifacts into the Open Package Convention (OPC).

4. It uninstalls the SharePoint App.

5. It installs the SharePoint App (OPC) using the life cycle API.

6. It updates the Hosts file if Peer Name Resolution Protocol (PNRP) is not used.

7. It launches the Web Application Project in IIS or IIS Express if there is one.

8. It updates the web.config with the correct client ID.

9. If the LaunchUrl in the App manifest is set to a site page in the App Project, then launch the browser to the LaunchUrl. If not, Visual Studio just launches the All apps page.

10. Visual Studio attaches the script debugger or Silverlight debugger.

The debugging experience will be familiar to any ASP.NET developer with the web application projects. Because there may be a large portion of the code in JavaScript, it is nice to have the script debugger automatically attached and ready. The experience with the SharePoint-hosted apps contains more files to work through because all the JavaScript files will be loaded from the SharePoint page. A good strategy for quickly building your app would be to develop any of the Web Application components that do not rely on other frameworks first and then add the dynamic functionality after you have the code ready to go. It is a great debugging experience as long as the development environment and server locations are correctly configured. Make sure to do the pre-planning to set up your environment, and you can quickly build powerful apps and debug them by simply using F5.

Classic SharePoint Solutions

Using Classic SharePoint Solutions, you can allow debugging support by setting a breakpoint and starting the debugger by pressing F5. The same experience is provided if you select the Farm or Sandbox solution from the Visual Studio projects. The first time you debug a SharePoint solution in Visual Studio, you will be asked to automatically configure your web.config on the SharePoint server to support the debugging sessions. This is done to prevent the need for manual changes to the server for every development environment. Also, this helps reduce the mistakes and frustration of not remembering every change needed to begin debugging. These steps also include recycling the app pool, retracting the solutions, deploying the solution, and activating the required features. This entire behavior can be modified from the Visual Studio properties and editors.

> **NOTE** *You need administrative permissions to the server to change web.config from Visual Studio, and these changes should not be done on a production server.*

Visual Studio takes three steps on your behalf. First, it turns on the call stack in the web.config by adding the line CallStack=true. Second, it disables custom errors in ASP.NET so that you receive detailed error information if there is an error, using `<customErrors mode="Off"/>` in your system.web section. Lastly, Visual Studio enables complication debugging, which makes ASP.NET compile your binaries with additional information to make debugging easier using `<compilation debug="true"/>`.

Besides making these changes, Visual Studio performs a number of steps when you start the debugging session from deployment to attaching the debugger as follows:

1. It runs your predeployment commands that you can customize.

2. It creates your WSP using MSBuild places in the bin\<build> directory.

3. If you deploy to the farm, Visual Studio recycles the IIS application pool to free resources.

4. If you deploy a new version of an existing solution, it deactivates your feature, uninstalls your existing solution, and deletes the existing solution package on the server. If you have feature receivers, your code will be executed.

5. It installs your new solution and features onto the server.

6. If you build a workflow, Visual Studio installs your workflow assemblies.

7. It activates your Site or Web features. You need to activate Web Application or Farm features. Again, the feature receivers will be executed to run the code.

8. For workflows, Visual Studio associates your workflow with the list or library you selected in the Workflow Wizard.

9. It runs your post-deployment commands.

10. It attaches the debugger to the SharePoint process (w3sp.exe) for Full Trust solutions and to the SPUCSPUWorkerProcess.exe for Sandbox Solutions.

11. If you deploy to the farm, Visual Studio starts the JavaScript debugger.

12. Visual Studio launches your browser and displays the correct SharePoint site for your solution.

A few notes about these steps. First, if you debug a workflow, you need to trigger the workflow through the web browser, the client applications, or custom code that you have written. Visual Studio doesn't automatically trigger your workflow. Also for workflows, any additional assemblies you reference must be in the global assembly cache (GAC).

Second, if you work with feature event receivers, don't have Visual Studio activate that feature event receiver for you. Instead, manually activate your feature event receiver so that it is in the same process as the debugger. You can disable activation in your deployment in your project settings.

Because SharePoint builds on many layers below it, such as Windows Communications Framework (WCF), you may want to enable advanced debugging in your Visual Studio environment. To do this, go into the Registry Editor, find `[HKEY_CURRENT_USER\Software\Microsoft\VisualStudio\10.0\SharePointTools]`, and change the DWORD value for EnableDiagnostics from **0 to 1**. If the DWORD value does not exist, create it as a new DWORD value. When you set this value, you see in the output window in the Visual Studio all the information that Visual Studio gets form SharePoint via the stack trace.

Debugging Using the Developer Dashboard

The Developer Dashboard has become a must-have tool for any user of SharePoint. A total redesign of the Developer Dashboard was required to make it easier to use and to provide better performance. Now the Developer Dashboard is not just for developers but can be used by IT professionals because of the diagnostic information provided from the dashboard. The main use of the Developer Dashboard still remains to provide diagnostic information for the page that is rendered. The information can range from basic page information to the ULS logs associated with the page. One of the major changes is how the Developer Dashboard displays and how it gathers the information. Figure 3-19 shows the Developer Dashboard and its components.

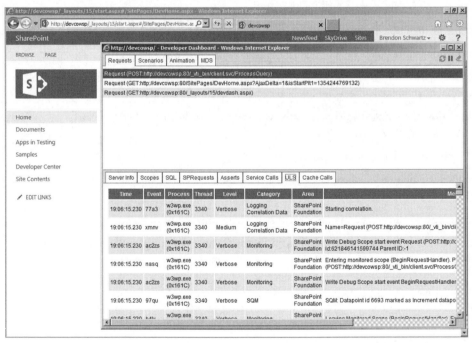

FIGURE 3-19

A number of tabs can now provide more detailed information about each request, and all the information is not in a single page. The trace information provides more information when available, such as the SQL tab, which enables you to click any request to see the detailed SQL command and analytics on each call. Also, you can see the ULS logs for the correlation ID for the page directly from the browser. The data that populates the browser pop-up window comes from a dedicated WCF service named *diagnosticsdata.svc*. This service was designed specifically for the Developer Dashboard and provides tracing information.

> **NOTE** *Diagnostic data is dependent on the Usage and Health Data Collection Service Application, which must be created and running.*

By default, the Developer Dashboard is off but allows a few options to turn it on. In the previous version of SharePoint, you could select three options, but SharePoint 2013 has only two modes, which are on or off. The On option is now equivalent to the On Demand option that places the icon on the page. The reason that there are only two options now is because the control is not embedded in the page, which means you don't need to worry about the control affecting content on the page. To enable the Developer Dashboard from PowerShell, you can use the following lines of script; just make sure to turn it off when you finish using it in production:

```
$contentService = ([Microsoft.SharePoint.Administration.SPWebService]::
   ContentService)
$devDashboardSettings =$contentService .DeveloperDashboardSettings
$devDashboardSettings.DisplayLevel =
   [Microsoft.SharePoint.Administration.SPDeveloperDashboardLevel]::On
$devDashboardSettings.Update()
```

This same script could be written in code because the PowerShell script and code use the same set of APIs. This depends on the usage you need to turn on the Developer Dashboard. For example, you might turn on the Developer Dashboard anytime you throw an exception in your code but turn it off on any other page render. As you can see, you need to add a reference and Using statement to Microsoft.SharePoint.Administration in your code. The code also needs to be run with the correct security context because the Developer Dashboard is a farm-wide setting.

Debugging Using SharePoint Logs

With the changes to the Developer Dashboard, you no longer need to go to the Unified Logging System (ULS) for a page. However, if you have other SharePoint Solutions or need to understand other actions happening at the same time as a page render, you still must use the SharePoint logs. The ULS logs contain logging information about actions that happen within SharePoint, so you might not see any logs related to the new apps for SharePoint. If you write apps hosted in SharePoint, you could still take advantage of logging to the ULS. Although, you could browse the ULS logs, using your favorite text editor. One great tool to check out is the ULSViewer, which is a free download from MSDN at `http://code.msdn.microsoft.com/ULSViewer`. It is an unsupported tool, but it is good at parsing the ULS logs and provides real-time viewing, smart highlighting (in which it highlights similar log entries when you hover over them), and a number of other features.

Debugging Silverlight Code

Visual Studio enables script debugging by default. If you want to debug a Silverlight application that runs in SharePoint, you need to change the properties under your project in the SharePoint section to check the Enable Silverlight Debugging check box.

Silverlight does not allow cross-domain scripting by default. If you make calls across domains, such as copying from one SharePoint site to another that may be in a different farm or uses a different URL, you need to become familiar with the *clientaccesspolicy.xml* file that you can use with Silverlight to override this policy. This will become common for developers building apps and including Silverlight on the web pages. You must place this file in the root of your SharePoint web server in the filesystem so that Silverlight has access to the new policy file.

> **NOTE** *MSDN has good resources to understand these restrictions at* `http://msdn.microsoft.com/en-us/library/cc645032(VS.95).aspx`.

Other Useful Tools for Debugging and Testing

Many community members have built tools for SharePoint since SharePoint 2007. Although these tools have not always been upgraded, many of the APIs in SharePoint have not changed, which means the tools may still work. Beyond Visual Studio, other useful tools can help you with debugging and testing in SharePoint. Following are some recommend ones, but there are more on popular sites such as CodePlex (`www.codeplex.com`).

SPDisposeCheck

One of the primary tools used for classic SharePoint solutions has been SPDisposeCheck. This tool enables scanning of code to determine if there are any memory leaks based on known patterns. The SharePoint APIs allocate COM-based memory that the Common Language Runtime (CLR) garbage collector does not release. For this reason, you need to explicitly call the `Dispose()` method on certain objects such as the `SPSite` and `SPWeb` objects. If you don't dispose of them, you get memory leaks in your application, and it can be hard to track down which pieces of your code are causing the leaks.

For this reason, Microsoft released a tool called SPDisposeCheck, which scans your code to tell you where you are not releasing this memory because of not calling the `Dispose()` method. This tool saves you a lot of time and heartache in tracking down memory leaks. You can download SPDisposeCheck from `http://code.msdn.microsoft.com/SPDisposeCheck`.

Internet Explorer Developer Tools

Sometimes the best debugging tools are the ones built right into the product. Internet Explorer provides you the ability to browse your HTML, script, and Cascading Style Sheets (CSS) code inside of its developer tools. To get to the developer tools, press F12 in the browser. You can debug your HTML and CSS by using the tree view and editing both sources on the fly. It also has a built-in debugger for JavaScript so that you can set a breakpoint and have the tools break when they hit your breakpoint. You get watch windows, local variables, call stacks, and an immediate window called the console. IE also includes a JavaScript profiler that shows you the performance of your script code, including the number of times a function was used and the amount of time it took. With these tools, you can track down any issues in your client-side code.

Firefox and Firebug

If you use Firefox as your browser, you can use Firebug as your HTML development and debugging tool. Firebug provides similar functionality to the IE developer tools in the Firefox environment.

Visual Round Trip Analyzer

The Visual Round Trip Analyzer (VRTA) sits on top of the network monitor tool from Microsoft and is a free add-on. It provides a graphic representation of how long it takes a client to talk to a server. This information can then be used to determine whether you are making excessive round trips, if your code is slowing down the pages (for example, because of loading many small JavaScript or CSS files), or if there are network issues causing any problems between your application and the server. You can download VRTA from `http://www.microsoft.com/downloads/details .aspx?FamilyID=119f3477-dced-41e3-a0e7-d8b5cae893a3`.

Fiddler

No discussion of debugging tools would be complete without mentioning Fiddler (`www.fiddler tool.com`). Fiddler is a web debugging proxy that logs all HTTP and HTTPS traffic between your computer and the Internet. Fiddler enables you to inspect all HTTP traffic, set breakpoints, and view your incoming and outgoing data. It is an essential tool to help you understand what server variables are coming back from your server, what their payload is, how many calls your client-side code took, and other factors that provide insight into your applications.

SUMMARY

This chapter introduced the existing tools as well as new tools that accompany SharePoint 2013 and the changes to the app model. There are more options for OOB developer experiences from adding apps to building them with no installed tools. Each option for development has value and should be used together correctly to quickly build the applications needed. SharePoint has evolved into a developer platform with full tool support for almost every scenario. These tools were introduced to help you understand what is needed from a SharePoint developer to build compelling applications. Finally, you reviewed how debugging can now be performed with both the classic SharePoint Solutions and new app model as well as other tools that assist in tracking down the issues.

Application Lifecycle Management in SharePoint 2013

Before you skip to the next chapter, consider this. SharePoint 2013 provides extensive capabilities to customize your new or existing production farms. This introduces many challenges in how to govern, monitor, operate, and introduce "change" to your production environment, in the shortest time possible, at the lowest risk, and in a manner that does not bring down your production environment.

Added to this challenge is that SharePoint 2013 provides a variety of powerful customization development and deployment models, features, and product capabilities. Coupled to this is that the complexity and solution key design decisions vary based on whether your target hosting location is on-premise or in a cloud-hosted environment.

Other important factors, including your application packaging model, your production application governance policies, and acceptance or "gate" criteria can affect your ability to deploy your customizations into your SharePoint 2013 production environment.

It doesn't matter if you are part of a customer or Microsoft partner development team, or even an independent software vendor (ISV) developing an app for the Microsoft Office Store. Without a sturdy, well-thought-out, and consistent Application Management Lifecycle (ALM) process, your SharePoint team might struggle. This chapter provides detailed guidance to help you overcome these challenges.

GETTING STARTED WITH APPLICATION LIFECYCLE MANAGEMENT

Application Lifecycle Management (ALM), as defined by Wikipedia, is the continuous process of managing the life of an application through governance, development, operations, and maintenance.

David Chappell, a well-respected author and speaker of numerous ALM whitepapers and books, provides unique insights in his whitepaper titled "What is ALM?" He defines it as more than just the Software Development Lifecycle (SDLC), but the entire time during which an organization is spending money on the software asset, from the initial idea to the end of the application's life. You can read Chappell's full whitepaper at `http://www.davidchappell.com/WhatIsALM--Chappell.pdf`.

ALM facilitates and standardizes the process of developing customizations (from idea to working software), supports the transition through your SharePoint environments to your production environment, and supports standard operational activities such as maintenance, upgrade, and patching until the end of life occurs. A consistently applied ALM process improves the governability of applications and customizations introduced to your SharePoint 2013 production environment.

This section further describes the three core aspects of ALM, as well as the supporting tools required and processes to be followed within your particular SharePoint 2013 project.

Three Application Lifecycle Management Perspectives

Application Lifecycle Management can be looked at from three core perspectives. These are the governance, development, and operations perspectives. Figure 4-1 provides an overview of each of these perspectives.

> **NOTE** *Although each of these perspectives is absolutely critical, this chapter focuses exclusively on the development aspects of your application life cycle.*

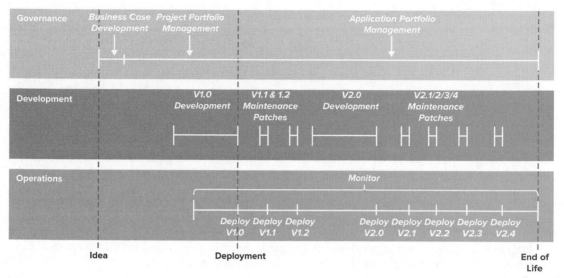

FIGURE 4-1

The governance perspective largely deals with:

➤ Project management, planning, coordinating, managing changes, and improvements to applications, and solutions in your SharePoint 2013 environment.

➤ Key decision making during the life cycle of your customizations and the SharePoint 2013 environments, from inception to end of life.

➤ Development of the business case to justify and get approval for the investment.

➤ Standard application project management to manage the application over the course of its development.

➤ Application portfolio management of the suite of applications and solutions in your SharePoint 2013 environments, including deciding on new applications that are required, which should be improved or retired.

The development perspective is focused on the activities that make up the typical development and maintenance/patch life cycle, including:

➤ Following a software development methodology, most commonly based on Agile or waterfall-based approaches. Common methodologies and frameworks include SCRUM, MSF, RUP, and Kanban.

➤ Requirements definition, design, development, testing, quality assurance, and deployment and release packaging.

➤ Developing maintenance fixes to resolve defects and developing new features and enhancements to release to your production environments.

The operation perspective, in relation to customizations, is focused on:

➤ Understanding, learning, rehearsing, and preparing to deploy new customizations and maintenance releases through your successive SharePoint 2013 environments until they are safely released and deployed to your production environments.

➤ Monitoring customizations in your production environment and reporting issues to the governance and development teams.

➤ Improving and tweaking the configuration of applications and production environments.

As a developer, you may think, that's interesting, but I am interested only in the development perspective. Well, the reality is that each of these perspectives is symbiotic, complementary, and dependent on each other. Poor performance in operations and governance teams and roles can cause problems for the development team and roles. Similarly poor development processes can cause headaches for operations and governance teams and roles.

A mature and well-defined application life cycle management process, which encompasses these three perspectives, can help your SharePoint team overcome these issues.

Application Lifecycle Management Tools

Microsoft Team Foundation Server (TFS) is the application life cycle management tool at the heart of most SharePoint projects. Microsoft Team Foundation Server 2012 provides the following "must-have" features for a team considering major development projects for the SharePoint 2013 platform:

➤ *Methodology or process templates* — Team Foundation Server 2012 supports various agile and waterfall methodologies through the use of process templates. TFS provides out-of-the-box process templates, including Microsoft Solutions Framework (MSF) for Agile Software Development (v6.0), MSF for CMMI Process Improvement (v6.0), and Visual Studio SCRUM (v2.0). In addition, you can use a number of third-party templates, such as Kanban. See the MSDN Article "Choose a Process Template" for more details at `http://msdn.microsoft.com/en-us/library/ms400752.aspx`.

➤ *Source code management* — Team Foundation Server enables development teams to work on the same code project at the same time. It includes features such as check-ins, code branching, merging, shelving, labeling, concurrent check-outs, check-in policies, and the association of check-ins to work items.

➤ *Work item tracking* — Work items consist of requirements, tasks, bugs, issues, and test cases. Team Foundation Server enables flexibility for how these work items are managed via an extensible work item tracking system. This tracking system controls the states a work item can be in and how the state transitions should occur. This results in better documentation, commenting, visibility of the history of issues, productivity, and discipline for the members of the project team.

➤ *Build automation* — Team Foundation Server provides great build management tools. *Build management* refers to the automatic creation and processing of new builds based on updates to code projects. Team Foundation Server supports manual builds, continuous integration, rolling builds, gated check-in, and scheduled builds. For example, you can schedule a nightly build, deploy this build to a virtual machine, and run a series of tests ready to be analyzed in the morning.

➤ *Project management and reporting* — Team Foundation Server 2012 provides reports and dashboards for you to use to assess and report on various aspects of your project's progress. For example, if you have implemented the agile process templates, you can track the progress of the iteration backlog and plan items for the next sprint.

Your project manager and technical lead must be sufficiently skilled in the configuration, optimization, and use of Team Foundation Server 2012. For example, if the customer demands an update on your team's progress, can your project manager instantly generate a report to provide an update? If your developers haven't been updating their work items, or your testers haven't been logging and tracking defects, you won't have the data to show your customer. If you don't have the data, you will struggle to report on any part of your team's progress. Team Foundation Server won't solve bad management, bad judgment, and bad developer habits or traits. Therefore, your project manager and technical lead must instill discipline and structure in your development, test, and release packaging team.

Understanding Key Development Tools

SharePoint 2013 has evolved, improved, and extended many of the existing development tools used by SharePoint developers today. New development tools have also been provided to develop SharePoint apps.

At the heart of the SharePoint 2013 solution development is Microsoft Visual Studio 2012. Microsoft Visual Studio 2012 is a powerful, integrated, and mature development environment that caters for the full development life cycle of customizations produced for your SharePoint 2013 farm. It provides a number of starting-point solution templates to begin development of SharePoint customizations, combined with deployment packaging tools to create Windows solution packages required by SharePoint to deploy fully and partially trusted assemblies and artifacts to your various environments.

Microsoft Visual Studio 2012 provides extensive support for the full application development life cycle. This includes features to plan and track your project, design functionality, code development tools (write, unit test, debug, analyze, and profile), build, testing (manual and automated tests, performance and stress tests), and deployment into virtual environments for further testing.

Visual Studio 2012 extensions are available to provide new SharePoint development tools, namely the Microsoft Office Developer Tools for Visual Studio 2012. See the Downloads section on the MSDN site at `http://msdn.microsoft.com/en-us/office/apps/fp123627`.

Based on my previous experience using the SharePoint toolset in Visual Studio, it provides a great starting point to learn about new types of customization options of SharePoint 2013. In larger projects and teams, depending on the type of customization, other approaches may be preferable. It depends on what customization you are developing.

SharePoint Designer 2013 is a WYSIWYG (what-you-see-is-what-you-get) tool that enables power users to configure elements of SharePoint sites. Although you could argue that this is not a true development tool, it does provide a deep level of support for customizing sites without requiring any code to be written. It's great for small changes, tweaks, modifications, and extensions to existing site features. In addition, SharePoint Designer 2013 changes are scoped automatically to a single site collection and not your entire farm.

Finally, the new Office 365 development tool enables developers to start building apps for Office or SharePoint directly out of a browser window. To get access to these tools, Microsoft requires you to sign up for an Office 365 Development site. This site provides features to help you develop and publish apps to your corporate catalog or Office Store. For more information, see `http://msdn` `.microsoft.com/en-us/library/jj220038(v=office.15).aspx`.

UNDERSTANDING THE SHAREPOINT 2013 DEVELOPMENT MODELS

The SharePoint 2013 platform supports three solution models for the now bewildering number of customization opportunities on the SharePoint 2013 platform.

This section provides an overview of these three models along with real-world guidance that you should consider when deciding which model to use.

The three solution models can be summarized as follows:

➤ *Farm solution model* — The farm solution model, also known as the *Fully Trusted Solution (FTS) Model*, enables you to deploy customizations directly to global assembly cache (GAC) and web front end 15 hive or SharePoint Root folders. This option provides the greatest power and flexibility in developing solutions for your SharePoint 2013 environment. This model was introduced in SharePoint 2007.

➤ *Sandboxed solution model* — The sandboxed solution model, also known as *Partially Trusted Solution (PTS) Model*, enables you to deploy customizations directly to an individual site collection. Partially trusted assemblies are executed in a separate isolated process, called the user code service. This model was introduced in SharePoint 2010. Microsoft has indicated that the sandboxed solution model is available in SharePoint 2013, but has been deprecated. This means you can still develop and use sandboxed solutions, but that they may not be upgradeable to SharePoint Next. Microsoft recommends moving away from the sandboxed solution model wherever possible and using the new app model in conjunction with client object models and out-of-the-box web services.

➤ *SharePoint app model* — The SharePoint app model is a completely new model provided by SharePoint 2013. It enables you to develop solutions that can be hosted in a corporate catalog and on the Microsoft Office Store Catalog.

To help you decide on the most appropriate model, look at the over-arching considerations when deciding between each model, followed by a side-by-side comparison of these models.

The over-arching considerations are as follows:

➤ *Factoring in cloud-hosted farms* — The hosting location of your farm directly affects the solution models available to you. For most cloud-hosted shared environments, the partially trusted model and new SharePoint app model are your available options. For cloud-hosted environments that take advantage of Microsoft dedicated hosted offerings, all three models are available to you.

➤ *Adhering to application governance policies* — It's a tough job balancing the risk of a site outage (and end users howling at you in frustration) versus allowing change to occur freely and spontaneously to your production sites. Over time, especially in large, mature SharePoint deployments, your SharePoint Application Managers develop an appreciation and risk profile (based on experience, wisdom, and pain) for the types of solutions and customizations they support. These form the basis for application governance policies that need to be adhered to.

➤ *Supporting increased speed of change* — In some process-laden business environments, getting new solutions to customers and end users deployed to your SharePoint 2013 farm can take a long time. The design and model you employ directly affects the length of time to get your customizations into production.

➤ *Incorporating existing architectural approaches* — Many SharePoint 2013 deployments are the result of an upgrade from a SharePoint 2010 environment. The upgraded customization and code base will most likely come from 2007 and 2010 environments, and may influence your approach to maintain existing solutions as fully trusted solutions, while developing some of the new solutions (where possible) using the new SharePoint app model.

A more detailed look at the strengths and weaknesses of each of these models are summarized in Table 4-1.

TABLE 4-1: Solution Models Side-by-Side Comparison in SharePoint 2013

FACTOR	SANDBOX	FARM	SP APPS
Overview	Supports declarative elements and user code service	Supports fully trusted solutions; filesystem-based customizations	Client-side orientated solutions; deployed from corporate catalog or Microsoft Office Store catalog
When to use	Deprecated	Create farm solutions when you can't achieve what you require using SP app model	Use wherever possible
Requires server side code	Runs under a Code Access Security (CAS) Policy and limited access to SharePoint Server APIs	Execute full trusted or partially trusted code; full access to SharePoint, third-party and custom APIs	No server-side code is supported
Resource Throttling	Yes	No	No, although model encourages distribution of effort to client side

continues

TABLE 4-1 *(continued)*

FACTOR	SANDBOX	FARM	SP APPS
Execute cross-domain	No; code executes within the user code service	No; code executes in the farm	Yes
Efficiency and Performance	Sandboxed architectural overhead; efficiency and performance limited to compute resources made available to user code service	Depends on your scenario, how you designed it, concurrent load, and a number of factors	Efficient as performance is distributed to the client side
Security	Secure	Secure, but is influenced by your scenario, design, custom code, and customizations	SP apps rely on OAuth 2.0; OAuth 2.0 is a standard framework and needs time to mature before you can safely assess it to be secure
Risk	Low risk, if you do not circumnavigate the sandbox (which many do)	Higher risk; In some case, no other alternative model may be available; requires deeper testing and quality assurance	Early days; risk profile has yet to be assessed; runs on the client-side, taking advantage of the client-side object model, so risk is expected to be low

Source: Microsoft TechNet Article - `http://social.technet.microsoft.com/wiki/contents/articles/13373.sharepoint-2013-what-to-do-farm-solution-vs-sandbox-vs-app.aspx`

In summary, Microsoft recommends, for the right reasons, that you brush up on your JavaScript skills and leave the beauty, cleanliness, and power of C# code in favor of the SP app model wherever it makes sense. For lovers of JavaScript, this is your time to jump for joy. Until the JavaScript development tools improve, and new toolsets (such as TypeScript) mature, some people will shed a tear or two.

The cold, hard reality is that many existing on-premise deployments have invested a significant amount of time, energy, and money, over many years, developing customizations that will *still* require server-side execution. There is also no getting around it that a vast number of customizations still require server-side code execution. Based on this, the most reasonable, balanced, and sensible approach is to slowly reduce your reliance and dependence on full-trust and sandboxed solutions over time, and cautiously introduce the new SP app model for new customizations where possible.

PLANNING YOUR CUSTOMIZATION MODEL AND RELEASE PACKAGING APPROACH

One of the key considerations for any SharePoint farm is the overall planning and design for the customizations and underlying components, and the solution packaging approach to deploying these customizations and components successfully through your environments into your production environment.

Customization Models

Now take a look at some of the common customization and component models available for SharePoint development.

Custom Component Development Model

During the planning of the SharePoint solution development, special attention should be given to the design of the customizations, and strategic design decisions related to the makeup of each of the solution packages. Unfortunately, relatively often, code architecture and structural planning in SharePoint projects is often an afterthought.

Your design defines the way your different components work, such as how web parts are developed, and how the overall code and Visual Studio project structure are created and developed. Your Visual Studio code projects structure, in turn, influences what is deployed in each solution package.

A lack of architectural and design planning can severely decrease the reusability of code inside of your project. The lack of proper design manifests itself later when it becomes difficult to test and later difficult to patch in your production.

As a rule of thumb, similar to any development work, code should be structured into different layers to provide flexibility and promote reusability of the code. Layering and structuring your code and code projects efficiently makes it easier to test, deploy, and maintain and update safely in your production environment.

You have numerous approaches to planning code architecture. The decision on the correct approach should be based partly on the skill of your development team and partly on maintainability and updatability considerations. The development skills at your disposable help guide your decision making as to whether advanced architectural patterns should be used, instead of simpler patterns.

Another key aspect to consider relates to the maintainability and future upgradeability of your code base. Will your maintenance developers be the original developers, or will they make up a slightly less-skilled team? Will new developers understand your code base when you or your original team is no longer on the project?

Most important and critically, and more often than you think, SharePoint development teams make the common mistake of putting all their customizations into one or two code projects (and solution packages). What starts as one or two web parts in one or two solution packages ends up with every customization ever built for their SharePoint deployment existing in a few solution packages.

Initially everything seems okay, but then after successive releases, each release takes longer and longer to get to production. As more and more code and customizations are added, the cost and risk profile for each production update goes up. What then occurs is the following:

➤ Quality assurance, using unit, regression, and integration testing become much bigger jobs than they need to be.

➤ Unnecessary complexity increases, and the frequency of trade-off type design decisions to keep all your components working goes up.

➤ Issues relating to your components in production take forever to be rectified.

➤ The customer or business gets annoyed and frustrated with the long time scales required, which in their eyes are simple changes that make a difference to their end-user experience.

These factors contribute to the long-term success of your code architecture, performance of your SharePoint environments, and, ultimately, the end-user experience.

If there is one lesson you take away from this section, it is *always* better to have a high number of relatively small solution packages in your production, as opposed to one or two massive solution packages. Now look at how you can achieve that.

Designing Reusable Frameworks in SharePoint

Reusable frameworks for SharePoint provide a cost-efficient way to reuse code for multiple projects without requiring recoding for each project. Common patterns and code classes will emerge during the creation of your initial release. These features can benefit your current and future SharePoint projects. Where possible, these should be included in separate framework-type code projects from the start.

As shown in Figure 4-2, look at a real-world example of how it is possible to split up your code and components into a structure that is easy to maintain, update, and grow.

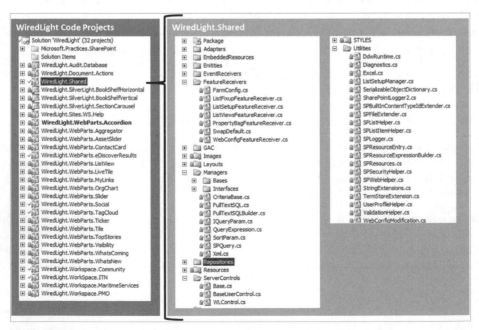

FIGURE 4-2

Now look at this example in more detail:

➤ *Microsoft.Practices.SharePoint* — Microsoft provides a number of common components, including logging, that can be used across all your code projects.

➤ *WiredLight.Shared* — To facilitate reuse, a shared code project (and component) houses all shared functionality. All changes to this code project are closely monitored.

➤ *Numerous web part projects* — Each web part is in its own code project, and, therefore, can be maintained and updated in an isolated fashion to the rest of the solutions.

➤ *Publishing sites* — Publishing sites, along with associated deployment and assembly artifacts, are deployed using isolated solution packages.

Using the preceding model and example, new solutions are easy to add to the overall portfolio of solutions. Defects are much easier to analyze, triage, maintain, and update in production.

Another good example of a reusable framework is Microsoft's patterns and practices guidance package for SharePoint. This package contains a lot of reusable generic code, which would be beneficial for multiple projects. Commonly, this type of code can either be copied to the project or used directly from its own packages.

The usage also depends on the skill level of the developers involved in the project. Writing generic reusable code could be difficult for less-experienced developers and could increase the overall work required for the project. However, reusable frameworks can be created relatively easily by an experienced team of developers, and the code can be used for multiple projects.

Following are some examples of common features included in reusable SharePoint frameworks:

➤ Logging

➤ Configuration management

➤ Caching

➤ Service locator model

➤ Generic list management

➤ Content type management

➤ Site provisioning management

The packaging and dependency planning of this type of framework-level code is examined in more detail in the "Large Project Considerations" section later in the chapter.

Third-Party Component Considerations

One way to decrease the amount of custom code required for your SharePoint-based solutions is to use third-party components. Great components and apps are available that can help fulfill your project objectives without implementing customizations. Aim to use your development resources and focus your development effort on activities that are not available out-of-the-box, or where third-party solutions are not available. Remember, your goal is to deliver business value, not to develop features that can already be met by affordable third-party solutions.

Another reason to prefer third-party solutions is that the developers of these solutions provide continual support and enhancements over time to their products. They worry about the testing and development resources to maintain these products. This helps your development team focus on delivering business-specific customizations and value.

Key considerations with third-party components include ensuring that your project will have sufficient legal rights to the usage and source code to avoid any additional costs throughout the project. This is especially true for community code projects made available on sites such as CodePlex. For these types of projects, review the license and ensure that source code is acquired to enable you to maintain and enhance if the third-party component vendor closes, or the community code project is no longer available. Your SharePoint deployment should not be dependent on custom code that cannot be supported, or for which your business is not correctly licensed.

> **NOTE** *You must ensure that third-party components do not impact your upgrade experience to future versions of SharePoint. Always attempt to ensure that the source code for the third-party components is available. This enables you to make changes required to upgrade to the next version of SharePoint. If not available, this may affect your future upgrade project. When source is not available, decisions to use components should be carefully analyzed because this can have a long-term impact for the future of your deployment.*

Release Packaging Approach

Solution and apps packages are used to deploy and release customizations to your SharePoint 2013 farms. You should always package your code and other customizations in solution or app packages, and use them to deploy your customizations. In SharePoint 2013, you have three different kinds of solution packaging types that can be used: fully trusted solutions, user (sandboxed) solutions, and as an app. Each type has specific behaviors and implications.

Fully Trusted Solutions

As in SharePoint 2007 and 2010, SharePoint 2013 supports fully trusted solutions that can be deployed at the farm level to provide any customizations required for your projects.

Fully trusted solutions are deployed by adding them to the farm solution store located in the configuration database using Windows PowerShell. When the solution is available, it can be deployed to your farm.

Fully trusted solution customizations are deployed to the filesystem of each server and can be considered to be deployed at the farm level, not simply for an individual web application. The web application choice in Central Administration affects only which web.config files are actually updated based on the configurations defined in the solution package. This also means that when the solution package contains features, these features are visible in multiple web applications, which can lead to confusion.

The biggest advantage to using fully trusted solutions compared to deploying customizations manually is the automation of customization deployment. You can ensure that each server in your farm is a completely identical set of deployed customizations. Another advantage is that if you reinstall one of your servers or add a new server to your SharePoint farm, all customizations are automatically deployed, without any manual intervention.

One of the most important things to consider is that deployment or upgrade of a fully trusted solution requires downtime, as shown in Figure 4-3. This service break may not be long, but it can have an impact on users accessing the portal at the time the new package is deployed. This downtime is required to refresh the assembly from the IIS worker process, and, in practice, requires either an IIS reset or application pool recycle.

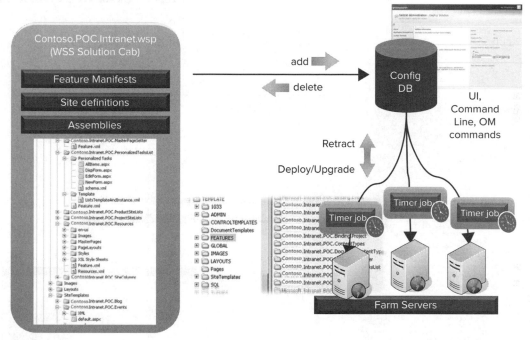

FIGURE 4-3

User (Sandboxed) Solutions

Sandboxed solutions, initially made available in SharePoint 2010, deploy customizations at the site-collection scope and safely execute customizations in a dedicated worker process. This enables a greater degree of flexibility when deploying small customizations and does not require an administrator to perform deployment on the server side.

> **NOTE** *Although user solutions are supported in SharePoint 2013, Microsoft recommends that you use the new SharePoint app model for new development. Microsoft has indicated it has deprecated user solutions in SharePoint 2013 in favor of the new app model. See* http://msdn.microsoft.com/en-us/library/ office/apps/jj163114(v=office.15).

Sandboxed solutions are deployed to a sandboxed solution gallery located in each site collection, and their usage can be monitored and controlled using an out-of-the-box monitoring system.

As shown in Figure 4-4, SharePoint 2013 imposes limitations on the types of solutions that can be created. This is to avoid code causing issues in the farm. Common usage scenarios include simple web parts and feature-based deployment of artifacts (such as master pages and page layouts). Sandboxed solutions are a great way to provide either department-level customizations or customizations to cloud-based environments such as Microsoft Online.

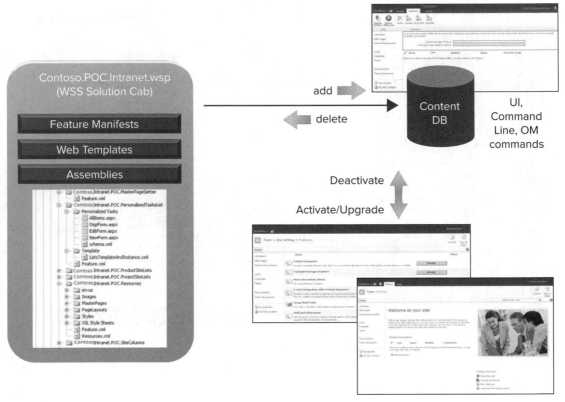

FIGURE 4-4

SharePoint 2013 Apps

Apps created using the new SharePoint app models are packaged in a file called *.APP. This file is composed of many of the files you see in a solution package, including the app manifest, SharePoint solution packages, custom actions and/or app parts, localization resource files, data tier application packages, web deploy packages, and any app office manifests.

When the app is ready, as shown in Figure 4-5, it can be published to the Microsoft Office Store or alternatively to your organization's corporate catalog of SharePoint apps.

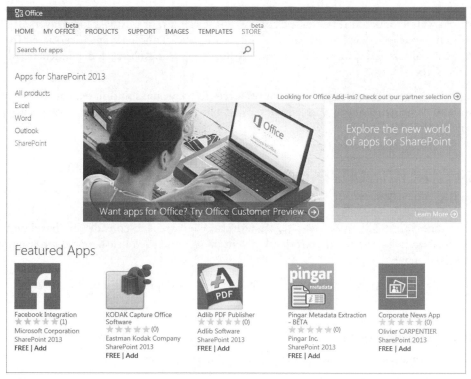

FIGURE 4-5

Design Practices

Because all SharePoint customizations are deployed using either solution packages or apps, planning your deployment is extremely important. A well-planned deployment provides flexibility for testing and reduces the impact on the costs of subsequent maintenance phases.

As discussed earlier in this section, one of the key considerations for the deployment architecture is the granularity of your customizations in each of the solution packages. Strike a balance between having too many solution packages versus placing all your customizations in one or two solution packages. Unnecessary regression testing is a waste of your budget, pushes out your timelines, and can be avoided. As shown in the real-world example, it is possible to structure your customizations into multiple solution packages based on their usage and functionalities. This structuring makes them easier to update.

Figure 4-6 shows a commonly used model, where features are divided based on their usage. As you can see, all commonly used features are placed in a common or shared solution package, and each keyfeature area has a dedicated package. This way, individual features (such as search or My Site) can be developed and tested without affecting other customizations.

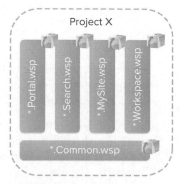

FIGURE 4-6

One challenge with solution packages relates to shared resources between multiple packages — for example, third-party assemblies, utility classes, common base classes, or business logic layers. If two different solution packages deploy the same resource, and the second package is retracted from the SharePoint farm, the shared resources are retracted. SharePoint doesn't track dependencies on individual artifacts and solutions.

This can be mitigated by using common or shared resources in a specific solution package. This way, all shared resources (such as third-party assemblies) are deployed centrally for the different services in the SharePoint farm.

PLANNING YOUR KEY DEVELOPMENT PHASES AND RELEASE MODEL

One of the most important (and, unfortunately, often overlooked) areas to consider in SharePoint deployments is the detailed planning of your development phases and the release model required to support each of these key phases.

This section discusses the key development phases and takes an in-depth look into the common releases used in SharePoint projects.

Key Development Phases

Most, if not all, SharePoint projects can be divided into three key stages:

➤ *Initial iterations* — New code project, developed over a series of sprints or iterations, that culminates in working software ready to be released to quality assurance environments.

➤ *Content creation starts* — Working (quality-assured) software is released to production environments and is available to site owners and content authors to begin using. Site and content preparation can now begin.

➤ *Release models after production use starts* — Software has been configured by site owners and content authors have finished creating the initial content. End users are now using the site (and working software) in production. Any software updates must be carefully planned and tested against copies of production data.

Now look at each of these key development phases in more detail.

Initial Iterations

The development phase will be divided into a number of iterations or subphases, regardless of the development methodology used in the project. This way, you can more easily plan the tasks based on priorities and follow up on development progress.

New SharePoint projects tend to start with a proof of concept (POC) to ascertain the feasibility and suitability of using SharePoint 2013. When projects progress to the next stage, the POC is often used as a starting point and code for your project team. The quality of most POCs is not adequate to directly continue to development. You must start discussions with the customer to ensure that the development assumptions and requirements gathered to this point are correct. This can ensure that the implementation moves in the right direction.

Most project teams prefer detailed technical specifications to be in place before code is developed. This is a difficult challenge to tackle up front in complex developments and requires a waterfall approach to development. More often than not, especially if your customer is not familiar with SharePoint, the customer knows only what he or she wants when he or she sees it. Using an Agile-based development methodology and philosophy helps to balance the amount of documentation required in the initial iteration.

> **NOTE** *Regardless of your methodology, always document your requirements and use cases. Failure to do this makes it harder for your development to estimate work effort, harder for your test team to produce test cases, and easier for your customer to scope-creep, and therefore harder for you to estimate the impact of additional effort required. Yeah, documentation is painful exercise, but it is this documentation that can help you get a sign-off from the customer.*

Another important consideration is the design of your Visual Studio project and code structure. Visual Studio structure defines solution names, features, and their behaviors. Take the time to design a proper Visual Studio structure because this can save rework and development effort later in the project.

Assuming that your Visual Studio code and project structure are planned and available, the developer can start implementation. This means that each of the web part classes and all feature definitions have been created based on the specification, but actual business code from the classes is missing. This way, you avoid issues in the structure deployment caused by changed feature associations or new solution packages.

Figure 4-7 demonstrates common development stages.

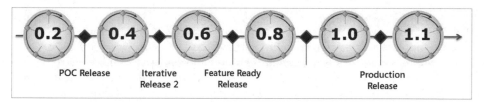

FIGURE 4-7

Content Creation Starts

One of the most important and critical milestones in a SharePoint project is when content creation starts. From this phase forward, daily or weekly builds cannot just re-create the site collection using scripts. You must start using an upgrade model to your environment because you don't want to lose content that the content editors have already created.

An important consideration related to content creation is deciding on and finalizing the data structure (for example, site columns and content types) of your deployment. Although these can be changed after the initial release, their update requires additional work and potential content patching to ensure no content is lost.

Whenever content creation starts, the development model must be switched to a maintenance-and-upgrade model. For smaller projects with few customizations, this is not a difficult change. But if a solution consists of numerous site definitions or web templates, the change is much more dramatic and must be carefully planned.

Release Models After Production Use Starts

When production use starts, you have additional considerations. All changes to your code base must be evaluated so that they don't cause any issues with the already deployed features. Therefore, your production upgrade model should be carefully planned.

Similar to SharePoint 2007 and 2010, downtime is required when new full-trust solutions are deployed to SharePoint 2013. If you use the rolling release life-cycle model, a service break is not required. User (sandboxed) solutions can be updated without requiring a service break, as long as the interfaces and features do not change too much. SharePoint apps do not require server downtime but are temporarily unavailable to end users while they are updated. See the MSDN app for SharePoint update process at `http://msdn.microsoft.com/en-us/library/ fp179904(v=office.15).aspx`.

The most important consideration when releasing new customizations is to ensure that a proper rollback strategy is available. Although SharePoint 2013 does not provide built-in, rollback functionality for farm or sandboxed solution package deployment failures, the new app model does provide extensive update and rollback support. For more information on the app update process, see the MSDN app for SharePoint update process article at `http://msdn.microsoft.com/en-us/ library/fp179904.aspx`.

In the case of failed farm and sandboxed solution deployments, depending on the issue encountered, either redeploying a previous version of the solution or restoring database backups are the only solutions to move forward.

> **NOTE** *Remember that if there's a need to restore database backups, both configuration and content databases must be restored. This is because the solution store for full-trust solutions is located in the configuration database. It's also important to synchronize the files in the filesystem because a full-trust solution is extracted to each of the servers in the farm. User (sandboxed) solutions are stored only in the content database, so their restoration is straightforward.*

Because there are many considerations for the maintenance phase deployments, a detailed road map and process for the upgrades should be created. This is quite common for larger projects that release new versions of your customizations after the initial release.

Figure 4-8 shows a deployment plan where, after the initial release, deployments are done on a quarterly basis.

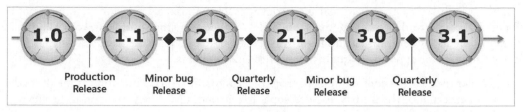

FIGURE 4-8

Release Models

The release model can be described as the process and flow from development to your production environment and includes implementation and maintenance time. It also includes the planning of the processes for maintenance of the servers and software, not just the flow of the customizations, solution packages, and apps.

This section examines several release models, including the following:

➤ Direct release

➤ Phased release

➤ Rolling release

Direct Release Model

One of the models used to ensure flexible SharePoint usage is to use SharePoint Designer in the production environment to customize the portal behavior based on business requirements. The *direct release model* requires one client environment and your production environment. This approach carries a higher risk of causing issues to end users in your production environment because changes made may impact end-user productivity.

Even though SharePoint Designer provides the flexibility to customize your environment, it may still require some custom code or XML configurations. This would require separate environments to ensure that SharePoint Designer customizations don't break anything in already-deployed customizations. There is no way of recording the SharePoint Designer customizations to enable you to apply them to multiple site collections. For example, if you have hundreds of different collaboration sites, this model is definitely not the most cost-efficient and is, therefore, not recommended.

Interestingly, sandboxed solutions and apps also fall under the direct release model. Site owners can upload a sandboxed solution to the User Solution gallery and can add an app from the corporate app catalog or, if it has been enabled, from the Microsoft Office Store catalog.

The risk of sandboxed solutions and apps causing catastrophic issues is greatly reduced. Speaking frankly and honestly, although it is highly unlike that these two solution models will result in downtime of your SharePoint 2013 farm, they may result in downtime of a critical site that is key and central to all users in your SharePoint 2013 farm. The key issue here is that a layer of governance is required to protect critical sites from apps and sandboxed solutions that have not been developed and tested to the same exacting standards of the core customizations in your SharePoint 2013 environments. Where feasible, do not directly release to a critical site. Always test your sandboxed solution or app in your quality assurance environments.

A final consideration, when consuming apps from the Microsoft Office App Store, is the dependence created on an external or third-party app developer to respond, in a timely manner, to produce updates for issues reported with their app. It is this loss of control to respond timely that degrade the end-user experience of carefully thought-out SharePoint 2013 deployments.

Phased or Gated Release Model

The *phased release model* (shown in Figure 4-9) uses separate environments for different phases of the project and incorporates clear decision criteria, which are essentially phases or "gates" that control how releases progress through your environments. Various criteria must be met before a release can proceed through a gate. This model is the most commonly used model in the SharePoint 2007 and 2010 environments because it provides the most opportunity for your operations and governance teams to pick up any issues before the release is installed in production environments.

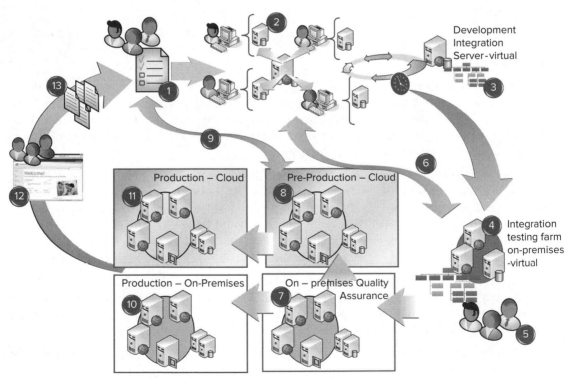

FIGURE 4-9

Figure 4-9 includes the following numbered tasks:

1. All requirements are transferred to tasks and assigned to project members.

2. Developers use their own standalone environments for development and store all customizations in the source control system.

3. A separate environment is used for integration testing.

4. An optional build verification or test farm is commonly used in large projects. This farm has multiple servers, mimicking the key facets of production and in preproduction farms architecture.

5. Before builds are released to production, they are approved.

6. In this phase, you must test and report defects before moving forward.

7. A preproduction farm is used for final verification and to verify that the customizations work in a production environment configuration. As mentioned earlier in this chapter, it's highly recommended that the preproduction environment mimics the production environment (including, for example, patching and configuration levels).

8. All feedback and bugs are collected from the quality assurance environment and reported back to the development team.

9. The production environment is used for the actual production usage.

10. End users can access the production environment.

11. End users provide additional feedback for future development phases.

The biggest challenge in the phased or gated release model is to keep the preproduction environment up to date with the production environment updates. This model requires following a process as strictly as possible, and all configurations are first tested in preproduction.

Quite often the preproduction user acceptance test (UAT) and testing (QA) farm do not mimic the production environment infrastructure. This makes it difficult to truly verify the deployment actions against production configurations of existing sites and customizations. Although developers may have superhero powers, they still rely on integration, smoke testing, and user acceptance testing of their software release against existing sites that may be touched by the release. It doesn't need to be all sites, but a good representative sample of sites that will be affected by the software release. This requires a well-maintained and regularly refreshed QA, UAT, and preproduction environment.

> **NOTE** *If the preproduction environment does not use an infrastructure similar to the production environment, and you are required to perform load testing, you must use the* baseline testing model. *This means that when the initial deployment of the customizations is done, load testing is performed in the preproduction environment. In subsequent releases, all load testing results are compared to the initial test results from the preproduction environment. This way, you get an indication of the performance implications of your latest changes.*

Rolling Release Model

The *rolling release model* (shown in Figure 4-10) uses two primary environments in turn for production and QA environments. This model provides extreme flexibility and increases the overall quality of the released iterations. Basically, the development is phased similarly as with a fully phased model, but the QA and production environments switch their roles during each release.

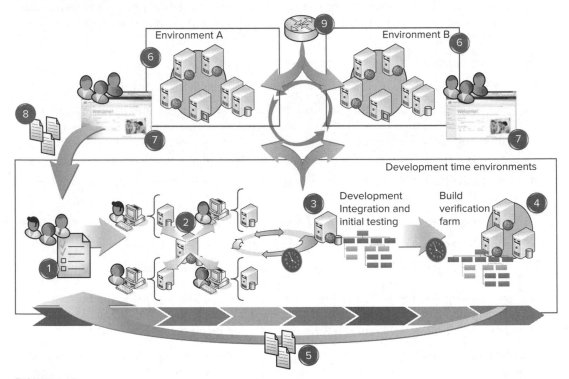

FIGURE 4-10

Figure 4-10 includes the following numbered tasks:

1. All requirements are transferred to tasks and assigned for the actual project members.

2. Development is done by using a standalone SharePoint deployment, and all customizations are stored in the source control system.

3. Integration and automated testing happen in separate virtualized environments so that testing does not interfere with actual development time activities.

4. Like in the phased model, depending on the project size, development style, and QA requirements, an additional build verification or test farm could be used for final acceptance testing before builds are transferred to the actual production environment. This environment is also used by the actual project testers to verify features.

5. All issues and possible improvement ideas are reported back to the task log for prioritization and bug fixing.

6. The production environment consists of two dedicated SharePoint farms, which act as the preproduction (or QA) and production environments.

7. End users access the different available services.

8. End users report possible feedback and additional ideas for the project team.

9. Load balancer or DNS routes request between multiple different environments.

Before customizations are deployed to the preproduction environment, content databases are copied from the production environment so that initial deployment actions can be verified. Final acceptance testing (which optionally includes load testing) can be conducted in the preproduction environment before the decision is made to move to production. For most flexible deployments, these environments should be virtualized so that you can easily increase hardware if new customizations have some additional requirements.

The switch between the environments is done at the load-balancer or DNS level. Before it's done, content databases in the current production environment are set to read-only mode, which disables all editing options from the SharePoint 2013 UI. (For example, Ribbon buttons are disabled and grayed out.) The portal behaves otherwise as planned, but there's no way to add any new content. Afterward, the content databases of the currently used production environment are copied one more time to the preproduction environment. When all required databases are available, traffic is switched between the environments from the network load balancer, and the roles of the environments are switched.

The rolling release model decreases downtime required for the releases and ensures that there's also a backup environment available if something critical happens on the farm (which is acting as the primary farm at the particular time). This not only improves the release model of the customizations, but also helps to minimize downtime during patching of the operating system and SharePoint 2013.

The rolling release model has obvious advantages with the SharePoint deployment. In many enterprise projects, there's a specific dedicated preproduction or QA environment, which mimics the production environment. Using the rolling release model, this environment and the investments done for the deployment are utilized more efficiently. In cases in which the production environments are virtualized, you can more efficiently use the virtualization platform to provide flexibility between the environments, meaning that you can definitely scale down the hardware capacity of the current preproduction or QA environment and scale up just before the traffic is switched again.

The rolling release model increases the availability of the services because when using this model, no service breaks are required during customization deployment, SharePoint patching, or even operating system patching. Depending on the virtualization platform architecture, the patching of the virtualized hosts may not even cause service downtime. Using Windows PowerShell, you could relatively easily automate the whole process of getting databases between environments and deploying customizations to a farm.

> **SHAREPOINT 2013 PATCHING CONSIDERATION WITH THE ROLLING RELEASE MODEL**
>
> Similar to SharePoint 2007 and 2010, every time you deploy full-trust customizations to a SharePoint 2013 farm, the IIS worker process is recycled. This causes downtime for the service. Depending on the deployment, this can have an impact on the actual end users. If only sandboxed solutions are used, there's no downtime for the customization deployment.
>
> SharePoint 2013 also supports phased patching of the actual SharePoint services. This means that you can take individual servers offline from the farm and update the SharePoint services individually. SharePoint patches are backward-compatible so that even though some of the servers are patched with newer versions in the farm, the primary version is still used. The actual upgrade to the latest version still requires downtime for the whole farm. This is because there might be database-level changes, which would not work with the previous version. So, patching has been improved, but an actual upgrade to the latest version (for example Service Pack 1) still requires downtime.

PLANNING YOUR UPGRADE AND PATCHING APPROACH

After a customization has been deployed to your SharePoint 2013 deployment, upgrade and patching considerations come into effect. This section discusses strategies and recommendations to upgrade customizations, and update sites, content, and code in your SharePoint 2013 farms.

Upgrading Solutions and Features

SharePoint provides features for solution and feature upgrade models that should be utilized in customization projects. These make the versioning of the customizations easier and remove the complexity required to modify existing sites.

The solution package manifest supports applying assembly redirections to the `web.config` file of the web applications. This helps to make the required changes to the applications, if assembly versioning is used as the versioning model for code.

feature framework provides extensive support for versioning features. This provides a method to update existing sites. This can be used not only for updating customizations, but also to manipulate content. There are a number of declarative and imperative code options to upgrade features that are already activated in various sites of your SharePoint 2013 farm.

From a development perspective, you should start using the versioning option as soon as content creation starts, especially when you can no longer delete and re-create site collections and sites. After this key milestone, all new versions of the features must be specifically planned, especially if any changes are required to existing sites.

As previously mentioned, the new app model provides extensive support for updating apps. The update process facilitates two key scenarios. The first scenario is where you need to update an existing App to add new functionality to fix a defect or security issue. The second scenario relates to replacing and migrating from an old app to an entirely new one. The following MSDN article provides in-depth information on updating an app in SharePoint: http://msdn.microsoft.com/en-us/library/fp179904(v=office.15).aspx.

Patching Your SharePoint 2013 Environment

Patching your production environments can be complicated. From a code perspective, this is primarily limited to how you deploy bug fixes to existing customizations and how new customizations are deployed to your environment.

From a content and farm perspective, after your initial code release and when production use begins, users create content; set up and complete workflows; customize and configure sites, lists, and items; fill in meta data based on existing content types; create their own content types; and so forth. Your production environment takes on a life of its own.

Patching

Patching of the code in SharePoint is relatively easy and can be done by updating the solution package (which already exists in the farm). From a code perspective, the only major thing to remember in SharePoint 2013 is that if you have newer versions of features developed, you must remember to increase the feature version and provide the required definitions for the feature upgrade actions.

When new versions of the feature are deployed as part of a new solution package version, the features are not automatically upgraded to the newest version. The feature framework follows the same patching model as other SharePoint patching, in that you can add newer versions of the definitions, but the upgrade doesn't have to be applied immediately.

The upgrade of feature definitions is performed either by using the PSConfig tool or by using SharePoint APIs, which provides more granular options for the upgrade. Running PSConfig results in downtime for the whole farm, so upgrading using that method is not always the best option. The SharePoint API can be used to upgrade individual features in a site collection or in the whole farm, and this approach doesn't require any downtime.

Content

Patching SharePoint content means patching or changing already provisioned sites in a production environment. Changing content types of individual list items can be a complex task and requires detailed planning. A *content type* defines the data structure of an individual data object in SharePoint 2013 that is stored in a SharePoint content database. Modification to existing content types should be carefully considered. SharePoint 2013 supports adding new fields to existing content types as part of the feature framework upgrade functionality. But if you must change content types of existing items, this must be developed as custom code or a PowerShell extension.

Complicated scenarios exist in which code and content updates need to be deployed to your production environment at the same time. For example, an upgraded site definition may now include a new site collection scoped feature. For new sites, this isn't a problem because the updated site definition activates the feature automatically. However, if the business requires the feature in existing sites, this requires code to activate the feature based on a specific site definition. These types of updates require careful planning to coordinate content or code changes across your farm.

Another example that may require an update to a content type is a base business document type, specifically developed for a business, which is already in use in all sites in production. If the update requires new fields, and moving content between fields, this requires code to update each item that uses the outdated field.

In these scenarios, IT professionals typically request a custom PowerShell extension or custom feature to perform these operations.

The recommended option is to use the new feature upgrade options, which can also provide support for feature versioning for existing sites. You can use this functionality to modify site structures and content in structured ways without any custom methodology, which would cause project-specific processes to be created. A feature framework versioning model can be also extended by using custom code to fulfill additional capabilities.

Other content considerations may also include the existence of different lists and web parts on sites. These can be relatively easily modified using the new feature framework upgrade functionality, which provides the capability to execute any custom code as part of the feature upgrade. This custom code can be then developed to do required changes for the existing structures based on new requirements.

In the following section you concentrate more on practical considerations for your development team planning.

PLANNING YOUR SHAREPOINT TEAM ENVIRONMENTS

The discussion in this section examines the environments required for SharePoint projects and how your solutions flow between these environments.

Environments for Large Projects

In large projects, more environments are required than your production environment. The main reason for additional environments is to provide a reliable QA process to avoid downtime and lost business productivity in your production environment. Figure 4-11 shows the common stages most large projects use to verify the quality of the solution.

FIGURE 4-11

Automated Build Environment

The automated build environment or *daily build environment* is used for daily automated integration testing. This environment is built automatically with the latest code from the source code system and, combined with virtual machine snapshots, can be used for daily testing and verification, depending on your environmental usage model.

The automated build environment is usually created from scratch on a daily or weekly basis using your customizations. Where your customizations include site definitions or web templates, these can be created relatively easily as large site hierarchies to mimic your future production environment. Therefore, you can smoke-test your project code and customizations before they are released to the next stage (for example, to your dedicated test environments).

Testing Environment

The *testing environment* is either the same environment used for automated builds, or, in larger projects, it is a large, dedicated SharePoint testing farm where specific release builds can be tested. For example, the test environment can be used for weekly builds to enable business and other stakeholders to keep track of development progress.

Similar to the automated build environment, you can start by re-creating the site hierarchy on each release. After your initial production release, your test environment would be used to mimic the upgrade of the customizations already in production.

Although separate testing environments are typically used in larger projects, a dedicated testing environment is highly recommended for all projects that use third-party solutions or development customizations.

Quality Assurance Environments

The *quality assurance (QA) environment*, the *User Acceptance Testing (UAT) environment*, and the *preproduction environment* should mimic the production environment from the point of view of a server layout and configuration so that each of these environments can be used to carry out the required testing. The environment should follow the same guidance for accounts and network-level configuration. This way, you can use this environment to ensure that, if customizations work in this environment, they should be fine for production usage as well.

Identifying the Environments Your Developers Require

There are various adaptations of setting up team development environments for SharePoint 2013 development. However, this depends heavily on the project size and requirements. Development environments should be standardized between the developers to avoid any issues with different versions of SharePoint 2013 or with any other third-party extensions. Standardization also helps to avoid unexplained issues occurring on a developer's machine.

If virtualization is used, you can quite easily create new development environments for developers. These can be hosted on beefy servers, or alternatively, depending on your virtualization software, hosted on your developer's machine. It is often more time-efficient to create a new environment (from an image), rather than trying to solve the issues caused by developer tinkering.

Generally, the setup of development environments should be automated as much as possible using scripting and other automation so that new environments can be created as fast as possible.

It is strongly recommended not to share a single SharePoint environment between developers. SharePoint development involves IIS application pool recycles, repeated WSP builds, and code debugging against SharePoint. These cannot be isolated in a shared SharePoint instance. Overall developer productivity will suffer.

Virtualized Dedicated Environments

This model is based on using virtualization software on the development computers to host an instance of the SharePoint and development environments.

Development environment isolation avoids any issues with developing multiple projects at the same time. You can use a native server operating system during the development phase, which minimizes any issues caused by the operating system platform. This increases the overall knowledge of developers about the native operating systems used in SharePoint production environments.

Windows 8 now supports client-side Hyper-V and can host a virtualized instance of your SharePoint 2013 development environment. For users using Windows 7 and Windows Vista (SP2) operating systems, other virtualization vendors provide software to virtualize and host the SharePoint development environment. In this scenario, a local instance of SQL Server, SharePoint 2013, Visual Studio, and any other tools are installed on the virtual machine and hosted on the developer's computer.

> **NOTE** *Setting up development using this model requires good hardware and lots of RAM! See TechNet (*`http://msdn.microsoft.com/en-us/library/ee554869(v=office.15).aspx`*) for Microsoft development recommendations.*

Figure 4-12 shows an example of a virtualized dedicated environment as described here:

- ➤ Each developer requires a powerful computer to host the virtualization environment. According to the Microsoft recommendation, at least 16 GB of RAM is required for your virtualized instance.

- ➤ A SharePoint development environment hosted on the developer computer can be accessed either by using remote connections and a desktop or by using Hyper-V. Virtual environments are either located directly in the corporate network to facilitate access to enterprise resources (such as Team Foundation Server) or environments that have two network cards (one for the internal domain and environment and another for accessing corporate resources).

- ➤ A centralized source code repository (such as Team Foundation Server) is used to store all developed source code.

- ➤ Physical servers (or set of virtualization host servers) host testing environments and other services.

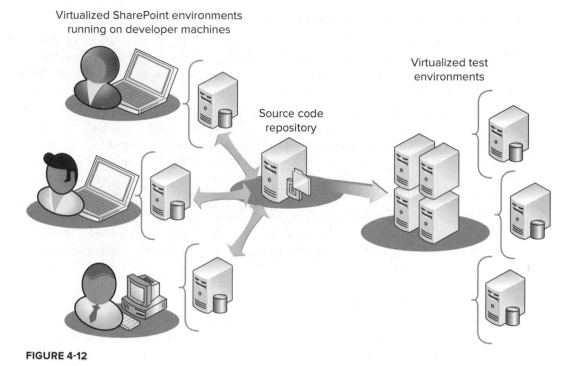

Virtualized SharePoint environments running on developer machines

Source code repository

Virtualized test environments

FIGURE 4-12

From the developer's point of view, this is a flexible model because all other applications used in daily work (for example, Office client applications) can be easily accessed and used, and the virtual instance of your development environment can be turned off when not required.

Another benefit of this model is the ability to snapshot your development instance after it has been configured. This enables the developers to roll back to a previous state or alternatively a clean state before starting a new project.

A key consideration is whether the development machine's main purpose is for development associated with a single project, or if it will be used across a number of clients or projects. If the physical machine is based on an image and is solely for use on one project, the risk is reduced. With constant development, the quality of a SharePoint 2013 instance degrades and becomes "fragmented." Even with a re-install, these problems may not be easy to eradicate (for example, Registry edit problems).

Dedicated computers require sufficient hardware to host the virtualized environments. Lack of sufficient hardware can impact the virtual SharePoint machine's performance and may impact development productivity. If the virtualized development environment creation is automated, overall productivity will be better because developers can take new, clean development environments when needed. An automated, virtualized environment configuration can ensure that there's a new, clean environment available (with the latest source code) within 15 minutes.

Numerous different virtualization techniques are available to choose from:

➤ Because SharePoint 2013 is 64-bit only, it must support hosting 64-bit operating systems. According to Microsoft, this model requires a minimum of 16 GB (24 GB is preferable) of memory to ensure that both client and host operating systems perform adequately. More memory equates to better productivity for each of your developers.

➤ Ensure that you provide hard disks that perform because these will host the virtual machines. If your organization still uses Windows 7, one option with Windows 7 is the Boot from VHD option, which enables the virtualization environment to be loaded as the primary operating system when the computer is started. With this option, the overall hardware requirements can be lower than mentioned previously. Nevertheless, the storage capacity must be sufficient to host multiple virtualization environments for different purposes.

One of the advantages of this kind of model is that individual developers don't need to have connectivity to the corporate network during development. This model enables easier and more flexible development, regardless of the developer location.

Centralized, Virtualized Environments

A centralized, virtualized environment is a development environment model where development environments are hosted on the centralized virtualization platform, and developers use remote connections to access these environments.

This model provides numerous advantages compared to environments hosted in the computers used by developers because this model provides centralized management of the development environments. Individual computers used by the developers in their daily work do not require powerful hardware. These computers are only for hosting client-side applications (such as Office clients and other productivity applications).

Figure 4-13 shows an example of a centralized, virtualized environment. Note the following in the figure:

➤ Individual developers don't have SharePoint installed on their local computers. They connect to the development environments using remote connections.

➤ Development environments are hosted in a centralized virtualization host.

➤ All active developers have their own development environment, which can be accessed using a remote connection. The environment is located either directly in the corporate network, or it has two network cards for having an internal domain and still can connect to the corporate network.

➤ Source code and other artifacts are stored in a centralized source code repository.

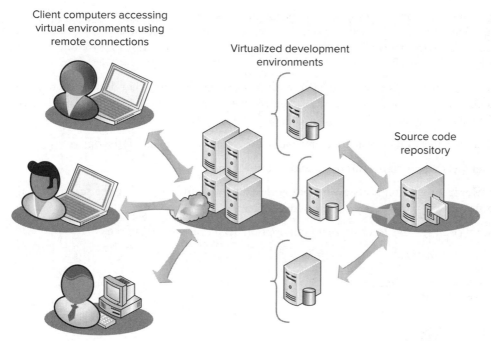

FIGURE 4-13

Because virtualized environments are centrally managed, they can be easily and efficiently used based on the current usage requirements. When they are not needed, this hardware can be dedicated to other environments. This results in cost-savings based on the efficient utilization of your available hardware. Similar models can be used to suspend development environments while spinning up testing environments and performing overnight tests. Ensure that individual developers are not blocked because of a lack of access to their centrally hosted virtualized SharePoint environment.

Individual virtualized development environments should still have at least 16 GB of memory dedicated to them. However, overall memory can be more efficiently used by the physical virtualization host machine.

In large projects, centralized virtualization platforms are often nevertheless used to enable integration testing and QA environments.

Hosting development machines requires expensive hardware for the centralized virtualization hosts. In many projects, these environments have been purchased as part of the project setup phase. After the primary development phase has ended, the same host can be used for hosting maintenance development environments, or, alternatively, for other projects.

Cloud Environments

In this model, development environments are placed and hosted in the cloud and accessed from developer computers using remote connections. The biggest advantage of this model is that there's no requirement to invest in on-premise expensive hardware, but rather to rent and consume from cloud-based services for the duration of the project.

Depending on service provider, the costs may be based on usage (in other words, the actual time when the cloud services are accessed). This minimizes secondary costs because you pay only for the time you use your environments. Using this model, you can spin-up your testing environments in the cloud whenever required.

From cost-management perspective, the biggest advantage is quite simply that developers need to have only a computer with Internet access and use remote connections to access the cloud-hosted development environments.

Figure 4-14 shows an example of a cloud environment. Note the following in the figure:

➤ Developers work from a computer with Internet access.

➤ Development environments are hosted in the cloud and are assigned to the same network segment as the cloud-located source code system.

➤ Source code systems (such as Team Foundation Server) are hosted in the cloud.

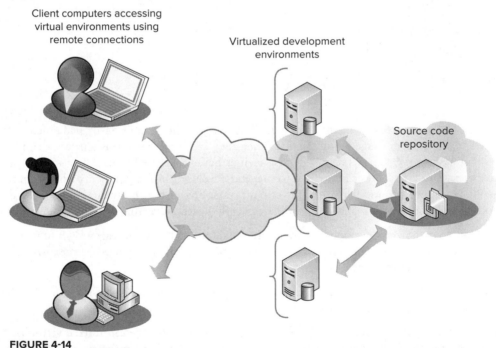

FIGURE 4-14

Development environments set up based on this model are extremely interesting options because they provide the potential for endless hardware capacity for your project and can be easily scaled up and out.

Identifying the Environments Your Testers Require

Efficient testing and QA require consistent and stable testing environments. Multiple testers can conduct testing in a single test farm because all are accessing the environment as users of the SharePoint 2013 system.

Testing is critical to the success of your project. Testers shouldn't need to worry about setting up environments or configuring preliminary settings as long as documentation and configuration of environments is not part of the quality assurances tasks to be taken.

All configurations required for the testing environment should be automated as much as possible. This way, the tester can concentrate on manual tests and verifying that your customizations work properly, rather than spending time on nonproductive actions.

Ensure that testers perform tests on machines that reflect the operating system, Office System Suite, and browser version of the business. For example, different defects will be picked up on a Windows Vista, Office 2007, Internet Explorer 8.0 browser build as compared to a Windows 7, Office 2010 and Internet Explorer 8.0/ 9.0/ Firefox or Windows 7/8, Office 2013, and Internet Explorer 8.0/ 9.0/ 10.0/ Chrome/ Firefox/ Safari.

> **NOTE** *For more information on what setups SharePoint 2013 supports, see*
> `http://technet.microsoft.com/en-us/library/cc263526(v=office.15)`
> `.aspx.`

Testers should be able to access the daily build environment to follow up on the progress of task and defect resolution so that all code is immediately available for testing. This way, developers can receive feedback on their enhancements and bug fixes. This enables issues to be resolved as soon as possible before a build is available to a wider audience.

MANAGING SHAREPOINT 2013 DEVELOPMENT TEAMS

Each SharePoint development project is made up of a unique team of talented individuals, each with their own preferences, code patterns, preferences, and style of working.

This section covers a number of important areas:

- ➤ Selecting software development methodology
- ➤ Setting development standards and best practices
- ➤ Managing, tracking, and recording key design decisions
- ➤ Planning for regular code reviews
- ➤ Large project considerations
- ➤ Large project life-cycle models
- ➤ Departmental teams
- ➤ Offshore teams

It is fundamental to set up the development team properly to ensure your SharePoint 2013 project will be successful.

Selecting Software Development Methodology

Usually, SharePoint projects are based on Agile development methodologies. Development occurs iteratively, and deliverables are divided into a smaller set of entities, which can then be delivered at different times. These methodologies are popular because they provide visible progress on the project. By splitting projects into smaller iterations, you can track the individual tasks more easily and follow up on the overall progress of your project.

The selection of a software development methodology may also be influenced by whether the project is in-house, offshore, or a partner lead delivery. In-house or partner-led deliveries will more than likely use a methodology the team has already adopted and can understand. Although offshore development and test teams may use an Agile or Scrum-orientated approach, they benefit greatly from an onshore waterfall process that require rock-solid requirements, technical specifications, and as little ambiguity to ensure the business or supplier receives the level of quality the first time around. Using the incorrect methodology with an offshore team may decrease the commercial viability of using an offshore team.

One of most well-known methodologies or frameworks for iterative projects is Scrum. Scrum can be a useful model for development but requires adequate resources to use effectively. The core plank of Scrum is to develop in iterations and have regular follow-up meetings on progress and next tasks. If the development team does not have good development leadership, or individual team members cannot plan their work adequately, this strict methodology can cause additional resource requirements and confusion for the project team members.

The software development methodology must include activities and processes that ensure and maintain the highest level of security. Retrofitting security into existing solutions is more costly to introduce, it increases the cost of ongoing maintenance, and it increases the likelihood of vulnerabilities being introduced when subsequent changes are made.

SharePoint solutions, in my experience, do not often start out as business critical solutions, but they always invariably end up as business critical. As a rule, never accept a portal deployment or custom development into a production that cannot show it has strived for and adheres to security best practices. This includes ensuring your team members have the training and support to produce code that is secure and is not vulnerable to standard attacks.

Regardless of the methodology employed, each member should always have clear responsibilities, estimate accurately, and report risks and issues early to the development lead and project manager. Development teams must be able to break their work into tasks that can be managed against a project schedule. Methodologies can help projects move forward, as long as project members realize that methodology is not the objective of the project, and they concentrate on the deliverables. Unfortunately, for some projects, intense focus is placed on following a methodology rigidly, which can be a detriment to the project delivery and real business value.

Lastly, using a methodology provides an industry-proven process and team structure, with clear guidelines, responsibilities, and activities. This is highly beneficial to managing scope, avoiding cost, and schedule overruns.

Setting Up Development Standards and Best Practices

It is vital that the SharePoint architect, technical architect, or development lead plan document and share a set of development team standards and best practices. As a Microsoft Gold Partner or supplier, always attempt to understand if the customer has existing policy documentation related to acceptable development standards, and make sure your team adheres to these standards.

Development standards include the following areas:

➤ Plan a consistent set of development environments for your development team.

➤ Develop a code project solution organization and management of the code project structure.

➤ Plan and set up your application life cycle management tools such as Team Foundation Services (TFS). This includes configuration of the source code control system to set up versioning (numbering), branching policies, and any add-on packs required to support your development methodology; for example, Scrum or Agile add-on packs.

➤ Plan your build process for development and integration builds on the build server.

➤ Configure TFS to kick off builds on the build server on check-in of any source code. In addition, ensure developers are alerted to any failed builds so that they can fix them as quickly as possible.

➤ Decide on the level of automation required for your project. For example, mature development teams deploy nightly builds to a snapshotted SharePoint 2013 environment and kick off a batch of tests for developers and testers to review in the morning.

➤ Plan and ensure quality of source code commenting and code style using source and style analysis tools available for Visual Studio and TFS.

➤ Set out a consistent set of patterns you want developers to follow relating to the development of common SharePoint 2013 customizations. Consistent code patterns drive high quality and reduce your bug count.

➤ Think about the level of code layering you require for your project. Do you plan to interface directly with the SharePoint object model or abstract some of the direct interaction to the manager and entity classes?

➤ Set out the types of unit tests, mocks, or coded UI tests you expect the development team to create.

➤ Plan up front what type of documentation is required by the customer and the deployment team to support, deploy, and maintain any code solutions in the production environment. This may include use cases, use case realizations or technical specifications, component maps, application architecture document, readme, and deployment configuration guides.

➤ Set out what coding standards should be adhered to. Examples include namespaces, exception handling (no empty try catches!), and user interface logic. Ensure the build process performs SPDisposeCheck!

Managing, Tracking, and Recording Key Design Decisions

Each key design decision should be tracked in a SharePoint list or Excel spreadsheet. The same applies to key software and infrastructure design decisions. Without a formal process, the same decision tends to get rehashed over and over again. When a key decision is made, it must be documented. This ensures traceability back to the original decision. When future projects occur and people ask why the architect designed the solution in a certain way, often the information and clear-headed reasoning is lost in the shifting sands of foggy memory.

Planning for Regular Code Reviews

Your development lead or SharePoint technical architect must plan time into the schedule to perform regular (weekly or sprint) code reviews to ensure code produced adheres to SharePoint 2013 development best practice.

- ➤ Code has been packaged for deployment so that it can be deployed to various development, testing, user acceptance testing, preproduction, and production environments.

- ➤ Code revisions have a revision history and appropriate comments in TFS.

- ➤ Code revisions have associated tasks, and the developer has not overridden your check-in requirements.

- ➤ Code has an appropriate level of logging and instrumentation.

- ➤ Using statements have been appropriately applied to release resources as early as possible.

- ➤ Code performs in run-time conditions when a component is hit; for example, 1,000 times a second. Does the code hit a shared component that will not cope under the load?

- ➤ Code profiling tools, such as ANTS Performance Profile, do not pick up badly performing code.

- ➤ Exception handling is present and appropriate. No empty "try catch" blocks, and preferably "try catch finally" code blocks exist.

- ➤ Security-related checks include any code that runs with elevated privileges and require elevated permissions. Ensure that sufficient defensive checks have been put in place to reduce the attack surface.

- ➤ Code is written once and reused as much as possible.

- ➤ Code is not overly complex. It should not require a genius to decipher and maintain. The ACID test for any code is, "Can someone else maintain the code after the individual is no longer on the project?"

- ➤ HTML code complies with validation tools and meets the accessibility requirements of the customer.

All code must be peer reviewed, and final code should be signed off by your development or team lead.

Large Project Considerations

Large SharePoint projects have challenges similar to any large project in which many people work on the same goals. For example, these challenges may include unclear (undefined) responsibilities, tasks, schedules, roles, and so on. Challenges must be addressed by proper planning of not just the project deliverables, but also the development, testing, and release process.

Large Project Life-Cycle Models

Especially with large projects, you must have clear responsibilities and development processes defined for the different features that are developed. The most common way to handle large development projects in SharePoint is to divide the features into multiple code projects and solution packages. That way, each feature project can consume common and shared services from one common framework. This means that, from a solution perspective, the design would be similar to the one shown in Figure 4-15.

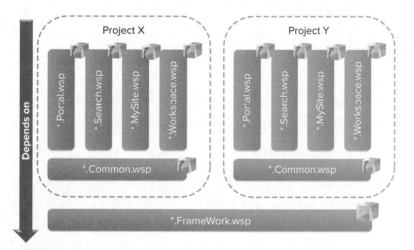

FIGURE 4-15

Figure 4-15 demonstrates how code and features could be efficiently divided between multiple different Visual Studio projects and solution packages. `Framework.wsp` contains abstract code, which can be used in any SharePoint deployment. Good examples for this kind of code would be logging, caching, and configuration services. Copying this kind of general code to each Visual Studio project or code structure is a waste of resources because it could be deployed and versioned as an individual package and then used by different projects.

Individual projects (Project X and Project Y) are large projects that provide different features (refer to Figure 4-15). Having a general, common solution package or code layer, you can easily share project-dependent features between different individual features. A good example of this kind of functionality would be custom master pages, which are used in different site definitions or web templates. This way, you could easily maintain and update UI-dependent functionality without, for example, being forced to do changes on the new feature or solution package.

Individual features in projects are divided into individual Visual Studio projects and solution packages to maintain and upgrade them individually. This way, these features could be individually tested and verified, even if other functionality is not available.

Customization architecture and deployment architecture have a direct impact on the overall maintenance costs and processes. Therefore, your model should be carefully planned based on your requirements. The example in Figure 4-15 is suitable for independent software vendors (ISVs) that develop many services for multiple customers. By separating framework layer code at the deployment level, each project can take advantage of any new base services introduced. Possible fixes can be performed to multiple projects by updating an individual package. As a result, individual project developers can concentrate on solving business logic requirements.

Figure 4-16 demonstrates the flow of development in larger projects where the framework-level code is separated into its own layer.

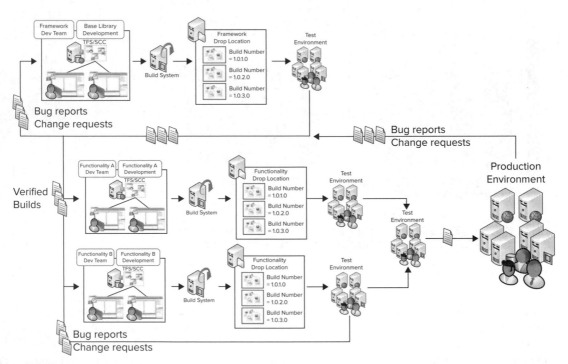

FIGURE 4-16

In this model, development teams are responsible for their own features, and dependencies are created for specific versions. For example, a framework-level development team has its own versioning model, and the team releases tested and verified versions on a weekly or monthly basis. Individual feature development or projects reference and use these stable and tested versions as their building blocks.

feature teams can use any suitable version of the framework that matches their requirements and schedule. This kind of approach provides flexibility for the individual feature teams when planning their development iterations and road map. If multiple features or projects are deployed to the same target environment (such as a SharePoint farm), projects must use the same platform-level version. But if the features are deployed to multiple targets (such as an intranet farm and Internet farm), features can use different versions of the platform-level services.

From a road map-level planning point of view, this kind of model requires a little bit more coordination to implement. But in the long term, it will definitely produce a return on investment by increasing productivity and decreasing time required in the maintenance model.

This model doesn't require tens of developers on the team. This model is also suitable for smaller development teams, where developers are shared between framework- and feature-orientated projects.

Decentralized Development Teams

One of the growing development models is the decentralized development team-based model, where IT provides a centralized platform for the individual features, and departments or decentralized development teams are responsible for (or in charge of) individual features introduced for end users. These kinds of models are great and flexible as long as the platform and environment are carefully managed.

If the decentralized development teams require only small customizations (such as branding changes), Apps and sandboxed solutions in SharePoint 2013 provide an extremely flexible platform to introduce changes and customization at the site-collection level.

By providing a centralized IT-driven platform, organizations and departments can take full advantage of the flexibility of the platform. IT may also provide centralized services to be available to decentralized development team releases, such as fully trusted proxies for sandboxed solutions if there are requirements to access some secured resources (which normally are not available from the sandboxed solution code). Additionally, the apps model caters to many new scenarios that were previously only accomplished using the sandboxed model. Apps can be developed by the decentralized IT team and submitted to the central IT team for deployment and inclusion on the internal app Corporate Catalog.

Offshore Teams

If offshore models are utilized properly, they can provide significant cost-savings in the development stage. Often, however, organizations do not completely understand the implications and what is required to use an offshore team.

For example, what methodology is suitable, what level of technical specifications are required, what onshore and offshore resources are required, what subtle cultural issues must be understood, QA, onsite development leadership, offsite project management, and planning and guidance for the customizations to be implemented all must be considered.

Efficiently utilizing offshore development teams and enabling individual features to be developed unfortunately tends to require a waterfall-based approach, where a great deal of upfront planning, thinking, designing, and documenting is required. There must be little to no ambiguity in any documentation. Your user experience and portal brand design must be completed earlier on in the process to enable offshore developers to avoid delays and ambiguity during the development.

For example, this means good documentation of any platform-level services and details concerning individual styling of the customizations (such as web parts). If roles and responsibilities are defined properly, and there's constant follow-up on the customizations, offshore development can be extremely cost-efficient. It requires extremely good project management and QA on the onshore end to ensure that features work is specified in the documentation.

Other considerations for offshore development are the customization ownership and how the source code is secured. If development occurs both onshore and offshore, access to the same centralized source code system must be provided. Figure 4-17 shows one model of having development synchronized between onshore and offshore teams. Note the following in reference to the figure:

➤   The onshore development team uses remote connections to access centrally deployed development environments.

➤   A centralized virtualization host is used for development and QA environments.

➤   Individual development environments are included.

➤   A source code system (such as Team Foundation Server) is included.

➤   A virtual private network (VPN) or other remote connection port provides access to corporate resources from external networks.

➤   Offshore developers have their own development environments connecting to Team Foundation Server from Visual Studio.

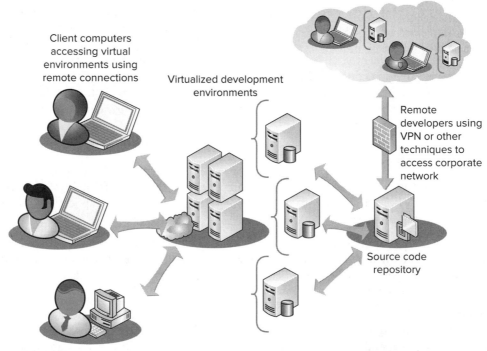

Client computers accessing virtual environments using remote connections

Virtualized development environments

Remote developers using VPN or other techniques to access corporate network

Source code repository

FIGURE 4-17

Optionally, you could also provide individual development environments for the offshore team, which would also be hosted in the centralized virtualization host. This could be possible as long as the offshore team could access the corporate network.

In this kind of model, the integration point of the onshore and offshore customization is the source code system from where actual builds can be then created.

MANAGING SHAREPOINT 2013 TESTING TEAMS

Testing practicalities depend on the project size and objectives. Unfortunately, projects quite often do not always concentrate on these topics enough during the development phase. A key indicator symptomatic of not understanding the value of testing is the time your project has reserved for it. This is a classic mistake in research and development, as well as in customer-oriented projects, which often delays the deployment to your production environments.

Setting Up a Testing Strategy

Set out a test strategy, or plan for your test manager to produce a test strategy that describes the approach that will be used to test the solution and the areas that will be tested. The test strategy should cover the following areas:

> *Human Resource* — How many resources are required to test the solution?

> *Hardware requirements and environments* — This covers the hardware requirements and environments required to adequately test your SharePoint 2013 platform and solution.

> *Software requirements and specialist testing tools* — This covers what software is required for the hardware and the software testing tools needed to adequately test the solution.

> *Test case creation process* — This covers what test cases will be written and the steps required for each test.

> *Types of functional and nonfunctional tests* — This covers how common SharePoint 2013 customizations will be tested, as well as the nonfunctional tests that will be performed. For example, this may include tests related to accessibility, localization, security, compatibility, performance, maintainability, and data migration.

> *Testing stages* — This should cover the unit, component, integration tests, system, regression, and user acceptance tests.

> *Defect tracking* — Defect tracking specifies what tool will be used to track defects. In Microsoft-orientated projects, Team Foundation Server (TFS) is often used as the tool to track defects.

> *Defect classification strategy* — The defect classification strategy ensures each defect is uniformly categorized and prioritized based on an agreed set of severity definitions. Examples include 1-Critical, 2-Major, 3-Minor, and 4-Trivial. This is important because customers often stipulate test exit criteria in the commercial contract that specify the maximum number of defects allowed for each severity definition.

➤ *Triage strategy and triage process* — This process is used to classify and prioritize defects. This meeting occurs regularly during the development stages of the project and daily during the stabilization phase near the end of a milestone.

One final area to plan is the test team roles and responsibilities; that is, the responsibilities of the test lead and the test team members.

Unit Testing

Unit testing is used to ensure that individual units of source code work as expected. Unit testing can be performed either manually or using automation by writing code-based tests to verify the code works properly.

For unit testing, one of the challenges in SharePoint development is the nature of SharePoint code and how developers implement logic in the user interface (UI) classes (such a web part or custom control). This makes it difficult to test business logic residing in the UI class, and this makes it even more difficult to ensure that your automated unit tests cover the majority of your code base.

If your customizations implement well-known patterns such as model-view-controller (MVC) or Model-View-ViewModel (MVVM) patterns, this can make it easier to test the logic of your UI classes.

Automated Builds and Integration Testing

Automated builds are used to automate integration testing of the customizations using a daily schedule, or whenever a developer checks in code. The objective is to ensure that code created by your development team integrates without any issues. This prevents large integration phases where overlapping code requires fixing and rework, and enables you to take a build at any time to deploy to other environments (such as your test environment).

Often, automated builds are extended to include other activities, such as unit testing or automated functional testing. By scheduling these to be actioned automatically, you can save on overall costs concerning quality assurance (QA). You can provide a new fully working version of the latest checked-in developer customizations in your test environment daily. When the customer or the tester arrives at work in the morning, results and indications of the expected test result will be available to analyze.

For example, say that you have already deployed a release of your solution to your customer (internal or external), and you want to ensure that the following iterations or maintenance builds could be easily deployed or actually upgraded over the existing environment.

In this kind of scenario, you can use the model defined in Figure 4-18. Here, you test the upgrade actions that must be performed as part of your automated build. Combining virtualization techniques, you mimic your production environment against your daily build. In a best-case scenario, you would have a legacy copy of your customer content databases from the production environment to perform this daily test.

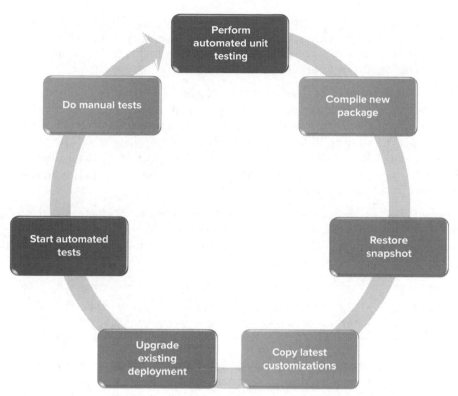

FIGURE 4-18

Understandably, it is not always possible to have a copy of production data in your test environments. You can still complete the following steps in Figure 4-18:

1. *Perform automated unit testing* — Before moving to the following steps, verify that the customizations actually work as expected. To verify business logic handling of the solutions, you create unit tests, which are automatically executed as part of your automated build. This way, any business-level issue can be identified as early as possible in your development cycle without requiring manual testing.

2. *Compile new package* — The automated build compiles the code stored in your source control system (optimally based on labeled status) to enable you to use the latest stable build, rather than simply the latest source code version. This avoids code that is in flux and is labeled as not ready to be released. This requires minor tweaks to your automated build configuration files (MSBuild scripts). This helps ensure that only correct source code versions are used.

3. *Restore snapshot* — Because automated builds are executed on a daily basis, you must restore your test environment to a base configuration that mimics the state of your current production environment, ready for your new build. Depending on your virtualization platform, this could be difficult to establish. With Microsoft Hyper-V, you can perform this action easily (using Windows PowerShell, for example) so that it can be easily automated and included in the build process.

4. *Copy the latest customizations* — After the testing environment has been restored to the point that matches the production environment (SharePoint and production customization version), you can start the server and copy the latest solution packages (WSP) and any other customizations for deployment purposes.

5. *Upgrade the existing deployment* — In this phase, you perform the upgrade of the environment with your latest build. Upgrade actions to perform depend on the project, solution artifacts, and your development model. However, upgrade solution commands are commonly performed from Windows PowerShell (as done during the production environment upgrade). If new site structures are required for the new customizations, you create the necessary scripts to make these structures available for testing purposes, and these scripts will be executed in this phase.

6. *Start automated tests* — In this phase, start any automated test scripts that verify the functional integrity of the code. Multiple different tools are available for recording this kind of web test. If you use Visual Studio, you can integrate the tests and results directly with the source code projects.

> **NOTE** *Visual Studio 2012 Team System provides project templates and test tools to create, automate, and execute tests against your test environment.*

7. *Do manual tests* — All the previous steps can be automated to be performed every night, or even multiple times each day. After automated testing has been performed, you can continue performing manual tests. In larger projects, dedicated test resources are responsible for reporting daily build results and performing the manual actions required. If automated builds are performed during the night, the latest version of the package installed would be ready for the tester to continue testing the next morning.

Automated builds can provide much more than just integration testing of the customizations and code. You can use a similar model before the initial version is available to re-create the portal on a daily basis. For example, you could create Windows PowerShell scripts that would create the initial hierarchy for the future intranet. After developers update the web templates with the latest changes, you would test the latest features on a daily basis. However, the primary purpose for this kind of daily build environment is not to create content because all content would be deleted or re-created every day.

The overall life-cycle models are examined earlier in this chapter in the "Planning your Customization Model and Release Packaging Approach" section. However, if you have requirements in your projects to provide a long-term testing environment for your customer, a target server for your daily builds would not be it. Good practices for these kinds of requirements would be to have a separate weekly release cycle for the environment, which can then be used for functional testing by your customer.

Test Case Planning

Test cases should be documented based on the original business requirements to verify the features of the individual elements and customizations. Test case documentation should be written at a level that people who are not technical or part of the implementation phase can perform the testing by following the documented test cases.

Where possible, some of the test cases can be recorded as web tests using Visual Studio Team System. These can be automatically executed as part of your daily build. This way, you can decrease the amount of overall resources required for actual testing.

Test cases should always be created for your development customizations. At the highest priority, they should concentrate on verifying the customizations, not out-of-the-box features, which have already been tested and are supported by Microsoft. If customizations include highly customized master pages, it is good practice to verify the standard out-of-the-box features because heavily customized master pages may break out-of-the-box features.

A common mistake with test case creation is that they are written based on already developed customizations. This results in a low-quality test case that tests the current outcome, not the original business requirement. You should test based on the original business requirement!

Each test case should have a high coverage of main and alternative outcomes of the individual feature. Another common issue is overly automating the setting of properties (for example, web part properties) in your script. This may lead to false verification because each test is testing only success cases and does not verify issues related to wrong property values.

You should consider the following when planning test cases:

➤ Missing configurations in SharePoint for checking error handling of the web part

➤ Invalid entries as configuration values for the web part with expected error handling

➤ Using a web part in alternative places, not only in the planned location

Each test case should include a clear definition of what is and is not tested. This helps a tester focus on the relevant issues. For example, a separate test should be used to check UI consistency across a number of customizations, rather than in a specific test case focused on the features provided by the customization. Each test case should have clear passing or failing criteria. This requires the expected outcome to be defined in detail.

Because many of the SharePoint customizations are based on some out-of-the-box features or services, each test case should also include the prerequisites from an environment and resource point of view. For example, testing a custom search results web part requires the correct configuration in your testing environment.

Performance Testing

Performance testing can be considered from either the IT professional or development point of view. From the IT professional point of view, performance testing ensures that the hardware is adequate for the planned usage and identifies performance bottlenecks. From the development perspective, performance testing focuses on reducing the impact on server resources per page request, the page payload size reduction for first and subsequent requests, and, lastly, the efficiency of client-side code.

A common mistake made by many development teams is a failure to use .NET code-performance profiling tools to proactively analyze and optimize the efficiency of their code during the project development cycle, rather than reactively when an issue is reported by the IT professional team, or, even worse, in production.

Following are some other performance testing considerations:

➤ *Mature test environments* — To get repeatable results, the environment should be stabilized and documented so that in subsequent releases a similar setup can be created. Ensure that the environment does not have any other load so that results and metrics are comparable to previous test results.

➤ *Population of test data set and information* — Create scripts and tools to populate the required information, which mimics the production usage. There's no point testing intranet performance if it actually doesn't have any content or site structures.

➤ *Deciding the adequate stress level for testing* — Plan your stress test usage models based on available capabilities of the tools you use, such as how many concurrent users access the site.

Performance testing activities depend on the life-cycle stage of your project and deployment. You can conduct performance testing in this environment before the initial release or public release is done to your production environment. Because you most likely cannot repeat a performance test in your production environment in later releases, it's beneficial to conduct a test also in an alternative environment, which can then be used in future phases as your baseline test environment. This means that if in the following phase performance decreases 10% in your reference environment, it will do the same in production.

Test results with this kind of baseline testing are not precise but can provide you a clear indication on the performance impact of the changes applied in a particular version.

Multiple simulated performance tests should be performed before the implementation phase of the project starts. Identify performance bottlenecks as early as possible to avoid development rework in later iterations. A good practice is to conduct performance testing as soon as you have a feature-ready release. Continue to repeat performance tests to demonstrate improvements against your initial performance benchmark. Continue repeating performance testing for maintenance releases done after the initial release of the customizations.

For example, say a previous intranet project follows the release cycle defined in Figure 4-19. As you can see from Figure 4-19, there were five iterative releases during development, and after that, development was changed to a quarterly release mode with optional bug-fix releases between quarterly releases.

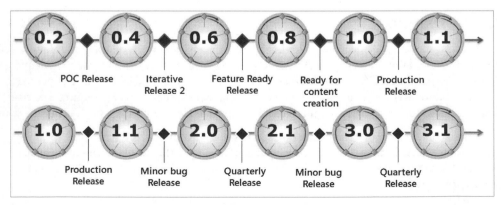

FIGURE 4-19

Version 1.0 of the performance tests was created at the same time as the feature-ready release, meaning a release when all functionalities have at least high-level functionality available based on requirements, but when implementation has not yet been polished for actual production usage.

These tests were updated and performed three times before the actual production release to identify possible issues as early as possible and to ensure that any fixes do not degrade performance. Each new major release provided updated performance tests. More important, the original performance tests used against Version 1.0 are performed to compare previous and current results.

By including performance tests in the portal life-cycle model in the maintenance phase, you can test the implication of changes to your production environment (such as patches to an operating system, a SQL Server, SharePoint cumulative updates, and service packs) and your customizations.

Functional Testing

Functional testing should be performed in an environment that simulates your production environment to ensure that your features and customizations are working properly. Even though SharePoint 2013 can be deployed to a client operating system, do not use this as your testing platform because the behavior will differ from a server-side test environment.

For midsize or large deployments, you should use a separate QA environment that mimics the production environment. You must realize that a testing environment should be based on multiple servers and not one server. For example, multiple Web Front Ends (WFEs) and load balancing cause a user's page request to behave differently than that of a single server.

Functional testing should be based on the test cases representing the business requirements to ensure features are properly verified before moving to the next stage in the deployment process. If automated tests are used in the project, manual functional testing should concentrate on areas and features that cannot be tested reliably using automation.

In SharePoint deployments, functional testing contains both solutions testing and UI styling verification. For example, issues related to UI rendering is a good example of a test that is quite often not precisely tested in projects.

User Acceptance Testing

User acceptance testing is the final verification of the version or deployment before it is deployed to the production environment. Quite often, business and key stakeholders are involved in the execution of the tests. This involves a combination of manual execution of "use cases" and test cases produced in previous steps of the project life cycle. User acceptance testing is a key milestone that helps the business and project stakeholders decide whether to move forward with your latest solution.

User acceptance testing should always be conducted for any solutions moving from preproduction to the production environment. It should also be conducted by the "customer" of the project and not by the developers. You must document the findings to enable project stakeholders to decide on the next actions. For example, these might include signoff or acceptance of your release and possible remaining issues to be fixed.

From a project management point of view, always remember that a completely bug-free solution is rare. In most projects, the project and business teams have decided on the maximum number of bugs at each severity level. Ensure that you provide enough time to respond to issues that may be picked up in user acceptance testing. Therefore, do not schedule user acceptance testing too close to your release date. Ensure that you have a buffer.

Defect Tracking

Numerous methods exist to manage *defect tracking*, and many different tools can be used. At a minimum, all relevant project team members should have access to enter and edit defects in one centralized location. In SharePoint projects, defects are usually tracked within SharePoint or using Team Foundation Server.

SharePoint provides issue tracking lists that can be further customized based on project need. The challenge with using a SharePoint-based tracking list is that developers would have two different tools to use. Team Foundation Server is the preferred approach, which provides nice centralized task lists directly in Visual Studio for developers. All other project team members could use the Team Foundation Server web access to manage issues and bugs.

When testing is planned, it's also important to agree on the process of handling defects and how they should be documented. Following are some key considerations for the creation of defects:

➤ *Priorities* — Each defect should be prioritized so that bug fixing can start from the most-critical issues and move to less-important issues. Prioritization should be agreed on by team members for the project to avoid all defects being prioritized too high.

➤ *Descriptions* — Each defect should have a detailed description of the issue. There should always be some business requirement or specification pointer, which justifies why it is a defect. Defects shouldn't be used to sneak enhancements into your project scope. Only use defects for existing features. The description should provide enough detail to reproduce the issue; otherwise, it will get lobbed back to the tester as Unable to Reproduce. If the issue cannot be reproduced, there's no way to ensure that it's fixed after code changes.

➤ *Screen shots* — Screen shots provide a simple and efficient way to provide more information on the encountered issues.

➤ *Time* — SharePoint has extensive logging, which provides additional information on an encountered error, or it can even be used directly to solve the root cause of the defect. If there's no exact time on when the bug or issue was encountered, there's no way to use this valuable information. Remember that your development team may work in different time zones.

Other Testing Considerations

Testing should be planned carefully to ensure that the required quality level is met. Testing should be a clear phase in the overall project plan and not considered as a buffer for development.

Because testing is based on requirements of the project, test planning can be started at the same time as the planning of the technical architecture or customization architecture.

When testing is conducted, ensure that user accounts with different levels of permissions are used to identify any permission issues in the code or configuration. Ensure that your developers verify that their code works in their development environment using different users and permissions before checking in their code.

SUMMARY

Many considerations that (unfortunately) are quite often overlooked in large SharePoint projects can help your project teams become more successful during the development, testing, and deployment phases of your project. This chapter discussed many of these considerations, and especially focused on a detailed look at what is required in large projects.

What does a large project actually mean? When should you follow this guidance? The answers to these questions are based on many factors, such as the size of your SharePoint farms; the degree of customization; the priority of your project to the business; the quality you require of the development, testing, and deployment deliverables; and your future road map. Many of the concepts discussed in this chapter apply to projects of all sizes and should be followed to improve the maturity and discipline of your development, testing, and deployment teams.

Future maintenance requirements should weigh heavily on your architecture patterns and key design decisions. Ensure key development through deployment processes are set up and followed. Consider that, after your initial version has been deployed, it is so much more expensive to fix than if you get these right in your initial version.

Unfortunately, there is no silver bullet to enable you to select the correct model for each project. Even though you may not plan processes and architecture in detail, you must make an informed choice, rather than making a decision with no understanding of the impact.

Throughout the rest of the book, you learn more details about these new features and learn how to program against these features to build robust and capable SharePoint 2013 applications.

Introducing Windows Azure and SharePoint 2013 Integration

WHAT'S IN THIS CHAPTER?

- ➤ Learning about cloud computing solutions
- ➤ Understanding the different approaches to buying and hosting SharePoint online
- ➤ Discovering Azure integration options and the new Azure workflow

MOVING TO THE CLOUD

For the past 20 years, corporate IT departments have focused on developing redundant infrastructures and developing a critical line of business applications to meet strategic business objectives. Over this period in time, the price, availability, and interconnectedness of computing has changed dramatically. Computing devices have moved from the desks of the privileged to the pockets of the masses. The ubiquity of wireless connectivity and the advent of entire new computing paradigms such as the Internet and tablets have strained the traditional IT organization's capability to flex and adapt. Two decades ago, business reports were delivered on paper. Ten years ago a line of business application could generate reports that worked on any machine with the correct OS and had the client application installed. Today, executives expect to operate their company from their iPhone and iPad. The days of Bring Your Own Device (BYOD) have definitely arrived.

On top of this increasing pace of technology change and the convergence of the consumer and corporate technology stacks, the world has suffered a tremendous financial setback. IT departments around the world and at every size organization are searching for ways to reduce or eliminate expenditures. This "doing more with less" mentality pushes IT managers and application developers to constantly look for cheaper ways to do things.

Outsourcing IT systems was identified as a formal business strategy in 1989, a revolutionary step taken first by Eastman Kodak but quickly adopted by dozens of major companies. *Outsourcing* is defined as the strategic use of outside resources to perform activities traditionally handled by internal staff and resources. With this definition, it is easy to see that companies have been doing this forever, whether in the form of leveraging contractors to smooth out the peaks and valleys of a variable workload or in the form of purchasing the services of another business such as a parts manufacturer supplying widgets to a consumer products manufacturer.

Outsourcing has primarily been adopted as a business strategy to secure some or all of the following benefits:

➤ Reduce and control operating costs

➤ Improve capabilities by focusing on core competencies and rely on world-class partners

➤ Share risks and resources with partner organizations

Although outsourcing has historically connoted the reduction of operating costs through the elimination of head count, IT organizations have stretched that definition to include a number of IT-specific initiatives designed to gain all of the previously listed benefits. Data centers have long been moved outside of corporate office buildings to reduce risk and achieve economies of scale. The evolution of hosting began with the movement of servers to data centers. The introduction of virtualization and its capability to maximize computing efficiency ushered in an era of multitenancy, or sharing of physical computing resources. Spurred on by the plummeting cost of hardware and suites of powerful virtualization technologies, grid computing enabled allocated computing resources to flex up and down, meeting demand without squandering capacity. Large organizations such as Amazon.com, Salesforce.com, IBM, Google, and Microsoft built massive data centers that leverage this foundation of shared resources and economies of scale to introduce commercially available outsourced computing capabilities called *cloud computing* (so named because of the cloud-shaped symbol used to reflect complex computing infrastructures such as the Internet).

What Is the Cloud?

Cloud computing is essentially a new business model: IT as a service. Organizations facing pressured budgets are attempting to reduce on-premise investments while still having access to the capabilities. One of those mechanisms to achieve these goals is to leverage the power and promise of the wave of cloud computing vendors offering competitive IT outsourcing options. The siren song of cloud computing is indeed hard to resist. Much in the same way an organization can benefit from moving a server from physical to virtual, the organization saves money in operating costs, electricity, and potentially even head count by outsourcing elements of the IT infrastructure.

Cloud computing comes in a variety of flavors; the three most significant are infrastructure as a service (IaaS), platform as a service (PaaS), and software as a service (SaaS). Each offering consists of the cloud vendor offering to take more responsibility in exchange for a reduced amount of flexibility. Figure 5-1 details the major stack elements involved in each flavor of cloud computing.

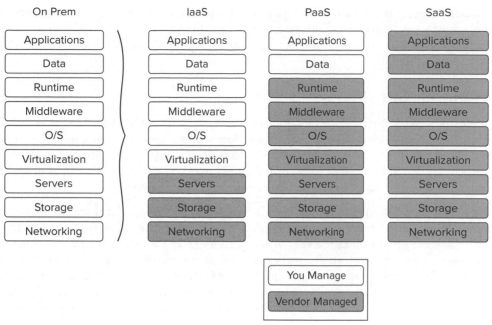

FIGURE 5-1

Moving from an on-premise environment to an IaaS provider such as Amazon's EC2 enables an organization to eliminate the need to have internal servers, storage components, and networking (refer to Figure 5-1). The full control of the virtualized IaaS environment remains in the hands of the customer, not the vendor. Although this level of flexibility may be exactly what is needed in some cases, it does come with an additional level of responsibility because the IaaS layer is currently programmatic. Consider the recent success story of Netflix weathering the Amazon.com cloud outage that brought down so many other online applications. To successfully remain online despite the outage, Netflix was required to write a large amount of networking code. Software applications built on top of IaaS layers often end up with a surprising amount of "infrastructure" code that contributes little-to-no business value.

Moving up a level from IaaS to a PaaS approach means that the customer accepts the cloud vendor's control of the run time and the operating system upon which it runs. For example, with Microsoft's Windows Azure platform, developers simply write functions that are delivered to the cloud. These developers are freed from worrying about the lower-level infrastructure code, and the customer organization doesn't need to worry about O/S upgrades, and so on. In exchange for this level of optimization and focus, the customer must accept the platform vendor's restrictions for development languages and capabilities. Should the customer organization want to make a strategic shift, such as one that takes them away from .Net to Java, the current cloud platform might possibly need to be abandoned and all logic reimplemented.

At the top of the cloud stack is the decision to fully outsource all components of an IT solution to a SaaS vendor. SaaS vendors offer an application or applications, typically web-based, which enables the customer organization access to functionality without concerns about stability, upgrades, or capacity. Users simply pay for their use. Consider Salesforce.com and its Chatter platform for enterprise social connectedness. Users of the application can chat, exchange files, and even extend the web application's core capabilities with custom functionality when necessary. Of course, in the walled garden of a SaaS vendor, moving to a different vendor is often a complex and costly migration.

Why Companies Care

Given an understanding of basic cloud computing concepts, the question usually asked is given a set of specific target benefits of cloud computing, "When does it make sense for an organization to consider cloud computing alternatives to in-house IT services?" Is the organization seeking to manage expenses for hardware investments? Beyond the potential financial benefits of cloud computing, why should a company with in-house IT expertise care about cloud computing?

It is difficult to give a one size fits all answer to this question. Instead, consider the types of issues and scenarios facing the particular organization in question. Some organizations are so large and process-driven that interactions with the various teams inside of IT take large amounts of valuable time. Other organizations are worried about the capability to minimize expense while still being in position to handle large, infrequent spikes in demand as is frequently true of web and mobile application vendors. Still other organizations may look to bring exceptional capabilities into their organization, capabilities that would otherwise be prohibitively expensive to develop and maintain internal to the organization.

Integrating cloud technologies into the standard set of IT services is an undeniable wave of change sweeping through corporate IT. The question faced by many then becomes, "What are the specific benefits my IT organization seeks to secure with this new technology?" The answers to this question typically depend on who is asking and what the individual yardstick for success looks like.

A chief information office (CIO) or chief technology officer (CTO) is typically concerned with the cost and speed of delivery and whether or not their people are focused on the right things. A CIO looks at the cloud as an Innovation Enabler, a platform that helps companies focus on innovation because it eliminates the infrastructure of getting up and running. Not only is the cost of delivery through the cloud typically much lower, but also the cloud by its very nature enables significant agility. Agility in the cloud is defined by the capability to quickly add and remove capacity, capabilities, and even entirely new solution offerings.

A chief marketing officer (CMO) or chief financial officer (CFO) usually has different concerns. Candidly, a CMO or CFO is typically motivated by the historical relationship with the IT organization. The cloud offers an opportunity to side-step around IT to accomplish business goals with fewer obstacles. The cloud is a *Business Enabler* because it is a platform with little to no dependence on existing enterprise infrastructures, full flexibility of technology stacks, and no limitations on capacity. Cloud vendors of PaaS and IaaS can usually accommodate a multitude of technologies and programming languages. For example, the Force.com platform now supports Java, the Windows Azure platform now supports PHP, and Amazon.com offers both Windows and LAMP platforms as EC2 Reserved Instances.

It is impossible to read a business or technology magazine or website without seeing cloud computing advertisements. All of the large technology vendors have or are introducing their cloud services. Even Dilbert has devoted comic strips to cloud computing. Companies are actively investigating the technologies, seeking some way to turn the best-in-class capabilities of cloud vendors into competitive advantages. Consider Netflix, a DVD subscription service that transformed its business and an entire industry by building a movie streaming service on top of Amazon.com's cloud services.

Why Developers Care

Given the ringing endorsement in the previous section for why a company should consider moving to one of the many cloud computing options available, it may seem redundant to say that developers should care about cloud computing. However, simply because management says to do something doesn't convey the depth of power and flexibility a single developer or a team of developers can have by incorporating cloud computing into their software development process. The rest of this section discusses some of the legitimate reasons why individual developers should pay attention to cloud computing.

The first reason is that cloud computing is an undeniable emerging force in software development, a sea change on the same magnitude as the Internet was in the mid-1990s. Where the Internet required developers to learn new skills to take advantage of the new methods to reach users, cloud computing comes with a similar offer. In exchange for picking up cloud computing capabilities, developers can reach infinite numbers of users with new functionalities across an ever-widening set of access points. Mobile devices and smartphones regularly rely on cloud services. Corporate infrastructures are migrating into the cloud. One of the best ways to future-proof a career as a software developer for the next several years is to incorporate cloud computing technologies into your software development toolkit.

Software delivery becomes easier than ever before with the power of the cloud at your back. Not only is it remarkably easy to provision a development environment or a development/integration environment in the cloud in minutes compared to the time it may take for corporate IT to respond, the skill bar for software delivery is actually lower. Cloud companies offer services that a developer can simply hook into, replacing what may otherwise take tremendous amounts of effort. For example, Microsoft's Azure service offers Media Services for streaming media from the web. Salesforce.com offers an API to its full suite of service objects so that the developer never again needs to create a "customer object" or worry about how to tie a customer to an order in the database. Cloud Foundry can help your applications reach web scale with MongoDB! Not only does the cloud offer new services that may otherwise require herculean efforts to build and deploy as an individual or small team, the immense power and elasticity of the cloud means that developers can write less code that is more efficient. For example, a constrained environment may lead a developer to conclude that vector graphics are more memory-efficient, but with the flexible power of the cloud, a developer can opt for the much easier to code bitmap graphic. Developers can focus on creating solutions rather than on performance tuning. Although cloud computing offerings do lower the skill bar, those technologists who are truly skilled are the ones excelling and setting trends in the industry.

The modern software environment is frequently a story of interconnected and integrated applications. In the cloud, the integration story is usually clear and easier to achieve than in a standalone environment. Cloud vendors have frequently created connections between major service offerings or have provided connections and APIs for connections as opposed to the tightly coupled code more frequently encountered inside of enterprises. In addition to API-based approaches to integrating services, cloud-based data integrations are an equally compelling story. Hadoop is an open-source distributed application designed to enable data operations such as search or format conversion across dissimilar unstructured data stores. Developers seeking to produce the best performance or analytical results for their application understand that more is better for available computing power.

Software developers ignore cloud computing at their peril. Regardless of the chosen platform, the environment is rapidly evolving, and being left behind is a real possibility. Even if the individual company a particular developer works for has no stated intention to move to cloud computing, the benefits for individual developers may still apply to internal applications or development processes. To an individual developer, the cloud means freedom! Freedom from IT administrator-induced delays, freedom to access some of the world's most powerful applications, freedom from worrying about hardware or infrastructure architectures, and freedom to focus on finding solutions to business problems.

Cautions for Cloud Adopters

The previous two sections and every cloud vendor on the planet will have you believing that the cloud is the future and that to ignore it is to be left behind. Although there is certainly some truth to the overall direction, there will always be exceptions and exceptional circumstances that prove that not every cloud has a silver lining. Here are a few legitimate reasons to pause and consider fully before diving headlong into production cloud deployments. Specifically, the concerns discussed include:

- ➤ Cost of development
- ➤ Security and data ownership
- ➤ Skill requirements
- ➤ Learning curves

First and foremost among concerns when moving to cloud-based platforms is the paradigm shift that development and testing in the cloud is no longer free. Every time the developer presses F5 to test an application, a bandwidth fee and a computer processing fee may be charged. The costs of development may vary greatly between vendors based on published fee structures. A real-world example of the development costs is that it took a monthly $10 investment of cloud computing services to spin up two Amazon Micro instances, leveraging both the LAMP and Windows stacks to act as SVN, database, and web servers. The costs are not large, but as development teams scale up, so do the costs. It is an unfortunate reality today that there are not good cloud simulation environments that enable developers to work locally while building applications for the cloud. Software developers working in the cloud may need to develop habits that involve debugging by hitting F5 less frequently and potentially not having access to continuous integration build processes. Without leadership commitments to cloud-based development and acceptance of the associated costs, the quality of development may suffer.

Continuing the conversation about costs, a move from the traditional on-premise experience to a cloud approach entails an organizational shift from capital expenditures (CapEx) to operational expenditures (OpEx). Given these different types of budgets and their different impacts on cash flow, organizations that are used to amortizing large IT CapEx expenses away from the bottom line may be resistant to larger OpEx commitments. The cost model of the cloud is based on the pay-for-use model. This model is somewhat unpredictable, especially with new offerings or offerings that are new to a population segment. This uncertainty may make cost predictions unreliable and can further challenge the decision-making dynamic as companies begin to have a truer understanding of this cost model. For example, a large Salesforce.com SaaS deal was scuttled by a recognizable company's CFO despite buy-in from the CIO and the CMO because the CFO was unwilling to commit to an annual $3 million operational expense. Part of the reason for the CFO's decision was due to the financial consideration of OpEx versus CapEx. The other part of the CFO's reasoning was that existing applications would need to be rewritten or heavily modified to work with the chosen cloud vendor, a hidden cost that the CFO was savvy enough to understand.

The security of the cloud and a lack of ownership of cloud data is a frequently discussed weakness of some cloud offerings. Although IaaS providers lay no claim to your proprietary application data, SaaS vendors store and manage the application data. Although some of the security concerns are legitimately misplaced, industries such as financial services and Big Pharma are skittish about who has access to their data and are unlikely to trust multitenant solutions from the cloud. For those organizations committed to cloud-based solutions but are nervous about security, a number of security vendors are happy to sell extra layers of security.

With PaaS and SaaS vendors, the OS and run time are abstracted away from the developer. This may be considered a freeing experience on the part of the architect and developer, or it may become an unbridgeable skills gap for software designers and developers. Turning to IaaS vendors brings back the ability to manage servers in a traditional sense but comes with a price. IaaS layers are currently programmatic, requiring significant amounts of code to manage network stuff. Consider the example of the 2012 Netflix outage due to weather causing an outage of Amazon.com. Although Amazon.com did its own analysis of the issue, Netflix documents on its tech blog stated that the reason for its extended three-hour downtime on June 29, 2012 relates to networking code failures in mid-tier load balancing causing unreachable network segments. Fascinating reading, but the referenced plumbing code is not related to the business objectives of Netflix other than "be a reliable platform." This example demonstrates that the learning curve to get from zero to hero is still a steep curve, even though some of the areas of the platform's stack may be abstracted away from the developer. In an on-premise deployment, developers with a traditional software engineering background typically understand how to handle load and contention given the expected load and target user population. The concern essentially boils down the question, "As things scale up, what are the *new* concerns I have to worry about?"

In addition to the learning curve related to large-scale deployments, the amorphous nature of cloud computing introduces a learning curve that may be uncomfortable for some individuals and organizations — questions such as whether or not the distinction between traditional infrastructure/application hosting and IaaS/SaaS is well understood. The evolution from hosting to IaaS/SaaS involves a move from individual instances to multi-occupancy and Multitenancy. Another question frequently asked is whether or not the particular cloud platform is mature enough to have stabilized in terms of its evolution of features, and whether or not the individual or organization can keep up with the pace of change. One of the learning curve complications for the cloud computing environment is the rapid change due to the consolidation of vendors through acquisition. Salesforce.com is particularly guilty of the vendor acquisitions, snapping up capabilities such as Rypple, Assistly (now Desk.com), Heroku, and Radian6.

Taken together, these listed risks indicate that IT departments are facing a steep learning curve. Not only are new capabilities available in the market that require investigation, but also those capabilities are elastic and change frequently. IT must grapple with the security implications that some cloud-based solutions mean that the company will no longer own its own data because it will live on a vendor's servers, an especially troubling restriction for health care and financial services firms. IT must also understand that it may be limited to the types of or amounts of usage available on third-party cloud systems. For example, to prevent one organization from thrashing a multitenant system, limits on API calls may be enforced.

Managing the cloud can become a new point of concern and specialization inside of an organization. Tools have been created by a number of third-party vendors for every stack, but this extra layer of cloud management may eventually become regulated by corporate IT departments in such a way as to remove some of the flexibility of the cloud through otherwise onerous procedures.

Finally, although cloud computing solutions offer tremendously attractive benefits for access and reach, a number of restrictions in online environments do not exist in on-premise environments. Informatica is one such vendor, placing restrictions on its OnDemand cloud solution that do not exist in local installs. Similarly, Microsoft's Office 365 SharePoint environment offers a reduced feature set when compared to on-premise installations.

Introducing and incorporating cloud computing is clearly not as effortless as the various vendors would have you believe. It behooves developers and technical business analysts to diligently gather high-level business requirements and work through them to find show-stoppers that preclude cloud-based solutions. The upside for IT departments is that the removal of typical infrastructure and platform requirements means that IT can focus more on how its business operates by learning more about its business data and business processes.

INTRODUCING WINDOWS AZURE

Microsoft offers IaaS and PaaS in its public cloud offering, Windows Azure, although the Microsoft Online suite of applications is considered to be a SaaS offering. Azure is effectively a specialized operating system that offers the following capabilities, as shown in Figure 5-2:

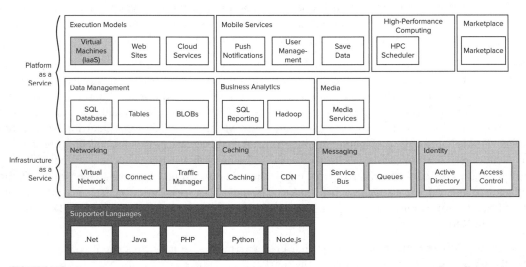

FIGURE 5-2

➤ *Websites* — Create websites in PHP, .NET, and Node.js, or pick from a gallery of open source applications.

➤ *Virtual Machines* — IaaS offering to create and host VMs running Windows Server 2008, 2012, or Linux.

➤ *Cloud Services* — Containers of hosted applications such as supported languages include Python, Java, Node.js, and .NET.

➤ *Data Management* — Offers SQL Database, tables, and BLOB storage.

➤ *Business Analytics* — Offers SQL Reporting, the Data Marketplace, and Hadoop.

➤ *Identity* — Offers Active Directory and Microsoft's Access Control Service.

➤ *Messaging* — Offers a service bus and queues for developers.

➤ *Media Services* — Offers streaming media services.

➤ Other infrastructural components including networking and caching.

Microsoft provides an excellent in-depth introduction to each of the components on its Intro to Windows Azure page (`https://www.windowsazure.com/en-us/develop/net/fundamentals/intro-to-windows-azure`). A brief overview of each component is presented next.

Execution Models

Virtual Machines, Web Sites, and Cloud Services are each distinct approaches a developer or service consumer can take to execute applications. The *Virtual Machines* capability abstracts a server-based infrastructure and enables users to create VMs ondemand based on a library of standard images or custom user-provided images. The VMs operate in the cloud as they would in an on-premise VM server, persisting changes and supporting the capability for the entire image to be moved to different (locally downloaded) servers.

Web Sites remove the requirement that customers administer the VM(s) but enable hosting of web applications on familiar IIS environments. Azure Web Sites environments are so similar to on-premise web server environments that the Azure service supports existing IIS websites being copied to the cloud with no change, including support for open source web applications such as WordPress, Joomla, and Drupal. Load balancing Web Sites is done dynamically by simply adding or removing instances.

Cloud Services is the original Azure AppFabric concept — a scalable, reliable, and low-admin environment for application development. Cloud Services applications are built by compositing virtual machine roles (instances) such as web and worker roles. These stateless roles are entirely managed by Azure for lower administrative responsibilities but offer added levels of flexibility over Web Sites. Cloud Services instances can independently be scaled up or down to manage reach and cost.

Mobile Services

Windows Azure Mobile Services are an encapsulation of several other Azure capabilities discussed later to enable app developers to quickly spin up a mobile app back end. Azure Mobile Services includes a *user management capability* based on Azure Active Directory, which streamlines away the need for an app developer to manage authentication. *Push notifications* are also included because of Windows Azure server-side scripting and integrated push support. Data from mobile apps is stored in the cloud because of the Azure data management capabilities described next.

High-Performance Computing

The power and promise of the cloud is that many computers can work together to solve problems faster. To truly enable multiple computers to work together to solve a problem, the application must support *parallel programming* so that more than one computer can execute the same code. Microsoft's High Performance Computing is just such a parallel programming environment. The Azure *HPC Scheduler* enables HPC applications to work on complex problems such as medical research or the rendering logic required to animate the next Pixar blockbuster.

Marketplace

The *Azure Marketplace* is a place to buy and sell SaaS applications and datasets. This market-place currently supports applications from vendors including Microsoft, AppDynamics, Cad Cam Systems, and more. Datasets are available for inclusion in applications, including such diverse options as demographics data, currency exchange data, air traffic data, and more.

Data Management

Given the Virtual Machine execution model previously described, a customer of Windows Azure can install any database technology on a VM, including open source or NoSQL databases such as MySql and MongoDB, respectively. For those not looking to administer their own cloud-based data center, Windows Azure offers cloud-based applications' three different methods to store and retrieve data.

Formerly known as SQL Azure, *SQL Database* is a relational database PaaS service. SQL Database supports ANSI SQL, T-SQL, transactions, and concurrent data access via Entity Framework, ADO. Net, JDBC, and other access technologies. Windows Azure SQL Database can even be accessed by SQL Server Management Studio.

Windows Azure Tables step down the capabilities of SQL Database by focusing on fast access to typed data such as a key/value store. Windows Azure Tables don't support complex operations such as joins and SQL queries, but they are cheap and scale to support a terabyte of data in a single table!

The third data storage and management option is *Windows Azure Blobs*. BLOB storage is ideal for longer-term file storage such as video or document files.

Business Analytics

Given the diverse and infinitely scalable nature of Windows Azure applications, traditional analytics offerings may have challenges integrating cloud-based data. To assist with business analysis of cloud-hosted data, Windows Azure offers two analytics options.

SQL Reporting works against SQL Database data in much the same way SQL Server Reporting Services works against SQL Server data. SQL Reporting is a traditional approach to data reporting that supports output formats including HTML, XML, PDF, and Excel, and can be built with traditional on-premise SQL Server Reporting Services tools such as the Report Builder and Visual Studio-based Business Intelligence Development Studio (BIDS) and SQL Server Data Tools (SSDT).

Announced in October 2011, Microsoft introduced the Apache open source, big data analytics capabilities of Hadoop to Windows Azure. Hadoop offers users the ability to analyze large quantities of unstructured, nonrelational data. Hadoop technologies on Azure support distributed MapReduce jobs and Hadoop-based technologies such as Hive and Pig.

Media

Media, specifically audio and video, are a tremendously important part of the rich Internet experience and are ever more frequently targets of corporate application development. Building on Microsoft's Media Platform for streaming audio and video, Azure Media Services makes cloud-based capabilities such as encoding, format conversion, content protection and more available to developers. With this service offering, developers can integrate media operations to workflows and Azure's extensive content distribution networks (CDN) for flawless worldwide delivery.

Networking

When building an application designed to reach a geographically distributed audience, it is frequently advantageous to build components in data centers near to the consumers to reduce network lag time. Microsoft supports this geo-distributed architecture by hosting customer applications in Windows Azure data centers located in the United States, Europe, and Asia. Application developers can take advantage of this geographic distribution yet build interconnected apps by leveraging the Windows Azure networking services.

Windows Azure Virtual Network combines a VPN gateway to connect Azure virtual machines to an organization's data center. This enables VM-based applications such as SharePoint and Active Directory to scale up and down as needed yet work with internal IP addresses to simplify access and management.

A step down from a full Windows Azure Virtual Network configuration, *Windows Azure Connect* is an on-premise installation that enables a local machine to communicate with cloud-based machines and applications through a secure, configuration-free connection. Connect is aimed at individual development teams that need to connect Azure applications to local databases without going to IT's network administration team.

In a global scenario, users of Azure applications can leverage the load-balancing capabilities of the *Windows Azure Traffic Manager* to ensure that they always access an application instance loaded in a geographically nearby data center. This load balancing helps to ensure that users experience the minimum amount of lag in application response time.

Caching

Caching is a common application performance improvement technique, where frequently accessed content is stored in memory rather than a slower read-access medium such as spinning disk storage. Windows Azure-based applications can take advantage of *Windows Azure Caching* if the data is persisted to any of the Azure Data Management components previously described. A *CDN* or content delivery network is a specially designed geographically distributed cache that enables frequently accessed BLOB data to be readily available worldwide. Some of the most frequently delivered BLOB files include the jQuery JavaScript libraries leveraged by millions of websites.

Messaging

Windows Azure messaging services are designed to support code interacting with code. Specifically, Windows Azure supports simple message queuing and complex service bus interactions.

Windows Azure Queues enable the pooling of messages by a receiver without requiring that the processing engine code immediately accept the message. This message queuing activity is frequently seen when large numbers of endpoints, such as sensors or distributed mobile applications, deliver details to the central server. The queue builds up as the central processing engine moves queued data through a logic engine into the appropriate long-term storage. This type of asynchronous application is especially common in web and worker role applications.

More complex than the simple queuing mechanism previously described, the *Windows Azure Service Bus* operates as a central messaging hub that any application can subscribe to. Messages are published onto the service bus, and all subscribed applications may receive the communicated message. The goal of any service bus is to enable loosely coupled application designs, and as such a service bus is extremely useful when interconnecting applications from different organizations.

Identity

Identity Lifecycle Management and Single Sign On are significant concerns for enterprises of all sizes. Knowing a user's identity is important to both authentication and authorization. In the cloud, Microsoft's identity and access control components are offered by *Windows Azure Active Directory*. Windows Azure Active Directory supports federation of identity information from on-premise Active Directory environments and Open-ID providers such as Facebook, Google, and Windows Live.

Although Windows Azure Active Directory supports federation with local AD environments, the user object is not the same as the local user and is a poor choice for applications leveraging Connect or Azure VPN to extend enterprise data centers. In this instance, should scaling Active Directory be necessary, the solution should leverage an Azure Virtual Machine running an installed and managed instance of Windows Active Directory.

SHAREPOINT AND MICROSOFT'S CLOUD OFFERINGS

SharePoint 2010 offered a number of integration points where Windows Azure could be plugged in by enterprising developers to customize and extend the platform's capabilities. Where SharePoint 2010 could be extended to the cloud, SharePoint 2013 was designed specifically with cloud computing and Windows Azure in mind. The remainder of this chapter explores those integration points, extension options, and more.

Before diving into the specific integration profiles between SharePoint 2013 and Windows Azure, it is worth reiterating the basic organizational and application benefits that can be attained as a result of integrating SharePoint and the cloud. The basic combination of broadening reach, reduced storage costs, and access to reusable application components can be composited together with a SharePoint 2013 installation to change and improve an organization's capability to meet customer and user needs.

SaaS Licensing for SharePoint

Microsoft has a number of service tiers and price points inside of its Office 365 SaaS offering. Each of the various service tiers effectively constitutes a license to use Office 365, with each tier stacking additional workloads onto the license. At its most basic and cheapest, the Office 365 Email plan is a $4 monthly cost per user plan that offers each user a 25 GB e-mail mailbox. Moving up to the Small Business P1 plan at $8 per user up to 50 users, organizations have access to the 25 GB mailbox, Microsoft Lync for IM and chat, Office Web Apps, and an online SharePoint collaboration environment with a single subsite. Near the top of the line, the E3 service plan costs $20 per user per month and offers unlimited e-mail storage for Lync, SharePoint with 300 subsites, Office Web Apps, and downloadable Office clients for installation on up to five workstations per user.

The following list contains a few of the SharePoint Online improvements now available in SharePoint 2013:

➤ Because of default external sharing, site owners can easily share sites and content with external users without requiring internal Active Directory accounts. For more on managing external users, check Microsoft's guidance article at `http://office.microsoft.com/en-us/office365-sharepoint-online-enterprise-help/manage-external-sharing-for-your-sharepoint-online-environment-HA102849864.aspx`.

➤ SharePoint Online's social features have been spread throughout the product, including activity tracking via the personal Newsfeed, file sharing through SharePoint's SkyDrive Pro, and a centralized favorite Sites page.

➤ Optional integration of Exchange Online enables SharePoint Online to centralize task assignments across sites and even Outlook tasks that would otherwise never hit SharePoint.

➤ As with on-premise installations, SharePoint Online 2013 offers new site templates, including the Community Site and Project Site designed to speed collaboration.

➤ Subscribers of E3 and E4 plans or SharePoint Online for Enterprise have access to premium capabilities such as the Discovery Center site template designed to deal with legal matters and content retention.

➤ SharePoint Online for Enterprise also supports Excel services-based business intelligence, a new workflow engine based on Windows Workflow Foundation 4 that supports loops and a number of new actions in SharePoint Designer 2013, and enhanced video management capabilities complete with search integrations.

The following list contains a few of the capabilities from SharePoint Online 2010 that have been discontinued:

➤ Several site templates including the meeting and document workspace templates, the group work site template, and personalization site template have been discontinued as the capabilities are now in other 2013 site templates.

➤ Several information management policies have been discontinued for lack of adoption or failure to meet expectations.

➤ Web Analytics has been discontinued in favor of a new analytics service that leverages the Search system.

➤ The SharePoint Chart Web Part, Status List, and Status Indicators have been deprecated in favor of Excel Services 2013.

➤ Search results no longer support RSS feeds; instead users should turn to Search alerts for an improved experience.

PaaS Licensing for SharePoint

If SharePoint 2013 is to be installed on Windows Azure Virtual Machines or is to be integrated with other Azure-based services such as Media Services or the Windows Azure SQL Database, pricing is the standard Windows Azure pricing. SharePoint 2013 is licensed by instance, much the same way that other Microsoft products are licensed. Thus, if a development team wants to leverage a pair of Windows Azure Virtual Machines to stand up a SharePoint 2013 development environment, the licensing must include

➤ Two instances of the Windows Server 2012 operating system.

➤ One instance of SQL Server 2012.

➤ Two instances of SharePoint 2013.

  ➤ Two servers are required for SharePoint 2013 because Windows Azure Workflow cannot be installed on a domain controller, and the Office Web Apps cannot be installed on a domain controller OR a SharePoint server.

➤ One instance of Visual Studio.

➤ One instance of local Office client applications.

➤ Windows Azure services priced according to the Windows Azure pricing calculator (`https://www.windowsazure.com/en-us/pricing/calculator/`). There are no specific price breaks for SharePoint implementations, including SharePoint Online implementations.

  ➤ Windows Azure offers a free trial that can help developers get acclimated to the new app and workflow models at no additional cost.

Integration Models

Stepping away from the SaaS offering, SharePoint 2013 (both SharePoint online and on-premise) offers a number of opportunities to leverage or integrate to components of the Windows Azure platform for enhanced reach and access. Beyond the normal application development scenarios that offer an opportunity to build on top of cloud platforms, SharePoint 2013 offers a pair of tremendous new development models that natively integrate with Windows Azure. The first and perhaps most significant of these new development paradigms is the cloud app model. The second is the new workflow infrastructure that leverages the Azure workflow manager.

Apps for SharePoint

Apps for SharePoint are the new mechanism for delivering functionality to SharePoint and a major new development target. Apps are distinct from Solutions for SharePoint in a number of ways, including the approach to acquiring, deploying, managing, and removing custom functionality. Apps are completely stand-alone applications that can be hosted in SharePoint or hosted externally in Windows Azure or other systems such as an on-premise web server. Deployment of app packages involves registering an app package with an app store. SharePoint 2013 offers a pair of app store options: the Internal App Catalog that is a private organization's apps or the public SharePoint Store. Apps in the public SharePoint store are available for any organization to purchase and are supported by the vendor organization. Apps in the Internal App Catalog are supported by the organization's IT department.

Contrast the new model with the SharePoint 2010 development option: solution packages. A *solution package* is a package that is either a full trust solution that is deployed directly to a SharePoint farm and requires an administrator to install, manage, and remove, or the alternative to full trust solutions is partial trust solutions that must be installed to a sandbox inside of the SharePoint environment. The solution package enables a developer to create a number of functional components, including web parts, custom controls, pages, event handlers, and back-end timer jobs. The solutions available in 2010 through the solution package delivery mechanism offer a tremendous amount of flexibility but do require a significant amount of knowledge about the SharePoint run time and development methodologies. Limitations of the run time prevented access to a number of modern web development technologies such as ASP.NET MVC or Test Driven Development.

One important distinction between the two models is the location of executing code: outside of SharePoint for apps, inside of the SharePoint run-time for solutions. This isolation is done to improve the stability of the core SharePoint environment. Another major distinction is the development approach. Because apps run outside of SharePoint, they can be built with any technology capable of invoking web service calls, including .NET, PHP, Ruby, Java, and JavaScript. Although the new app model is compelling on the face of its many benefits discussed here and in Chapter 6, "Getting Started with Developing Apps in SharePoint 2013," all SharePoint 2010 development techniques and approaches have been carried forward into SharePoint 2013. For all existing customization investments, no change is required to continue to take advantage of that investment.

Apps for SharePoint can be built with the Napa Office 365 development tool that builds code-free applications in the browser. Napa apps can be imported into Visual Studio 2012 if more powerful functionality becomes necessary. Of course, Visual Studio 2012 is the core development tool for SharePoint apps.

The new app experience offers three different app hosting options for developers, as shown in Figure 5-3.

➤ Apps for SharePoint can be hosted by Windows Azure as part of the cloud-hosted model for SharePoint apps. Azure-hosted apps take advantage of the Windows Azure Web Sites component to host web applications that leverage any ASP.NET technology (ASP.NET Web Form, ASP.NET MVC, and ASP.NET Web Pages). Apps designed for Office 365 authenticate with Windows Azure Active Directory and OAuth 2.

➤ Apps can be hosted by a developer's own server infrastructure, whether that infrastructure is an on-premise infrastructure or a cloud-based infrastructure.

➤ The final option is to deploy the app directly into SharePoint for internal hosting.

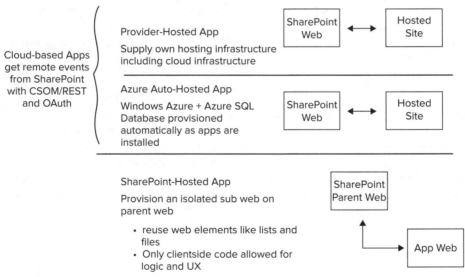

FIGURE 5-3

Chapter 6 is dedicated to diving deeper into apps from a development perspective.

Azure Workflows

In addition to a new development model for SharePoint app functionality, SharePoint 2013 introduces a new model for developing workflows. SharePoint 2013 offers the .NET 4.5 Windows Workflow Foundation as a new approach to enacting custom logic inside of a SharePoint site. The .NET 4.5 Workflows are hosted outside of SharePoint on Windows Azure Workflow service. Office 365 uses this new Azure service automatically, not requiring developers to acquire a Windows Azure account. The integrations in Office 365 are provided automatically.

The benefits of including .NET 4.5 Workflows include a number of new workflow capabilities such as stages and loops, the ability to invoke web services, and, of course, the scalability and performance benefits to run on the Azure platform. Table 5-1, re-created from an MSDN article, describes the new workflow activities available in SharePoint 2013. Notice that the final five activities deal with Microsoft Project. New in SharePoint 2013 is integration with Project 2013, complete with Project-based workflows.

TABLE 5-1: SharePoint 2013 Workflow Activities

ACTION	DESCRIPTION
Assign a Task	Assigns a single workflow task to a user or group
Start a Task Process	Initiates execution of a task process
Go to This Stage	Specifies the next stage in a workflow to which flow control should be handed
Call HTTP Web Service	Functions as a method call to a Representational State Transfer (REST) endpoint
Start a List Workflow	Starts a list-scoped workflow
Start a Site Workflow	Starts a site-scoped workflow
Build DynamicValue	Creates a new variable of type DynamicValue
Get Property from DynamicValue	Retrieves a property value from a specified variable of type DynamicValue
Count Items In DynamicValue	Returns the number of rows in a variable of type DynamicValue
Trim String	Removes all leading and trailing white-space characters from the current string
Find Substring in String	Returns 1-based index of the first occurrence of one or more characters, or the first occurrence of a string, within a string
Replace Substring in String	Returns a new string in which all occurrences of a specified character or string are replaced with another specified character or string
Translate Document	Functions as a wrapper around the HTTP activity that calls the synchronous translation API. You must configure a Machine Translation Service Application for the SharePoint site on which you run the workflow
Set Workflow Status	Updates workflow status as specified in message string

continues

TABLE 5-1 *(continued)*

ACTION	DESCRIPTION
Create a Project from Current Item [Microsoft Project]	Creates a Project Server project based on the current item
Set the current project stage status to this value [Microsoft Project]	Sets the two status fields within the current stage of the project
Set the status field in the idea list item to this value [Microsoft Project]	Updates the status field of the original SharePoint list item
Wait for Project Event [Microsoft Project]	Pauses the current instance of the workflow to await a specified Project event: Project checked in, Project committed, Project submitted
Set this field in the project to this value [Microsoft Project]	Sets the value for the enterprise custom field for a specified project

Table source: `http://msdn.microsoft.com/en-us/library/jj163177(v=office.15)`

As developers and site owners approach creating workflows for SharePoint 2013, they have two choices of platforms: the new platform leveraging Windows Azure Workflow Services and .NET 4.5 or the old SharePoint 2010 platform. As with other SharePoint 2010 customizations, the entire 2010 workflow platform was brought forward into SharePoint 2013 so that no existing investments need change.

Workflows can be built with the Office SharePoint Designer or with Visual Studio 2012. In either case, workflows are declarative-only constructs that rely on XAML files to define and frame the execution of the logic. The implication of this change is that workflows are no longer compiled but are instead interpreted. This interpretive approach is what enables workflows to be executed outside of the SharePoint run time and offers opportunities for numerous visualization and editor tools.

Chapter 15, "SharePoint 2013 Workflow Development," dives deeper into workflow development and how workflows can be used to extend SharePoint 2013.

SUMMARY

This chapter introduced you to core cloud concepts and benefits. Cloud offerings such as IaaS, PaaS, and SaaS bring fantastic levels of flexibility and capability to organizations, usually at compelling pricing options. However, everything is not always rosy in cloud-land. Pay attention to legitimate company constraints that may preclude production cloud-based deployments such as regulatory restrictions. Following the introduction to cloud computing, the chapter delved into Microsoft's Windows Azure platform and its integration points with SharePoint 2013, introducing you to key concepts, components, and usage patterns. Given the extremely easy access to unlimited scalability and the ability to host SharePoint functionality in Azure for new customizations, it is not unreasonable to expect that organizations worldwide that leverage SharePoint will be leveraging Windows

Azure. As will be discussed in Chapter 6, auto-hosting code in Azure is the default development experience! As a developer, this represents a huge opportunity for future skills growth and continued relevance in a competitive jobs marketplace.

Of course, it bears repeating that SharePoint 2010 methods for development, including full trust solution packages, continue to be valid options for SharePoint developers. All existing code-based customizations should continue to work in SharePoint 2013, but all new development exercises should look seriously at the new app model approach.

The next chapter expands on this chapter's introduction to Azure with a look at developing apps for SharePoint 2013. In the next chapter you learn how to develop for SharePoint's new app model, including how Azure service components may be incorporated.

Getting Started with Developing Apps in SharePoint 2013

ARCHITECTURAL OVERVIEW OF SHAREPOINT APPS

Chapter 5, "Introducing Windows Azure and SharePoint 2013 Integration," introduces the benefits of cloud computing. Chief among these benefits is the ability to separate portions of responsibility to different services or providers. This decoupled approach is as familiar to anyone used to a services-based approach to application development as it is to infrastructure architects who leverage a mix of hosted and on-premise servers. Microsoft Office 2013 and SharePoint 2013 leverage the capabilities of the cloud within the new app experience.

An *app* is a self-contained functional application, complete with user experience, data storage, and business logic. Anyone familiar with modern mobile devices is familiar with the concept of an app. Apps for Office and SharePoint combine the power of enterprise software with the flexibility of the Web. Apps are specifically targeted to solve specific business scenarios, and due to their self-contained architecture are easy to manage. The portability of apps is such that an app for Office 365 works in an on-premise installation and that apps developed for SharePoint may even work as apps for Office. The rest of this chapter and Chapter 7, "Further Developing Apps in SharePoint 2013," focus on SharePoint apps; the development story for Office apps is introduced in later chapters.

SharePoint 2013 adopts this decoupling approach with the new app model known as *app isolation*, a clear separation of core portal functionality and extensions to that functionality plugged into the SharePoint user interface while being hosted on alternative infrastructures. By adopting this new app model, SharePoint is a big winner in a number of ways:

> ➤ Apps are self-contained and independent of SharePoint server deployments. This means that any SharePoint environment can install and host an app without worrying about farm deployments or administrator approvals.

> ➤ Apps reduce platform risks, freeing the platform from worrying about app-based customizations during service packs and updates. Because the app is effectively an external web application running in an iFrame, SharePoint doesn't need to worry about putting customizations at risk when an approved Microsoft service release makes changes to the server.

> ➤ Apps are deployed by default to isolated subsites within a specialized domain. This domain isolation leverages modern web browser technologies to prevent cross-site scripting attacks, whereas the external hosting model prevents unauthorized or incorrectly written code from executing on the SharePoint server.

> ➤ Apps are designed to support multitenant installations. The site administration-controlled approach to installing and managing functionality eliminates unintentional farm-level customizations, allowing numerous distinct tenants to occupy the same farm.

> ➤ Apps lower the bar for developers by supporting any web technology that can emit HTML, CSS, and JavaScript. This includes any flavor of ASP.Net, Java, Ruby, PHP, CoffeeScript, TypeScript, and more.

Programming Model Overview

An app for SharePoint is any focused, secure solution that connects to the SharePoint server via client-side APIs, either CSOM or REST. The app is either entirely client-side code embedded in a SharePoint page or a wholly contained application that resides on independent hardware and authenticates to the portal through the OAuth 2.0 protocol in a manner familiar to users of Facebook applications. Apps that connect to an instance of SharePoint are managed by that instance's App Management Service. The App Management Service is designed to centrally manage, secure, and license apps.

> **NOTE** *Notice several specifically chosen words and phrases in the text: instance of SharePoint and license apps. The app experience is designed from the ground up to work within the multitenant management experience of Office 365. It is precisely this architecture that enables one customer or team to install an app without impacting any other tenant and without impacting the stability of the environment.*

Most apps for SharePoint 2013 will be developed as web applications; although, an application for a desktop or mobile device such as an iPad also qualifies. Because the interconnection to SharePoint is managed with an OData-compliant REST interface, remote .NET client APIs, and OAuth security protocols, an app can be developed in any language with any development tool. Furthermore, this standards-compliant REST interface enables the development of apps that expose interfaces in varied and diverse environments such as iOS apps. To learn more about the OData standard, refer to the OData site at http://www.odata.org. As stated in Chapter 2, "What's New in SharePoint 2013," the promise of having both OData (as the protocol and enabler) and REST (as the design pattern) is to make SharePoint Data accessible to almost any other platform and any type of device via URL and standard HTTP verbs.

Microsoft has included a number of enhancements in Visual Studio 2012 that specifically target the SharePoint app development experience. For Office 365 apps, a web-based development environment called the Napa Office 365 Development Tools is available free of charge.

Comparing Apps and Solutions

An app is a standalone application, with all that it entails. Because it stands alone, the infrastructure, management, and upgrades for apps happen outside of SharePoint. Although the hosting options for apps will be examined more closely in the next section, you must understand that an app that requires server-side code must be installed on its own web server infrastructure, apart from SharePoint. Apps that exclusively leverage client-side scripting for logic may be hosted in SharePoint, but no app code can be installed on a SharePoint server. Apps are acquired by site administrators and farm administrators from the public SharePoint Store or from an internal corporate App Catalog.

Solutions are different from apps in that they are rarely completely standalone applications. Instead, solutions are usually packages intended to customize or extend the functionality of one or more SharePoint sites. Solutions are almost always custom development exercises by either third-party developers or an internal development team. Code is installed into SharePoint either by administrators as a full trust solution or by site administrators as a partial trust or sandboxed solution.

Where both full trust and sandbox solutions are managed by farm administrators, apps enable greater administrative flexibility. Apps are designed for multitenancy, meaning that one site owner can add a specific app, whereas another may choose not to. When an app developer releases an upgrade to the SharePoint Store or App Catalog, each individual site administrator is notified of the available update and can independently upgrade the app on their sites. Because an app is an entirely self-contained application, if a site administrator decides to remove a particular app from a site, the app instance and all of its data are deleted from the site. Administrators can watch for app errors and issues; site owners have the ability to add and delete apps from their sites. Microsoft has created an App Overview for IT Pros poster, which details the delineation of app management capabilities, as shown in Figure 6-1.

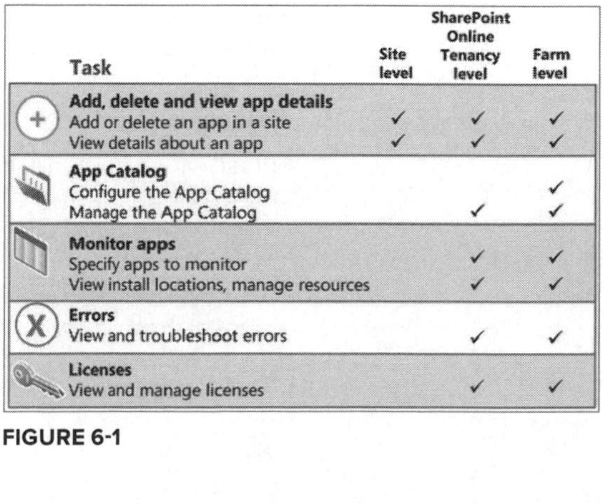

Task	Site level	SharePoint Online Tenancy level	Farm level
Add, delete and view app details Add or delete an app in a site View details about an app	✓ ✓	✓ ✓	✓ ✓
App Catalog Configure the App Catalog Manage the App Catalog		✓	✓ ✓
Monitor apps Specify apps to monitor View install locations, manage resources		✓ ✓	✓ ✓
Errors View and troubleshoot errors		✓	✓
Licenses View and manage licenses		✓	✓

FIGURE 6-1

To monitor and manage apps, farm administrators leverage Central Administration's General Application Settings page. SharePoint Online administrators leverage the SharePoint Online Application Center's Apps page. Site owners use their site's All Site Content page.

> **NOTE** *SharePoint Store administrators have the ability to identify an app as unsafe and remove it from the store. Should this happen, all apps are disabled and removed but that app's data is preserved for independent recovery.*

Hosting Options

As previously mentioned, a core decision of the app programming model is where to host the code and data. The user interface is typically presented to SharePoint users as HTML, CSS, and JavaScript in the browser, whereas the independent back end may be hosted in SharePoint or on some other infrastructure. The app model supports three app hosting options, which replace the farm and sandbox solutions of SharePoint 2010. Sandbox solutions and farm solutions continue to be viable development targets in 2013, but all new development should leverage the app model instead. This is the only mechanism to leverage the App Store for Office 365. The three app hosting options include the SharePoint hosted app, the provisioner hosted app, and the Azure auto-hosted app. The differences between these models are defined by their different deployment stories. Figure 6-2 summarizes the three hosting options.

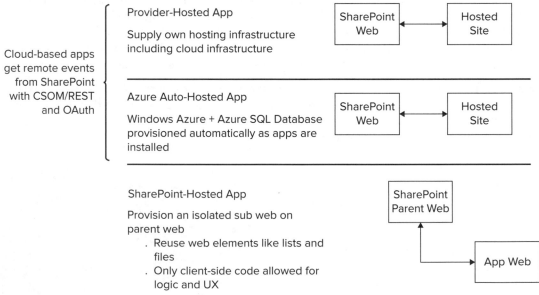

FIGURE 6-2

The *SharePoint-hosted app* is an app manifested inside of SharePoint and lives only inside of SharePoint. You must understand that even with a SharePoint-hosted app, there is no code running on the server; all code must run in the client. A SharePoint-hosted app is effectively an .aspx page full of JavaScript that implements the wanted behavior via client-side script and service calls.

Cloud-hosted apps are actually any app hosted outside of the SharePoint server, including those hosted on a local IIS server in the same data center. Because the app is hosted off of the SharePoint server, the app can be developed and hosted using any technology the developer cares to choose, such as PHP or Java. Cloud-hosted apps enable server-side code that communicates with SharePoint via the same client-side script and service calls as SharePoint-hosted apps. Due to the external hosting, the OAuth 2 protocol is used to provide the authentication mechanism that is required to allow access.

Cloud-hosted apps include two distinct deployment models, the *provisioner-hosted app* and the *Azure auto-hosted app*. The provisioner-hosted app enables the developer to define his own infrastructure, regardless of whether this infrastructure is a local server or a cloud service provider such as Amazon .com or even Azure (which a developer may choose to have much more explicit control over the behavior of the Azure-based management experience). You must understand that the selection of a provisioner-hosted app deployment model means that additional servers are required to meet the needs of the SharePoint environment. Be sure to include this extra server in infrastructure planning phases.

An Azure auto-hosted app is an app created in SharePoint that includes a web project and a SQL project. When the app is installed from either of the two market places, the app's web deployment manifest is automatically delivered to Azure, which automatically and invisibly provisions an Azure website service and an optional Azure SQL database instance. The application's back-end infrastructure and server-side code is completely abstracted away from the developer and the user. Both cloud-hosted app options enable the creation of extremely rich and fully featured application experiences in contrast to a SharePoint-hosted app.

As an Office 365 customer, integration to Azure is automatically wired up when an Azure auto-hosted option is selected for deployment. When an end user installs an Azure auto-hosted app, Office 365 automatically deploys and provisions a copy of the app as a Windows Azure website, and Office 365 then manages it on behalf of the end user who installed it.

Regardless of how an app is developed and deployed, after installed into a SharePoint instance, the SharePoint app management engine secures the app and the underlying platform by enforcing a level of isolation. Any time an app executes, it actually executes on a unique app domain with a unique, generated URL. This is done to prevent deliberate and accidental cross-site scripting attacks. The other benefit of this approach is that each tenant is isolated from every other tenant during execution.

EXAMINING AN APP

Now you will quickly visit a SharePoint site to understand a bit more about apps before jumping into the actual development of apps. Begin by opening a default SharePoint site. The default home-page for a SharePoint team site offers a number of navigation options and an enticing interactive Get

Started app in the middle of the screen. Along the left side of the screen is the familiar contextual Quick Launch menu, complete with the familiar Site Contents link. Click the Site Contents menu option to see the lists, libraries, and other apps.

Notice that the Site Contents page refers to all site contents as Lists, Libraries, and other Apps, as shown in Figure 6-3. All items, including document libraries, image libraries, and task lists are considered to be apps that store their data in a list. Although the rest of this chapter discusses how to create custom apps with code that resides outside of SharePoint, you must understand that default SharePoint constructs are the exact same things that they were before. Calling these familiar SharePoint concepts "apps" is just a change in vocabulary. This change in vocabulary cleans up the experience for an end user who may not understand the difference between a document library (app) and a custom solution with code running on Azure. The core set of SharePoint functionality does not change; it does not get a dedicated tenant-based URL in an auto-created subweb or any special permissions.

FIGURE 6-3

You also need to understand that the new app-centric SharePoint 2013 experience does not eliminate web parts as an important development target. You simply need to put the default homepage of a team site into edit mode to see that the interactive Getting Started page component is actually a web part that can be placed on any page. Figure 6-4 demonstrates exactly that scenario.

Hover over an app to see the region highlight on mouse over. In addition to the mouse-over-text highlighting, an ellipsis or three dots indicating a hover card context menu appear in the top-right corner. Click this ellipsis to see that the management for an app is easily accessible from the Site Contents page, as shown in Figure 6-5. From this experience you can manage the settings and permissions of an app.

FIGURE 6-4

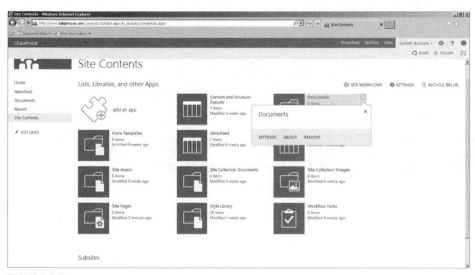

FIGURE 6-5

Adding an App

Click the Add an App button seen in Figure 6-5 to examine the native apps and the app store experiences. Native apps, as previously mentioned, are essentially nothing more than the lists, libraries, and web parts which were available in the SharePoint 2010 environment. However, in addition to the native apps, a default installation and Office 365 environments also have access to the SharePoint Store. The SharePoint Store is a public app marketplace where end users can find free and premium apps built by hundreds or thousands of enterprise application developers. Figure 6-6 illustrates the SharePoint Store experience.

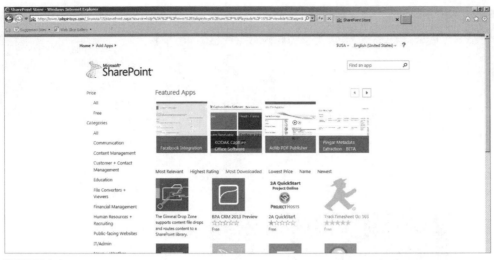

FIGURE 6-6

DEVELOPING YOUR FIRST APP

To create apps, the first thing to do is create a developer site collection that accepts deployments of apps from Visual Studio. To create a developer site, simply create a new site collection in Central Administration, and select the Developer Site template from the Collaboration tab, as shown in Figure 6-7.

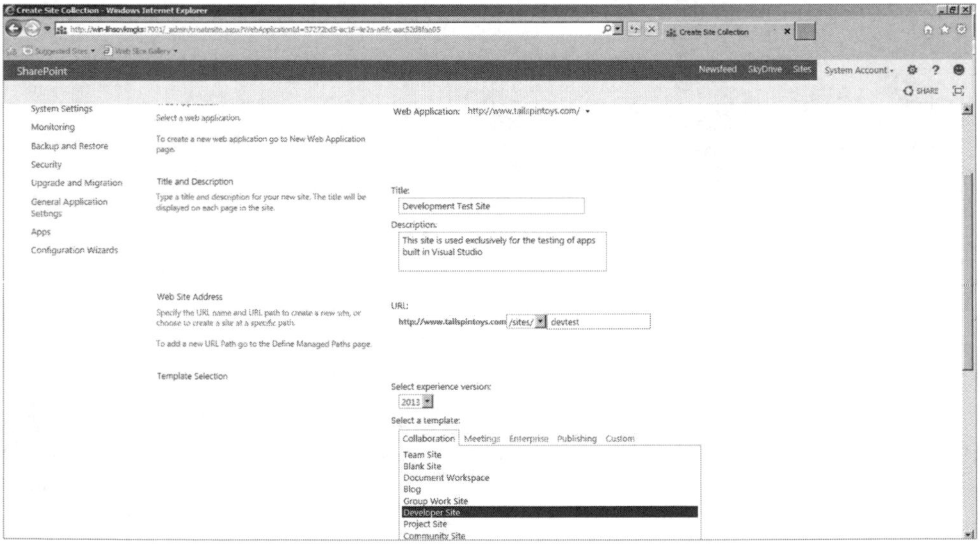

FIGURE 6-7

After the developer site is in place, open Visual Studio 2012 and follow these steps to create a simple SharePoint 2013 app. A rite of passage for all new systems and development methodologies is to first create a Hello World app, and this is no exception.

1. In Visual Studio, select File ⇨ New Project ⇨ App for SharePoint 2013, and name it **SharePointHosted_HelloWorld**, as shown in Figure 6-8.

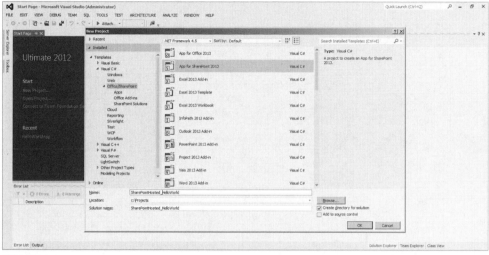

FIGURE 6-8

2. The next screen is a wizard screen with three questions. The first question asks for the name of the new app. Use easy-to-read language here because this is what end users will see; liberal use of spaces for improved readability is encouraged. The second question is asking for the URL of the development site. When copying and pasting from the browser, be sure to stop the URL at the _layouts path (that is, `http://www.tailspintoys.com/sites/devtest` instead of `http://www.tailspintoys.com/sites/devtest/_layouts/15/start.aspx#/SitePages/DevHome.aspx`). A Validate button is available to test the connectivity to the specified URL. The final question asks for the preferred hosting model. Because this is a SharePoint-hosted example, change the selection from the default auto-hosted to SharePoint-hosted. Figure 6-9 illustrates the appropriate values.

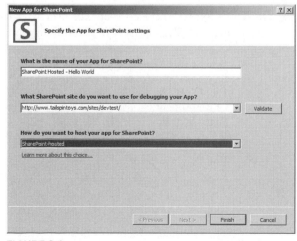

FIGURE 6-9

3. Visual Studio processes for a few moments as it creates the new project and communicates with the SharePoint Developer site. When the new project has been created, expand the Pages folder in the Solution Explorer, and double-click on the Default.aspx page to begin looking at the contents of the default project template, as shown in Figure 6-10. Notice that while the page extension is .aspx, there is no associated code-behind file. Recall that because this is a SharePoint-hosted app, there cannot be server code deployed with this app.

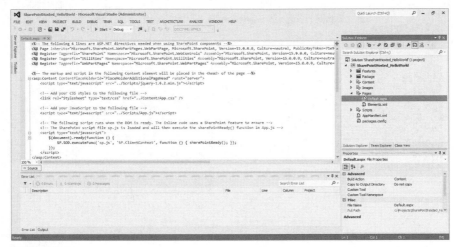

FIGURE 6-10

Near the bottom of the Default.aspx page is div inside of the PlaceHolderMain content place holder. This div leverages the JavaScript code in App.js (found in the Scripts folder in the Solution Explorer) to identify the current user. Add the following line above the div:

```
<h1>Hello World! This is my first SharePoint 2013 app!</h1>
```

This is the extent of the code change necessary to demonstrate a working SharePoint 2013 app hosted inside of SharePoint. However, before launching the app and marveling at the successful first app, it is worth briefly examining the other components of the Visual Studio solution to understand the contents of the App for SharePoint 2013 project template.

➤ The Features folder contains the SharePoint Feature packaging, which is required to activate and provision the files associated with the new SharePoint-hosted app. As in 2010, the Feature designer in Visual Studio supports explicit inclusion and exclusion of items in the Solution, Feature Activation Dependencies, and access to the Element Manifest.

➤ The Package folder contains the new SharePoint 2013 App Package designer, which sports a user experience similar to the Feature designer. This Package manifest contains details for a SharePoint-hosted app, which indicate a clear lineage from the older SharePoint Solutions such as a Manifest, which includes a Solution node with a `SolutionId` attribute.

➤ The Content folder currently contains the app's App.css style sheet and is the ideal location for other content items in future apps. In addition to the app's content files, an Elements.xml manifest is present. Double-clicking the Content folder opens this `Elements.xml` file.

> ➤ The Images folder is the clearly named repository of app images such as the AppIcon.png. An Elements.xml manifest file keeps track of items that need to be deployed.

> ➤ The Pages and Scripts folders previously have been described. Like the Images folder, they are clearly named, and each contains an Elements.xml manifest.

> ➤ The last two items in the default template include an AppManifest.xml and a `packages` `.config` file. Double-clicking the AppManifest.xml opens a specific designer that guides the developer through making changes to the app such as managing the title, name, and icon for the app as well as manipulation of permission requests, prerequisites (features or capabilities), and adjustment of the query string. For now the default selections work, and these options are examined in more detail later in the "Developing a Provider-Hosted App" section.

At this point, the "development" tasks are complete, and the project template has been briefly discussed. Press the Start button in Visual Studio to deploy the app to the developer site. After the app has been successfully deployed, the web browser opens and automatically navigates to the Site Contents page. Here, as shown in Figure 6-11, the new SharePoint Hosted - Hello World app is now present as an installed app. Although this is a developer site, the installation is complete, and the app exposes monitoring and permissions via the ellipsis in its top-right corner.

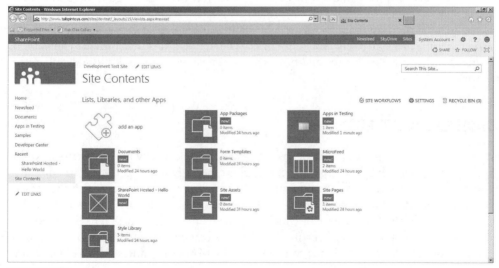

FIGURE 6-11

Notice the app isolation as executed by a distinct URL. The developer site lives at the original URL (`http://www.tailspintoys.com/sites/devtest`) but when the new app is opened, the browser goes to a new URL (`http://app-d2dcbf5e27c6cd.apps.tailspintoys.com/sites/ devtest/SharePointHostedHelloWorld`). The bolded alphanumeric code in the URL is unique to the specific site. The rest of the new app URL would be consistent for any other site that is in the TailSpinToys domain that launches this app. The SharePointHostedHelloWorld keyword at the end of the URL is actually the name of the app that was coded into the AppManifest.xml in Visual Studio. Your browser also contains additional details in the URL bar, standard tokens such as the host URL and the language/culture pair. Figure 6-12 demonstrates the successful Hello World app.

FIGURE 6-12

This concludes the Hello World app demonstration. Granted, this was a simple demonstration, but consider what has been covered in this example. From this example, you now understand that a dedicated development SharePoint site collection must exist with its top-level site based on the Developer Site template. You now know how to create a project in Visual Studio 2012 and know the basic structural components of the default project template. Finally, you understand that although no code is allowed on the server for a SharePoint hosted app, a savvy web developer with access to jQuery can create extremely compelling HTML5 applications that provide tremendous business value across a range of devices and browsers. The next sections look more deeply into developing apps.

CLIENT-SIDE OBJECT MODEL

Now that the Hello World application has been completed, a quick review of the client-side object model (CSOM) is in order. The client-side object model is especially important to SharePoint apps developers because it is the only mechanism with which an app can interact with the server to perform remote communication and control tasks. As with SharePoint 2010, there is actually more than one version of the CSOM, one of which is designed to work with .NET clients such as Windows Forms, WPF, and Silverlight because .NET clients can understand results as .NET objects. The other version of the CSOM is designed to work with ECMAScript callers such as JavaScript, and results are returned to callers as JSON.

There is also a difference in the namespaces provided by the .NET and ECMAScript object models. Because you extend the Ribbon using script, the ECMAScript OM has a Ribbon namespace, whereas the managed client OM does not. Plus, there is a difference in naming conventions for the foundational part of the namespaces. For example, if you want to access a site, in the .NET API you would use the `Microsoft.SharePoint.Client.Site` object, but in ECMAScript you would use SP.Site. Table 6-1 shows the different namespaces for the two client OMs.

TABLE 6-1: Supported Namespaces in Client OMs

.NET MANAGED	ECMASCRIPT
Microsoft.SharePoint.Client.Application	N/A
N/A	SP.Application.UI
N/A	SP.Ribbon
N/A	SP.Ribbon.PageState
N/A	SP.Ribbon.TenantAdmin
N/A	SP.UI
N/A	SP.UI.ApplicationPages
N/A	SP.UI.ApplicationPages.Calendar
Microsoft.SharePoint.Client.Utilities	SP.Utilities
Microsoft.SharePoint.Client.WebParts	SP.WebParts
Microsoft.SharePoint.Client.Workflow	SP.Workflow

To show you how to map your understanding of server objects to the client, Table 6-2 shows how server objects would be named in the client OMs.

TABLE 6-2: Equivalent Objects in Server and Client OMs

SERVER OM	.NET MANAGED	ECMASCRIPT
Microsoft.SharePoint.SPContext	Microsoft.SharePoint.Client.ClientContext	SP.ClientContext
Microsoft.SharePoint.SPSite	Microsoft.SharePoint.Client.Site	SP.Site
Microsoft.SharePoint.SPWeb	Microsoft.SharePoint.Client.Web	SP.Web
Microsoft.SharePoint.SPList	Microsoft.SharePoint.Client.List	SP.List
Microsoft.SharePoint.SPListItem	Microsoft.SharePoint.Client.ListItem	SP.ListItem
Microsoft.SharePoint.SPField	Microsoft.SharePoint.Client.Field	SP.Field

Before diving into writing code with the client OM and adding references in VS, you first need to understand where these DLLs are located and some of the advantages of the DLLs, especially size.

As with other SharePoint .NET DLLs, you can find the .NET DLLs for the client OM located under `%Program Files%\Common Files\Microsoft Shared\Web Server Extensions\15\ISAPI`. Where SharePoint 2010 offered two DLLs for the managed OM, `Microsoft.SharePoint.Client` and `Microsoft.SharePoint.Client.Runtime`, SharePoint 2013 offers nine DLLs including

➤ `Microsoft.SharePoint.Client`

➤ `Microsoft.SharePoint.Client.DocumentManagement`

➤ `Microsoft.SharePoint.Client.Publishing`

➤ `Microsoft.SharePoint.Client.Runtime`

➤ `Microsoft.SharePoint.Client.Search.Applications`

➤ `Microsoft.SharePoint.Client.Search`

➤ `Microsoft.SharePoint.Client.ServerRuntime`

➤ `Microsoft.SharePoint.Client.Taxonomy`

➤ `Microsoft.SharePoint.Client.UserProfiles`

If you look at these DLLs in terms of size, combined they are at 1.6 MB. Compare that with `Microsoft.SharePoint`, which weighs in at more than a hefty 25 MB.

Because the ECMAScript implementation is different from the .NET one and needs to live closer to the web-based code for SharePoint, this DLL is located in `%Program Files%\Common Files\ Microsoft Shared\Web Server Extensions\15\TEMPLATE\LAYOUTS`. There, you can find four relevant JS files: `SP.js`, `SP.Core.js`, `SP.Ribbon.js`, and `SP.Runtime.js`. Of course, when you debug your code, you use the debug versions of these files, such as `SP.debug.js`, because the main versions are minified to save on size and bandwidth. Also, you can set your SharePoint deployment to use the debug versions of these files automatically by changing the `web.config` file for your deployment located at `%inetpub%\wwwroot\wss\VirtualDirectories\80` and adding to the system.web section the following line: `<deployment retail="false" />`. Again, these files are less than 1 MB.

Finally, Silverlight is a little different in that it has its own implementation of the client OM for Silverlight specifically. You can find the Silverlight DLLs at `%Program Files%\Common Files\ Microsoft Shared\Web Server Extensions \15\TEMPLATE\LAYOUTS\ClientBin`. You can find two files, `Microsoft.SharePoint.Client.Silverlight` and `Microsoft.SharePoint.Client .Silverlight.Runtime`. Combined, the files also come in under 1 MB in size.

Microsoft has redistributable versions of the .NET and Silverlight object models to install on your client machines. If you have Office 2013 installed on your machine, you don't need the redistributable version, and if you don't, you can retrieve the 32-bit and 64-bit versions of the redistributable installer at `www.microsoft.com/downloads/en/details.aspx?FamilyID=b4579045-b183-4ed4- bf61-dc2f0deabe47`. Given the long URL, it is probably easier to search for "SharePoint Server 2013 Client Components SDK."

CSOM Improvements over SharePoint 2010

Although the introduction of the client-side object models in the 2010 product changed how developers access SharePoint functionality, it was not always easy to use. As mentioned earlier, CSOM coverage of SharePoint 2010's capabilities was quite limited. The client-side development experience was frequently frustrating, in part because of those limitations and because of the limited support for non-.NET languages. Although CSOM was introduced to SharePoint developers in SharePoint 2010 as a significantly reduced set of capabilities when compared to server-side code, SharePoint

2013's CSOM has had a significant amount of work put into it by Microsoft. Although the CSOM is not yet at 100-percent parity with the server-side object model, it has significantly more coverage in the 2013 product than in the 2010 product. In addition to deeper access to some commonly used namespaces, some significant new capabilities are now accessible from client-side code including

- Social
- Search
- Managed meta data
- BCS
- Activity feeds
- User profiles

Microsoft has made commitments to improve the reach and accessibility of SharePoint APIs and has chosen to do so from the same web service platform. In addition to the new APIs available in the client object models, a new Representational State Transfer (REST) service has been made for each API. This new REST service enables developers to use any technology that supports REST web requests when creating apps. At a high level, Figure 6-13 shows the .NET/Silverlight and ECMAScript object model interactions. The client object models are all built to interact with the client.svc web service, which handles batching, serialization, and parsing of requests and replies (refer to Figure 6-13).

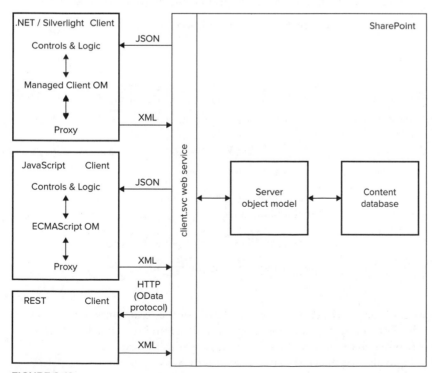

FIGURE 6-13

RESTful SharePoint 2013

SharePoint 2010 introduced REST services for SharePoint, but SharePoint 2013 offers a number of improvements. First, understand the core capabilities of the REST interface. SharePoint 2013's REST service endpoints enable HTTP-based CRUD (Create, Read, Update, and Delete) operations on most of the SharePoint client object model types and members. This new capability grants REST access to objects such as lists, sites, and more. To read from a SharePoint type or member, use HTTP GET commands. To insert, use HTTP PUT commands. To update a SharePoint type or member, use HTTP POST commands. You can also use the POST command to create new structural elements in SharePoint such as lists and sites. And you can use the HTTP DELETE command to remove or recycle SharePoint content.

SharePoint 2013 follows the OData specification and uses the Atom protocol to respond to REST service requests; although, you can use the Accept header to request JSON formats instead of Atom formats.

REST service URI endpoints correspond to the client OM API in most cases, leveraging the following structure: `Http://servername/site/_api/namespace/object|property|indexer(index)| method(parameters)/?$ODataOperation/`.

For example, `http://server/site/_vti_bin/client.svc/web/lists` can accept POST commands to create new lists in the specified SharePoint site. To shorten the preceding URL, `http://server/ site/_api/web/lists` reaches the same endpoint. Because Microsoft recommends that URLs are kept below a 260-character limit, the use of the `_api` convention is the preferred URI notation.

Table 6-3 identifies a number of REST service endpoints in addition to /web.

TABLE 6-3: SharePoint 2013 REST Service Endpoints

AREA	CLIENT OM	REST ENDPOINT	SERVER OM
Lists	ClientContext.Web.Lists	http://server/site/_api/web/lists	SPList
Site	ClientContext.Site	http://server/site/_api/site	SPSite
Web	ClientContext.Web	http://server/site/_api/web	SPWeb
User Profile		http://server/site/_api/Sp.UserProfiles. PeopleManager	
Search		http://server/site/_api/search	
Publishing		http://server/site/_api/publishing	

As noted in the description of the REST service structure, REST service endpoints support calls similar to the CSOM calls. For example, you can leverage an indexer and pass in a GUID to retrieve a specific item or to search for an item in a list by its title with the `_api/web/lists/ getbytitle`('item title') equivalent of the GetByTitle from other CSOM methods.

The following example demonstrates how you can use REST to query the Contacts list and retrieve an item with ID equals of 1:

```
http://Tailspintoys.com/_api/web/lists/getByTitle('Contacts')/
   getItemByStringId('1')
```

The following code snippet is an example of how to leverage the REST services in C# to get all of the lists in the site. First, the code creates the request to the lists REST endpoint and retrieves the details in an Atom format.

```
HttpWebRequest listRequest =
    (HttpWebRequest)HttpWebRequest.Create(sharepointUrl.ToString() +
      "/_api/Web/lists");
listRequest.Method = "GET";
listRequest.Accept = "application/atom+xml";
listRequest.ContentType = "application/atom+xml;type=entry";
listRequest.Headers.Add("Authorization", "Bearer " + accessToken);
HttpWebResponse listResponse = (HttpWebResponse)listRequest.GetResponse();
StreamReader listReader = new StreamReader(listResponse.GetResponseStream());
var listXml = new XmlDocument();
listXml.LoadXml(listReader.ReadToEnd());

var titleList = listXml.SelectNodes("//atom:entry/atom:content/m:properties/
    d:Title", xmlnspm);
var idList = listXml.SelectNodes("//atom:entry/atom:content/m:properties/
    d:Id", xmlnspm);
```

The previous code snippet assumes that an accessToken has already been retrieved by the application.

Table 6-4 is a tiny slice of the power available to users of the REST service.

TABLE 6-4: Helpful REST Commands

METHOD	REST COMMAND	DESCRIPTION
POST	http://server/site/web/doclib/_api/contextinfo	Retrieves a SPContextWebInformation structure with the following properties: ➤ webFullUrl ➤ siteFullUrl ➤ formDigestValue ➤ LibraryVersion ➤ SupportedSchemaVersions
POST	http://server/site/_api/web/webinfos/add	Creates a site.
POST	http://server/site/_api/web/lists/getbytitle('Shared Documents')/rootfolder/files/add(url='a.txt', overwrite=true)	Uploads a file to the Shared Documents root folder.

continues

TABLE 6-4 *(continued)*

METHOD	REST COMMAND	DESCRIPTION
PUT	http://server/site/_api/web/Lists/ GetByTitle('RestTest')	Updates an existing SharePoint object. All writable properties must be specified or the request will fail.
PATCH (POST with a separate X-Http-Method header specification)	http://server/site/_api/web/Lists/ GetByTitle('RestTest') Header: X-Http-Method: PATCH	Updates an existing SharePoint object. Any writable properties that are not supplied in the PATCH have their values preserved. PATCH and MERGE commands behave the same, but Microsoft recommends the use of PATCH because MERGE has been deprecated.
GET	http://server/site/_api/web/ GetFileByServerRelativeUrl('/ Shared Documents/myDocument. docx')/$value	Get the contents of a file stored in the root folder of a Shared Documents library.
DELETE (POST with a separate X-Http-Method header specification)	http://server/site/_api/web/Lists/ GetbyTitle('RestTest') Header:X-Http-Method: DELETE Header: IF-MATCH = "ETagValue"	Delete a SharePoint list. The ETag must be used to meet the OData specification for optimistic concurrency control. See the OData specification for more details on ETags.

Microsoft has produced an MSDN article about programming using the SharePoint 2013 REST service that covers the REST programming interface in greater depth. The article can be found online at `http://msdn.microsoft.com/en-us/library/fp142385(v=office.15).aspx` and is titled "Programming using the SharePoint 2013 REST service" for those who prefer to leverage search rather than attempting to type obscure alphanumeric codes into the URL bar.

DEVELOPING EXTERNALLY HOSTED APPS

JavaScript-driven HTML5 apps can certainly be extremely powerful, but there are occasions in which server-side code is required. Although SharePoint is no longer a candidate host platform for compiled application code, the available hosting options include provider-hosted and auto-hosted (Azure-hosted) apps. A provider-hosted app is one where the developer defines the infrastructure as opposed to the auto-hosted app, where the infrastructure decisions are removed from the developer.

High-Trust Apps for Single Server Development Environments

If you, as a developer, attempt to create a single server development environment as is the case with many portable virtual machine-based development environments, there are a number of special considerations for provider-hosted apps. The problem with running both SharePoint and the provider infrastructure is that SharePoint requires a number of special steps including the presence of a certificate and the creation of a unique client ID to use a server-to-server (STS) communication protocol. Apps that use this STS protocol are known as high-trust apps because the app is allowed to assert any user identity because the app creates the user portion of the access token. The STS protocol is a generic protocol used by Microsoft applications including Exchange, Lync, and other applications that require temporary access tokens. SharePoint provider-hosted apps that are created for on-premise cannot use a context token to identify the user as an app in the cloud would. What a high-trust app is NOT is a full-trust app. A high-trust app must still be coded to ask the installing user for explicit permissions.

MSDN has an excellent article detailing the steps required to configure a provider-hosted app as a high-trust app. You can find the article online at `http://msdn.microsoft.com/en-us/library/office/apps/fp179901(v=office.15)`, which has been replicated in part here for the sake of completeness.

1. Create a public and private test certificate (commercial or self-signed as described here):

    a. In IIS manager, select the ServerName node in the tree view on the left.

    b. Select the Server Certificates icon.

    c. Select the Create Self-Signed Certificate link from the set of links on the right side.

    d. Name the certificate HighTrustSampleCert, and then choose OK.

    e. Right-click the certificate and then select Export.

    f. Export the file to your project folder (usually, this is in the Visual Studio 11\Projects\ProjectName folder in your My Documents folder) and give it a password such as `'Password1'`.

2. Create a corresponding test .cer file using the following steps:

    a. In Server Certificates view, double-click HighTrustSampleCert to display the certificate details.

    b. Next, on the Details tab, choose Copy to File to launch the Certificate Export Wizard.

    c. Choose Next.

    d. Use the default value No, do not export the private key, and then choose Next.

    e. Use the default values. Choose Next.

    f. Choose Browse, name the certificate HighTrustSampleCert, and then save it in a location of your choice. It is saved as a .cer file.

    g. Choose Finish.

> **NOTE** *The .pfx file must be on the same computer where Visual Studio is running. The .cer file must be on the same computer where SharePoint 2013 is installed. The .pfx file must be deployed to the web server that is hosting your web application, at the same file path as the computer running Visual Studio. Alternatively, the path can be adjusted in the web.config file, as shown in this article (see the MSDN article "How to: Create high trust apps for SharePoint 2013 using the server-to-server protocol (advanced topic)" at* `http://msdn` `.microsoft.com/en-us/library/fp179901(v=office.15).aspx`*).*

3. Generate a client ID, and create a GUID with Visual Studio. Ensure all letters are lowercase.

4. Configure services in SharePoint 2013 for server-to-server app use. Ensure that the app management service and user profile application are configured. The steps are as follows:

    a. In Central Administration, under Application Management, select Manage service applications.

    b. On the Service Applications page, ensure that the User Profile Service Application and App Management Service services are started.

    c. Under Application Management, select Manage Services on Server.

    d. On the Services on Server page, ensure that the User Profile Service is started.

5. Configure SharePoint 2013 apps (per-app configuration required). Build and execute the following pieces as a single PowerShell script:

    a. Identify the .cer file:

```
$publicCertPath = "c:\Projects\HighTrustSampleCert.cer"
```

    b. Use the client ID previously created, and ensure all letters are lowercase:

```
$appId = "4ed7b623-a09f-4b5d-9ff6-8e48a9c5c049"
```

    c. Identify the SharePoint 2013 URL. Point to a Developer Site for the greatest likelihood of success; although, single server installs do not require this:

```
$spurl = "http://www.tailspintoys.com/sites/devtest"
```

    d. Get the SPWeb object for the site:

```
$spweb = Get-SPWeb $spurl
```

    e. Get the authentication realm for the SharePoint site:

```
$realm = Get-SPAuthenticationRealm -ServiceContext $spweb.Site
```

    f. Identify the .cer file previously created:

```
$certificate = Get-PfxCertificate $publicCertPath
```

g. Get the app ID together with the realm value:

```
$fullAppIdentifier = $appId + '@' + $realm
```

h. Create the trusted security token service:

```
New-SPTrustedSecurityTokenIssuer -Name "High Trust Sample App"
-Certificate $certificate -RegisteredIssuerName $fullAppIdentifier
```

i. Register the app principal with the app management service:

```
$appPrincipal = Register-SPAppPrincipal -NameIdentifier $full
AppIdentifier -Site $spweb -DisplayName "High Trust Sample App"
```

6. Create a provider-hosted app.

All of these steps are required to get the environment into shape for an internally produced yet externally hosted app.

Developing a Provider-Hosted App

The following steps walk through the process of creating a simple provider-hosted app.

1. In Visual Studio, select File ⇨ New Project ⇨ App for SharePoint 2013, and name it **ProviderHosted_SimpleExample**.

2. In the New App for SharePoint Wizard, ensure the developer site URL is correctly selected, and be sure to identify that the app is to be provider-hosted instead of auto-hosted or SharePoint-hosted.

3. The last screen of the New app for SharePoint Wizard enables the selection of the previously exported certificate and asks for the password previously used to encrypt the certificate. The Issuer ID is the same as the app ID previously used, as shown in Figure 6-14.

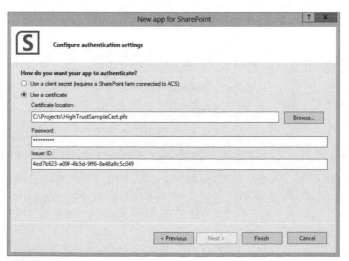

FIGURE 6-14

4. After the new project has been created, examine the Permission requests section of the AppManifest. It is now both possible and logical to ask for permission to the various SharePoint CSOM endpoints. Permissions for apps must be granted at the time of installation based on requests made by the developer in the AppManifest. The user who chooses to install an application can grant only the permissions she has available, and all permissions must be granted at that time. Apps cannot function with a partially available set of permissions. Table 6-5 lists the available endpoints that can be configured inside of the AppManifest designer, whereas Figure 6-15 shows the interface.

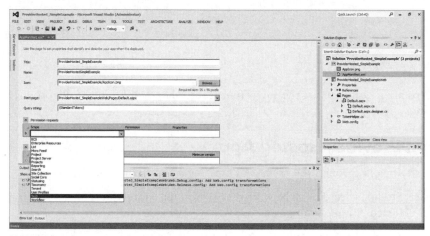

FIGURE 6-15

5. At this point, testing the application is as simple as pressing F5. In the event that a security warning pops up asking about the validity of the certificate from localhost, be sure to click Yes.

6. After the certificate trust questions have been answered, the web browser will open and ask the installing user for permission to install the new app.

TABLE 6-5: Development Endpoints

SCOPE	AVAILABLE PERMISSIONS	NOTES AND SCOPE ATTRIBUTE URL
BCS	Read	http://sharepoint/bcs/connection
Enterprise Resources	Read, Write	Part of the Project Server 2013 features. Not installed by default: http://sharepoint/projectserver/enterpriseresources
List	Read, Write, Manage, FullControl	Supports an additional property called BaseTemplateId, which is an integer where the value matches the type of the List Element such as 101. This property enables filtering of list types. http://sharepoint/content/sitecollection/web/list

Micro Feed	Read, Write, Manage, FullControl	Part of the SharePoint 2013 social features and services: http://sharepoint/social/microfeed
Project	Read, Write	Part of the Project Server 2013 features. Not installed by default: http://sharepoint/projectserver/projects/project
Project Server	Manage	Part of the Project Server 2013 features. Not installed by default: http://sharepoint/projectserver
Projects	Read, Write	Part of the Project Server 2013 features. Not installed by default: http://sharepoint/projectserver/projects
Reporting	Read	Part of the Project Server 2013 features. Not installed by default: http://sharepoint/projectserver/reporting
Search	QueryAsUserIgnoreApp Principal	http://sharepoint/search
Site Collection	Read, Write, Manage, FullControl	http://sharepoint/content/sitecollection
Social Core	Read, Write, Manage, FullControl	Part of the SharePoint 2013 social features and services: http://sharepoint/social/core
Statusing	SubmitStatus	Part of the Project Server 2013 features. Not installed by default: http://sharepoint/projectserver/statusing
Taxonomy	Read, Write	http://sharepoint/taxonomy
Tenant	Read, Write, Manage, FullControl	Part of the SharePoint 2013 social features and services: http://sharepoint/social/tenant
Web	Read, Write, Manage, FullControl	http://sharepoint/content/sitecollection/web
Workflow	Elevate	Part of the Project Server 2013 features. Not installed by default: http://sharepoint/projectserver/workflow

Developing an Azure Auto-hosted App

Before beginning the conversation about Azure auto-hosted apps, you must understand that auto-hosted apps in SharePoint 2013 can be installed only on SharePoint Online websites. This is because SharePoint Online accounts can bundle in pricing for Azure apps, making them free to developers and users.

The steps to build an Azure auto-hosted app are nearly the same as the steps to build a provisioner-hosted app. Follow these steps to get started:

1. In Visual Studio 2010, create a new project based on the App for SharePoint 2013 template. In the New App for SharePoint Wizard, leave the hosting option set to the default selection, auto-hosted. Name the project **AutoHosted_SampleProject**, as shown in Figure 6-16.

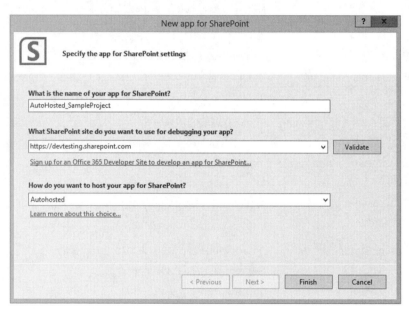

FIGURE 6-16

2. Click Finish in the wizard, and Visual Studio creates a pair of projects inside the solution, the app for SharePoint, which largely consists of deployment packaging XML, and the ASP .Net web application.

3. In the AppHosted_SampleProject C# project, open the AppManifest.xml, and change the Title and Name of the project to friendlier names. Title is what users see, whereas Name is an internal name that should contain no spaces.

4. In the AppHosted_SampleProjectWeb C# project, open the web.config, and add this element to the <system.web> element to simplify debugging:

```
<customErrors mode="Off"/>
```

5. Press F5 to deploy and debug the application. Even though there is no custom code in place yet, this step helps to validate that all setup steps have been properly performed. The web browser should automatically open to ask if the AutoHosted Sample Project should be trusted and installed. With no code changes, the browser screen should look like Figure 6-17. At this point in the development of the solution, the web application is being hosted on your local development machine's instance of IIS Express. (The URL bar points to http://localhost:[portnumber]/....) Configuring the app for auto-hosting occurs in a later step.

FIGURE 6-17

6. Assuming that testing has been successful to this point, the ASP.Net web application is now ready for customization. Every SharePoint 2013 site ships by default with a number of themes, available in the Change the Look under the site's Settings gear icon. The code below leverages REST API calls to access the list of available themes.

7. Open the Default.aspx file, and replace the body tag and its contents with the following HTML to add a button and a grid to the screen:

```
<body style="font-family:'Segoe UI'">
    <form id="form1" runat="server">
    <div>
    <h2>Available Themes</h2>
    </div>
    <asp:Button ID="Button1"
        runat ="server"
        OnClick="Button1_Click"
```

```
        Text="List Available Themes"
        BackColor="#FFFFFF"
        ForeColor="Black"
        Font-Size="Medium"
        Style="border-style: solid;"
        Height="50px"
        Width="180px" />
    <asp:Literal ID="Literal1"
        runat="server"><br /><br /></asp:Literal>
    <asp:GridView ID="GridView1"
        runat="server"
        BackColor="LightGray"
        BorderStyle="None"
        Caption="Themes"
        CaptionAlign="Left"
        CellPadding="5"
        GridLines="None"
        HorizontalAlign="Left">
        <AlternatingRowStyle BackColor="White"
            ForeColor="Black" />
    </asp:GridView>
    </form>
</body>
```

8. Open the Default.aspx.cs code behind, and replace the existing using statements with the following list to add necessary XML and SharePoint capabilities while eliminating unnecessary references:

```
using Microsoft.SharePoint.Client;
using System;
using System.Collections.Generic;
using System.Linq;
using System.Net;
using System.Web.UI.WebControls;
using System.Xml.Linq;
```

9. Add the following three variables to the class above the Page_Load function to make them available across multiple methods:

```
// members
SharePointContextToken contextToken;
string accessToken;
Uri sharepointUrl;
```

10. Replace the Page_Load method with the following code. This code leverages the TokenHelper class (included by default in the web project) to grab an OAuth access token necessary for all web service calls. This token validates the calling user's identity to the server. To ensure the button's OnClick code has access to the token, it will be passed in as a string via the button's optional CommandArgument parameter:

```
protected void Page_Load(object sender, EventArgs e)
{
    // request the access token
    TokenHelper.TrustAllCertificates();
```

```
string contextTokenString = TokenHelper.GetContextTokenFromRequest(Request);
if (contextTokenString != null)
{
    // Get context token
    contextToken = TokenHelper.ReadAndValidateContextToken(contextTokenString,
    Request.Url.Authority);
    // Get access token
    sharepointUrl = new Uri(Request.QueryString["SPHostUrl"]);
    accessToken = TokenHelper.GetAccessToken(contextToken,
    sharepointUrl.Authority).AccessToken;

    // Pass the access token to the button event handler.
    Button1.CommandArgument = accessToken;
}
}
```

11. Add the following method to grant behavior to the button click event. This code leverages the access token to make a RESTful request for the contents of the Composed Looks list, the list that stores the themes available to the site. Given the JSON response, the results will be parsed into a grid for display:

```
protected void Button1_Click(object sender, EventArgs e)
{
    // retrieve the user's access token
    string accessToken = ((Button)sender).CommandArgument;

    if (IsPostBack)
    {
        sharepointUrl = new Uri(Request.QueryString["SPHostUrl"]);
    }

    // REST/OData section.
    string oDataUrl = "/_api/Web/lists/getbytitle('Composed
      Looks')/items?$select=Title,AuthorId,Name";

    HttpWebRequest request =
      (HttpWebRequest)HttpWebRequest.Create(sharepointUrl.ToString() + oDataUrl);
    request.Method = "GET";
    request.Accept = "application/atom+xml";
    request.ContentType = "application/atom+xml;type=entry";
    request.Headers.Add("Authorization", "Bearer " + accessToken);
    HttpWebResponse response = (HttpWebResponse)request.GetResponse();

    // Response markup parsing section.
    XDocument oDataXML = XDocument.Load(response.GetResponseStream(),
      LoadOptions.None);
    XNamespace atom = "http://www.w3.org/2005/Atom";
    XNamespace d = "http://schemas.microsoft.com/ado/2007/08/dataservices";
    XNamespace m = "http://schemas.microsoft.com/ado/2007/08/dataservices/
      metadata";

    List<XElement> entries = oDataXML.Descendants(atom + "entry")
                            .Elements(atom + "content")
                            .Elements(m + "properties")
```

```
                        .ToList();

        var entryFieldValues = from entry in entries
                               select new
                               {
                                   Title = entry.Element(d + "Title").Value,
                                   AuthorId = entry.Element(d + "AuthorId").Value
                               };

        // Bind data to the grid on the page.
        GridView1.DataSource = entryFieldValues;
        GridView1.DataBind();
}
```

12. Press F5 and test the code to ensure everything is working smoothly before moving ahead with the final auto-hosting configurations. The functioning application should look like Figure 6-18.

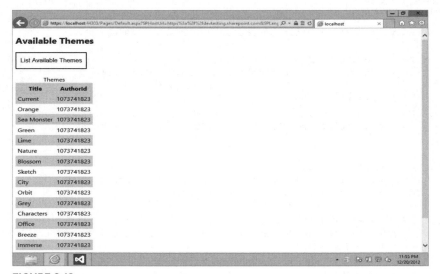

FIGURE 6-18

13. To configure the app to be auto-hosted, open the web project's References node, and set the Copy Local property to True for each of the following assemblies to ensure they are installed to the new Azure virtual machine.

➤ Microsoft.IdentityModel.dll

➤ Microsoft.IdentityModel.Extensions.dll

➤ Microsoft.SharePoint.Client.dll

➤ Microsoft.SharePoint.Client.Runtime.dll

➤ System.IdentityModel.dll (By default, this is set to False.)

14. Right-click the SharePoint app project (AutoHosted_SampleProject) and select Publish to create the app.publish folder inside of the bin\Debug or bin\Release folder of the project. Inside of this app.publish folder will be the app package file, which contains the Azure Web Site package. The contents of the .app cabinet file will be described in more detail in Chapter 7.

The app has now been packaged and is ready for installation in the App Catalog. Installing an app to the App Catalog is a simple process for a tenant administrator:

1. Log into SharePoint Online as the administrator.

2. Open the SharePoint Administration Center page by selecting SharePoint from the Admin menu at the top of the screen.

3. Inside of the administration center, select the apps category, and choose the App Catalog to make apps available to your organization. If you have not identified an App Catalog for your tenant yet, this screen prompts you to create a new one or select an existing App Catalog URL. If an App Catalog has already been defined, choose the Distribute Apps for SharePoint option to view the Apps for SharePoint list. Drag the app package previously created onto the screen to make the app available.

4. Click the Edit icon for the newly added app to manage properties visible to end users such as the app's category and publisher name.

5. The app is now available to be installed inside of any site in this organization's SharePoint Online tenancy. Navigate to a site and Add an App via the Site Contents link. Select the AutoHosted Sample Project to answer the trust question, and add the app to the site.

SUMMARY

This chapter introduces developers to the new wide world of Apps for SharePoint. New development targets and deployment models combine to make this chapter more of a gentle introduction to the new technology landscape of apps development than a deep dive into any specific capability. The goal of this chapter is to accelerate you through the necessary plumbing of apps development and to allow you to concentrate on the development of business functionality. Be aware that additional research will be required to truly master any of the concepts introduced in this chapter.

The following chapter takes you deeper into the world of apps development. Next up are the critical topics of designing the user experience for apps and the management of deployments and upgrades.

Further Developing
Apps in SharePoint 2013

WHAT'S IN THIS CHAPTER?

➤ Extending the user experience into remotely hosted apps

➤ Understanding the packaging and deployment process, including deployment to the public SharePoint Store

➤ Choosing between Provisioner-Hosted and Autohosted apps

WROX.COM CODE DOWNLOADS FOR THIS CHAPTER

The wrox.com code downloads for this chapter are found at www.wrox.com/remtitle .cgi?isbn=1118495829 on the Download Code tab. The code is in the chapter 07 download and individually named according to the names throughout the chapter.

DEVELOPING YOUR APP USER EXPERIENCE

When considering SharePoint 2013 apps, there are three main options for exposing app functionality to users. These options include the immersive app, which offers a full screen experience, and a partial screen option, which behaves much in the same manner as a web part does. The final option is for an app to embed itself into the SharePoint UI as a custom action, which kicks off a process that has no significant user interface. Figure 7-1 illustrates the different options.

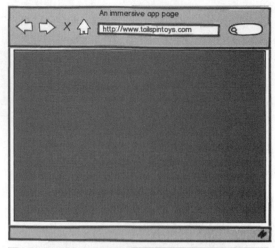

Immersive App - app is shown full screen in a separate page

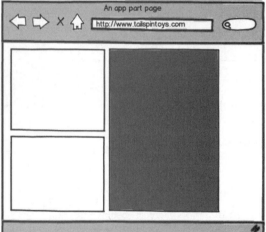

Part - App is shown as a part on the SharePoint page - similar to a web part

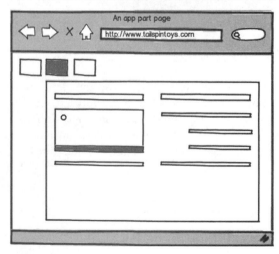

UI Custom Actions - it is possible to make the app available through the Ribbon or menu actions for documents and items

FIGURE 7-1

The intention of the three different interaction options is to grant developers flexibility in integration options coupled with flexibility in the look-and-feel user experience department. One of the core questions for the three design options has to do with the type of chrome and branding that the developer wants SharePoint to provide versus what the developer provides:

➤ Full-screen apps are ASPX pages hosted in SharePoint. These apps should leverage the app template.

➤ HTML pages are hosted in SharePoint or outside of SharePoint. These apps should use the chrome control.

➤ Completely custom pages are offered as an option for developers to completely control their own branding experience.

Planning for an app's UX is a complex set of decision points and options based on the number of different deployment options. Building the UX for a full-screen app may be different if that app is cloud-hosted versus a SharePoint-hosted app. If the app is run in an isolated subweb, how does the developer connect an app to the host web's UX?

Cloud-hosted apps can leverage the chrome control to incorporate the host web's navigation header and branding. This control requires the presence of a SharePoint JavaScript library and a placeholder `<div>` tag. When the chrome control is available in the app, it can be customized by developers.

When an app is deployed to its own isolated subweb, SharePoint leverages an HTTP handler to merge the CSS in place on the main site with the CSS inside of the app's isolated subweb. If the IE toolbar is opened on an app site and the CSS tab is clicked, notice that the first CSS file entry is a reference from the developer site and then the `_layouts/15/defaultcss.ashx`. This file is the `ASP.Net` HTTP handler, which ensures that app sites retain the same look and feel as the rest of the SharePoint site. This is inclusive of site images and CSS for HTML structures, such as the H1 tag used in the SharePoint-hosted Hello World app created in Chapter 6, "Getting Started with Developing Apps in SharePoint 2013."

1. To examine the chrome control in action, return to the Azure auto-hosted application created in Chapter 6. Open the `ApManifest.xml` and add a parameter to the Query string element so that it reads:

```
{StandardTokens}&SPHostTitle={HostTitle}
```

2. Replace the `<head>` tag and its contents with the following HTML and JavaScript. This code loads the appropriate JavaScript resource files and controls from the Microsoft CDN:

```
<head>
    <title>Chrome control host page</title>
    <script
        src="//ajax.aspnetcdn.com/ajax/4.0/1/MicrosoftAjax.js"
        type="text/javascript">
    </script>
    <script
        type="text/javascript"
        src="//ajax.aspnetcdn.com/ajax/jQuery/jquery-1.7.2.min.js">
    </script>
    <script
        type="text/javascript"
        src="ChromeLoader.js">
```

```
    </script>
<script type="text/javascript">
    "use strict";

    var hostweburl;

    //load the SharePoint resources
    $(document).ready(function () {
        //Get the URI decoded URL.
        hostweburl =
            decodeURIComponent(
                getQueryStringParameter("SPHostUrl")
        );

        // The SharePoint js files URL are in the form:
        // web_url/_layouts/15/resource
        var scriptbase = hostweburl + "/_layouts/15/";

        // Load the js file and continue to the
        //    success handler
        $.getScript(scriptbase + "SP.UI.Controls.js")
    });

    // Function to retrieve a query string value.
    // For production purposes you may want to use
    //   a library to handle the query string.
    function getQueryStringParameter(paramToRetrieve) {
        var params =
            document.URL.split("?")[1].split("&");
        var strParams = "";
        for (var i = 0; i < params.length; i = i + 1) {
            var singleParam = params[i].split("=");
            if (singleParam[0] == paramToRetrieve)
                return singleParam[1];
        }
    }
</script>
</head>
```

3. Insert this placeholder into the top of the `<body>` tag:

```
<body style="font-family:'Segoe UI'">
    <form id="form1" runat="server">

        <!-- Chrome control placeholder -->
        <div
            id="chrome_ctrl_container"
            data-ms-control="SP.UI.Controls.Navigation"
            data-ms-options='{
                "appHelpPageUrl" : "Help.html",
                "appIconUrl" : "siteIcon.png",
                "appTitle" : "Wrox Press Sample chrome control app",
                "settingsLinks" : [
                    {
                        "linkUrl" : "Account.html",
```

```
                              "displayName" : "Account settings"
                    },
                    {
                        "linkUrl" : "Contact.html",
                        "displayName" : "Contact us"
                    }
                ]
            }'>
        </div>


    <div>
    <!-- The chrome control also allows access to the
        host web's stylesheets -->
    <h2 class="ms-accentText">Available Themes</h2>
    </div>
    <asp:Button ID="Button1"
        runat ="server"
        OnClick="Button1_Click"
        ….
```

4. Deploy and view the results; now the app page looks more like a SharePoint page. The IIS Express dev server may not have access to site assets such as the app icon image, but this resolves itself when deployed to the App Catalog. Your app should look something like Figure 7-2.

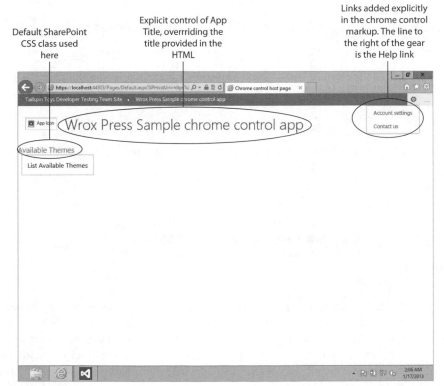

FIGURE 7-2

Now that the control is in place, modifying the behavior of the chrome is a matter of explicitly defining the behavior of the chrome control in the placeholder `<div>` previously added.

Now that the chrome control grants insight into how to design a full screen app, it is time to turn your attention to the cases of app parts and custom actions.

Developing an Embeddable App or App Part

An app part is similar in terms of user experience to a web part in that users can experience the app inside of the host web. The app part actually leverages an iFrame to display remote content and provide the same level of isolated subweb runtime protection. End users have access to custom property settings, which are passed to the app part via the query string.

The following steps walk you through the important distinctions that must be taken into account when developing an app part instead of a full-screen app experience.

1. Create a new app with Visual Studio, and select either auto-hosted or provisioner-hosted as you see fit; this example uses an auto-hosted app. Give your new project a name such as **SampleAppPartProject** and click Finish on the wizard.

2. In the SharePoint project, right-click the project, and add a new item. Select a Client Web Part (Host Web) from the list, and name the web part something easy to distinguish, such as **SampleAppPart**, as shown in Figure 7-3.

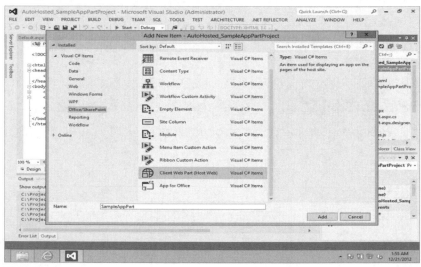

FIGURE 7-3

3. The act of adding a client web part can add an `Elements.xml` to the SharePoint project and an `ASPX` page of the same name to the web project. Open the `Elements.xml` to see that it's currently fairly empty. The empty `<Properties/>` tag is where custom properties can be passed via the query string to the `ASPX` page. These properties are interactive for end users in exactly the same way web part properties are. Add a few sample properties to the web part with the following XML:

```
<Properties>
  <Property
      Name="strProp"
      Type="string"
      RequiresDesignerPermission="true"
      DefaultValue="String default value"
      WebCategory="Tailspin Toys Custom Apps"
      WebDisplayName="A property of type string.">
  </Property>
  <Property
      Name="intProp"
      Type="int"
      RequiresDesignerPermission="true"
      DefaultValue="0"
      WebCategory="Tailspin Toys Custom Apps"
      WebDisplayName="A property of type integer.">
  </Property>
  <Property
      Name="boolProp"
      Type="boolean"
      RequiresDesignerPermission="true"
      DefaultValue="false"
      WebCategory="Tailspin Toys Custom Apps"
      WebDisplayName="A property of type boolean.">
  </Property>
  <Property
      Name="enumProp"
      Type="enum"
      RequiresDesignerPermission="true"
      DefaultValue="1st"
      WebCategory="Tailspin Toys Custom Apps"
      WebDisplayName="A property of type enum.">
    <EnumItems>
      <EnumItem WebDisplayName="First option" Value="1st"/>
      <EnumItem WebDisplayName="Second option" Value="2nd"/>
      <EnumItem WebDisplayName="Third option" Value="3rd"/>
    </EnumItems>
  </Property>
</Properties>
```

4. The top of the `Elements.xml` defines the URL of the web page to be displayed in the app part. Given that there are now custom properties, the URL needs to be modified to handle those new properties. Update the `Src` value to match the URL here:

```
<Content Type="html" Src="~remoteAppUrl/Pages/SampleAppPart.aspx?{StandardTokens}
  _&amp;strProp=_strProp_&amp;intProp=_intProp_&amp;boolProp=_boolProp_&amp;
  enumProp=_enumProp_&amp;editmode=_editMode_" />
```

5. Now that parameters are being passed from the app part framework to the page via the query string, it's time to do something with those parameters. Open the `SampleAppPart.aspx` file, and place the following control into the empty `<div>` tag on the page:

```
<asp:Literal ID="Literal1" runat="server" Text="Hello to the world from an app
  part"></asp:Literal>
```

6.   Open the `SampleAppPart.aspx.cs`, and replace the `Page_Load` function's contents with the following code. This simple code can grab each parameter from the query string and display the values to end user. Changing values in the web part properties dialog updates the values shown in the app part.

```
protected void Page_Load(object sender, EventArgs e)
{
    var intParam = Request.QueryString["intProp"];
    var strParam = Request.QueryString["strProp"];
    var boolParam = Request.QueryString["boolProp"];
    var enumParam = Request.QueryString["enumProp"];
    var editMode = Request.QueryString["editMode"];

    if ("true" == editMode)
    {
        Literal1.Text = "App Part is in edit mode";
    }
    else
    {
        Literal1.Text = "intProp = " + intParam + "<br>" +
                        "strProp = " + strParam + "<br>" +
                        "boolProp = " + boolParam + "<br>" +
                        "enumProp = " + enumParam;
    }
}
```

This is a relatively trivial example of functionality, as shown in Figure 7-4, but it effectively demonstrates how the app part framework leverages the query string to exchange configuration information. Armed with this and access to SharePoint's client object model, a savvy developer should now understand how similar the traditional web page development experience is to the new app part development experience.

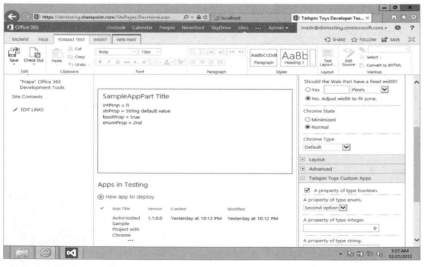

FIGURE 7-4

> **NOTE** *As of this writing, using static HTML files instead of ASPX pages cause IIS Express and Azure websites to return a 405 Method Not Allowed error instead of the app part page. To remedy this, an HTTP Handler must be added to the web project's* web.config *file. This allows the app part page to work but seems to break any ASPX page hosted by that isolated subweb. ASPX pages are rendered to the browser as text files.*
>
> ```
> ...
>     <system.webServer>
>       <handlers>
>         <add name="AspNetStaticFileHandler" path="*" verb="*"
>         type="System.Web.StaticFileHandler" />
>       </handlers>
>     <system.webServer>
> </configuration>
> ```

Developing a Custom Action App

Custom actions are the SharePoint Ribbon buttons and edit control block (ECB) actions available from an item's context menu (seen as three dots in SharePoint 2013). Apps of this type are usually designed to interact with list items. Beyond a few configuration elements described in more detail next, developing a custom action app is substantively the same experience as developing an app part. List item details are passed via the query string to an externally hosted page, which performs whatever actions might be relevant.

1. Create a new app with Visual Studio, and select either auto-hosted or provisioner-hosted as you see fit; this example uses an auto-hosted app. Give your new project a name such as **SampleCustomActionProject** and click Finish on the wizard.

2. Add a new web form to the web project and name it **CustomActionTarget**. This file must be in place before you can proceed to the steps of adding ECB or Ribbon actions.

3. Open the new CustomActionTarget.aspx page, and add the following ASPX markup into the empty <div>:

```
<asp:Literal ID="Literal1"
    runat="server"
    Text="Hello to the world from a custom action app">
</asp:Literal>
```

4. Open the CustomActionTarget.aspx.cs file, and replace the Page_Load method with the following code to print each query string parameter to the screen:

```
protected void Page_Load(object sender, EventArgs e)
    {
        Literal1.Text = string.Empty;
        foreach (string queryStringParam in Request.QueryString)
        {
```

```
Literal1.Text = Literal1.Text + "<br>" + queryStringParam +
" = " + Request.QueryString[queryStringParam];

        }
    }
```

5. In the SharePoint project, right-click the project, and add a new item. Select a Menu Item Custom Action from the list, and name the web part something easy to distinguish, such as **SampleCustomActionApp**, as shown in Figure 7-5. A wizard pops up asking for the following details:

   a. Where do you want to expose the custom action? **Host Web**

   b. Where is the custom action scoped to? **List Template**

   c. Which particular item is the custom action scoped to? **Document Library**

   d. Click <Next> to see the next screen.

   e. What is the text on the menu item? **Invoke Sample Menu Item Custom Action**

   f. Where does the custom action navigate to?
   SampleCustomActionAppWeb\CustomActionTarget.aspx ?HostUrl={HostUrl}& Source={Source}&ListURLDir={ListUrlDir}&ListID={ListId}&ItemURL={ItemUrl}& ItemID={ItemId}

FIGURE 7-5

6. In the SharePoint project, right-click the project, and add a new item. Select a Ribbon Custom Action from the list, and name the web part something easy to distinguish, such as **SampleRibbonButton**. A wizard pops up asking for the following details:

   a. Where do you want to expose the custom action? **Host Web**

   b. Where is the custom action scoped to? **List Template**

    c. Which particular item is the custom action scoped to? **Document Library**

    d. Click <Next> to see the next screen.

    e. Where is the control located? **Ribbon.Documents.Manage**

    f. What is the text on the menu item? **Invoke Sample Menu Item Custom Action**

    g. Where does the custom action navigate to?
SampleCustomActionAppWeb\CustomActionTarget.aspx ?HostUrl={HostUrl}& Source={Source}&ListURLDir={ListUrlDir}&ListID={ListId}&ItemURL={ItemUrl}& ItemID={ItemId}

7. The act of adding these two custom actions to the SharePoint project causes a pair of `Elements.xml` to be added to the SharePoint project. You can open each `Elements.xml` to see the content, but there is no need to change anything here. The last question of the wizards allowed for the input of the URL parameters, which your app uses to achieve its wanted level of functionality.

8. Run the app and navigate to any document library in the host web. Add content if none exists, and invoke the custom action either via the Ribbon button on the Files tab or via the ECB menu, as shown in Figure 7-6.

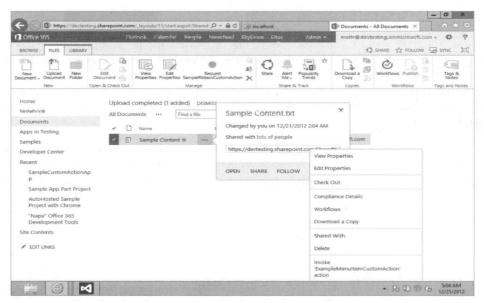

FIGURE 7-6

This is again a relatively trivial demonstration of functionality, but it does effectively demonstrate how the Custom Actions approach leverages the query string to exchange configuration information, as shown in Figure 7-7. Armed with this and access to SharePoint's client object model, a savvy developer should now understand how similar the traditional web page development experience is to the new app part development experience.

HostUrl = https://devtesting.sharepoint.com
Source = https://devtesting.sharepoint.com/Shared Documents/Forms/AllItems.aspx
ListURLDir = Shared Documents
SelectedListID = {FFCD03F0-289F-4CE2-A156-5085BE65737A}
SelectedItemID = 1

FIGURE 7-7

App Design Guidelines

Apps that are developed for use on the public market place must go through approval by Microsoft in much the same way an app approval process for a phone store works, such as the iPhone or Windows Phone app stores. The apps that are submitted to the approval process must adhere to the SharePoint UX design guidelines, available in full at `http://msdn.microsoft.com/en-us/library/jj220046(v=office.15).aspx` in an MSDN article titled "Apps for SharePoint UX Design Guidelines."

The crux of the design guidelines includes instructions for consistent styling and a review of CSS styling guidelines. SharePoint 2013 takes a number of visual cues from the design language formerly known as Metro, and Microsoft wants apps created by its partners and customers to mesh well with that design paradigm.

The details in this article are important but are not specifically developer activities as opposed to designer activities, so this chapter won't dwell on visual styling guidance.

DEVELOPING YOUR APP PACKAGING

As shown in the previous Azure auto-hosted example, publishing a solution with Visual Studio results in the project's bin directory containing an app package in the form of an `.app` file. This `.app` file is actually a `.zip` format and can be investigated by renaming the extension to `.zip`, as shown in Figure 7-8.

Notice the presence of the `app.manifest` inside of the `.app` deployment package. This manifest describes where the app is hosted and the start page of the website being rendered:

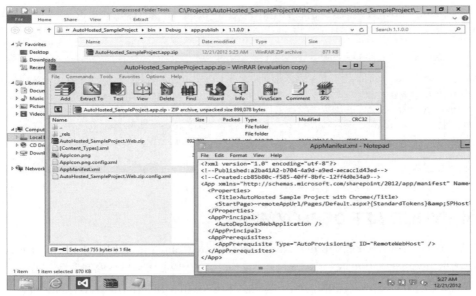

FIGURE 7-8

```xml
<?xml version="1.0" encoding="utf-8"?>
<!--Published:a2ba41A2-b704-4a9d-a9ed-aecacc1d43ed-->
<!--Created:cb85b80c-f585-40ff-8bfc-12ff1d0c34a9  >
<App xmlns="http://schemas.microsoft.com/sharepoint/2012/app/manifest"
  Name="AutoHostedSampleProjectWithChrome"
  ProductID="{42580491-4e33-4f6c-8d4b-4cbd939fe65f}"
  Version="1.1.0.0" SharePointMinVersion="15.0.0.0">
  <Properties>
    <Title>AutoHosted Sample Project with Chrome</Title>
    <StartPage>~remoteAppUrl/Pages/Default.aspx?{StandardTokens}&amp;
SPHostTitle=
    {HostTitle}</StartPage>
  </Properties>
  <AppPrincipal>
    <AutoDeployedWebApplication />
  </AppPrincipal>
  <AppPrerequisites>
    <AppPrerequisite Type="AutoProvisioning" ID="RemoteWebHost" />
  </AppPrerequisites>
</App>
```

Beyond this simple set of details are the included permission requests that the app requires to success-fully be installed. It is this simple collection of data elements that make up the extent of SharePoint's knowledge of the app. This separation of concerns enables developers to leverage any language they prefer, including node.JS or Ruby, as well as any application design paradigm such as MVC.

An app for SharePoint can either be uploaded to an organization's private App Catalog or submitted for review and inclusion in the public SharePoint app marketplace. If the app is submitted to the public app marketplace, Microsoft runs some validation checks on it to ensure that all elements meet certain design criteria. For example, app manifest markup must be valid XML, and no delivered feature can be targeted above the Web scope. After the code package passes all of the requisite testing stages, the package is signed by Microsoft and made available within the app store.

> **NOTE** *The code quality checks that Microsoft runs on the delivered code is not included in any of the native Visual Studio quality checks. Microsoft has currently identified 62 policies across 10 categories, identified in detail online in an MSDN article titled "Validation policies for the apps submitted to the Office Store"* (`http://msdn.microsoft.com/en-US/library/office/apps/jj220035`).

DEVELOPING YOUR APP DEPLOYMENT

The app code has been developed and tested. Now you need to deploy the code package to production. The deployment conversation now diverges based on the hosting option selected.

> ➤ SharePoint-hosted apps may simply be files that can be uploaded to the server. No server-side code means there's no need to manage app packaging unless that app packaging is wanted for code reuse.

> ➤ Auto-hosted and SharePoint-hosted apps are self-contained solutions published in the manner described next.

> ➤ Provisioner-hosted apps not only include the SharePoint component that must be deployed and maintained, but also the web project that must be deployed to its own infrastructure. This chapter assumes that any organization electing to build on top of its provisioner infrastructure does not need advice on how to deploy web applications. This chapter addresses only the SharePoint components.

In addition to diverging based on the selected hosting option, another deployment decision point is the choice of app stores: the public Office Store or the private app catalog.

Publishing to the Office Store

Before attempting to publish an app to the Office Store for broad availability, you must have a Microsoft Seller account and have access to the Microsoft Seller Dashboard. For references on how to accomplish this prerequisite step, refer online to Microsoft's How To article titled "Create or edit your seller account in the Microsoft Seller Dashboard," found online at `http://msdn.microsoft.com/en-us/library/jj220034.aspx`.

Apps being submitted to the Office Store for publication are uploaded via the Microsoft Seller Dashboard. Microsoft then runs the verification process to ensure the app adheres to the content and behavior guidance previously identified. After the app is clear of all validation hurdles (a process that may take more than one iteration of the review process) Microsoft digitally signs the app package and places it into the public Office Store.

Part of the public app publishing process includes the ability to specify an app licensing scheme. The publisher can determine the price of the app (free, trial, or for purchase) and whether a license is per user or per site. SharePoint doesn't actually enforce the licensing terms; this code is up to you. However, SharePoint does provide a licensing framework leveraging callbacks that you can take advantage of with custom code in your app to enforce your wanted licensing scheme.

> **NOTE** *Public app store validation policies are defined at* `http://msdn` `.microsoft.com/en-us/library/office/apps/jj220035(v=office.15).aspx`.

Publishing to an App Catalog

As shown in the "Developing an Azure Auto-hosted App" section of Chapter 6, creating and publishing to an internal App Catalog is a trivial task for a SharePoint administrator (on premise or as a cloud tenant). Microsoft takes no responsibility for the quality of the code delivered to the internal app store. Code quality procedures are left up to the individual organization.

Table 7-1 compares the attributes of the Office Store and the App Catalog in a way that may help you decide which way to go. Microsoft's recommendation is to understand the publishing direction before coding begins so that capabilities such as the licensing framework can be baked in versus ignored.

TABLE 7-1: Office Store and App Catalog Comparison

OFFICE STORE	APP CATALOG
App is publically available.	App is available to users with access to this SharePoint deployment.
Licensing framework available.	Licensing framework is not available for use.
App package verified by Microsoft for technical and content adherence to policies.	App package verification performed by SharePoint when app is uploaded.
You must be signed up with Microsoft Seller Dashboard to upload apps.	No registration with Microsoft is required.

Table source `http://msdn.microsoft.com/en-us/library/office/apps/jj164070.aspx`

DEVELOPING FOR APP UPGRADEABILITY

Microsoft applied a great deal of its experiences in mobile application stores when the app experience was designed. Chief among those lessons learned was the recognition of the need for a robust application update system. App designers need the ability to update an app, regardless of whether that update is to add new capabilities or to fix problems in existing capabilities. The centralized hosting model for apps makes app updates a much easier process than the distributed nature of web parts seen in past versions. Updates are essentially redeployments of existing apps, but the app update process ensures that app data hosted in SharePoint is preserved even if the app update fails.

Updating SharePoint Apps

SharePoint app manifests contain two important identifiers, a product ID and a version number. To update an app, ensure that the product ID remains constant and the version number increments. Adjust the functionality as wanted, and deploy the app package to the public or private app store it previously was deployed to.

After an app update is delivered to the app store, an update notification appears with the app in the Site Contents page of any site where the app is installed. In addition, tenant and farm administrators are notified of app updates in their respective administration UIs.

When a user clicks on a link to update an app, the app is installed again. The user is prompted to approve the changes along with approval of permissions required by the app (even if they do not change between versions). While the app is being upgraded, it is temporarily rendered inaccessible. Auto-hosted apps have the entire infrastructure (Azure websites and SQL Azure databases) locked for upgrade.

> **NOTE** *Auto-hosted apps that upgrade SQL Azure database schemas automatically make a backup of the database before any schema change is applied. The same is true of Azure website components; transaction-protected component swaps automatically roll back in the event of failure.*

For custom upgrade logic, four hooks are available in the event that an upgrade must make changes to computed fields or other customizations:

➤ A data script may be added to an app package.

➤ PostDeployment scripts may be added to a DACPAC (a data-tier application schema package) that is run as part of a data application component upgrade.

➤ The upgrade process calls out to a PostUpdate web service, which is available for the developer to create and register inside of the app manifest.

➤ The app could contain some staging logic to ensure the proper changes have been made before normal execution of the app commences.

If an app leverages provider-hosted components, those components are not managed by SharePoint. It is easy to envision the upgrade process for those web components being kicked off by the PostUpdate web service.

App Migration

One scenario not directly supported by Microsoft is the app migration scenario, where the "update" of an app is actually the wholesale replacement of that app with entirely new components. In this case, a new Product ID must be specified inside of the app manifest, and any required data migrations must be handled by the app's first run or by a remote service monitoring the feature installed event receiver via SharePoint's remove event receiver framework.

ADDITIONAL CONSIDERATIONS FOR APPS DEVELOPERS

The following considerations can be important when developing apps:

➤ Recall that the CSOM grants access to the Site Collection and below; farm solutions are required for access to farm capabilities.

➤ Apps cannot directly communicate with each other because they are completely isolated from each other. This is similar to the way apps work on tablets and phones. An approach is to have the app have a footprint outside of SharePoint, such as in Azure. This external footprint could expose a web service such as a WCF service endpoint that could be the communication mechanism for one app to talk to another app. This is effectively like a proxy mechanism that gets around app isolation.

➤ Silverlight has not been officially deprecated and still works complete with access to the client object model. However, even Microsoft recognizes that JavaScript and HTML 5 reach the widest audience.

➤ DNS entries per app are not required. The recommendation is to create a wildcard DNS entry for a target app's domain. Visual Studio can handle this for you.

➤ Apps can support their own authentication, meaning that they support windows auth or forms auth/claims auth based on the development targets.

➤ One consideration for app development that must be recognized is that no custom server-side code can be delivered to SharePoint, including custom server controls. All custom server-side code must be hosted outside of the SharePoint environment for apps. Server-side code is, of course, still a development target for on-premise developers. Web parts, timer jobs, and more are still valid approaches for SharePoint developers. The apps infrastructure was created to widen the field for developing business functionality, but Microsoft openly recognizes that the app framework will not meet every need.

➤ A remote event receiver is similar to standard event receivers, but the code runs in an external service. Remote event receivers can be tricky to develop, but they are available to apps, whereas normal event receivers are not.

KEY RECOMMENDATIONS

As this chapter draws to a close, several questions may arise:

➤ SharePoint developers with experience in previous versions will want to know when should traditional server-based solutions be used, if ever?

➤ What drives the choice for a SharePoint-hosted app versus a cloud-hosted app?

➤ What drives the choice for a provider-hosted app versus an Azure auto-hosted app?

The following sections answers these questions.

Decision Criteria for Cloud-hosted Apps Versus SharePoint-hosted Apps

Apps are clearly Microsoft's definition of the future of SharePoint code. Sandboxed solutions have been deprecated in SharePoint 2013. With this deprecation, apps are the only option for users to add functionality in a self-service manner. The prevalence of the SharePoint Store and the corporate App Catalog will blur the lines between native capabilities and customizations in a way SharePoint hasn't seen before.

When considering app hosting options, Table 7-2 defines some design recommendations to help developers choose between cloud versus SharePoint-hosted apps.

TABLE 7-2: Cloud and SharePoint Hosted Apps Comparison

CLOUD-HOSTED APPS	SHAREPOINT-HOSTED APPS
The most flexible option, capable of supporting any type of app code	Best suited for smaller apps based on inline JavaScript code requirements
Offers developers the option to create their own infrastructure and to use any development technology	SharePoint-based JavaScript code, no server-side code of any sort
May require handling of Multitenancy and explicit permissions management	Inherits the Multitenancy capabilities and permissions of the page or site

Decision Criteria for Developing Apps Versus Farm Solutions

The goal of this incredible investment and shift in approach to SharePoint development by Microsoft is clear. Microsoft wants developers to focus on apps as the preferred default choice in development approaches. The question then becomes, when should a developer turn to alternative, legacy development approaches such as farm solutions?

The generic advice from Microsoft is to develop an app whenever possible because apps offer a number of advantages over farm solutions:

➤ End users:

    ➤ Because of the SharePoint Store and Corporate Catalog, end users can find apps to be the easiest to discover, purchase, and install.

    ➤ Apps offer the write once, run *almost* everywhere promise of running equally well in on-premise environments, Office 365 environments, and possibly even Office client tools (as Agave apps).

➤ Administrators:

    ➤ Apps go beyond sandbox solutions in giving SharePoint administrators the safest way to extend SharePoint.

➤ Developers:

    ➤ Apps lower the bar for developer skills requirements and learning curves because they enable non-SharePoint programming skills.

    ➤ Apps are easier than farm solutions to build on top of cloud-based flexibility and scalability.

    ➤ Unlike farm solutions that tend to be written to either use the permissions of the logged in user or elevate to system-level permissions, apps can leverage the permissions of the installer because of the explicit OAuth permissions request approach.

    ➤ Apps enable developers to leverage cross-platform standards, including HTML, REST, OData, JavaScript, and OAuth.

➤ Companies:

    ➤ Compared to setting up a business to market and sell a SharePoint solution, apps are extremely easy to market and sell to the public via the Microsoft SharePoint Store. They maximize your flexibility in developing future upgrades.

Despite these advantages, there are also times when a business problem can be solved only with code executing on the server. When deciding between SharePoint Apps and SharePoint Solutions, there are several factors that can help you decide whether you should develop and app or a solution:

➤ Does the code require the server-side object model because of incomplete coverage by the CSOM? If so, farm solutions are the only option because sandbox solutions have been deprecated.

➤ Does the code require access to SharePoint objects outside of the site collection (SPSite) hosting the site (SPWeb) in which the app is running? If so, farm solutions are the only option.

➤ Is the code designed to assist an end user or an administrator? Administrative tasks are not available in the CSOM API and therefore must leverage the server-side OM in farm solutions.

➤ Is the code a standalone application or does it have inherent dependencies that require careful management of the platform, such as how the SharePoint Publishing Infrastructure requires content types, workflows, page elements, and other functional components to all be present for the entire business solution to work? If a complex set of interconnected functionality is required, farm solutions are the best choice because apps are by design isolated and independent.

Farm solutions are still the only answer to adding functionality to the SharePoint farm that must live inside of SharePoint. Service applications and timer jobs are clear examples of SharePoint functionality that does not belong in an app. Although, the technique of offloading work to a scalable cloud infrastructure works with the more traditional remote procedure calls of a server-side application. There are many reasons to turn to farm solutions only as a last resort, including:

➤ Farm solutions are available to all web applications on a server. (There's no such thing as Multitenancy here!)

➤ Farm solutions are almost always deployed with full trust and as such offer no protections to stop bad code from overwhelming a server. A single misplaced while loop can bring a server to its knees.

➤ Farm solutions require administrative access to the server for installation and upgrade, requiring IT participation and outages. Enterprise IT shops take a dim view of this type of infrastructure management when more elegant options are available.

Sandbox solutions offer some improvements to these aforementioned problems, but they are not without issues of their own. Sandbox solutions are an attempt to create a self-service user management model for deployed code. Sandbox solutions even offer to protect the server from bad code with a built-in resource management capability. It is true that sandboxed solutions have been deprecated, but existing solutions may still be installed in SharePoint 2013. The deprecation status indicates that Microsoft recommends that new development efforts be directed toward apps instead of sandbox solutions. The reason for ending the life of sandbox solutions as a valid development target is related to a number of issues that cramp a sandbox solution's capability to deliver true business value, including the following:

➤ No access to `SharePoint.WebControls`, which means that developers do not have access to native controls, including the SharePoint Ribbon. This significantly constrains a developer's ability to create consistent user interfaces.

➤ Code can do only what the executing user can do. Unlike apps that require the installation user to have the requisite permissions, sandbox solutions operate as the current browsing user. This limits the capability for sandboxed code to hide back-end data stores.

➤ Sandboxed code can't interact with SharePoint's notification and messaging capabilities, including a complete inability to send e-mail with the configured SMTP server that works for all other SharePoint e-mail functionality.

➤ Sandbox solutions lack access to a number of core capabilities, such as access to SharePoint's mapped folders (`_layout`), programmatic workflows, timer jobs, `ADO.Net`, and more.

SharePoint apps offer to solve a significant number of the problems previously listed.

➤ Where farm solutions are installed farmwide and are thus available to all web applications, apps are multitenant.

➤ App code cannot be installed on a SharePoint server farm; therefore, the full-trust scenarios are simply not a factor for apps.

➤ Apps are deployed to the corporate app store by IT, but after that registration process has been accomplished, IT is no longer a bottleneck in the installation and use of an app inside of a site.

➤ Apps enable access to a consistent SharePoint user experience because of the general shift to HTML-, CSS-, and JavaScript-powered user experiences.

➤ As previously mentioned, apps get past the sandbox solution's inability to elevate privileges by leveraging the permissions available to the installing user, not the executing user. The use of OData permissions defined in an `AppManifest.xml` allows for an explicit definition of required permissions, which are acknowledged at the time of installation.

Unfortunately, there are some scenarios that will likely cause developers to ignore apps as the preferred development scenario. The first and foremost of these is that the CSOM is not as feature rich or as easy to work with as the server-side object model. SharePoint MVP Doug Ware has done an in-depth analysis of the available CSOM classes and compared these with the server-side OM. In Doug's analysis, more than 6,800 properties and methods across 96 core classes were examined and found that the CSOM is missing approximately 4,000 members of the server-side OM. Doug is quick to point out that some of the difference is due to equivalent functionalities in the CSOM with different naming conventions, but the impression that the CSOM has less than full parity with the server-side OM is the obvious and correct deduction. Find the results of Doug's investigation along with a downloadable Excel comparison of classes on his Elumenotion blog at `http://www.elumenotion.com/Blog/Lists/Posts/Post.aspx?ID=159`.

Table 7-3 describes approaches for developing apps first and farm solutions second.

TABLE 7-3: Overall Development Design Criteria

FUNCTIONALITY NEED	SUGGESTED APPROACH
Custom web parts	Apps support remote pages with embedded web parts or the exposure of remote web applications in an app part.
Event receivers and feature receivers	Apps for SharePoint support the equivalent remote event receivers through CSOM.
Custom field types or list columns	Apps can create lists with columns based on existing fields, including the calculated and computed field types. Furthermore, creating an entirely custom grid or remote page gives developers even more explicit control.
Custom web services for SharePoint built on the service application framework	It is possible to create custom web services as remote services.
Application pages	Remote web pages are the way to go here. Expose remote pages through apps.
Custom site definitions	Farm solution only: No app approach is available.
Delegate controls	Farm solution only: No app approach is available.
Custom themes	Farm solution only: No app approach is available.
Custom action groups and custom action hiding (modifying the SharePoint Ribbon)	Farm solution only: No app approach is available.

Decision Criteria for Developing Provider-hosted Versus Azure-hosted Apps

When approaching cloud-hosted apps' development options, what exactly is the difference between developing for Azure and determining your own infrastructure in a provider-hosted app? The difference is the level of control you have in designing and defining the scalability of the solution. Azure abstracts all of this away from the developer, which is freeing at small scale but may be a problem at extremely large scales. At an extremely large scale, things such as CDNs, geographic distributions, and edge nodes become important to meet performance requirements. As a developer, you may not trust Azure's auto-hosting to handle your specific needs as you scale past small-and-medium to web-and-super-web scales (50,000,000+ users).

SUMMARY

Where Chapter 6 introduces the major concepts of hosted apps, this chapter has focused on the surrounding development activities beyond the functionality of the app itself. Building a powerfully functional app is not very compelling to users if it doesn't look attractive and easy to use. A powerful, attractive, and easy-to-use app is not very effective if it can't be delivered to a SharePoint server for use. Finally, this chapter provides the reader with a number of decision-making criteria that help guide developers to the right hosting approach for their app.

The following chapters dive into the specialty capabilities of SharePoint, such as workflow, search, and web content management. Some truly exciting changes have occurred in each of these workloads, so keep reading!

Developing Social Applications in SharePoint 2013

WHAT'S IN THIS CHAPTER?

➤ Discovering new APIs for customization and integration

➤ Accessing the Community template programmatically

➤ Accessing user data with SharePoint My Sites and the User Profile API

➤ Enhacing the social feeds from the Social API

WROX.COM CODE DOWNLOADS FOR THIS CHAPTER

The wrox.com code downloads for this chapter are found at www.wrox.com/remtitle .cgi?isbn=1118495829 on the Download Code tab. The code is in the chapter 08 download and individually named according to names throughout the chapter.

Many psychological and educational theories attempt to explain how a person's environment impacts his ability to learn and understand. A person's social connections form an environment that has become a focus in educational institutions and learning organizations. For example, the developmental theory of social constructivism suggests that a person's culture and context in social settings allow groups to construct knowledge jointly for the benefit of the group. This concept was further expounded in the *IBM Systems Journal* article titled "Communities of Practice and Organizational Performance" where the authors identify a community as "a group whose members regularly engage in sharing and learning, based on their common interests," or a *community of practice*. The authors conclude that:

. . . communities play a significant role in the development of social capital, which in turn influences organizational outcomes. These findings provide us with guidance to using communities as a vehicle for improving performance. However, the real challenge is to identify the management actions that will build the social capital necessary to achieve these goals.

(LESSER AND STORCK, 2001)

Organizations that seek to foster the growth of communities or teams of like-minded individuals working together toward common goals often turn to software applications to assist with the cultivation of organizational relationships. These applications fall into the broad category of social software and are usually identifiable by the techniques they use to share information between users.

This chapter examines the technical capabilities of SharePoint 2013 and how you can use them to produce the social capital mentioned by Lesser and Storck. SharePoint 2013 offers the following application areas that are of special interest in the social software category:

➤ *User-generated content and participation* — Taking advantage of SharePoint 2013's new community features along with the tagging and rating, infrastructures work together to unify SharePoint users into communities of practice.

➤ *Social feeds* — SharePoint 2013 builds brand-new activity feed and microblog capabilities into each user's My Site and team site. These new capabilities work to keep each user more informed of the user community around them, enabling them to better identify communities of practice that the user may wish to join.

This chapter ends with a quick look at a suggested governance model, which organizations may choose to adopt as a set of guide rails designed to prevent their SharePoint installation from going off the tracks and turning into something other than what the organization intends.

NEW AND IMPROVED SOCIAL FEATURES IN SHAREPOINT 2013

The following overview outlines the numerous enhancements to SharePoint that speak specifically to the social software space.

New User Experience

SharePoint 2013 has been enhanced with a new user experience to enable users to quickly find information and more easily interact with data. The look and feel of SharePoint 2013 sites has been refreshed and enhanced with HTML5 to enable capabilities such as drag and drop of documents from the desktop into the browser. SharePoint Search, discussed in Chapter 9, "Building Search-Based Applications in SharePoint 2013," has been integrated with the FAST search engine technology such that FAST is now a core part of the product, complete with its enhanced user experience. Users can more easily leverage their My Site to keep track of their interests and happenings around the organization.

Multiple Supported Browsers

SharePoint 2013 allows you to create web pages that work in today's most popular web browsers and mobile browsers. The browsers that are supported include:

➤ Microsoft's Internet Explorer versions 8 and later (6 and 7 are not supported)

➤ Mozilla Firefox (latest released version)

➤ Google Chrome (latest released version)

➤ Apple Safari (latest released version)

➤ Windows Phone 7.5 or later

➤ iOS 5.0 or later (Office web apps full functionality supported on iPad 2 and later with iOS 6.0 or later)

➤ Android 4.0 or later

The new user experience has been designed to target a broad set of standards-based browser capabilities while providing an excellent experience. Figure 8-1 demonstrates this new user experience on a mobile device with high-fidelity browsing on one side of the image and the easy-to-use navigation menu available for mobile devices on the other side of the image.

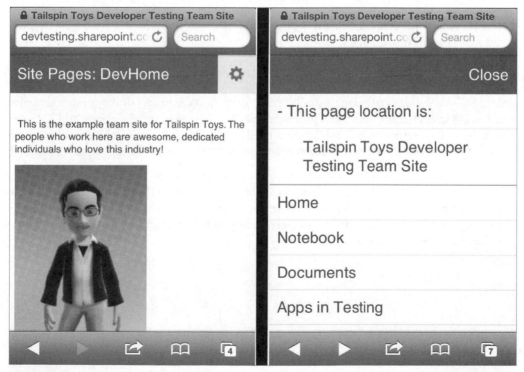

FIGURE 8-1

Rich Text Editor

Editing SharePoint content is similar to editing Office document content, thanks to the rich text editor. This rich text editor enables dragging and dropping of page content, familiar keyboard shortcuts such as Ctrl+Z multistep undo, and CSS-compliant styling selections such as Address and BlockQuote. Furthermore, the page-editing experience uses the ubiquitous SharePoint Ribbon and in-line content-editing capabilities to make manipulating SharePoint content even more familiar.

➤ *The Ribbon* — Office applications, including SharePoint, offer an extremely rich user experience with dozens, if not hundreds, of optional settings and application interaction points. This array of options can be dizzying and difficult to navigate to unfamiliar users. The Ribbon brings application functions and options together into a logically grouped, context-sensitive tab interface. SharePoint 2013 offers an enhanced Ribbon experience complete with the capability to "focus on content" and hide extraneous site elements, such as the quick launch menu.

➤ *In-line content editing* — A major enhancement that has been improved for the editing experience is in-line content editing. With SharePoint 2013 you do not leave the page to edit or add content; a content-editing box appears on top of the current page you are editing and goes away when the content has been added. Aside from ease of content editing, this also helps with navigation because you never have to return to the page you started creating content on, because you never left. Improved over SharePoint 2010 is the 2013 in-line content editor's capability to strip formatting from Office applications to ensure consistency of user experience. Now in 2013, if a user pastes content from a Word document, the formatting of the Word document is discarded and styles from the wiki's CSS are applied for headings and paragraph text.

Enterprise Social Networking

Although the words *social networking* usually strike terror into the hearts of corporate executives, SharePoint again takes the Internet concepts popularized by Myspace and Facebook and pulls the best features into an enterprise-class application. Inside of SharePoint, the following features help stitch a collection of users into a rich social fabric.

➤ *My Sites and User Profiles* — The core of any social application is the user profile (see Figure 8-2). Here is where all users can define their personal attributes and whether or not these attributes are public available or should be private. A user's My Site is a secure site that exposes their profile details and a host of social functionality, such as a new newsfeed, colleagues, contacts, and more.

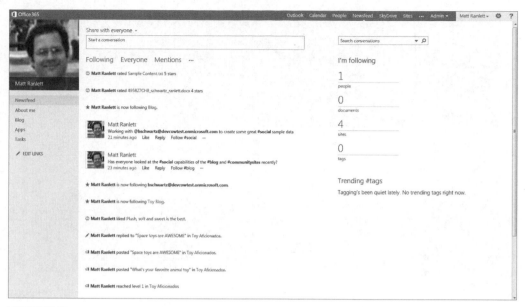

FIGURE 8-2

➤ *Expertise and Ask Me About* — Users can identify which keywords or tags they are interested in keeping track of and which keywords or tags they are willing to speak to others about. SharePoint 2013 users can proactively represent a level of knowledge about or interest in a topic by offering visitors the ability to Ask Me About a topic or tag. The Ask Me About tags and phrases are displayed on a user's profile page and are exposed via the search engine. By mining a SharePoint site for expertise, a user can see which individuals are associated with a particular tag and which tags any individual has associated with their profile.

Sharing Content

SharePoint 2013 introduces a new approach to sharing sites and documents with others. Content can now be easily shared via the Share button on the Ribbon, which pops up a simple sharing dialog box, as shown in Figure 8-3. Users of Office 365 can even share content with external partners without requiring any preexisting portal user identity because of Office 365 integration with the Windows Live identity management platform.

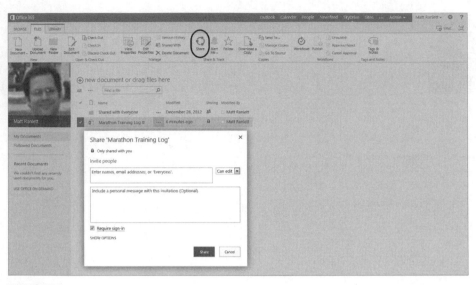

FIGURE 8-3

Enticing User Contributions with Blogs, Wikis, and Discussions

Returning from previous versions of SharePoint, blogs and wikis are easily visible social features of SharePoint 2013.

➤ *Blogs* — A blog is an application generally featuring owner-written content that is open for public comment. Blogs can be incredibly useful to an individual or team attempting to communicate to an otherwise disconnected audience of readers. SharePoint 2013 refreshes the concept of corporate blogs with new features and a fresh look and feel, as shown in Figure 8-4.

FIGURE 8-4

➤ *Wikis* — Complementing blogs in the user-generated content category are wikis. Although wikis as a concept have been around since 1995 and available in SharePoint since 2007, the simple concept is deceptively difficult to employ in organizations used to working with documents as the primary means for disseminating information. The hallmark features of wikis include simple data entry and ease of linking content inside of the wiki. SharePoint 2013 takes the concept of a wiki and simplifies SharePoint page editing and creation by offering wiki functionality in every page. The net effect of this change is a simplified SharePoint page-editing experience that lends itself to an organic growth combined with the traditional list and library-based information management capabilities familiar to users of previous versions of SharePoint.

➤ *Communities* — With SharePoint 2013, Microsoft demonstrates an understanding of the power of Internet discussion forums in a way not previously available in earlier versions of SharePoint. To build on the power of discussions, SharePoint offers a new community site template. In 2013, the community site template focuses less on the one-way communication of information and instead emphasizes more the quantity and quality of feedback. The new community site template treats every post as a discussion in a discussion board, where responses to the initial discussion item can be liked and voted as the best reply, as shown in Figure 8-5.

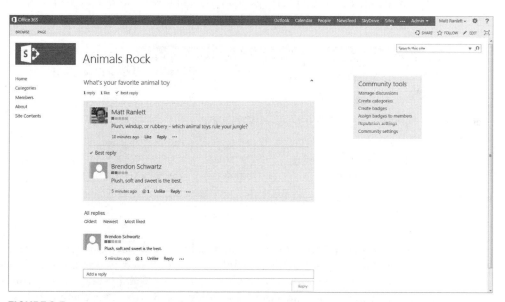

FIGURE 8-5

Socializing Categorization and Feedback

Tags and social feedback not only make enterprise content easier to manage, but they also enhance user participation and interaction by enabling users to discover content and what other users think of that content. SharePoint 2013 takes that socialization of content to greater heights with features including the newsfeed and the content-following capability.

➤ *Tags* — The act of tagging content is the assignment of descriptor words or categories to that content. There are two types of tagging: social tagging and expertise tagging. *Social tagging* refers to content and adds meta data to content to describe what it is, what it contains, or what it does. *Expertise tagging* is related to people and describes what they do, which projects they work on, or what skills they have. Where social tagging of content allows users to organically flex and grow a portal's information architecture over time, expertise tagging helps build relationships and connections to other people in the organization. Learn more about tags in the "Managed Meta Data" section of Chapter 12, "Enterprise Document Management."

➤ *Bookmarks* — Bookmarks enable a user to define how a link is shared and categorized. SharePoint bookmarks even support the inclusion of non-SharePoint content. Microsoft continues to support external bookmarks via the tagging engine but has refocused this capability with the new Following architecture, described in more detail in the "My Sites in Depth" section.

➤ *Feedback* — A popular social Internet activity is to rate and comment on the activities and contributions of other users. SharePoint 2013 incorporates the optional capability to enable content ratings with either a five-star system, as shown in Figure 8-6, or a likes rating. To activate this capability in any list or library, simply turn the capability on (off by default) inside of the library's Rating Settings Management screen, found on the List Settings screen.

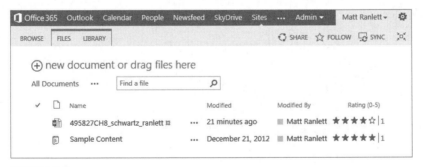

FIGURE 8-6

➤ *Newsfeed* — Users of Facebook can recognize how easily they can communicate with each other via the Wall. SharePoint 2013 builds this concept of a communication accelerator into its newsfeed capability, which combines a user's recent portal activities with the user mentioning @[user name] and Twitter-like #hashtag syntax. This combination enables a single newsfeed to serve as both a microblog such as Twitter and an activity feed such as a Facebook wall. Newsfeeds are available for use on an individual user's profile page (refer to Figure 8-2), and team sites, which activate the Site Feed feature.

➤ *Following* — As with people on Twitter, users of SharePoint 2013 have the opportunity to follow the people they find interesting. Not only can people be followed, but also sites, documents, and tags can be followed. When something has been followed, information starts to appear in the user's newsfeed. Users manage their followed content via their My Site, and an administrator can define governance for following content in Central Administration.

Enterprise Taxonomy

A special mention of the enterprise taxonomy or meta data feature set is required at this point. Microsoft SharePoint Server 2013 includes a feature that enables a company to centrally define its classification taxonomy. An information architect or librarian can select a set of categories into which all content in the enterprise falls. These categories can then be applied to an element of content in the portal. The enterprise taxonomy differs from social tagging in that the enterprise taxonomy is a formally designed and approved view of the organization and can be consistently applied to all of the content in the portal. Social tagging, as discussed in the earlier "Social Categorization and Feedback" section, creates an informal folksonomy, which helps users find the content they're interested in faster but does not replace the formal corporate information architecture. The enterprise taxonomy capabilities are discussed in the "ECM Features" section of Chapter 12.

TRADITIONALLY SOCIAL USER-GENERATED CONTENT EXPERIENCES

Corporate intranets have historically been an asset controlled by the IT and Corporate Communication departments. The purpose of a corporate intranet has traditionally been to disseminate information from the top down. The Human Resources department has an area in which users can download approved HR documents and forms. The Marketing department has an area in which it can post approved logos and letterheads. The IT department may even offer an electronic form that submits trouble tickets to the company help desk. When SharePoint entered the company landscape, it offered users the ability to easily contribute their own content to the intranet. Most frequently, this has been in the form of project team sites where a community of people work together to produce and share document-based work products. Occasionally user contributions have been in the form of a knowledge-based or wiki-based dynamic document. SharePoint discussion lists keep threaded conversations out of e-mail and available on the portal for everyone to consume. SharePoint 2013 continues the trend of previous versions of focusing on users with an updated team sites concept that has become even easier to update and maintain than before, as well as the new community site template discussed in the "Communities" section. One of the smallest and yet most significant changes to the default team site template in SharePoint 2013 is the default inclusion of the easily removable Get Started with Your Site web part that helps new users understand the realm of possibilities available to them. SharePoint 2010 team sites used to start with a blank page that would frequently leave novice site owners confused as to where they should start.

Wikis Everywhere

A wiki is a collection of web pages that makes it easy for people to edit and cross-link information to organically grow and refine content based on contributions of multiple people. One of the best aspects of SharePoint wikis is the feature affectionately known as Wikis Everywhere. Now, every SharePoint team site is a wiki site by default! Editing the content on a page becomes as simple as clicking the Edit tab and typing in the page that contains the rich text page editor previously described. Creating a new page is as simple as using the familiar double bracket enclosure [[ ]] to create a link to the page that doesn't yet exist. SharePoint creates a stub page or placeholder to the new page, creating the page after the link is clicked for the first time.

Wiki pages are not restricted to sites based on the team site template. Any site can add a specialized wiki page library that stores wiki publishing pages. To present users with the easiest possible page creation experience, consider the following recommendations for wiki page library management:

➤ *Do not enforce check-in or check-out requirements to prevent a user from accidentally locking a page.* This does give rise to the possibility of one user overwriting another user's content, but SharePoint's inherent content-versioning capabilities provide users with the ability to roll content back on demand.

➤ *Do not enforce content approval on wiki pages.* Wiki pages are meant to be quickly edited and posted for peer review and edit. Scenarios that call for content approval on wiki content may be better suited for SharePoint's ordinary web content management functionality.

➤ *Consider the use of an open term store local to the site containing the wiki library.* This enables users to create new terms and doesn't lock them to the corporation's taxonomy. To keep a consistent experience, seed the local term store with preset terms from the formal taxonomy.

Blogs

SharePoint 2013 provides familiar blog functionality such as authoring posts, reader comments, and content categorization, but it has further enhanced the experience by adding theme and post ID capabilities. Refer to Figure 8-4 to see a blog that has the theme changed and post layout updated.

The blog site template in SharePoint 2013 features a refreshing UI template that would be acceptable on any public internet site without modification. Navigation elements have been enhanced to allow sorting content by category and date. The content features an Ajax-based page experience when toggling the comment view on and off. The blog is described by an About This Blog content area. Owner-specified related links are also available for readers of the blog. Finally, the Share & Track Ribbon tab offers readers the familiar notification, sharing, and social capabilities.

Adding posts to and editing posts on a SharePoint 2013 blog takes advantage of the rich text editor seen on team site pages. The author can use the SharePoint Ribbon complete with Live Preview functionality and streamlined image-insert capabilities to write and edit content online. Should the online editing experience not meet the user's needs, the ability to launch an external blogging program such as Microsoft Word is available as a link in the owner tools section.

Public-facing blogs are a familiar phenomenon, but some of the uses for internal blogs may be less apparent. Internal blogs are written by company employees for company employees and are often a valuable tool for promoting organizational awareness. Examples of internal blogs include:

➤ Executive blogs from the CEO featuring posts about the company

➤ Product managers blogs advertising product changes

➤ HR blogs intended to keep people up to date with company policy changes

➤ IT blogs from technology workers posting software tips

Blogs are written either from a bottom-up perspective or a top-down perspective. Bottom-up posts are written from the perspective of the line workers and low-to-mid-level managers. These blogs are written to express ideas or experiences they have had. Top-down blogs are a way to deliver executive messages, such as strategic direction, corporate status, and announcements. Blogs act as a record of lessons learned, experiences, events, successes, and failures. The numerous benefits of internal blogs include knowledge sharing and team building:

➤ *Knowledge sharing* — Knowledge sharing occurs when information, experience, skills, or expertise is exchanged among people or friends or within a community or an organization. By its nature, the act of blogging is a way to share information with the blog's readers. The writers take the time to think about the message they want to deliver and attempt to express the message in a clear and understandable fashion so that it can be consumed by many readers.

➤ *Team building* — Blogs help to strengthen teams by allowing ongoing and constant communication between team members, regardless of distance. Blog posts and associated comments enable group communication of ideas and questions without the intrusive effects of e-mail distribution lists. As team members continue to communicate, bonds of trust between members are built on the spirit of collaboration, which helps make the team stronger. This kind of communication works inside of a single team or department and across multiple teams; internal blogs enable geographically distributed teams to easily communicate with each other in an easy and open way, whether that geographic distribution is around the world or just in the next room.

COMMUNITIES

Recalling the words of Lesser and Storck, a community of practice is a group whose members regularly engage in sharing and learning, based on their common interests. Inside of an organization, the groups can be team focused, department focused, and even activity- or work-product focused. A key point to think about when building communities is that they shouldn't become a distraction for people during their common work activities. An ideal corporate community is one that enhances the work experience and makes it easier to quickly accomplish tasks.

One of the major pillars of a community is collaboration. Collaboration can be something as straightforward as a discussion board or be as complex as tagging content or assignment of meta data. Meta data is anything that describes the actual data, such as the author, the last edited date, the organizational department that owns the content, and the customer to whom the content is pertinent. By encouraging community members to add content to their various communities, they can stay current on a given topic and can be more in touch with how that content is viewed and used throughout their community. Wikis, blogs, and discussion forums are great ways for members to collaborate and get feedback from other participants in the community.

Collaboration can be successful only with good communication; this is what ties the community together. Communication requires that the technology enables members to interact and also expects the members to clearly convey their ideas with the tools provided to them. With SharePoint 2013 there is a wide selection of tools such as microblogs and discussion forums with Best Reply voting that can be used to communicate the ideas of community members to their peers and the world. The "Community Site Template," "Discussions," and "Newsfeed in Depth" sections of this chapter introduce each of these tools and how they can be independently and jointly leveraged to create a thriving online community.

An online corporate community should be a secure and safe place for teams of people to work together. It should provide the tools that enable the team to collaborate and communicate effectively with each other, regardless of each team member's physical location. Building an online community may have proven to be difficult in the past, but with Microsoft SharePoint 2013, it has become a much easier task. With SharePoint 2013, community creators are given the opportunity to set up their community however they see fit, organically grown from a variety of the community site template. When created, the community can have open or private group membership, as well as the ability to control access to information within the membership of that community through extremely flexible and granular security configurations.

Creating a new community is as simple as creating a new SharePoint 2013 site. You can use the community site template or add the community features to an already-created site.

The first step of building a successful community is defining the topic of interest for the community. A vibrant community is one that has contributions from many people on a regular basis. Choosing a topic that many people will be interested in will usually get a lot more repeated and regular interaction, enriching the overall content. If the topic is predetermined, a good plan is to have a content owner or subject matter expert drive some of the early conversations. By adding dedicated owners and perhaps seeding the site with a few conversation starters, the community will likely grow and remain active for a longer time. However, communities and the associated SharePoint sites do not last forever, especially in the fast-paced corporate environment of today. When a community becomes stale, it should be decommissioned and removed to prevent the overall online corporate ecosystem from bogging down with old and out-of-date material. For example, it is now easy for a SharePoint 2013 site owner to set the closure and deletion settings to mark a site as read-only and leave it for archive purposes until such time as it is no longer needed and can be deleted.

The second task is to determine if the community is open or private. An open community is one that allows any member to join and usually displays the community in a directory listing. For example, most communities that focus on common interests such as company events will be an open community. There is also the option of having a private community with a closed membership. A closed membership might be appropriate to a community focused on nonpublic matters such as the concerns of the company's financial decision makers. The decision between an open or private community depends on the need of the community and the type of content that should be available to that community.

To help grow the community, the right tools are needed to engage users of all types. These tools can include both off-line and online capabilities such as a web browser or using the Microsoft Office Suite. Such a wide range of available tools enables all members to personalize their unique style of interaction with the communities they belong to. Many members find that instead of using one tool for maintaining their community contributions, they actually use many tools. For instance, members might usually use Microsoft Outlook as their reader for conversations and documents when traveling or on the go and they cannot access the computer that they use regularly. Then, they may turn to an Internet browser such as Microsoft Internet Explorer to view, edit, and respond to the community when they get back online for a full set of capabilities.

Community Site Template

The community site template incorporates all of the features together into a single site template. This template has all of the lists and libraries needed for enhanced discussions and blogs, as well as member involvement with badges, replies, and member reputation. This template brings together many features that add the custom actions, lists, and web parts to use all of the community enhancements. You can see in Figure 8-7 that when created, the site will have social features, the membership list, and the administrative links.

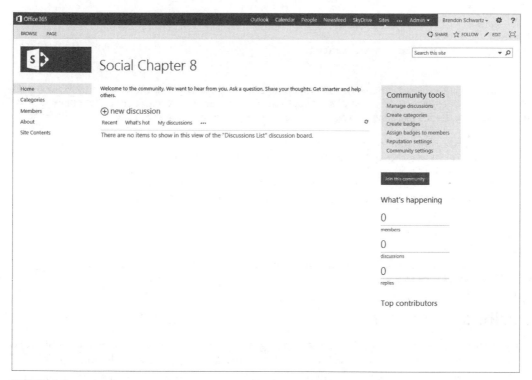

FIGURE 8-7

As you can see, the community site template is a normal site template just like a team site. The community components do not interact with a central service application such as My Sites. Therefore, there is no specific API for the community features, but rather you can access all of the elements in the site just as you would with any other code for sites. The community site template is not available in SharePoint Foundation 2013. This means that you can still use components such as discussion boards, but you will not have the added automated community features. Listing 8-1 shows some of the values stored in the property settings of the web for each community. The code also determines if the site is community-based on the selected templates.

LISTING 8-1: Community Site Template Properties

```
SPWeb web = site.RootWeb;
//Check if this is a community site
if (web.WebTemplate == "COMMUNITY")
{
    //Get the Community Established Date
    DateTime CreatedDate;
    if (web.AllProperties.ContainsKey("vti_CommunityEstablishedDate"))
    {
        CreatedDate = (DateTime)web.AllProperties["vti_CommunityEstablishedDate"];
    }
    else
    {
        CreatedDate = web.Created;
    }

    string RepliesCount = web.AllProperties["Community_RepliesCount"].ToString();
    string TopicsCount = web.AllProperties["Community_TopicsCount"].ToString();
    string MembersCount = web.AllProperties["Community_MembersCount"].ToString();

    //Display Values of the Community
    Console.WriteLine("Community Created On {0}", CreatedDate);
    Console.WriteLine("Number of Replies Count {0}", RepliesCount );
    Console.WriteLine("Number of Topics Count {0}", TopicsCount);
    Console.WriteLine("Number of Members Count {0}", MembersCount);

}
else
{
    Console.WriteLine("This is not a community template, this is the {0} template",
    web.WebTemplate);
}
```

Discussions

The discussion boards are one of the major lists to get improvements with this version of SharePoint. The discussion boards list has been one of the primary list templates since the beginning of SharePoint. Over the years the way discussion boards have been used has changed based on the impact of how data is communicated. The new features include a cleaner user interface for creating a reply to a post, being able to mark a discussion as a question, and being able to use metrics from discussions to determine a person's reputation.

To assist with moderation of the content, SharePoint 2013 provides a link to a Manage Discussions web page and a web part that shows a summary of the number of discussions and replies. If you use the community template, you can notice that the default list has a different title than the URL, so be careful to know which one you need if you use the API. Listing 8-2 shows the interaction with the Community Discussion.

LISTING 8-2: Community Discussion

```
SPWeb web = site.RootWeb;
string discussionURL = web.Url + "/Lists/Community Discussion";
SPList communityDiscussion = web.GetList(discussionURL) ;

//Create a new discussion topic
string discussionTitle = "New Discussion Created" + DateTime.Now;
SPListItem discussion =
    SPUtility.CreateNewDiscussion(communityDiscussion.Items,  discussionTitle);

discussion[SPBuiltInFieldId.Body] = "Creating discussion in API";
discussion.Update();
web.Update();

//Display all of the discussions and posts
SPListItemCollection discussionTopics =
communityDiscussion.GetItems(new SPQuery());
foreach (SPListItem discussionTopic in discussionTopics)
{
    Console.WriteLine("Discussion: " + discussionTopic.DisplayName);

    object BestAnswerID = discussionTopic[SPBuiltInFieldId.BestAnswerId];
    if (BestAnswerID != null)
    {
        Console.WriteLine("Discussion has Best Answer ID =" + BestAnswerID);
    }

    SPQuery query = new SPQuery();
    query.Folder = discussionTopic.Folder;
    SPListItemCollection posts = communityDiscussion.GetItems(query);

    foreach (SPListItem post in posts)
    {
        Console.WriteLine(post[SPBuiltInFieldId.Body]);

    }
}
```

REPUTATION

SharePoint 2013's reputation system is a site-level calculation of the achievements that a person has earned on a given community. The settings are completely configurable and designed to allow for different types of calculations. The ability to select if the items in the lists can be rated provides for community interaction and contribution. This is especially important in a system that uses the question-and-answer features of the discussion posts. The SharePoint team did not stop at being able to rate the content; actually, they added the ability for users to select between rating and liking content. This complete rating system provides the foundation so that you can build complex community applications. To modify these settings you can click the link on the homepage of the community or navigate to the Site Settings menu that also provides the administrative links. Figure 8-8 shows the Community Reputation Settings page.

FIGURE 8-8

In the reputation settings, user ratings are only a small portion of the overall way that a person creates achievements. There are four items that allow a user to create points if the achievement point system is enabled. These are Creating a new post, Replying to a post, Member's post or reply gets liked or receives a rating of 4 or 5 stars, and Member's reply gets marked as "Best Reply." You can provide your own unique values to how much weight these areas count for. After you determine the point values that each item will receive when created, you can use five different point levels to display where a user currently is ranked. This ranking appears on each member's profile of the site, which is also configurable. You can either display the point level as a set of images from 1 to 5, or you can use text to display what the level means. For instance, in your site you might configure level 5 to be listed as an Expert and Level 1 to be a Contributor.

Gifted Badges

The reputation system automatically recalculates your reputation based on the selected values previously detailed, but SharePoint 2013 also provides a new way to give users a badge on their profile. The badges are defined in a list on the site called /Lists/Badges, which provides a Lookup field to the Community Members list of whom the badge is given. After you define the values of the badges, you can then select members and assign them badges — hence the name "gifted badges" because you are gifting the badges to them.

When you give a badge to a user, the badge shows up on the user's profile card. The badge displays in place of the reputation settings. This means that if you give someone a badge, her profile will show only the badge and not the level received on the site. If you remove the badge from the user, she can then show her point level again. When building your site, consider which one of these you would like to display, or you could create a new query to the Community Membership list to display both. Remember the values are stored in a SharePoint list that you can access through the SharePoint standard API. Some of the fields might not show up if they are hidden, but you can still access them in the API.

Best Replies Used with Question and Answer

As previously mentioned, one of the metrics for building reputation is based on the number of replies a user enters that are marked as the best reply for a discussion. The way to indicate a reply is the best is done by the moderator and owner of the discussions. Only one reply can be marked as the best reply, but this post gets moved to the top of the discussion list and highlighted with the discussion that started the thread.

The best-reply field that is called BestAnswerID in the Discussion board schema.xml is the ID of the corresponding post. This field is marked as read-only, which means you must update the field using the user interface or directly from the API. Keep in mind that if you change the value, that only one person will get a reputation score based on the currently selected best reply, but the previous person will not lose reputation points.

To help determine which questions have been answered, there is an option to mark a discussion as a question. After it has been marked as a question, a flag is set for the views to show the discussion if it is not answered. There is an Answered questions view and an Unanswered questions view. This Q-and-A feature takes advantage of the best-replies option, and a discussion is considered answered if a moderator has marked a post as a best reply.

Members Page

The members of a community are what help it to succeed. Administrators help manage the community and keep it on track. For these reasons there is a new membership page and administration experience for the members of the community. The membership page describes the community members. Because these members are users of the SharePoint farm, the membership page will provide a subset of the user profile details plus list any externally invited users. It is important to know that because the community features and template are not allowed to be used on externally facing websites, the membership page is available to authenticated users only.

On the membership page you can find that you can sort the members by top contributors, new members, or A–Z and Z–A. When the members are shown in the membership list, you can see their details about them, such as their picture, name, reputation, and standard metrics about their reputation. You can also see information about yourself on the page. In your information you can find your reputation score, how many points are needed to get to the next level, and the ability to leave the community if you no longer want to participate.

MY SITES IN DEPTH

SharePoint 2007 and SharePoint 2010 both used the My Site feature to create a single central location for users to manage their profile details, store personal and publically available content, and in 2010, microblog and communicate via the Note Board. SharePoint Server 2013 expands this existing feature set with an emphasis on simplifying the user experience through a clean and uncluttered UI and a unified navigation. 2013 My Sites also offer a centralized list of assigned tasks across sites and even applications, thanks to the new Work Management service application, which can integrate SharePoint, Project Server, and Exchange tasks. New features, including the Newsfeed, allow enterprises to host internal Twitter-style conversations, which leverage a familiar hashtag vocabulary to keep employees in touch and up to date with each other.

User Profile

User profiles in SharePoint contain the details about individuals in the organization. Properties like first and last name, title, e-mail address, and department are but a few of the fields that are stored in a user's profile available by default. User profiles are also easily extended to store customized information.

There are three methods to populate the profile database in SharePoint:

➤   Import through Active Directory (AD) or an LDAP server via the User Profile Synchronization service.

➤   Manually add and edit profiles either centrally or by each user individually.

➤   Other business systems can augment AD data with Business Connectivity Services (BCS).

Organizations that have committed to technologies such as Active Directory will have an easier time populating their profile database because of native integrations, but other user directories and databases are valid options. After a user profile is created, a basic profile page for that user will be created. This page is a placeholder that contains core information. Apps and web parts that reference the user's profile, such as the results of a people search, point to this placeholder page until the My Site has been provisioned for the user.

Programming the User Profile

Microsoft makes several APIs available for accessing and manipulating user profile data including several client object models and REST services. Microsoft recommends leveraging your choice of CSOM to reduce the amount of code installed on a server. When leveraging the .NET client object model, the primary object is the `PersonProperties` object inside of the `Microsoft.SharePoint.Client.UserProfiles` namespace.

To create a simple application that reads a specific user's profile properties using the best practices CSOM API, follow these simple steps:

1.   Create a new Visual Studio 2012 Console Application project, and give it an easily identifiable name such as **UserProfileReader**.

2.   Add references to the following assemblies:

```
Microsoft.SharePoint.Client
Microsoft.SharePoint.ClientRuntime
Microsoft.SharePoint.Client.UserProfiles
```

3. Add the following code to the Main method:

```
// Update constants with real values.
const string serverUrl = "http://tailspintoys.com/";
const string targetUser = "tailspin\\mattr";

ClientContext clientContext = new ClientContext(serverUrl);

// Get the PeopleManager
PeopleManager peopleManager = new PeopleManager(clientContext);
// Get the user's properties
PersonProperties personProperties = peopleManager.GetPropertiesFor(targetUser);

// Load and run the request for AccountName and UserProfileProperties
clientContext.Load(personProperties, p => p.AccountName, p =>
p.UserProfileProperties);
clientContext.ExecuteQuery();

foreach (var property in personProperties.UserProfileProperties)
{
    Console.WriteLine(string.Format("{0}: {1}",
        property.Key.ToString(), property.Value.ToString()));
}
Console.ReadKey(false);
```

Notice in the object relationships for the PersonProperties parent and child objects in the code snippet that PeopleManager.PersonProperties.UserProfileProperties<iEnumerable> grants access to each available property name and value for a user's profile.

To learn more about user profiles in SharePoint 2013 including common programming tasks such as how to create and change user profile properties, review the MSDN article "Work with user profiles in SharePoint 2013" at http://msdn.microsoft.com/en-us/library/office/jj163800(v=office.15).aspx.

> **NOTE** *Administrators will rejoice upon learning that there is no difference between the setup and configuration of the User Profile Synchronization service in SharePoint Server 2010 and SharePoint Server 2013. Everything from setup requirements to configuration options and implications remains the same. The UI has, of course, changed in 2013, as well as an internal component called the Management Agent Run Configuration for both AD and SharePoint agents. The impact of these core component changes is faster synchronization performance.*

My Site Document Libraries and SkyDrive Pro

SharePoint 2013 automatically provisions every user's My Site with an access-restricted document library called My Documents. By default, items in this document library are access restricted, but a folder inside the library called Shared with Everyone offers everyone read access. This experience, clearer in intent than 2010's pair of distinct libraries named Personal and Shared, is also the home location for SkyDrive Pro. SkyDrive Pro is SharePoint 2013's new content synchronization experience that enables easy off-line access to content via Windows Explorer integration in the same manner as Dropbox and SkyDrive. Unlike those public services, however, SkyDrive Pro is secured and backed up by corporate IT (or Microsoft for Office 365). To access SkyDrive Pro via the browser, simply click the SkyDrive link in the top navigation. To synchronize content to a new computer, click the SYNC button in the right corner on the Ribbon, as shown in Figure 8-9. Clicking the SYNC button installs a small program to continuously keep content synchronized between that PC and the My Site SharePoint document library. Mobile applications are also available to quickly access SkyDrive Pro content on the go.

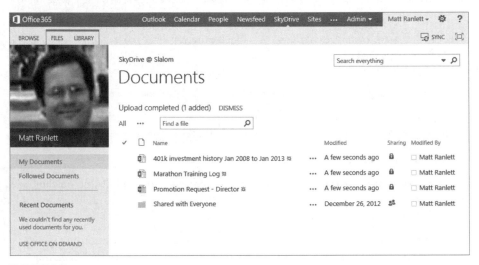

FIGURE 8-9

Following Content and People

Following content in SharePoint 2013 is the user-initiated act of indicating interest in a specific document, person, site, or tag. By following portal content or users, normally accomplished via a Ribbon button, the user's newsfeed can receive updates about that content or user. When a user creates a site, interest in that site is inferred by SharePoint, and that user is automatically marked as following that site. The same is not true of tags or documents; when users apply a tag or upload a document, they are not automatically assumed to be interested in either the tag or document.

NEWSFEED IN DEPTH

SharePoint 2013's most visible enhancement in upgrading SharePoint's social awareness is in the new newsfeed architecture. The newsfeed is made up of two social-feed components:

➤ *Microblogs* — Twitter-style interactions between users

➤ *Activity feeds* — Facebook-style automated application notifications about the interactions of users with documents and content

To meet the reliability and performance requirements of these two social feeds, SharePoint leverages a distributed cache service built on top of the Windows Server AppFabric Distributed Caching architecture. This distributed caching service not only speeds the performance of social feeds, but also assists in the caching of authentication tokens. By default the distributed cache service is active on all web and application servers in a farm, but administrators have the ability to consciously dedicate specific machines in a farm to the caching service. The total maximum size of the cache is the sum of the memory allocated to the Distributed Cache service on each of the servers running the service. Figure 8-10 shows how the architecture of newsfeed and the Distributed Cache service work together to provide SharePoint 2013's social awareness. The Distributed Cache service is a fundamental component not only of the social feeds but also to 10 other caching services, such as the Search Query Web Part and the Security Trimming Cache.

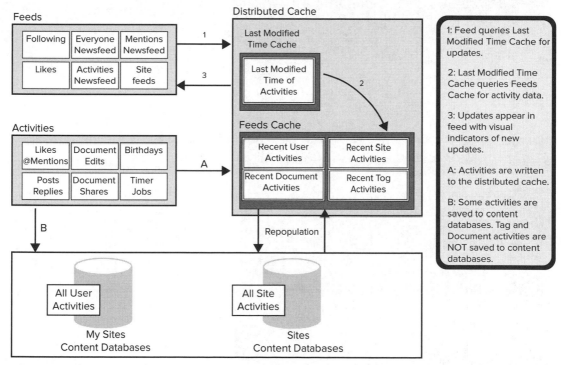

FIGURE 8-10

Microblogs

Microblogs are positioned to be the internal Twitter of an organization, designed to allow for short status updates. SharePoint 2013's microblogs are designed for public peer-to-peer interactions via the @mention syntax. The centralized access to the microblog via a My Site newsfeed allows for easy generation of interest in public dialogue. To assist users in applying context to a conversation, Microsoft adopted the #hashtag syntax popularized by Twitter. Hashtags work like any other meta data tag, complete with tag profile pages and inclusion in a user's My Site page's Trending Tags.

Users can post updates to their microblog via their My Site and via a number of mobile applications, as shown in Figure 8-11. After a user has posted a message, it can no longer be edited but it can be deleted. The maximum length of an individual post is 512 characters, and an individual post can receive a maximum of 100 replies. In addition to text, @mentions, and #hashtags, a user can enter URLs, pictures, and videos. HTML syntax is not supported.

FIGURE 8-11

Activity Feed

SharePoint considers an activity to be potentially any action, either user generated or system generated. Out of the box, SharePoint 2013 recognizes four broad categories of activities including:

➤ Microblog activities such as posts, likes, mentions, and tagging

➤ Following activities such as when a user follows people or documents

➤ User profile activities such as a user's birthday or changes to Ask Me About

➤ Document activities such as editing or sharing a document

These activities are stored in the Distributed Cache and content databases (refer to Figure 8-10). When an activity has been recorded, it becomes eligible for display on any of the available feeds in SharePoint, including the following My Site feed views:

➤ *Newsfeed* — A user's default My Site feed view, showing the 20 latest details from people followed by the user.

➤ *Everyone* — A feed view of the 20 latest activities of all users.

➤ Activities — The most inclusive and accurate view of a user's activities, including system-generated activities. The Activities view is not limited to 20 items.

➤ *Mentions* — A view of all posts or replies where the user was @mentioned.

➤ *Likes* — A listing of all microblog posts or replies that the user has liked. This is separate from the I Like It tagging feature originally introduced in SharePoint 2010.

In addition to the feed views available on a user's My Site, a site feed is also available on a team site. A site feed functions like a user's My Site newsfeed except that it can be secured to a restricted group of users. Site feeds are accessible through search, but security trimming is enforced such that a user without access to the site containing the feed will not receive feed activities in their search results.

For more information on the SharePoint 2013 microblogs, feeds, and Distributed Cache service, refer to the TechNet article, "Overview of microblog features, feeds, and the Distributed Cache service in SharePoint Server 2013," available online at `http://technet.microsoft.com/en-us/library/jj219700(office.15).aspx`.

PROGRAMMING WITH THE SOCIAL API

Writing code for SharePoint 2013's My Sites and Newsfeeds leverages the SharePoint Social API. Microsoft has made significant investments since the 2010 version to open functionality and lower the development bar. To that end, Microsoft offers no fewer than six distinct options for working with the My Site social features defined in Table 8-1.

TABLE 8-1: Social API Programming Models

API Name	Class Library and Path/Schema
.NET client object model	Microsoft.SharePoint.Client.UserProfiles.dll in %ProgramFiles%\Common Files\Microsoft Shared\web server extensions\15\ISAPI
Silverlight client object model	Microsoft.SharePoint.Client.UserProfiles.Silverlight.dll in %ProgramFiles%\Common Files\Microsoft Shared\web server extensions\15\TEMPLATE\LAYOUTS\ClientBin
Mobile client object model	Microsoft.SharePoint.Client.UserProfiles.Phone.dll in %ProgramFiles%\Common Files\Microsoft Shared\web server extensions\15\TEMPLATE\LAYOUTS\ClientBin
JavaScript object model	SP.UserProfiles.js in %ProgramFiles%\Common Files\Microsoft Shared\web server extensions\15\TEMPLATE\LAYOUTS
Representational State Transfer (REST) service	`http://<mySiteUri>/_api/social.feed` `http://<mySiteUri>/_api/social.following` `http://<siteUri>/_api/SP.UserProfiles.PeopleManager`
Server object model	Microsoft.Office.Server.UserProfiles.dll in %ProgramFiles%\Common Files\Microsoft Shared\web server extensions\15\ISAPI

With the Social API, developers can write code to read and write to a user's social feed, follow people or content on behalf of the user, or retrieve various user profile properties. Follow these instructions to create a sample application that manipulates a user's social feed.

1. Create a new Visual Studio 2012 Console Application project, and give it an easily identifiable name such as **SocialFeedPosts**.

2. Add references to the following assemblies:

    ```
    Microsoft.SharePoint.Client
    Microsoft.SharePoint.ClientRuntime
    Microsoft.SharePoint.Client.UserProfiles
    ```

3. Add the following using statements:

    ```
    using Microsoft.SharePoint.Client;
    using Microsoft.SharePoint.Client.Social;
    ```

4. Add the following code to the Main method:

    ```
    // Update constants with real values.
    const string serverUrl = "http://tailspintoys.com/";

    ClientContext clientContext = new ClientContext(serverUrl);

    // Write the post's text.
    ```

```
SocialPostCreationData feedMessage = new SocialPostCreationData();
feedMessage.ContentText = "This is an automated post from sample code";

// Get the SocialFeedManager.
SocialFeedManager feedManager = new SocialFeedManager(clientContext);

// Publish the post.  The first param is null because this is not a reply
feedManager.CreatePost(null, feedMessage);
// Update the user's newsfeed
clientContext.ExecuteQuery();
```

This is an extremely simplified example designed to introduce you to the `SocialFeedManager` object. This object is responsible for accessing a user's feed for read/write purposes. For more information on developing applications that leverage the SharePoint 2013 Social API, refer to the MSDN article titled "Work with social feeds in SharePoint 2013," available online at `http://msdn.microsoft.com/en-us/library/jj163237.aspx`.

SUMMARY

Microsoft has dramatically overhauled the accessibility and utility of SharePoint's social capabilities with the release of SharePoint 2013. SharePoint 2013 is now a first-class competitor in the social enterprise application space with new features such as microblogs and badging. This chapter covered the existing and new capabilities, including consumption-centric features such as the new multidevice user experiences and newsfeeds, as well as the content-contribution–centric features such as enhanced content editing and social feedback. This chapter introduced you to key concepts and architectures, as well as the new Social API. Armed with this knowledge, you created several prototype applications such as one to manipulate discussion forums and one to access a user's profile details.

The next chapter focuses on discovery and content awareness through the new SharePoint 2013 search engine, now based on the FAST technology.

Building Search-Based Applications in SharePoint 2013

WHAT'S IN THIS CHAPTER?

➤ Customizing search results by extending the UI or creating your own

➤ Creating queries and working with rules, result templates, and CSOM

➤ Developing connectors, content processing, and result sources

➤ Creating rank profiles and managed properties

➤ Recognizing common patterns for developing search extensions and search-based applications

WROX.COM CODE DOWNLOADS FOR THIS CHAPTER

The wrox.com code downloads for this chapter are found at `www.wrox.com/remtitle .cgi?isbn=1118495829` on the Download Code tab. The code is in the chapter 09 download and individually named according to names throughout the chapter.

Search is now everywhere, and most people use it numerous times a day to keep from drowning in information. Enterprise search provides a powerful way to access information of all types, and it enables you to bridge across the information silos that proliferate in many organizations. Perhaps because of the simplicity and ubiquity of the search user experience, the complexity of search under the hood is rarely appreciated until you get into it. Developing with search and SharePoint 2013 is rewarding and not difficult; although, it requires an understanding of search and sometimes a different mindset.

Chapter 1, "Architectural Overview of SharePoint 2013," covered an overview of the new architecture of search. Chapter 2, "What's New in SharePoint 2013," included a quick overview of the new search features. This chapter focuses on the development aspects: what you can customize and extend. You go through search from front to back; starting with the UI and formatting, next covering how to work with queries, and then covering content acquisition and enrichment. After you have explored these, you learn about the "systems" aspects of search such as relevance, linguistics, and packaging, with a focus on what you can change. The goal is to give you all the tools you need to build search-based applications.

Learning to develop great applications, including search, can serve you and your organization well. In SharePoint 2013, search has become one of the primary ways to access information. You can build more flexible, more powerful applications that bridge different information silos while providing a natural, simple user experience.

SEARCH ARCHITECTURE AND EXTENSIBILITY

SharePoint 2013 has a single core search engine. Though this might seem natural, it is a big departure from the search architecture in SharePoint 2010, where the integration of FAST produced a hybrid architecture. With SharePoint 2010, there were multiple, different codebases involved in search — primarily FAST — but SharePoint 2010 Foundation had different search code than SharePoint 2010 Server; Search Server 2010 had a different variant; and so on. With SharePoint 2013 there is only one code base: Different capabilities are enabled at different licensing tiers, and some capabilities are not available online, but it's all the same engine. There is one installer, one Search Service Application (SSA), and one farm.

The search engine core in SharePoint 2013 is a brand new one, originating from years of advanced research and development; it is not directly derived from any of the SharePoint 2010 search offerings. There are lots of high-end search features that show the FAST heritage, and you can think of this as bringing high-end FAST search features to all SharePoint customers. But there are lots of new concepts and new mechanisms under the hood, as well as a brand-new face.

New Search Architecture

An overview of the new search architecture (from a developer's point of view) is shown in Figure 9-1.

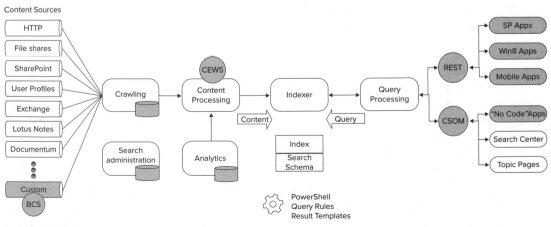

FIGURE 9-1

The components of this architecture were described in Chapter 1, from a functional point of view; this information isn't repeated here. Referring to Figure 9-1, you see the shaded components are the ones you can extend or customize. The circles in this diagram are the APIs you can use directly:

➤ New REST and CSOM APIs for working with queries (typically with JavaScript and C#).

➤ BCS for creating new indexing connectors. (BCS is covered in Chapter 13, "Introducing Business Connectivity Services," and Chapter 14, "Advanced Business Connectivity Services," but you see how to use BCS specifically with search in this chapter.)

➤ A new Content Enrichment Web Services (CEWS) API for extending content processing.

Of course, PowerShell is available for everything in search. Search-based applications, like all SharePoint 2013 applications, can be SharePoint-hosted, provide-hosted, or auto-hosted (see Chapter 7, "Further Developing Apps in SharePoint 2013"). A facility for exporting and importing search settings makes it easy to package applications that use search.

Implications of the New Search Architecture

There are a few essential things to understand about this architecture:

➤ It's **new**. As previously mentioned, the search core is quite different from anything in the 2010 wave; so are the query processing, content processing, and analytics subsystems. You can find lots of new things to learn. If you have developed a search-based application on SharePoint 2010, you can likely get it to run reasonably easily, but you should not expect exactly the same behavior.

➤ There is a **distributed dataflow engine** that runs nearly all of the search components. You'll see NodeRunner if you look at a process monitor, and this could be running many different search instances. This gives some great scaleout and fault-tolerance capabilities, but it takes some getting used to.

➤ It's **multitenant**. With some exceptions (notably the content-processing extensibility mechanism or CEWS API), every part of the search engine is built to be multitenant from the ground up. This was driven by the need to serve Office 365, but there are benefits for on-premise SharePoint deployments as well.

➤ It's **fully fault-tolerant** and highly scalable. SharePoint 2010 was close, but the search administration component was not redundant, which could be problematic.

➤ The **search product lineup has changed dramatically** with SharePoint 2013. In SharePoint 2010, there was a complex lineup with nine different options; in SharePoint 2013, there are the normal three tiers. If you want to create a pure search application, you can do this: Create a services farm with search, but also include the MMS (term store) and User Profile service. If you want to create a customer-facing search application, you have a nice surprise — the licensing changes make this a fraction of the cost.

➤ Search takes **lots of resources** (CPU, RAM, and disk). This isn't new, and the footprint of search with SharePoint 2013 has some improvements. But those new to search typically underestimate what is needed.

➤ There are **multiple databases** under the hood. The Analytics Reporting database is particularly of interest to developers, especially because web analytics has now been subsumed into search. But the Search Admin database is something you may be working with. These two as well as the Link database and the Crawl database are all scalable, and you can partition and mirror them, host them on your SQL cluster, and more. The Crawl database tends to be the largest and scales with the amount of content crawled.

If you are familiar with FAST Search for SharePoint, you will notice that there are many new concepts and constructs. This is not derived directly from the FAST code line. In fact there are a number of FAST Search Server 2010 for SharePoint deprecated features, which are listed at `http://technet.microsoft.com/en-us/library/ff607742(v=office.15)#section4`. Don't let this discourage you, as there are many exciting capabilities in the new search architecture.

Extensibility Points for Search

There's a variety of extensibility points for search, and you may use just a few or all of them. Here are the main areas meant to be extended:

➤ UI level

  ➤ Web parts (notably the new Content Search Web Part)

  ➤ Result templates

  ➤ Navigation settings

➤ Query level

  ➤ Query syntax (KQL and FQL)

  ➤ Query APIs (REST and CSOM)

  ➤ Query rules

➤ Content and meta data

  ➤ Search schema

  ➤ Result sources

  ➤ Content crawling and connectors (BCS)

  ➤ Content processing (CEWS)

➤ Relevance and linguistics

  ➤ Rank profiles

  ➤ Authorities

  ➤ Term sets and dictionaries (such as refiner sets and synonyms)

  ➤ Linguistics (such as custom word-breakers)

  ➤ Analytics (such as recommendations)

You cover each of these through the chapter, roughly in this order.

Top Customization Scenarios

There's a wide range of customization available with search. You may configure a search vertical using only simple query rules and result templates, or create a completely custom solution with your own connectors, content processing, relevance, and UI.

There are no hard rules here: General-purpose search applications, such as intranet search, can benefit from custom code and might be highly customized in some situations, even though intranet search works with no customization at all. However, most customization tends to be done on special-purpose applications with a well-identified set of users and a specific set of tasks they are trying to accomplish. Usually, these are the most valuable applications as well — ones that make customization well worth it.

Although there are no hard rules, there are common patterns found when customizing Enterprise Search. The most common customization scenarios follow:

➤ *Modify the end-user experience to create a specific experience and/or surface specific information* — Examples: Add a new refinement category, change the result set format or layout, show results from a federated location, add a promoted result for an upcoming sales event, and configure different rankings for the human resources and engineering departments.

➤ *Create a new vertical search application for a specific industry, department, topic, or role* — Examples: Reach and index specific new content, design a custom search experience, and add Audio/Video/Image search.

➤ *Create new visual elements that add to the standard search* — Examples: Show location refinement on charts/maps, show tags in a tag cloud, enable "export results to a spreadsheet," and summarize financial information from customers in graphs.

➤ *Query and indexing modifications* — Add terms and custom information to the search experience. Examples: Expand query terms based on synonyms defined in the term store, augment customer results with project information, show popular people inline with search results, or show people results from other sources. Both the query rules and the connector framework provide a way to write *shims* — simple extensions of the .NET assembly where a developer can easily add custom data sources and do data mash-ups.

➤ *Create new search-driven sites and applications* — Create customized content exploration experiences. Examples: Show reports as a results, create drawing file previews, index content from custom repositories such as SAP or Siebel, and create content-processing plug-ins to generate new meta data.

SEARCH DRIVES APPLICATIONS

Search-based applications are found throughout most enterprises — both in obvious places (such as intranet search) and in less visible ways. (Search-driven applications often don't look like "search.") Search shows up throughout SharePoint 2013. It's where you expect it: search centers, the search capabilities on every site and every page, people search, and more. It's behind in social features such as mySites, myTasks, and mySiteView. It's behind many of the ECM features, notably the e-Discovery Center. And it is the underpinning of the new Web Content Management (WCM) capabilities. There are built-in search-based applications, such as video search, as well.

Developing search-powered applications has been a difficult task. Some of this is the complexity that comes with any software dealing with human language. Some of it is the general lack of understanding of how search works. But some of this came from the way SharePoint 2010 and other enterprise search platforms were built. With SharePoint 2013, developers have a development platform that is *much* more powerful and simpler to work with than SharePoint 2010. That fact extends to search-based applications as well.

SharePoint 2013 is built as a platform for developing applications — as you learn throughout this book. It is designed to run search-based applications and to run multiple such applications on the same platform. As shown in Figure 9-2, there are built-in search-based applications as well as facilities for partner-built and custom-built search-based applications.

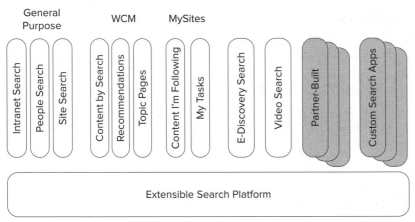

FIGURE 9-2

This search-as-a-platform approach isn't a new thing. It has been powerfully applied at quite a number of organizations. But prior to SharePoint 2013, the cost and complexity of creating and managing these applications was prohibitive for many organizations.

Out-of-the-box Search Applications

Before you get into creating your own search-based applications, it's useful to play with the out-of-the-box ones. These include standard intranet search, people search, site search, and video search. When you stand these up and work with them, you can get a sense of how the new search capabilities work — from the UX to the content crawling.

These applications are meant for general audiences; everyone in your organization might use them. Many successful search applications are targeted for specific roles, topics, or industries. But the same patterns apply, and the same techniques are used to build them.

Naturally, you can also extend the out-of-the-box applications. For example, you might bring information from external sources and directories into people search or extend the way the video search tab works. It's easy to do and worth doing even as part of a much larger search project. Actually, it's a good practice to start a search project with an out-of-the-box application, add in content from a set of sources, and use this as a rapid prototyping platform.

Search-driven Web Content Management

Web content management (which is covered in Chapter 10, "Web Content Management") is essentially built on top of search in SharePoint 2013. There is a new search-driven publishing model, which serves up the appropriate content dynamically — separating the creating and management of content management and the publishing of it. Delivering online experiences, including scenarios such as online catalogs, was a key goal for SharePoint 2013. There are several features worth highlighting:

➤ *Search-engine optimization (SEO)-friendly* — SEO has been quite hard with SharePoint, but there is big news here. "Friendly URLs" (without the arcane syntax added by SharePoint 2010) make a SharePoint site work like any normal site. Topic pages (which are designed to pull public search traffic to a given page) are generated automatically.

➤ *Taxonomy-based navigation* — Pages and page hierarchies can be created using taxonomies from the SharePoint term store. This makes it straightforward to have consistent search and navigation — a proven advantage for online sites. You can also specify which meta data is available for navigation from each page in a hierarchy — for example, to show the weight and battery life of laptops but the cooling power of air conditioners. This is called *faceted navigation*" as distinct from *refinement*.

➤ *Dynamic Content presentation* — Instead of creating static content, links, and so on, the new paradigm for online sites is dynamic and centered around the new Content Search Web Part (CSWP), as shown in Figure 9-3. Users don't know this is search-powered; it just looks like well-presented content. But the content is selected dynamically using a search query. It can take context into account, simply by using it as part of the search query behind the scenes. Content can come from any site collection. For a case like online catalogs, this is an essential mechanism. But as you'll see, the CSWP is an incredibly useful tool for lots of scenarios.

➤ *Recommendations* — We are all familiar with recommendation features online — suggestions based on your history, other shoppers, and so on. These are now included with SharePoint 2013. Surfacing suggestions based on what others searched or used (popularity) or on similar items to what you are looking at (correlation between items) is straightforward to configure. This is driven by search, specifically by the analytics capability.

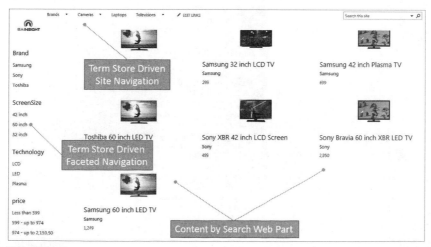

FIGURE 9-3

Social Features — Driven by Search

Chapter 8, "Developing Social Application in 2013," discussed building social applications; here you focus on what is search-driven, so you can see how to extend it. Search drives several key social features in SharePoint 2013, even ones where it's not apparent that search is used under the hood.

SharePoint 2013 adds several new social features to those that were introduced with SharePoint 2010. For example, clicking a hash tag in a post or discussion shows a list of all conversations about that topic enterprise-wide, done via a search query. You can follow content as well as people; the view of "Docs I'm Following," as shown in Figure 9-4, is the result of a search query as well. Another example is in "My Docs: Shared with Me," which shows you all the documents shared with you from everyone's My Documents. It looks like a form view but, in reality, it uses search underneath to

FIGURE 9-4

aggregate content from all MySites across site collections. Under the hood, there's a query against a ShareWith field for your name, which also filters out docs shared with everyone.

e-Discovery — Driven by Search

Electronic discovery, or e-Discovery, is the process of locating and managing content that you might need to provide as part of a legal case or an audit. e-Discovery is an important and sophisticated area, and it includes a number of steps, as shown in Figure 9-5.

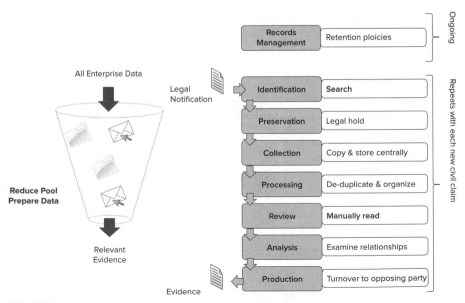

FIGURE 9-5

The e-Discovery functionality in SharePoint Server 2013 is a big step up from SharePoint 2010 and is probably the first time you could consider this to be a full application. There is now unified discovery across Exchange, SharePoint, and Lync, as shown in Figure 9-6. Exchange now has the same search infrastructure as SharePoint, which makes unifying the search much easier. Lync archives via Exchange, and Lync messages and chat logs show up in Exchange mailboxes, so Lync content is discoverable via the search in Exchange 2013.

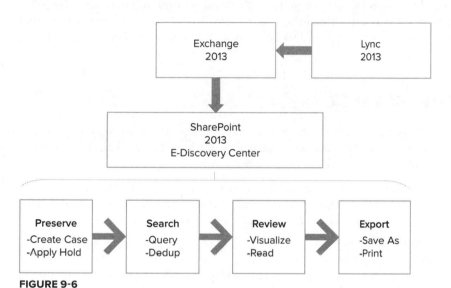

FIGURE 9-6

There are several parts to e-Discovery with SharePoint 2013:

➤ The **e-Discovery Center** is a site collection where you perform e-discovery queries across multiple SharePoint farms and Exchange servers, and preserve the items that are discovered. The *e-Discovery Center* site template creates a portal for discovery cases and lets you conduct searches, place content on hold, and export content. For each case, you create a new collaboration site that uses the *e-Discovery Case* site template.

➤ **In-place holds** preserve Exchange mailboxes and SharePoint sites — including SharePoint list items and SharePoint pages — while still allowing users to work with site content. The state of the content at the time of preservation is recorded. If a user changes the content or even deletes it, the original, preserved version is still available. Users may not be aware that a document is on hold, which is a powerful and distinctive capability. For scenarios in which you want to be sure the original is removed and not available for changing, you can accommodate that as well.

➤ Support for searching and exporting **external content** from file shares and other sources. Any content from SharePoint 2013, Exchange 2013, or a file share or website that is indexed by Search or by Exchange Server 2013 can be discovered from the e-Discovery Center. For example, to implement e-Discovery across an enterprise, you configure SharePoint 2013 Search to crawl all file shares and websites that contain discoverable content, and configure the central Search service application to include results from Exchange Server 2013.

➤ The ability to **export discovered content** from Exchange Server 2013 and SharePoint Server 2013. Within the e-Discovery Center, just export the results of an e-Discovery search for later import into a review tool.

There's more to e-Discovery than search, of course — preservation, holds, policy management, and export. But search is the cornerstone and is what makes it possible to recall all the information needed to react to legal actions, without getting irrelevant information that you have to sift through. As a developer, you can extend the e-Discovery capabilities — adding new content sources, presentation format, workflows, and so on — using the same techniques covered in the rest of this chapter.

WORKING AT THE UX LAYER

With SharePoint 2013, working at the user interface level is dramatically easier than it was with SharePoint 2010. Search is no exception. Actually, search benefits much more than many other areas of SharePoint because it is such a dynamic user experience.

One of the challenges with most search UIs is that all of the search results look the same. The user has to look at each result, or jump to the result itself to see if that is what they are looking for. This is one of the reasons so many people still feel their search experience is poor.

In SharePoint 2013, you have the ability to control the look of the search results on a granular level, using result types and display templates. For each type of content, you can control how to display it — what meta data to show, what icons or previews to display, and what layout to use. If you have a mix of different types of content (for example, people, documents, and e-mails) together in the same result set, displaying them differently is important. Users can distinguish them much more easily and will see only the meta data that is useful for each type. Some types of content (such as pictures) work best laid out in a grid rather than a list, others (such as database records) call out for a presentation in a tabular format.

Tailoring search results in this way was possible with SharePoint 2010, but it was incredibly hard. It meant working with large, complex XSLT files, with little tooling support, in an error-prone process. If you have done this with SharePoint 2010, you will be happy to work with result templates. If you haven't, you've dodged a bullet. With SharePoint 2013, there is a great framework for tailoring search results, along with tooling support and wizards such as the query builder. Everything is based on HTML and JavaScript, so you can control things directly as much as you need to, using familiar tools and techniques.

Components of the Search Center

As with SharePoint 2010, the search center is composed of web parts, and you can create and include your own web parts. But the action happens in a new results framework that provides a remarkable amount of control over search presentation without the complexity and difficulty encountered with SharePoint 2010 (and basically every search engine on the market).

The results framework is composed of three parts:

➤ A **rules engine** manages a set of query rules to determine if the result type should be triggered.

➤ A **property list** associates the rule to document type, content type, or other managed property within SharePoint search.

➤ **Display templates** define how a particular result will be displayed.

This model is a huge improvement. In SharePoint 2010, if you wanted to render a particular item differently, you were working in XSLT and modifying a monolithic document that styled the core results web part. This was a painful and error-prone process. In addition, it wasn't uncommon for several different packages to want to modify the core results web part, so integrating multiple search add-ons was a nightmare. With SharePoint 2013, you work in HTML, using your favorite web design tools, and you can design each result template separately and install them without stepping over each other.

Search Web Parts

The search web parts in SharePoint 2013 are much simpler. As you can see in Figure 9-7, there are only four web parts provided by default with a search center:

➤ Refinement

➤ Search Box

➤ Search Navigation

➤ Search Results

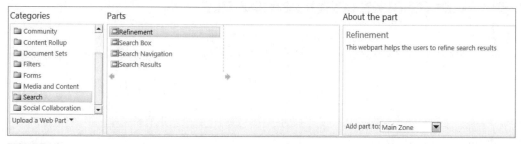

FIGURE 9-7

Gone are the complications of working with separate parts for search statistics, and so on. SharePoint 2010 had 17 web parts for search! The functions of most of these are now handled by display templates. To add an additional tab to a search center, it is as easy as adding another URL to the search navigation, as shown in Figure 9-8.

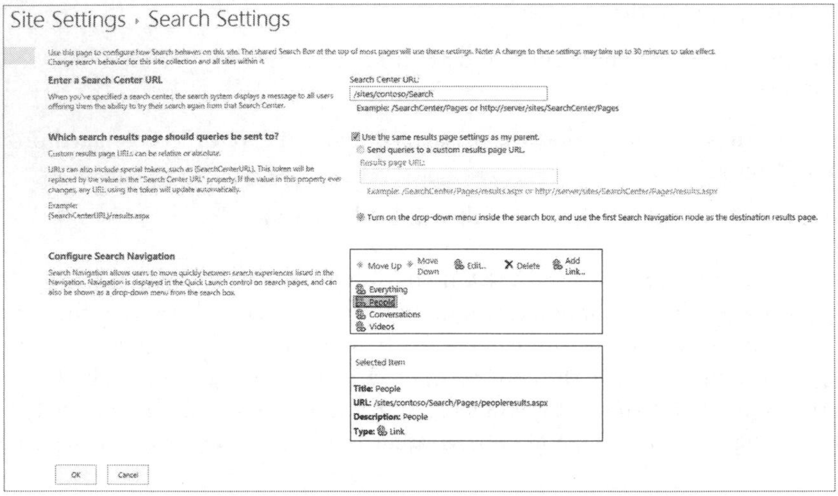

FIGURE 9-8

The Content Search Web Part

In addition to the search web parts, there are a number of new web parts that are powered by search. Foremost among these is the Content Search Web Part (CSWP), which is essentially the Core Search Results web part made simple. A CSWP can be placed anywhere (shown in Figure 9-9) to easily display content.

The CSWP is an addition to the Content Rollup category web parts. Note that it is not currently available with Office 365, only in on-premise instances of SharePoint 2013.

FIGURE 9-9

You can use a CSWP to create no-code solutions in many cases that you would have needed custom code before. A classic example is to create a simple address book widget — this is now just a CSWP using people search! The CSWP can return any content from the search index.

The CSWP is both easy and powerful, but there are a few gotchas. The CSWP returns content that is as fresh as the latest crawl of your content; it does not provide instant refresh of new content. And these are only the major versions because search crawls only the major versions of content, never the minor versions. Lastly, you can get content only from a search index, and some site collection administrators mark sites to not be indexed. If any of these are major issues for your situation, use a Content Query web part instead.

You can change the CSWP's look easily using another new construct: result types and display templates.

Result Types and Display Templates

There's a new concept in SharePoint 2013 search, called *result types*, which is at the heart of tailoring search results. You can think of a result type as a type of content; you might have a different result type for e-mails, for best bets, for reports, and so on. A result type is bound to a given result source (which is covered in the section "Working with Content") such as the local SharePoint index or an Exchange 2013 index. A result type is defined by a rule and is associated with a display template.

Display templates, also new in SharePoint 2013, define how a particular result type displays. They are sometimes called Result templates. Each one is an HTML file that references Managed Properties. The HTML file can contain inline JavaScript, or it can call external JavaScript and CSS.

Result types and display templates take some getting used to, but you can quickly find them easy and fun to work with. They open up a new world in which search results are compelling, easy to understand, and natural. This kind of experience is becoming more and more common in online sites or apps, but few people actually did the work necessary to pull this off with SharePoint 2010. With SharePoint 2013, this is easy — and a little bit of customization goes a long way in creating a great search experience.

Result Types

A result type consists primarily of a set of rules that describe which of the items in the search results match that result type. When a user issues a query, the results come back, and each result is evaluated against the rules in the result types. A display template is then applied to the result based on the type that it matches.

In addition to the rules, there is a property list, which associates the rule to document type, content type, or other managed property within SharePoint search.

Result types can be simple, but there are a lot of options, and you can make them quite advanced. For example, rules can use criteria and boolean logic on any managed property. A result type specific to sales reports would have a rule like `ContentType="sales report"`.

You can set the result type in a web part, change it in a query rule, and manipulate it along the way.

With each result type, you determine which managed properties you would like to have returned. (There must be at least one to use a result template.) There is a large set of prebuilt result sources, so in most cases this is a matter of tailoring and not a lot of work.

Each result type has a corresponding HTML rendering template. Inside the template, you set how property items display using a specific tag set (`-#= myitem =#-`). You can set specific graphics, icons, styles, and so on, and preview the results on the spot.

Display Templates

Each part of the result set can be controlled by a different display template. There are display templates for each of the different results types within the search results, the hover panel for each result type, and each of the refinement controls.

Figure 9-10 shows an example search result using multiple result types. Each type of result has a different layout (via a display template). Most of these are simple (just title and link), leaving more meta data to the hover panel. From the top of the screen moving down, there are types of results: recommendations; a spotlighted image (formerly called a visual best bet); my queries ("looking for these again?"); a custom content type (projection analysis), which displays links to related material; default results (a Word document and a PowerPoint, using the same display template); and videos (using a grid layout).

FIGURE 9-10

From this example you can get a sense of the power of display templates. Results of similar types are displayed together (in Result Blocks). One word of warning: Too many result types can get out of hand. Users can typically find results on the first page, and result blocks help provide focus and attention to the entire page, not just the first few results. But too many result blocks can interfere with a natural sense of relevance and with the guided exploration provided by refinement.

A display template retrieves managed properties and displays them. Figure 9-11 shows an example search result with five managed properties displayed: title, file extension, path, document summary, and preview image. Display templates use HTML and JavaScript.

With a display template, there are four main things to work with:

➤ *Managed properties* — You specify what managed properties you need retrieved at query time, using the `mso:ManagedPropertyMapping` tag. You can then use those properties in your HTML.

➤ *External JavaScript and CSS* — You can externalize JavaScript or CSS files you may have and then add them to your display template. (This is optional.)

➤ *Inline JavaScript* — You can also use inline JavaScript in your display template. You just need to make sure that it is below the first `<div>` in your display template.

➤ *HTML* – This is where you create the actual HTML for your display template that will render the results.

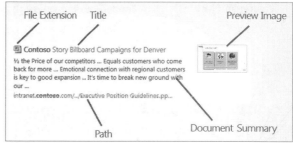

FIGURE 9-11

Execution Order and Logical Model

To the site administrator, display templates are straightforward; you simply associate a result type with a template, and there are many of these provided OOB. As a developer, it's worth understanding the logical model and how the display templates fire.

The logical model has three main parts:

➤ *Web part* — This specifies the query and templates to use and triggers templates when search results are available. There are multiple web parts per page.

➤ *Control template* — Determines how to lay out the items on the page and controls the execution of the Item templates. There is one Control template per web part instance. For the search result page, for example, the pagination, result count, and preference controls are in the Control template. (In SharePoint 2010 these required separate web parts.)

➤ *Item template* — Determines how each item looks. There can be different templates for different types of items, so there can be multiples per web part.

There are also templates for filter, group, and the new hover panel.

Display templates are executed in the browser (client-side), which enables rich interaction with the local environment. OnPostRender fires after both Control and Item templates finish rendering, so you can use this to initialize information that is not dependent on individual result data.

Example: Custom JavaScript in the Control Template

Creating display templates is straightforward. There are lots of OOB templates, so it's a good idea to copy one of these as a starting point. Use your favorite HTML editor. Place your template in the Master Page Gallery. Then it executes whenever referenced.

Start with a simple example, some JavaScript that makes a standard "Hello World" message. You can find this in a JavaScript file named `SearchRocks_DisplayTemplate.js` from this book's downloadable files:

```
<script type="text/javascript">
  document.write('<b>Search Rocks</b>');
</script>
```

Inside the first <Div> in the Control template; you can call this JavaScript as follows:

```
$includeScript(this.url, "~sitecollection/_catalogs/masterpage/DisplayTemplates/
Finished/Control_jSearchRocks_Script.js");
```

Now you see this in your search results.

Example: Adding to an Item Template

After you get used to using display templates, you'll find it easy to make search results exactly the way you want them. For example, say you want to highlight results that are new (without sorting or ranking them). This is a small change to an existing template. Try this using a display template file named `Item_DisplayTemplate_DocumentsWithDates.html` from this book's downloadable files. This file has a display template with inline JavaScript.

Place this file anywhere in the master page gallery, and it appears in the drop-down for item display templates in the CSWP tool pane. This file was created by copying and changing the "Item_TwoLines.html" display template. The action is just in two lines:

```
var modifieddate = $getItemValue(ctx, "ModifiedDate");
if (new Date(modifieddate) > new Date("12/4/2012"))
    modifieddate = "<b>NEW! </b>" + modifieddate;
```

Note that special tokens are required when working with inline JavaScript. The ability to use inline JavaScript in a display template is fabulous, but it is a bit tricky. The code *must* be placed after the first DIV tag in your display template. Any JavaScript logic needs to be surrounded by a "pound underscore" (#_ ... _#) token inside a comment. Assigning values to your variables uses an "underscore pound equals" (_#= ... =#_) token. To emit a managed property or variable from any inline JavaScript you've created, it needs to be enclosed in this tag set. Inside a display template, the managed properties are all available in the `ctx.CurrentItem` object. For example, to emit the SearchRocks managed property, you add this tag: _#= ctx.CurrentItem.SearchRocks =#_ .

Working with Managed Properties

Managed Properties are an essential element throughout SharePoint search. On the query side, these hold the information for each returned item. With SharePoint 2013 there are a new set of properties for each Managed Property:

➤ *Alias* — Friendly name for referencing this Managed Property.

➤ *Multivalued* — Managed Property can have multiple values.

➤ *Queryable* — Managed Property can be used in property-based searches.

➤ *Refinable* — Managed Property can be used as a refiner.

➤ *Retrievable* — Managed Property can be returned in the results.

➤ *Searchable* — This includes the value of the Managed Property in the search index.

➤ *Sortable* — Managed Property can be used for sorting results.

➤ *Type* — This is the data type of the Managed Property.

These are largely self-explanatory, but a few of them are worth describing for developers. You cover some of these distinctions in the section about working with queries. (For example, if a Managed Property is queryable but not searchable, it will cause a hit only when the value is explicitly included in a property search.) When working on the UI, there are two tricky things:

➤ A multivalued Managed Property can return several values in one item, which means you should decide how to accommodate when there are 0, 1, or more values to display. Multivalued properties can also mean that refiner values don't sum to the number of hits, which is a common source of confusion. If you know that a property is a multivalue property, you can also set up a fallback scenario for the case in which the first one does not contain a value. This can be done like this: `'Price':'BasePrice';'NormalPrice';'TotalPrice'`.

➤ With some templates, in particular the hover panel, inputs are all treated as strings, so you should validate data before using it.

In display templates, inputs are filled in with search managed properties specified by default, for example:

```
<mso:ManagedPropertyMapping msdt:dt="string">
'Link URL'{Link URL}:'Path'
</mso:ManagedPropertyMapping>
```

However, a user can change the property mappings within a web part, as shown in Figure 9-12. This is a great benefit in many ways, but it also means you should think through dependencies carefully.

This makes templates easy to understand, and easy to configure, but it also means that you should think of result types and display templates as tightly bound.

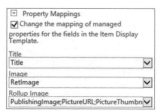

FIGURE 9-12

Example: Working with Managed Properties in Item Templates

An example of Item templates works heavily with managed properties. For many custom Item templates, you add managed properties in the mso:ManagedPropertyMapping tag.

To understand how to use managed properties, try the code in the project named SalesReport.zip. This example (courtesy of Steve Peshka) shows a Sales Report template. This adds the attributes from a custom sales report content type you created and shows them directly in the search results. This is done by modifying the default Excel File Item template, Item_Excel.htm. You can download SalesReport.zip from this book's downloadable files. It contains five files: a CSS file and an HTML file that provide the display template, two PNG files used in the design, and a Word document that highlights the steps to create and deploy this display template.

The full set of properties in this example gives you a sense for a typical result. The search engine provides a number of OOB Managed Properties, such as HitHighlightedSummary and CollapsingStatus, which are worth learning:

```
<mso:ManagedPropertyMapping msdt:dt="string">'Title':'Title','Author':'Author',
'Size':'Size',
'Path':'Path',Description':'Description',
'LastModifiedTime':'LastModifiedTime',
'CollapsingStatus':'CollapsingStatus','DocId':'DocId',
'HitHighlightedSummary':'HitHighlightedSummary',
'HitHighlightedProperties':'HitHighlightedProperties',
'FileExtension':'FileExtension','ViewsLifeTime':'ViewsLifeTime',
'ParentLink':'ParentLink','ViewsRecent':'ViewsRecent',
'FileType':'FileType','IsContainer':'IsContainer',
'ServerRedirectedURL':'ServerRedirectedURL',
'ServerRedirectedEmbedURL':'ServerRedirectedEmbedURL',
'ServerRedirectedPreviewURL':'ServerRedirectedPreviewURL',
'AccountManager':'AccountManager', 'SalesRegion':'SalesRegion',
'TotalAccounts':'TotalAccounts', 'TopAccounts':'TopAccounts',
'DirectReports':'DirectReports', 'ContentType':'ContentType'
</mso:ManagedPropertyMapping>
```

This has several custom managed properties, such as AccountManager and SalesRegion. To use these in the HTML for the Item template is straightforward:

```
<!-- Account Manager -->
<span class="ReportHeading ReportText">
  Account Manager:
</span>
<span class="ReportText">
  _#= ctx.CurrentItem.AccountManager =#_
</span><br/>

<!-- Sales Region -->
<span class="ReportHeading ReportText">
  Sales Region:
</span>
<span class="ReportText">
  _#= ctx.CurrentItem.SalesRegion =#_
</span><br/>
```

To render these into the display, the example uses a CSS file, called `SalesReport.css`, and a new script tag to invoke it from the display template. The new script tag needs to be added within the template. This should be below the `<body>` tag and above the first `<div>` tag.

```
<body>
    <script>
        $includeCSS(this.url, "./styles/SalesReport.css");
    </script>

    <div id="Item_SalesReport">
```

Finally, to use this requires a matching result type, which can be configured simply, as shown in Figure 9-13.

FIGURE 9-13

The Hover Panel

The hover panel is an exciting addition to this release, and it is controlled by another template. The basic idea of the hover panel is to simplify the inline meta data into compact, streamlined results and put richer meta data and actions into a separate dialog box. When users want to learn more about a result, they can hover their cursor over that result to see the Hover Panel dialog box and investigate a result more thoroughly, without having to click through and load the document.

The OOB Hover Panel dialog box is shown in Figure 9-14.

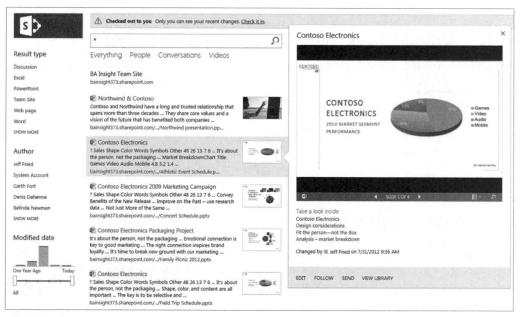

FIGURE 9-14

It has a preview, a set of meta data, and some actions you can take. This presentation is quite rich, and putting items in the hover panel keeps the main search results much cleaner.

The hover panel can be completely customized, using result types, just as the result templates customize the search results. It is controlled by its own template, but you customize it with the same techniques described for Result templates.

The OOB Web Application Viewer or Preview is available for all Office documents saved to SharePoint. This is driven from the Office Web Apps Server and doesn't work for content outside SharePoint or file formats such as PDF or DWG. But with some work, you can create your own previews and integrate them into the hover panel.

You can also leverage the OOB preview. In many cases you may want to show a scaled image of the document. GetPictureMarkup returns an image rendition based on dimensions: `Srch.ContentBySearch.getPictureMarkup()`.

The OOB hover panel contains "deep links," which are clickable headings and titles generated from the document structure. These take you directly to that part of the document. They are not a "search inside" and aren't aware of the context that got the user to this document, but they are nevertheless a cool, useful, and distinctive feature.

Adding actions to the hover panel is also done via HTML and JavaScript. The OOB actions (follow, edit, view library, and e-mail) give you a sense of the utility of acting directly on a given result. Customizing these is straightforward. For example, to add a "find on map" action, you would check that the meta data has valid geocoordinates and call your favorite map component.

Summary – Using Result Types and Display Templates

You've seen some examples of customizing search displays. The steps for this overall are quite simple:

> ➤ Plumb any properties you need into search.

> ➤ Create the look you want with a display template.

> ➤ Hook up the template to a result type.

> ➤ Try it out with a search.

WORKING WITH QUERIES

Search engines have two "doors:" a back door where content goes in and is indexed and a front door where queries go in and results come out. This simplistic view can be quite helpful when you develop search-based applications. You can work with each "door" nearly independently to speed and simplify development.

The back door (the content side) is covered in the section "Working with Content." The front door (the query side) includes the presentation (web parts, result types, display templates) just discussed, but it also includes a sophisticated capability for managing and processing queries. SharePoint 2013 adds a powerful query processing framework, as shown in Figure 9-15.

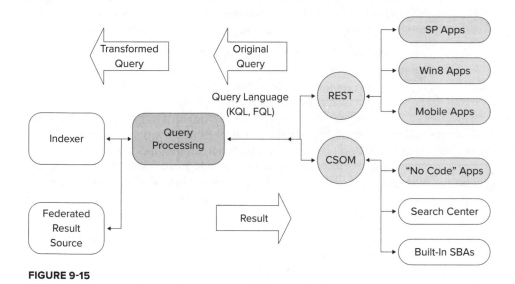

FIGURE 9-15

Queries may come into the query-processing component from many different sources — from the built-in search center and search-based applications, from programs you develop, or even from any source of URIs. (Because a search query is "just" a URL, you can treat a query URL as a link to set precanned queries into your solutions.) The CSOM and REST APIs are the ways to work with queries and query suggestions programmatically.

Queries have a specific syntax and follow a specific query language: either keyword query language (KQL) or FAST query language (FQL). You create and modify queries using these languages in web parts, query rules, and result sources, in addition to fully custom programs. The query side of search has a remarkable amount of power, and customizing search with queries in SharePoint 2013 is remarkably simple. By learning the query languages and APIs, you'll be well on your way to building great search-based applications.

Query Processing

Queries are processed under the hood of the search engine, and there are some remarkable facilities for query processing. Deep under the hood, queries are processed in data flows that go through many steps. These flows aren't available to you as a developer, but you can accomplish essentially anything you might want to do through the query APIs, query syntax, and query rules in SharePoint 2013.

If you're familiar with SharePoint 2010, think of query processing as the evolution of search scopes, federated locations, and best bets. However, in SharePoint 2013, all three of these are now deprecated in favor of result sources, query rules, and result blocks.

➤ *Result sources* — Enable you to focus searches to a subset of the total information accessible in your organization by applying extra conditions to the search queries on behalf of the end user. Stated as such, they sound much like 2010 search scopes. The key difference here is that the extra conditions enabled in 2013 go far and beyond what 2010 could do. SharePoint 2013 comes with a strong query builder to apply conditions based on the user, the search page URL (or any parameter found in it), the site, or the current date. Result sources can also be used to return results from remote content such as federated locations in SharePoint 2010.

➤ *Query rules* — Enable conditional transformation of queries and results based on custom logic. (These were mentioned when introducing the new Results Framework earlier.) Imagine you want to simplify searching budget spreadsheets in your organization. Using query rules, you can type simple search queries such as **budget spreadsheet project foo,** and behind the scenes the request can be transformed into something more elaborate. The query rule might recognize the terms Budget and spreadsheet in the search query and rewrite the query so that the document content type must be budget, the file type must be Excel, and the file content must match the project name you specified in the search keywords. In addition, the results would be sorted from the most recently modified file so that the freshest information is returned first. It is worth noting that the same Query builder functionality used for result sources is also available here as a means to define conditions on query rules or transform user queries.

➤ *Result bocks* — Are groups of results of the same type using the same result template, as covered in a previous section. All results from a given content source are presented together in a block. For example, the "best bet" construct is handled by a query rule that promotes specific items, and a corresponding result template.

Query processing includes a number of techniques for understanding the intent behind the query and mechanisms to reformulate the query to get closer to matching the intent. Queries typed by users tend to be short (averaging ~2.4 words per query), and in many applications you may be creating queries without a user typing anything (sometimes called *zero-term search*). But there is a lot of information and context available, including:

➤ *Where the query originated from* — For example, if you run a search from your company's helpdesk intranet site, you are likely to be looking for FAQs, how-to's, or IT specialists. To create more targeted results, you might use a specific result source (similar to how you might use a search scope with SharePoint 2010).

➤ *Who launched a query* — If you are based in the United States and searching for employee benefits, you are more than likely looking for U.S. employee benefits than for Canada or United Kingdom. To handle this, a query rule might bias the results from the user's home locale higher, or might filter out other results entirely.

➤ *What concepts or entities can be recognized in the query* — For example, if you were searching for an expense report form, the search engine could return the Excel spreadsheet, InfoPath form, or web page, which enables you to file your expense report (rather than a set of already-created expense reports).

Links with Predefined Queries

An essential thing to understand is that a query is just a link. The URL:

```
http://server/site/_api/search/query?querytext='trombone'
```

is a search query, against the REST API:

```
http://server/site/_api/search/query?querytext='trombone'&sortlist=
    'LastModifiedTime:descending,Rank:ascending'
```

is the same query with a two-level sort added.

If you want to understand how a given search works, it usually helps to look at the URL involved because the search parameters are there in plain sunlight.

A simple technique for using search is to simply grab the URL from a query you like and save it as a link. Following that link will then run the query and give you the results. You can use this as a static link, as a favorite, inside a program, and so on.

Using REST and CSOM to Query Search

With SharePoint 2013, there are two APIs available for queries: the Client Side Object Model (CSOM) and a REST API. You can use any language with either of these. However, it is often most natural to use JavaScript with the REST interface and to use the CSOM from managed code (such as C#).

Using the REST API with JavaScript

As described earlier, the REST API takes the form of a search URL, such as:

```
http://server/site/_api/search/query?querytext='{KQL Query}'
```

With JavaScript you can use this URL with an HTTP GET and get results via JSON. The action is all in a simple `ajax` call:

```
$.ajax(
        {
            url: Results.url,
            method: "GET",
            headers: {
                "accept": "application/json;odata=verbose",
            },
            success: Results.onSuccess,
            error: Results.onError
        }
    );
```

You can use the REST API with managed code including C# as well; though, it's slightly more involved. You don't see the code for that here, but following are code samples available via MSDN.

The REST API has three calls for search, as shown in Table 9-1.

TABLE 9-1: REST API's Search Calls

METHOD	REST URL	DESCRIPTION
query	`http://host/site/_api/search/query`	Uses HTTP Get Used to retrieve search results
postquery	`http://host/site/_api/search/postquery`	Uses HTTP POST Used to retrieve search results with URIs longer than you can do with "query" (> 4096 character query)
suggest	`http://host/site/_api/search/suggest`	Uses HTTP GET Used to retrieve query suggestions

If you were using the Query Web Service with SharePoint 2010, it is deprecated and replaced with the REST API. This SOAP web service uses the `search.asmx` page, and it works only when running in "14 mode".

Using the CSOM API with C#

To use the CSOM with C# is straightforward. You create a client context, and specify the site and query string:

```
ClientContext cctx = new ClientContext("http://site");
KeywordQuery query = new KeywordQuery(cctx);
query.QueryText = "{KQL}";
```

Then to execute the query is a CSOM call, as follows:

```
SearchExecutor executor = new SearchExecutor(cctx);
ClientResult<ResultTableCollection> results = executor.ExecuteQuery(query);
cctx.ExecuteQuery();
```

The results appear in a table that you can iterate over:

```
ResultTable result = results.Value[0];
foreach (var r in result.ResultRows)
{}
```

You can also use JavaScript with the CSOM; though it applies only to SharePoint-Hosted apps. If you are self-hosted (running remote applications), C# is recommended with the CSOM.

As with the REST API, the CSOM enables you to get query suggestions and search results. (You can get either prequery suggestions or post-query suggestions.)

Search Query Syntax

The REST and CSOM APIs are the methods for submitting queries. But what do you put in the query strings? The query string is where the action is, and the syntax is important to know.

A query request from a query client normally contains the following main parts:

➤ *The user query* — This consists of the query terms that the user types into a query box found on the user interface. In most cases, the user simply types one or more words, but the user query may also include special characters such as "+"and "−". The user query will normally be treated as a string that is passed transparently by the query client on the interface.

➤ *Property filters* — These are additional constraints on the query that are added by the query client to limit the result set. These may include filters limiting the results by creation date, file type, written language, or any other meta data associated with the indexed items.

➤ *Query features and options* — These are additional query parameters that specify how a query is executed and how the query result is to be returned. This includes linguistic options, refinement options, and relevancy options.

Search in SharePoint 2013 supports two search syntax types for building search queries:

➤ *Keyword Query Language (KQL) syntax* — The syntax that users typically see. KQL in SharePoint 2013 is a continuation of KQL from SharePoint 2007 and SharePoint 2010, with some additional capabilities.

➤ *FAST Query Language (FQL)* — A more powerful, more complex syntax appropriate for programmatic query creation. FQL is a continuation of the FQL syntax from FAST ESP and FAST Search for SharePoint 2010; although, there are fewer operators and fewer capabilities exposed via FQL in SharePoint 2013.

You can create queries in either syntax on any edition of SharePoint 2013.

SQL syntax, which was available with SharePoint 2007 and 2010, has been dropped. If you have an application that used SQL for search queries, it won't run on SharePoint 2013. Everything you could do with SQL queries you can do with FQL queries now, but you need to rewrite the queries in the new syntax.

Keyword Query Language (KQL)

Keywords can be a word, a phrase, or a prefix. These can be simple (contributes to the search as an OR), included (must be present — for example, AND, denoted by +), or excluded (must not be present — for example, AND NOT, denoted by −).

Property filters provide you with a way to narrow the focus of the keyword search based on managed properties. These are used for parametric searches, which allow users to formulate queries by specifying a set of constraints on the managed property values. For example, searching for a wine with parameters of {Varietal: Red, Region: France, Rating: ≥90, Price: ≤$10} is easy to achieve with property filters and easy to explore using refiners.

KQL supports using multiple property filters within the same query. You can use multiple instances of the same property filter or different property filters. When you use multiple instances of the same filter, it means OR; for example, `author:"Charles Dickens" author:"Emily Bronte"` returns results with either author. When you use different property filters, it means AND; for example, `author:"Isaac Asimov" title:"Foundation*"` returns only results that match both. Property filters also enable you to collapse duplicates; for example, `duplicate:http://<displayUrl>` requests duplicate items for the specified URL (which would otherwise be collapsed).

KQL was enhanced with SharePoint 2010 to support wildcard suffix matching, grouping of query terms, parentheses, and logical operators, such as AND, OR, NOT, and NEAR. With SharePoint 2013, the only additions to KQL are for ranking. The dynamic ranking operator (XRANK) is now available with KQL, as is the WORDS operator, which are covered shortly. The KQL syntax reference is at `http://msdn.microsoft.com/en-us/library/sharepoint/ee558911.aspx`.

Search query syntax is generally straightforward, but there are several tricky things to watch out for. First of all, the entire query is a string, so property filters must not have white space. The query `author:"John Smith"` does not return the same results as the query `author: "John Smith"` (with a space after the colon). Instead, it returns items that contain "John Smith" where the author is blank. Secondly, queries are literal and may miss content. For example the query `"northeast sales pptx"` won't match Office 2007 documents, whose file extension is ppt. In addition, there are many operators and parameters that may not have obvious use until you gain some experience with them.

FAST Query Language (FQL)

The FAST Query Language (FQL) is intended for programmatic creation of queries. It is a structured language and not intended to be exposed to the end users. FQL has more operators than KQL and has a set of parameters that modify the operators. Like KQL, you can work with properties, but there is a lot more you can do. The basic syntax of an FQL query looks like this:

```
[property-spec]:operator(operand [,operand]* [, parameter="value"]*)
```

In addition to the KQL operators, FQL provides a number of additional operators, more wildcard capabilities, and more relevance control. The operators include:

➤ Numeric operators (FLOAT, INT, and DATETIME)

➤ Strong operators (WEIGHT, WILDCARD, and MODE)

➤ Boundary matching (STARTS-WITH, ENDS-WITH, and EQUAL)

➤ More wildcard options (? and postfix * and ?)

➤ Complex combinations of query operators, such as nesting of boolean operators

FQL syntax enables nested expressions, so you can wrap queries with other operators. For example, if you want to limit items to particular languages, you could leave the original query expression intact and use:

```
and(filter(languages:or("en", "de"))),
    <your query expression>)
```

To limit results to a particular price range you can use:

```
and(price:range(100, 200) <your query expression>)
```

FQL opens a whole world of search operations to the developer. The full set of capabilities is too long to cover in this book, but you can refer to the FQL syntax reference at `http://msdn.micro` `soft.com/en-us/library/sharepoint/ff394606.aspx`.

Affecting Relevance via a Query

It may seem like there are a lot of weird query operators that overlap, for example OR, ANY, and WORDS. The reason for this is relevance control. There are cases in which you want to affect relevance in different ways, and you can do this in your query through the choice of operators and through the specification of a rank profile in the query.

For example, the WORDS operator provides ranking in the same manner as synonyms. For example, the query:

```
WORDS(Dog, Mutt, Cur)
```

retrieves the same items as the query:

```
Dog OR Mutt OR Cur
```

But the ranking counts the WORDS example so that a document containing four occurrences of Dog, three occurrences of Mutt, and two occurrences of Cur would rank the same as a document with nine occurrences of Dog, higher than it ranks with the OR example.

STRING operators in FQL enable you to explicitly put a ranking weight on a term to emphasize an operand that would otherwise get "lost" in the results.

```
string<"operand">[,weight=<value>]
```

The query:

```
or(string("Linq", weight=200), jquery, ajax)
```

can find documents on Linq, JQuery, or Ajax but put particular emphasis on Linq and put these at the top of the results.

XRANK

Changing relevance using queries is an incredibly powerful technique and enables you to easily create search experiences that account for a user's context, preferences, and choices. You may want to bias results, for example, based on a selection of authors the user has chosen but without filtering out other items completely. This technique is sometimes called using *influencers* as opposed to *refiners*.

You get detailed control of ranking at query time using the XRANK operators.

```
xrank(<match expression> [, <rank-expression>]*, rank-parameter[, rank-parameter]*)
```

XRANK was available for FAST Search for SharePoint but the syntax has changed a bit with SharePoint 2013.

XRANK and WORD are now available for both KQL and FQL queries. This makes it straightforward to take an end user query and add an XRANK operator for ranking control without needing to reformat it into FQL syntax.

For example, say you want to boost results from either of two people, Diane Talbot or Mary Baker. Using XRANK, you would form this query:

```
xrank("SharePoint 2013 Development", person:"diane talbot", person:"mary baker"),
nb=1.5)
```

You can use XRANK for managed properties, not just for the full-text index. Using a set of parameters, you can influence ranking in a wide variety of ways.

Examples Using Query Customization

This section shows how to apply query customization through a few examples with simple applications.

Picture Search Example

Imagine you wanted to implement an image search where pictures display if they match a query but only if they are in a picture library. You do this simply by using a KQL query with property filters:

```
{query-string},
isDocument:1, ContentClass:STS_ListItem_PictureLibrary
```

In this case, the properties are built-in managed properties. `isDocument` indicates whether this item is a container (such as a folder in a document library) or not, so `isDocument:1` tells search not to return folders. `ContentClass` describes what kind of content this is, and in this case you ask only for members of picture libraries.

One of the great things about learning and using query customization is that it can be applied easily. In this example, the property filters could be specified as a fixed part of the query simply by configuring the search results web part. A final touch for this application would be to create XSLT that formatted the search result to display pictures and their meta data in an appealing UI.

Topic Page Example

You can use a similar approach to create topic pages, where content around a particular topic is gathered even if the content is in different site collections or even different farms. The KQL query:

```
{topic-query-string},
isDocument:1, ContentClass:STS_ListItem_DiscussionBoard
```

handles items from any discussion board. For a topic page, a useful technique is to have the whole query be a fixed query and let the page-load event, which loads the web part, fire the initial query. It is straightforward to modify the content query web part to use enterprise search queries and format and display enterprise search results. There are several blog postings on this subject and commercial web parts available that do this.

Query Builder

SharePoint 2013 provides a new tool that helps users to visually build complex queries, called the Query Builder. The Query Builder shows up throughout the admin interface (as shown in Figure 9-16) when there's an option to manipulate or transform the search query. It is found in several places – in Query Rule configuration, Result Source configuration, and in the CSWP. This means that complex queries will be more common because they can come from programs, advanced search, or the Query Builder. This Query Builder is used pervasively, for example, when you edit query rules or result blocks. It shows you results, including refiners and sorting, so you can use it to test queries as well.

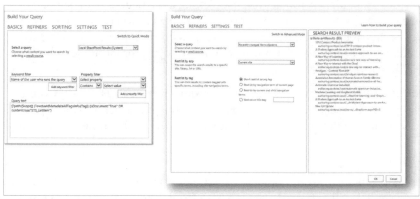

FIGURE 9-16

For developers, testing queries via the Query Builder is useful, but often insufficient. There is a great separate query test tool available on Codeplex at `http://sp2013searchtool.codeplex.com`. As shown in Figure 9-17, this tool provides precise control of the many different flags and options for search queries, and it lets you see results, refinements, query suggestions, and more directly in the tool. It's a handy utility, and you will use it heavily if you develop with complex queries.

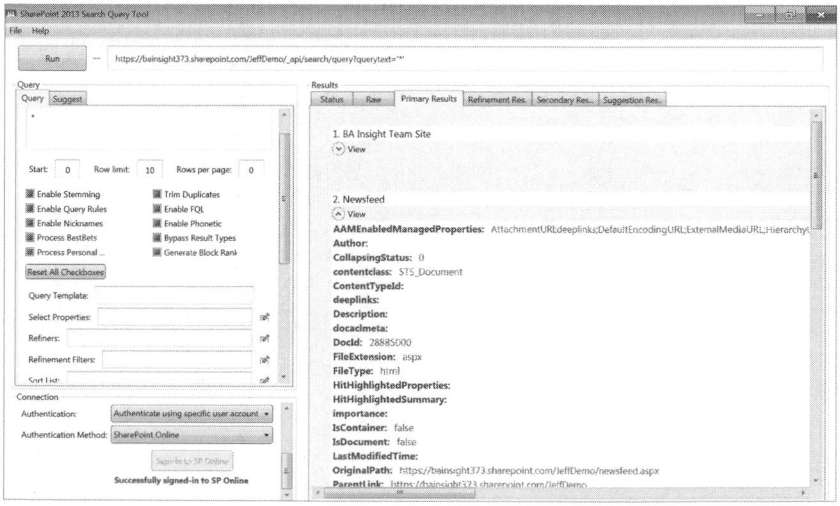

FIGURE 9-17

Query Rules

Query rules are a new feature in SharePoint 2013 that is designed to make query processing easy. There are limitations to query rules: For example, you can't call an external program from a query rule. But they give you a lot of power without a lot of complexity. You have access to lots of context that lets you infer the intent of a query. You have a remarkable amount of control over how the query is handled — how it is expanded or rewritten, what result sources it is applied to, and so on. And you can easily control how results display, as already covered.

In a query rule, you specify conditions and correlated actions. The actions specified in the rule change the search results; for example, narrowing results, picking a particular result source, or changing the order in which results display. Say you have an intranet site where all company events are maintained in a library that you have shared as a catalog, and you want to promote a particular seminar. To do this, you create a query rule that boosts that event to the top of the search results when someone searches for **seminar** or **event**.

There were some capabilities in SharePoint 2010 that processed queries, such as the keyword features that applied to synonyms, best bets, and promotions/demotions; these are all now replaced by query rules. When you become familiar with this new feature, you will find you can work wonders.

Query Rules Framework

The Query Rules framework is quite powerful but also straightforward to understand. The configuration UI, as shown in Figure 9-18, illustrates the main parts of this framework. You can also configure these via PowerShell.

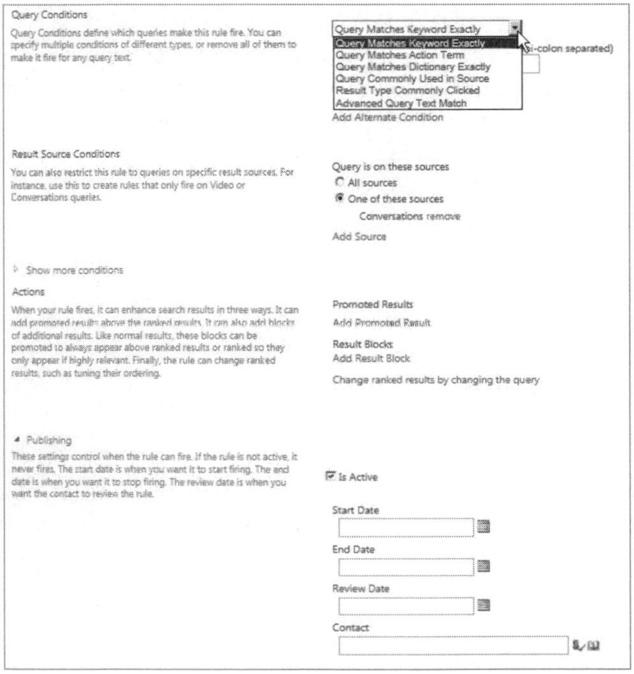

FIGURE 9-18

Query Conditions range from simple ones (query contains a specific word), through more sophisticated ones (query is common in a particular source), to advanced rules that can match across a set of terms, a dictionary, regular expressions, and so on.

Result Source Conditions control where the query is applied (discussed later in this chapter); in a nutshell they are the systems or types of content being searched. This lets you steer queries to different sources based on the query conditions.

Query Actions control what happens when the conditions are met. This enables you to add results or result blocks and to control ranking or query processing through changes to the query. There are three main parts to this:

➤ *Promoted results* — You can specify if the returned action should be treated as a hyperlink (behaving like a Best Bet) or as a fully formatted HTML block (behaving like the Visual Best Bet feature from FAST Search).

➤ *Result blocks* — As described earlier in this chapter, a result block is essentially a result set that is displayed all together; multiple result blocks can be used with different query conditions on each if wanted.

➤ *Change the ranked results by changing the query* — Sometimes known as query rewriting, this is powerful. You can add terms to the query or change them. By using XRANK you can also change the result ranking without changing the selection of results. For example, if the condition of the rule is met, boost the result's relevance ranking by a specific number of points.

You use publishing to control when a rule applies. For example, a benefits enrollment that is available for a limited time might be promoted through a visual best bet — but only during the enrollment period.

Query rules are typically quite simple and intuitive. They can also get fairly complex because you can have multiple query conditions, multiple result sources, and multiple result blocks and query transformations. As a developer, you can create some exciting things using query rules, especially when combined with display templates. Often the techniques you will use are heuristic — the trick with query processing is that you are trying to figure out what the user wants from a small query and a set of limited context. There are some inspiring examples at `http://blogs.msdn.com/b/carloshm/archive/2012/12/16/how-to-use-query-rules-and-display-templates-to-detect-the-intent-of-your-users.aspx`.

Query Transforms and Query Variables

Queries can be modified in a number of places in SharePoint 2013. These include web parts, query rules, and result sources, as shown in Figure 9-19. Each of these enables the user to launch the Query Builder. Each of these places transforms the query. The transformation is conditional in query rules, depending on the query and many other contextual variables.

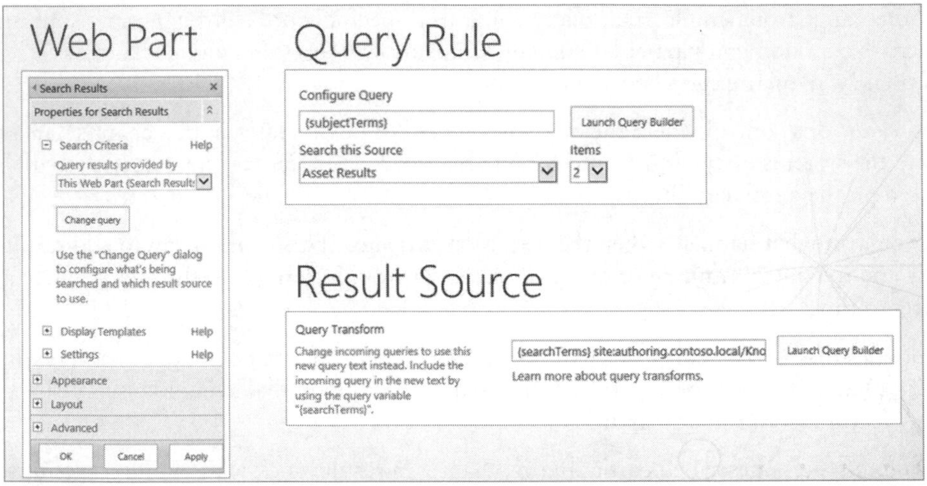

FIGURE 9-19

The interactions between Query conditions and actions are done through query variables. There are a number of variables, which can be modified by web parts, by query rules, or by custom code. For example, a Search web part might have a static query store configured. A user typing **laptop** sets the `searchBoxQuery` variable to "laptop," and the web part modifies the `searchTerms` variable to "laptop store."

A query rule modifies these query variables. This can be as direct as selecting a result source. For example, this query rule selects the product results source (for example, for an online shopping site):

```
searchTerms := {searchTerms} site:…
result source := Product Results
```

Imagine you have a query rule such as:

```
Matches Action Term ProductType
    actionTerms := match
    subjectTerms := remainder
```

And you have a termset ProductType that contains various products, including Laptop. A query `Laptop battery` would set `actionTerms` to `Laptop` and `subjectTerms` to `battery`. A query action such as:

```
Result Block with
  {subjectTerms}
  contenttype:{actionTerms}
from Product Results
```

selects the Laptop result template and sets `contenttype` to `battery`, triggering a displayed result that is tailored, as shown in the section on Result templates.

Query variables cover a wide range and provide the developer an enormous amount of power. You can control the interactions between query rules (stop/continue) and also steer actions toward web parts. (This is particularly visible in the CSWP.) There are many available query variables that provide context when you get into creating more complex query actions or result templates, including:

➤ *Site and site collection properties* — URL, site.ID of the site, and essentially any property from the site where the query was issued are available to you as query variables.

➤ *Page, query string, and request properties* — The URL is parsed for you as query variables. You also can access the URL of the page where the query was issued and the fields on the page, as well as the usage analytics for that page.

➤ *User properties* — If the query is on behalf of authenticated users, you get the users' name, e-mail, locale, preferred language, and any property from their user profile. This enables you to create contextual search experiences — as personalized as you like.

➤ *Term and term set properties* — Because site navigation in WCM is now controlled by the term store, you can use this to understand where you are in the site or catalog.

➤ *List and list item properties* — For queries against "this list," you can access the URL and any property of the current list or current list item.

A note on syntax: Spaces matter, and multiple-valued query variables are tricky. Query variables may contain spaces (such as "Mark Twain") but spaces are used to tokenize queries provided by users. Multiple tokens that aren't in double quotes are taken as OR'd values. With query variables you use special syntax to get around the gotchas in this area:

➤ Use the escape character when concatenating multiple values. For example: `customProperty:"{\User.Name};{\User.ZipCode}"` would become `customProperty:"Mark Twain;90210"`.

➤ Some query variables may return multiple values; you should explicitly OR these: `{|ManagedProperty:{QueryVariable}}`. Multivalued variables work properly only or columns of type Managed Metadata, and you cannot use ANDs, only ORs.

Example with Localized Results

You may want to display results that are personalized to each user's department and office location. Someone searching for **cafeteria menu** most likely wants to see what's for lunch in the office where she works.

This can be done by using query variables, in particular looking at fields in the user's profile (from the SharePoint profile store). `{User.LCID}` will be the numeric value of the locale from the user's profile, and you can use this as a filter in the query.

The query rule conditions to do this are simple (with `Lunch_Topic` containing a set of synonym terms, and the content tagged with locale IDs):

```
Matches Lunch_Topic Exactly
    searchTerms := all
        location:{User.LCID}
```

To boost results requires slightly more finesse. For example, the Finance Department may want to see results that have "finance" in them ahead of others.

However, you wouldn't want to simply add the term "finance" into the query in this case. Adding it via "AND finance" would remove many wanted results; adding it via "OR finance" would bring back many things that matched only the term "finance" and weren't what the user was looking for in his or her query.

You can use query rules to select a result source with particular content types (such as Excel files) ahead of other types, or use query actions to promote particular file types. Either of these might be enough. But you can also use code to apply XRANK to change the relevance ranking of the results. The query:

```
XRANK(query-string,"finance")
```

will have the wanted effect. Only results that match `query-string` will be returned, but those that contain the word "finance" will show up higher on the list. XRANK can apply to properties, as well as allowing an explicit boost parameter.

Summary — Working with Queries

The query side of search has a remarkable amount of power, and customizing search with queries in SharePoint 2013 is remarkably simple. It is important to understand the basic query syntax (KQL and FQL) because you modify queries in web parts, query rules, and result sources in addition to fully custom programs. The CSOM and REST APIs are the ways to work with queries and query suggestions programmatically. You can also treat a query URL as a link to set precanned queries into your solutions.

WORKING WITH CONTENT

There are two ways to get content into a search application: indexing and federation. Both of these show up as result sources in SharePoint 2013; though, the mechanisms are quite different. Indexing involves crawling content, doing linguistic processing and content enrichment on that content, and then creating a complex internal set of data structures (called an index) optimized for retrieval. The index is kept within the farm as a set of index partitions, and queries are matched against that index. Federation sends queries to other search instances (either SharePoint search or other forms) and may send queries to multiple search instances and then combine the results.

As a developer, you can find reasons to use both of these techniques. In the rest of this section, you walk through content capture for indexing, content processing, and then federation using result sources.

Content Capture — Crawling and Connectors

The "Back Door" to search engines — the content side — is as important as the query side. Capturing content is fundamental to search. If it's not crawled and indexed, you can't find it!

You can get a big win quickly in a search project, often simply by bringing in additional content. Typical enterprises have hundreds of repositories of dozens of different types, and accessing this content easily and securely is a huge problem — one that is easy to solve using search. Bridging content silos in an intuitive UI is one of the primary benefits of many search applications.

SharePoint 2013 search can access content from anywhere, not just content from within SharePoint. This is supported through a set of pre-created connectors, plus a framework and set of tools that make it possible to create and administer connectivity to whatever source you like. There is already a rich set of partner-built connectors to choose from, and as a developer, you can easily leverage these or add to them.

Crawling and Connectors Fundamentals

The process of connecting to content sources, crawling them to get content, and making that content searchable is far more complex than most people realize. It was also one of the most frustrating areas to manage with SharePoint 2010.

The high-level steps involved in crawling are shown in Figure 9-20. A connector establishes secure access to a particular content source (usually on a read-only basis). All the content to be indexed is extracted from the source system, and the meta data fields are mapped into crawled properties. The first crawl, called a *full crawl*, is the most onerous. It enumerates all the content, extracts it, and maps it. (This can take significant time if the content is large, especially because the goal is usually to have no operational impact on the source system.) Subsequent crawls, called incremental crawls, extract only information that has changed since the last crawl — usually a tiny fraction of the full crawl.

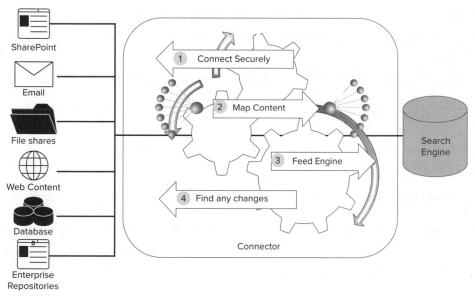

FIGURE 9-20

This basic process is standard for all search engines. The factors that differ between different search engines are:

➤ Number and range of prebuilt connectors for different source systems

➤ Support for different security models (which can get quite complex)

➤ Throughput (documents per second)

➤ Latency (freshness — the time from when content changes to when it is searchable)

➤ Robustness and fault tolerance

➤ Ease of administration

➤ Mechanisms and tooling for extending connectors and building custom connectors

SharePoint 2013 is strong in all of this; although, most connectors are supplied by Microsoft's partners, not Microsoft.

Using Out-of-the-box Connectors

SharePoint 2013 supports multiple crawl components, crawl databases, and content sources, as shown here. There are a number of connectors included out-of-the-box:

➤ *SharePoint Connector* — The most heavily used connector. This supports crawling older versions of SharePoint as well as SharePoint 2013. It now has a continuous crawling feature, which provides great freshness.

➤ *Web crawler (HTTP)* — For getting at websites (both external and internal)

➤ *File System Crawler* — Which supports a variety of filesystem types

➤ *Business Data Connectivity (BDC) Framework* — The primary way to create new connectors.

SharePoint 2013 also includes several OOB connectors that are built on the BDC framework:

➤ Taxonomy Connector (connects to MMS)

➤ People Profile Connector

➤ Exchange Public Folders Connector (does not access private mailboxes)

➤ Lotus Notes Connector

➤ Documentum Connector

The capabilities of the different OOB connectors and the connector framework are shown in Figure 9-21.

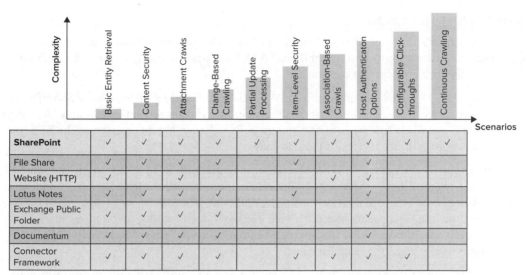

	Basic Entity Retrieval	Content Security	Attachment Crawls	Change-Based Crawling	Partial Update Processing	Item-Level Security	Association-Based Crawls	Host Authenticaton Options	Configurable Click-throughs	Continuous Crawling
SharePoint	✓	✓	✓	✓	✓	✓	✓	✓	✓	✓
File Share	✓	✓	✓	✓		✓		✓		
Website (HTTP)	✓		✓				✓	✓		
Lotus Notes	✓	✓	✓	✓		✓		✓		
Exchange Public Folder	✓	✓	✓	✓				✓		
Documentum	✓	✓	✓	✓				✓		
Connector Framework	✓	✓	✓	✓		✓	✓	✓	✓	

FIGURE 9-21

Most of the connectors are basically the same connectors from SharePoint 2010. The BDC framework and crawler infrastructure are also basically the same as SharePoint 2010 — an exception since most of the rest of search in SharePoint 2013 is brand new. There are, however, a few notable changes:

➤ *Continuous Crawling (SharePoint connector)* — Previously, SharePoint crawls could previously have a freshness (latency) of several minutes, even for incremental crawls. Crawls could also get backed up, and there were situations in which freshness could spike to hours. Continuous crawling addresses this, essentially by spawning threads to crawl as needed, so content is much fresher (tens of seconds) and consistently fresh.

➤ *Anonymous Crawl for HTTP (web crawler)* — SharePoint 2010 used the spsearch account to log into sites, which stymied many people trying to crawl SharePoint sites with anonymous access, public websites, and the like. SharePoint 2013 now offers a pain-free way to perform this task.

➤ *Asynchronous Web Part Crawl (web crawler)* — SharePoint sites that load web parts asynchronously (which dramatically speeds up the first display of the page) posed a problem for the crawler in SharePoint 2010, and search delivered incomplete information for these sites as a result. In SharePoint 2013 search, the crawler now gets a full rendering of the page to index them. This doesn't work for all asynchronous pages, just for most out-of-the-box web part content. But it takes care of the vast majority of problems in this area.

➤ *Claims support via the BDC* — For developers, the most important changes to connectors are in security. The BDC-based connector framework provided only AD ACLs with SharePoint 2010, and it now supports claims with SharePoint 2013. There is also a new security trimmer interface to handle complex security scenarios, which are covered a bit later.

FAST Connectors Removed

This area is one in which people coming from FAST Search for SharePoint will notice the most changes. Unfortunately, a number of capabilities FAST users have enjoyed are not in SharePoint 2013. The notable ones for content capture are

➤ *Content API* — This was an API from FAST (both ESP and FAST Search for SharePoint) that is removed. There is no API to push content into the SharePoint 2013 index. As a developer you can likely find ways to fit a system with a change-log mechanism to the BCS, but there is no way to truly create a push-to-index.

➤ *Enterprise Web Crawler* — The web crawler in SharePoint 2013 is essentially the same as the SharePoint 2010 one. FAST provided an additional crawler with a variety of high-end features. These included high performance, rendering of dynamic sites (executing JavaScript while crawling, and so on), pluggable seed and crawl frameworks, and a large number of operating parameters. These features can be important for large-scale crawling, public-content-harvesting, or other scenarios.

➤ *Java Database Connectivity (JDBC) connector* — FAST provided a direct connection to databases with SQL plug-ins; for many FAST developers this was a Swiss Army knife. Most of the scenarios covered by this connector, however, can be supported via the BCS.

➤ *Lotus Notes connector* — There is a Notes connector available from Microsoft with SharePoint 2013, the same as the SharePoint 2010 one. FAST provided a higher-end connector for Notes with the ability to handle dynamic security, change meta data, and work with higher performance.

Many of these gaps are covered via software from Microsoft partners.

Indexing Changes Improve Content Capture

The core indexing engine is radically different with SharePoint 2013. The indexer is higher performance, has lower latency, and is much more robust. As a developer, the indexing process is opaque to you. You can't access or change it, and there isn't an intermediate form you can easily access (as there was with FAST FixML previously). But you should be aware of these changes because they can make your life easier.

There are several examples in connectors and crawling where these changes are evident. Continuous crawling, for instance, is made possible partially by the lower latency of the indexing process. The robustness of the indexer, and in particular the atomicity of the indexing process, alleviates many of the strange issues seen with crawling in SharePoint 2010, especially those caused by items left in the index after outage events that were no longer in the crawl database (or vice versa). Schema management is much simpler (and also multitenant), and this benefits connectors because meta-data mapping is one of the functions of connectors. And the powerful content processing available with SharePoint 2013 is experienced by end users as better content.

Connectors and Connector Framework

SharePoint Server 2013 still supports existing protocol handlers (custom interfaces written in unmanaged C++ code) used since MOSS 2003. However, the protocol handler interface has been deprecated for a long time, and the BCS is the recommended way to create indexing connectors. If you have a legacy protocol handler, this is the time to rewrite it.

The Connector Framework uses .NET assemblies and supports the BCS declarative methodology for creating and expressing connections. It also enables connector authoring by means of managed code. This increased flexibility, with enhanced APIs and a seamless end-to-end experience for creating, deploying, and managing connectors, makes the job of collecting and indexing data considerably easier. See Chapters 13 and 14 for more information on BCS overall.

Creating an indexing connector using BCS does require some special attention. If you create an external list using BCS, you don't automatically get an indexing connector. And you don't need all the capabilities of BCS to create indexing connectors. (For example, usually indexing connectors read only; they don't create, delete, or update source information.)

The scenarios for creating indexing connectors are summarized in Figure 9-22. There are two parts to a connector: the connector code, which handles the connectivity and the connector methods, and the model file, which describes the structure of the host system. The connector framework uses the model file to connect the connector code to the crawling subsystem in search.

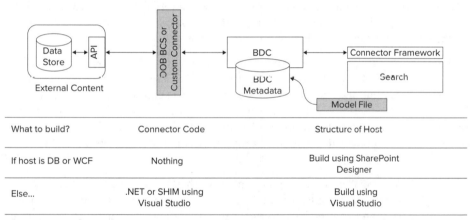

What to build?	Connector Code	Structure of Host
If host is DB or WCF	Nothing	Build using SharePoint Designer
Else...	.NET or SHIM using Visual Studio	Build using Visual Studio

FIGURE 9-22

Model Files

Every indexing connector needs a *model file* (also called an *application definition file*) to express connection information and the structure of the back end, and a BCS connector for code to execute when accessing the back end (also called a *shim*). The model file tells the search indexer what information from the repository to index and any custom-managed code that developers determine they must write (after consulting with their IT and database architects). The connector might require, for example, special methods for authenticating to a given repository and other methods for periodically picking up changes to the repository.

You can use OOB shims with the model file or write a custom shim. Either way, the deployment and connector management framework makes it easy — crawling content is no longer an obscure art. SharePoint 2013 also has great tooling support for connectors.

Using OOB shims (Database/WCF/.NET) is straightforward with SharePoint 2013. OOB shims are most appropriate when connecting to "flat" data structures for read-write or flat views for read-only look-ups, and custom shims often become necessary when connecting to complex data types (for example, multilevel hierarchies or tables with multiple relationships), or when fault tolerance logic needs to be applied (for example, to provide resiliency against source schema changes).

Chapters 13 and 14 provide examples of creating model files and deploying them. This chapter provides some indexing connector projects, to give you a sense of how they work. You can use two projects from this book's downloadable files to try out some BCS connectors. FlatFileBCSConnector. zip provides a simple BCS connector with a model file. XmlFileBCSConnector.zip gets a little more sophisticated and provides a connector for XML files.

For a database or a WCF source, you don't need to write connector code; the methods are all built in for you. For complex repositories, custom code enables you to access line-of-business data and make it searchable.

Writing Custom Connectors — Custom Shim

For complex repositories, custom code enables you to access line-of-business data and make it searchable. There are two types of custom connectors: a managed .NET Assembly BCS connector and a custom BCS connector. In this case, you use the .NET BCS connector approach. You need to create only two things: the URL parsing classes and a model file.

The code is written with .NET classes and compiled into a Dynamic Link Library (DLL). Each entity maps to a class in the DLL, and each BDC operation in that entity maps to a method inside that class. After the code is done and the model file is uploaded, you can register the new connector either by adding DLLs to the global assembly cache (GAC) or by using PowerShell cmdlets to register the BCS connector model file. Configuration of the connector is then available through the standard UI; the content sources, crawl rules, managed properties, crawl schedule, and crawl logs work as they do in any other repository.

If you chose to build a custom BCS connector, you implement the `ISystemUtility` interface for connectivity. For URL mapping, you implement the `ILobUri` and `INamingContainer` interfaces. Compile the code into a DLL and add the DLL to the GAC, author a model file for the custom back end, register the connector using PowerShell, and you are done. The SharePoint crawler invokes the `Execute()` method in the `ISystemUtility` class (as implemented by the custom shim), so you can put your special magic into this method.

A Few More Tips on Custom Connectors

The new connector framework takes care of a lot of things for you, but there are many elements you may want to take advantage of. Here are a couple more key capabilities worth knowing:

➤ *To create item-level security* — Implement the `GetSecurityDescriptor()` method. For each entity, add a method instance property:

```
<Property Name = "WindowsSecurityDescriptorField"
  Type ="System.Byte[]"> Field name </Property>
```

➤ *To crawl through entity associations* — For association navigators (foreign key relation-ships), add the following property:

```
<Property Name="DirectoryLink"
    Type="System.String"> NotUsed </Property>
```

Planning for Connector Development

Connector development is harder than it looks. If you are considering developing a connector, there are some factors worth your consideration:

➤ *Size of content source* — For small content sources, a straightforward implementation such as a custom BCS connector is fine. For large sources, optimizing the throughput makes a big difference in the time it takes to do a full crawl. The difference can be orders of magnitude for some systems.

➤ *Impact on the source system* — Some source systems are fragile, and a continual crawl may have an impact on production systems. You can mitigate this through crawl plans and exclude rules, but your connector may need to throttle its operations. You should also understand the maintenance windows for the source system in production and schedule crawling around these windows.

➤ *Security mapping* — Each system may have its own security, and mapping that security can be challenging. SharePoint 2013 enables claims information with content outside of SharePoint, which is a significant improvement over SharePoint 2010. However, accessing security claims from a source system is not simple, and mapping security entitlements across multiple systems is one of the most challenging aspects of indexing connectors. Some security schemes may push you toward real-time security trimming, which requires more development and has a significant performance impact on search performance; you cover custom security trimming shortly.

➤ *Data schema and APIs* — Systems with a static schema and direct database access are generally straightforward to write connectors for; a BCS connector fits this model well. Systems that have dynamically changing schemas, user-specific views, complex APIs, and so on become more challenging.

➤ *Maintenance* — If you connect to a commercial system (rather than one you have built), you may need to update your connector when there are updates to the system. Support and maintenance is ongoing and can be a significant effort.

The bottom line is that you shouldn't underestimate the effort involved in connector development and deployment. There are third-party connectors you can buy, and the growth of search with SharePoint and has grown this market — so there are options to buy or use third-party frameworks rather than build your own. Don't fear connector development, especially for moderate-scale systems with straightforward security and data schema. But watch out for the classic trap: a development project that gets to basic connectivity quickly but struggles to achieve security and scale and is then dragged further down in troubleshooting and maintenance as the source system changes. Plan your development carefully to avoid this trap.

Security Trimming

Enterprise Search must be secure. By design, search results match the entitlements on the indexed items. If you can't read it, you won't see it in your search results. When you use OOB connectors, this all "just works." But if you write your own connectors, it's important to be mindful of how search security works and to make sure your connectors handle security correctly.

Search Security Principles

Security is a deep subject, well beyond what you will cover here. But there are a few principles of security you need to keep in mind that are specific to search.

➤ *Authentication versus authorization* — Authentication, which is focused on "who are you?" is not the responsibility of search. SharePoint handles authentication at sign-on, and the user credentials are a given at query time. Authorization, which defines the access policy ("what can you see?") is the main focus in securing search items.

➤ *Level of granularity* — You can consider data access security at several levels: repository, item, or sub item. For the most part, search is focused on per-item security. Also, the entitlement that matters for search is whether the user has read access or not because search does not write to the source system. These are simplifying factors; you need to test only whether the search results accurately reflect the read access in the source system, on a per-item basis.

➤ *Crawling accounts* — Indexing connectors crawl once, in the context of a service account, rather than crawling in the context of each user. This is one of the reasons that OAUTH is not typically used for connectors. The crawling account must have read access to all the information you want to crawl, and the connector must access and transmit the entitlements on each item.

➤ *Timing and updates* — Unlike access in the source system, search captures the document entitlements at time A (crawl time) and uses them at time B (query time). This is a major complicating factor because it means that you have to provide security updates, and that the security entitlements may be stale until an incremental crawl has taken place.

➤ *Heterogeneous systems* — You may be crawling many different systems, each with its own security model. There has to be a correspondence somewhere, a mapping of all systems to a common security model. This isn't something you do when you write the connector, but it's one of the challenges in deploying a connector in the field.

The search index contains information for all users; but selecting only the results that a given user is entitled to read is called *security trimming*. There are two ways to handle security trimming:

➤ *Early binding* — The search engine index includes ACL information put into special fields at crawl time. These are matched at index time by ACLs created from the user authentication. The user credentials become another query term so that only the authorized results are returned. Figure 9-23 illustrates the matching done with early-binding security.

➤ *Late binding* — ALL security work is done at query time. A result set containing all matching results (independent of the user) is traversed as it's returned from the search index, and any results that aren't authorized for the current user are removed.

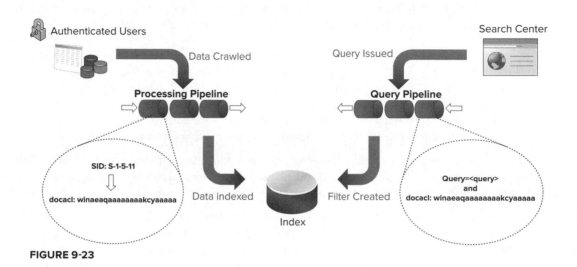

FIGURE 9-23

Generally speaking, early-binding security is much better than late-binding security, and SharePoint 2013 takes an early-binding approach as much as possible. Late binding carries a significant performance impact, because a much larger set of results may need to be returned (with many of them discarded on the fly). As a result, query latency with early binding is slow. Secondly, deep refiners are impossible with late binding. When some (or most) of a result set is thrown away, any deep refiners (which are created in a specialized index structure) no longer match the results. SharePoint 2010 search used a form of late binding, which resulted in latency and scale issues, and restricted it to shallow refinement. FAST used early binding, which is reflected in SharePoint 2013.

The main downside of early binding is complexity. Extra work is done by the connectors, crawler, and indexer, which also means that the indexing latency is somewhat longer and that the index is slightly larger. The BCS connector framework takes care of most of this complexity for you. But there are cases in which the source system security is complex enough that you have to do extra work, or where early binding alone just cannot do the job. This is where you need custom security trimming.

Custom Security Trimming

SharePoint 2013 provides APIs for two kinds of custom security trimmers:

➤ *Pre-trimmer* (`ISecurityTrimmerPre`) — This is a new capability, which rewrites the query prior to sending it to the index (much like the techniques explored in the subsection on working with queries).

➤ *Post-trimmer* (`ISecurityTrimmerPost`) — This implements late binding security, enabling you to remove items from the result set that don't match users' access rights. It is conceptually similar to the `ISecurityTrimmer2` interface from SharePoint 2010. Note that `ISecurityTrimmer2` is still supported but deprecated; this interface wasn't supported with FAST Search in 2010. If you are writing a new connector, you should definitely use `ISecurityTrimmerPost` and forget about `ISecurityTrimmer2`.

Each type of trimmer has an initialize method and a per-query method. The pre-trimmer uses `AddAccess` per query (before the query is executed) and the post-trimmer uses `CheckAccess` per query (after the query is executed). Trimmers are associated with a rule path (crawl rule) because you typically set up different security trimmers for different content sources. You can have multiple post trimmers associated with a crawl rule, which are executed in order. Deployment of security trimmers is a bit awkward; you have to restart the query component to register the rule.

As usual with security trimming, implementing the methods is not the biggest challenge. With claims types available in SharePoint 2013, the methods in the security trimmers can handle many security scenarios. Knowing what types of claims you have and what you want to change is the tough part.

Because post-trimmers add latency and make refiners inaccurate, they should be used carefully. A "last minute check" to double check results for high-security situations is one typical scenario. This overcomes the issue of stale entitlements due to crawl latency. It can ensure that users don't see results immediately if their entitlements were removed, but it can't make new results appear as soon as entitlements are added. Another scenario is handling the complex, dynamic security models, which are used in some source systems — ones where the security rights are encoded in dynamic or hierarchical rules, which can't be fully handled at crawl time.

Security trimmers are a specialized subject. In fact, they are among the most complex topics in search. In any scenario (pre-trimmer, post-trimmer, or combination), special care is recommended. There are some nice reference examples and walkthrough of custom security trimmers at `http://blogs.msdn.com/b/security_trimming_in_sharepoint_2013/`.

Customizing Content Enrichment

After capturing content securely, search processes that content in a variety of ways, preparing it for indexing. Understanding this processing and extending it allows you to create some remarkable search experiences.

Content Pipeline Processing

Human language is a tricky thing, and algorithms aimed at understanding it are complex and imperfect. Yet this is what makes it seems like "search just works" for end users. Linguistic processing, which aims to leverage the meaning of documents or words, is the "special sauce" of search — and one of the most mysterious and difficult to understand areas. The text analytic techniques are the realm of specialists, but as a developer you can integrate in a variety of techniques or create your own.

In preparing content for indexing, linguistics processing is applied in stages, each stage building on the previous one. Figure 9-24 gives an overview of the steps in what is often called the *content pipeline*. (The steps in gray are not OOB but illustrate some of what is possible by adding third-party components.)

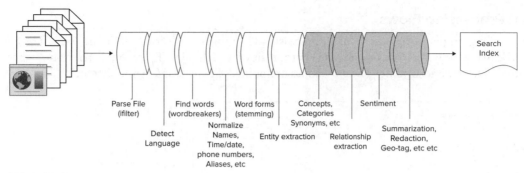

Parse File (ifilter) | Find words (wordbreakers) | Word forms (stemming) | Concepts, Categories Synonyms, etc | Sentiment

Detect Language

Normalize Names, Time/date, phone numbers, Aliases, etc

Entity extraction

Relationship extraction

Summarization, Redaction, Geo-tag, etc etc

Search Index

FIGURE 9-24

Document Parsing

SharePoint 2013 introduces a completely new document parsing facility, with some big improvements. These changes include:

➤ *Automatic file format* detection no longer relies on file extensions, eliminating the kind of errors that happened when users or applications do creative things like making .memo files.

➤ *Deep link extraction* works like a table of contents generator and allows you to click into previews for Word and PowerPoint formats.

➤ *Meta-data extraction* for titles, authors, and dates provides better meta data and is much easier to understand than the techniques used in SharePoint 2010 (where Optimistic Title extraction was one of the top sources of user confusion).

➤ *High-performance format handlers* for HTML, DOCX, PPTX, TXT, Image, XML, and PDF formats mean faster crawls and indexing.

This new parsing facility does not use the IFilter interface, which is a major change. The IFilter API is still supported and 64-bit IFilters will continue to work; though, there are some minor changes in behavior of this API. There's a large number of third-party IFilters available, and these will continue to be a key tool for you if you develop search solutions with different file formats (for example, DWG files). To make content in a particular file format searchable, that file format must be covered by the new document parsing facility or by an IFilter.

The 2010 Microsoft Filter Pack (which is also used by Exchange 2010, Windows Desktop Search 4, and SQL 2008, and 2010) isn't needed with SharePoint 2013. All 15 of the formats it supports are built in, plus 40 more (including PDF, Montage, Visio, and OneNote). For most scenarios this is plenty. However, you should still look at the need for IFilters (third party or custom) with any sophisticated search applications. There are hundreds of different file formats in the world — the Advanced Filter Pack for FAST Search supported 422 file types. Note that the Advanced Filter Pack is not supported for SharePoint 2013, so if you are migrating from FAST, you are more likely to need a third-party IFilter.

Content Processing Flows

There's a lot going on inside the Content Processing Component, as shown in Figure 9-25. The content processing flow populates the managed properties for each item. There are different branches for Insert, Delete, and Update. The gray boxes are points of extension/customization.

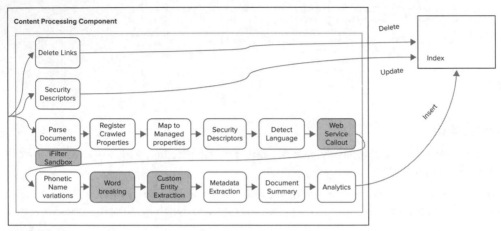

FIGURE 9-25

All of the content processing extensibility is currently limited to OnPremise deployments. This includes Entity Extractors, Custom word-breakers, Custom IFilters, and the Content Enrichment Web Service (CEWS). This means that they are not available via O365.

Content Enrichment Web Services (CEWS)

SharePoint 2013 provides a new way for developers to extend content processing, called the *Content Enrichment Web Service (CEWS)*. This API is a simple, high-performance mechanism to add linguistic processing. If you need summarization, geotagging, concept extraction, relationship extraction, and regular expression matching, it can be added via CEWS. If you want to add specialized low-level linguistics, this is a job for CEWS as well.

CEWS calls an external web service, as shown in Figure 9-26, using SOAP via a proxy. This is the only way to modify all content during indexing, independent of source.

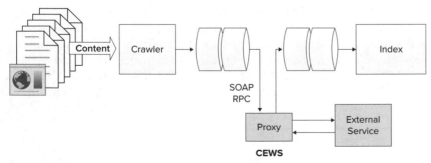

FIGURE 9-26

Using a web service callout opens up many options and removes some of the difficulties in writing pipeline extension stages (compared to previous FAST versions). FAST Search for SharePoint supported a content processing extension mechanism, which called an executable (running in a sandbox) with every item indexed, just before the end of the content processing pipeline. This mechanism was quite slow (because it called an executable each time), limited (because it could access only crawled properties and could not change any properties), and cumbersome (because it ran in a limited sandboxed environment with little tooling or diagnostics). Using a web service is far better.

With CEWS, the processing pipeline passes designated managed properties (including document text) to the remote service. There are hidden and read-only properties, but many managed properties (such as Title) can be modified.

The mechanism for CEWS is simple:

➤ The content processing component sends a SOAP RPC call to a configurable endpoint over HTTP.

➤ The payload contains an array of property objects.

➤ The web service performs some custom logic on the array of property objects and returns an array of modified or new property objects.

➤ The web service must send a response to the web service client within a given timeout.

No specific authentication or encryption mechanisms are supported as part of the contract. You can, however, apply your own security on the transport mechanism.

A trigger condition is registered in the ContentEnrichmentConfiguration object, which allows control of when the content flow calls out to an external web service. A set of PowerShell commandlets control the configuration, and there are robust error handling mechanisms built in.

Example CEWS Application

To understand how CEWS works, let's look at an example that implements a movie-rating program in a web service called by the CEWS mechanism. Given a set of content and managed properties (set up in the example), this takes you through creating a service and configuring it via PowerShell. Follow this using the file MovieService_CEWS_Example.cs from this book's downloadable files.

The web service implements the IContentProcessingEnrichmentService and first creates variables that will be populated by the web service. The CEWS provides managed properties to the web service and expects managed properties back. processedItemHolder is what the web service returns; it contains the managed properties:

```
namespace PopularMovieService
{

    public class PopularMovieService : IContentProcessingEnrichmentService
    {
        // Define variables to hold the managed properties that the
        //  web service will populate.
        private Property<Int64> NewIntegerMP = new Property<Int64>();
```

```
private Property<DateTime> NewDateTimeMP = new Property<DateTime>();

private readonly ProcessedItem processedItemHolder =
    new ProcessedItem
{
    ItemProperties = new List<AbstractProperty>()
};
```

Parsing the managed properties and creating new ones is a matter of iterating through the item properties. This is a simple service; you normalize the title by putting it in title case and calculate how long it has been since the release date. You also add a new managed property, which indicates when the item was processed by the web service:

```
foreach (var property in item.ItemProperties)
    {
        var s = property as Property<string>;
        if (s != null)
        {

            // The value of the new text managed property is the
            // string in title case.
            CultureInfo cultureInfo =
                Thread.CurrentThread.CurrentCulture;
            TextInfo textInfo = cultureInfo.TextInfo;
            string normalizedString =
                textInfo.ToTitleCase(s.Value.ToLower());
            s.Value = normalizedString;
            processedItemHolder.ItemProperties.Add(property);
        }

        var l = property as Property<Int64>;
        if (l != null)
        {
            // The value of the new integer managed property is the
            // number of years since the release date.
            int CurrentYear = DateTime.Now.Year;
            NewIntegerMP.Name = "YearsSinceRelease";
            NewIntegerMP.Value = CurrentYear - l.Value;
            processedItemHolder.ItemProperties.Add(NewIntegerMP);
        }

        // Set the time for when the properties where added by the
        // web service.
        NewDateTimeMP.Name = "ModifiedByWebService";
        NewDateTimeMP.Value = DateTime.Now;
        processedItemHolder.ItemProperties.Add(NewDateTimeMP);
    }
```

To activate the callout, create a configuration that includes the endpoint (this service), the input managed properties, and the output managed properties. This is done via PowerShell and looks like this:

```
$config = New-SPEnterpriseSearchContentEnrichmentConfiguration
$config.Endpoint = "http://localhost:817/PopularMovieService.svc"
$config.InputProperties = "Director", "Title", "ReleaseYear"
$config.OutputProperties = "Director", "Title", "YearsSinceRelease",
"ModifiedByWebService"
```

To bind this configuration to the wanted search application takes one more line of PowerShell. Note that there can be only one content enrichment configuration active on a search application at a time:

```
Set-SPEnterpriseSearchContentEnrichmentConfiguration
        -SearchApplication $ssa
        -ContentEnrichmentConfiguration $config
```

Now, content from crawls will be sent to this web service. Via the CEWS, three managed properties will be transmitted to the web service, and four will be returned.

Working with Federation and Result Sources

As mentioned earlier, there are two ways to get content into a search application: indexing and federation. Indexing was described and you saw how to create indexing connectors, how to handle security trimming, and how to extend the content processing that happens during indexing. But what about federation?

Principles of Federation

In addition to indexing information, search can present information to the user via federation. This is a "scatter-gather" approach: The same query is sent to a variety of different places, and the results display together on the same page. Federation is not a replacement for indexing, but it is an essential tool for situations in which indexing is impossible (web search engines have the whole web covered; you don't have the storage or computer power to keep up with that) or impractical. (You have an existing vertical search application that you don't want to touch.) Federation can also be a great mechanism for migration.

Figure 9-27 shows some of the situations in which you might use indexing and federation. The truth is indexing, if possible, is always better. If you index the content you can, among other things, control relevancy, freshness, performance, faceted navigation, and filtering for the end users. You add meta data or structure via content processing when you index. When you federate search indexes, you essentially relinquish control of these and become dependent on what the other system is capable of. With federation, the results are only as good as the "weakest link." Your results will be as slow as the slowest search engine queries and as relevant as the weakest search engine queried, and they won't have consistent meta data.

When to Use Indexing

- If there is no way to search a repository.
- You want common relevance ranking.
- You want to extract full text and metadata.
- You want to be able to scope to an arbitrary subset of content.
- The source search performance/reliability is insufficient.

When to Use Federation

- You need a quick, powerful way to bring together results across multiple search systems.
- Data is distributed across multiple repositories.
- Search already exists in the repository.
- Crawling is not feasible...
  - Cost or integration difficulty
  - Geo-distribution of systems
  - Proprietary / Legal restrictions on source content access

FIGURE 9-27

However, federation is an important technique and essential when indexing isn't possible. These cases are when there is too much content (federating to Bing or Google is sensible because you aren't going to recrawl the entire web) or when there is subscription content or other limited access (as found with many information services). It can also include cases with distributed content, rather than crawling from a central place or farm across a limited-bandwidth WAN. You can use federation to create a unified view across different systems.

OpenSearch

Microsoft has embraced federation wholeheartedly, in particular the OpenSearch standard. Microsoft began supporting OpenSearch in 2008 with the introduction of Search Server 2008. All of Microsoft's Enterprise Search products support OpenSearch, as does desktop search in Windows 7 and Windows 8, and Internet Explorer versions 8, 9, and 10.

OpenSearch is a standard for search federation, originally developed by Amazon.com for syndicating and aggregating search queries and results. It is a standard used throughout the industry, and new OpenSearch providers are created every day.

The operation of OpenSearch is shown in Figure 9-28. The basic operation involves a search client, which could be a desktop (Windows 8), a browser (Internet Explorer 10), or a server (SharePoint 2013). It also involves a search provider, which is any server with a searchable RSS feed, meaning that it accepts a query as a URL parameter and returns results in RSS/Atom.

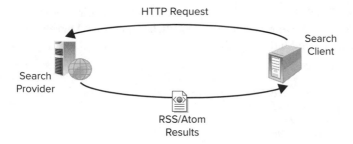

- HTTP Request with query in the URL:
  - http://www.site.com/srchrss.aspx?q={search Terms}
- RSS/Atom results:
  - RSS results with <title>, <Link>, <description>
  - Best sources also include:
    <pubdate>, <author>, <category>, <media:thumbnail>
  - Optionally include custom metadata:
    <recordid>, <projectname>, <contactnumber>

FIGURE 9-28

Example OpenSearch Provider

Let's see how a custom OpenSearch provider works. Try this using the file `OpenSearchProvider_AdventureWorksDB.zip` from this book's downloadable files. The project contains a number of files that comprise a product search and inventory search from the AdventureWorks database, several OSDX files, and OpenSearch providers for product search.

This code creates a simple RSS feed from the result of a database query, built on the AdventureWorks database:

```
resultsXML.Append("<rss version=\"2.0\"
xmlns:advworks=\"http://schemas.adventureworks.com/Products/Search/RSS\"
xmlns:media=\"http://search.yahoo.com/mrss/\">");
resultsXML.Append("<channel>");
resultsXML.AppendFormat("<title>Adventure Works: {0}</title>", queryTerm);
resultsXML.AppendFormat("<link>{1}?q={0}</link>", queryTerm, RSSPage);
resultsXML.Append("<description>Searches Products in the Adventure Works
database.</description>");
while (sqlReader.Read())
{
    ...
    resultsXML.Append("<item>");
    resultsXML.AppendFormat("<title>{0}</title>", sqlReader[0]);
    resultsXML.AppendFormat("<link>{1}?v={0}&amp;q={2}</link>", sqlReader[1],
    RSSPage, query);
    resultsXML.AppendFormat("<description>{0} ({1}) has {2} units of inventory and
    will need to order more at {3} units.</description>", sqlReader[0],
    sqlReader[1], sqlReader[2], sqlReader[4]);
    ...
    resultsXML.Append("</item>");
}
resultsXML.Append("</channel></rss>");
```

The behavior of this is described in an OSDX file, which is shown next. An OSDX file is simple XML, and clients such as Windows 8 can incorporate this with one click. Of course, SharePoint 2013 also acts as an OpenSearch client (as did SharePoint 2010):

```
<?xml version="1.0" encoding="UTF-8"?>
<OpenSearchDescription
xmlns:ms-ose="http://schemas.microsoft.com/opensearchext/2009/"
xmlns="http://a9.com/-/spec/opensearch/1.1/">
   <ShortName>ProductsSearch</ShortName>
   <Description>Searches the Adventure Works Products database.</Description>
   <Url type="text/html" template="http://demo/sites/advsearch-
prod/Pages/productresults.aspx?k={searchTerms} "/>
   <Url type="application/rss+xml"
template="http://demo/_layouts/adventureworks/productsearch.aspx?q={searchTerms}"/>
</OpenSearchDescription>
```

Understanding Result Sources

With SharePoint 2010, it was difficult for some organizations to provide organization-wide search. The standard way to do this was to centrally index all content in a large central farm, if the latency allowed. For global organizations, this was often not feasible. The only alternative was to field pages with multiple separate query boxes and result sets, which was not what users wanted.

SharePoint 2013 has a new mechanism called result sources, which enables you to federate across farms and support many distributed scenarios. Rather than crawling across the WAN, you can consider using remote result sources. If you have separate search systems on your site (for customers) and on your intranet (for employees), think about using result sources to include site search results in the intranet search.

There are four built-in result sources, as shown in Figure 9-29.

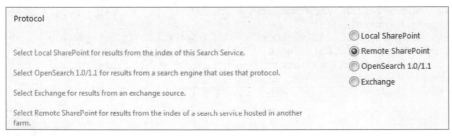

FIGURE 9-29

➤ *Local SharePoint (the default)* — Serves results from the search SSA serving this farm.

➤ *Remote SharePoint* — Serves results from another SharePoint 2013 SSA. This can be another on-premise system in a distributed configuration, or it can be SharePoint in O365. Hybrid configurations (SharePoint online can federate with the on-premise search engine or vice versa) are a primary focus for this capability.

> ➤ *OpenSearch* — Serves results from OpenSource providers. This can be an existing provider (there are several hundred) or one that you develop, as previously described. You can cover a wide range of systems with this technique. Note that refiners are not supported by OpenSearch.

> ➤ *Exchange* — Serves results from and Exchange 2013 instance so that users can search through their mailboxes along with SharePoint content. This is feasible because Echange 2013 uses the same core search engine as SharePoint 2013.

When combining result sources and result blocks, administrators can offer their users a single list of results composed of both local and remote results. Result sources are used to select result templates; OOB remote results are shown as result blocks (one per source) either above all results or merged within the local results returned.

In addition to handling federation, result sources also take over the function of scopes from SharePoint 2010. Result templates are bound to specific result sources, and result sources also are used in query actions, as shown in previous sections.

When considering result sources for your search application, there are a few factors you should be aware of:

> ➤ Result sources work only with SharePoint 2013; every federated farm must upgrade.

> ➤ Results are presented in result blocks, not interleaved.

> ➤ Refiners are not combined; they are driven by local content only.

For situations that require more, you can develop alternatives or extensions. However, this is a difficult area, and there are some partner-built alternatives that may be worth considering before delving too deeply. Despite these limitations, result sources are an important tool for creating search applications. There is a lot you can do simply with the OOB result sources, including support of hybrid and distributed configurations, and you can add your own using OpenSearch.

Summary — Working with Content

Search starts with content, and there is a lot to deal with on the development on the content side of SharePoint 2013 search. Even though the crawling and connector subsystem is the part of search that changed the least with SharePoint 2013, there are some significant enhancements, such as continuous crawling, web crawler improvements, and support of claims through BCS. A new set of security trimming APIs provides an ability to do pretrimming (a form of query modification, specifically for complex security scenarios) as well as post-trimming (late security binding).

The Content Processing component is new with SharePoint 2013 and provides four main extensibility points: IFilters, custom word-breakers, custom entity extractors, and the CEWS. Of these the CEWS is the most significant; it supports a wide range of content enrichment scenarios with a much cleaner, higher performance mechanism than the one provided with FAST Search for SharePoint. All content processing extensions are restricted to on-premise installations and are not available with Office 365.

Federation provides a mechanism for surfacing search content in situations in which you can't index or in which indexing is prohibitive. Federation and scopes are subsumed by a new SharePoint 2013 mechanism called *result sources*, which include local SharePoint, Exchange (opening up several scenarios with e-mail search), remote SharePoint (supporting distributed as well as hybrid cloud/on-premise configurations), and OpenSearch result sources.

TAILORING RELEVANCE

Search relevance is a deep subject encompassing many aspects. Although relevance is most formally focused on the order of search results in the result set, it encompasses the whole result experience — all the aspects of search quality. This includes the refinement or faceted navigation experience, and things like best bets and recommendations.

Tuning and tailoring search relevance has been a bit of a black art. Relevance is intrinsically hard because it is subjective (different people often have different "right" answers to the same query), because it is dealing with the vagaries of human language, and because the underlying optimization problem search attempts to solve is so hard that approximations and heuristics are required.

SharePoint 2013 makes search management much easier, including control of relevance, and this is a boon to the developer and the IT pro.

Managing Relevance via Queries and Content

Many of the mechanisms you have already covered are used in managing relevance. These include both query-side and content-side techniques.

Query-side Relevance Tools

Query rules are one of the prime mechanisms for controlling search quality (aka relevance). For example, query rules control best bets as well as setting content types and terms. They enable dynamic reordering, such as preferring a document from a specific source. Some of the key query-side tools in relevance management are:

➤ *Synonyms* — Using a set of synonyms, you can expand queries to improve the recall of items. Synonyms are deployed via a thesaurus (one per farm) and can also be supplied in query rules.

➤ *Query spelling correction* — Built from user behavior but can also be controlled via include and exclude terms kept in the SharePoint term store. For example, a query of "razar blades" will be spell-corrected to "razor blades," but if you want to exclude the brand name "RAZAR" so that you search for it without correction, simply go to the Search Dictionaries menu in the Term Store Management Tool, click on Query Spelling Exclusions, and create RAZAR as a term.

➤ *Query suggestions* — Added by default when users have clicked the results for that query at least six times; can also be seeded with phrases that always or never are used as query suggestions.

➤ *Query rules* — A key tool in controlling and managing relevance. This includes dynamic reordering rules that are translated under the hood into XRANK in queries. An example of this is shown in Figure 9-30.

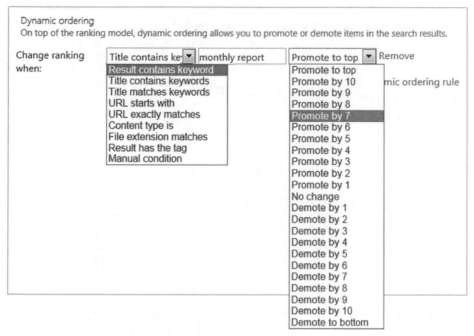

FIGURE 9-30

Some of the more sophisticated query rules are aimed at relevance. These include regex matching or dictionary matching.

Content-side Relevance Tools

The primary way to improve relevance via content-side work is by improving the content, so content enrichment plays a big role. Entity extraction, in particular, provides meta data for search and refinement. Custom entity extractors (created from the term store) and company name extraction are available as part of content processing for this.

Scoping a query to a specific source (either a content type or a result source) provides a higher-precision result. Historical (log-based) matches, including likely sources and likely content types, provide a way to open the rules up to the crowdsourcing behavior that is used to improve the base relevance.

Result Sources and Authorities

Result sources can scope or federate searches, and are a core tool for adjusting relevance. Authorities, which identify important data hubs, are another one.

Authorities are set on an SSA basis and enable you to configure the sites that are most important and the sites with low intrinsic relevance, as shown in Figure 9-31. The distance of an item from an authority that matches the query is an important ingredient in relevance.

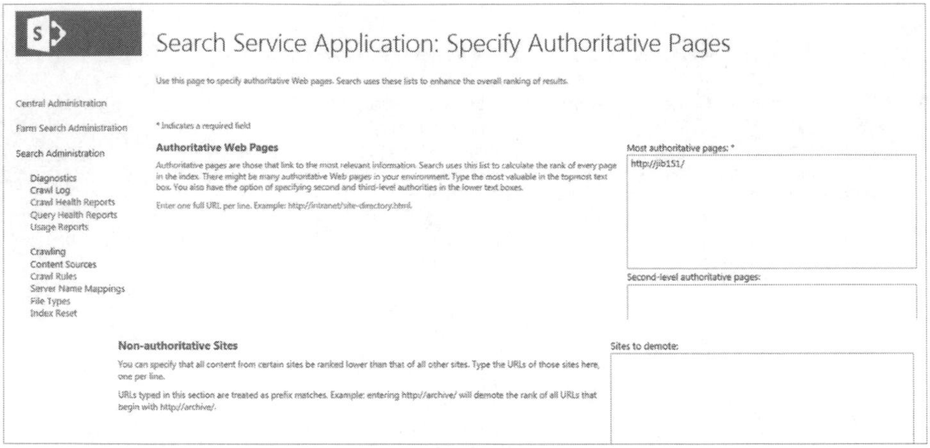

FIGURE 9-31

Rank Profiles

A rank profile is a construct that sets the weight of ranking for the fields in a search schema. There can be multiple rank profiles, and you can select a rank profile from a query. There is a new tuning tool, which helps you improve an existing ranking model or construct a new one.

Custom ranking models, with which you build relevance from ground zero, are not for the faint of heart. They should be used only after simpler options (authorities, thesaurus, query rules, dynamic rules, and so on) have been considered. But a custom rank profile can be an important part of a packaged search application or vertical. Because you can bind ranking models to sources with query rules, you can isolate any relevance changes to specific sources.

There are two predefined full-text indexes other than the default full-text index: the SharePoint Terms full-text index (SpTermsIdx) and the People index (PeopleIdx). This means that different relevance applies for WCM and for people search, versus content search, even though these are all provided by the same underlying search engine.

As a developer, you have two main ways of creating rank profiles: PowerShell and the SharePoint Administrative OM. Because SharePoint 2013 has good tools importing and exporting search settings, you can also create a rank profile and then import it on a new system.

Note that importing and exporting customized search settings is a great way to package your search solutions generally. You can do this through the CSOM, through the Site Settings page, or through PowerShell.

SharePoint 2013 has a new analytics component, which drives several parts of SharePoint. This replaces the web analytics and search reporting functions of SharePoint 2010. Note that this is one of the few areas in which running SharePoint 2013 in "14 mode" loses major functionality; there is no web analytics if you run in 14 mode.

Analytics uses information about user behavior (queries, clicks, and so on), which are derived from log information. Unlike SharePoint 2010, the search logs can be correlated with the web logs, and you can see how people got to searches and where they went after searches. Analytics also uses information about the relationships between content from the link database (created as part of content processing). Finally, there is information about system operations, which is grist for the mill.

You will notice analytics in two direct ways: the reports that are provided by SharePoint 2013 and the recommendations provided. You can leverage or extend both of these in your code.

One way to do this is to create your own analytics events, using the SPAnalyticsUsageEntry class. For example, if you wanted to track when users took a particular action, then you would create an event type around this, and then use one of the LogAnalyticsEvent() methods to log that action. To see it in a report, you would need to create a custom report; you can also use these events in other ways, as you will see. For example, if you want to log when people tweeted about an item, you would create a custom analytics event. By default, events are processed daily, so you would see this in each day's reports.

There are several ways to apply or influence recommendations in your application. Recommendations use the managed property recommendedfor, so you can configure a CSWP with recommendations in the query; for example, recommendedfor:printer would display recommendations for printers that would be of interested to the user. The "recommended for you" list generated with OOB configurations is a CSWP preconfigured with this kind of query.

To make effective personalized recommendations, you use the UserHistoryWebPart, which tracks the browsing history for the user and makes this available in the context. This can be combined with a CSWP, as shown in Figure 9-32. The popularity of documents is tracked internally by views and also by unique viewers. This same data is available within a document library using the Popularity Trends button in the Share and Track group on the Ribbon.

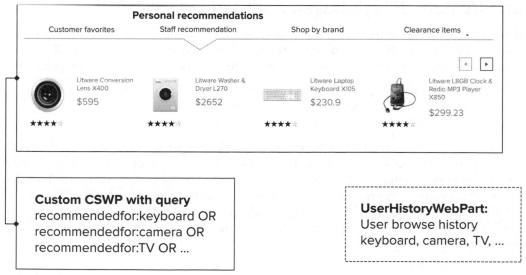

FIGURE 9-32

There are less direct ways that analytics information is used. In particular, analytics processing influences search relevance. If many users click through on an item, that item can move up the list. This is an effective and proven approach for fielding good relevance without extensive tuning — a self-adjusting mechanism. You can extend this mechanism as well, though this is an advanced topic. One way to do this is by creating a custom analytics event, making it part of an update group (so that information is pushed into the search index when the statistics on this event change) and using this in rank profile.

TYING IT ALL TOGETHER

This chapter has covered the layers of search customization from front to back: user experience, queries, content, and relevance. A typical development project with search will use several of these. Tying it all together is a matter of applying these tools and techniques in combination.

Building Quick Search Verticals

Simple search verticals may not need custom content sources. With SharePoint 2013, you can create a smart search vertical remarkably easily using a few steps:

1. Create a result source specific to the targeted information (by content type, for example).

2. Set up a search center site and configure the Search Result and Refiner web parts.

3. Create a few query rules, which define any special behavior (such as promotions and demotions or Visual Best Bets).

4. Customize a Result template for the particular content type and meta data.

Building Custom Search-based Applications

SharePoint 2013 is designed to support a variety of search-based applications on the same search platform. There are a number of OOB applications, such as e-Discovery, video search, WCM, people search, and so on. You can create your own search-based applications to go along with these.

Figure 9-33 shows some examples of search-driven applications. These are applications like any other, except that they take advantage of search technology in addition to other elements of SharePoint 2013 to create flexible and powerful user experiences.

There is a wide diversity of search-based applications, which are often specific to role, topic, task, and industry, and some organizations have dozens of search-based applications running. But there are common patterns, as illustrated in Figure 9-34. The same type of application is used by different roles, sometimes under a different name. For example, a "wealth management portal" for a financial advisor is quite similar to an "analyst workbench" for a homeland security analyst. The styling, the specific content sources, the specific content processing, and the names will be different, but the application pattern is the same.

Customer Service 360 Client Matter 360 Sales Manager

Analyst Workbench Research Portal Intelligence Dashboard

FIGURE 9-33

	Sales	Marketing	Research & Development	Customer Support	Professional Services	Manufacturing/Operations	Finance	Legal	Human Resources	IT	Executive
Knowledge Base (example: consultant KM, collateral library, ...)	✓	✓	✓	✓	✓	✓	✓	✓	✓	✓	✓
Research (example: legal research, product research, ...)		✓	✓	✓	✓	✓	✓	✓			
Information Discovery (example: pub center, library, ...)	✓	✓	✓	✓	✓		✓	✓		✓	✓
Analyst Workbench (example: fusion center, wealth management advisor)		✓	✓			✓	✓	✓			
360° view (example: Voice of the Customer, Matter Dashboard)	✓	✓	✓	✓	✓					✓	✓
Action Environment (example: Call Center Advisor, Proposal Center)	✓			✓	✓	✓	✓	✓	✓	✓	
Situational Awareness (example: Competitor tracking, fusion center)	✓	✓	✓			✓	✓	✓	✓	✓	✓
Pattern Detection (example: Fraud detection, AML)		✓		✓	✓		✓			✓	
Logistics & Planning (example: Production planner, inventory management)	✓	✓				✓				✓	

FIGURE 9-34

SharePoint 2013 is designed to support a wide range of search-based applications on a single platform. Some of these work out-of-the-box, some of these will be no-code customizations, and others are sophisticated applications requiring significant development. As you have seen, you can work with many different areas of search:

➤ User interface (theming, web parts, and templates)

➤ Queries and results (CSOM and REST APIs, query languages, query rules, result templates, and refinement)

➤ Content (connectors, crawling, content processing, and managed properties)

➤ Relevance (rank profiles, analytics, and recommendations)

SharePoint 2013 is a great platform for building search-based applications. You may work with only one of the areas covered or with all of them in the same project. As you become more familiar with developing with search in SharePoint 2013, you'll also find yourself combing search with other parts of SharePoint in interesting ways.

Combining Search with Other Workloads

Search is pervasive in SharePoint 2013 and underlies the social and WCM workloads in many ways. Search is nearly always used along with sites in SharePoint 2010. The search center is a site, for example, and there is a small search box on the majority of sites.

But search can also be combined with all the other parts of SharePoint to build powerful capabilities and applications. Search combines with all the forms of content management: ECM, RM, and WCM. By extending SharePoint you can use search technology to add machine-generated meta data to content, which makes amazing applications possible.

Search combines with Insights (BI) in several ways, from simple co-existence in information centers, to complex text analytics, search analytics, and unified information access. Search can combine with composites, with workflows, forms, and "codeless" application development. Some of these combinations are out of the box, but many of them require you to extend SharePoint and perform innovative development work.

As you become fluent in developing applications with search and SharePoint 2013, keep these patterns and combinations in mind. You will discover many ways to apply them.

SUMMARY: BUILDING SEARCH-BASED APPLICATIONS IN SHAREPOINT

With a new development model for SharePoint 2013 and particularly for search, the capability to extend search is much more accessible. Search has generally not been well understood or fully used by developers, but SharePoint 2013 is changing that. By making search pervasive throughout SharePoint, making it much easier to own and use high-end search capabilities, and by including tooling and hooks specifically for application developer, Microsoft has taken a big step forward in helping developers do more with search.

Search has taken a big step toward being "normal" with SharePoint 2013. At one level, a search app is just another SharePoint app, and a search solution is just another SharePoint solution. Using search from a REST API, pulling in results from remote SharePoint and Exchange farms, incorporating search results in an app for Office — all of these have become possible.

There are still plenty of complexities to search. There are search-specific areas, such as connector development, or customizing linguistics and content processing, which require experience (and can look much easier than they actually are). There are tricky techniques to query rules (inferring what people are looking for) and to search relevance (because the "right" answer is subjective). However, search with SharePoint 2013 has brought a whole new set of tools to the SharePoint developer. The CSWP, for example, is a great all-purpose component. In many situations, instead of working with CAML and SPSiteDataQuery, it is much simpler to drop in a CSWP.

Building powerful search applications is easier than ever in SharePoint 2013. You can create a wide range of applications based on search at various levels of customization. You can also combine search with other parts of SharePoint (Insights, Social, Composites, Sites, and Content) to create compelling solutions.

The high-end capabilities from FAST Search are now integrated into the SharePoint platform as a single search technology. Developers of search-based applications can create some remarkable solutions with the new APIs and mechanisms. Search is quickly becoming the primary way developers surface unstructured information in their applications.

10

Web Content Management

WHAT'S IN THIS CHAPTER?

➤ Designing your taxonomy with SEO and meta data navigation

➤ Consuming content from multiple sites with search-driven publishing

➤ Using APIs to access content programmatically

➤ Using the new Design Manager to brand your site

➤ Working with usage analytics and multilingual support

WROX.COM CODE DOWNLOADS FOR THIS CHAPTER

The wrox.com code downloads for this chapter are found at www.wrox.com/remtitle
.cgi?isbn=1118495829 on the Download Code tab. The code is in the chapter 10 download
and individually named according to the names throughout the chapter.

The Web Content Management (WCM) features touch many aspects of SharePoint. There
have been significant changes to the way WCM works inside of SharePoint 2013 especially in
regards to content authoring and rendering that content. There are three major roles that each
plays equally in the development of your WCM site. These roles are Information Architects,
designers, and developers. Each role has actions highlighted on the homepage of the publishing
site except for the developers who would deploy their modifications through SharePoint
packages or with the JavaScript of the pages.

The primary goal of WCM sites is to enable users to create rich, dynamic websites. These
sites can be customized for their design aspects and provide solutions for scenarios such as
intranets, company websites, or e-commerce sites. Before the creation of WCM systems,
websites consisted of static web pages that included the styling, layout, and content combined
together on each page. This made it difficult to make changes to sites. Today's WCM systems
such as SharePoint 2013 provide a full feature set for maintaining these high traffic and visually
pleasing sites. These sites also now serve multiple devices such as smartphones and tablets.

To create a WCM site you must ensure the WCM features are turned on. These features are called the publishing site features. When creating the site, you can select the Publishing Portal site that has the publishing features activated; although, you can manually turn them on within any SharePoint site. The publishing features add the WCM navigation links and required functionality to your site. To see if the features are enabled, you can look at the new Site Actions menu displayed with the gears similar to Internet Explorer. If there is a link for the new Design Manager, as shown in Figure 10-1, then the publishing features are turned on.

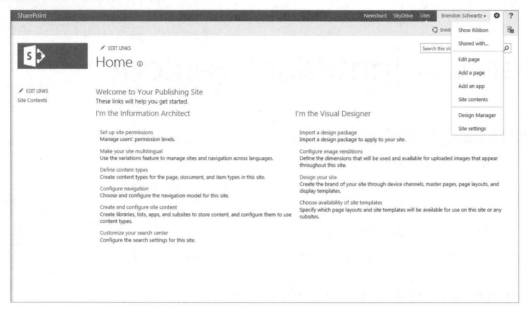

FIGURE 10-1

SharePoint 2013 provides a major overhaul of many of the WCM features from previous versions of SharePoint that are welcome. There have been updates to the way that content and data display on the page, as well as many additions to the publishing classes. The Publishing sites now leverage many of the features that have been enhanced in SharePoint 2013 such as the Managed Metadata Service and Search Service.

TAXONOMY AND THE INFORMATION ARCHITECT

The new features in SharePoint 2013 highlight the role of the Information Architect as a primary participant in WCM sites. The actions associated with the Information Architect are highlighted on the homepage of publishing portals with quick links to the actions they perform (refer to Figure 10-1). The role of the Information Architect within SharePoint sites focuses on three major areas: administration, content, and site navigation.

These major areas defined for the Information Architect center around the concept of the taxonomy of a site. The definition of *taxonomy* is to define a platform agnostic classification and definition of information as it relates to the content and consumption by end users. In plain English this means that taxonomy provides details for the terms, navigation, search, site structure, and content classification. The Information Architect is the planner of your site and defines what will be built with taxonomy that describes how things are organized and what fields are displayed.

There are entire practices around user experience and techniques that you can use to drive a good site design. When planning for the taxonomy of a site, you can use many techniques; some common tasks are as follows:

➤ Define a concept map.

➤ Perform a content audit of key information.

➤ Review search terms required for the site.

➤ Identify the vocabulary (that is, Terms) based on the site content.

Administration

The administration tasks required to be performed by an Information Architect are critical to the site and how the content displays to users. These tasks require clear planning around the permissions of the content and when it can be viewed. You must manage which apps are built for the site, such as e-commerce apps for online payments. Along with the permissions and apps, the Information Architect must plan the content for the site using the content types and the search settings.

New Management Pages

There are number of new management features provided at the Site Collection level that enable Information Architects to perform their jobs. Many of these pages were available at the Farm level previously, such as the Term Store Management pages, but have been moved to the Site Collection level to support the new WCM features added in SharePoint 2013.

Planning for WCM Sites

You can design a SharePoint site in many ways. You need to make sure that you determine the architecture and the plan for cross-site publishing if you want to use this new feature. This book focuses on the development aspects of SharePoint 2013 WCM, but Microsoft TechNet provides planning worksheets and guidance if you are interested in the architecture components.

> **NOTE** *Find planning worksheets and infrastructure guidance at Plan for Internet, intranet, and extranet publishing sites in SharePoint Server 2013 at* `http://technet.microsoft.com/en-us/library/jj635878(v=office.15).aspx.`

Site Navigation

The majority of the sites using WCM features heavily rely on site navigation. This requires a structured global navigation within the Site Collection and a way to provide users with links to both site pages and subsites. Microsoft has made major improvements within these features to now use a dynamic set of navigation links defined within a Term Set.

SEO Improvements

The sites built with WCM features require a high-level discoverability for users to quickly consume pages. Actually, many external-facing websites on the Internet need a high level of search engine optimization (SEO) to help their pages to rise in search results of major providers such as Bing and Google. This was difficult in SharePoint 2010 and earlier due to the path that web content was stored in.

You have probably seen a site that has the /Pages in the URL that was a trademark of many SharePoint sites. The Pages library is still a part of the site structure for publishing sites, but the new managed navigation enables you to separate the content and the navigation of the site to provide excellent SEO for your publishing sites. The new pages created using the user interface create SEO structured URLs automatically for you.

Each page now has a set of SEO properties that are editable from the Edit SEO Properties menu. Figure 10-2 shows what items can be modified such as the Browser Title, Meta Description, and Keywords. The other options apply to the Sitemap settings, and you can even define if the page should be exposed to search engines.

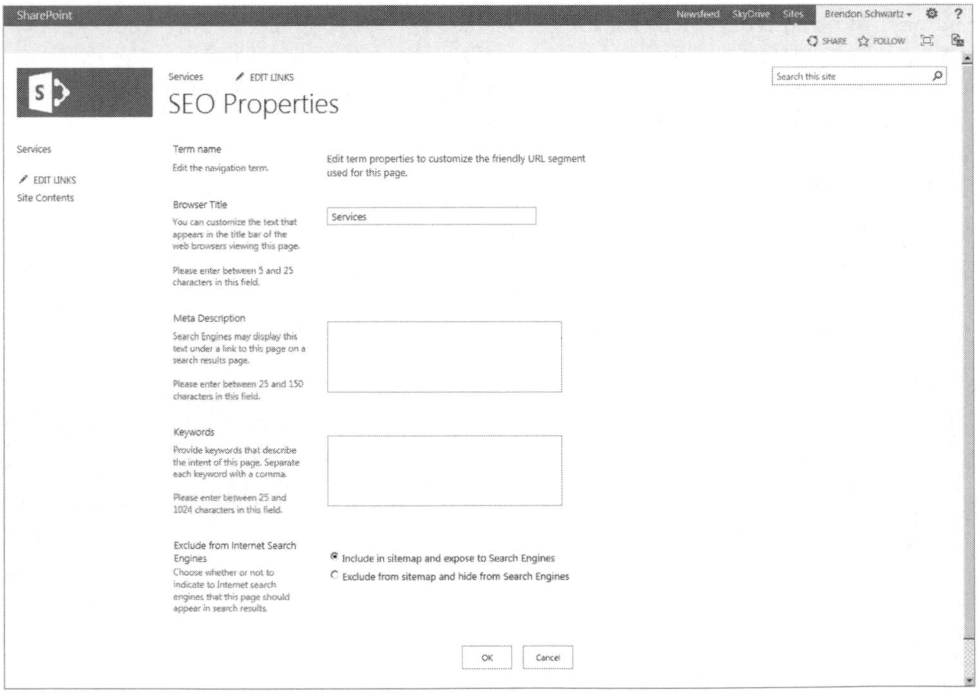

FIGURE 10-2

In addition to the visible enhancements to the clean URLs on each page, the homepage now provides a clean redirect code. This redirect now provides a status update of HTTP 301 instead of the HTTP 302 that was returned in SharePoint 2010. This provides search engines with a better understanding of why the redirect occurs and can improve the ranking of pages because the search engine knows that the page is supposed to be redirected.

Managed Navigation Using Term Sets

The new managed navigation in SharePoint provides the site taxonomy within each site using the term store and managed meta data introduced in SharePoint 2010. There were improvements within the term store to enable each site to manage the navigation for that site. The ability to now select the inherited navigation from the parent and structural navigation is still available for use, but using the new managed navigation for top-level sites gives you full control of how the pages display no matter where the content is stored. This concept of separation of content and navigation is the key reason for the managed navigation. All of the options are clearly identified in the Navigation settings, as shown in Figure 10-3.

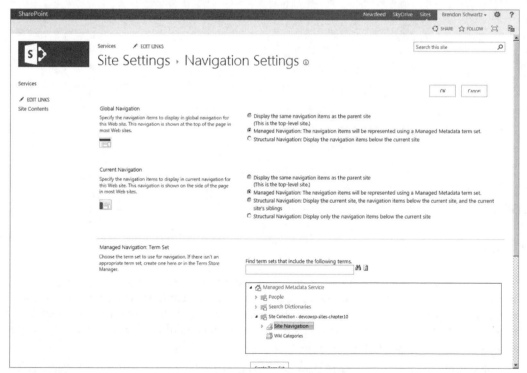

FIGURE 10-3

Terms' Intended Use

With the addition of terms for navigation, Microsoft also added the ability to define what a term could be used for. Figure 10-4 shows this new concept of intended use. Each new term that is not part of the site navigation can now be designed for the type of intended use the Information

Architect plans and how users can interact with the new defined terms. There are three ways that a term could be used when you create them. The first is for use as a tag, which was introduced in SharePoint 2010. The next two are with navigation, using the term for site navigation or faceted navigation. When selecting these check boxes, the term can then be incorporated into the navigation elements on the site.

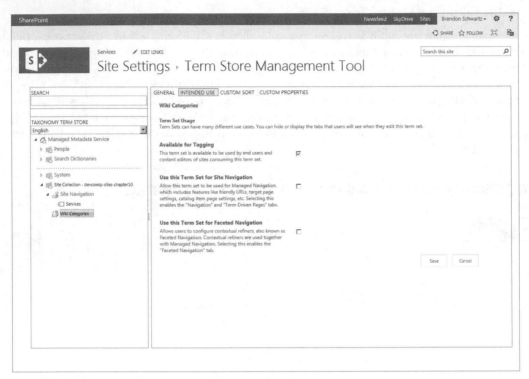

FIGURE 10-4

PAGE CREATION

The page creation process used in SharePoint 2013 is designed for end users to build pages just as they would in a tool like Microsoft Word. You can paste your content directly into the site or convert file types to web content. The easiest way to create a page is by using the user interface. This creates the page directly on the site so make sure you publish content only if you are ready for it to be consumed. To create a page, use the following steps:

1. Click the Site Actions icon, and then select New Page.

2. In the Add a Page dialog, provide the name of the page, and then click create.

3. This opens a newly created page using the default Page Layout. Add your content, and press the Save and Publish button.

> **NOTE** *You can select which page layout to use with the New Page button under Site Actions ⇨ Site Settings ⇨ Page layouts and site templates in the New Page Default settings.*

The Add a Page dialog uses the Article Page with a Body only as the default option when you enable the publishing features. This dialog is responsible for also creating the URL that the page is now associated with. The URL now displays as you type in the wanted page name and is added to the Site Navigation Term Set when you click the Create button. You can see an example of the new, friendly URLs that are generated for you in Figure 10-5.

FIGURE 10-5

In addition to the friendly URL, the generated URL does not have the /Pages or .aspx path for the SEO reasons previously discussed. This means that any time you create a new page you can assume you have clean URLs as you are generating the site. The structure of the navigation can be changed after the pages are created, and they do not have to all be structured as top-level sites from the pages library.

To make it easier for content owners to create and publish content, there is now a Save and Publish button. This enables you to quickly create a page, add content, and publish the content for viewing with a single-click. You no longer have to worry about the content not being shown due to it being in draft status. Many users didn't even realize that the content they were creating was not published and they needed to perform any action on the Publish tab.

SEARCH-DRIVEN PUBLISHING

The introduction of search-driven publishing enables you to design pages and sites that can provide dynamic and rich pages generated based on tags. This style of displaying content has proven to be useful on sites that have changing content and need to change where the content is displayed. With this new type of publishing, all of the content is pushed into the search index and then displayed on the page with queries to the SharePoint search index. This ability to show content from the search index allows you create content in a single location and publish it to multiple places.

Catalogs for Site Publishing

A new concept introduced with this version of SharePoint 2013 to assist with publishing content across site collections is called a *catalog*. The catalog is a list that has been designated as a location for storing content that will be reused through the Cross-Site Collection Publishing features to present the same content somewhere else in the site.

You can create as many catalogs within your farm as you want. For an intranet with multiple departments publishing information, each site for the departments could have content it tags for publishing to the homepages. The architecture options are limitless and can be secured and distributed based on the Information Architecture you have defined.

Creating a catalog on a site requires that you define the meta data you will use for indexing in the search engine and selecting a list or library that will store the content. If you use the new template called Product Catalog, you already have a list that has been established for you; otherwise, you must enable the Cross-Site Collection Publishing feature. In the list or library settings, you will have the Catalog Settings menu in the general settings, as shown in Figure 10-6.

FIGURE 10-6

The ability to publish and unpublish catalogs can be done from within the user interface, but you also can control the site with a class called `PublishingCatalogUtility`. This class is responsible for providing access to the collection of catalogs on the server and providing statues about the catalogs. This class can also be used to start or stop sharing of the catalog and provide information about the lists that are connected to them. Table 10-1 shows the class members.

TABLE 10-1: `PublishingCatalogUtility` Class Members

NAME	DESCRIPTION
GetCatalogConfiguration	Provides the current configuration of requested catalog along with any of the shared settings
GetIsFieldValueFriendlyForUrl	Called to validate that the Field Value will be safe for use in URLs such as search results, REST requests, and URL strings
GetIsPublishingCatalog	Used to determine if an SPList is already a catalog in the global list
GetPublishingCatalog	Returns the publishing catalog requested
GetPublishingCatalogs	Provides a collection of the publishing catalogs available to the users
PublishCatalog	Adds the catalog to the globally defined list of available catalogs
UnPublishCatalog	Removes the specified catalog from the future use

Cross-Site Collection Publishing

The ability to display content from other site collections is based on the cross-site publishing features, sometimes referred to as XSP informally. When the content has been added to a catalog and then searched, it can then be consumed by a publishing site that can display that information on any page.

Cross-site collection enables true content reuse that can be added to the page either through a query, automatically generated based on the page name, or using a set of APIs. The primary class that manages the connections to the catalogs is the `CatalogConnectionManager`. This class enables you to consume catalogs from a search as well as provides information about the connections provided into the search. The manager is the central point to add or remove a catalog to be used for consumption. Just like many of the classes in SharePoint, you must call the Update method for any data to be changed on the server. Table 10-2 lists the class members.

TABLE 10-2: `CatalogConnectionManager` Class Members

NAME	DESCRIPTION
`AddCatalogConnection`	Adds a new catalog connection to the managed collection, you must call `Update` for the catalog to be stored.
`Contains`	Checks if a catalog connection is already used for the path to a specified catalog.
`DeleteCatalogConnection`	Removes the connection on the site to the catalog.
`GetCatalogConnectionSettings`	Returns the settings for the connection to the catalog as a `CatalogConnectionSettings` object that contains all of the details.
`Update`	The `Update` method must be called when making an action on the catalog connections; the action will not be completed until Update is called.
`UpdateCatalogConnection`	Allows you to update the catalog connection information after it has been added to the manager.

CREATE AND EDIT CONTENT

Every WCM site is based on rich and well-designed content with the site pages. SharePoint provides a set of pages to accomplish this with a variety of layouts. The pages created with the publishing infrastructure have content types associated to them that define the content that will be input in the layout. The content types provided by SharePoint are Article Page, Catalog-Item Reuse, Enterprise Wiki Page, Error Page, Project Page, Redirect Page, and Welcome Page. The SharePoint publishing infrastructure provides fields that can be edited on a web page just like Microsoft Word.

Ribbon Enhancements

The Ribbon was introduced with previous versions of SharePoint but has been enhanced with SharePoint 2013. The key focuses are around ease of use and more single-click actions. This means that for content editors there is a closer experience to Microsoft Word with content they create on the web. There is also the ability to easily hide the Ribbon from the content viewing area now. This enables content editors to open the Ribbon as needed and to move it out of the way when displaying the content.

The new styles menu provides a quick and visual way of changing the text just like Microsoft Word. This helps to know what the page should look like and not just rely on HTML styles that might not have a direct mapping to Microsoft Word. You can even copy and paste your content from Microsoft Word directly into the Rich Text Editing area resulting in cleaner content. The new styles used on the page can be seen in Figure 10-7, providing the Microsoft Word-like editing experience within the Ribbon.

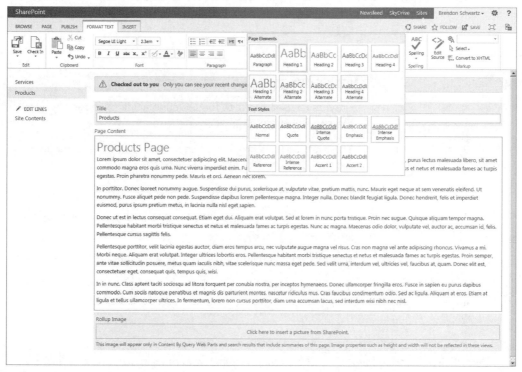

FIGURE 10-7

Publishing Field Controls

The page layouts define a set of content that is stored in the list and can be edited when creating a page. The most common type is the Publishing HTML Field control. You can see this control when you create an article page, which is the default, in the main Page Content area. These controls provide the rich editing experience without having to create an additional code, such a rich text editor.

These controls are not movable and require that they be placed on the page with the article type. You can think of these controls as editors to the list data that is contained on the page, which means you get versioning and approval of the content. If you have worked with web parts in the past, you will notice that the control feels similar to a web part, but the web part is strictly a control that is not directly tied to a list like the Field controls.

The controls are part of the `Microsoft.SharePoint.Publishing.WebControls` class, which contains many controls and web parts used within publishing for almost any type of interaction needed with the user. Table 10-3 shows some of the highly used controls.

TABLE 10-3: `WebControls` Class Members

TYPE	DESCRIPTION
AssetUrlSelector	Provides a user interface for selecting a link or image URL from the site collection.
ContentByQueryWebPart	This web part has been used as the primary content roll-up web part and has multiple options.
MediaFieldControl	Used to display media such as a media player.
RichHtmlField	Provides an Editor like Microsoft Word for entering text and HTML-based content.
RichImageField	Enables selection and displaying of an image field.
TableOfContentsWebPart	Provides the table of contents web part used for the roll-up of site structure.

> **NOTE** *These are some of the more common used Field controls, but you can find a full list of objects in the class at* `http://msdn.microsoft.com/en-us/library/ microsoft.sharepoint.publishing.webcontrols(v=office.15).aspx.`

To add fields to your pages with the Publishing Field types, you need to create a site content type using site columns. This means that the WCM data must be predefined prior to the page layout being created. Figure 10-8 shows the fields in the site columns that can be added as part of the publishing infrastructure.

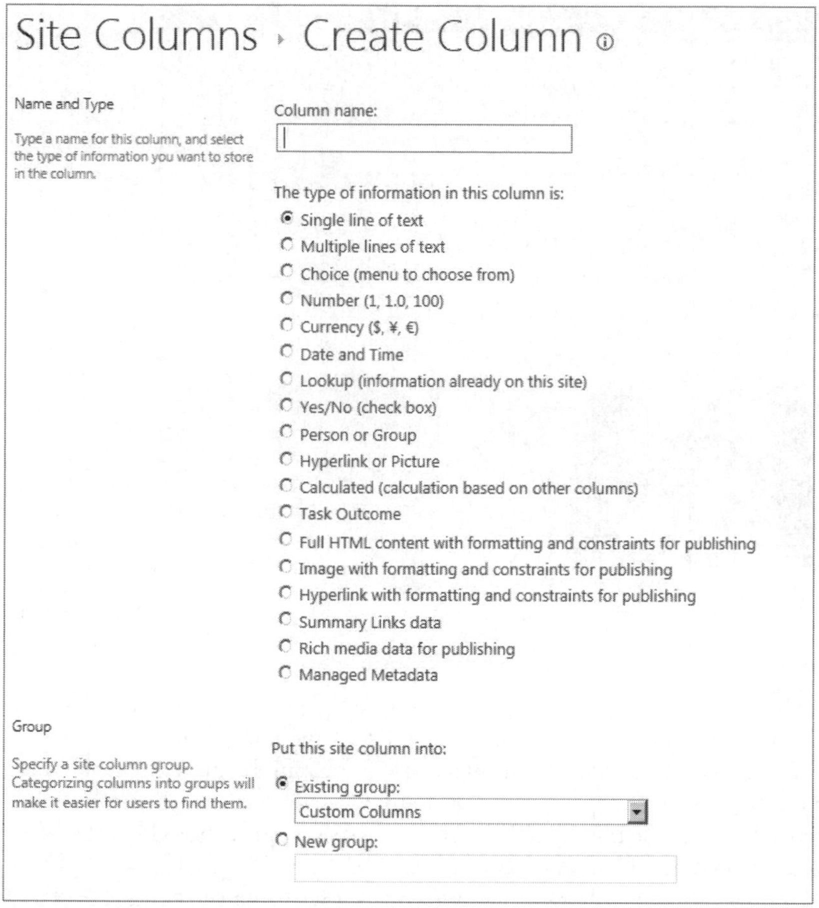

Site Columns › Create Column ⓘ

Name and Type

Type a name for this column, and select the type of information you want to store in the column.

Column name:

[   ]

The type of information in this column is:

- ⦿ Single line of text
- ○ Multiple lines of text
- ○ Choice (menu to choose from)
- ○ Number (1, 1.0, 100)
- ○ Currency ($, ¥, €)
- ○ Date and Time
- ○ Lookup (information already on this site)
- ○ Yes/No (check box)
- ○ Person or Group
- ○ Hyperlink or Picture
- ○ Calculated (calculation based on other columns)
- ○ Task Outcome
- ○ Full HTML content with formatting and constraints for publishing
- ○ Image with formatting and constraints for publishing
- ○ Hyperlink with formatting and constraints for publishing
- ○ Summary Links data
- ○ Rich media data for publishing
- ○ Managed Metadata

Group

Specify a site column group. Categorizing columns into groups will make it easier for users to find them.

Put this site column into:

- ⦿ Existing group:
  [Custom Columns   ▾]
- ○ New group:
  [   ]

FIGURE 10-8

Image Renditions

The introduction of image renditions provides a way to control the look of the web content you are creating when using images. Images on the web have always displayed in their default size format unless you specify a predefined width and height. This works if you can resize every image placed into content, but many times there is a predefined size that is wanted or mandated by style guides. This becomes difficult to manage when you want to use the same image using different sizes within the site. To assist with the challenges of image sizes on pages, SharePoint introduces image renditions. After you add an image to the page, you can then select the image rendition that you want using the Ribbon and the Image tab menu, as shown in Figure 10-9.

FIGURE 10-9

The image renditions are placed on the page using the same URL of the image with a query parameter added for the image rendition to use. This means that you can dynamically create URLs in your code to place the wanted image rendition using JavaScript or using the new device channels. To specify the URL use the `RenditionID` query string parameter. This ID and all image renditions are stored in a file named `http://<site>/_catalogs/masterpage/PublishingImageRenditions.xml`. The following sample code shows using the `RenditionID` of 2 that is listed in the xml file and defined using the Image Rendition site settings page:

```
http://www.wintiptoys.com/SiteCollectionImages/PR.gif?RenditionID=2
```

The BLOB cache is used to create multiple sizes of the image dynamically and must be enabled to use image renditions. To turn on the BLOB cache, set the enabled value to true in the `web.config` of the web application your site is in. In addition to enabling the BLOB cache, you should also select a good location for storing the images as they could increase in size quickly and take up valuable space on the default location. You can see in the list of file types that this does not apply only to images but could also be used with videos:

```
<BlobCache location="C:\BlobCache\14" path="\.(gif|jpg|jpeg|jpe|jfif|bmp|dib|
tif|tiff|ico|png|wdp|hdp|css|js|asf|avi|flv|m4v|mov|mp3|mp4|mpeg|mpg|rm|rmvb|wma|
wmv|ogg|ogv|oga|webm|xap)$" maxSize="10" enabled="true" />
```

The image renditions are exposed through the SharePoint API using the static class `Microsoft.SharePoint.Publishing.SiteImageRenditions` and providing the site collection you want the renditions from. This class uses the `ImageRenditionCollection` class and the `ImageRendition` class to add, remove, and update image renditions on the site. To add a new image rendition, use the following code:

```
ImageRenditionCollection siteRenditions =
    SiteImageRenditions.GetRenditions(SPContext.Current.Site);

ImageRendition addRendition = new ImageRendition();
addRendition.Name = "New Product Image";
addRendition.Width = 100;
addRendition.Height = 100;

siteRenditions.Add(addRendition);
siteRenditions.Update();
```

DYNAMICALLY DISPLAYING CONTENT

Displaying content is one of the core principles for WCM, and this has been accomplished through publishing pages and Content by Query web parts in previous versions of SharePoint. You can still use those same techniques, but SharePoint 2013 introduces some additional capabilities that are designed to make it easier to build the pages using search and client-side techniques.

Building rich pages that have updated content requires that you build the WCM site correctly as well as construct the content correctly. The content needs to be tagged or labeled for you to programmatically find the data. You can do this by placing content in a specific location, giving the content a specific name, or adding common attributes such as tagging a document. With WCM the term *document* is a reference to any set of content you display on the web. The actual type of documents could be anything from web-based content (HTML) to Word documents or PDFs.

Content by Search Web Part

The new Content by Search web part provides the easy-to-use web part configuration of the Content by Query web part from the search index. You can think of this as the Core Search Results web part with easy-to-use and preconfigured results. The new Content by Search web parts have their own Query Builder user interface to make it easy to select the content you want with fine granularity. This also allows users that might not know search query syntax to use the wizard to pull back the correct data onto the page.

The Content by Search web part is an addition to the Content Rollup category web parts. You can still use the Content by Query web part if you want to use content that is located within the site collection. If you want to use content that is reusable across sites, you can use the new Content by Search web parts. Figure 10-10 shows how you can build your own query quickly within the user interface and see a preview of the results.

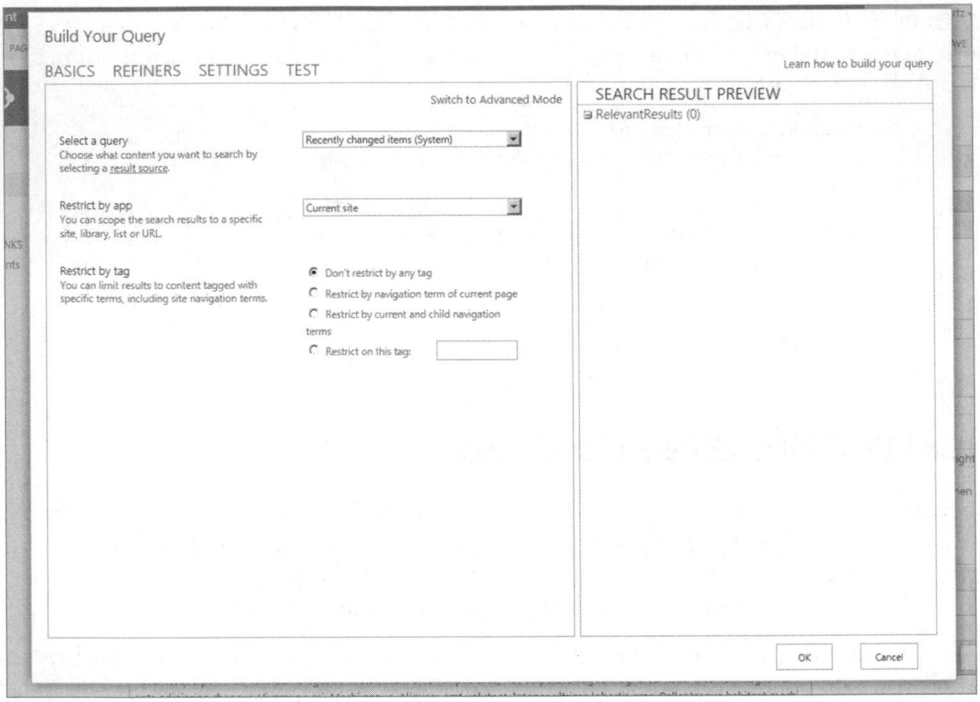

FIGURE 10-10

Search-Driven Web Parts

There are a number of web parts provided as part of the Search-Driven web parts category. These are web parts that have predefined search results already configured in their configuration and can be added to the page by end users. All of the web parts use the Content by Search web part with the custom query. You could create your own Search-Driven web part if you have a specific catalog or query that you would like on multiple pages. The current list of Search Driven web parts is shown here:

➤ Articles

➤ Catalog-Item Reuse

➤ Items from a Catalog

➤ Items Matching a Tag

➤ Pictures

➤ Popular Items

➤ Recently Changed Items

➤ Recommended Items

➤ Videos

➤ Web Pages

➤ Wiki Pages

ACCESS CONTENT PROGRAMMATICALLY

The entire SharePoint platform has provided more ways to connect to APIs and content of the site over the years. SharePoint 2013 continues to improve access by maintaining classes and adding new API methods. The publishing infrastructure builds on the core classes and adds publishing-specific APIs. The APIs available are Server Side, Client-Side Object Model (CSOM), and REST. This enables you as the developer to decide what languages and platforms you would want to use when building sites and content. There is a chance that you would use more than one of these APIs in your solution because they each have a different role. Table 10-4 shows what languages would be best for the development task at hand.

TABLE 10-4: API References for Publishing

NAME	LANGUAGE	REASON	TASKS
Server Side API	C# or VB.NET	If you write code that can be deployed to the server and you are familiar with the Microsoft .NET Framework	Publishing Field controls and server-side processing
CSOM	C#, VB.NET, Silverlight, JavaScript	Used for remote development including on SharePoint web pages, client applications, and SharePoint apps	Server generated web controls and Silverlight apps
REST	JavaScript, C#, VB.NET	Primarily used in loosely typed languages such as JavaScript but can be consumed from any location that can make a call to a URL	AJAX updates, remote websites, and OData requests

Server-Side API

The Server-Side APIs are the most commonly used and have been around since SharePoint 2007 for the publishing infrastructure. The components provided by these APIs deliver the user interface, controls, and pages for creating WCM sites. To access these APIs you need to write code in Managed .NET using either Visual C# or Visual Basic. The code can run on the server and must be in a trusted location such as the GAC or the Bin. To access the classes for SharePoint publishing, reference the server DLLs in your project in addition to the SharePoint core DLL. The `Microsoft .SharePoint.Publishing.dll` contains the public classes specifically for the publishing framework. Here is the location of the server-side API DLL:

```
C:\Program Files\Common Files\Microsoft Shared\Web Server Extensions\15\ISAPI\
Microsoft.SharePoint.Publishing.dll
```

To access content from the publishing pages, you can use the built-in `PublishingWeb` class that is a wrapper for the `SPWeb` object on sites that have the publishing infrastructure enabled.

The first thing to do is create your project and add the SharePoint Publishing DLL as a reference. The following steps show how to do that:

1. Right-click the References folder in your project; select Add Reference.

2. Click the Extensions category if it is not already selected. You could also type Publishing into the search box.

3. Hover over `Microsoft.SharePoint.Publishing` and click the check box. Don't just click and highlight the item because this will not add the reference.

4. Click OK to add the reference to the project.

With the project set up, you can now use the code in Listing 10-1 to display the pages in a publishing library. You will use the static methods from the `PublishingWeb` class and show the values on a web page.

LISTING 10-1: Display Pages in the Publishing Page Library

```
//Check if the Current Web is a Publishing Web
if (PublishingWeb.IsPublishingWeb(SPContext.Current.Web))
{
    //Get the Publishing Web Object
    PublishingWeb pubWeb = PublishingWeb.GetPublishingWeb(SPContext.Current.Web);

    //Loop through each Publishing Page to display information about the page
    PublishingPageCollection pubPageCollection = pubWeb.GetPublishingPages();
    lstPublishingPages.Rows = pubPageCollection.Count;

    foreach (PublishingPage pubPage in pubPageCollection)
    {
        //Display Info about the publishing Page
        lstPublishingPages.Items.Add(
            String.Format("{0}({1})", pubPage.Name, pubPage.Url));
    }
}
```

There are many classes within SharePoint for different purposes. When creating sites and content, there are a few other libraries that you can reference when working with WCM. The other Server-Side APIs that support the publishing framework are listed here:

➤ *Document Management API* — `Microsoft.Office.DocumentManagement.dll`

➤ *Records Management API* — `Microsoft.Office.Policy.dll`

➤ *Search API* — `Microsoft.Office.Server.Search.Applications.dll`

➤ *Taxonomy API* — `Microsoft.SharePoint.Taxonomy.dll`

> **NOTE** *For a full list of namespaces of objects that are used with sites and content visit* `http://msdn.microsoft.com/en-us/library/jj193044(office.15)` `.aspx.`

Client-Side Object Model (CSOM)

The Client-Side Object Model (CSOM) provides a managed wrapper class that can make calls from the client using JavaScript. This is done through a WCF web service hosted on the server named _ vti_bin/client.svc. This service is used for all client-based calls no matter which library you use. The libraries built for WCM publishing features are used in .NET, Silverlight, and Windows Phone. Referencing and using the .NET CSOM is just like referencing the Server-Side API. The major difference between the two is that the .NET CSOM must get a context object before making calls to the objects. This is because the code is translated into JavaScript and does not have the server-side objects readily available. The .NET CSOM DLL is located here:

```
C:\Program Files\Common Files\Microsoft Shared\Web Server Extensions\15\ISAPI\
Microsoft.SharePoint.Client.Publishing.dll
```

You can use the Client Publishing CSOM objects by adding the core SharePoint Client and Runtime DLL references. After you add these classes, you can add the Publishing Client DLLs and use the classes alongside the core CSOM classes. The following code shows how you can get the site image renditions and display the name of each:

```
ClientContext context = new ClientContext(url);
IEnumerable<ImageRendition> siteRenditions =
        SiteImageRenditions.GetRenditions(context);

context.ExecuteQuery();

foreach (ImageRendition imgRendition in siteRenditions)
{
    Console.WriteLine(imgRendition.Name);
}
```

REST CSOM

Part of the new API set provided by SharePoint 2013 is an implementation of REST-based services using the CSOM server framework. This enables applications to make calls directly to a RESTful endpoint, which is especially useful in languages such as JavaScript; although, you can also use it from server code. The REST API provides new features around OData and maps the _api/ path to the _vti_bin/client.svc. Also, you should try to use the new API instead of the .asmx files for new development. The location for the Publishing and Search classes is shown in Table 10-5.

TABLE 10-5: Location for REST API

NAME	LOCATION
Publishing	http://server/site/_api/publishing
Search	http://server/site/_api/search

BRANDING SITES

Creating your own brand or look and feel of sites has been a goal for many organizations. You might even often hear someone ask, "How do I make this site not look like SharePoint?" There are now many options for achieving a fully branded site that is easy to build. There are full set of APIs and user interfaces to help designers build and deploy these packages. The APIs also enable developers to build rich content using the server or client-side programming using the Server API, .NET client object model (CSOM), JSON, JavaScript, and REST.

To build your own branding, use Master Pages and page layouts to design the look and feel of the site. These pages along with any automatically generated pages take the content stored in the content database and combine them together for the output to the browser. SharePoint combines the page layout with the Master Page to render the page to the browser. This means the page layout consists of content placeholder elements that instruct SharePoint where to place elements on the page inside the Master Page.

Master Pages

The global design elements along with the global controls such as navigation, search, and content area are defined in the Master Page. Each page can have a master page defined, but SharePoint makes it easy to assign Master Pages per site. The Master Page combined with a Page Layout can provide the entire site layout. This is where you would define your Cascading Style Sheets (CSS) as well as the HTML and content areas for all of your pages. When creating the Master Page, remember the file maintains the consistent user experience across your site. In SharePoint 2013, creating Master Pages has become easier with the introduction of the Design Manager and HTML Master Pages.

Page Layouts

The Page Layout is a template that is used to author content in your site. The template is designed to have two modes: a display mode and an edit mode. The display mode simply takes the data in a list item (that is, row of data) and maps the fields to the right location on the Page Layout. This means that you can have multiple Page Layouts for the same set of content and can change the Page Layout without modifying the underlying data.

You can modify the data by navigating to the page and using the Edit Page button to change the page into edit mode. This provides a way to modify the data that is stored in the content database but does not let you modify the page HTML. The Page Layout must be defined and created prior to the data being stored in the site, enabling separation of the content and layout. The advantage is that the author can edit content on the same location that the page will be rendered to visitors, and the designer can update the Page Layout as needed.

From a content-authoring perspective, the Page Layout dictates how the authoring experience functions. It accomplishes this in two ways. First, every Page Layout must be associated with a content type that is available in the Pages library and inherits from the Page content type. Second, the Page Layout implements editable fields that provide authoring areas on the page. These fields match up with the site columns defined in the content type. The HTML Page Layout enables you to quickly build page designs using the content types.

Composed Looks

Many sites such as intranets want to change the way the sites look but are not interested on taking on a fully branded project for their sites. The new Composed Looks feature brings together many concepts that were already provided to create a single point that users can use to modify the look of their site. This enables you to have more power directly within SharePoint and provide branding in a supported and structured way.

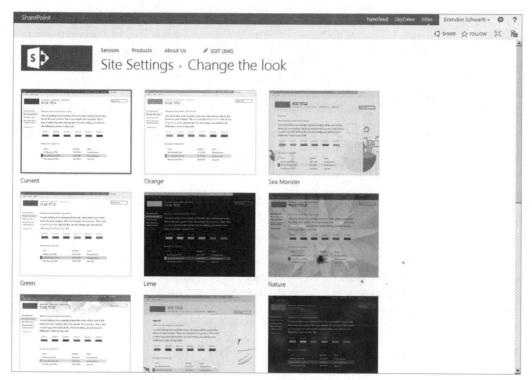

FIGURE 10-11

The Composed Looks provided with SharePoint 2013 use a combination of settings and show what your site could look like, as shown in Figure 10-11. Although this might look similar to the SharePoint 2010 Office Theme files (.thmx), the new engine separates the color palette and the fonts used on the site. The composed looks change the default look and feel by using different layouts, colors, images, and fonts. Table 10-6 shows the items used to create Composed Looks.

TABLE 10-6: Composed Looks File Types

ITEM	EXTENSION	TYPE	DESCRIPTION
Title	N/A	String	The display name you want to provide for users to select from.
Master Page URL	.master	HTML Master Page	The Master Page defines the global layout of the page and can be now created in the designer manager if v15.master does not fulfill the needs.
Theme URL	.spcolor	XML Color Palette File	Provides the color palette to be used with a composed look and defines the color values for each location.
Image URL	.jpg or image file	Image File	This is the background image file for the entire site. The default types provided by Microsoft are .jpg files using dimensions of 1024 x 768.
Font Schem URL	.spfont	XML Font File	Enables designers to provide their own fonts that might not be included in the default set of fonts.
Display Order	N/A	Number	This defines where the Composed Look will be shown in order when the user is looking at all of the options.

The Composed Looks are just a starting point for users to brand their sites. When a look is selected, the Change the Look page will be provided for users to modify any of the elements they want to be different than the defined Composed Look.

To change the Color Palette or Font file, download one of the default files, and modify the colors or fonts that you would like to change. This would need to be done only if you want to deploy a Composed Look for multiple sites or automate applying the Composed Look on the site. Listings 10-2 and 10-3 show samples of the two files.

LISTING 10-2: From colorscheme0001.spcolor

```xml
<?xml version="1.0" encoding="utf-8"?>
<s:colorPalette isInverted="false" previewSlot1="BackgroundOverlay"
  previewSlot2="BodyText" previewSlot3="AccentText"
xmlns:s="http://schemas.microsoft.com/sharepoint/">
    <s:color name="BodyText" value="444444" />
    <s:color name="SubtleBodyText" value="777777" />
    <s:color name="StrongBodyText" value="262626" />
    <s:color name="DisabledText" value="B1B1B1" />
    <s:color name="SiteTitle" value="262626" />
    <s:color name="WebPartHeading" value="444444" />
    <s:color name="ErrorText" value="A83238" />
    <s:color name="AccentText" value="0072C6" />
    <s:color name="SearchURL" value="338200" />
...
```

LISTING 10-3: From fontscheme001.spfont

```
<?xml version="1.0" encoding="utf-8"?>
<s:fontScheme name="Bodoni" previewSlot1="title" previewSlot2="body"
xmlns:s="http://schemas.microsoft.com/sharepoint/">
    <s:fontSlots>
        <s:fontSlot name="title">
            <s:latin typeface="Bodoni Book" eotsrc="/_layouts/15/fonts/
            BodoniBook.eot" woffsrc="/_layouts/15/fonts/BodoniBook.woff"
            ttfsrc="/_layouts/15/fonts/BodoniBook.ttf"
            svgsrc="/_layouts/15/fonts/BodoniBook.svg"
            largeimgsrc="/_layouts/15/fonts/BodoniBookLarge.png"
            smallimgsrc="/_layouts/15/fonts/BodoniBookSmall.png" />
            <s:ea typeface="" />
            <s:cs typeface="Segoe UI Light" />
            <s:font script="Arab" typeface="Segoe UI Light" />
            <s:font script="Deva" typeface="Nirmala UI" />
            <s:font script="Grek" typeface="Segoe UI Light" />
            <s:font script="Hang" typeface="Malgun Gothic" />
            <s:font script="Hans" typeface="Microsoft YaHei UI" />
    ...
```

Custom Branding in Expression Web

Because users want to brand SharePoint sites and create a brand without SharePoint Designer, SharePoint includes that ability to use any web design tool or HTML editor to create the branding for your WCM site. One tool you can consider is Microsoft Expression Web when working with the web pages. This is one of the tools for designers that come with Expression Studio for taking your concept from design to HTML.

> **NOTE** *For more on the Microsoft Expression products, visit the homepage at* http://www.microsoft.com/expression/.

Install Microsoft Expression Web; then you can start creating your HTML from a blank page or download a style as a starting point from a website such as http://www.freecsstemplates .org. Make sure to check out the licensing restrictions with any web pages you download or plan to purchase before using them. When the page HTML and design are complete, you can transform it into a SharePoint design using the Design Manager.

Microsoft Expression Web refers to the collection of files as a site. You can use the site as a container for all of your branding elements, including your HTML Master Page. The site points directly to a set of files on the file system that can be mapped directly to the files in the Master Page gallery. To create your first brand with Microsoft Expression Web, follow these steps:

1. To start building a site brand, open Microsoft Expression Web.

2. Click the Site tab and select New Site.

3. Within the New Site dialog, pick the type of site to create. In this case use a prebuilt empty site, so select General ➪ Empty Site.

4.   Select the location to deploy the files; for now select somewhere on your hard drive.

5.   To make it easier to open in the future, keep the check box for Add to Managed List selected, and provide the name of the site design.

6.   The first file to add to your site is the HTML Master Page. Select File ➪ New ➪ Page.

7.   Then select CSS Layout and the type of layout you are looking for. For this example you can use Header, nav, 2 columns, footer; then click OK.

8.   Click Save, and give the file the name **simpledesign.html**. At this point you also want to update the page title by clicking Change Title.

9.   After the HTML Master Page is saved, you must also save the CSS file. Name it **simpledesign.css**.

10.   Now you can add any HTML elements and images you want to make the site design specific to you.

Your HTML Master Page should now look like the following code. The text that will be replaced was added to help show you where to replace content when adding the dynamic content later:

```
<!DOCTYPE html PUBLIC "-//W3C//DTD XHTML 1.0 Transitional//EN"
"http://www.w3.org/TR/xhtml1/DTD/xhtml1-transitional.dtd">
<html dir="ltr" xmlns="http://www.w3.org/1999/xhtml">

<head>
<title>Wrox Chapter 10 Branding with Expression Web</title>
<meta content="text/html; charset=utf-8" http-equiv="Content-Type" />
<link href="simpledesign.css" rel="stylesheet" type="text/css" />
</head>
<body>

<div id="masthead">//Replace with Header HTML
</div>
<div id="top_nav">//Replace with Global Navigation
</div>
<div id="container">
<div id="left_col">//Replace with Quick Launch Menu
</div>
<div id="page_content">//Replace with Page Contents
</div>
</div>
<div id="footer">//Replace with Footer HTML
</div>

</body>
</html>
```

If you are not a designer and want a great look and feel to your site, you can start with online templates. Download or purchase a site that is strictly CSS and HTML; then you can just open the site using the Site menu and the Open Site option. Ensure that any code or forms are removed from pages before you upload them, but this is a great way to quickly have your design in place. Some of the content you download might be in Adobe Photoshop (.psd) files because many designers develop the site as an image and then provide it to the developer to convert into the true HTML.

Microsoft Expression Web provides the ability to import an Abode Photoshop file directly into your site design. These options provide you as the developer with many options and team structures for building your site design.

The finished site design will contain static content without any HTML form elements and would be viewable in an HTML browser such as Internet Explorer. Figure 10-12 shows what a branded site design might look like in Microsoft Expression Web. This shows how easy it is to create a brand even without being connected to SharePoint using tools already familiar to you and your team.

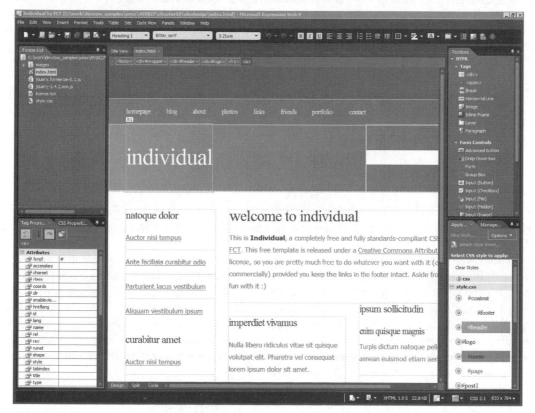

FIGURE 10-12

Even though tools such as Visual Studio and Microsoft Expression Web enable you to create rich web pages such as Master Pages and Page Layouts as well as add ASP.NET controls to your page, you will not want to add them at this time. The Master Page that this template will be transformed into will not have a code behind, and the server-side code you might write will not be uploaded with the files.

By using rich design tools such as Microsoft Expression Web that contain support for HTML5 and previewing pages in Internet Explorer 9 and Google Chrome, you can quickly build Internet-facing websites that users will appreciate.

DESIGN MANAGER

The Design Manager provides a set of steps that help you create a unique site design without installing any additional tools. Each step in the process provides information on what the step requires and links to the actions. The Design Manager is designed to enable you to create your brand for all devices and package the site design when you finish. You can see the Welcome page, which is Step 1, in Figure 10-13.

FIGURE 10-13

The Design Manager has changed the paradigm that SharePoint designers have used for years. Previously, designers for SharePoint would open a Microsoft SharePoint Designer (SPD) and directly modify the pages on a live site. This meant that you had to know about the specific SharePoint controls that were needed on the page and that you could use the simple drag-and-drop user interface to design. Some designers would just export the SharePoint Master Pages or start with the minimal set of controls required, called the Minimal Master Page. This meant there was little support for users that exported the site and many restrictions if you used SharePoint Designer. The change now aligns with many other website designs by enabling the design to be created outside of SharePoint and converted when it is ready for viewing. Keep in mind this does mean that the drag-and-drop functionality that many designers have used for many years will not be available in the new version of Microsoft SharePoint Designer 2013.

Using Device Channels for Mobile Experiences and Device Targeting

Over the past few years, devices of all shapes and sizes have become popular. From smartphones to tablets, users are now browsing the web in new ways. This market continues to be ever-changing and new devices such as the Microsoft Tablet are introduced frequently. This makes it extremely hard to create websites to fulfill the needs of both current and future devices, especially if you are not aware of what might be on the horizon.

Approximately 15 to 20 percent of web browsing is done from mobile devices, and the trend for mobile devices is going to increase over the next few years. In addition to the form factors, mobile devices have introduced multiple platforms and browsers. This means to account from all of the combinations of devices, platforms, and browsers, you must make many adjustments to site design.

Even large organizations have started to use tablets on a more regular basis, and many executives have tablets as their primary devices. This means that your WCM sites for the Internet or intranet must have the capability to provide an experience designed for the intended device — or as close as possible.

To deal with the growth of mobile devices for your WCM sites, you can use a new feature called Device Channels. This is a way to target the branding, content, and layout of your site to the type of browsers and devices defined in your site. There are two primary components for Device Channels to work. The first is defining the Master Page of the site that will be rendered when a mobile device makes a request. The second is to define which content will be displayed for each type of device based on available screen real estate.

Device Channels

The Device Channel is a list of settings that determines which Master Page to show based on user agent strings from their device. The Device Channel is set up to check if the device inclusion rules contain any of the elements in the user agent string and use the first channel found in the ordered list. The Design Manager provides a step to define and order your sites' Device Channels.

The *user agent string* is a string defined in HTML browsers to describe to the web server information about the system viewing the data. There have been many changes over the years, but most browsers have the same common elements in the user agent string. Many of them have the following format:

```
Mozilla/[version] ([system and browser information]) [platform]
([platform details]) [extensions]
```

When looking at the user agent string for Internet Explorer, you might find the following depending on if you are on the desktop or mobile browsers. To learn about the history of the user agent string and how it has evolved, go to http://www.nczonline.net/blog/2010/01/12/history-of-the-user-agent-string/.

```
Mozilla/5.0 (compatible; MSIE 9.0; Windows NT 6.1; Trident/5.0)
```

```
Mozilla/5.0 (compatible; MSIE 9.0; Windows Phone OS 7.5; Trident/5.0;
IEMobile/9.0)
```

> **NOTE** *If you want to know what your current user agent string is, you can use Fiddler or use the website at* http://www.useragentstring.com/. *The site also has a list of most user agent strings listed at* http://www.useragentstring.com/pages/useragentstring.php.

Creating a Device Channel requires setting a few values and then ordering the channels in which they should be executed. After the Device Channel is created, you can set a new Master Page to the channel when applying the site designs with the Design Manager. Use the following steps to create a Device Channel:

1. Click Step 2. Manage Device Channels; then click Create a Channel.

2. Provide a display name in the Name text box and description.

3. Add a unique alias for access to the channel in code.

4. Add one or more Device Inclusion Rules, which is a part of a user agent string. Enter only one per line, such as IEMobile/9.0.

5. Check the Active box and click Save.

Device Channel Panel Control

To control the data on the page, you can use the new Device Channel Panel Control by specifying which channel you want to make specific changes for. This control can be added from the Snippet Gallery discussed in the "Snippet Gallery" section later in the chapter or as a SharePoint control. This could be useful if you want to display only a limited amount of content for a mobile browser but want more content added for the full desktop browser.

The Device Channel panel enables you to create HTML content that can be included in as many channels as needed by using the `IncludedChannels` attribute. The `IncludedChannels` attribute uses the Alias and not the display name of the Device Channels you defined earlier. You can use multiple channels by adding a comma in between the channels in the attribute. To use the control add the following code to your Master Pages or Page Layouts:

```
<PublishingWebControls:DeviceChannelPanel runat="server"
IncludedChannels="SmartPhones">
  <!-- Enter HTML in this section -->
  <div>This content only displays on the SmartPhone Device Channel</div>
```

When everything is configured you can test what the design looks like by forcing the site to use the desired Device Channel with a query string parameter. Using the Device Channel Alias again, you can specify which channel displays in the browser.

The query string template is located here:

```
http://<site>/products/?DeviceChannel=<DeviceChannelAlias>
```

Here is an example of a query string Device Channel:

```
http://tailspintoys.com/products/?DeviceChannel=SmartPhones
```

Working with Design Files and Assets

Every design is defined as a set of HTML, CSS, JavaScript, and image files, as well as any other supporting files. To create a design you need at least one HTML page that represents your Master Page known as your global layout.

One of the first thing you will do as a developer or designer of web pages is map the Master Page Gallery to the a network drive. SharePoint 2013 has enhanced the Master Page Gallery to work over WebDav and provide a filesystem interface for tools such as Microsoft Expression Web, Visual Studio, and Dreamweaver. This mapped drive enables you to edit any of the files from within Windows Explorer and especially the Master Pages and Page Layouts now.

> **NOTE** *If you use a Windows Server, make sure to enable the Desktop Experience feature to get the WebDav options that are provided with the service WebClient.*

To set up a connection to the Master Page Gallery, you could just click the link provided by the URL, which opens in your network drive locations. It is recommended that you create a mapped network location by following these simple steps. Included are steps from KB article 2445570 (http://support.microsoft.com/kb/2445570) for resolving slow responses on Windows Vista and Windows 7:

1. Start by opening the Design Manager of the site you are interested in.

2. Click Step 3, Upload Design Files.

3. There you see the link to the Master Page Gallery; right click it and select Copy Shortcut. The URL looks like this: http://intranet.devcow.com/_catalogs/masterpage/.

4. Click the Start menu of Windows and then Computer.

5. In Windows Explorer for Computer, select Map network drive from the options.

6. Choose the drive letter you want, paste the location you copied from the Design Manager, and leave the check box marked for Reconnect at Login.

7. Now verify your Internet Explorer options by opening Internet Explorer.

8. Click the Gears icon (Tools menu); then click Internet Options.

9. Click the Connections tab, and then select the LAN Settings.

10. In the LAN Settings dialog box, uncheck Automatically Detect Settings. Then click OK.

Now that you have designed your site and mapped the folder location, you next need to edit the files you created and modify them with the correct SharePoint elements. Using the Design Manager Wizard, you need to select the name of the file you created as your global brand and let SharePoint add the required elements. The name of the file is common across all of the pages, so you want to name it something unique. It is a good idea to store your files in a folder to keep them located together.

Converting HTML Master Pages

When you are at Step 4 Edit Master Pages, you have already created your HTML Master Page and the supporting files that will be converted using the Design Manager. The Master Page editor is a power tool that enables you to upload your HTML Master Page and provides information on the status of the conversion. If there are errors, the Design Manager displays them to you and enables you to try the conversion again when corrected.

Convert your HTML Master Page to a SharePoint Master Page by following these steps:

1. Copy the files you create to the new mapped Master Page Gallery.

2. Start the Design Manager if it is not already open, and click Step 4, Edit Master Pages.

3. Click Convert an HTML File to a SharePoint Master Page.

4. This brings up the Select an Asset dialog; now select your HTML Master Page. (The authors' page is located in /_catalogs/masterpage/chapter10/ewSiteDesign/ simpledesign.html.)

5. Click Insert to start the conversion process; wait for the page to refresh and show a status of Conversion Successful.

6. Click the Conversion Successful to bring up the Preview Mode of the Designer Manager.

In the Design Preview you can change the page content that is being displayed to help see what elements need to be updated as you build your site. You also see a large, yellow rectangle explaining that there is a <div> tag that is automatically placed on the page to show the content of the Page Layouts. This is just a starting place for the HTML Master Page, and you need to make sure to add all of the dynamic content now as well as any styling you want to match the SharePoint design. Make sure to create a test page to display the content, and make sure your site design converted correctly.

The conversion of the HTML file added HTML to the file it converted, so you can update the elements already provided on the page. To edit the files, you need to open them in the HTML editor if they are not already open there. Navigate to the mapped path and create a site that opens directly from that location. Move the content placeholder to the correct location as well as any other HTML elements. As you edit the file, the SharePoint Master Page will also be updated, but you cannot directly modify the SharePoint Master Page file. To add the dynamic content, you need to use the Snippets link, which brings up the Snippet Gallery.

> **NOTE** *If you use Microsoft Expression Web, make sure to copy the path name such as* `Z:\chapter10\ewSiteDesign`, *or the tool converts the location to the HTTP path to the SharePoint site and notifies you that it cannot edit SharePoint sites.*

Snippet Gallery

Creating static site designs that require dynamic content or server tags creates an interesting problem. The Snippet Gallery assists in resolving this issue by enabling you to create dynamic content controls that can display in static HTML. The controls and their settings can be configured using an online form that can then be copied to HTML pages for your site design.

The Snippet Gallery works for both HTML Master Pages and HTML Page Layouts. The code that is generated can be edited prior to copying it, so you can adjust the components and their previews as needed. You can even fully brand the component in the Snippet Gallery that will be copied with the control when it is generated. After the pages are converted to SharePoint Master Pages and Page Layouts, the components will be converted into the actual controls.

The Snippet Gallery provides HTML markup for your HTML Master Page for many of the page elements. There is even an option to create your own snippet from custom ASP.NET controls. All of this is done through HTML comments that are marked up with special characters and sample HTML for the previews. Figure 10-14 shows the Snippet Gallery and what displays when Top Navigation is selected.

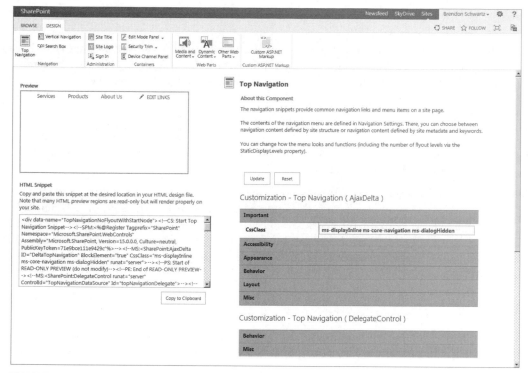

FIGURE 10-14

Each control has a unique set of customization options, and they each render differently. The rendering and conversion is done by using a set of HTML comments that have a SharePoint-specific token to notify the conversion engine on what action to take. The Snippet Gallery provides a standard interface no matter which control is selected.

➤ *Design tab* — This tab selects which control is being selected and edited by the Snippet Gallery. There are groupings for all the major components and even a Custom selection if a control is not listed.

➤ *Preview window* — The preview areas shows what the tag will look like in your HTML pages; it is not editable.

➤ *HTML snippet* — This snippet provides an area to view the HTML that is generated by the Snippet Gallery and provides a Copy button.

➤ *Control description* — This shows the name of the control and provides a description in the About this Component section.

➤ *Customization options* — You can see the set of HTML, CSS, Ajax, .NET, or Web Part settings depending on what the control provides.

The easiest way to understand how to use the Snippet Gallery is to try it. Using the following steps you can add the top navigation (ASP.NET control) and Search box (Web Part Control) to the `simpledesign.html`.

Start by navigating to the Snippet Gallery, which is located inside the Design Manager Preview Mode:

1. Open your site and navigate to the Design Manager located in the Site Settings gear. (Notice that each time you open Design Manager, Preview Mode, or Snippet Gallery, a new tab opens so that you don't need to navigate around the site to get between them.)

2. Click the Step 4. Edit Master Pages link.

3. Click the simpledesign link, and verify the status is Conversion Successful.

4. In the Preview Mode click the Snippets link in the top left; this takes you to the Snippet Gallery for this HTML Master Page.

With the Snippet Gallery open, you can now select the controls you want and add them to your HTML Master Page. As soon as the control is updated on the WebDav location, the Master Page will also be updated. You can use the generated HTML snippets in any HTML web design tool; the output HTML is not specific to any Microsoft product. You can use the Microsoft Expression Web Design HTML editor, but there is nothing special between using this tool or NotePad in regards to the Snippet Gallery.

1. If the Microsoft Expression website is not open, open Microsoft Expression Web, and open the WebDav site created earlier.

2. Now switch back to the Snippet Gallery, and select Top Navigation if it is not selected. You can verify that the control in the top right of the content area displays the control's name.

3. Look at the customization area, and notice that there is a section for the AspMenu because this control is based on that control. Make any changes and click the Update button.

4. You can see in the preview what the changes will look like. For example, if you change the AspMenu ⇨ Layout ⇨ Orientation to Vertical, you see that it is now Vertical in the preview as well.

5. After you modify the control, click Copy to Clipboard. You will most likely get the Internet Explorer dialog asking to make sure you are allowing access to your Clipboard. Click Allow Access.

6. Again, switch back to the Microsoft Expression Web tool to find the section you marked as //Replace with Global Navigation. Remove that text and paste the contents of your Clipboard into that section.

7. Save the page and refresh it in the Design Preview. Depending on your preview mode of the HTML editor, there might be small differences between the HTML editor and Design Preview page.

8. After you verify your page works, navigate back to the Snippet Gallery and click the Search Box button.

9. If you look closely at the HTML snippet, you can notice that a namespace is being registered as well as adding the web part. This is to make sure the control classes are available.

10. Again, make any changes to the properties. They are Web Part properties this time; click the Update and then Copy to Clipboard buttons.

11. Paste the Search Box HTML snippet into the page in the left column, and click Save.

12. Refresh the page in the Design Preview, and you now have navigation and the search box.

As you added the controls to the page, you probably noticed the use of the HTML comments and that each snippet is self-contained. This means that if the control required a delegate control or a register tag they were added with the control in the HTML snippet. To complete your page, finish adding all of the components you want to the page such as the site title, site logo, any device-specific containers, and any predefined web parts. If you look through all of the web part options, you can see the options for your pages are almost limitless, and you can create any page you could use with the user interface. The following code block shows what some of the snippet will look like:

```
<div id="top_nav" xmlns="http://www.w3.org/1999/xhtml">
<div data-name="TopNavigationNoFlyoutWithStartNode">
<!--CS: Start Top Navigation Snippet-->
<!--SPM:<%@Register Tagprefix="SharePoint" Namespace=
  "Microsoft.SharePoint.WebControls" Assembly="Microsoft.SharePoint,
  Version=15.0.0.0, Culture=neutral, PublicKeyToken=71e9bce111e9429c"%>-->
<!--MS:<SharePoint:AjaxDelta runat="server" CssClass="ms-displayInline
  ms-core-navigation ms-dialogHidden" BlockElement="True"
  ID="DeltaTopNavigation">-->
<!--PS: Start of READ-ONLY PREVIEW (do not modify)-->
<!--PE: End of READ-ONLY PREVIEW-->
<!--MS:<SharePoint:DelegateControl runat="server" Id="topNavigationDelegate"
  ControlId="TopNavigationDataSource">-->
<!--PS: Start of READ-ONLY PREVIEW (do not modify)-->
<span style="display: none">
<table cellpadding="4" cellspacing="0" style="font: messagebox; color: buttontext;
  background-color: buttonface; border: solid 1px; border-top-color:
  buttonhighlight;
  border-left-color: buttonhighlight; border-bottom-color: buttonshadow;
  border-right-color: buttonshadow">
<tr>
<td nowrap="nowrap"><span style="font-weight: bold">PortalSiteMapDataSource</span>
- topSiteMap</td>
```

All of the controls are easy to use and straightforward, but you should spend some time learning what you can do with the Custom ASP.NET Markup control. This snippet wraps the ASP.NET elements in the blank text into the properly commented snippet. The following code is from an ASP. NET AdRotator control that can be added to the left navigation directly under the search box. All of the HTML snippets are just text and can be edited or created by hand, but make sure to create invalid HTML or the HTML Master Page will have conversion errors and won't display. If this happens the Design Preview tells you exactly which line of the HTML Master Page has the issue and what the problem is.

```
<!--CS: Start Create Snippets From Custom ASP.NET Markup Snippet-->
<!--SPM:<asp:AdRotator runat="server" id="AdRotator1"
  AdvertisementFile="~/Documents/adFile.xml">-->
<!--SPM:</asp:AdRotator>-->
<!--CE: End Create Snippets From Custom ASP.NET Markup Snippet-->
```

Package for Deployment

The last step in the process is to package your files for deployment on another server. This could be moving the files from development to production or providing them for download to other people. The packaging process takes the files you have created and puts them into a WSP file that can then be uploaded to any other SharePoint site.

To make sure that you can package files, you need to publish them in the Master Page Gallery. You should also test your files by assigning them to the wanted device channels of the site. All of the files from the Master Page Gallery are placed into the package. You should try not to add any files for testing or that you do not want distributed to others in the library if you are packaging the files. The packages are versioned, and you can update the name of the package at any time without affecting the files inside of them. Figure 10-15 shows Step 8. Create Design Package after the package has been created. This is the last step in Design Manager, but you can navigate to any step at any time.

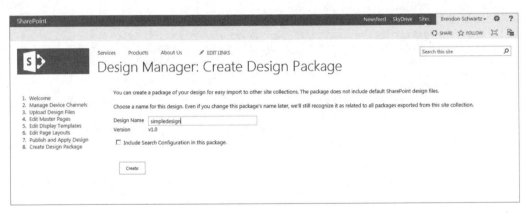

FIGURE 10-15

USAGE ANALYTICS

The ability to know what is working on your site and what is not is powerful. This ability allows you to have insight into how the content is used, what pages people visit, and how your site is consumed. This data is rolled up into 15 days' worth of data, and user information is removed from the reports. To keep the servers running well, the daily data is purged from the system periodically.

All the data from the Usage Analytics is created from user actions such as clicks or viewed items. Due to the size of the reported data, the reports automatically trim the least-visited content and show the most recent data in the reports. The data that is aggregated together is moved to the reporting database for future reports. If you want the detailed data, you must store it in another location. These reports can easily be exported to Excel. The reports in Excel can be configured for either 15 days or 36 months depending on the settings configured for the report. The usage reports to use with your WCM site are Popularity Trends and Most Popular Items.

Architecture and Improvements

The Usage Analytics components are designed to work with the Search Analytics processing. To support the analytics architecture, there is a component to run the analytics processing jobs. These jobs process the information and store it in the correct locations. To store the content the Analytics architecture uses the Analytics reporting database. This database stores information such as usage event counts and views that provides the data to generate Excel reports.

The engine for analytics has been greatly improved on the Analytics Processing Component to scale with the farm and content. The new improvements to usage analytics include the ability to scale on collecting data, search relevance, and reporting size. These improvements allow the system to make search more relevant not only based on the content but also with the usage of the data. You will see the search relevance of your items improve over time without any changes to the Search settings.

The data that is stored in the Analytics database is also processed into the search engine to assist with search queries. The data affects the search rankings that are used for relevance, and you can directly call each item from the search index in your queries because they are sortable managed properties. The combination of the two sets of information, content, and usage makes it possible to determine the importance of your WCM content on the site. There are predefined usage events that SharePoint uses when you configure a site with default settings.

The default usage events in SharePoint 2013 are:

➤ Views

➤ Recommendations Displayed

➤ Recommendations Clicked

Using Usage Events in Code

Calling the default usage events can be done by adding the event into the HTML where it occurs. These events are defined by SharePoint 2013, and these events are used for the data in the reports created out of the box. There are classes in the Server-Side APIs, Client APIs, and JavaScript to enable you to create the events. There are also a number of default events that you must know the name and ID for in order to make the correct calls. The number order is important because you will use the integer for the one you want.

The default usage event types are:

➤ View

➤ Recommendation View

➤ Recommendation Click

➤ Search

The following code shows how you can add an event of Recommendation Click to an item when clicked. There are two areas where you need to add code. The first is the function to add the usage event, and the second is on the page when the item is clicked. First, here is the JavaScript function to add the event:

```
window.Log<RecommendationClick>ToEventStore = function(url)
{
    ExecuteOrDelayUntilScriptLoaded(function()
    {
        var chpt10_clientContext = SP.ClientContext.get_current();
        SP.Analytics.AnalyticsUsageEntry.logAnalyticsEvent(chpt10_clientContext,
        3, url);
        chpt10_clientContext.executeQueryAsync(null,
                    Function.createDelegate(this, function(sender, e)
                                        {
                                            //Add Error message to page
                                            e.get_message()
                                        }
                                    )
                                );
    }, "SP.js");
}
```

Here is the button to click to add the usage event:

```
<input id="btnAddUsageEventClick" type="button" value="button"
onclick="Log<RecommendationClick>ToEventStore('http://www.bing.com')" />
```

Extending Usage Events

The usage architecture enables you to customize your WCM solutions by adding your own custom event types that can be recorded into the usage data. There can be up to 12 custom events per tenant that you are running. In addition to the custom usage events you can also influence the level of importance submitted to search when sending an event. The custom events you create can track metrics on pages, documents, catalog items, or even sites that users interact with. You could also incorporate third-party usage tracking applications but also have the option of using the custom events based on your needs.

To create the custom usage event, you must add the event to the Analytics Tenant Configuration. This can be done through any of the APIs, but you must have database access to write the event to the database. Here is how you create a custom usage event type:

```
SPServiceApplicationProxy proxyService =
    SPServiceContext.Current.GetDefaultProxy
        (typeof(SearchServiceApplicationProxy));
SearchServiceApplicationProxy proxySearch = proxyService as
    SearchServiceApplicationProxy;

AnalyticsTenantConfig config =
    proxySearch.GetAnalyticsTenantConfiguration
        (SPContext.Current.Site.SiteSubscription.Id);

config.RegisterEventType(Guid.NewGuid(), "CustomEvent", "Chapter10");
config.Update(proxySearch);
```

MULTILINGUAL SUPPORT

Many sites using WCM features need the capability to support displaying content to many people with many languages. There have been updates to content translation along with the new Content by Search web part on how to create and manage multiple translations of content. There are a number of improvements that have been introduced in SharePoint 2013. The primary enhancements are around the stability and speed to the services, and the ability to replicate an entire list or library — not just the pages libraries.

You can create multilingual sites using the Site Variations feature in SharePoint 2013. If you used SharePoint Variations in SharePoint 2010, the features are still available to provide any needed modifications to your content. Site Variations provide a way to create a single source of content called a Source Variation label that can be copied to multiple target variation labels. When working with variations, you can create content that can be imported or exported using a third-party format called the XLIFF file format for content translation.

Navigation for a site with multilingual support previously required using a variation label or constructing your own redirection page at the variation root. The Host Header Site Collections provides a way to create unique URLs per language while still easily reusing content from a Site Variation label or search-driven content. This makes it easy to have a site that ends with a .com address as well as one from another top-level domain such as a German site of .de.

One major improvement with multilingual is the new Machine Translation Services that are now introduced into SharePoint 2013. This service enables you to automatically translate files using a Microsoft cloud-hosted translation service. The requests sent to the translation service can be done either synchronously or asynchronously. The APIs for this service can be used from a server-side object model, client-side object model, REST, or using the JavaScript API. Table 10-7 lists the APIs and the files to include when using them.

TABLE 10-7: Translation Service APIs

API	REFERENCED FILENAMES
Server-Side Object Model	Microsoft.Office.TranslationServices.dll
.NET Client-Side Object Model	Microsoft.Office.TranslationServices.Client.dll
Silverlight Client-Side Object Model	Microsoft.Office.TranslationServices.Silverlight.dll
REST Client-Side Object Model	`http://serverName/_api/TranslationJob` `http://serverName/_api/SyncTranslator` `http://serverName/_api/TranslationJobStatus`
JavaScript Client-Side Object Model	SP.Translation.js

The three primary arguments you need for making a translation are the input file or file path, output file or file path, and the language to translate the content into. If you are not sure which language you are looking for, use the following code to determine which languages are supported:

```
protected void lnkShowLanguages_Click(object sender, EventArgs e)
{
    SPServiceContext serviceContext =
        SPServiceContext.GetContext(SPContext.Current.Site);
    StringBuilder sb = new StringBuilder();
    foreach (CultureInfo item in
      TranslationJob.EnumerateSupportedLanguages(serviceContext))
    {
        sb.AppendFormat("<li>{0} - {1}</li>", item.DisplayName,item.Name);
    }
    litLanguages.Text = String.Format("<ol>{0}</ol>", sb);
}
```

> **NOTE** *Use the NLS API Reference for a full list of languages supported on the operating system:* `http://msdn.microsoft.com/en-us/goglobal/bb896001 .aspx.`

To add a job to the translation queue using the asynchronous actions, you need to provide the input file that will be used for translation and an output file that will be modified with the translated content. The following code shows how this is done using the Server-Side Object Model:

```
protected void btnTranslate_Click(object sender, EventArgs e)
{
    String strTargetLanguage = "de";
    SPServiceContext serviceContext =
        SPServiceContext.GetContext(SPContext.Current.Site);
    TranslationJob job =
        new TranslationJob(serviceContext,
            CultureInfo.GetCultureInfo(culture));
    job.AddFile(txtInputFile, txtOutputFile);
    job.Start();
}
```

SUMMARY

Web Content Management in SharePoint 2013 has undergone some major changes that now provide compelling reasons that can be used for many scenarios. There are new techniques for creating, displaying, and editing content on the site as well as less restrictions on what content can be used. The WCM and publishing APIs have been extended for the new features and provide you with the ability to select the best API for the task. The new Design Manager and HTML design tools bridge the gap between HTML tools and SharePoint pages, enabling a more open and inviting environment. Finally, the services for Usage Analytics and multilingual support build on the foundation for improving your sites with a full set of developer APIs.

11

Using InfoPath with SharePoint 2013

WHAT'S IN THIS CHAPTER?

➤ Designing InfoPath forms

➤ Using features in InfoPath and InfoPath Forms Services 2013

➤ Applying InfoPath best practices

➤ Programatically working with InfoPath Forms

WROX.COM CODE DOWNLOADS FOR THIS CHAPTER

The wrox.com code downloads for this chapter are found at www.wrox.com/remtitle
.cgi?isbn=1118495829 on the Download Code tab. The code is in the chapter 11 download
and individually named according to the names throughout the chapter.

Capturing and displaying data is a critical part of SharePoint. InfoPath helps end users modify
those views quickly. The key advantage of InfoPath is that it provides an easy-to-use interface
for structured forms and provides rich developer functionality for adding business logic.

To create and display forms, SharePoint 2013 uses a service on the server called InfoPath
Forms Services. This service is designed to enable end users to use their browsers to fill out
InfoPath forms and enable administrators to manage those forms. SharePoint provides a full
object model for the InfoPath client, InfoPath forms, and InfoPath server administration. This
enables developers to build enterprise business processes and forms that can be sophisticated
yet easy to create. This has enabled the development of powerful business applications such as
dashboards, data capture forms, and many more.

InfoPath continues to improve the integration with the other Office 2013 products with changes
to the look and buttons like the Insert Image location. No new functionality or scenarios have
been introduced, but InfoPath 2010 and SharePoint 2010 features are still supported and highlighted for InfoPath 2013 and SharePoint 2013 developers.

The biggest change in InfoPath 2013 is the new way to write and edit code. When writing code for InfoPath 2013, InfoPath now requires Visual Studio 2012 with the Microsoft Visual Studio Tools for Applications 2012 add-on to be installed. You will quickly notice that you need these components as soon as you try to open the code editor. The programming experience and assembly references have not fundamentally changed, but you now have the benefits of the most up-to-date version of Visual Studio when developing InfoPath forms.

INTRODUCING THE TRAINING MANAGEMENT APPLICATION

In this chapter, you use an example of a Training Management application built for a fictitious company named Adventure Works, which illustrates the capabilities of InfoPath 2013 and Forms Services 2013. There have not been many large changes between InfoPath 2010 and InfoPath 2013, so many of these examples would work in both systems. First, walk through the application and how it works from the user's perspective.

Scenario: The Human Resources (HR) Department at Adventure Works uses SharePoint and InfoPath to implement a training-course system. You can think of the Training Management application as a set of three use cases as follows:

➤ New training creation use case

➤ Training registration use case

➤ Increment stat counter use case

The Adventure Works staff can perform various activities in this application. For example, the training coordinator can create training events and add them to a SharePoint list named Trainings. This list will be customized and enhanced by InfoPath 2013 to facilitate the training creation use case.

Also, the HR Department at Adventure Works allows its employees to register for a training class. The training registration form is designed in InfoPath and can be hosted inside the InfoPath Form web part on a web part page. The training registration form must be rendered in a typical desktop web browser and in browsers on handheld or mobile devices.

After a training request is filled out and saved, the result is stored in a form library named Registrations, and an event handler associated with the Registrations form library updates a counter in another custom SharePoint list, named Stats. The Stats list is hidden from employees so that its content can't be modified and it does not clutter navigation.

Creating the Sample List

To create powerful forms with SharePoint and InfoPath you need to create the SharePoint lists and libraries that you can work with. To create the training list, start by creating a new custom list and add the following fields:

➤ *Title* — A title for the training events; a single line of text.

➤ *Class Code* — Each class has a unique identifier for the training class (unique eight-character fixed); a single line of text.

➤ *Description* — The description of the training; a single line of text.

➤ *Start Date* — The training start date; date and time.

➤ *End Date* — The training end date; date and time.

➤ *Cost* — The cost of the training (in dollars); currency.

➤ *Level* — The difficulty level associated with the training (a number from 1 to 5); number.

➤ *Enrollment Deadline* — The date that enrollment ends; date and time.

➤ *Address* — The address of the training facility (multiple lines of text); multiple lines of text.

➤ *Additional Information* — Optional information about the training itself (enhanced rich text with pictures, tables, and hyperlinks); multiple lines of text.

Figure 11-1 illustrates all the fields of the new Trainings list, their types, and whether they are required when submitting to the list.

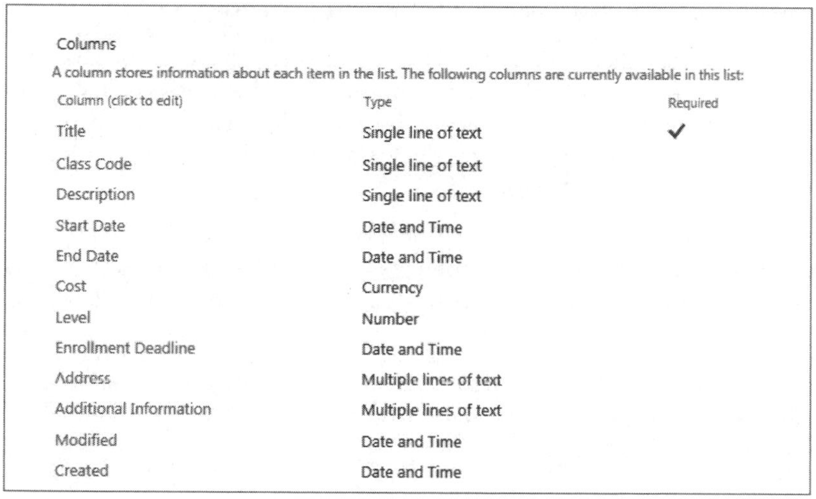

Columns

A column stores information about each item in the list. The following columns are currently available in this list:

Column (click to edit)	Type	Required
Title	Single line of text	✔
Class Code	Single line of text	
Description	Single line of text	
Start Date	Date and Time	
End Date	Date and Time	
Cost	Currency	
Level	Number	
Enrollment Deadline	Date and Time	
Address	Multiple lines of text	
Additional Information	Multiple lines of text	
Modified	Date and Time	
Created	Date and Time	

FIGURE 11-1

CUSTOMIZING SHAREPOINT LIST FORMS

SharePoint 2013 provides a simple and easy-to-use way of customizing SharePoint list forms. The forms created in InfoPath 2013 can be used and embedded into SharePoint to build dynamic sites. One of the exciting features in InfoPath 2013 is the ability to extend or enhance the forms used by SharePoint lists for creating, editing, or showing list items. You can modify list form layouts, set validation rules, or create additional views using little or no code. When you finish modifying the list forms, reflecting your changes back to SharePoint is just a matter of using the one-click publishing capability that comes out of the box with the list form.

Customizing SharePoint List Forms

To customize the list forms in SharePoint 2013, navigate to a list or library, and click Customize Form in the Customize List section of the List tab that appears on the Ribbon, as shown in Figure 11-2.

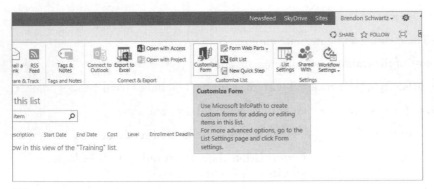

FIGURE 11-2

This launches InfoPath Designer in SharePoint list mode, and a basic form is auto-created from the fields specified in the list's schema. You can see the fields in the Fields task pane on the right side of the design canvas in which mandatory fields are designated with a red asterisk.

When you click one of the existing form fields, the control tools' contextual Ribbon appears on the top and gives you the ability to interact with the list columns inside of InfoPath Designer. Any changes at this point will be persisted later to the SharePoint list when the form is published. For example, if you change a control's binding to a new field, that field will be automatically added to the list's schema when the form template is published to SharePoint.

The controls placed on the forms are selected based on the field type of that column. Figure 11-3 shows the sample list created with text and Date/Time columns already added to the form for each field. The Date and Time Picker control enables you to type a date and time or selects a date from a calendar display.

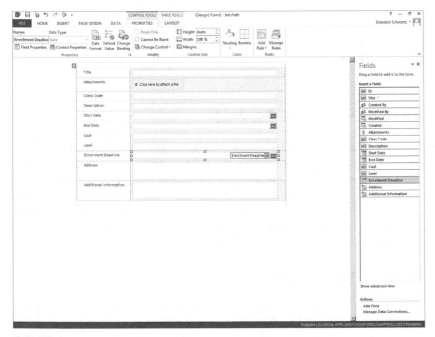

FIGURE 11-3

In addition to auto-generating the form through the SharePoint Ribbon buttons, you can launch InfoPath Designer by going to the New tab on the File menu and choosing SharePoint List as the template. You then enter the URL of the wanted list and the same InfoPath form auto-generates for you.

InfoPath Controls

A number of InfoPath controls can be placed into your form with InfoPath 2013. Each field type maps to one of the InfoPath controls when the form generates. The controls are part of categories that define how they work on your form; these categories are Input, Objects, and Containers. The controls used to map to fields will be from the Input category. You can see all the Input category controls listed here.

➤ Text Box

➤ Rich Text Box

➤ Drop-Down List Box

➤ Combo Box

➤ Check Box

➤ Date Picker

➤ Date and Time Picker

➤ Multiple-Selection List Box

➤ List Box

➤ Person/Group Picker

Changing the form and controls is easy as you can see by extending the form based on the scenario. By using a container called a Section or Optional Section, you can group controls together. For this example, you create an Optional Section to meet the requirements that the training coordinator will want to save real estate on the form, and only enter the information if needed. Add the Optional Section to your form using the following:

1. Click the auto-generated Rich Text Box next to the Additional Information text, and press Delete. (The control will have a label of Additional Information.)

2. In the Fields task pane, click Show Advanced View.

3. Then click the drop-down menu next to the Additional Information field, and choose Optional Section with Controls.

Now you have the Optional Section and the same Rich Text Box bound to the Additional Information file inserted into the form, as shown in Figure 11-4.

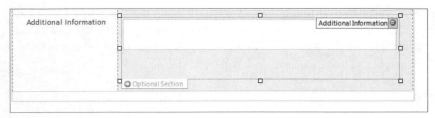

FIGURE 11-4

Creating Business Logic with Rules and Views

Programming has evolved dramatically over the last decade with technologies like XML and XSD. These standards have made it possible to separate data and presentation layers, especially on the web. This is the foundation that InfoPath is built on, and two components of InfoPath use these technologies to help build the business logic of the InfoPath forms. These technologies are called Rules and Views that together create the User Interface for displaying data, and the logic to make the user interface and data behave as needed.

Rules

Rules in InfoPath are a set of one or more actions used to create a dynamic experience for the users of the form when they fill it out. There is always an event that triggers a rule, and in response, the rule performs some action such as a format change or a validation check:

Adding rules to a form is straightforward. You use the following sample rules based on the scenario to build some sample rules on your form:

➤ If End Date < Start Date, show a validation error message.

➤ If Enrollment Deadline > Start Date, show a validation error message.

➤ Only the Address and Additional Information fields can be edited after the training is created.

To add these rules follow these steps:

1. Click the End Date control (Date Picker) to select it.

2. Next on the Home tab in the Ribbon, click Manage Rules. (This will open the Rules task pane.)

3. Click the New button and then Validation.

4. Give the rule a name such as RuleEndDate.

5. Click the None hyperlink in the Condition section.

6. Define the rule to run when the condition in Table 11-1 is true.

TABLE 11-1: Rule

RULE NAME	CONTROL TRIGGER	CONDITION	VALUE
RuleEndDate	End Date	Is less than	Start Date
RuleEnrollmentDeadline	Enrollment Deadline	Is greater than	Start Date

7. Enter a ScreenTip for the error message.

Repeat the steps for the Enrollment Deadline control using Table 11-1. Figure 11-5 shows what the RuleEndDate Condition will look like.

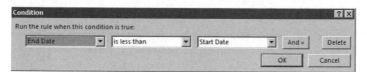

FIGURE 11-5

BEST PRACTICE #1

InfoPath rules and formulas (referred to as declarative logic) are powerful ways to add intelligence to your InfoPath forms. You should always use declarative logic instead of custom code unless the declarative logic cannot perform the needed logic.

Views

Views provide a way to have different layouts of the same information in a single form, and depending on the view shown to the user, they see the layout for only that view. Views are just a presentation of the data in the form, and the same fields can be displayed in multiple views using separate controls. Views are a great way to present your form differently to the users based on different states that the form is in. The view can be changed based on rules or actions triggered by the user during run time of the form.

You can create a new view from the Page Design tab, but you need to add the controls and layout to the new form after it is created. Using the scenario, you will make the fields that need not be edited read only. To do this you will create a different view that will be used when the user edits a list item. To create the views follow these steps:

1. Click the Page Design tab on the Ribbon, and in the Views group, click New.

2. Enter a name for the view; for the example, use Edit Training and click OK.

3. To re-create the default controls and layout, copy (Ctrl+C) the entire layout and controls, and paste (Ctrl+V) them onto the second view.

4. Add a meaningful title to the top of the form for both the default and Edit Training views (that is, New Training and Edit Training).

5. In the Edit Training view, remove the attachment row.

6. Change the Date Picker controls to Text Box controls because the Date Picker control cannot be set to read-only. Right-click Start Date ⇨ Change Control, and then select the Text Box control, as shown in Figure 11-6.

7. Repeat step 6 for Start Date, End Date, and Enrollment Deadline.

8. Right-click the Title Text Box. Click Text Box Properties ⇨ Display tab. Then check the Read-only check box.

9. Repeat step 8 for the following fields: Title, Class Code, Description, Cost, and Level.

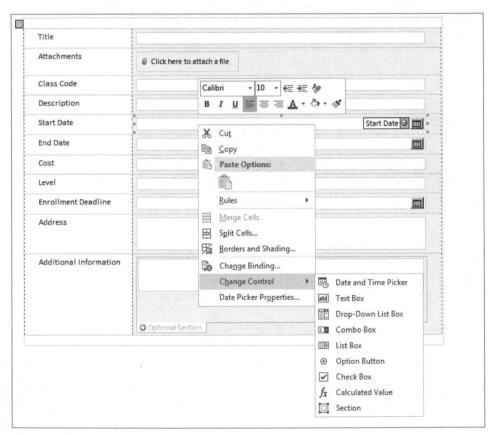

FIGURE 11-6

At this point your Edit Training view should look like Figure 11-7.

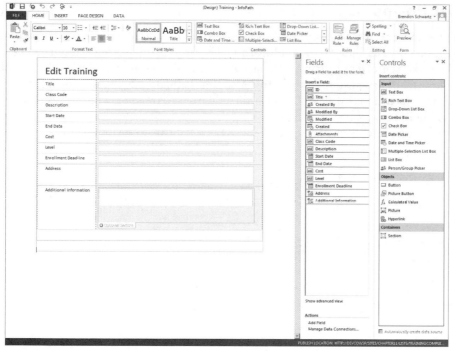

FIGURE 11-7

To change between the views using the form, you need to set up the actions to change between the views based on the conditions set. After you perform the following steps, you have a rule that runs when the form loads:

1. Navigate to the Data tab; then click the Form Load button. This brings up the Rules menu again with the Form Load as the rule type.

2. Click the New button and select Action.

3. Then type an appropriate name for the rule; use RuleSwitchToEditView.

4. Change the condition of the rule to show the Edit page when the list item has an ID assigned to it. By setting the rule to ID, the comparison to it is not blank.

5. Click the Add button to set the condition, and select the Switch Views action.

6. In the View drop-down box, specify Edit Training view.

Now you have customized the input form and provided the needed logic for the training form.

> **NOTE** *Because external lists are just like lists with some extra hooks added to the Business Connectivity Services data source, they can be treated like typical lists in InfoPath. However, the steps you need to take to customize external list forms are different from those for typical list forms. External list form customization is mostly done with SharePoint Designer.*

Publishing List Forms

When you finish designing your forms, you need to publish them to SharePoint. This is the step that creates the connection between SharePoint and InfoPath. The form that has been created can be published directly to the SharePoint list generated using the File tab, and then the Info tab or Publish tab. Figure 11-8 shows the current state of the form. Also, InfoPath already knows which list to publish to because you opened the InfoPath Designer directly from SharePoint. This means that there is no additional configuration required when publishing this form to SharePoint. Just verify that the publishing location is correct, click the button that says Quick Publish, and you are done.

FIGURE 11-8

After a form is published to a SharePoint list you may want to save the form locally. In this case do not close the form, but instead click the Save As option, and save the template to your local drive. The important point to remember here is that saving a form template locally or on a network share is a totally different process from publishing it. Publishing versus saving a form template is covered in greater detail in the section "Publishing InfoPath Forms," but for now know that there are two types of finalized forms: Publishing and Saving.

After the form has been successfully published and its template is locally saved, you can test that all the design and dynamic logic work as expected in SharePoint. Return to the SharePoint list in the site, and create a new list item to view the recently published forms. The default ASPX page is replaced with the default view of the form template you just customized and published. After filling out the form (see Figure 11-9), you can submit it by clicking Save on the top of the Ribbon. At this point, the form applies the appropriate rules to validate your input and adds a new list item to the SharePoint list.

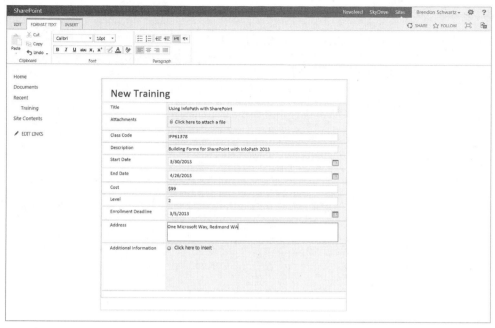

FIGURE 11-9

If you closely look at the URL of the rendered form, you see that the form, unlike uncustomized list forms, is not loaded by the NewForm.aspx page. Instead, it is loaded by another out-of-the-box web part page called newifs.aspx.

The newifs.aspx, displayinf.aspx, and editifs.aspx pages are part of the list's infrastructure in SharePoint 2013. These pages were added in SharePoint 2010 to provide tighter integration with InfoPath forms directly into lists. They are all web part pages that can be customized via the browser. All three pages are accessible from the List tab ⇨ Form Web Parts drop down on the Ribbon, as shown in Figure 11-10. Each page hosts an instance of the InfoPath Form web part that knows how to locate and load the form template associated with the SharePoint list.

FIGURE 11-10

When editing an existing list item, you see that the rule you placed in the Load event of the form kicks in and switches the view from New Training to Edit Training (see Figure 11-11), where you can edit the last two fields of the form only.

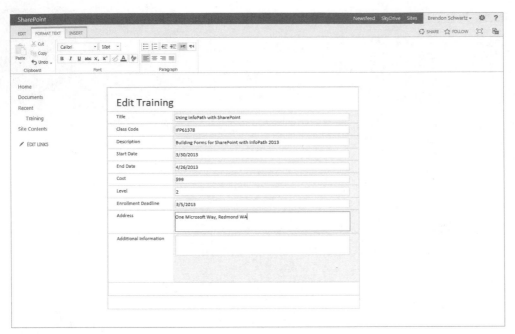

FIGURE 11-11

> **NOTE** *You can find this form template (Training.xsn) in the code download for this book.*

If you want to undo everything and revert to the out-of-the-box ASPX forms after you have customized the forms, you can do this quickly without any issues. Browse to the List Settings page of the SharePoint list, click Form Settings, select Use the Default SharePoint Form, and click OK. Optionally, if you leave the Delete the InfoPath Form from the server unchecked, the InfoPath form you customized remains on the server. The next time you click Customize Form, the saved InfoPath form will be used in the InfoPath Designer instead of a new one being auto-generated from scratch.

Two things about SharePoint list forms to consider: First, custom code is not supported in a customized list form using InfoPath 2013. If you open any of the forms that have been auto-generated from a SharePoint list, there is no Developer tab on the Ribbon to launch the coding tools. Second, you can publish a list form only to the list it belongs to. This also means that converting your list form to a form library is not possible.

DESIGNING INFOPATH FORM TEMPLATES

InfoPath separates data from schema and presentation. This means that the form you design to be used as a Form Template can store only a reference to your design and keep the data separate from the presentation layer. Each form template will be used in a form library and also store the data in that library.

To build upon the scenario, create a form library named Registrations that will be used to store the form template and completed forms (the data). Every time the form is filled out, an instance of the form template is stored in the form library. The result is just an .xml file that contains the data that was entered into the form and a reference to the form template. Everything else that makes up the form is provided by its form template.

Unlike the list form, Form Templates can be filled out using two form entry options. One option is to browse directly to the SharePoint form library and click the New Form button. The other option is to navigate to a web part page where an InfoPath form web part has been added that references the form template. Both options open the forms for users to fill out. After you press the Save button, the results are saved in the SharePoint form library.

What Is a Form Library?

A form library is a specific type of document library that includes an InfoPath form as its primary template and easily allows users to fill out a new InfoPath form or edit an existing one. Instead of storing documents, the form library is designed to save the InfoPath form XML and open it with the right version of the InfoPath form template.

Although InfoPath Designer 2013 enables you to create a form library on a SharePoint site when you publish your form template, there are situations in which you may want to create the form library beforehand. For example, you may want to create the form library, change its settings such as versioning, and set up permissions to it before publishing the form template, simply because people who publish may not have enough permission to complete such a task. Follow these steps to create a form library:

1. Click the Site Setting gear icon ⇨ Add an App.

2. Select the Form Library app.

3. In the Name box, type **Registrations**.

4. Click Create.

After the form library is created, you can specify how its form templates should be opened. Browse to the Form Library ⇨ Form Library Settings, and select Advanced Settings. These settings are listed under Opening Documents in the Browser, as shown in Figure 11-12. The default behavior when you create the form library from within SharePoint is to open the forms in the browser, but nothing stops you from changing it to InfoPath Filler 2013 (by selecting Open in the client application).

Opening Documents in the Browser
Specify whether browser-enabled documents should be opened in the client or browser by default when a user clicks on them. If the client application is unavailable, the document will always be opened in the browser.

Default open behavior for browser-enabled documents:
- ○ Open in the client application
- ○ Open in the browser
- ● Use the server default (Open in the browser)

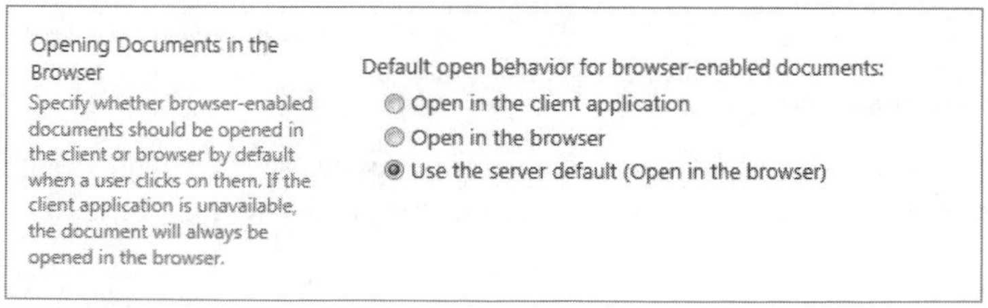

FIGURE 11-12

Designing Your Form Template

Building a form template is similar to building a form for a SharePoint list except you start with an open canvas and do not have an auto-generated form based on fields. Start by opening InfoPath Designer 2013 from your local machine. On the New menu select the type of form you want to design. InfoPath makes this process easy by providing a form template called SharePoint Form Library. When selecting a template to start from, InfoPath Designer provides descriptive text in the top-right corner of the New page to help describe what the form provides, as shown in Figure 11-13. It is important to take a moment and review prebuilt templates, their concepts, the matching color schemes, and the optional layout used in each.

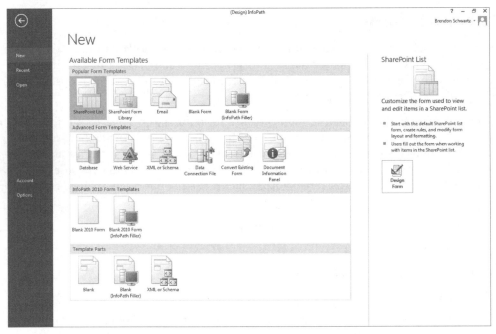

FIGURE 11-13

BEST PRACTICE #2

Using prebuilt templates accelerates the form creation process and saves you a considerable amount of time if you are new to InfoPath 2013.

All available form templates are grouped into four main categories:

➤ *Popular Form Templates* — A wide range of popular form templates to start your design. When customizing SharePoint lists and document libraries, this is the category that you want to focus on.

➤ *Advanced Form Templates* — This category covers templates for more advanced scenarios, mostly for querying and submitting data to databases, web services, or other external data sources.

➤ *InfoPath 2010 Form Templates* — Form templates that also work in InfoPath 2010 in backward-compatible mode.

➤ *Template Parts* — Contains three templates for building reusable components — also known as mini-form templates. When built, mini-form templates can simplify the creating of more complex forms, much like splitting the page into user controls in classic ASP.NET.

From Available Form Templates, choose the SharePoint Form Library template, and click Design Form on the right side of the dialog box.

After you open InfoPath Designer 2013, you may notice that laying out your form to get a professional look and feel is now easy. InfoPath uses page layouts as a framework to organize your form's content, including controls, graphics, and tables (which include section layouts).

Building a Form Template

Now that you understand what the form library and form template are, you can create a form to upload to the library based on the training scenario. First, you need to replace the page layout that InfoPath gives you by default with something more appropriate for the Training registration form. Just delete everything you see on the form (Ctrl+A/Delete). On the Page Design tab, select one of the five page layout templates, for example Color Bar. Add an appropriate title, and adjust the form so that it is centered. At this stage, your form contains only one page layout and a title, as shown in Figure 11-14.

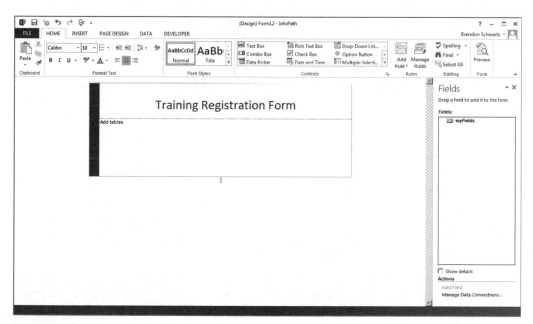

FIGURE 11-14

Next, you need to add a section layout to the form to create a logical grouping of information that you want to collect in your form. From the Insert tab under the Tables gallery, choose Single Column Stacked 4 — No Heading, and insert it where it says Add Tables, right underneath the title.

The template adds three rows by default, and you need to add three more rows so that the following controls can be placed on the form:

➤ *Event Name* — A required Drop-Down Listbox control linked to the Trainings list

➤ *Alternate Email* — A required text box with validation rules

➤ *Emergency Contact Name* — A required text box

➤ *Emergency Contact Phone Number* — A required text box with validation rules

➤ *Short Bio* — An optional text box

➤ *Manager* — An optional People/Group Picker control

From the new Controls gallery on the Home tab, add the required controls to the main section layout on the design canvas. You can set the controls to be required by right-clicking each control and selecting the Cannot Be Blank check box in the control's Properties dialog box (Validation section). Because each control on the form and its auto-generated field represent the data on the form, give them more descriptive names. To do that, name the controls and the fields (field1 to field6) as described in the preceding bulleted list.

> **NOTE** *It is a common misconception in InfoPath that fields, controls, and groups are interchangeable terms. A field represents the data collected by your form. All the fields available in your form can be accessed from the Data tab ⇨ Show Fields ⇨ Fields task pane. A group is an element in the data source that can contain fields or other groups. A control can be bound to a field or a group. When bound, the data collected by a control is saved in the form's underlying XML file. However, a control can also be left unbound, meaning that it doesn't save any data.*

Applying Themes

InfoPath 2010 introduced the ability to quickly change the look and feel of your form just like the other Office products with themes. If you need to change the overall look of your form, you can simply apply a new theme to the entire form. To do this, look on the Page Design tab in the Themes gallery. You can select an appropriate style that best describes your form needs. Pick a color scheme that matches your site or company colors.

If you still have your cursor within a table cell on your form, on the Layout Contextual tab, click the Borders button, and make some adjustments to the form so that there is a border around the entire layout page. When these steps are complete, the form should look like the one in Figure 11-15.

FIGURE 11-15

To complete the form, you need to add some rules to the form template just like you did with the SharePoint list form. Follow these steps to add the needed rules.

1. Click the Emergency Contact Phone Number text box.

2. From the Controls Tools/Properties tab, click the Manage Rules button to launch the Rules Manager.

3. Click New ➪ Validation to create the rule.

4. Provide a name for the rule such as **PhoneNumberIncorrect**.

5. Create a condition with EmergencyNumber, which does not match a pattern.

6. Then select the Phone Number pattern.

7. Add the ScreenTip of Please enter a phone number.

Repeat these steps for the Alternate Email Address field, but change the Data Entry pattern from the Phone Number pattern to the Email pattern.

Many validation rules require specific common patterns used in many forms. As you can see in Figure 11-16, there are many ready-to-use data entry patterns that you can choose from. You can even customize each pattern's associated regular expressions and create your own customized pattern.

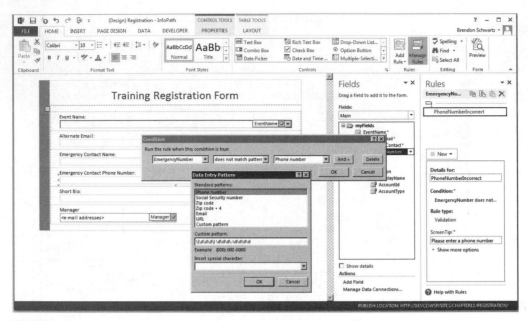

FIGURE 11-16

> **NOTE** *InfoPath Designer 2013 enables the option to copy and paste rules in the Rules task pane. This was added with InfoPath Designer 2010 to help save time and work more efficiently when designing your forms for complex rules. Copying and pasting rules doesn't work across multiple forms.*

People and Group Picker Control

You can use the People and Group Picker control to provide the person selection in SharePoint. Notice how, by adding this control to the design canvas, a group has been added in the Fields task pane containing three fields: DisplayName, AccountID, and Account Type.

To see the SharePoint related properties, go to the People Picker control's Properties dialog box, and on the SharePoint Server tab, specify the SharePoint site URL to query for people and groups. Notice in the General tab how you can narrow down the people/group picking query to choices like People Only, People and Groups, Allow Multiple Selections, or even a specific SharePoint group, as shown in Figure 11-17.

If you added a People/Group Picker control to a customized SharePoint list form (such as the Trainings list forms), you don't need to go through all these additional steps to set it up. The control is smart enough to pick the right context for you.

Querying SharePoint Lists in Forms

Almost every form connected to SharePoint uses list data in the form. Querying SharePoint lists is a built-in feature of InfoPath with wizards to guide you through the process. To add a SharePoint list connection to a form, use the Data tab, and click the From SharePoint List in the Get External Data gallery. On the first page of the Data Connection Wizard, type the full URL of the SharePoint list, and click Next. The second screen in the wizard enables you to select the SharePoint list you will get data from. After you click Next, the third screen of the wizard is where you select the fields that must be included in the data source.

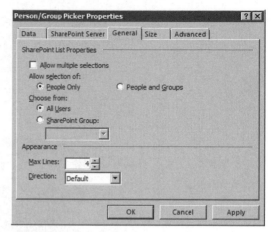

FIGURE 11-17

The wizard provides the option Store a Copy of the Data in the Form Template. Use this if you are building the form offline or need to work with the data in the form, even if a connection cannot be made. Also, you can provide the option Automatically Retrieve Data When Form Is Opened, which provides a rule on when the data source should be called.

> **BEST PRACTICE #3**
>
> Before selecting Automatically Retrieve Data When Form Is Opened, when creating a data source with the Data Source Wizard, consider the following two tips: Loading large data sources can significantly increase your form's initial rendering time and should be avoided if possible. You should postpone such queries to a later time during the form's life cycle or make them on demand, based on user-initiated actions. One solution is to create wizards (using views) and have a splash screen in the default view that loads the required data sources in subsequent views. This option should not be selected if either data source changes frequently or it contains sensitive information that must not be included in the form's schema (for offline use).

To connect a field using the example, click in the Event Name control's Properties dialog box, select Get Choices from an External Data Source, and in the data source, select the secondary data source. Click the XPath image next to the Entries box, and choose the data fields of the data source, which will be `d:SharePointListItem_RW` element. Set the Value to the Class Code field, and the Display to the Title field, as shown in Figure 11-18, and then click OK.

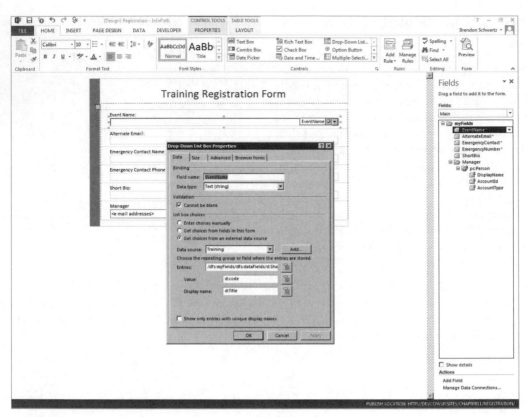

FIGURE 11-18

With many data sources, you need only a subset of data that's relevant to the users, but the data source fetches all the list items. As many list items are created over time, there is a chance that the items could become irrelevant or simply not used anymore. To address this issue you can use a filter that enables the users to view only relevant list items.

Using the example, the Training list has a column that you can use to filter the Enrollment Deadline that indicates when the registration for the training is due. This is the column to use to define the filter by following these steps:

1. In the Event Name control's Properties dialog box, click the button next to the Entries box.

2. Select the d:SharePoint ListItem_RW group as the group to apply the filter to.

3. Click the Filter Data button to load the Filter Data dialog box.

4. Click the Add button to show the Specify Filter Conditions dialog box.

5. Select Enrollment Deadline, is greater than.

6. Then select Use a Formula and use the now() function in the Insert Function button under Date/Time.

Querying REST Web Services

In the previous section, you used the traditional technique for querying SharePoint lists. Alternatively, you can query data including SharePoint lists using REST Web Services with a capability called WCF Data Services.

WCF Data Services is a framework that enables interactions with SharePoint data in a RESTful manner. With SharePoint 2013 there are also new OData RESTful endpoints that provide data in either Atom or JSON formats.

> **NOTE** *REST Web Services are not a one-way data collection for browsing only data; they can provide full Representational State Transfer (REST) over HTTP support for browsing data and manipulating it using regular HTTP verbs (GET, PUT, DELETE, and so on), which WCF Data Services supports.*

Everything starts with a URL because REST is all about using URIs to identify resources, modify them, and transfer them using a representation of the resource. The most obvious advantage of using REST is simplicity. Anyone who can craft a URL can work with REST APIs, which makes REST even more powerful compared to other data access methodologies. Because InfoPath 2013 supports connecting to REST APIs, you can query the SharePoint lists (a resource in the REST context) using SharePoint's REST Web Services.

To add a REST connection to a SharePoint list, navigate to the Data tab in the InfoPath Ribbon. In the Get External Data gallery, click From Web Service, and then click From REST Web Service.

The REST URL would be formatted as follows:

```
http://<site>/_vti_bin/ListData.svc/<list>
```

Such as:

```
http://devcow.sharepoint.com/_vti_bin/ListData.svc/Trainings
```

Type the URL in the Address text box, and click Next in the wizard. In the next step, give the new data source a name and check the Automatically Retrieve Data When Form Is Opened option to create a secondary data source.

Before you consume this feed in your InfoPath form, examine the XML output from the endpoint by typing the feed URL in the browser and pressing the Enter key. This is a simple way to see what the returned results are. If you use Internet Explorer, you may need to turn off the feed reader view in the browser to see the returned raw XML. In Internet Explorer this option can be turned off by unchecking the Turn on Feed Reading View option in the Tools ➪ Internet Options ➪ Content Tab ➪ Feed and Web Slices ➪ Settings.

One great advantage of using REST data sources is that you can easily restrict the returned entities by applying the $filter expression to the entity set, identified in the last segment of a REST URI. In other words, you filter data right in the source instead of using form-level filtering.

The $filter can be difficult to figure out so look at an example. On the Data tab, click Form Load from the Rules category. This opens the Rules task pane in which you can create rules that will run when the form is opened. Create a new rule and leave the condition section empty. This runs the rule whenever your form loads and is not based on a specific condition.

Next, click the Add button and select Change REST URL (see Figure 11-19). This action makes it easier to change the filters of REST URLs such as SharePoint. The Change REST URL action enables developers to change the REST URI dynamically when an event is triggered, such as Form Load or Submit. This brings up the Rule Details dialog box, which gives you more options for manipulating the URI you initially set for the data source, as shown in Figure 11-20.

FIGURE 11-19

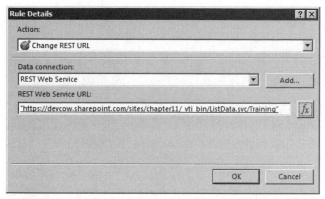

FIGURE 11-20

To implement the filter, click the function (fx) button next to the URL and insert the following:

```
concat("https://devcow.sharepoint.com/_vti_bin/ListData.svc/Training",
"?filter=EnrollmentDeadline gt datatime'", now(), "'")
```

To make the REST Web service call, you need to add
another rule to the form load that runs the action.
To add this action, click the Add button in the Rules
task pane again, but this time choose Query for the
data rule action. As shown in Figure 11-21, in the
Rule Details dialog box, you just need to click OK
because the Action and Data Connection values
have already been set. Figure 11-22 shows both rules
and their order in the Rules task pane for the Form
Load event.

FIGURE 11-21

Using the REST web services, you can now change
the Event Name drop-down list box to be bound to the new data source.
In the Control's Properties dialog box, select Get Choices from an External
Data Source, and in the data source, select the secondary data source.
Next, click the XPath image next to the Entries box, and choose the entry
element. The entry element represents an individual list item in the returned
feed and acts as a container for meta data and data associated with each
list item. Set the Value to the Code field, and the Display to the Title field;
then click OK.

A great feature with InfoPath is that you can use the Preview form without
publishing it to a SharePoint site. Press F5 and preview the form. Your form
should load only the trainings in which the enrollment deadline is greater
than today. Using these techniques shows how easy it is to combine the
power of REST data sources with formulas in InfoPath 2013 to create
filters using absolutely no code.

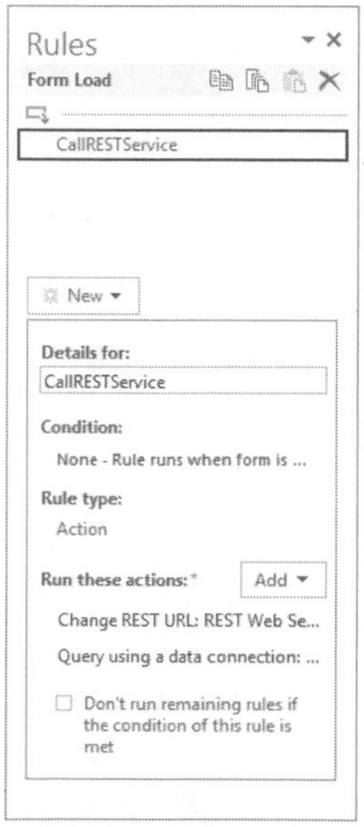

FIGURE 11-22

BEST PRACTICE #4

Use query parameters to stop loading unnecessary data in your data sources. If you can't filter data at the source, at least filter your data at the form level if possible. Filtering data saves rendering time and boosts the overall performance of your form when the underlying data sources contain a lot of data.

Submit Behavior

Submitting forms in InfoPath is a powerful capability. Submitting provides the ability to control the behavior of the form and where the collected data ends up. Submitting an InfoPath form is different from saving it, and these two actions shouldn't be confused. The most obvious difference is that you cannot submit a form that has validation errors, but that is not the case when you save the form. Another difference is that when you save an InfoPath form, the results are saved as XML in the form library. When you submit the form, not only do you have the option of saving the results as XML, but you also have plenty of other options, such as closing the form or running rules without writing any custom code. In many scenarios, the level of control you get out of the box for submitting your forms is what makes it a more appealing option than just saving the form.

If you go to the Data tab and select the Submit Options button, you will find several settings to define the submission behavior of the form. You can design your form to submit to a series of powerful connection points, such as the SharePoint form library, e-mail, a web service, a web server, a DCL connection, or even a hosting environment. Finally, if you want to satisfy complex submission requirements, you can write custom code by selecting the appropriate option, as shown in Figure 11-23.

Also, you can define your own Submit button. Simply add a regular button, and in the Control Properties tab, set its action to Submit, as shown in Figure 11-24. Alternatively, you can click the button and choose Submit Data from Add Rule in the Control Tools Properties contextual menu (see Figure 11-25). Both actions result in the same behavior for the button.

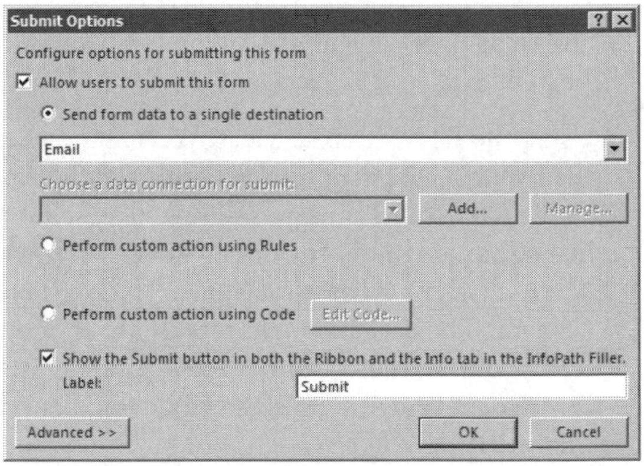

FIGURE 11-23

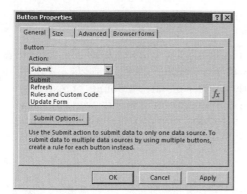

FIGURE 11-24

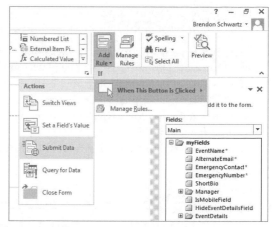

FIGURE 11-25

After Submit is enabled in a form and all the properties are set, a Submit button appears on the SharePoint Ribbon next to the Save and Save As options when the form is first opened, as shown in Figure 11-26.

FIGURE 11-26

Some of the buttons in the SharePoint Ribbon are customizable from within the form template (Form Options ⇨ Web Browser). For example, you can hide the Save button and leave Submit as the only option to persist the form's data.

Form Programming

One of the most used classes is the Environment variable to determine if the form is displayed in the browser and if the form is displayed on a mobile platform. Using the Environment variable, you can implement a mobile-friendly form. Using the scenario for the chapter, you can build a mobile-friendly form using custom code that is in the form's load event to detect whether the form is rendered in the a mobile browser, and then switch the default view to a lighter view accordingly.

The mobile view of a form starts with a new form called Mobile View and hiding any controls that would not be a good fit for mobile platforms. The controls that would not be a good fit are any that require a large amount of input, due to the difficulty of entering large amounts of text. Also, controls like the People Picker control that is just rendered as a text box in mobile web browsers without the search for a user capability. A good practice is to have a way to tell if the data were entered from a mobile browser, and you can do that by storing the value in a field to indicate that the form was submitted using a mobile browser.

BEST PRACTICE #5

Since InfoPath 2010, every form can be viewed on mobile devices by default. The key differences in rendering between desktop web browsers and browsers on mobile devices require taking into account the size and data entry limitations. There are also limitations on the behavior of some controls when rendered in mobile web browsers. There are unsupported controls and controls that are rendered as plain text boxes such as the Date/Time Picker and People/Group Picker.

To write custom code in your form and work with the InfoPath object model, the minimum requirements are:

➤   Microsoft .NET 4.0

➤   Microsoft Visual Studio 2012

➤   Microsoft Visual Studio Tools for Applications 2012

➤   Selection of the default programming language (C# or VB.NET) to use when writing the code for the form. This can be set on the Developer tab using the Language button. The programming language can be changed only before any code has been written for the form; so, for example, you cannot mix and match VB.NET and C# code in one form.

To begin implementing the mobile view, you need to create the mobile field. In the Fields task pane, click Add Field and define a field named IsMobileField of type True/False (Boolean). Next, create a new view in the registration form named Mobile View; the steps to create the view can be reviewed from earlier in the chapter. Simply copy and paste everything from the default view into the new view, and change the title to Mobile Training Registration. In the mobile view, delete the entire rows that contain Short Bio and Manager controls to make the form more compact. Next, you need to select the On Load Event from the Developer tab. This launches the code editor, and you will be ready to start developing in Microsoft Visual Studio, as shown in Figure 11-27.

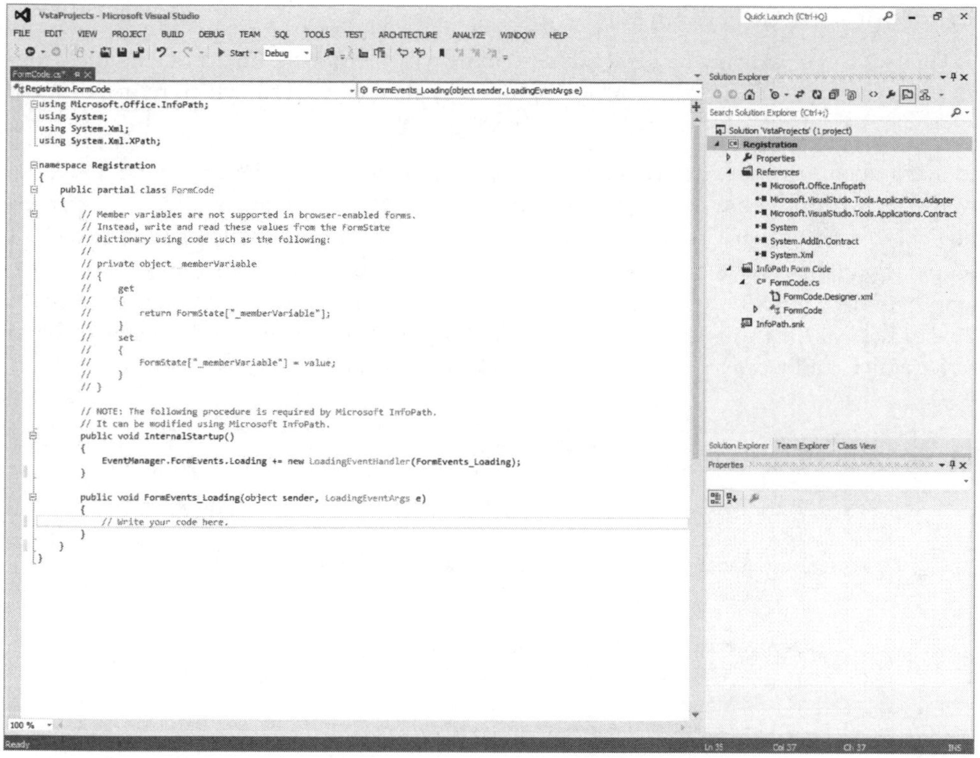

FIGURE 11-27

Although it is entirely possible to write the code for the event handlers beforehand and wire them up manually later by changing the form definition file (.xsf), the approach recommended by Microsoft is to create the event handlers in design mode just as you did for the Form Load event. This way, InfoPath automatically creates the declarations of the event handlers in the code and makes the required modification to the form definition file that enables a form template to use those event handlers. The form definition file (.xsf) is covered in greater detail in the "Form Anatomy" section later in this chapter.

Adding Event Handlers

To detect the mobile browser and set the fields in InfoPath, complete the `FormEvents_Loading` event handler, as shown in Listing 11-1. The event handler uses the `MainDataSource` property of the `XMLForm` class to call the `CreateNavigator` method to return an instance of the `XPathNavigator` class. The returned object defines a random and read-only access cursor model over the form's underlying XML data, which at this point is positioned at the root node.

Using the InfoPath object model, you can access and change almost everything in the form at run time. You just need to know how to get a reference to the element you want to change. This is made possible because the underlying data in InfoPath is all XML, so the `XPathNavigator` and `XmlForm` classes can be easily used for interacting with the form's data. The `XMLForm` object is initialized in the form load, so you don't need to use the `this` keyword in C# (or the `Me` keyword in Visual Basic) to access its members, such as `MainDataSource` or `NamespaceManager`.

Using the Environment Class Object

Next, the code uses the Environment object to determine which run-time environment and program was used to open the form. This class provides a property called IsMobile, which returns true if the form is viewed by a mobile browser.

Finally, the overloaded SelectSingleNode method is used to navigate to the IsMobielField field. Then, the code uses the SetValue method of the second XPathNavigator object to set the value of the field to true; otherwise, it is set to false. The SelectSingleNode method takes an XPath expression (string) and a resolver parameter for resolving namespace prefixes (via the NamespaceManager property of the XmlForm class). To determine the absolute XPath to the IsMobileField field in the SelectSingleNode method, right-click the field in the Fields task pane in InfoPath Designer, and from the context menu, click Copy XPath.

LISTING 11-1: Code for Setting the IsMobileField Value

```
public void FormEvents_Loading(object sender, LoadingEventArgs e)
{
    XPathNavigator rootNav = MainDataSource.CreateNavigator();
    if (Environment.IsMobile)
    {
        XPathNavigator mobileFieldNav =
            rootNav.SelectSingleNode("/my:myFields/my:IsMobileField",
            NamespaceManager);
        mobileFieldNav.SetValue("true");
    }
}
```

Another common programming task that you can use is to change data on the form when a field changes. To do this you need a new section on the Registration form that displays the training details such as cost, start date, and address. Only add this section and its contents to the default view, to keep the mobile view as light as possible. This section should appear only when an employee selects a training opportunity from the Event Name drop-down list box control; otherwise it remains hidden.

To implement this dynamic behavior, use the following steps. The registration form will look like Figure 11-28 with the changes applied:

1. In the Fields task pane, click Add Field, and create a field named HideEventDetailsField of type True/False (Boolean). Use this field to show/hide the Event Details section in the default view.

2. Next, add a new row to the form's main table after the People Picker control.

3. Insert a section from the Controls gallery on the Home tab to the new row just created named EventDetails.

4. Add a new table to the section, and insert three text boxes with the following names in each row to host the Start Date (EDStartDate), Cost (EDCost), and Address (EDAddress) controls.

Training Registration Form

Event Name:

Alternate Email:

Emergency Contact Name:

Emergency Contact Phone Number:

Short Bio:

Your Manager
<e-mail addresses>

Training Details

Cost:	
Start Date:	
Address:	

Section

FIGURE 11-28

To hide the form you can use the dynamic logic with the conditional rules. With formatting in InfoPath 2013, you can apply text formatting and background shading to controls, and disable or highlight controls based on user input or a condition. Use the following steps to add the conditional formatting to your forms.

1. In InfoPath Designer, select the Event Details section, and click Manage Rules if the Rules task pane is not already visible.

2. Then from the Rules task pane, click New ⇨ Formatting to add a new conditional formatting rule.

3. Name the rule HideOnLoad.

4. Click the hyperlink for the Condition, and set the formatting condition to HideEventDetailsField, which is equal to TRUE.

5. Click the check box for Hide This Control, as shown in Figure 11-29

At this point, the formatting rule you just created, with the custom code to add to your form's Load event in Listing 11-2, ensures that the Event Details section is hidden when the registration form loads in the default view.

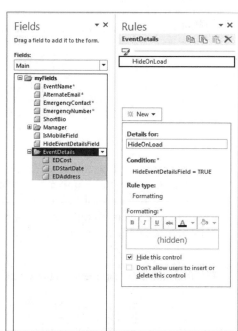

FIGURE 11-29

LISTING 11-2: Code for Setting the HideEventDetailsField Value

```
        public void FormEvents_Loading(object sender, LoadingEventArgs e)
        {
            XPathNavigator rootNav = MainDataSource.CreateNavigator();
            if (Environment.IsMobile)
            {
// Code Omitted for brevity
            }
            else
            {
                XPathNavigator hideEventDetailsFieldNav =
                rootNav.SelectSingleNode("/my:myFields/
                my:HideEventDetailsField", NamespaceManager);
                hideEventDetailsFieldNav.SetValue("true");
            }
        }
```

With the Event Details section hidden at the form's startup, now you need to add the necessary logic to show this section and populate its content when the Event Name drop-down list box changes. To create a new event handler for the drop-down list, first save the form and then right-click the EventName field. From the Context menu, select Programming ➪ On After Change Event to launch Visual Studio if it is not already open.

InternalStartup() Function

As you can see in the following code snippet, the event binding code is placed in the InternalStartup() method of the FormCode.cs (or FormCode.vb) file in your form template project. The binding is done using the XmlChangedEventHandler delegate that represents the method that will handle the changed event of the EventName field.

```
       public void InternalStartup()
       {
           EventManager.FormEvents.Loading += new
           LoadingEventHandler(FormEvents_Loading);
           EventManager.XmlEvents["/my:myFields/my:EventName"].Changed += new
           XmlChangedEventHandler(EventName_Changed);
       }
```

The EventChanged event handler is auto-generated with no code in it. The code you write in this event handler uses the training class code the employee selects from the Event Name drop-down list box as a key to select the rest of the training details. After the matching training is found, your code populates the Event Details section with the rest of the details so that the employee can review the form before saving it, as shown in Listing 11-3.

LISTING 11-3: Code for EventName_Changed Event Handler

```
        public void EventName_Changed(object sender, XmlEventArgs e)
        {
            XPathNavigator rootNav = MainDataSource.CreateNavigator();
            XPathNavigator hideEventDetailsFieldNav =
```

```
        rootNav.SelectSingleNode("/my:myFields/my:HideEventDetailsField",
        NamespaceManager);
hideEventDetailsFieldNav.SetValue("false");
XPathNavigator eventNameNav =
        rootNav.SelectSingleNode("/my:myFields/my:EventName",
        NamespaceManager);
XPathNavigator trainingsNav =
DataSources["Trainings"].CreateNavigator();
trainingsNav.MoveToRoot();
XPathNodeIterator codeSelectionIterator =
        trainingsNav.Select("//*[local-name() = 'Code']");
while (codeSelectionIterator.MoveNext())
{
    if (codeSelectionIterator.Current.InnerXml.Equals(eventNameNav.
        Value)
        && !codeSelectionIterator.Current.InnerXml.Equals(""))
    {
        XPathNavigator matchedTraining = codeSelectionIterator.Current;
        matchedTraining.MoveToParent();
        XmlDocument training = new XmlDocument();
        training.LoadXml(matchedTraining.OuterXml);
        XPathNavigator detailsNav = training.CreateNavigator();
        XPathNavigator domNav = MainDataSource.CreateNavigator();

        //Populate the Cost Field
        XPathNavigator detailNav =
            detailsNav.SelectSingleNode("//*[local-name() = 'Cost']");
        XPathNavigator formNav =
            domNav.SelectSingleNode("/my:myFields/my:EventDetails/
            my:EDCost", NamespaceManager);
        formNav.SetValue(detailNav.Value);

        //Populate the Start Date Field
        detailNav =
            detailsNav.SelectSingleNode("//*[local-name() =
            'StartDate']");
        formNav =
            domNav.SelectSingleNode("/my:myFields/my:EventDetails/
            my:EDStartDate", NamespaceManager);
        String eDate = detailNav.Value;
        eDate = eDate.Substring(0, 10);
        formNav.SetValue(eDate);

        //Populate the Address Field
        detailNav = detailsNav.SelectSingleNode("//*[local-name() =
        'Address']");
        formNav =
            domNav.SelectSingleNode("/my:myFields/my:EventDetails/
            my:EDAddress", NamespaceManager);
        formNav.SetValue(detailNav.Value);
        break;
    }
}
}
```

The first three lines of the code set the `HideEventDetailsField` field to false so that the formatting rule in the form kicks in and the Event Details section is toggled so that it is visible.

Navigating Elements in the Form

As discussed the data is XML, and using the built-in .NET classes for navigating through elements is critical. To create the navigation objects, notice the first bolded lines in Listing 11-3 where a reference to the secondary data source is constructed and an `XPathNavigator` object is created for accessing the data source. Next, the cursor is positioned at the root of the data source and an iterator (of type XPathNodeIterator) over all the Class Code nodes is returned. Because the returned `XPathNodeIterator` object is not pointing to the first node in the selected set of Class Code nodes, a call to the `MoveNext` method must be made to position the cursor on the first node in the selected set of nodes. This is done in the `While` expression.

The rest of the code is simply looping through the selected nodes and finding the one that matches the training class code selected by the user. When the control flows into the `while` loop, two conditions are checked in the beginning:

➤ The training class code in the current context node equals the training code selected by the user.

➤ The user has not selected a blank value from the Event Name control.

If both of these conditions are met, this means that a node in the data source with matching training code has been found. Notice the second bolded lines. The matching node is stored in the `matchedTraining` variable, and the corresponding `XPathNavigator` is moved to the parent node of the current Class Code node, which is the node that contains all the information about the training. The `outXML` of the parent node is stored in the training object of type `XMLDocument`, and a navigator (detailsNav object) is created for it. Another navigator (domNav object) is created to access the fields in the Event Details section of the form.

The rest of the code uses the elements to populate the information. The controls in the Event Details section are populated with information retrieved from the `detailsNav` navigator object.

BEST PRACTICE #6

As demonstrated in this chapter, the code for an event handler associated with the changed event that uses the `XmlChangedEventHandler` delegate should be auto-generated only from within InfoPath Designer 2013. Writing the event handlers beforehand and manually modifying the form definition file (.xsf) to wire them up is not a best practice. This is mainly because changes made to this file outside of InfoPath Designer 2013 might be lost if the form template is modified in InfoPath Designer 2013.

Now, the additional information section and all its contents show up only if an employee selects a training opportunity; otherwise, they are hidden. In general, showing and hiding parts of your forms help you design organized forms in which only relevant information is shown to the users.

Click the Preview button (from the Quick Access Toolbar) to test your form before publishing it. Typically, the Preview button is a powerful tool that can be used when designing InfoPath forms; use it as much as needed to verify forms before they are published.

Publishing InfoPath Forms

InfoPath is all about collecting, parsing, and validating data from multiple sources. The data that's collected in a form needs to be persisted somewhere. In the design phase of your forms, it's important to know where the form eventually ends up because determining the final destination of your form defines your form's publishing model.

Again, just as with submitting a form versus saving it, publishing and saving a form template are not identical processes. Saving a form template is just saving it so that it can be reopened for further changes. However, publishing a form template refers to a process that prepares the form for distribution. If you do not publish a form template, you haven't distributed it properly, and users cannot fill it out. Unlike list forms, form templates created by InfoPath Designer can be published to a variety of destinations. You can publish them to a SharePoint Server, a list of e-mail recipients, a network location, or a shared folder on a computer, as listed in the Publish tab in the File tab menu.

Although SharePoint 2013 makes it easy to change the out-of-the-box SharePoint list forms to custom InfoPath forms, the traditional approach of publishing to form libraries is still available for many scenarios. This can be a good option when you need to abstract complex logic in your form by using custom code. As discussed previously, the SharePoint list forms do not support custom code.

Publishing to a Form Library

To publish your form to a form library, open InfoPath to the File menu tab, and click Publish. Then click the SharePoint Server button to launch the Publishing Wizard. The wizard is similar to InfoPath 2010. First, you choose the location of the SharePoint site. Next, you select Enable This Form to Be Filled Out by Using a Browser, and choose the Form Library option, as shown in Figure 11-30.

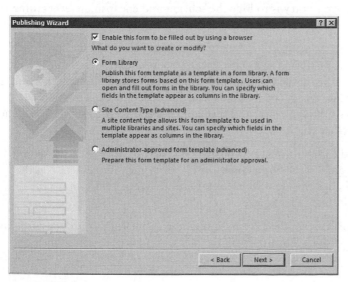

FIGURE 11-30

> **NOTE** *This section assumes that you already have Sandboxed solutions config-ured. If you don't, you might run into an error.*

In the next wizard, specify that the form template should be updated in an existing form library, and from the available libraries choose a SharePoint form library on your site. Click Next to proceed to the next step.

The next step of the wizard offers two important options:

➤ *Property Promotion* — This option enables you to set specific fields in your form to be vis-ible as columns in the SharePoint library, which can be used in SharePoint as meta data or workflow variables.

➤ *Web Part Connection Parameter Promotion* — InfoPath 2010 introduced forms that can participate in the web part connections. Unlike SharePoint list forms in which every field is, by default, available to participate in a web part connection scenario, when you publish a form to a SharePoint form library, you need to take explicit actions to determine what fields are available to be used in a web part connection. You also need to specify whether a promoted field is used as a subscriber (Input), publisher (Output), or subscriber/publisher (Input/Output) parameter. Obviously, subscriber parameters can receive data only from other web parts but cannot send data. Publisher parameters can send data to other web parts but cannot receive data.

Both of these options are also available in the Property Promotion category in the Advanced form options dialog in the File menu tab.

Although it's entirely possible to promote all the fields inside an InfoPath form and make them available as columns, in forms with complex schemas, this technique may not be efficient. Again, remember that one reason to use a form library is to hide the schema and encapsulate everything in the form itself. The last step in the wizard presents a summary of some of the information collected throughout the Publishing Wizard.

Unlike with list forms, when a form is published to a form library, it cannot be accessed using Form Options on the library settings page or from the Customize Form in SharePoint Ribbon. Instead, it is configured in the Document Template section of the Advanced Settings option in the library settings page. Click the link that says Edit Template, and this launches InfoPath Designer 2013 and downloads the form template for further changes.

With the form successfully published to the InfoPath forms library, you can now open the form in your web browser of choice. Navigate to the SharePoint form library, click Documents on the Library Tools contextual menu, and click the New Document button. Figure 11-31 shows the selected form opened and filled out in Internet Explorer.

When you complete filling out the form, press the Save button, and give the form a proper name to save it in the InfoPath forms library. Notice that the Event Details section is not visible when the form loads up or in editing mode, which is exactly what you coded before.

FIGURE 11-31

> **NOTE** *You can find this form template in the code download for this book, in the Chapter 11 zip file. It is called Registration.xsn.*

Publishing to a Content Type

When publishing a form template to SharePoint, you have another option, which is publishing to a content type. Binding a form template to a content type allows the template to be reused in other form libraries.

During the Publishing Wizard when you promote fields, always make sure that mappings between the promoted fields and the site columns are exactly what you expect them to be. Otherwise, you may end up causing duplicate site columns and making the previously published site columns orphaned. In the Publishing Wizard, select each field name, and click Modify to see the mapping with the site column. Typically, the first time you publish the form template to a server, you expect fields to be promoted to new site columns labeled with None: Create New Site Column. However, in subsequent republishing processes, you want to map to an existing site column (This Content Type) rather than creating another new column.

If you continue to publish to the same server, the association is remembered in the form's schema, and you don't need to take any further action. When you publish a form template to multiple servers and then you come back, make some changes to the form template, and republish it again to the first server. In this case, your promoted site columns are re-created multiple times under the Microsoft

InfoPath site column group with the same name but different IDs. Remember, always check the mappings before pressing the Publish button in the last step of Publishing Wizard.

Form Security

The last page of the Publishing Wizard provides the ability to manage the security level of the form. Each form template created in InfoPath 2013 should have one of the available three security levels:

➤ Restricted

➤ Domain

➤ Full Trust

By default, InfoPath Designer 2013 adjusts the security level of your form according to the functionalities included in the form template, and that is the recommended option, as shown in Figure 11-32. When you start, all new blank form templates come with the Restricted security level, meaning that the form can access content only inside the form. As you complete the form and add functionality, such as querying SharePoint lists, scripts, or HTTP submit, the security level of the form will be automatically raised to Domain. The Domain security level is the maximum trust level that can be set automatically by InfoPath Designer 2013. This security model allows access outside of the form, but only within the domain in which the form template physically resides. Keep in mind that InfoPath Designer 2010 added the ability to create forms that run inside sandboxed solutions that are tied to the form templates with the Domain security model. Sandboxing forms are covered in the next section.

If you need to do things that the Domain security level doesn't allow (for example, deploying certificate-signed form templates), then you need to manually set the security level to Full Trust. Note that the Full Trust security level requires your form to be administrator approved. This means that the form template must first be reviewed and approved by the farm's administrator and then deployed through the Central Administration site.

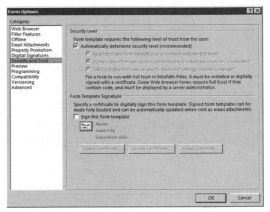

FIGURE 11-32

Sandboxing Your Forms

Like rules and formulas, writing custom code enables form developers to greatly enhance the functionality of their forms with managed assemblies that become part of the form template.

Sandboxed solutions introduced with SharePoint 2010 allow form developers to create their forms with managed code and directly publish them to a form library while the security level of the form is still set to Domain. This greatly increases the number of options for creating forms and allows more users to safely create power forms.

A unique characteristic of sandboxed solutions is that they run in partially trusted mode. So, using them doesn't conflict with the Domain security model of the form. This means that the form can be deployed using the site collection administrator privilege and right from within the InfoPath Designer, instead of through the Central Administration site.

The sandboxing infrastructure comes from the core platform and is widely used to limit the security vulnerabilities of the farm, while giving developers easy deployment of their code to any site collection. After a form with custom code is published to a SharePoint form library, it ends up in the site collection's User Solution gallery and is activated by default.

Form Anatomy

The result of saving an InfoPath form template is a file with an .xsn extension. An XSN file is a kind of compressed CAB (cabinet) file that contains other XML files. If you change the extension to .CAB and double-click the file, it opens the form template as an archive file. Alternatively, you can select Export Source Files from the Publishing tab on the File tab menu to export the source files of the form template. Figure 11-33 shows the exported files of a form template.

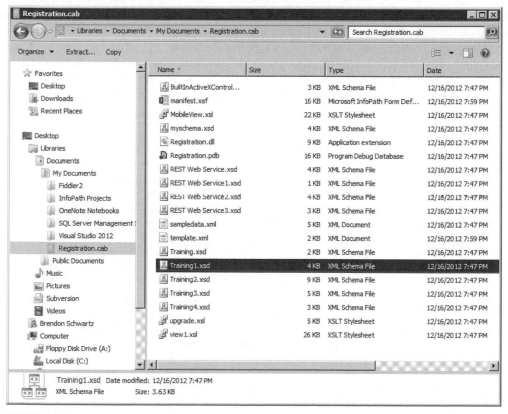

FIGURE 11-33

The form definition file (manifest.xsf) contains a listing of all other files that make up the template, as well as other information, including views used in the form, external data sources, and error messages. If you open this file in a text editor such as Notepad and scan it, you soon realize why this file is considered the heart of the form template.

Scroll through the XML code until you locate the `xsf:extensions` element. This element is used to specify properties and features of the form templates such as managed code form template project settings for Visual Studio, settings for the views included in the form, and whether the form should be browser-compatible. If the form includes any property promotion or if the form is published to a content type, then relevant child elements appear in the `xsf:extensions` element to instruct SharePoint how to perform the bindings.

As you complete your form design, you should examine the content of the `manifest.xsf` often to become familiar with the different parts of the form template and the underlying hooks to the form library.

Toward the end of the `manifest.xsf` file content, there is an `xsf:dataObjects` element used to define all the secondary data sources in the form. This element contains a collection of `xsf:dataObject` child elements.

Notice the bolded section in the following code snippet. Within the parent collection, each `xsf:dataObject` element is an in-memory representation (XML document object model) of the associated external data source. The XML Document Object Model (DOM) programming interface enables form developers to traverse the secondary data source's tree-like structure and manipulate its nodes. The association between the `xsf:dataObject` element and the secondary data source is created via the `xsf:dataObject` element. In this particular example, a SharePoint adaptor that points directly to the Trainings list is used to query for data. The `xsf:dataObject` element also has a `schema` attribute that references the schema file used for the data object. The schema file is also part of the form template (refer to Figure 11-33).

```xml
<xsf:dataObjects>
<xsf:dataObject name="Trainings" schema="Trainings.xsd" initOnLoad="yes">
<xsf:query>
<xsf:sharepointListAdapterRW queryAllowed="yes" submitAllowed="no"
  siteURL="https://devcow.sharepoint.com/sites/chapter11/"
  sharePointListID="{CC157A05-5592-41F4-A448-DA002F54405D}" name="Trainings"
  contentTypeID="" sortBy="ID" sortAscending="yes" relativeListUrl="Lists/
  Training/">
<xsf:field internalName="Title" required="yes" type="Text"></xsf:field>
<xsf:field internalName="code" required="no" type="Text"></xsf:field>
<xsf:field internalName="Description" required="no" type="Text"></xsf:field>
<xsf:field internalName="start" required="no" type="DateTime"></xsf:field>
<xsf:field internalName="end" required="no" type="DateTime"></xsf:field>
<xsf:field internalName="Cost" required="no" type="Currency"></xsf:field>
<xsf:field internalName="Level" required="no" type="Number"></xsf:field>
<xsf:field internalName="deadline" required="no" type="DateTime"></xsf:field>
<xsf:field internalName="Address" required="no" type="FullHTML"></xsf:field>
<xsf:field internalName="info" required="no" type="FullHTML"></xsf:field>
<xsf:field internalName="ID" required="no" type="Counter"></xsf:field>
</xsf:sharepointListAdapterRW>
</xsf:query>
</xsf:dataObject>
```

> **NOTE** *Data connections inside the InfoPath form template have a relative URL and are not hard-coded to only one library.*

In addition to the schema files created for each secondary data source, the form template maintains a schema for the main XML data that it recognizes in a file named `myschema.xsd`. Listing 11-4 shows the schema file for the Registration Form template.

LISTING 11-4: Training Registration Form Schema

```xml
<?xml version="1.0" encoding="UTF-8" standalone="no"?>
<xsd:schema targetNamespace="http://schemas.microsoft.com/office/infopath/2003/
  myXSD/2012-09-20T03:11:21" xmlns:xsi="http://www.w3.org/2001/XMLSchema-instance"
  xmlns:pc="http://schemas.microsoft.com/office/infopath/2007/PartnerControls"
  xmlns:ma="http://schemas.microsoft.com/office/2009/metadata/properties/
  metaAttributes"
  xmlns:d="http://schemas.microsoft.com/office/infopath/2009/WSSList/dataFields"
  xmlns:q="http://schemas.microsoft.com/office/infopath/2009/WSSList/queryFields"
  xmlns:dfs="http://schemas.microsoft.com/office/infopath/2003/dataFormSolution"
  xmlns:dms="http://schemas.microsoft.com/office/2009/documentManagement/types"
  xmlns:xhtml="http://www.w3.org/1999/xhtml"
  xmlns:ns1="http://schemas.microsoft.com/ado/2007/08/dataservices"
  xmlns:m="http://schemas.microsoft.com/ado/2007/08/dataservices/metadata"
  xmlns:ns2="http://www.w3.org/2005/Atom"
    xmlns:my="http://schemas.microsoft.com/office/infopath/2003/myXSD/
  2012-09-20T03:11:21" xmlns:xd="http://schemas.microsoft.com/office/infopath/2003"
  xmlns:xsd="http://www.w3.org/2001/XMLSchema">
  <xsd:import schemaLocation="BuiltInActiveXControls.xsd"
   namespace="http://schemas.microsoft.com/office/infopath/2007/PartnerControls"/>
  <xsd:element name="myFields">
  <xsd:complexType>
  <xsd:sequence>
  <xsd:element ref="my:EventName" minOccurs="0"/>
  <xsd:element ref="my:AlternateEmail" minOccurs="0"/>
  <xsd:element ref="my:EmergencyContact" minOccurs="0"/>
  <xsd:element ref="my:EmergencyNumber" minOccurs="0"/>
  <xsd:element ref="my:ShortBio" minOccurs="0"/>
  <xsd:element ref="my:Manager" minOccurs="0"/>
  <xsd:element ref="my:IsMobileField" minOccurs="0"/>
  <xsd:element ref="my:HideEventDetailsField" minOccurs="0"/>
  <xsd:element ref="my:EventDetails" minOccurs="0"/>
  </xsd:sequence>
  <xsd:anyAttribute processContents="lax"
    namespace="http://www.w3.org/XML/1998/namespace"/>
  </xsd:complexType>
  </xsd:element>
  <xsd:element name="EventName" type="my:requiredString"/>
  <xsd:element name="AlternateEmail" type="my:requiredString"/>
  <xsd:element name="EmergencyContact" type="my:requiredString"/>
  <xsd:element name="EmergencyNumber" type="my:requiredString"/>
  <xsd:element name="ShortBio" type="xsd:string"/>
  <xsd:element name="Manager">
  <xsd:complexType>
  <xsd:sequence>
  <xsd:element ref="pc:Person" minOccurs="0" maxOccurs="unbounded"/>
```

continues

LISTING 11-4 *(continued)*

```
    </xsd:sequence>
  </xsd:complexType>
</xsd:element>
<xsd:element name="IsMobileField" nillable="true" type="xsd:boolean"/>
<xsd:element name="HideEventDetailsField" nillable="true" type="xsd:boolean"/>
<xsd:element name="EventDetails">
  <xsd:complexType>
    <xsd:sequence>
      <xsd:element ref="my:EDCost" minOccurs="0"/>
      <xsd:element ref="my:EDStartDate" minOccurs="0"/>
      <xsd:element ref="my:EDAddress" minOccurs="0"/>
    </xsd:sequence>
  </xsd:complexType>
</xsd:element>
<xsd:element name="EDCost" type="xsd:string"/>
<xsd:element name="EDStartDate" type="xsd:string"/>
<xsd:element name="EDAddress" type="xsd:string"/>
<xsd:simpleType name="requiredString">
  <xsd:restriction base="xsd:string">
    <xsd:minLength value="1"/>
  </xsd:restriction>
</xsd:simpleType>
<xsd:simpleType name="requiredAnyURI">
  <xsd:restriction base="xsd:anyURI">
    <xsd:minLength value="1"/>
  </xsd:restriction>
</xsd:simpleType>
<xsd:simpleType name="requiredBase64Binary">
  <xsd:restriction base="xsd:base64Binary">
    <xsd:minLength value="1"/>
  </xsd:restriction>
</xsd:simpleType>
</xsd:schema>
```

The schema file contains a set of predefined types such as `boolean` and `string`, as well as new `complexType` and `simpleType` based on the data source. In addition to the type declarations, the schema imposes some constraints on the structure and content of the form's data. For example, the `my:requiredString` type means the element cannot be blank, and the `xsd:sequence` element defines a specified sequence within the containing element, such as the `myFields` element.

Notice the first bolded line in Listing 11-4. This line identifies the `http://schemas.microsoft.com/office/infopath/2007/PartnerControls` namespace and schema components (inside the `BuiltInActiveXControls.xsd` file) referenced in the `myschema.xsd` file. This is because of the Manager People Picker control you placed on the form.

Also, notice the `myFields` bolded section in Listing 11-4, which appears to be the first element in the `myschema.xsd` file. This element references other elements that each represent a control in the form template.

> **NOTE** *The form's schema file provides a view of the underlying data that the form recognizes at a relatively high level of abstraction. By scanning the schema, you can quickly see that the data is structured in a hierarchy of data types and exactly as they appear in the Fields task pane.*

The next fields to analyze in Figure 11-33 are the view<name>.xsl files. These XSL-based files are the views that you created in the form template. Most of the formatting rules or form-level filters you apply to data end up as XSL code and are placed in the respective view file.

Three more files in Figure 11-33 warrant some attention.

First, The <formname>.dll file is the generated assembly for the code you added to EventName Changed and FormEvents_Loading event handlers in the Form Programming section. Second, the template.xml file contains the actual XML data that is edited by InfoPath. By default, when debugging or previewing a form template, the data in the template.xml file is used. Optionally, you can create your own data file and instruct InfoPath Designer 2013 to use it when previewing the form in InfoPath Designer 2013. The third file is sampledata.xml. This file specified the default values of the fields when the form opens in the client or browser application. This file is not used for previewing or debugging purposes, as the template.xml file is. In this file, you can find only the field definitions, type, and option to supply a default value and the actual value.

Working with the Form XML in Code

The XML data stored in the form library conforms to the form's schema (myschema.xsd), so you can write or generate code that conforms to this schema to load the XML and interact with it. Recall from an earlier discussion that one of the primary reasons for using a form library is to easily access all the data stored within the InfoPath form without promoting any fields.

Generating Wrapper Classes for Form XML

One tool that can help generate the class files from XML is called XSD.exe. You can use the XSD. exe utility to generate a wrapper class that represents the data elements. This generated class enables you to access the form's data using a strongly typed object instead of parsing the XML data by using XPath (like all the other samples so far). To perform the steps to generate the class file, navigate to the location of the extracted form's exported files (see the previous section) and run the following command using the Visual Studio Native Tools command prompt:

```
Xsd.exe /c myschema.xsd BuiltInActiveXControls.xsd
```

The XSD.exe utility is not following the imports and/or includes in the myschema.xsd file, so you need to specify the BuiltInActiveXControls.xsd schema file directly on the command line, too. Otherwise, the utility throws a missing element exception. The generated file is named after the schema files used in the command line, myschema_BuiltInActiveXControls.cs. Change the filename to RegistrationsSchema.cs instead. Note that the generated partial classes in this file are given the same name as the root elements, as shown in Listing 11-5.

LISTING 11-5: Partial myFields Class

```csharp
using System.Xml.Serialization;

public partial class myFields {
    private string eventNameField;
    private string alternateEmailField;
    private string emergencyContactField;
    private string emergencyNumberField;
    private string shortBioField;
    private Person[] managerField;
    private System.Nullable<bool> isMobileFieldField;
    private bool isMobileFieldFieldSpecified;
    private System.Nullable<bool> hideEventDetailsFieldField;
    private bool hideEventDetailsFieldFieldSpecified;
    private EventDetails eventDetailsField;
    private System.Xml.XmlAttribute[] anyAttrField;

    /// <remarks/>
    public string EventName {
        get {
            return this.eventNameField;
        }
        set {
            this.eventNameField = value;
        }
    }

    /// <remarks/>
    public string AlternateEmail {
        get {
            return this.alternateEmailField;
        }
        set {
            this.alternateEmailField = value;
        }
    }

    /// <remarks/>
    public string EmergencyContact {
        get {
            return this.emergencyContactFicld;
        }
        set {
            this.emergencyContactField = value;
        }
    }

    /// <remarks/>
    public string EmergencyNumber {
        get {
            return this.emergencyNumberField;
        }
        set {
```

```csharp
                this.emergencyNumberField = value;
        }
    }

    /// <remarks/>
    public string ShortBio {
        get {
            return this.shortBioField;
        }
        set {
            this.shortBioField = value;
        }
    }

    /// <remarks/>
    [System.Xml.Serialization.XmlArrayItemAttribute("Person",
    Namespace="http://schemas.microsoft.com/office/infopath/2007/PartnerControls",
    IsNullable=false)]
    public Person[] Manager {
        get {
            return this.managerField;
        }
        set {
            this.managerField = value;
        }
    }

    /// <remarks/>
    [System.Xml.Serialization.XmlElementAttribute(IsNullable=true)]
    public System.Nullable<bool> IsMobileField {
        get {
            return this.isMobileFieldField;
        }
        set {
            this.isMobileFieldField = value;
        }
    }

    /// <remarks/>
    [System.Xml.Serialization.XmlIgnoreAttribute()]
    public bool IsMobileFieldSpecified {
        get {
            return this.isMobileFieldFieldSpecified;
        }
        set {
            this.isMobileFieldFieldSpecified = value;
        }
    }

    /// <remarks/>
    [System.Xml.Serialization.XmlElementAttribute(IsNullable=true)]
    public System.Nullable<bool> HideEventDetailsField {
        get {
```

continues

LISTING 11-5 *(continued)*

```
                return this.hideEventDetailsFieldField;
            }
            set {
                this.hideEventDetailsFieldField = value;
            }
        }

        /// <remarks/>
        [System.Xml.Serialization.XmlIgnoreAttribute()]
        public bool HideEventDetailsFieldSpecified {
            get {
                return this.hideEventDetailsFieldFieldSpecified;
            }
            set {
                this.hideEventDetailsFieldFieldSpecified = value;
            }
        }

        /// <remarks/>
        public EventDetails EventDetails {
            get {
                return this.eventDetailsField;
            }
            set {
                this.eventDetailsField = value;
            }
        }

        /// <remarks/>
        [System.Xml.Serialization.XmlAnyAttributeAttribute()]
        public System.Xml.XmlAttribute[] AnyAttr {
            get {
                return this.anyAttrField;
            }
            set {
                this.anyAttrField = value;
            }
        }
    }
}

//Code Omitted For Brevity
```

With the wrapper class generated by the XSD.exe tool, you can add the file to any Visual Studio project and access the objects through class references. To use the file in a SharePoint project, start Visual Studio 2013 and create a new project using the SharePoint 2013 project template.

Working with Form XML Data in SharePoint Code

Next, choose Deploy as a farm solution, and click the Finish button. The SharePoint 2013 project needs the event receiver added to the project by adding a new item. Click Add Item and select event receiver in the template gallery; give the event receiver a name. In this example, your code should be able to respond to "An item was added" event of type List Item Events for a Form Library, as shown in Figure 11-34.

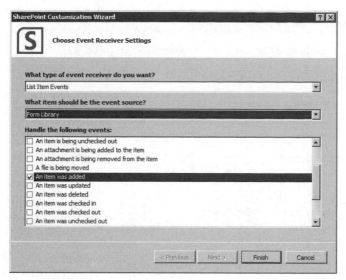

FIGURE 11-34

After you finish the wizard, Visual Studio stubs out all the necessary code and the Feature and Solution package necessary to deploy this event handler as a farm WSP solution. At this point, you can add to your project the wrapper class (RegistrationsSchema.cs) that the XSD.exe utility generated.

> **WARNING** *If you ever make a change to the form's schema, you need to rerun the XSD.exe utility against the new schema file, delete the old wrapper class, and add the new one to the project.*

When the package is deployed and the associated feature is activated, the callout code in Listing 11-6 is used to access and increment the counter value in the Stats list for a particular training. Next, rename EventReceiver1.cs to UpdateStatSink.cs, and add the callout code within the class to override the ItemAdded method.

In the code, notice the first bolded section. In this section, the InfoPath form that was just added is retrieved and stored in a variable of type SPFile. Next, InfoPath's XML file is deserialized into a strongly typed C# object of type myFields. This is done via a call into a helper method called DeserializeFormData (SPFile, Type), which is covered a bit later in this section. If the returned object is not null, a LINQ query is used to see if the selected training code exists in the Stats list.

The second bolded section indicates if the Count function returns a number greater than zero, meaning the matching training code is found in the Stats list. Then, the code continues with incrementing its Counter field by one. This is all done through a call to a second helper method named IncrementCounter (SPListItem). On the opposite, if the matching training code is not found, a new list item is added to the Stats list, and the Code and Counter columns are set accordingly.

LISTING 11-6: UpdateStats Event Receiver ItemAdded Method

```
public override void ItemAdded(SPItemEventProperties properties)
{
        SPFile ifpFile = properties.ListItem.File;
        myFields fields =
(myFields)DeserializeFormData(ifpFile, typeof(myFields));
        if (fields != null)
        {

            SPLinqDataContext cdc =
new SPLinqDataContext("http://dev.devcow.com/sites/hr");


            var result = from trs in cdc.Stats
                         where trs.Title.Equals(fields.EventName)
                         select new { trs.Id };

            SPList statList = properties.Web.Lists["Stats"];
            if (result.Count() > 0)
            {
                SPListItem matched =
                statList.GetItemById((int)result.First().Id);
                IncrementCoutner(matched);
            }
            else
            {
                SPListItem newItem = statList.Items.Add();
                newItem["Title"] = fields.EventName;
                newItem["Counter"] = 1;
                newItem.Update();
            }

        }

}
```

Listing 11-7 demonstrates the DeserializeFormData() helper method called from the ItemAdded method, which demonstrates how to change the InfoPath XML data into the strongly typed classes. This method starts with receiving two parameters of type SPFile and Type. In the code, the SPFile parameter is opened in binary format, and the actual content is stored in a byte array, which is read into a memory stream a bit later.

Notice the highlighted lines in the code. First, a new instance of the XMLSerializer class is initialized, and an object of type rootElementType is serialized into it. The rootElementType parameter is of type myFields because that is what was passed in from the ItemAdded code. In the next line, a new XmlReader instance is created using the memory stream and, in the line after, it is deserialized into the result variable. Finally, the result variable is returned to the caller, which contains the actual content of the form data in a strongly typed object.

LISTING 11-7 DeserializeFromData Helper Method

```
private object DeserializeFormData(SPFile ipfFile, Type rootElementType)
{
    byte[] xmlFormData = ipfFile.OpenBinary();
    object result = null;
    if (xmlFormData != null)
    {
        using (MemoryStream fileStream = new MemoryStream(xmlFormData))
        {
            XmlSerializer serializer = new XmlSerializer(rootElementType);
            XmlReader reader = XmlReader.Create(fileStream);
            result = serializer.Deserialize(reader);
            fileStream.Close();
        }
    }

    return result;
}
```

Listing 11-8 demonstrates the second helper method used in the ItemAdded method. The only thing that needs to be highlighted about this method is the extra logic that is written to handle the race condition when multiple instances of the event handler try to update the Counter column in the Stats list. This condition can occur when two or more registration forms are saved at the same time by different users.

The SharePoint object model automatically locks the list item when retrieving and incrementing the Count field's value, so all you need to do is to place your code in a try/catch block. If the race condition occurs, the SharePoint object model throws an exception, meaning the existing counter value is dirty. If the value is considered dirty, the code has logic to make three attempts to retrieve and increment the value again. If all three attempts fail, the exception will be logged, and the update won't happen.

LISTING 11-8: IncrementCounter Help Method

```
private void IncrementCoutner(SPListItem item)
{
    int retryUpdate = 0;

doUpdate:
    try
    {
        int currentCounter = int.Parse(item["Counter"].ToString());
        item["Counter"] = currentCounter + 1;
        item.Update();
    }
    catch (Exception ex)
    {
        retryUpdate += 1;
        if (retryUpdate <= 3)
```

continues

LISTING 11-8 *(continued)*

```
                    {
                        System.Threading.Thread.Sleep(3000);
                        goto doUpdate;
                    }
                    else
                    {
                        // Log the exception
                    }
                }
            }
```

The last step to getting your event handler to work is to update the Class node in the `Elements.xml` to include the changes you have just made to the project. Listing 11-9 shows the `Elements.xml` file of the feature that has been added to the project by Visual Studio 2012. This file identifies the assembly's fully qualified name, class (`UpdateStatSink`), and `ItemAdded` method to implement in the event handler.

In this example, the event handler is associated with all the form libraries of the site as specified by the `ListTemplateID` attribute in the bold line. In general this not an ideal situation; instead, the event handler should be associated with a content type or a particular custom form library so that it is not kicked off on every form library in the site.

LISTING 11-9: Elements.xml file

```
<?xml version="1.0" encoding="utf-8"?>
<Elements xmlns="http://schemas.microsoft.com/sharepoint/">
  <Receivers ListTemplateId="115">
    <Receiver>
      <Name>UpdateStatERItemAdded</Name>
      <Type>ItemAdded</Type>
      <Assembly>$SharePoint.Project.AssemblyFullName$</Assembly>
      <Class>UpdateStatsEventHandler.UpdateStatER</Class>
      <SequenceNumber>10000</SequenceNumber>
    </Receiver>
  </Receivers>
</Elements>
```

To deploy and debug the solution, press F5, and Visual Studio deploys the WSP package as a farm solution and activates the features. Visual Studio also associates the event handler with all the form libraries on the site. Navigate to the Central Administration site under Solution Management, and verify that the solution has been successfully deployed, as shown in Figure 11-35.

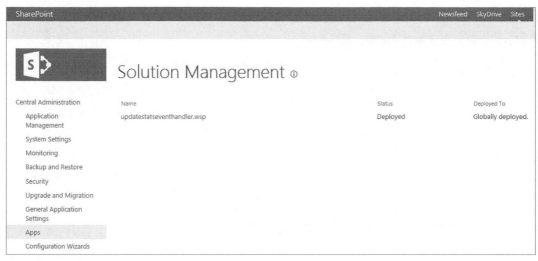

FIGURE 11-35

Try the code by browsing to the form library and creating a new form, such as the Registration form. You should now have a fully functional solution so that when forms are saved to the Registration form library, the even handler is kicked off to update the related counter in the Stats list.

TOOLS FOR FORM DEVELOPERS

As you have seen so far, InfoPath 2013, along with Form Services 2013, provides a highly extensible platform on which you can build electronic forms that play an important role in various business processes across your organization. You can use a number of tools and utilities to make form development easier. Now have a quick look at a few of the tools that you can leverage when working with InfoPath forms.

The Rule Inspector

When adding declarative business logic (dynamic logic) or even custom code (imperative logic) to your form, it is often challenging to keep track of all fields and groups that invoke this logic or how this logic may affect other fields, groups, or logic in the form template.

To address this challenge, InfoPath Designer 2013 includes a tool called the Rule Inspector. When you access this tool, you initially see either the Overview pane alone or both the Overview pane and the Details pane, depending on how the tool is accessed, as shown in Figure 11-36.

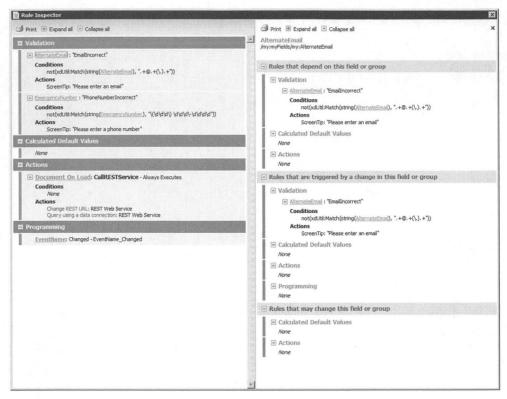

FIGURE 11-36

The Overview pane on the left lists all the business logic currently used in the form template, grouped into four categories: Validation, Calculated Default Values, Actions, and Programming. This grouping enables you to easily see what fields or groups contain the business logic, the type of the logic, and some information about each rule. If you click any orange links in the Overview pane, the Details pane expands with more specific information, mostly about the dependencies on other fields, groups, or rules in the form. Although the imperative logic in the Programming group is not disassembled, it is still helpful to know what is going on in the code behind in a high-level view without having to launch Visual Studio.

For many form developers, when troubleshooting or reviewing an InfoPath form, the Rule Inspector is a helpful tool, and the first place they go after they open the form in Design mode.

The Design Checker

In InfoPath 2013, one of the driving forces behind browser-enabled forms is to have parity with the InfoPath client and parity with forms online in SharePoint. A good practice to verify that the forms are valid is to run the Design Checker to identify incompatibility issues and ensure that your form template works correctly. This tool can be found in the File tab on the Info page. The text in the middle indicates that the form template is currently compatible with Forms Services as a web browser form.

With the compatibility settings applied, you can click the Design Checker button on the Info page of the File tab to bring up the Design Checker task pane. At that point all local and online checks are performed, and potential errors or warnings are revealed in the Task pane, as shown in Figure 11-37.

Typically, errors prevent the form template from being published as a browser-enabled form. However, warnings can be discarded, which may result in a nonworking, browser-enabled form. Simply go through the list of issues, review them, and take appropriate actions to resolve them.

FIGURE 11-37

InfoPath JavaScript Tool

In addition to the tools discussed so far, there are tools that can be executed right from within Internet Explorer when the form first loads:

➤ IP_DebugComplexity.ComposeSummary()

As the name implies, the first tool provides a summary of the following counters in the browser-enabled forms:

➤ View Data Tree Node

➤ Include Hidden Controls

➤ HTML InfoPath Controls

➤ HTML Elements

As shown in Figure 11-38, to run this tool, you should type the following JavaScript code into the address bar of the browser, and press Enter:

```
javascript:alert(IP_DebugComplexity.ComposeSummary())
```

The Compose Summary tool doesn't fix anything in the form, nor does it give you guidelines on how to fix the issues. It just provides some facts that can be used to reduce the form's complexity. The total number of HTML elements that a form produces is an important factor in measuring the form's complexity.

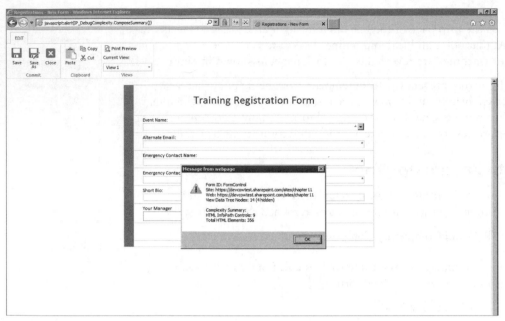

FIGURE 11-38

SUMMARY

This chapter introduced to you new ways to work with InfoPath Designer and SharePoint. You were introduced to building rich business applications that can be built with SharePoint lists. You can use the tools learned in this chapter to make small changes to a single list or build an entire application that requires rich forms to present and collect data.

The topics covered in the chapter were customizing SharePoint list forms with InfoPath Designer using the Customize Form button from SharePoint. You learned how to add views, rules, actions, and formatting to the form to make a powerful form with little-to-no coding. Then you took the form a step further and learned how to integrate complex logic using Visual Studio and managed code to the form. Knowing that you have full control of the form in managed code provides the power to build any solution. The code from the chapter showed how to navigate the XML that is the data structure of the InfoPath form and data.

Finally, you looked at what makes the InfoPath form and all the files created when building a form. Then you looked at ways to consume the InfoPath form in other applications such as SharePoint. The code used tools to help build the auto-generated code and files for using strongly typed classes, and you looked at tools that you can use to review your form when publishing it to a SharePoint location. All these tools together can help you build the applications of your organization.

12

Enterprise Document Management

WHAT'S IN THIS CHAPTER?

➤ Exploring document and records management features

➤ Managing a flexible taxonomy for your organization through managed meta data and centralized content type publishing

➤ Discovering new ECM features including standards-compliant eDiscovery across SharePoint, Exchange, and file servers

➤ Creating custom solutions that extend the ECM Framework via new CSOM APIs

WROX.COM CODE DOWNLOADS FOR THIS CHAPTER

The wrox.com code downloads for this chapter are found at www.wrox.com/remtitle .cgi?isbn=1118495829 on the Download Code tab. The code is in the chapter xx download and individually named according to names throughout the chapter.

Every organization leverages SharePoint's ubiquitous file and data storage capabilities in innumerable team and department sites. This easy access to theoretically limitless web-based content storage poses a special problem for those responsible for organizing, categorizing, and securing that content, especially legally sensitive content. This chapter explores SharePoint's content management capabilities targeted at the needs of the enterprise as opposed to the needs of the team. You explore content types, document sets, records management, eDiscovery, and the expanded Enterprise Content Management (ECM) object model designed to work programmatically with these capabilities.

SharePoint Server 2013 provides rich new features that enable organizations to define a flexible yet powerful information architecture. With proper planning of content types, libraries, and managed meta data, you can secure improved manageability as you accumulate content of all types, both structured and unstructured. You can use the ECM object model to extend this capability to existing applications and create custom solutions hosted in and outside of SharePoint.

Today, there is an explosion in the types of content that exist in organizations. Examples include documents, digital assets, reports, web content, and social content. ECM is the process of making sense of and bringing compliance to the massive amount of this electronic content that is stored on internal networks, external networks, the cloud, and SharePoint Server.

THE DOCUMENT MANAGEMENT MINDSET

The most frequently heard complaint about corporate content stores, regardless of whether those content repositories are intranets or file servers, is that relevant content is difficult if not impossible to find. Users are familiar with the powerful search experiences of the public Internet, but a corporate intranet's mix of structured (database-like) and unstructured (document-like) content requires both rich search and contextual navigation. Allowing users to filter and navigate based on common terms and taxonomy provides an interface that is more suitable to hosting large numbers of corporate libraries and lists.

Companies are tasked with managing more content than ever before. Security, rules, and accountability requirements are becoming more complex. This pattern will continue for the foreseeable future. As you prepare for an explosion of content, the new developer tools and features in SharePoint Server should ease this transition.

ECM Features

SharePoint Server has a rich set of features to support document management. However, in addition to managing traditional document artifacts, you can manage social content, including tacit updates from users, microblogging, wikis, blogs, and discussion forums. What makes SharePoint different from most other ECM systems is how it layers social technologies on top of the ECM features, while enabling you to manage this social content.

SharePoint Server provides features to make managing large numbers of complex content types easier. Some of these features include unique document IDs, document sets, and a global taxonomy. In this chapter, you cover these welcome additions, while exploring how you can use new collaboration features in the context of document management. Table 12-1 identifies the existing baseline document management features from SharePoint 2010 that still exist in SharePoint 2013.

TABLE 12-1: Baseline ECM Features Carried Forward from SharePoint 2010

FEATURE	DESCRIPTION
Managed Metadata Service Application	Features that enable global meta data to be shared and managed across farms, site collections, sites, and libraries.
Content Type syndication	A subset of the Managed Metadata Service that enables content types to be published to and then disseminated from a hub.
Unique Document ID Service	Creates a static URL for items.

Content Organizer	Provides document routing within any site.
Document Sets	Provide compound document support.
Meta-data navigation and filtering	Filter and navigate based on predefined tags and taxonomy.
Document libraries	List definitions with features added to support document management.
Document Center	Site definition with structures in place to manage large amounts of documents.
Recycle Bin	Two-stage recycle bin enables recovery of deleted documents without using backups.
Versioning	After versioning is enabled, drafts and major versions are stored as separate items in a library. The versions can be restored at any point in time.
Information policies	Farm, site-collection, site, content-type, and library-level information management policies. Built-in policy features include labels, bar codes, expiration, and auditing.
Records Center	Site definition used for retention and document routing.
Item-level permissions	Individual documents can be secured.
Content Types	An abstraction layer fostering manageability of content and meta data. Settings, properties, and functionality can be defined for types of content rather than individual items.

The bulk of Microsoft's investment in the ECM space has gone to eDiscovery, but as noted in Table 12-2, new capabilities have been added for content managers in a number of places. Microsoft published a high-level list of new 2013 eDiscovery features online at `http://technet.microsoft.com/en-us/library/fp161513.aspx`.

TABLE 12-2: New ECM Features in SharePoint Server 2013

FEATURE	DESCRIPTION
In-place retention/preservation of SharePoint and Exchange content	eDiscovery is simpler with the identification and management of records across integrated server systems.
Integrated eDiscovery case-management portal site template	Extending across SharePoint, Exchange, Lync, and file server content, SharePoint's eDiscovery case management toolset enables a single eDiscovery experience.

continues

TABLE 12-2 *(continued)*

FEATURE	DESCRIPTION
Team folders	Mail and documents merge in SharePoint's team folder, a common location for working on mail and documents. The team folder is accessible from SharePoint, Outlook, and Outlook Web Access. Documents are stored in SharePoint, and e-mails addressed to the dedicated team folder e-mail address are stored in Exchange; however, SharePoint can create and apply a compliance policy.
Open standards-compliant content interactions	Content Management Interoperability Services (CMIS) 1.0 is built into SharePoint 2013. (2010 offered an add-on for CMIS 1.0.) CMIS enables non-native applications such as Adobe Photoshop or Documentum to access hosted content in an integrated manner without requiring a web browser. As of this writing, CMIS is only available in on-premise installations.
Open standards-compliant eDiscovery content export	The content results of a query-based discovery set can be exported from SharePoint in a zip file with an XML manifest file that conforms to the Electronic Discovery Reference Model (EDRM) specification.
In-place record holds	SharePoint 2010 enabled in-place content holds, but a record hold would lock content and prevent editing. SharePoint 2013 enables In-Place Holds on live content that can still be edited. Each site contains a secret library that stores preserved content that has been locked before changes are made to it. This approach minimizes content duplication by preserving at an item level yet enables end users to continue to see current versions of a document.
Managed meta data enhanced for new usage models	Meta data can now be used for navigation as well as term and search driven pages. Term sets can independently be configured for use in site navigation, search navigation, and faceted content filtering. In addition, term sets can now be shared across site collections, pinned for use in specific locations, and even identified as the only term set available to users.
Multilingual meta data	Unlike SharePoint 2010, which offered languages only after a language pack had been installed, SharePoint 2013 enables the use of any LCID as a language identifier without requiring the installation of that language pack as a prerequisite.

FEATURE	DESCRIPTION
.NET client object model (CSOM) support for managed meta data APIs	SharePoint 2013 introduces the ability to write CSOM and JavaScript against the taxonomy. Customizations require references to the new `Microsoft.SharePoint.Client.Taxonomy.dll`.
Cross-site content publishing	By leveraging built-in search capabilities, SharePoint 2013 introduces the ability to create sites that reach across site collection boundaries or even across farms to share content.
Site policies, closure, and deletion	SharePoint 2013 now offers the ability to create automated site closure and deletion retention policies. Site closure means that the site's content is removed from search indexes but is still accessible (and editable) to site members and administrators. When a site is deleted, all content including shared mailboxes are eliminated. Site retention policies enable date-based closure and deletion as well as workflow-driven closure and deletion.
Shredded storage of documents in SQL Server	Not technically a developer feature or even a capability that will be noticed by end users, shredded storage is a SQL Server feature used by SharePoint to break a document up into pieces inside of SQL Server to reduce the size of content traveling across the wire. Because the files can now be invisibly broken into pieces, only the bits that were changed are updated in SQL Server.
Office web apps (OWA) have normalized URLs	You can now open an Office document in the browser, read, and even understand the URL. Simply append `"?Web=1"` to the URL of a document in a library to open the file in the appropriate OWA editor.
Enhanced document sets	New support for OneNote and folders within document sets. Document sets that show up in SharePoint search results now leverage a new icon to better identify themselves as document sets. Versioning improvements now capture the entire document set as a versioned "file," rather than just the interior contents as was done in SP2010.

Microsoft keeps an updated list of deprecated SharePoint 2010 features online at `http://technet.microsoft.com/en-us/library/ff607742`, but Table 12-3 mentions those deprecated features most closely related to the topic of content management.

TABLE 12-3: Deprecated ECM Features in SharePoint Server 2013

FEATURE	DESCRIPTION
Document Workspace site templates	Document collaboration scenarios are now answered by the team site, so Microsoft removed the Document Workspace template to simplify the list of templates available for new site collections.
Visio Process Repository site templates	Never a widely used template, the Visio Process site template has been removed from the list of available site collection templates. It will still be supported for 2013 sites (just not site collections).

Expanded ECM Object Model

You can use the ECM programming model to extend the functionality of the new ECM features and create custom solutions. The programming model includes support for three types of programming: the server-side object model for server-side programming, a client object model, and RESTful web services for client-side programming. The number of namespaces and types is vast; however, Table 12-4 illustrates some of the primary namespaces and some prominent types that are commonly used. In this chapter, there is sample code showing how some of the members might be used. The actual assembly files are located in the SharePoint root in the ISAPI folder.

TABLE 12-4: The ECM Object Model

NAMESPACE	DESCRIPTION
`Microsoft.Office.DocumentManagement`	Provides types and members for managing documents.
`Microsoft.Office.DocumentManagement.DocumentSets`	Provides types and members for managing document sets.
`Microsoft.Office.DocumentManagement.MetadataNavigation`	Provides types and members for managing meta data navigation.
`Microsoft.Office.DocumentManagement.Server`	Contains the Multilanguage document library event receiver.
`Microsoft.Office.DocumentManagement.VideoSets`	Provides types and members for managing video assets.
`Microsoft.Office.RecordsManagement.Holds`	Provides types and members for applying holds to documents and updates the status of those holds.
`Microsoft.Office.RecordsManagement.InformationPolicy`	Provides types and members for creating and administrating information management policies.

Microsoft.Office.RecordsManagement .OfficialFileWSProxy	Provides the result of a GetFinalRouting DestinationFolderUrl operation performed asynchronously.
Microsoft.Office.RecordsManagement .PolicyFeatures	Provides access to records management policy classes such as ExpirationTask and Barcode.
Microsoft.Office.RecordsManagement .RecordsRepository	Provides access to content routing classes.
Microsoft.Office.RecordsManagement .Reporting	Provides access to classes that enable developers to generate audit reports.
Microsoft.Office.RecordsManagement .SearchAndProcess	Provides types and members to define and initiate search and process operations.
Microsoft.Office.Server.Discovery	Provides access to eDiscovery classes such as Case, Source, and ExportCollection.
Microsoft.SharePoint.Taxonomy	Includes classes that provide the basic functionality for enterprise meta-data management. Examples include types for managing terms, term sets, groups, keywords, term stores, and meta data service applications.
Microsoft.SharePoint.Taxonomy .ContentTypeSync	Includes classes that manage synchronization of content types between site collections.
Microsoft.SharePoint.Taxonomy.Generic	Includes classes for collections of generic taxonomy items.
Microsoft.SharePoint.Taxonomy .WebServices	Includes classes for the web services used to manage taxonomies included in rich and web client applications.

Source: SharePoint 2013 SDK - http://msdn.microsoft.com/en-us/library/sharepoint/jj193044.aspx

GETTING THE MOST FROM THE DOCUMENT CENTER

The Document Center in SharePoint Server is a site definition that can be used in combination with a content type hub to manage hundreds of millions of documents and act as a large archive. Of course, in a large system with hundreds of millions of items, many instances of a Document Center might be provisioned, each with its own content database supporting up to 1 terabyte of content. When millions of documents are involved, the ideal management scenario is to separate the collaboration from finalized storage. Scale is achieved by using a distributed architecture.

Although the constructs included in a Document Center are useful for large repositories, smaller teams can use a single Document Center instance to serve as a starting point for document management for smaller deployments. Therefore, the Document Center site template supports both the read-mainly and collaborative in-place authoring scenarios.

By design, the Document Center is meant to be easy to use, while also being easy to administer. Everyone can have access to its features, and everyone can see as much as they need to within the security defined by administrators and content stewards. It is worth noting that although the Document Center is easy to use because it is preconfigured with the constructs needed to manage large sets of documents, you can also turn these features on in any team site.

The new Document Center in SharePoint 2013, as shown in Figure 12-1, and has been enhanced to include:

➤ Meta-data navigation features and taxonomy capabilities

➤ A Document ID Service

➤ Integration with Office Client New, Open, and Save functions

➤ Multistage retention policies

➤ Folder-based information policies

➤ Location-based meta-data defaults and metadata–driven navigation

➤ Integration with the Records Center site definition

➤ A configuration to act as a template that enables organizations to quickly start managing documents

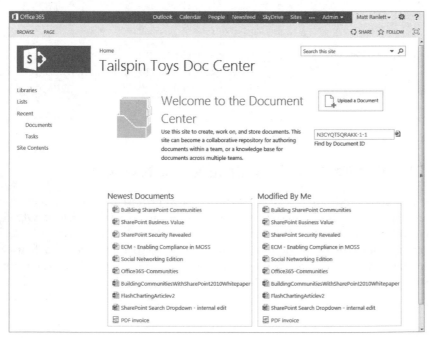

FIGURE 12-1

Note the Document ID search web part. Documents can be located using a unique ID that is assigned when they are created. As in SharePoint 2010, all documents in a Document Center template based site collection can automatically receive a unique ID. This feature can be enabled or disabled by the site administrator.

When designing a document management strategy using SharePoint 2013, it is helpful to acknowledge that users generally fall into three roles:

➤ Visitors are individuals who have read-only access to documents. Common tasks for visitors include browsing documents, searching, and reading documents.

➤ Contributors are individuals responsible for creating documents or document sets and participating in workflows.

➤ Content Stewards maintain document libraries and Document Centers and may be responsible for creating libraries, views, and subsites. They configure meta data, navigation, and security, and act as nontechnical administrators.

Visual Studio and the Document Center

Developers can use the `SetupDocSiteFeatureReceiver` class in the `Microsoft.Office .DocumentManagement.DocSite` namespace to customize how the Document Center is created. The feature receiver is inherited like any other feature receiver. The feature events can use the object model to customize new Document Centers as they are created.

CONTENT ROUTING

Architecting large document repositories requires advanced planning and possibly a team of content stewards. Uploading, navigating, and finding content become tricky when scaling for millions of items. SharePoint 2013 leverages capabilities introduced in the previous version to provide features that assist content stewards in managing large repositories, as well as making repositories easier to use. One of these site-level features is the Content Organizer (CO).

Often, when users are adding content to a large repository, there is this sense that they are handing the content off to the content stewards. Most of the time, the content found in these larger repositories is in a finished state and ready for storage and consumption. One use of the CO is to route documents to specific site collections or folders based on rules and meta data.

Managing the Content Organizer

The CO is activated using the Site Features list. After the feature is activated, you configure the CO using the Content Organizer Setting and Content Organizer Rules links under Site Administration. The CO is the evolution of the Routing Table web part and the related document routing features in the SharePoint 2007 Document Repositories site definition.

The Drop Off Library

When the Content Organizer (CO) feature is activated, a special document library—the Drop Off Library (see Figure 12-2)—is created and added to the Quick Launch navigation. Any content that derives from the Document content type and is received by the Drop Off Library can be routed to alternative locations without user intervention. The location that the content is routed to is determined by rules that the content stewards create. Content can be routed to other site collections, libraries, or folders within libraries. The CO can be configured to force all content to be uploaded to the Drop Off Library. After this is configured, it can act as a holding area for documents that do not have the required meta data needed for rule processing.

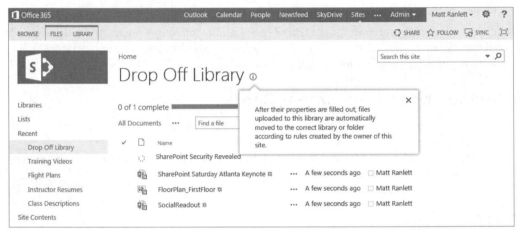

FIGURE 12-2

There are several scenarios for using the Content Organizer:

➤ Masking upload complexities from contributors

➤ Delivering content flagged as confidential to secure locations

➤ Submitting content to large repositories

➤ Moving content to folders with specific Document Information Policies

➤ Creating new folders as needed and then moving content to them

Documents may be sent to document libraries via different pipes. For example, you can use the context menu Send To pipe, manual uploads, workflows, and the object model. Because the Drop Off Library is a standard library, all of these submission pipes are supported.

Creating Rules

Typically, content stewards are responsible for adding rules to route content around the organization. Before creating rules, the CO should be configured using Site Settings. There are several useful options available during configuration:

➤ The Redirect Users to the Drop Off Library option redirects users' content to the Drop Off Library if they try to upload content to a library that is associated with rules.

➤ When the Sending to Another Site option is enabled, content can be routed to other site collections. This is useful when the content stewards are responsible for lots of content that needs to be distributed across many site collections.

➤ Folder provisioning settings allow new folders to be created when certain thresholds are reached. This is another useful feature in repositories that contain a large number of documents. Folders can be provisioned, allowing you to maintain fewer than 5,000 items in a given folder.

> **NOTE** *The List View Threshold is a setting in SharePoint that represents the maximum number of items retrieved in one request. The default value is 5,000 and the minimum is 2,000.*

➤ The Duplicate Submissions setting enables you to allow versioning or provide unique filenames so that files are not overwritten.

➤ Role managers will be notified if files have been submitted to the Drop Off Library but have not been routed for various reasons.

Rules List

The content stewards add rules using the Content Organizer Rules link (see Figure 12-3), which you can access using the link in the Site Administration section on the Site Settings page. When content is received by the CO, rules are processed by priority and can assist the content stewards in making sure that content is stored in the appropriate place.

To create a new rule, you must provide the following information:

➤ **Rule name:** A user-friendly name, which may be exposed in the File Plan report.

➤ **Rule Status and Priority:** Set a value between 1 and 9 with 1 having the highest priority. Having a higher priority means the rule executes before rules with a lower priority.

➤ **Submission's Content Type:** The selected content type properties will be exposed to condition logic. If the rules are met, the content assumes this content type.

➤ **Conditions:** Enables configuration of up to six logical comparisons of content type properties.

➤ **Target Location:** The location the content will be moved to if it matches all of the conditions defined. This location can be another site or site collection.

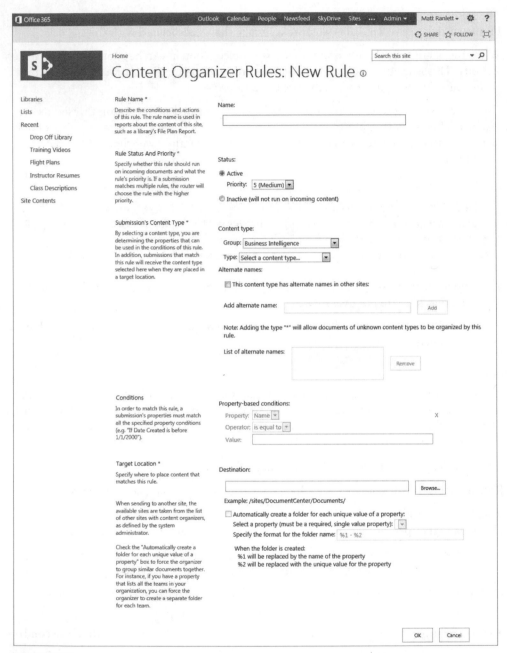

FIGURE 12-3

In summary, the Content Organizer feature is available for any site template, not just Record or Document Centers. You create rules that help the CO decide where the various types of content should be stored. This enables you to enforce security and information policies. The CO can route content based on properties as well as content type.

USING DOCUMENT LIBRARIES IN THE DOCUMENT CENTER

Like the previous version of the Document Center, there is one default document library contained in any newly provisioned Document Center sites. Of course, it is possible to add libraries as needed. Many of the features explored in this chapter are managed at the document-library level. Although large organizations may require many site collections and Document Centers to manage hundreds of millions of documents, smaller teams may be able to achieve their document management goals using a single document library. A single library can contain large numbers of documents. However, generally speaking, if you need to manage many items, you should distribute the items across multiple libraries or sites for various reasons.

Folders in a document library can be based on business needs. With the release of SharePoint 2013, you must understand that the folders contained in libraries serve many purposes outside the traditional use, assisting with categorization. Because you can manage information policies at the folder level and these policies are inherited similarly to security policies, you can use folders as a means of maintaining and organizing retention policies. Document meta data can be automatically populated according to the location of the document, allowing folders to play a role in meta data as well. Table 12-5 is a list of the default settings for the document libraries provisioned using the Document Center site definition.

TABLE 12-5: Default Document Library Settings for the Document Center

LIST SETTING	DOCUMENT LIBRARY DEFAULT	SHAREPOINT SERVER 2010 DOCUMENT CENTER SETTING	SHAREPOINT SERVER 2013 DOCUMENT CENTER SETTING
Content Approval	No	No	No
Version History	No versioning	Creates major and minor versions	Creates major and minor versions
Draft Item Security	Not available	Read permissions (minimum)	Read permissions (minimum)
Require Check Out	No	Yes	Yes
Content Types	No	Yes	Yes
Document Template	`Template.doc`	`Template.doc`	`Template.dotx`
Browser-enabled Documents	Open in the client application	Open in the client application	Use the server default (Open in the browser)
Folders	Yes	Yes	Yes
Search	Yes	Yes	Yes

Because the Document Center is designed to manage a large number of documents, the ability to quickly sort and filter, as well as navigate to, content is important. SharePoint 2013 provides three quick ways to find the content needed: column-level filters, meta-data navigation, and key filters.

Meta-Data Navigation and Filtering

Metadata–based navigation helps users find documents quickly and explore unstructured content that might span many folders in a library. Content stewards define navigation hierarchies based on content types, single-value choice fields, or managed meta-data fields. The selected fields appear on the Quick Launch toolbar when the user browses inside of a properly configured document library and can be used to assist in navigating large amounts of documents.

Key filters can be defined (see Figure 12-4), allowing users to filter documents by terms entered in the Key Filters section of the Quick Launch toolbar. Both the navigation hierarchy and key filters are defined at the library level using Library Settings.

Field types that are available for key filters include:

➤ Content type

➤ Choice fields

➤ Managed meta-data fields

➤ Date and time fields

➤ Number fields

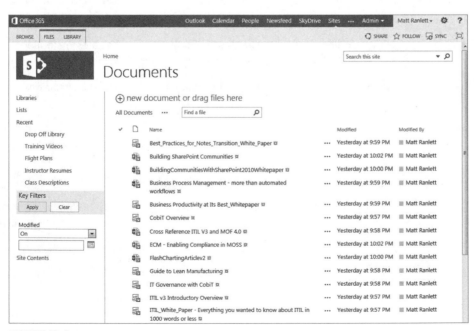

FIGURE 12-4

To enable meta-data navigation and filtering in a document library, follow these simple steps:

1. Open the library in question.

2. On the Library Ribbon tab, select the Library Settings action.

3. Click the Metadata Navigation Settings link in the General Settings list.

4. Configure the navigation hierarchies and key filter fields. By default the Document Center's Documents library has selected the Folders hierarchy field and the Modified key filter field.

5. It is considered a good practice to allow for automatic indexing of the library based on selected navigation and filter selections (a default setting).

The next section discusses this final meta-data navigation configuration choice in more detail, as shown in Figure 12-5.

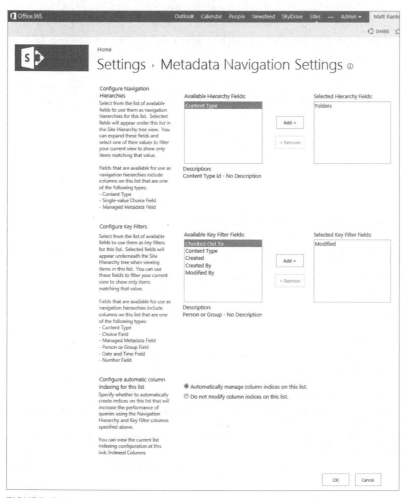

FIGURE 12-5

Queries and Indexes

When defining columns used for navigation, SharePoint defaults to automatically creating and managing the column indexes on the list. This setting, Configure Automatic Column Indexing for This List, can be seen in the meta data navigation settings screen above in Figure 12-5. The indexes are created using the data that will be used in queries as the tree is navigated and nodes are selected. As new nodes are selected, SharePoint decides if it can reuse an index from the last query. If the previous index can't be used, a new query will be created using another available index. If the query fails because of too many results being returned, a fallback query will be used to return top items from the list.

Visual Studio and Document Libraries

Much of what developers learned about document library definitions and Visual Studio in the previous version of SharePoint is still relevant today. Custom document libraries can be created using list definition templates found in Visual Studio 2013. You can use the various flavors of the object model to send and retrieve items to and from the document library. Custom fields and views can be added as part of any list definition. Listing 12-1 uses the object model to set options such as list throttling and synchronization properties.

LISTING 12-1: Document Library Manipulation Using the SharePoint Object Model

```
using System;
using Microsoft.SharePoint.Client;

namespace ECMSampleThrottling_Console
{
    class Program
    {
        static void Main(string[] args)
        {
            // Starting with ClientContext, the constructor requires a URL to the
            // server running SharePoint.
            ClientContext context =
                            new ClientContext("http://www.tailspintoys.com/");

            // The SharePoint web at the URL.
            Web web = context.Web;

            // Execute the query to the server.
            context.ExecuteQuery();

            // Define the list to be created
            ListCreationInformation listParams = new ListCreationInformation();
            listParams.Title = "Stuffed Bear Fabrics";
            listParams.Description = "Available fabric options for plush animals";
            listParams.DocumentTemplateType =
                            (int)ListTemplateType.DocumentLibrary;

            // add the list
```

```csharp
            List classList = web.Lists.Add(listParams);

            // Execute the query to the server.
            context.Load(classList);
            context.ExecuteQuery();

            Console.WriteLine("Library added...");

            Console.ReadLine();
        }
    }
}
```

Create a Document Library List Definition in Visual Studio

You can create a list definition and list instance using the templates that are included in Visual Studio 2012. The list definitions are created using project templates included in Visual Studio.

To create a list definition and list instance, follow these steps:

1. Create an empty SharePoint 2013 project, available on the Office/SharePoint ⇨ SharePoint Solutions menu.

2. Right-click the Project in the Solution Explorer, and select Add ⇨ New Item.

3. In the Add New Item window select List, and rename the default name from **List1** to **Model Airplane Assembly Plan**, as shown in Figure 12-6.

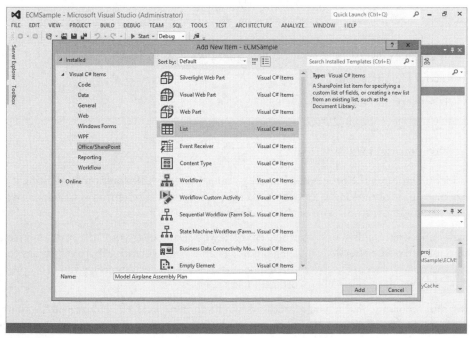

FIGURE 12-6

4. Click Add to bring up the SharePoint Customization Wizard.

5. Using the SharePoint Customization Wizard, do the following:

    a. Set the display name.

    b. Select the base template for the list definition.

After you click the Finish button, the new definition will be generated, and a new folder will be created under the Solution Explorer. After the list definition is generated, you can define custom fields as needed.

RECORDS MANAGEMENT

With the explosion of digital information and the requirements of keeping this information compliant with government and industry regulations, records management has become a critical component of any SharePoint deployment. If you haven't heard of records management, you will. Records management is the process of classifying, securing, discovering, and managing your information from creation to destruction. SharePoint provides numerous features that allow end users, developers, and IT pros to make their applications and information compliant.

> **NOTE** *Records management is a broad topic and always evolving with industry experts and new tools. There are a number of industry sites that are good to use for new trends in records management such as Association for Information and Image Management International (AIIM) at* www.aiim.org.

SharePoint provides records management using four key feature areas:

➤ Record identification

➤ eDiscovery and legal holds

➤ Auditing and reporting

➤ Retention and expiration

Record identification is the process of formally managing your information by making it an official record. As part of making it an official record, you specify a retention schedule, any auditing requirements, and how to dispose of the information.

eDiscovery and legal holds work together, enabling you to uncover your information assets using search no matter where they live, and legal holds enable you to create eDiscovery cases for legal requests and compliance. eDiscovery is tied to search, so if you are interested in eDiscovery, you should become familiar with Microsoft search services.

Auditing and reporting enable you to audit, down to an item level, the changes made to an item such as when and who modified the content. Combined with reporting, you can get a report out to Excel that shows you the details about your information across your site and also which content is following your information policies across your site.

Retention and expiration enable you to set policies for retention and expiration of your information. You can control this at the individual piece of content level or force policies based on the location the content lives in SharePoint. Expiration is the process of archiving or destroying your content when the content is no longer needed, or, for compliance reasons, when you want to remove the content from your system.

These four areas, when combined, provide you with a robust records management application and platform to control the flow of information assets in your organization.

Record Identification

Record identification is the process of turning information assets into declared records. Becoming a declared record has implications for activities such as managing the life cycle of the asset, making it discoverable, and archiving the record for longer term storage. SharePoint 2013 enables records management in either a staged process of moving records to a SharePoint Records Center or creating in-place records management. If you decide to use in-place records, you can leave the asset in place in the library and manage the information as a record. To get these features you need to make sure the In Place Records Management feature has been activated.

SharePoint provides the ability to declare many types of information as records. This means that you can create records for files, such as Microsoft Office documents, as well as social networking types, such as blogs and wikis. All content in SharePoint is considered content and can be used in records management.

Multistage disposition is a key feature in records management. You can have multiple stages based on different timeframes and criteria. This lets you set up policies, such as Check Legal Documents Every Year to See if They Have Expired or if the Conditions on the Contracts Have Been Met, while also having a policy that deletes a contract 7 years after the document is approved. This technology can work with nonrecords, so think about the scenarios in which you can use this technology even outside of records management.

Record Center Site Template

The Records Center template enables easier access for users submitting documents and records managers searching for documents based on document ID. The Records Center also uses some of the other Enterprise Content Management (ECM) features, such as meta data–driven navigation, to make it easier to browse the Records Center by meta data rather than by folder hierarchy. The last point about the Records Center template is that you can have multiple Records Centers in a single site collection. Rather than forcing you to use a single Records Center, SharePoint enables you to have multiple Records Centers to which you can point different sets of users or content.

You may be wondering when to use the Records Center versus in-place records management. The difference will be policy and preference. For example, if your company would rather manage active content separate from records content, using the Records Center makes sense. In addition, if you have a records manager for your organization and want centralized management of your records, rather than relying on individual groups to manage their policies, you will want to deploy the Records Center. If your users need access to their content after they declare it as a record, you will want to use in-place records management. Figure 12-7 shows the Records Center template.

FIGURE 12-7

Content Organizer

As part of organizing your records, SharePoint supports a Content Organizer and Content Organizer rules. These rules enable you to specify where content should go based on a number of criteria, including properties such as content type. By having these rules, end users or applications can submit their documents to the Records Center; and the Records Center, or any SharePoint site where the Content Organizer is running, can route the content to the right location. Using the Content Organizer settings, you can create customized content routing rules, both in the user interface and using the API.

The last feature in the records center is the hierarchical, meta data–driven file plan in the archive. Having the ability to set file plans through the meta data contained in the content makes administration easier. File plans enable different record actions according to location or content type.

Auditing and Reporting

With any records management solution, good auditing and reporting are critical. Auditing allows you to track what users are doing with the content and whether they are accessing, deleting, or moving it. SharePoint supports per item reporting, so you can see the actions performed on content at an individual item level. SharePoint also supports reporting using the file plan, so you can understand the compliance details for your content. By providing a simple user interface similar to the Properties interface, SharePoint makes it easy to understand the compliance details for your documents. Figure 12-8 shows the Compliance Details dialog box.

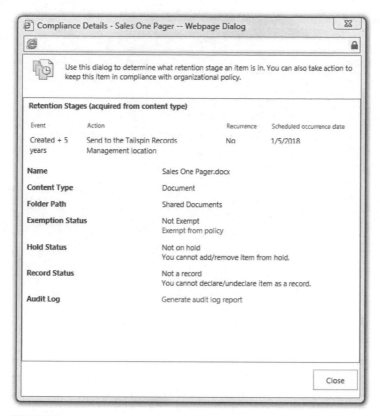

FIGURE 12-8

Records Management API

The SharePoint classes provide many methods for working with content that you will already be familiar with. These include accessing document libraries and sites to store and manage files. Most of SharePoint programming with records management involves accessing content, declaring records, creating new information management policies, performing discovery and holds, and generating reports. The following sections step you through performing actions using the different object models when working with records in SharePoint 2013. A full range of classes are in a number of namespaces and can be referenced from the following DLLs: `Microsoft.Office.Document Management` and `Microsoft.Office.Policy`.

Declaring and Undeclaring Records

One of the most common operations in records management is declaring and undeclaring records. If you want to declare records in place, you need to turn on the in-place records management feature for your site collection, and then the Record Declaration Settings window appears in your site collection administration web page, as shown in Figure 12-9.

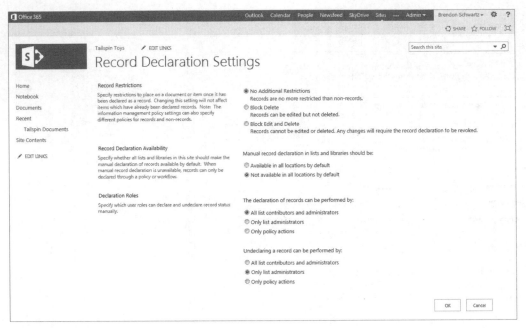

FIGURE 12-9

The classes needed for creating records are located in the `Microsoft.Office.RecordsManagement`
`.RecordsRepository` namespace. The primary methods are `DeclareItemAsRecord` and `Undeclare`
`ItemAsRecord`. To perform an action on an item, these methods pass an `SPListItem` object to the
static method. The method performs the entire action of declaring or undeclaring the item as a
record, respectively.

The following code in Listing 12-2 uploads a file to a document library. It uses the `IsInPlace`
`RecordsEnabled` method to check to see if in-place records management is enabled. Then it calls
`DeclareItemAsRecord` to declare the new document as a record. To make sure that the record is
declared, you have two options. You can check the expiration time to make sure that it was set to
the right date, or you can use the `IsRecord` method, which takes an `SPListItem` object and returns
a boolean indicating whether the item is a record or not.

LISTING 12-2: Upload File to Document Library

```
using (SPSite site = new SPSite(SharePointURL))
{
    SPWeb web = site.RootWeb;
    SPList list = web.GetList(SharePointListURL);

    Stream fileStream = File.Open(filePath, FileMode.Open);
    SPFile file = list.RootFolder.Files.Add(
```

```
fileSharePointURL, fileStream);

                SPListItem item = file.Item;
                file.Update();

                Console.WriteLine("In Place Records enabled: " +
Records.IsInPlaceRecordsEnabled(site).ToString());

                //Declare the item as a record
                Records.DeclareItemAsRecord(item);

                bool currentStageRecurs = false;
                DateTime? ExpireDT =
Expiration.GetExpirationDateForItem(item, out currentStageRecurs);

                //Make sure it declared
                if (ExpireDT == null)
                {
                    Console.WriteLine("Not declared!");
                }
                else
                {
                    Console.WriteLine("Declared Expiration Date: " +
                                        ExpireDT.ToString());
                    //Also show if Record using IsRecord
                    Console.WriteLine("IsRecord: " + Records.IsRecord(item);
                }

                //Undeclare the object
                Records.UndeclareItemAsRecord(item);
            }
```

Creating Organizer Rules

The Content Organizer enables SharePoint to route documents based on the rules you specify. Although you can create these rules through the user interface, as shown in Figure 12-10, you can also create rules through the object model. The object model offers a class called Microsoft.Office.RecordsManagement.RecordsRepository.EcmDocumentRoutingWeb. This is the base class that you will start working with, using the object model (OM). From this class, you can access the rules contained in the Content Organizer feature. One thing to remember is that you must activate the Content Organizer feature in your site feature settings. If you do not, you won't see the user interface for creating rules, and the object model won't work.

From the routing web object, you can access the RoutingRuleCollection that contains your EcmDocumentRouterRule. With the rule object, you can access the properties of an existing rule. To create a new rule, you create a new ECMDocumentRouterRule and pass the SPWeb object, which represents the SharePoint location where you want to create the rule.

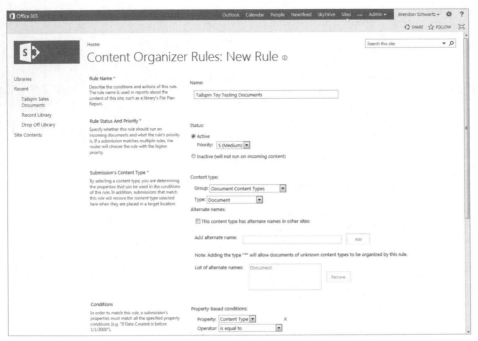

FIGURE 12-10

Because content rules require XML conditions, the easiest way to create a content rule is by using the user interface and then copying the XML from the rule. Table 12-6 lists the properties you need to set to create a rule, and Table 12-7 lists the operators.

TABLE 12-6: Properties to Create a Rule

NAME	DESCRIPTION
Name	Name of the rule.
Description	Description for the rule.
Priority	String that is the priority of the rule compared to other rules; 1 is highest, and 9 is lowest.
ContentTypeString	Content type string used to specify your content type. The format must be ID|Name.
TargetPath	Relative path to the target folder such as /Shared Documents.
ConditionString	XML fragment that contains the conditions that you want met before the rule fires. Table 12-7 shows the different Operator options for this property, but the general format is `<Conditions><Condition Column="Column ID|Column Internal Name|Column Title" Operator="Operator" Value="Value" /></Conditions>`.
Enabled	Boolean that specifies whether the rule is enabled.

TABLE 12-7: Operators for Content Organizer Rules

NAME	DESCRIPTION
IsEqual	Checks to see if the value of the column is equal to the value specified.
IsNotEqual	Checks to see if the value of the column is not equal to the value specified.
GreaterThan	Checks to see if the value of the column is greater than the value specified.
LessThan	Checks to see if the value of the column is less than the value specified.
GreaterThanOrEqual	Checks to see if the value of the column is greater than or equal to the value specified.
LessThanOrEqual	Checks to see if the value of the column is less than or equal to the value specified.
BeginsWith	Checks to see if the value of the column begins with the value specified.
NotBeginsWith	Checks to see if the value of the column does not begin with the value specified.
EndsWith	Checks to see if the value of the column ends with the value specified.
NotEndsWith	Checks to see if the value of the column does not end with the value specified.
Contains	Checks to see if the value of the column contains the value specified.
NotContains	Checks to see if the value of the column does not contain the value specified.
IsEmpty	Checks to see if the value of the column is empty. You specify a blank string for the value.
IsNotEmpty	Checks to see if the value of the column is not empty. You specify a blank string for the value.

If you want to enable autofoldering based on a unique property, use the DocumentRouterAutoFolder Settings class. This class contains a number of properties you need to set to make autofoldering work. Table 12-8 shows the properties for the DocumentRouterAutoFolderSettings class. The code in Listing 12-3 following the table shows how to set these properties and use them in your code.

TABLE 12-8: DocumentRouterAutoFolderSettings Properties

NAME	DESCRIPTION
Enabled	Boolean that specifies whether these settings are enabled.
AutoFolderPropertyInternalName	The internal name of the field to use for autofoldering.
AutoFolderPropertyId	The property ID of the field to use for autofoldering.
AutoFolderPropertyName	The property name of the field to use for autofoldering.
AutoFolderPropertyTypeAsString	The property type as a string of the field to use for autofoldering.
AutoFolderFolderNameFormat	The name format to use for the folder. By default, this will be %1 to %2. %1 will be replaced by the name of the property. %2 will be replaced with the unique value for the property.

LISTING 12-3: Using Content Organizer Methods in API

```
EcmDocumentRoutingWeb router = new EcmDocumentRoutingWeb(web);

//Output the values to the Console of each Rule and Settings
foreach (EcmDocumentRouterRule rule in router.RoutingRuleCollection)
{
Console.WriteLine("Name:" + rule.Name);
Console.WriteLine("Rule Info:" + rule.ConditionsString);

try
{
DocumentRouterAutoFolderSettings autoFolder = rule.AutoFolderSettings;

Console.WriteLine("AutoFolder Name: " + autoFolder.AutoFolderPropertyName);
Console.WriteLine("Internal Name: " + autoFolder.AutoFolderPropertyInternalName);
}
catch { }
}

//Create a new rule
SPContentType contentType = web.ContentTypes["ProductDocument"];
string contentTypeString =
          String.Format("{0}|{1}", contentType.Id, contentType.Name);

EcmDocumentRouterRule newRule = new EcmDocumentRouterRule(web);
newRule.Name = "Tailspin Document Route ";
newRule.Description = "Created by  Wrox Chapter 12 Samples";
newRule.Priority = "5";
newRule.ContentTypeString = contentTypeString;
newRule.TargetPath = "/ToySpecifications";
```

```
newRule.ConditionsString = @"<Conditions>
<Condition
Column=""8553196d-ec8d-4564-9861-3dbe931050c8|FileLeafRef|Name""
Operator=""Contains""
Value=""Specification"" />
</Conditions>";

//Create autofolder settings
//Get Field Properties (must be required and single value property
SPField customField = contentType.Fields["ProductName"];

DocumentRouterAutoFolderSettings aFolder =  newRule.AutoFolderSettings;
aFolder.Enabled = true;
aFolder.AutoFolderPropertyInternalName = customField.InternalName;
aFolder.AutoFolderPropertyId = customField.Id;
aFolder.AutoFolderPropertyName = customField.Title;
aFolder.AutoFolderPropertyTypeAsString = customField.TypeAsString;
aFolder.AutoFolderFolderNameFormat = "%1 - %2";

newRule.Enabled = true;
router.RoutingRuleCollection.Add(newRule);
```

eDISCOVERY AND COMPLIANCE

The entire Document and Records Management Systems in SharePoint 2013 have been improved with the capabilities in eDiscovery that are used for compliance teams. The new site template and eDiscovery features provide a platform that you can develop and extend. The platform and API is designed to allow companies to meet compliance and legal regulation requests by gathering information from multiple sources such as desktops, servers, and e-mail. When the information is collected and reviewed, the legal teams can act upon the content based on the legal needs.

The foundation for eDiscovery was introduced in SharePoint 2010 by allowing records managers to place a hold on SharePoint sites. There were some drawbacks around the Hold feature in sites that did not allow users to continue to use the files. And it was difficult to search across multiple platforms such as e-mail. There are many new improvements with Exchange 2013, but only the topics related to SharePoint 2013 will be discussed. If you are interested in a full review of Exchange 2013 features, you should review the material on for Microsoft TechNet.

eDiscovery Center Site Template

The new eDiscovery template is designed to be the central location for legal teams to manage the content and documents required for case management. This includes creating the set of content that will be held or used for preservation, providing quick visibility of all content surfaced through search and exporting the content as needed. The eDiscovery Center can be connected to both the SharePoint Farm and the Exchange Servers. To reduce the complexity of managing these two locations, SharePoint 2013 provides the same user interface and APIs used to manage SharePoint content as well as Exchange content. Figure 12-11 shows what the new eDiscovery Center looks like.

FIGURE 12-11

The new eDiscovery Center is easy to use and provides the steps a user should use to get started. Keep in mind that eDiscovery is powered by a SharePoint Search Service Application (SSA) and that the content is preserved using the Search Service Application proxy. This technique of using the Search Service also allows for the new feature called In-Place Holds. (In-Place Holds will be discussed further in the "eDiscovery in SharePoint 2013" section.) If you have multiple Search Service Applications, you need to create an eDiscovery Center for each one. To plan your Search and eDiscovery infrastructure as well as permissions, use the TechNet guidance and worksheets located at http://technet.microsoft.com/en-us/library/fp161512(office.15).

eDiscovery in SharePoint 2013

With the growing push toward compliance, eDiscovery continues to be a critical component of SharePoint deployments. eDiscovery enables you to discover information and capture content for use at a later date based on legal, compliance, or policies at your company.

Case Management for Discovery Sets, Queries, Sources, and Exports

Creating a SharePoint 2013 eDiscovery Case is the first step of the request for content in the eDiscovery process. All of the cases are stored in the eDiscovery Center where they can be managed and created as needed. The eDiscovery Case is a SharePoint 2013 subsite that will contain the sources and filters for request. The elements that make up the eDiscovery Case are as follows.

➤ Sources

➤ Filters

➤ Exports

To use these elements you need to create a Discovery set and query. These list items provide the needed configuration for the eDiscovery system to pull the right sources for the eDiscovery request. The eDiscovery set provides the details on the location of the records (source) and limits which records are returned from that source (filter). In addition to the settings for the documents, the eDiscovery set enables you to select if the set needs to mark the documents as held using the new In-Place Hold feature. You can see each of these in the following Figure 12-12.

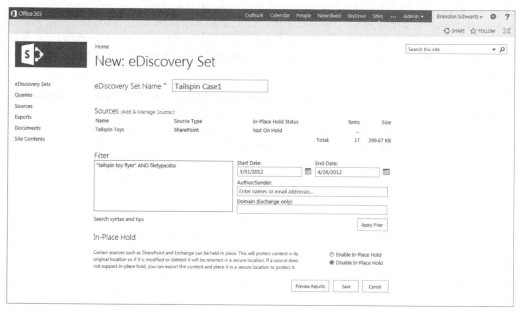

FIGURE 12-12

The major element of the eDiscovery set is the source configuration that defines where the content under review is being held. The sources can be defined from within the eDiscovery set and are the connections to the contents' In-Place Hold status. There are two types of content that can be scanned when performing the eDiscovery process, namely mailboxes and locations. The mailbox is a reference to a single mailbox set up in Exchange using the name of the user or the e-mail address. The locations refer to SharePoint sites or filesystems that are in the search index. Using the location for SharePoint sites and file shares, you will get all content at the root of the location and all subcontent.

No action is taken on the content unless you select In-Place Hold; until then, the system uses only the search results to show real-time metrics of the content. The In-Place Hold feature has been added to SharePoint 2013 to improve the Hold feature added in SharePoint 2010. Previously, when you set a Hold with the feature introduced in SharePoint 2010, users could not continue to work with the files that were in the Hold. This made it difficult to work with large eDiscovery cases and files on systems that needed to continue working, especially if the case took a long time to complete. The In-Place Hold resolves this issue by creating a snapshot of the content and allowing users to continue to work with the content by making changes or deleting files.

The way this works is through a document library that is created at the site that is marked for the In-Place Hold. A library called the Preservation Hold Library is created with security permissions set up for the site administrator to access the content. This library is hidden from all other users, who will not know if one of their files is currently under review in an eDiscovery case. There will be only one library created for all of the eDiscovery cases for that site that all files will be placed into. To allow the content to surface back to the eDiscovery case site, the library is set up to allow the search crawler to have special permissions to crawl the content. After the files are modified or deleted, they will be placed into the Preservation Hold Library if an In-Place Hold was requested. This allows the team to manage the content for the case, but also allows users to continue working with documents needed for business. The preservation hold library holds only files that have been modified, so you need to verify the file is in the Preservation Hold Library if you are programmatically accessing the library.

Using the eDiscovery sets you can create queries of relevant content as well as define the additional filters on content in the sources already defined. The query page provides the ability to see the content with details about the author and date created as well as a link to view or download the file. After the query has been completed, the set of files can be exported using the export file and Export Wizard.

The Export Wizard provides the steps needed to create a package that contains the items specified in the queries. SharePoint provides an option to remove duplicate exchange content (such as the same e-mail in two locations) as well as the option to include versions of the SharePoint documents in your packages. If there are files that are encrypted or have file formats that are unrecognized such as log files, they can still be added to the list of files added to the export. After you begin the export, a .NET application opens and performs the download to your desktop.

When you finish performing the export using the eDiscovery Download Manager, you see a folder with the name of the query that is configured as well as the files requested in the download. You also notice that there is a reports folder with some basic reports about the case and a summary of the export that has been performed. SharePoint 2013 has also provided a manifest.xml file, which is a load file for the export in an open standard format called the Electronic Discovery Reference Model (EDRM). The content is formatted according the EDRM format to allow it to be imported to any other review tool that also supports that format. Listing 12-4 shows an example of part of a manifest.xml file.

LISTING 12-4: Manifest.xml file from eDiscovery Export

```
<?xml version="1.0" encoding="utf-8"?>
<Root MajorVersion="1"
      MinorVersion="1"
      Description="Tailspin Budget Reports"
      DataInterchangeType="Update"
      CaseId="50437b7d-1b8c-45c5-a4a0-b724a7aee95a"
      xmlns:xsi="http://www.w3.org/2001/XMLSchema-instance"
      xmlns:xsd="http://www.w3.org/2001/XMLSchema">
  <Batch>
    <Documents>
      <Document DocID="34959672" DocType="File" MimeType=
```

```
 "application/vnd.openxmlformats-officedocument.wordprocessingml.document">
<Tags>
  <Tag TagName="#Title" TagDataType="Text"
            TagValue="Toy Flying Car Budget" />
  <Tag TagName="#Filename" TagDataType="Text"
            TagValue="Toy Flying Car Budget.docx" />
  <Tag TagName="#FileExtension" TagDataType="Text" TagValue="docx" />
  <Tag TagName="#Author" TagDataType="Text" TagValue="Brendon Schwartz" />
  <Tag TagName="#DateCreated" TagDataType="DateTime"
            TagValue="2013-01-05T23:21:20" />
  <Tag TagName="#DateModified" TagDataType="DateTime"
            TagValue="2012-08-07T09:44:00" />
  <Tag TagName="ModifiedBy" TagDataType="Text"
            TagValue="Brendon Schwartz" />
  <Tag TagName="#FileSize" TagDataType="LongInteger" TagValue="19505" />
  <Tag TagName="ContentType" TagDataType="Text"
            TagValue="application/vnd.openxmlformats-officedocument
                      .wordprocessingml.document&#xA;&#xA;Document" />
</Tags>
<Files>
  <File FileType="Native">
    <ExternalFile FilePath="Tailspin Toys\newtoys\Shared Documents"
              FileName="Toy Flying Car Budget.docx" FileSize="19505"
Hash="SHA256:1eb0009cbe3f778b10ea3d2d10d2d1527fa581bae033883f8dc92daa9a899d8f" />
  </File>
</Files>
<Locations>
  <Location>
    <Custodian>Tailspin Toys</Custodian>
    <LocationURI>https://tailspin.sharepoint.com/sites/newtoys/
              Shared Documents/Toy Flying Car Budget.docx</LocationURI>
    <Description>None</Description>
  </Location>
</Locations>
</Document>
```

> **NOTE** *For more details about this standard, visit the working groups site at* `http://www.edrm.net/projects/xml`.

Create Compliance with SharePoint 2013

Compliance features have become critical for many companies, especially with the amount of content they try to manage today. SharePoint 2013 continues to improve on the capabilities of compliance with a focus on the entire site. In previous versions of SharePoint, you could create policies on documents and content types, but you could not manage an entire site as a container for compliance of all the content inside of that site. The compliance features of records management still contain the ability to audit based on set documents and creates information management policies in addition to the new site level compliance.

Information Management Policies

Managing content can be difficult without some set of policies applied to the content. The policies help comply with any procedures in an organization, as well as allow you to comply with legally mandated requirements. These policies focus on three major areas: auditing, retention, and printing. The policy features can be accessed either through the user interface or API for automating your compliance. When using information management policies, you have the ability to set the policy at the site collection, list and library, or content-type level.

Site Compliance

Microsoft has provided many compliance options since SharePoint 2007, but many of the options were designed for individual documents. This meant that a company either could not force compliance on an entire site or had to purchase a third-party tool for compliance and archiving. SharePoint 2013 introduces features to provide the site-level compliance with the enhancement of site polices, closure, and deletion.

To use the closure and deletion features, you first need to set up a site policy. You can have as many named site policies within a site, but only one can be applied to the site at a time. Using the API you can change the policies based on changes in content, such as highly confidential information being added to a site. The site policy enables you to select the actions to perform on the site closure and deletion, as well as the ability to make the entire site collection read-only when an entire site collection is closed. Figure 12-13 shows the settings page for creating a new site policy.

FIGURE 12-13

After at least one site policy has been created, you can apply that policy to the site. When this is done using the user interface, the site settings page for site closure and deletion will be updated with the date on which the closure will occur as well as the deletion. From the site closure and deletion page you can close the site now as well as postpone the deletion of the site based on the set policy. The dates provided are based on the site creation date and the date that the site is closed. Figure 12-14 shows the site settings page with the policy applied.

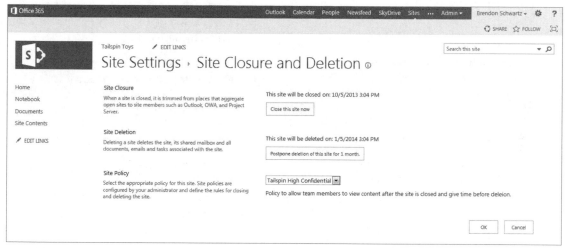

FIGURE 12-14

The addition of the new site policy, closure, and deletion feature helps maintain compliance around projects that have a set start and end date. To adhere to specific usage policies for users on projects, SharePoint can use the site closer and deletion options. The feature is not limited to projects but can specifically address this need in your sites used for projects. The internal name used in the API reflects this and uses the word Project instead of Site. When explaining the following class and code, the word Project is used to refer to a SharePoint site; although, the user interface uses the word Site.

The Microsoft framework has added the new `ProjectPolicy` class to manage the Site Policies and the site closure and deletion times. The class also provides static methods that enable you to perform Site Compliance programmatically on the site. The methods can be divided into two major categories: the methods that provide information about the Project and the actions you can perform on the Project. There is no way to create a new policy from code. The methods are provided to only perform actions on the Project (that is, Site) or update values of the current policies. Table 12-9 and 12-10 show the methods of the `ProjectPolicy` class separated into the two categories.

TABLE 12 -9: Methods to Return Information About the Project

METHOD	RETURN TYPE	DESCRIPTION
DoesProjectHavePolicy	Boolean	Determines if a site has a Site Policy currently set
IsProjectClosed	Boolean	Returns if the Site has been marked as closed already
GetProjectCloseDate	DateTime	Provides the date that the site will be closed based on the policy settings and the created by date of the site
GetProjectExpirationDate	DateTime	Provides the date the site will be deleted based on the site being closed
GetProjectPolices	List<ProjectPolicy>	Returns a list of the policies defined on the site

TABLE 12-10: Actions on the Project

METHOD	DESCRIPTION
ApplyProjectPolicy	Allows you to apply a site policy to the site based on one of the predefined site policies defined in the GetProjectPolices list
CloseProject	Marks the site as closed immediately
OpenProject	Marks the site as open again with the site policy still applied
PostponeProject	Uses the site policy to change the close date the specified amount of time that is listed

Using the methods is straightforward with a limited number of parameters. The key parameter is that you need the SPWeb object related to the Project Policy or Project. There is no constructor on the class, so if you want to create a Project Policy, you must do it through the user interface on the site first. Listings 12-5 and 12-6 show how you can use the methods to review the policies, apply them to the Project, check the status of the Project, and change the state of the Project. The API is available from both the server-side object model and the client-side object model using the proper DLL showing in Table 12-11.

TABLE 12-11: References Required to Use the ProjectPolicy Class

API	NAMESPACE	REFERENCE DLL
CSOM	Microsoft.SharePoint.Client.InformationPolicy	Microsoft.Office.Policy.Client.dll Microsoft.Office.Policy.Silverlight.dllMicrosoft.Office.Client.Policy.Phone.dll
Server Side	Microsoft.Office.Records Management.Information Policy	Microsoft.Office.Policy.dll

LISTING 12-5: Code to Apply a ProjectPolicy if One Has Been Created

```
if (ProjectPolicy.DoesProjectHavePolicy(web))
{
Console.WriteLine("Project already has a policy");
Console.WriteLine("ProjectPolicy::" +
          ProjectPolicy.GetCurrentlyAppliedProjectPolicyOnWeb(web).Name);
}
else
{
//The site must have at least one policy.
ProjectPolicy firstpolicy = ProjectPolicy.GetProjectPolicies(web).First();
ProjectPolicy.ApplyProjectPolicy(web,firstpolicy);
}
```

LISTING 12-6: Code to Postpone or Close Project Based on Policy Dates

```
if (     web.CurrentUser.IsSiteAuditor
    && ProjectPolicy.GetProjectExpirationDate(web).
              AddDays(10).CompareTo(DateTime.Now) < 1)
{
Console.WriteLine("PostPone the project for the auditor");
ProjectPolicy.PostponeProject(web);
}
else if(       web.CurrentUser.IsSiteAdmin
  && ProjectPolicy.GetProjectCloseDate(web).AddDays(5).CompareTo(DateTime.Now) > 1)
{
Console.WriteLine("Closing the project for the site admin");
ProjectPolicy.CloseProject(web);
}
```

Retention Schedules

Retention schedules are created by generating XML to describe the configuration of the schedule. After you understand the pattern of the XML, generating and applying retention is merely a few lines of code. To see what the XML of the retention schedule looks like, see Listing 12-7 that deletes content after 6 years. The retention schedule XML scheme will be discussed in detail after Listing 12-7, so just use it as a starting point to understand what the structure looks like.

LISTING 12-7: XML Retention Schedule

```
<Schedules nextStageId="2">
  <Schedule type="Default">
     <stages>
        <data stageId="1">
           <formula id="Microsoft.Office.RecordsManagement.PolicyFeatures
                    .Expiration.Formula.BuiltIn">
              <number>6</number>
```

continues

LISTING 12-7 *(continued)*

```
                    <property>Created</property>
                    <period>years</period>
                </formula>
                <action type="action" id="Microsoft.Office.RecordsManagement
                        .PolicyFeatures.Expiration.Action.Delete" />
            </data>
        </stages>
    </Schedule>
</Schedules>
```

Understanding Retention Schedule XML Scheme

In the XML, there is a top-level Schedules node that contains a property that is the ID of the next stage, even if that next stage does not exist. Below that, the `Schedule` node contains the multiple `stages` you want to occur on your content. To have multiple stages, you add multiple data nodes, each with a unique, incrementing integer in your `stageID` property. You can specify the `type`, which can be `Default` or `Record`. `Default` enables you specify custom actions to occur on any items, whereas `Record` performs the actions only on declared records.

From the `data` node, you see the `formula` node. The `id` of the `formula` node is the ID of one of the built-in formulas in SharePoint. You could point at your own custom class to implement your own formulas by specifying the class name in the `id` attribute. The built-in formulas enable you to add days, months, or years to the column you specify in the `property` node. In the example, the formula is calculated from the `Created` property, and 6 years are added to that property for the action to be triggered. The possible values for the `period` node are `days`, `weeks`, and `years`.

Next is the action you want to perform if the formula's criterion is met. In the sample, this means 6 years from the creation date has expired. To specify the action you want to perform, you specify the action in the `id` attribute for the `action` node. Again, you can use a custom action here by specifying your custom action class implementation for the `id` value. In the example, `Microsoft.Office` `.RecordsManagement.PolicyFeatures.Expiration.Action.Delete` is specified, which is a delete action. Table 12-12 gives you the possible built-in action values. For brevity, `Microsoft.Office` `.RecordsManagement.PolicyFeatures.Expiration.Action` has been removed from all of them, so make sure to add this back before using the actions in your XML.

TABLE 12-12: Records Management Actions

NAME	DESCRIPTION
Custom	Specifies the use of a custom action.
Delete	Deletes the content.
DeletePreviousDrafts	Deletes all drafts of the content except for the most recent.
DeletePreviousVersions	Deletes all previous versions except for the most recent.
MoveToRecycleBin	Moves the content to the recycle bin.
Record	Declares the content an in-place record.

`Skip`	Skips the step.
`SubmitFileCopy`	Submits the content to the records repository as a copy.
`SubmitFileLink`	Submits the content to the records repository and retains a link in the library.
`SubmitFileMove`	Submits the content to the records repository as a move that deletes the content from its current location.
`Workflow`	Triggers a workflow. You need to specify the GUID for the workflow in the id attribute for this action node. This action node does not need to be prefaced with `Microsoft.*` but instead should just be `<action type="workflow" id="GUID of workflow"/>`.

Creating and Applying Retention Schedules

With a good understanding of the XML scheme, you can create any retention schedules needed by simply building new XML nodes onto the previous simple example. To demonstrate a more complex retention schedule, the following XML sets three stages in Listing 12-8. The first stage recurs every 6 months and deletes the previous versions of the content. The second occurs 6 months from the modified date of the content and declares the content as a record. The last occurs 5 years from the created date and deletes the content.

LISTING 12-8: Complex Retention Schedule

```
<Schedules nextStageId-"4" default-"false">
  <Schedule type="Default">
    <stages>
      <data stageId="1" recur="True" offset="6" unit="months">
        <formula id="Microsoft.Office.RecordsManagement.PolicyFeatures
                    .Expiration.Formula.BuiltIn">
          <number>6</number>
          <property>
            Created</property><period>months</period>
        </formula>
        <action type="action" id="Microsoft.Office.RecordsManagement.
                    PolicyFeatures.Expiration.Action.DeletePreviousVersions" />
      </data>
      <data stageId="2">
        <formula id="Microsoft.Office.RecordsManagement.PolicyFeatures
                    .Expiration.Formula.BuiltIn">
          <number>6</number>
          <property>Modified</property>
          <period>months</period>
        </formula>
        <action type="action" id="Microsoft.Office.RecordsManagement.
                    PolicyFeatures.Expiration.Action.Record" />
      </data>
    </stages>
  </Schedule>
```

continues

LISTING 12-8 *(continued)*

```
    <Schedule type="Record">
      <stages>
        <data stageId="3">
          <formula id="Microsoft.Office.RecordsManagement.PolicyFeatures
                         .Expiration.Formula.BuiltIn">
            <number>5</number>
            <property>
              Created</property><period>years</period>
          </formula>
          <action type="action" id="Microsoft.Office.RecordsManagement
                         .PolicyFeatures.Expiration.Action.Delete" />
        </data>
      </stages>
    </Schedule>
  </Schedules>
```

To use the retention schedule, you can apply it to your site in one of two methods. You can attach the retention schedule to the content type, or you can attach it to the list. When attached to the content type, the retention schedule is followed regardless of where the content type is created. With the content type syndication functionality, your retention schedule can travel wherever a content type travels. If you associate the retention schedule with a list, the schedule works on content in only that list. With portability in mind you want to use the content type option so that your retention schedule works everywhere.

Programmatically checking and applying retention schedules can be done with built-in API classes. To check to see if you have a custom list policy, you can use the `ListHasPolicy` property on the `Microsoft.Office.RecordsManagement.InformationPolicy.ListPolicySettings` object. This boolean property returns whether the list has a custom policy or not. To set the list to use a custom policy, set the UseListPolicy boolean to `True` and then call `Update` on your `ListPolicySettings` object. Set this to `False` to use the content type retention policy. The constructor for your `ListPolicySettings` object takes an `SPList` object, which is the list you want to investigate. Listing 12-9 and Listing 12-10 show how to use these objects and properties.

LISTING 12-9: Change the List Policy Setting on a List

```
    SPWeb web = site.RootWeb;
    SPList list = web.GetList(SharePointListURL);

    ListPolicySettings policy =  new ListPolicySettings(list);

    if (!policy.ListHasPolicy)
    {
    //make the list use a custom list policy
    policy.UseListPolicy = true;
    policy.Update();
    }

    //Check to see if setting was successful
    Console.WriteLine("List Policy Set: " + policy.ListHasPolicy.ToString());
```

LISTING 12-10: Set a Custom Retention Policy on the List

```
using (SPSite site = new SPSite(SharePointURL))
{
SPWeb web = site.RootWeb;
SPList list = web.GetList(SharePointListURL);
SPFolder folder = web.Folders[SharePointListURL];
SPWeb parentWeb = list.ParentWeb;

SPList parentList = parentWeb.Lists[folder.ParentListId];
ListPolicySettings listPolicySettings = ListPolicySettings(parentList);

if (!listPolicySettings.UseListPolicy)
{
//Enable Location Based Policy if it isn't enabled
listPolicySettings.UseListPolicy = true;
listPolicySettings.Update();

//Refresh to get the updated ListPolicySettings
listPolicySettings = new ListPolicySettings(parentList);
}

listPolicySettings.SetRetentionSchedule(folder.ServerRelativeUrl,
policyXml, "My Custom Retention");
listPolicySettings.Update();

Console.WriteLine(listPolicySettings.
            GetRetentionSchedule(folder.ServerRelativeUrl));
}
```

To create the same policy on a content type requires a bit more code, but the process is similar. The code in Listing 12-11 is the same as the previous sample, but instead of getting the list policies, the code retrieves the content types in SharePoint, in particular the document content type. The code then uses the GetPolicy method to retrieve the expiration policy for the content type. If that policy does not exist, it creates the policy. Then, it sets the CustomData property for that policy and calls the Update method to set the retention policy for the content type.

LISTING 12-11: Create a Retention Policy on a Content Type

```
using (SPSite site = new SPSite(SharePointURL))
{
SPWeb web = site.RootWeb;
SPList list = web.GetList(SharePointListURL);
SPFolder folder = web.Folders[SharePointListURL];
SPWeb parentWeb = list.ParentWeb;

SPList parentList = parentWeb.Lists[folder.ParentListId];
ListPolicySettings listPolicySettings = new ListPolicySettings(parentList);

SPContentType contentType = web.ContentTypes["Document"];
Policy policy = Policy.GetPolicy(contentType);
```

continues

LISTING 12-11 *(continued)*

```
//Check to see if it exists, if not create it
if (policy == null)
{
Policy.CreatePolicy(contentType, null);
policy = Policy.GetPolicy(contentType);
}

PolicyItem retentionPolicy = policy.Items[Expiration.PolicyId];
//See if a policy already exists, if not create one
if (retentionPolicy == null)
{
policy.Items.Add(Expiration.PolicyId, policyXml);
policy.Update();
}
else
{
retentionPolicy.CustomData = policyXml;
retentionPolicy.Update();
}

//Display policy XML to validate it worked
retentionPolicy = policy.Items[Expiration.PolicyId];
Console.WriteLine("Policy XML: " + retentionPolicy.CustomData.ToString());
```

CONTENT MANAGEMENT INTEROPERABILITY SERVICES (CMIS)

The Content Management Interoperability Services (CMIS) is an open source standard used for interoperability with any ECM system that supports the standard. SharePoint has implemented and supported this standard since the SharePoint 2010 Administrative ToolKit. SharePoint 2013 redesigned the implementation and enhanced the interfaces to provide a more powerful experience. As of the writing of this book, SharePoint supported the released version of the standard, which is CMIS 1.0.

> **NOTE** *The full specification and updates for CMIS are located at* `https://www.oasis-open.org/committees/tc_home.php?wg_abbrev=cmis`.

One of the biggest challenges using an open standard is authentication since multiple types of platforms can implement the standard. Each platform might have their own type of authentication for accessing the content, and to seamlessly integrate with those systems, they must communicate using the same types of authentication. SharePoint 2013 provides the ability to use multiple types of authentication both native to Windows as well as open standards such as claims environments.

SUMMARY

In this chapter, you learned to use SharePoint to manage documents and artifacts for small teams, as well as hundreds of millions of documents for large organizations. You discovered the importance of using the SharePoint API to manage content and information architecture. Using SharePoint helps you eliminate information silos by using constant meta data and terms across site collections and farms.

You also have seen how you can use records management in SharePoint 2013. Declaring records and creating Content Organizer rules can be done directly in the user interface, but more importantly you can use the API to also manage the records. With the new eDiscovery Center, you can easily manage your compliance without affecting the document management of your sites. Combine the new records management features with the new document management features, and SharePoint becomes a capable information management system for handling large amounts of data. This combination also enables you to build powerful information management solutions with SharePoint.

13

Introducing Business Connectivity Services

WHAT'S IN THIS CHAPTER?

➤ Learning the basics of Business Connectivity Services

➤ Creating no-code BCS solutions

➤ Creating Office 365 solutions

➤ Using BCS solutions with SharePoint

WROX.COM CODE DOWNLOADS FOR THIS CHAPTER

The wrox.com code downloads for this chapter are found at www.wrox.com/remtitle
.cgi?isbn=1118495829 on the Download Code tab. The code is in the chapter 13 download
and individually named according to the names throughout the chapter.

Although Microsoft SharePoint Server 2013 is an excellent platform upon which to build
information solutions, it will never be the only system in an organization. Organizations will
always have additional systems, such as customer relationship management (CRM) and enterprise
resource planning (ERP) to target specific datasets and business processes. Organizations
may also have other custom applications, databases, and web services that are not part of
the SharePoint infrastructure. These *external systems* (external to SharePoint that is) contain
significant amounts of data and represent significant financial investments. As a consequence,
these systems will not soon be replaced by any solution created solely in SharePoint.

The challenge is that SharePoint solutions are often closely related to the data and processes
contained in external systems. For example, a document library containing invoices may contain
meta data also found in the ERP system or be addressed to a customer whose information is also
in the CRM system. Without some way to use data from the external systems, the SharePoint
solution is forced to duplicate the same information. This duplication can then lead to data
maintenance issues between the external system and the SharePoint solution.

In addition to the data challenges presented within SharePoint, there are challenges when integrating external data with Office 2013 documents. When salespeople create a quote, for example, they often look up customer contact information in a CRM system, copy it to the clipboard, and then paste it into the document. This duplication of effort obviously increases the time necessary to create documents. Furthermore, salespeople must be connected to the network to access the CRM system; they cannot easily create a quote while offline.

Failure to sufficiently integrate external systems with SharePoint solutions can slow the adoption of SharePoint within an organization. After all, the most important data used by information workers is often in external systems. Therefore, your solutions must consider how to integrate external data and that is where Business Connectivity Services (BCS) comes into play. This chapter is intended as an introduction to BCS technologies and is immediately followed by an advanced chapter on BCS development.

INTRODUCING BUSINESS CONNECTIVITY SERVICES

BCS is an umbrella term for a set of technologies that brings data from external systems into SharePoint Server 2013 and Office 2013. If you have worked previously with Business Connectivity Services in Microsoft SharePoint Server 2010, you will find only a few new things in the 2013 version, which are summarized in Table 13-1. If you have not previously worked with the BCS, don't worry; no prior experience is required to understand or use BCS in SharePoint solutions. Figure 13-1 shows a diagram of the major functional blocks that make up BCS.

TABLE 13-1: New Capabilities and Improvements

CAPABILITY/IMPROVEMENT	DESCRIPTION
OData Sources	Visual Studio 2012 supports tooling specifically designed to allow the creation of External Content Types (ECTs) against OData sources.
App-Level ECTs	External Content Types can be created that are scoped to a single SharePoint app.
REST and client-side object model (CSOM)	REST and CSOM programming interfaces against External Content Types, and external lists are new and improved.
Notifications and Event Receivers	External lists and External Content Types support event handlers and notifications such as Alert Me functionality.
Office 365 and SharePoint Online	New and improved support for using External Content Types with Office 365 and SharePoint online.
Sorting and Filtering	Improved sorting and filtering infrastructure to make external lists more efficient when querying external systems.

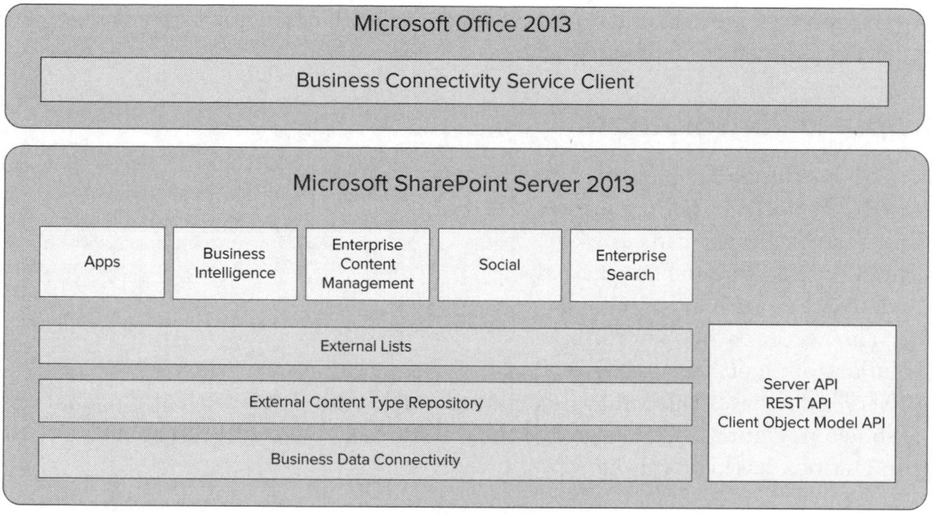

FIGURE 13-1

In the context of BCS, the term *external system* refers to any data source that is outside of the SharePoint infrastructure. As previously noted, this can include third-party software, custom applications, databases, web services, and even cloud computing solutions. BCS communicates with external systems through the Business Data Connectivity (BDC) layer. The BDC layer contains the plumbing, run-time API, and connectivity functionality necessary to communicate with external systems.

Although the BDC layer provides connectivity to the external system, it does not dictate what data is returned from the system. The operations and schema for the returned data is instead defined by an External Content Type (ECT). An ECT contains an entity definition that specifies the exact fields that should be returned from an external source. For example, a "Customer" ECT might specify that the `CustomerID`, `FirstName`, and `LastName` fields be returned from the CRM system. In addition, an ECT defines the operations that can be performed. The available operations include create, read, update, delete, and query (CRUD). Defining ECTs is one of the primary activities involved in creating a BCS solution and may be performed in either Microsoft SharePoint Designer 2013 (SPD) or Microsoft Visual Studio 2012 (VS2012). When completed, ECTs are stored in the External Content Type catalog.

Although you can create many different custom solutions using BCS, the simplest way to expose external data in SharePoint is to use an external list. An external list is a SharePoint list based on an ECT. Just as standard lists (tasks, announcements, calendars, libraries, and so on) are based on content types, external lists are based on External Content Types. External lists behave similarly to standard lists, support views, and item editing. You can use external lists in on-premises SharePoint farms and Office 365 (O365). External lists can be part of classic SharePoint solutions and the new SharePoint app model.

In Office 2013, the BCS Client layer can use External Content Types to display external data in Office clients. This data may be displayed in Outlook using standard forms such as contact lists or used in Word to support meta data and document creation. In all cases, you can make use of InfoPath to enhance the presentation of external data.

Creating Simple BCS Solutions

Although BCS solutions can be complex, they can also be created without code. Using the tools found in SPD and SharePoint, you can easily create an External Content Type and an external list. This data can then be edited in SharePoint or Office clients. This section walks you through a simple BCS solution for an on-premises farm based on a SQL Server database. The database contains a single table of marketing campaign information, as shown in Figure 13-2. The goal of the walkthrough is to create a list in SharePoint and a calendar in Outlook based on this data.

CampaignID	CampaignName	StartDate	EndDate
2	Contoso Celebrity Appearances	2013-05-01 00:00:00	2013-05-15 00:00:00
3	Summer Movie Tie-In	2013-07-04 00:00:00	2013-08-15 00:00:00
4	Holiday Sale	2013-11-01 00:00:00	2013-11-30 00:00:00
5	Vacation Seepstakes	2013-12-01 00:00:00	2013-02-01 00:00:00
6	Fantastic Fall	2013-10-15 00:00:00	2003-12-01 00:00:00

FIGURE 13-2

Creating External Content Types

The solution begins with the definition of External Content Types to define the schema and operations to perform on the data. Regardless of whether your BCS solution ultimately uses code, you almost always define the ECTs using the SharePoint Designer. The tooling in SPD for creating ECTs was designed to be sophisticated enough to be used by professional developers across all types of BCS solutions. To begin, you simply open a development site in SPD and click the External Content Types object under the list of Site Objects, as shown in Figure 13-3.

Clicking on New External Content Types in the Ribbon enables you to start defining basic ECT information. The basic ECT information consists of a Name, Display Name, Namespace, and Version. You can also select from a list of various Office Item Types, which determines what form will be used to render the information when it is displayed in Outlook. Figure 13-4 shows the basic ECT information for the walkthrough with the Appointment Office Item Type selected.

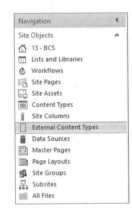

FIGURE 13-3

Clicking Operations Design View presents a form for defining connection information to an external system. Clicking the Add Connection button allows you to select from three types of connections: WCF, SQL, and .NET Type. Selecting WCF enables you to connect to a web service, SQL enables you to connect to a database, and .NET Type enables you to use a custom .NET Assembly Connector, which is covered in Chapter 14.

External Content Type Information	
Key information about this external content type.	
Name	Campaign
Display Name	Campaign
Namespace	http://www.contoso.com/campaigns
Version	1.0.0.0
Identifiers	There are no identifiers defined.
Office Item Type	Appointment
Offline Sync for external list	Enabled
External System	Click here to discover external data sources and define operations.

FIGURE 13-4

When connecting to various data sources, you must always be concerned with the principal used to authenticate against the external source. This principal may be the user's account or a service account. In addition, the account may use Windows authentications, claims authentication, or token authentication.

For this walkthrough, the service account running the associated SharePoint web application (aka the SharePoint system account) is used. This approach is known as *revert-to-self authentication*. Because the SharePoint system account is a powerful account, revert-to-self must be explicitly enabled using the following PowerShell script. The final SQL connection type information is shown in Figure 13-5.

```
$bdc = Get-SPServiceApplication |
        where {$_ -match "Business Data Connectivity Service"}
$bdc.RevertToSelfAllowed = $true
$bdc.Update()
```

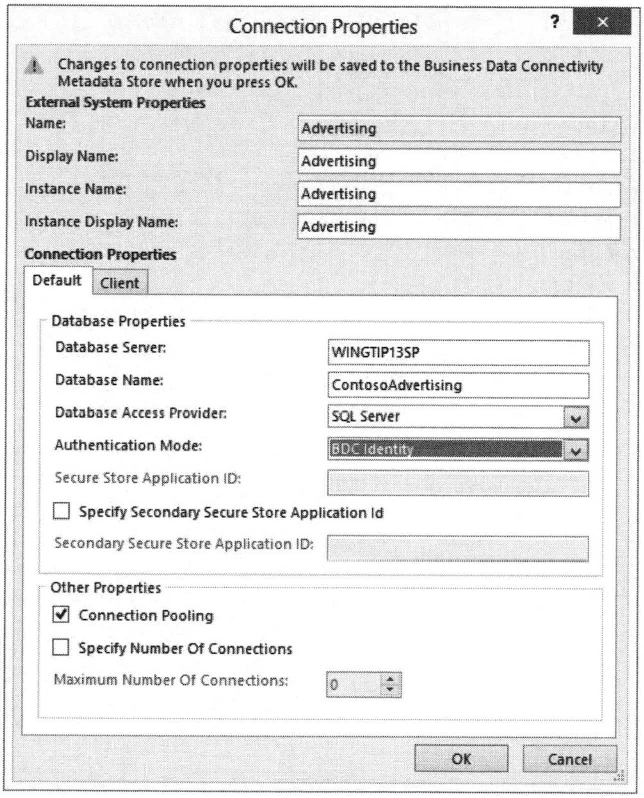

FIGURE 13-5

After the data source connection is made, SPD can create operations for the ECT. When using a SQL connection, SPD can infer a significant amount of information about the data source and the operations, so it is easier to create the entire set of CRUD operations. All you need to do is right-click the table in the connection and select Create All Operations from the context menu, which launches a wizard to collect the small amount of information required to complete the operation definitions. Figure 13-6 shows the context menu in SPD.

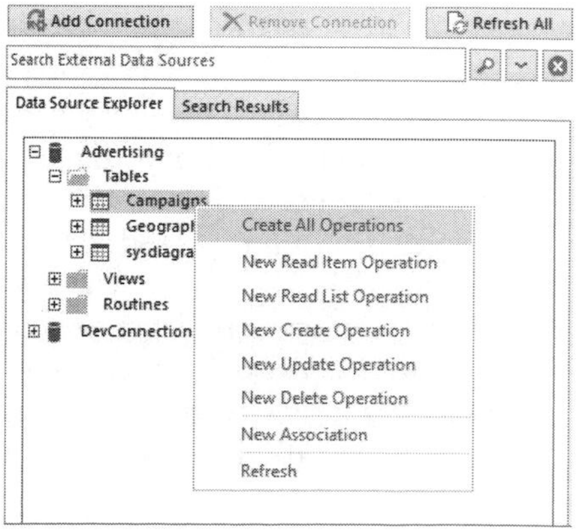

FIGURE 13-6

To complete the operation definitions, you must at least map fields from the ECT to fields in Outlook. This mapping determines how the ECT is displayed in Outlook form. In this example, the Subject, Start, and End fields in Outlook must be mapped to the ECT. This is because Appointment was selected as the Office Type. For this walkthrough, `CampaignName` is mapped to `Subject`, `StartDate` to `Start`, and `EndDate` to `End`. When the wizard finishes, the ECT definition is complete; you can save it in SPD by clicking the Save button. The ECT is then visible in the list of ECTs for the site.

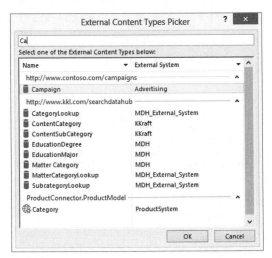

FIGURE 13-7

Creating External Lists

After the ECT is created, you can use it as the basis for an external list. External lists can be created directly in SPD or in the browser. For this walkthrough, a new external list was created by selecting the Lists and Libraries object from the list of Site Objects and then clicking the New External List button. When you create a new external list, the set of available ECTs is presented. Figure 13-7 shows the list of available ECTs with the new Campaign type visible.

After the new external list is created, you can view it immediately in the browser. Because all the CRUD operations were created, the list supports editing items, adding items, and deleting items. Figure 13-8 shows the new list in SharePoint Server 2013.

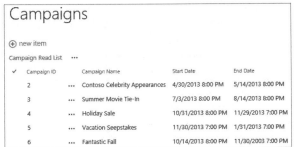

FIGURE 13-8

SharePoint Server 2013 supports taking lists offline through Microsoft Outlook if the site feature "Offline Synchronization for External Lists" is activated. For this walkthrough, the external list was defined as an Appointment Office Type, and it can be synchronized with Outlook by clicking Connect to Outlook in the List tab of the Ribbon within SharePoint. When this button is clicked, a Visual Studio Tools for Office (VSTO) package is accessed and an installation screen is presented. This VSTO package must be installed for synchronization to continue. Figure 13-9 shows the installation screen presented to the user.

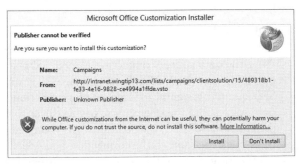

FIGURE 13-9

Creating Simple O365 Solutions

In addition to creating simple database solutions for on-premises farms, you can also create them for Office 365 (O365). Creating such a solution requires that you have both a Windows Azure account and an O365 account. You must then create your database in SQL Azure before creating your External Content Type in O365. This section walks you through the basic approach. If you do not have a SQL Azure account, you may sign up for one at `http://www.windowsazure` `.com/en-us/pricing/free-trial/`. If you do not have an O365 account, you can sign up for a developer account at `http://msdn.microsoft.com/en-us/library/office/apps/` `fp179924(v=office.15)`.

Creating SQL Azure Databases

If you have a Windows Azure account, you may easily create a SQL Azure database using some simple scripts. You can manage SQL Azure databases just like any on-premises SQL database by using the Microsoft SQL Server management tools. All you need is the name of the database server and administrator credentials, which you provide during the setup of a new SQL Azure database server. After the database is created, you can use scripts to create tables and populate those tables with data. If you have a lot of data to move, you can even create a SQL Server Integration Services package to move data from your on-premises development environment into the SQL Azure database.

Managing the Secure Store

The key to successfully creating a BCS solution in O365 is to set up the proper credentials for accessing the SQL Azure database. In the simple on-premises example, you use the SharePoint system account as the principal. This approach will not work for O365, however, because the database expects the solution to use a SQL Azure login and not a Windows account. Therefore, you must use the Secure Store to map the current user's credentials to the expected service account principal. The Secure Store Service is explained in detail in the section "Understanding the Secure Store Service." For this walkthrough, it's enough to say that all the accounts in the O365 installation have been mapped to the SQL Azure credentials that were set up when the SQL Azure database was created. Figure 13-10 shows the connection information for the ECT in O365. Note the name of the database server refers to the SQL Azure database, and the Secure Store Application ID refers to the Secure Store entry that maps user credentials to SQL Azure credentials.

FIGURE 13-10

Creating External Lists

After the ECT is created and the credentials properly mapped, you can create an external list in O365 the same way you do in an on-premises farm. This means that you can use either the SharePoint Designer or the browser. The external list behaves identically in O365 as it does in an on-premises farm.

UNDERSTANDING BCS ARCHITECTURE

BCS is made up of several components and interacts with several services within SharePoint. To create effective BCS solutions, you must understand the architecture, components, and service interfaces available for development. A detailed diagram of this architecture is presented in Figure 13-11.

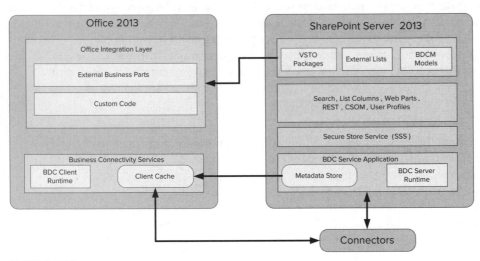

FIGURE 13-11

Understanding Connectors

As mentioned previously, BCS communicates with external systems using several connectors. The simple solution presented earlier utilized the SQL connector to access a SQL Server database, but BCS also supports a WCF connector for accessing general web services and an OData connector specifically designed for OData services. Together, these connectors cover a significant number of data sources, but they can't cover all possible scenarios.

In scenarios in which you need more flexibility than is provided by the out of the box connectors, you can build a .NET Assembly Connector instead. A .NET Assembly Connector is a project that you create in Visual Studio 2012 that contains the ECT definition and associated business logic for accessing a specific external system. This exposes the full power of the .NET Framework for accessing and manipulating data. The .NET Assembly Connector is covered in Chapter 14, "Advanced Business Connectivity Services."

Understanding Business Data Connectivity

As stated previously, BDC is the term that encompasses the plumbing and run-time components of BCS. Both the server and the client have BDC components. These components are complementary so that you can use a similar approach to creating BCS solutions whether you are focused on the server, client, or both. On the server, the BDC components consist of the ECT catalog and the server-side BDC run time. On the client, the BDC components consist of a meta data cache and the client-side BDC run time.

Managing the Business Data Connectivity Service

When you create ECTs in SPD and save them, they are stored in the ECT catalog (also referred to as the meta data catalog). This catalog is a database accessed through the Business Data Connectivity service application. Figure 13-12 shows the basic architecture of the BDC Service Application.

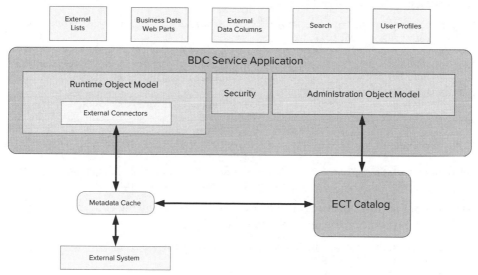

FIGURE 13-12

External connectors and ECT meta data are used to access the external systems and retrieve data through the run-time object model. The BDC Service Application then provides that data for use inside of SharePoint. A meta data cache is maintained in the service so that the ECT model is readily available. This meta data cache is updated every minute to ensure that the latest ECT model is available to the farm. Although BCS does cache the ECT model, external system data is never cached on the server. Each ECT operation is always performed directly against the external system.

Along with caching meta data to improve performance, BCS also can limit the connections and data size associated with operations. The BDC Service Application implements five throttle settings to limit the connections made and data returned from external systems. Table 13-2 lists the throttles and the default settings.

TABLE 13-2: BDC Service Application Throttles

TYPE	DESCRIPTION	SCOPE	DEFAULT	MAXIMUM
Connections	Total number of connections allowed to external systems	Global	100	500
Items	Number of rows returned from a database query	Database	2,000	25,000
Timeout	Database connection timeout	Database	60 sec	600 sec
Size	Size of returned data	WCF	3 MB	150 MB
Timeout	Web service connection timeout	WCF	60 sec	600 sec

Managing throttles is accomplished using PowerShell scripts. The following code displays the current throttle settings:

```
Add-PSSnapin Microsoft.SharePoint.PowerShell -ErrorAction SilentlyContinue
$bdc = Get-SPServiceApplicationProxy |
        Where {$_ -match "Business Data Connectivity"}
Get-SPBusinessDataCatalogThrottleConfig -ThrottleType Connections -Scope Global
                                        -ServiceApplicationProxy $bdc
Get-SPBusinessDataCatalogThrottleConfig -ThrottleType Items -Scope Database
                                        -ServiceApplicationProxy $bdc
Get-SPBusinessDataCatalogThrottleConfig -ThrottleType Timeout -Scope Database
                                        -ServiceApplicationProxy $bdc
Get-SPBusinessDataCatalogThrottleConfig -ThrottleType Size -Scope Wcf
                                        -ServiceApplicationProxy $bdc
Get-SPBusinessDataCatalogThrottleConfig -ThrottleType Timeout -Scope Wcf
                                        -ServiceApplicationProxy $bdc
```

You can modify each of the throttle settings using PowerShell. The following code shows how to change the number of items that can be returned from a database:

```
Add-PSSnapin Microsoft.SharePoint.PowerShell -ErrorAction SilentlyContinue
$bdc = Get-SPServiceApplicationProxy |
        Where {$_ -match "Business Data Connectivity"}
$throttle = Get-SPBusinessDataCatalogThrottleConfig -ThrottleType Items
            -Scope Database  -ServiceApplicationProxy $bdc
Set-SPBusinessDataCatalogThrottleConfig -Maximum 3000 -Default 1000
                                        -Identity $throttle
```

Alternatively, you can simply disable any throttle. The following code shows how to disable the connections throttle:

```
Add-PSSnapin Microsoft.SharePoint.PowerShell -ErrorAction SilentlyContinue
$bdc = Get-SPServiceApplicationProxy |
        Where {$_ -match "Business Data Connectivity"}
$throttle = Get-SPBusinessDataCatalogThrottleConfig -ThrottleType Connections
            -Scope Global -ServiceApplicationProxy $bdc
Set-SPBusinessDataCatalogThrottleConfig -Enforced:$false -Identity $throttle
```

The BDC Service Application is part of the service application framework in SharePoint. The management interface for the BDC Service Application is accessible through Central Administration by selecting Application Management ⇨ Manage Service Applications. Figure 13-13 shows the BDC Service Application in Central Administration.

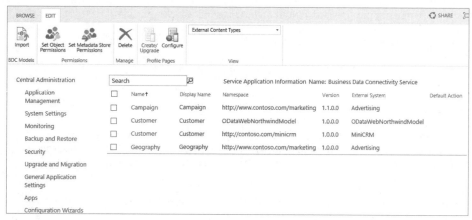

FIGURE 13-13

From the Service Applications page, you can click Properties in the Ribbon to see the basic service properties for the BDC Service Application. In the Properties dialog box, the name of the database where the ECTs are stored displays. This database is set up when the BDC Service Application is first created during farm installation and configuration. As with all services, from the Ribbon you can also set administrative and connection permissions for the service so that it can be used by other servers in the SharePoint farm.

Clicking the Manage button on the Service Applications page opens the View External Content Types page. This page lists all ECTs currently stored in the catalog. On the Edit tab, you can grant rights to manage the ECT catalog by clicking the Set Catalog Permissions button, and you can set rights for individual ECTs by clicking the Set Object Permissions button. This enables you to determine which users can use ECTs to access external systems.

On the Edit tab, there is also a drop-down list that determines how ECT information is presented on the page. Initially, the drop down is set to External Content Types, which shows the ECTs in a list. Selecting External Systems from the drop-down list shows all the available connections that are defined. Selecting BDC Models, on the other hand, lists the models that contain both connection and ECT information.

The list of BDC models is of special importance to the developer because the BDC model contains the reference to the ECT, the connection information for the external systems, security information, and more. Furthermore, the model can be exported using the drop-down menu on the list item and then subsequently imported into another catalog. When a model is exported, it is saved as an XML file known as a *BDC Metadata Model*. BDC Metadata Models can also be exported directly from SPD by right-clicking the ECT and selecting Export Application Model.

The following code shows part of a BDC Metadata Model based on the walkthrough earlier in the chapter. Take special note of the bolded code. In the `LobSystemInstance` properties, you can see the basic connection information for the external system. These values were all set when the external system connection was specified in SPD.

```xml
<?xml version="1.0" encoding="utf-16" standalone="yes"?>
<Model xmlns:xsi="http://www.w3.org/2001/XMLSchema-instance"
xsi:schemaLocation="http://schemas.microsoft.com/windows/2007/BusinessDataCatalog
BDCMetadata.xsd"
 Name="SharePointDesigner-CampaignsData-Administrator-92aec138-31d3-
4155-980f-db4c681c2260"
xmlns="http://schemas.microsoft.com/windows/2007/BusinessDataCatalog">
  <Properties>
    <Property Name="Discovery" Type="System.String"></Property>
  </Properties>
  <LobSystems>
    <LobSystem Type="Database" Name="SharePointDesigner-CampaignsData">
      <Properties>
        <Property Name="DiscoveryVersion" Type="System.Int32">0</Property>
        <Property Name="WildcardCharacter" Type="System.String">%</Property>
        <Property Name="Discovery" Type="System.String"></Property>
      </Properties>
      <LobSystemInstances>
        <LobSystemInstance Name="SharePointDesigner-CampaignsData">
          <Properties>
            <Property Name="AuthenticationMode"
                      Type="System.String">RevertToSelf</Property>
            <Property Name="DatabaseAccessProvider"
                      Type="System.String">SqlServer</Property>
            <Property Name="RdbConnection Data Source"
                      Type="System.String">localhost</Property>
            <Property Name="RdbConnection Initial Catalog"
                      Type="System.String">ContosoAdvertising</Property>
            <Property Name="RdbConnection Integrated Security"
                      Type="System.String">SSPI</Property>
            <Property Name="RdbConnection Pooling"
                      Type="System.Boolean">true</Property>
            <Property Name="Discovery" Type="System.String"></Property>
            <Property Name="ConnectionName"
                      Type="System.String">CampaignsData</Property>
          </Properties>
        </LobSystemInstance>
      </LobSystemInstances>
    </LobSystem>
  </LobSystems>
</Model>
```

Introducing the BDC Server Runtime

The BDC Server Runtime consists of the run-time object model, the administration object model, and the security infrastructure. The run-time object model provides access to ECTs, whereas the administration object model provides objects for managing the ECT catalog. The security infrastructure facilitates authentication and authorization for ECT operations and external system access.

Understanding the Client Cache

When BCS solutions are taken to Office clients, a client cache is used to store both the BDC Metadata Model and the external system data. The client cache is a SQL Server Compact Edition (SQLCE) database that is installed as part of the Office 2013 installation. The database is encrypted to prevent tampering, as there is no reason for developers to access the database directly.

A synchronization process (BCSSync.exe) runs on the client to synchronize the cache with the associated external systems. When CRUD operations are performed on data within the Office clients, the operations are queued inside the client cache and synchronized with the external system when it is available. The synchronization process also attempts to update data in the cache at various intervals from the external system depending on the user settings and availability of the external system. Conflicts between the cache and the external system are flagged for the end user so that they can be resolved.

Introducing the Office Integration Runtime

The Office Integration Runtime (OIR) is the set of components and associated APIs that bind the ECTs to the Office clients and your own custom solutions. The OIR loads whenever a host Office client is started. The OIR is installed on the client as part of the Office 2013 installation process.

Understanding the Secure Store Service

The Secure Store Service (SSS) is a service application that provides for the storage, mapping, and retrieval of credential information. Typically, the credentials stored by SSS are used to access external systems that do not support Windows authentication. This is accomplished by mapping the stored credentials to an existing Windows user or group.

To store credential sets for an external system, a new target application must be created in SSS. The target application acts as a container for credential sets mapped to an external system. The target application settings page contains a name for the application and a setting to specify whether each individual user has a separate set of mapped credentials or whether every user maps to a single common set of credentials. Figure 13-14 shows application settings mapping a single set of credentials to an Active Directory group.

Create New Secure Store Target Application ⓘ

Target Application Settings

The Secure Store Target Application ID is a unique identifier. You cannot change this property after you create the Target Application.

The display name is used for display purposes only.

The contact e-mail should be a valid e-mail address of the primary contact for this Target Application.

The Target Application type determines whether this application uses a group mapping or individual mapping. Ticketing indicates whether tickets are used for this Target Application. You cannot change this property after you create the Target Application.

The Target Application page URL can be used to set the values for the credential fields for the Target Application by individual users.

Target Application ID

ContosoDatabases

Display Name

Contoso Databases

Contact E-mail

administrator@contoso.com

Target Application Type

Group

Target Application Page URL

◉ Use default page

○ Use custom page

◉ None

FIGURE 13-14

After the target application is defined, credential fields are defined. In most cases, the target application saves a username and password, but SSS can save any text-based credential information. For example, a domain field could be added so that the credential sets consisted of a username, password, and domain. Figure 13-15 shows typical username and password fields defined for an application.

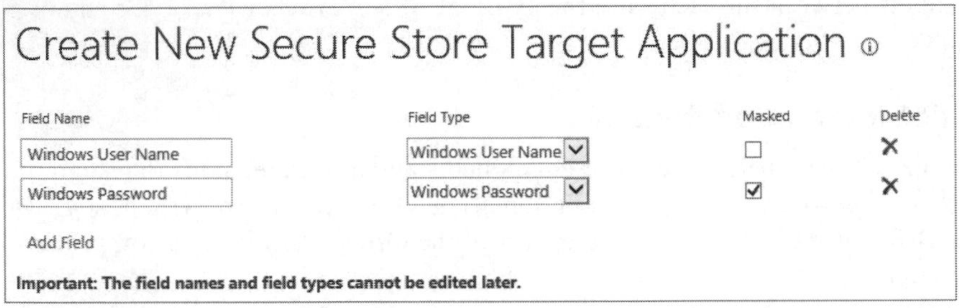

FIGURE 13-15

After the application and credential fields are defined, you must enter the actual credential information by right-clicking the application and going to Set Credentials. For each user or group that will access the external system, a set of credentials must be created using the field definitions for the application. Figure 13-16 shows credentials being entered for an application. After the credentials are in place, the application can be used during the definition of an ECT to allow access to the external system using the credentials stored in the SSS. If end users attempt to access the system without proper credentials in SSS, they will be directed to a login page so the credentials can be entered and stored.

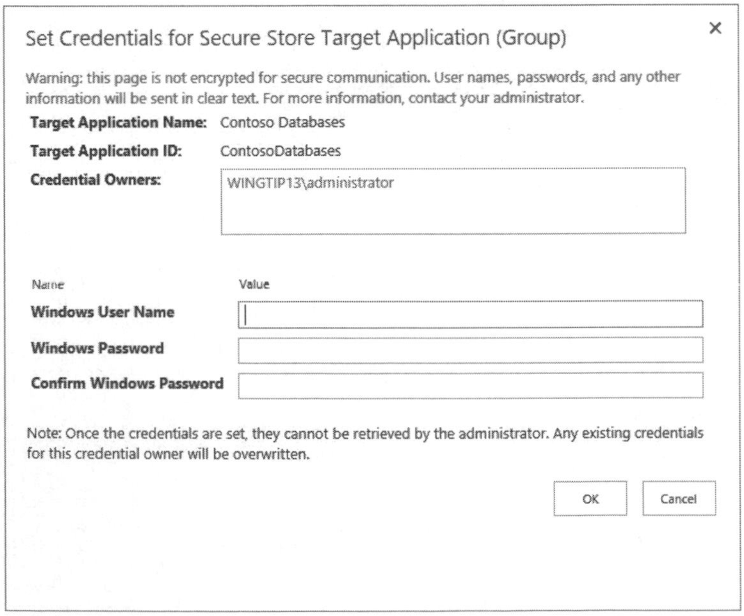

FIGURE 13-16

Although BCS and SSS work well together to provide authentication in many scenarios, there may be times when you want to utilize SSS in custom solutions. In these cases, you can access SSS programmatically to retrieve credentials. These credentials can then be used by your solution (such as a web part) to access external systems directly without using BCS. The following code shows how to access the credentials in the default instance of SSS:

```
ISecureStoreProvider p = SecureStoreProviderFactory.Create();
string username = string.Empty;
string password = string.Empty;
using (SecureStoreCredentialCollection creds =
        p.GetCredentials("ContosoDatabases"))
{
    foreach (SecureStoreCredential c in creds)
    {
        switch (c.CredentialType)
        {
            case SecureStoreCredentialType.UserName:
                username = c.Credential.ToString();
                break;
            case SecureStoreCredentialType.Password:
                password = c.Credential.ToString();
                break;
            case SecureStoreCredentialType.WindowsUserName:
                username = c.Credential.ToString();
                break;
            case SecureStoreCredentialType.WindowsPassword:
                password = c.Credential.ToString();
                break;
            case SecureStoreCredentialType.Generic:
                //Generic credentials
                break;
            case SecureStoreCredentialType.Key:
                //Key
                break;
            case SecureStoreCredentialType.Pin:
                //Pin
                break;
        }
    }
    //Log in using the credentials
}
```

Understanding Package Deployment

When an end user elects to synchronize an external list with Outlook or the SharePoint Workspace, BCS creates a VSTO click-once deployment package that contains all the elements necessary to work with the list on the client. The package is created by BCS just in time and is stored under the list in a folder named ClientSolution. After the package is created, the deployment starts automatically.

The package contains the BCS model defining the external system, ECTs, operations, and security information necessary to access and modify data. The package also contains subscription information, which tells the client cache what data to manage and how it should be refreshed. Finally, the package contains pre- and post-deployment steps that you should take, such as creating custom forms in the client application to display the data.

When deployed, the add-in can make use of *Office business parts* on the client to help render data. Office business parts are Windows form controls that display a single item or list of items in a task pane. These parts simplify the rendering process so that custom task panes do not need to be created for the client.

Understanding App Architecture

SharePoint 2013 introduces the new app model, which provides complete isolation of the code associated with custom solutions. To support this model, Business Connectivity Services introduces the capability to BDCM models directly within the app. These app-level ECTs do not reside in the BDC Service Application. Instead, they are isolated into an in-memory instance of the BDC Runtime, which loads the BDC Metadata Model deployed as part of the app. Figure 13-17 shows the high-level architecture supporting app-level ECTs.

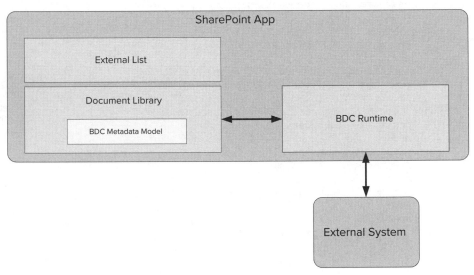

FIGURE 13-17

A SharePoint app that utilizes an app-level ECT can deploy the BDC Metadata Model as part of the app. This model is stored inside of a special document library as part of the solution architecture. When the app is accessed by a user, an instance of the BDC Runtime is spun up in memory and the model is loaded. The model can then be used to drive an external list within the app scope. When the app is closed, the BDC Runtime is torn down. This architecture means that the app-level ECT is completely isolated from the SharePoint server and the BDC Service Application. App-level ECTs are fairly easy to create, but the tooling is only present in Visual Studio 2012; they cannot be created in SPD. The exact process for creating these solutions is covered in Chapter 14.

WORKING WITH BDC METADATA MODELS

The BDC Metadata Model is an XML file that completely defines the ECT, its connection to the external system, and its operations. When creating BCS solutions using the SPD tooling, you are simply building up the XML contained in the BDC Metadata Model. This model is then stored in the Metadata Store.

Although you can create BCS solutions without looking at the XML contained in the BDC Metadata Model, professional solutions require a strong understanding of the elements in the model. When creating more advanced solutions in BCS, the BDC Metadata Model is often exported from SPD, modified, and imported when a wanted feature is not directly supported by the SPD tooling. Furthermore, it is educational to export the BDC Metadata Model and examine it as changes are made.

You export a BDC Metadata Model from the list of External Content Types. After selecting an ECT, you can click the Export BDC Model button, which brings up the Export BDC Model dialog box. In this dialog box, you can select to export the Default model or the Client model. The Default model is the one used on the server, and the Client model is the one stored in the client cache following list synchronization. The two models reflect any differences you made in the connection properties to be used on the server or client but have the same ECT definitions. The models are exported with a BDCM extension, which is the file extension for all BDC Metadata Models. Figure 13-18 shows the Export BDC Model dialog box.

FIGURE 13-18

When exported, the simplest way to work with the BDC Metadata Model is to change the file extension from `.bdcm` to `.xml` and open it in Visual Studio 2012. Although Visual Studio can open files with a `.bdcm` extension, doing so results in Visual Studio using its BCS designers instead of showing the XML directly. The BCS designers are covered in Chapter 14.

The schema file for the BDC Metadata Model is named `BDCMetadata.xsd` and can be found in the `/Program Files/Common Files/Microsoft Shared/web server extensions/15/Template/XML` directory. When working with exported models, you should copy the schema file into the directory where you exported the model. If you do this, you get IntelliSense support in Visual Studio when you open the file for editing.

You import a BDC Metadata Model through the BDC Service Application in Central Administration. When importing an edited model back into the BDC Service Application, you should be sure to update the ECT version, as a best practice. As an alternative, you can simply delete the existing model before importing the edited model.

Examining the BDC Metadata Model XML directly is an excellent way to learn the intricacies of the schema. Throughout this chapter, both the SPD tooling and resulting XML will be presented so that you can see exactly how the tools affect the model. As a starting point, the following code shows some of the basic elements used in the model:

```
<Model xmlns:xsi="http://www.w3.org/2001/XMLSchema-instance"
       xsi:schemaLocation="http://schemas.microsoft.com/.../BDCMetadata.xsd"
       xmlns="http://schemas.microsoft.com/windows/2007/BusinessDataCatalog"
       Name="My Model">
  <LobSystems>
    <LobSystem>
      <LobSystemInstances>
        <LobSystemInstance/>
      </LobSystemInstances>
      <Entities>
        <Entity Name="MyEntity"
                DefaultDisplayName="My Entity"
                Namespace="http://mynamespace"
                Version="1.0.0.0"
                EstimatedInstanceCount="10000" >
          <Methods>
          </Methods>
        </Entity>
      </Entities>
    </LobSystem>
  </LobSystems>
</Model>
```

The `Model` element is the root of the XML and contains the schema reference. This element also contains the `Name` attribute, which is displayed in the BDC Service Application. The `LobSystem` element is a container for the model associated with a particular external system. Notice that it is possible to have multiple external systems defined in the same model. The `LobSystemInstance` element provides connection information for a particular external system.

The `Entity` element begins the definition of an ECT for a particular external system. The `Name` attribute is the programmatic name of the ECT, and the `DefaultDisplayName` attribute is the display name that appears in the SharePoint UI. The `Namespace` attribute is used for disambiguation between ECTs that have the same programmatic name. The `Version` attribute is used to indicate the latest version of the ECT. All these attributes are entered in SPD when creating a new ECT.

The `EstimatedInstanceCount` attribute is used as a hint to BCS solutions as to how many entity instances can be expected from the external system. The `EstimatedInstanceCount` attribute cannot be edited through SPD, and its use is determined solely by the application consuming the model. You could use this attribute, for example, when creating a custom web part to determine whether to load all the data immediately or on demand. This is a good, albeit simple, example of why you might need to export a model, modify it by hand, and import it.

WORKING WITH EXTERNAL DATA SOURCES

External data sources contain the data from external systems and are the starting point for any BCS solution. An ECT must be associated with an external data source through one of five connector types: SQL Server, WCF Service, OData, .NET Assembly, or Custom. When creating BCS solutions in SPD, you primarily make use of the SQL Server or WCF Service connectors. The OData, .NET Assembly, and Custom connector types are typically part of a solution created in Visual Studio.

When creating a new ECT, you can associate an external data source by clicking the link titled Click Here to Discover External Data Sources. Clicking the link takes you to the Operation Designer, where you can see all the available external data sources. This view allows additional external data sources to be added or existing ones to be removed. The Operation Designer also allows the structure of external data sources to be searched using a keyword. This facility helps locate tables, views, and web methods by name, which is helpful if there are many external data sources available.

When working with an existing ECT, you can open the Operation Designer by clicking the Operations Design View button on the Ribbon. The Connection Properties dialog box can be opened by clicking the External System link in the ECT Information panel or by clicking the Edit Connection Properties button in the Ribbon. You can change the external data source associated with an ECT by clicking the Switch Connected System button in the Ribbon. Figure 13-19 shows the available buttons in the Ribbon.

FIGURE 13-19

Connecting with the SQL Server Connector

The SQL Server Connector provides connections to Microsoft SQL Server, Oracle, OLE DB, and ODBC databases. Because databases represent the bulk of the available external data, the SQL Server Connector is used frequently in BCS solutions. The SharePoint Designer provides tooling to support connections with Microsoft SQL Server, but connections to Oracle, OLE DB, and ODBC sources require hand editing of the BDC Metadata Model.

Connecting to Microsoft SQL Server Databases

When adding a new SQL Server Connection in the Operation Designer, you must fill out the SQL Server Connection properties dialog box with the required information to connect to the external system. The following code shows the `LobSystemInstance` element for a typical connection to Microsoft SQL Server using Microsoft's AdventureWorks sample database available at `http://msftdbprodsamples.codeplex.com`.

```
<LobSystems>
 <LobSystem Type="Database" Name="MySystem">
  <Properties>
   <Property Name="WildcardCharacter" Type="System.String">%</Property>
  </Properties>
  <LobSystemInstances>
  <LobSystemInstance Name="MySystemInstance">
   <Properties>
    <Property Name="AuthenticationMode" Type="System.String">
      PassThrough
    </Property>
    <Property Name="DatabaseAccessProvider" Type="System.String">
     SqlServer
    </Property>
    <Property Name="RdbConnection Data Source" Type="System.String">
     AWSERVER
```

```
      </Property>
      <Property Name="RdbConnection Initial Catalog" Type="System.String">
       Adventureworks
      </Property>
      <Property Name="RdbConnection Integrated Security" Type="System.String">
       SSPI
      </Property>
      <Property Name="RdbConnection Pooling" Type="System.String">
       True
      </Property>
     </Properties>
    </LobSystemInstance>
   </LobSystem>
  </LobSystems>
```

For the SQL Server Connector, a series of `Property` elements are used to specify the values that define the connection to the database. The `AuthenticationMode` property determines how authentication is performed to the external system. The possible values for `AuthenticationMode` are listed in Table 13-3.

TABLE 13-3: Authentication Modes

VALUE	APPLICATION	DESCRIPTION
PassThrough	Databases and Web Services	Connects to the external system using credentials of the current user
RevertToSelf	Databases and Web Services	Connects to the external system using credentials of the IIS application pool
WindowsCredentials	Databases and Web Services	Connects to external system using Windows credentials returned from the Secure Store Service
RdbCredentials	Databases	Connects to database using non-Windows credentials returned from the Secure Store Service
Credentials	Web Services	Connects to the web service using non-Windows credentials returned from the Secure Store Service

The `DatabaseAccessProvider` property specifies what type of database is targeted. This value may be set to `SqlServer`, `Oracle`, `OleDb`, or `Odbc`. Depending upon the value selected for this property, other properties may be required as children of the `LobSystemInstance` element. In the case of the `SqlServer` example, the `RdbConnection Data Source`, `RdbConnection Initial Catalog`, `RdbConnection Integrated Security`, and `RdbConnection Pooling` properties are required. You'll recognize each of these properties as a component of a standard connection string.

Connecting to Oracle Databases

Because there is no tooling support in SPD for connecting to Oracle data sources, creating models for Oracle databases can be difficult. One approach is simply to start from scratch with a blank XML file and then import the model into the BDC Service Application. Another approach is to model the ECT against a SQL Server database, export the model, edit the model, and import the changed model. Neither approach is ideal. If you start from scratch, you are more likely to commit typographical errors. On the other hand, modifying a SQL Server model is error-prone because the query syntax differs between SQL Server and Oracle. In any case, you must eventually end up with something that looks like the following code:

```
<LobSystems>
 <LobSystem Type="Database" Name="MySystem">
  <Properties>
   <Property Name="WildcardCharacter" Type="System.String">%</Property>
  </Properties>
  <LobSystemInstances>
   <LobSystemInstance Name="MySystem Instance">
    <Properties>
     <Property Name="AuthenticationMode" Type="System.String">
     RdbCredentials
     </Property>
     <Property Name="DatabaseAccessProvider" Type="System.String">
     Oracle
     </Property>
     <Property Name="RdbConnection Data Source" Type="System.String">
     MY_NET_SERVICE_NAME
     </Property>
     <Property Name="SsoApplicationId" Type="System.String">
     MY_SECURE_STORE_APP_ID
     </Property>
     <Property Name="SsoProviderImplementation" Type="System.String">
     Microsoft.Office.SecureStoreService.Server.SecureStoreProvider,
     Microsoft.Office.SecureStoreService, Version=15.0.0.0,
     Culture=neutral, PublicKeyToken=71e9bce111e9429c
     </Property>
    </Properties>
   </LobSystemInstance>
  </LobSystemInstances>
 </LobSystem>
</LobSystems>
```

BCS META MAN

Because the tooling in SPD does not support all data sources and operations, a third-party market has emerged for tools that create BCS models. A favorite third-party tool for creating BCS solutions is the BCS Meta Man. BCS Meta Man supports connections to Oracle and ODBC data sources along with other operations not supported by SPD. BCS Meta Man installs as an extension to Visual Studio 2012. Learn more at www.lightningtools.com.

The `AuthenticationMode` property is set to `RdbCredentials` for connections to Oracle. This means that non-Windows credentials supplied by the Secure Store Service are used to access the Oracle database. The `DatabaseAccessProvider` property is set to Oracle to indicate that Oracle is the target system. The `RdbConnection Data Source` property is set to the value of the `Net Service Name`, which is the alias for the database found in the `tnsnames.ora` file. The `SsoApplicationId` property is set to the name of the application in the Secure Store Service that is providing the credentials. The `SsoProviderImplementation` property refers to the implementation of the Secure Store Service. In the sample code, the property references the server-side Secure Store Service. If the model were used on the client, the following code should be substituted:

```
<Property Name="SsoProviderImplementation" Type="System.String">
Microsoft.Office.BusinessData.Infrastructure.
SecureStore.LocalSecureStoreProvider,
Microsoft.Office.BusinessData, Version=15.0.0.0, Culture=neutral,
PublicKeyToken=71e9bce111e9429c
</Property>
```

Connecting to ODBC Data Sources

Creating models for ODBC data sources is also not supported directly in SPD. Therefore, you must create the model from scratch and import it into the BDC Service Application. The following code shows what an ODBC connection looks like in the model XML:

```
<LobSystems>
 <LobSystem Name="ODBC" Type="Database">
  <LobSystemInstances>
   <LobSystemInstance Name="ODBCInstance">
    <Properties>
     <Property Name="AuthenticationMode" Type="System.String">
      PassThrough
     </Property>
     <Property Name="DatabaseAccessProvider" Type="System.String">
      Odbc
     </Property>
     <Property Name="RdbConnection Dsn" Type="System.String">
      MY_DSN_NAME
     </Property>
     <Property Name="RdbConnection uid" Type="System.String">
      MY_USERNAME
     </Property>
     <Property Name="RdbConnection pwd" Type="System.String">
      MY_PASSWORD
     </Property>
     <Property Name="RdbConnection Trusted_Connection" Type="System.String">
      yes
     </Property>
     <Property Name="RdbConnection integrated security" Type="System.String">
      true
     </Property>
    </Properties>
```

```
    </LobSystemInstance>
   </LobSystemInstances>
  </LobSystem>
 </LobSystems>
```

The `AuthenticationMode` property is set to `Passthrough`, but the credentials used to access the data source are provided in the `RdbConnection uid` and `RdbConnection pwd` properties. You can see how these properties build an ODBC connection string similar to the way it is done for Microsoft SQL Server.

Connecting to OLEDB Data Sources

Just like Oracle and ODBC, creating models for OLEDB data sources is not supported by the SPD tooling. The BDC Metadata Model must be created from scratch and imported into the BDC Service Application. The following code shows what an OLEDB connection looks like for a Microsoft Access database:

```
<LobSystems>
 <LobSystem Type="Database" Name="MySystem">
  <LobSystemInstances>
  <LobSystemInstance Name="MySystemInstance">
   <Properties>
    <Property Name="AuthenticationMode" Type="System.String">
      PassThrough
    </Property>
    <Property Name="DatabaseAccessProvider" Type="System.String">
     OleDb
    </Property>
    <Property Name="RdbConnection Data Source" Type="System.String">
     C:\Mydatabase.mdb
    </Property>
    <Property Name="RdbConnection Persist Security Info"
     Type="System.String">
     false
    </Property>
    <Property Name="RdbConnection Connection Provider" Type="System.String">
     Microsoft.ACE.OLEDB.12.0
    </Property>
   </Properties>
  </LobSystemInstance>
 </LobSystem>
</LobSystems>
```

The `AuthenticationMode` property is set to `Passthrough`. The `RdbConnection Data Source` refers to the location of the MS Access file. The `RdbConnection Connection Provider` specifies the OLEDB provider to use for the connection.

Connecting with the WCF Service Connector

The WCF Connector provides connections to web services, including Windows Communication Foundation (WCF) and ASP.NET web services. The SharePoint Designer provides tooling for connecting with web services and their associated meta data so that operations can be defined against the services. The key to using a web service as an external data source is for SPD to access the meta data of the web service that describes the available operations. SPD supports accessing service meta data through both Web Service Description Language (WSDL) and meta data exchange.

Connecting to ASP.NET Web Services

ASP.NET web services typically expose WSDL documents to describe the available operations. WSDL documents are accessed using the endpoint of the service appended with the query string ?WSDL. Figure 13-20 shows the Connection Properties dialog box with settings for an ASP.NET web service. Table 13-4 describes the settings in the dialog box.

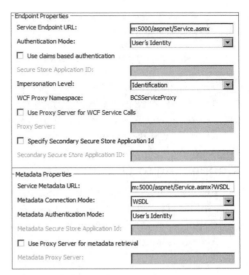

FIGURE 13-20

TABLE 13-4: Web Service Connection Settings

SETTING	DESCRIPTION
Service Endpoint URL	The base address of the web service.
Authentication Mode	Used to select a value from Table 13-3.
Use Claims Based Authentication	Selected if the web service supports claims authentication.
Secure Store Application ID	The name of the Secure Store Service application that provides credentials for accessing the web service.
Impersonation Level	Sets the Windows impersonation level as follows: None: No impersonation. Anonymous: The server cannot impersonate or identify the client. Identification: The server can identify the client but cannot impersonate the client. Impersonation: The server can impersonate the client on the server only. Delegation: The server can impersonate the client locally and during requests to remote resources.
WCF Proxy Namespace	The programmatic namespace used for the generated proxy class.

Use Proxy Server for WCF Service Calls	Specifies a proxy server to use when calling the web service.
Specify Secondary Secure Store Application ID	A secondary Secure Store Service application that supplies additional credentials. These credentials are used when a web service expects credentials to be passed as parameters in the method call.
Service Metadata URL	The address of the meta data document.
Metadata Connection Mode	Specifies whether to obtain meta data as WSDL or through a MEX endpoint.
Metadata Authentication Mode	Used to select an authentication mode from the values in Table 13-3 that will be used when accessing service meta data.
Use Proxy Server for Metadata Retrieval	Specifies a proxy server to use when returning service meta data.
Specify Number of Connections	The maximum number of connections allowed to the service.

The settings in the Connection Properties dialog box are used to generate the properties for the LobSystem and LobSystemInstance elements of the model. The exact properties presented in the model can vary according to the selections made in the dialog box. The following code shows how the settings in Figure 13-20 are translated into the BDC Metadata Model:

```
<LobSystems>
 <LobSystem Type="Wcf" Name="ASP.Net Web Service">
  <Properties>
   <Property Name-"ReferenceKnownTypes" Type-"System.Boolean">
    True
   </Property>
   <Property Name="WcfMexDiscoMode" Type="System.String">
    Disco
   </Property>
   <Property Name="WcfMexDocumentUrl" Type="System.String">
    http://webserver.aw.com:5000/aspnet/Service.asmx?WSDL
   </Property>
   <Property Name="WcfProxyNamespace" Type="System.String">
    BCSServiceProxy
   </Property>
   <Property Name="WildcardCharacter" Type="System.String">*</Property>
   <Property Name="WsdlFetchAuthenticationMode" Type="System.String">
    PassThrough
   </Property>
  </Properties>
  <Proxy>EABvmrlbJFsHTQdvYZp1cdN6TVqQAAMA...AAAAAA</Proxy>
  <LobSystemInstances>
   <LobSystemInstance Name="Item Service">
    <Properties>
     <Property Name="UseStsIdentityFederation" Type="System.Boolean">
     False
```

```
        </Property>
        <Property Name="WcfAuthenticationMode" Type="System.String">
         PassThrough
        </Property>
        <Property Name="WcfEndpointAddress" Type="System.String">
         http://webserver.aw.com:5000/aspnet/Service.asmx
        </Property>
        <Property Name="WcfImpersonationLevel" Type="System.String">
         Identification
        </Property>
       </Properties>
     </LobSystemInstance>
    </LobSystemInstances>
   </LobSystem>
 </LobSystems>
```

Along with the properties set in the model, you can also notice a `Proxy` element. This element has been significantly truncated in the code listing but will normally contain a large text string. This large text string is the serialized proxy class generated by the SPD tooling when connecting to the web service. This proxy class is used by BCS to communicate with the web service when calling methods. Serializing the class in the BDC Metadata Model makes the class portable and simplifies deployment to client applications.

Connecting to WCF Web Services

WCF web services expose WSDL just like ASP.NET web services but can also expose a meta data-exchanged (MEX) endpoint to describe the available operations. MEX endpoints can be used by SPD to support generating a proxy class against the service. Figure 13-21 shows the Connection Properties dialog box with settings for a WCF web service exposing a MEX endpoint.

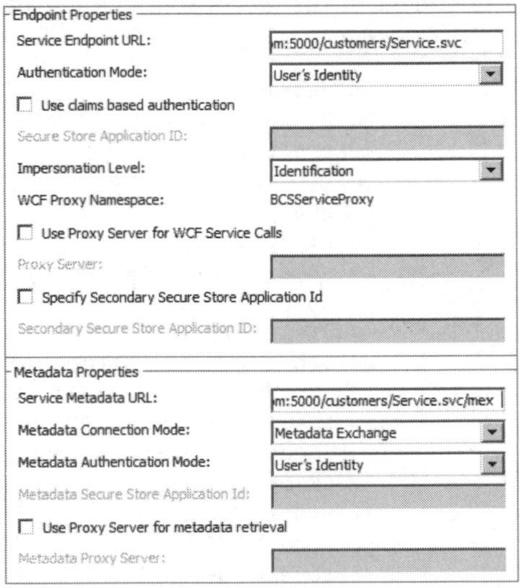

Just like ASP.NET web services, the values set in the Connection Properties dialog box are used to create the `LobSystem` and `LobSystemInstance` elements in the BDC Metadata Model. The properties in the model are the same as ASP.NET web services, but the values are set up to utilize a MEX endpoint instead of a WSDL endpoint.

FIGURE 13-21

CREATING METHODS

BCS method stereotypes define the operations that can be performed against an external system. The six method stereotypes supported by SPD are `Finder`, `SpecificFinder`, `Creator`, `Updater`, `Deleter`, and `AssociationNavigator`. These six method stereotypes are used to generate a view of many items, show details for a single item, create a new item, update an existing item, delete an item, and display data relationships, respectively.

Implementing Method Stereotypes

When implementing a method stereotype in the BDC Metadata Model, you use a `Method` and a `MethodInstance` element. The `Method` element defines the input parameters, output parameters, and filters that will be used with the method stereotype. The `MethodInstance` element defines the type of method stereotype to be implemented.

BDC Metadata Models typically consist of many `Method` elements defining operations against the external system. Each `Method` element can consist of one or more `MethodInstance` elements; however, it is typical to have a one-to-one relationship between `Method` and `MethodInstance` elements. This approach simplifies the model and makes it easier to develop the solution. The following code shows the basic XML schema to implement a method stereotype:

```
<Method Name=[Method Name]>
 <Properties>
  <Property>[Property Value]</Property>
 </Properties>
 <FilterDescriptors>
  <FilterDescriptor Type=["Limit", "PageNumber", "Wildcard", etc]
 </FilterDescriptor>
 <Parameters>
  <Parameter
   Direction=["In", "Out", "InOut", or "Return"]
   Name=[Parameter Name]
   AssociatedFilter=[Name of a FilterDescriptor]>
   <TypeDescriptor
    TypeName=[.NET Framework Type e.g, "System.Int32"] />
  </Parameter>
 </Parameters>
 <MethodInstances>
  <MethodInstance
   Type=["Finder", "SpecificFinder", "Creator", etc]
   Name="MyMethodInstance">
  </MethodInstance>
 </MethodInstances>
</Method>
```

Defining Properties

A `Method` element can contain one or more `Property` elements. These properties are specific to the method implementation and vary depending upon the connector type used to access the External System. Specific values are discussed in detail later in this chapter.

Defining Parameters

A `Method` element can contain one or more `Parameter` elements. Parameters are used as inputs and outputs to methods. Parameters are defined as `In`, `Out`, `InOut`, or `Return` types. The exact set of parameters required is based on the function signature of the method stereotype. For example, a `Finder` method might not have any `In` parameters and only a single `Return` parameter. A `SpecificFinder` method, on the other hand, might have a single `In` parameter representing the primary key of a record to return and a single `Return` parameter containing the record.

Parameter elements always contain one or more `TypeDescriptor` elements. `TypeDescriptor` elements are used to map data types in the external system to well-known .NET Framework types that can be used by BCS. The types may be single-value types such as a `System.String` or can be collections of types. Collections of types are required, for example, when the return value from an external system is a record that contains multiple fields.

Defining Filters

A `Method` element can contain zero or more `FilterDescriptor` elements. Filters are used by BCS to provide system or user input to methods. For example, you can set a filter in a view definition for an external list as a way to specify which entity instances to return from an external system. You can also set filters by system, such as when a filter is used to limit return data based on the identity of the current user. Filters are always associated with an input parameter. This association is how the filter value is transmitted to be received from the method implementation. Table 13-5 lists the filters supported by SPD.

TABLE 13-5: BCS Filters

NAME	SPD SUPPORT	DESCRIPTION
ActivityId	SpecificFinder Creator Updater Deleter AssociationNavigator	Used to pass the `CorrelationId` into an operation
Comparison	Finder	Used to specify a value that must exactly match a field to return items from a Finder operation (for example, `LastName='Hillier'`)
LastId	SpecificFinder Creator Updater Deleter AssociationNavigator	Used to pass the identifier of the last item read to an operation that is returning the data for the item in chunks
Limit	Finder	Used to specify a maximum limit on the number of items returned from an operation
PageNumber	Finder	Used to specify the zero-based page number that should be returned from a multipage operation
Password	SpecificFinder Creator Updater Deleter AssociationNavigator	Used to pass the password that was provided by the Secure Store Service to the operation for security checks

SsoTicket	SpecificFinder Creator Updater Deleter AssociationNavigator	Used to pass the SSO ticket that was provided by the Secure Store Service to the operation for security checks
Timestamp	Finder	Used to specify the last time a Finder operation was called so that only changed data is returned
UserContext	SpecificFinder Creator Updater Deleter AssociationNavigator	Used to pass the identity of the caller to an operation
Username	SpecificFinder Creator Updater Deleter AssociationNavigator	Used to pass the username that was provided by the Secure Store Service to the operation for filtering and security checks
UserProfile	SpecificFinder Creator Updater Deleter AssociationNavigator	Used to pass the profile of the current user to an operation
Wildcard	Finder	Used to specify a search pattern that can be used to return items from an operation (for example, `LastName LIKE 'Steve%'`)

Understanding Stereotype Requirements

The value of the SPD tooling is that it knows how to create the correct set of properties, parameters, and filters for the supported method stereotypes. In cases in which you implement method stereotypes by hand, however, you must be aware of the requirements implicit in each method stereotype. It is not enough to simply designate the `Type` attribute of a `MethodInstance` element; the parameters and filters must be defined so that an acceptable method signature results. Table 13-6 lists the parameters required for each method stereotype. Note that filters are generally not required but can be applied as an option to further refine an operation.

TABLE 13-6: Required Parameters

NAME	INPUT	RETURN
AssociationNavigator	Entity instance ID	Collection of entity instances
Creator	Collection of fields	None
Deleter	Entity instance ID	None
Finder	None	Collection of entity instances
SpecificFinder	Entity instance ID	A single entity instance
Updater	Entity instance ID Collection of fields	None

Creating Methods for Databases

Databases are the easiest external data sources to work with in SPD. Because databases have tables, views, stored procedures, primary keys, and foreign keys, it is easier for the SPD tooling to create valid BDC Metadata Models with less human input. After an ECT is created and associated with a database as an external system, the Operation Designer shows the available tables, views, and stored procedures with which to work. You can use any of these objects as the starting point for a method.

Creating Finder Methods

Finder methods return views of the external system. You can use these views to create views in external lists and the Business Data web parts, or to support search. As such, an ECT can support multiple Finder methods. To start creating a Finder method, you can right-click one of the available tables, views, or stored procedures and select New Read List Operation from the context menu. When you create a new Finder method, SPD starts the Read List Wizard.

The first step of the wizard asks for the Operation Name and Operation Display Name of the Finder method. When naming methods, you should adopt a standard and use it consistently. The names that you select appear in several places throughout SharePoint, so it's a good idea to use a naming standard that end users can read and understand.

The next step in the wizard enables you to set up filters for the Finder method. When you create the first Finder method, SPD automatically marks it as the default Finder method. The default Finder method is the default view used for external lists and is the default method called by the crawler during search indexing. This is important because you do not want to filter the default Finder method in any way so this step in the wizard would be skipped.

When you create subsequent Finder methods, you want to apply filters. Filters are important because they limit the amount of data that can be returned from the external system, thus making the solution more efficient. In the same way that you create views in a standard SharePoint list, you want to create filtered Finder methods in SPD.

In the wizard, you can add a new filter to a Finder method by clicking the Add Filter Parameter button. Clicking this button, however, results only in the creation of an undefined filter, which generates a warning in the wizard. To configure the filter, you must click the Click to Add link, which opens the Filter Configuration dialog. Figure 13-22 shows the wizard with the Filter Configuration dialog open.

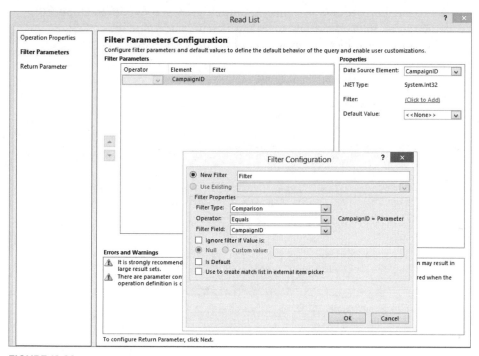

FIGURE 13-22

In the Filter Configuration dialog, you can select the type of filter that you want and set properties such as values to ignore. After you complete the settings in the Filter Configuration dialog box, you can close it, but the filter definition is still not complete. In the Properties section of the wizard, you must select the field to be associated with the filter and provide a default value for the filter.

The next step in the wizard asks you to configure the values returned from the external system. Here you will be asked to specify the Identifier for the ECT. The Identifier field is the field that has the value that uniquely identifies an entity instance in the external system. For databases, this is most often the primary key. Select this field and check the Map to Identifier check box.

In this step, you also are prompted to specify fields to be displayed in the External Item Picker dialog box. This dialog is the picker control that appears in Microsoft Word whenever a library uses a field based on an ECT. This is important because the user sees only the fields that you mark, so they should be the fields the end user needs to search. Select each of the fields, and click the Show in Picker check box.

In this step, it's also a good idea to take a close look at the display name for each field. Make sure that these values are readable because they appear as column headers in external lists. You can also uncheck any fields that you do not want to display in the view. Finally, if you have a DateTime field in the data source that represents the last time the record was edited, mark that field as the Timestamp field. This allows Search to use the field in support of incremental crawls.

Modeling Finder Methods

Using tables, views, or stored procedures as sources result in the creation of different models. This is expected as the syntax to query these sources is different. The following code shows an implementation of the same Finder method using each of the three sources:

```xml
<!-- Table -->
<Method IsStatic="false" Name="AllNamesTable">
 <Properties>
  <Property Name="BackEndObject" Type="System.String">
   Names
  </Property>
  <Property Name="BackEndObjectType" Type="System.String">
   SqlServerTable
  </Property>
  <Property Name="RdbCommandText" Type="System.String">
   SELECT [ID] , [Title] , [FirstName] , [MiddleName] , [LastName] ,
   [EmailAddress] , [Phone] FROM [MiniCRM].[Names]
  </Property>
  <Property Name="RdbCommandType"
   Type="System.Data.CommandType, System.Data, Version=2.0.0.0,
   Culture=neutral, PublicKeyToken=b77a5c561934e089">
   Text
  </Property>
  <Property Name="Schema" Type="System.String">
   MiniCRM
  </Property>
 </Properties>
 <Parameters>
  <Parameter Direction="Return" Name="AllNamesTable">
   ...
  </Parameter>
 </Parameters>
 <MethodInstances>
  <MethodInstance Type="Finder" ReturnParameterName="AllNamesTable"
   Name="AllNamesTable" DefaultDisplayName="All Names Table">
 </MethodInstance>
 </MethodInstances>
</Method>


<!-- View -->
<Method IsStatic="false" Name="AllNamesView">
 <Properties>
  <Property Name="BackEndObject" Type="System.String">
   vw_GetNames
  </Property>
  <Property Name="BackEndObjectType" Type="System.String">
   SqlServerView
  </Property>
  <Property Name="RdbCommandText" Type="System.String">
   SELECT [ID] , [Title] , [FirstName] , [MiddleName] , [LastName] ,
```

```
       [EmailAddress] , [Phone] FROM [dbo].[vw_GetNames]
      </Property>
      <Property Name="RdbCommandType"
       Type="System.Data.CommandType, System.Data, Version=2.0.0.0,
       Culture=neutral, PublicKeyToken=b77a5c561934e089">
       Text
      </Property>
      <Property Name="Schema" Type="System.String">
       dbo
      </Property>
     </Properties>
     <Parameters>
      <Parameter Direction="Return" Name="AllNamesView">
       ...
      </Parameter>
     </Parameters>
     <MethodInstances>
      <MethodInstance Type="Finder" ReturnParameterName="AllNamesView"
       Name="AllNamesView" DefaultDisplayName="All Names View">
      </MethodInstance>
     </MethodInstances>
    </Method>


    <!-- Stored Procedure -->
    <Method IsStatic="false" Name="AllNamesProcedure">
     <Properties>
      <Property Name="BackEndObject" Type="System.String">
       sp_GetNames
      </Property>
      <Property Name="BackEndObjectType" Type="System.String">
       SqlServerRoutine
      </Property>
      <Property Name="RdbCommandText" Type="System.String">
       [dbo].[sp_GetNames]
      </Property>
      <Property Name="RdbCommandType"
       Type="System.Data.CommandType, System.Data, Version=2.0.0.0,
       Culture=neutral, PublicKeyToken=b77a5c561934e089">
       StoredProcedure
      </Property>
      <Property Name="Schema" Type="System.String">
       dbo
      </Property>
     </Properties>
     <Parameters>
      <Parameter Direction="Return" Name="AllNamesProcedure">
       ...
      </Parameter>
     </Parameters>
     <MethodInstances>
      <MethodInstance Type="Finder" ReturnParameterName="AllNamesProcedure"
       Name="AllNamesProcedure" DefaultDisplayName="All Names Procedure">
      </MethodInstance>
     </MethodInstances>
    </Method>
```

The primary difference between each of the three implementations is the set of `Property` elements used in each. Tables and views, for example, use dynamic SQL statements, whereas the stored procedure uses a direct call to the procedure. Notice that none of the methods have any input parameters or filters defined. If parameters were defined, however, a new stored procedure would need to be defined because any input parameters must be reflected in the stored procedure definition, whereas the dynamic SQL statements written against tables and views can simply be changed in the model.

When a stored procedure with input parameters is used, the wizard presents a screen that enables you to assign filters to the parameters. These filter values can then be set in the view definition of the external list by an end user or as an input parameter in the Business Data web parts. The following code shows a stored procedure that supports a wildcard as an input parameter:

```
<Method IsStatic="false" Name="NamesByWildcardProcedure">
 <Properties>
  <Property Name="BackEndObject" Type="System.String">
   sp_GetNamesWildcard
  </Property>
  <Property Name="BackEndObjectType" Type="System.String">
   SqlServerRoutine
  </Property>
  <Property Name="RdbCommandText" Type="System.String">
   [dbo].[sp_GetNamesWildcard]
  </Property>
  <Property Name="RdbCommandType"
   Type="System.Data.CommandType, System.Data, Version=2.0.0.0,
   Culture=neutral, PublicKeyToken=b77a5c561934e089">
   StoredProcedure
  </Property>
  <Property Name="Schema" Type="System.String">
   dbo
  </Property>
 </Properties>
 <FilterDescriptors>
  <FilterDescriptor Type="Wildcard" FilterField="LastName" Name="Wildcard">
   <Properties>
    <Property Name="CaseSensitive" Type="System.Boolean">
     false
    </Property>
    <Property Name="IsDefault" Type="System.Boolean">
     false
    </Property>
    <Property Name="UsedForDisambiguation" Type="System.Boolean">
     false
    </Property>
   </Properties>
  </FilterDescriptor>
 </FilterDescriptors>
 <Parameters>
  <Parameter Direction="In" Name="@wildcard">
   <TypeDescriptor TypeName="System.String"
    AssociatedFilter="Wildcard" Name="@wildcard">
    <Properties>
```

```
  <Property Name="Order" Type="System.Int32">0</Property>
 </Properties>
 <DefaultValues>
  <DefaultValue
   MethodInstanceName="NamesByWildcardProcedure" Type="System.String">
   A
  </DefaultValue>
  </DefaultValues>
  </TypeDescriptor>
 </Parameter>
 <Parameter Direction="Return" Name="NamesByWildcardProcedure">
  ...
 </Parameter>
 </Parameters>
 <MethodInstances>
  <MethodInstance Type="Finder"
   ReturnParameterName="NamesByWildcardProcedure"
   Name="NamesByWildcardProcedure"
   DefaultDisplayName="Names by Wildcard Procedure">
  </MethodInstance>
 </MethodInstances>
</Method>
```

In the code, notice that a `FilterDescriptor` of type `Wildcard` has been added to the model. This filter is associated with the `LastName` field and the `@wildcard` input parameter. What this does is pass the value of the filter into the `@wildcard` input parameter. This means that the stored procedure must have a parameter by that exact name available, as shown in the following code:

```
CREATE PROCEDURE [dbo].[sp_GetNamesWildcard]
@wildcard nvarchar(10)
AS
SELECT ID,Title,FirstName,MiddleName,LastName,Suffix,EMailAddress,Phone
FROM MiniCRM.Names
WHERE LastName LIKE @wildcard + '%'
```

Remember that the purpose of filters is to retrieve input from either the end user or the system. In the case of the wildcard filter, the idea is to let the end user set up a view based on a partial string search of the last name. In the SharePoint interface, this appears as a value that can be set in the view definition of the external list.

Understanding the Default Finder

The default `Finder` method deserves special consideration in the design of any BCS solution. As stated previously, the first method `Finder` method created in SPD will be the default. When you create subsequent `Finder` methods, the wizard presents a check box that you can use to change the default `Finder`. If you do nothing, however, it will always be the first one created.

The default `Finder` method serves two important purposes. First, this is the method that generates the default view for an external list. Second, this method is used by the search indexer to retrieve records during the crawl process. The method is identified as the default `Finder` through the `Default` attribute of the `MethodInstance` element and the target of the crawl through the `RootFinder` property, as shown in the following code:

```
<MethodInstance
 Type="Finder"
 ReturnParameterName="AllNames"
 Default="true"
 Name="AllNames"
 DefaultDisplayName="All Names">
 <Properties>
  <Property Name="RootFinder" Type="System.String"></Property>
 </Properties>
</MethodInstance>
```

When SPD defines a Finder as both the default Finder and the root Finder, it can cause significant problems in your solutions. This is because the default Finder should be filtered, but the root Finder should not. Finder methods should generally have filters on them to limit the number of rows returned. If they do not have filters, BCS throws an error if they return more than 2,000 rows to an external list. However, root Finders should never be filtered because the filtering excludes items from the search index so that they never appear in search results. Therefore, you must manually edit the BDC Metadata Model to assign the default Finder and root Finder to different Finder methods unless you know that your data source will never exceed 2,000 rows, which is the limit for external lists.

Creating Other Methods

Creating SpecificFinder, Creator, Updater, and Deleter methods generally follows the same concepts as Finder methods. The wizard walks you through the steps necessary to define appropriate parameters and filters. In the case of stored procedures, remember that any required input parameters or filters must be explicitly available as parameters in the stored procedure.

Creating Methods for Web Services

Web services are generally more difficult to work with than databases because the form of the exposed methods in a web service can vary widely. There is no explicit schema available for tables and views, and there are no primary/foreign keys available for inferring relationships. Therefore, the design of a BCS solution that utilizes web services must be carefully considered.

Although you can use an existing web service as an external data source, the requirements of the method stereotypes more often lead to the creation of a custom service for a BCS solution. Custom services should expose methods that correlate closely to BCS method stereotypes. The following code shows the programmatic interface for a simple WCF service:

```
[ServiceContract]
public interface IService
{
    [OperationContract]
    List<Customer> CrawlCustomers();
    [OperationContract]
    List<Customer> GetCustomers(int Limit);
    [OperationContract]
    List<Customer> GetCustomersByRegion(string Region);
    [OperationContract]
    Customer GetCustomer(string Id);
```

```
        [OperationContract]
        void CreateCustomer(string FirstName, string LastName);
        [OperationContract]
        void UpdateCustomer(string Id, string FirstName, string LastName);
        [OperationContract]
        void DeleteCustomer(string Id);
    }
    [DataContract]
    public class Customer
    {
        [DataMember]
        public string Id { get; set; }
        [DataMember]
        public string FirstName { get; set; }
        [DataMember]
        public string LastName { get; set; }
    }
```

The exposed methods of the web service are designed in accordance with the requirements of Table 13-4. The Finder methods return collections of Customer entity instances, whereas the SpecificFinder returns only a single entity instance. The Creator, Updater, and Deleter methods return void.

Three Finder methods are exposed. The CrawlCustomers method has no filter and is intended for use by the indexer. The GetCustomers method accepts a limit filter to prevent causing errors in the external list if too many results are returned. The GetCustomerByRegion accepts a filter to limit the return results to customers in a given region. These parameters all appear in the SPD Wizard so that they can be mapped to the appropriate filter types.

Defining Associations

Associations are relationships between ECTs. SPD supports one-to-many, self-referential, and reverse associations. One-to-many associations return many related entity instances from a single parent entity instance. Self-referential associations return entity instances of the same type as the parent entity instance. Reverse associations return a parent entity instance from a single child entity instance. Associations created in SPD are of type AssociationNavigator.

Creating One-to-Many Associations

The most common type of association in BCS solutions is the one-to-many association, whereby a parent entity instance is related to many child entity instances. This type of association supports scenarios such as when a single Customer has many Orders or when a single Client has many Contacts. This design is identical to the way database tables are related.

To create a one-to-many association, you must first define both External Content Types. The child ECT should be defined so that it contains a foreign key related to the parent ECT. This means that the Order ECT would contain a CustomerID field or the Contact ECT would contain a ClientID field. If the relationship is based on a database table or view, nothing else needs to be done. If the relationship is based on a stored procedure or web service method, you must also create a stored procedure or method that accepts the parent entity instance identifier and returns the child entity instances.

After you have the ECTs defined, the new association can be created from the Operation Designer. If the relationship uses tables or views, select the child table or view. If the relationship uses stored procedures or web services, select the procedure or method that accepts the parent entity instance identifier and return the child entity instances. Right-click and select New Association in the context menu to start the Association Wizard.

In the Association Wizard, you map the child ECT to the parent ECT by clicking the Browse button and selecting the parent ECT from a list. After you select the parent ECT, you must map the identifier of the parent ECT to the foreign key in the child ECT.

In the next screen of the wizard, you map the input parameter of the child to the foreign key. Most of the time this field has the same name as the identifier that was selected in the first screen, but they can be different.

```xml
<Method IsStatic="false" Name="ContactsForClient">
 <Properties>
  <Property Name="BackEndObject" Type="System.String">
   ClientContacts
  </Property>
  <Property Name="BackEndObjectType" Type="System.String">
   SqlServerTable
  </Property>
  <Property Name="RdbCommandText" Type="System.String">
   sp_GetAllClientContacts
  </Property>
  <Property Name="RdbCommandType" Type="System.Data.CommandType,
   System.Data, Version=2.0.0.0, Culture=neutral,
   PublicKeyToken=b77a5c561934e089">
   StoredProcedure
  </Property>
  <Property Name="Schema" Type="System.String">dbo</Property>
 </Properties>
 <Parameters>
  <Parameter Direction="In" Name="@ClientID">
   <TypeDescriptor TypeName="System.Int32" IdentifierName="ClientID"
    IdentifierEntityName="Client"
    IdentifierEntityNamespace="http://clients_web"
    ForeignIdentifierAssociationName="ContactsForClient"
    Name="ClientID" />
  </Parameter>
  <Parameter Direction="Return" Name="ContactsForClient">
   ...
  </Parameter>
 </Parameters>
 <MethodInstances>
  <Association Name="ContactsForClient" Type="AssociationNavigator"
   ReturnParameterName="ContactsForClient"
   DefaultDisplayName="Contacts For Client">
   <Properties>
    <Property Name="ForeignFieldMappings" Type="System.String">
    &lt;?xml version="1.0" encoding="utf-16"?&gt;
    &lt;ForeignFieldMappings
    xmlns:xsi="http://www.w3.org/2001/XMLSchema-instance"
    xmlns:xsd="http://www.w3.org/2001/XMLSchema"&gt;
    &lt;ForeignFieldMappingsList&gt;
```

```
&lt;ForeignFieldMapping ForeignIdentifierName="ClientID"
ForeignIdentifierEntityName="Client"
ForeignIdentifierEntityNamespace="http://clients_web"
FieldName="ClientID" /&gt;
&lt;/ForeignFieldMappingsList&gt;
&lt;/ForeignFieldMappings&gt;
    </Property>
   </Properties>
   <SourceEntity Namespace="http://clients_web" Name="Client" />
   <DestinationEntity Namespace="http://clients_web" Name="Contact" />
  </Association>
 </MethodInstances>
</Method>
```

One-to-many relationships are used in the
SharePoint interface to display entity instances.
In an external list of child entity instances, the
foreign key for the parent entity instance can be
set using the picker, as shown in Figure 13-23.
If a profile page is defined for the parent ECT, it
automatically is created to contain a list of related
child ECTs.

Creating Self-Referential Associations

Self-referential associations are created
using the same approach as one-to-many
relationships. The difference is that a
self-referential relationship uses the same
ECT as the parent and the child. Therefore,
the ECT must have a separate field defined
that acts like the foreign key in a one-to-
many relationship but instead refers to an
entity instance of the same type.

FIGURE 13-23

For example, consider creating an organizational chart from a single table of employees. The table
contains an ID field as the primary key and a ManagerID field to relate the current record to another
record in the table. Using this information, an association can be created between the Employee ID
and ManagerID field, as shown in the following code:

```
<Method IsStatic="false" Name="EmployeesForManager">
 <Properties>
  <Property Name="BackEndObject" Type="System.String">
   Employees
  </Property>
  <Property Name="BackEndObjectType" Type="System.String">
   SqlServerTable
  </Property>
  <Property Name="RdbCommandText" Type="System.String">
   SELECT [ID] , [ManagerID] , [Title] , [FirstName] , [MiddleName] ,
   [LastName] , [EmailAddress] , [Phone] FROM [dbo].[Employees]
   WHERE [ManagerID] = @ID
  </Property>
```

```
<Property Name="RdbCommandType"
 Type="System.Data.CommandType, System.Data, Version=2.0.0.0,
 Culture=neutral, PublicKeyToken=b77a5c561934e089">
 Text
</Property>
<Property Name="Schema" Type="System.String">
 dbo
</Property>
</Properties>
<Parameters>
 <Parameter Direction="In" Name="@ID">
  <TypeDescriptor TypeName="System.Int32" IdentifierName="ID"
   ForeignIdentifierAssociationName="EmployeesForManager"
   Name="ManagerID" />
 </Parameter>
 <Parameter Direction="Return" Name="EmployeesForManager">
  ...
 </Parameter>
</Parameters>
<MethodInstances>
 <Association Name="EmployeesForManager" Type="AssociationNavigator"
  ReturnParameterName="EmployeesForManager"
  DefaultDisplayName="Employees for Manager">
  <Properties>
   <Property Name="ForeignFieldMappings" Type="System.String">
    &lt;?xml version="1.0" encoding="utf-16"?&gt;
    &lt;ForeignFieldMappings
    xmlns:xsi="http://www.w3.org/2001/XMLSchema-instance"
    xmlns:xsd="http://www.w3.org/2001/XMLSchema"&gt;
    &lt;ForeignFieldMappingsList&gt;
    &lt;ForeignFieldMapping ForeignIdentifierName="ID"
    ForeignIdentifierEntityName="Employee"
    ForeignIdentifierEntityNamespace="http://bcs/orgchart"
    FieldName="ManagerID" /&gt;
    &lt;/ForeignFieldMappingsList&gt;
    &lt;/ForeignFieldMappings&gt;</Property>
  </Properties>
  <SourceEntity Namespace="http://bcs/orgchart" Name="Employee" />
  <DestinationEntity Namespace="http://bcs/orgchart" Name="Employee" />
 </Association>
</MethodInstances>
</Method>
```

The key to creating the self-referential relationship is the SQL query that returns entity instances when the ManagerID=ID. Note that SPD does not always create this SQL query correctly when you are creating a new self-referential association in the tooling. Therefore, you should be sure to export and examine the query after the method is created. After it is created correctly, you can use the relationships like any other.

Creating Reverse Associations

Reverse associations return a single parent entity instance for a child entity instance. Reverse associations are not supported for tables and views but are supported for stored procedures and web services because the reverse association in not inherent in the database schema. It must be explicitly programmed through a stored procedure or web service. For example, you could create a stored procedure that takes the identifier for a Contact and returns the parent Client entity instance, as shown in the following code:

```
CREATE PROCEDURE sp_GetClientByContactID
@ClientContactID int
AS
Select Clients.ClientID, Clients.Name, Clients.Address1, Clients.Address2,
Clients.City, Clients.Province, Clients.PostalCode, Clients.Country,
Clients.Phone, Clients.Fax, Clients.Web
From Clients
Inner Join ClientContacts
On Clients.ClientID = ClientContacts.ClientID
Where ClientContactID = @ClientContactID
```

After the stored procedure is written, open the Operation Designer for the child ECT. Select the stored procedure, right-click, and select New Reverse Association from the context menu. As with the other associations, you can then browse and select the parent ECT.

WORKING WITH EXTERNAL LISTS

External lists support many of the same capabilities as standard SharePoint lists, such as custom list actions and custom forms. In SharePoint Server 2013, they have been enhanced to also support event handlers and notifications. This section takes a closer look at some of the capabilities of external lists.

Creating Custom List Actions

Custom list actions allow you to add a new button to the List Item menu, View Item Ribbon, New Form Ribbon, View Form Ribbon, or the Edit Form Ribbon. The target of the button can be an existing form or a URL. For standard lists, you can also initiate a workflow from the button, but external lists do not support this function.

New custom list actions are created from SPD by selecting the list and clicking the Custom Action button in the Ribbon. This button then opens the Create Custom Action dialog box.

Creating Custom Forms

For every standard and external list, a set of forms is created to display, edit, and add items. Using the SharePoint Designer, you can create and customize these forms as ASPX pages or as InfoPath forms. This capability helps you enhance data presentation and perform field-level validation on items.

Creating ASPX Forms

When you create an external list, new, edit, and display forms are automatically created as appropriate, based on the operations defined for the associated ECT. Using SPD, you can see these forms by clicking on the Lists and Libraries object followed by the list of interest. The existing forms are listed on the summary page.

The default forms created for the external list utilize the List Form web part (LFWP). The LFWP executes Collaborative Application Markup Language (CAML) queries against the external list to display items. Unfortunately, the LFWP does not support modifying its presentation; a new form must be created instead.

Clicking the New button above the form list in the summary page opens the Create New List Form dialog box. This dialog box is used to create new, edit, and display forms that are based on the Data Form web part (DFWP). The DFWP utilizes XSLT to transform list data into a display. Modifying this XSLT can easily change the presentation of list data.

For example, consider an external list that returns information about SharePoint images. The BCS solution has a column called Path that returns the path to the image. In a simple BCS solution, Path appears as a column and the user simply sees the text of the URL. A better experience, however, would be to show the image itself. This can be done by adding a new display form and modifying the XSLT, as shown in the following code.

```
<img>
 <xsl:attribute name="src">
  <xsl:value-of select="@Path"/>
 </xsl:attribute>
</img>
```

In addition to using SPD, you can also modify the list forms inside of the SharePoint 2013 interface. While viewing the external list, click the List tab on the Ribbon. The Modify Form Web Parts button enables you to select a form to modify. The difference is that you will be modifying the web part that is rendering the list using the Properties pane.

Creating InfoPath Forms

Instead of ASPX pages, you can choose to create custom InfoPath forms for the external list. InfoPath form creation can be initiated directly from SPD by clicking the Design Forms in InfoPath button from the List Summary page. This action opens InfoPath with a default form that you can edit.

InfoPath forms are easier to create and offer simpler styling and advanced controls. Using InfoPath, you can take advantage of lists and drop-downs as well as styles and themes. When the form is complete, you must save it and then execute a Quick Publish. Quick publishing is available by clicking the File tab in InfoPath. When published, the form is available on the new, edit, and display forms.

SUMMARY

Business Connectivity Services (BCS) provides the infrastructure and tooling necessary to bring external data into SharePoint. When creating BCS solutions for SharePoint 2013, the SharePoint Designer should be considered as your primary tool. The tooling support in SPD is easier to use than the equivalent tooling in Visual Studio. In addition, you can export the model and edit it by hand to include capabilities not supported in the SPD tooling. In short, you should use SPD for the majority of your solutions that are based on databases and web services. Complex solutions that use SharePoint apps or custom-coded connectors are covered in Chapter 14.

14

Advanced Business Connectivity Services

WHAT'S IN THIS CHAPTER?

➤ Creating BCS connectors

➤ Searching BCS systems

➤ Using the BCS object model

➤ Using BCS with SharePoint apps

WROX.COM CODE DOWNLOADS FOR THIS CHAPTER

The wrox.com code downloads for this chapter are found at www.wrox.com/remtitle
.cgi?isbn=1118495829 on the Download Code tab. The code is in the chapter 14 download
and individually named according to the names throughout the chapter.

Chapter 13, "Introducing Business Connectivity Services," discussed creating Business
Connectivity Services (BCS) solutions with little coding. This chapter explores custom coding
in BCS by presenting .NET Assembly Connectors and the BDC server object model, which
lays the foundation for custom BCS solutions.

CREATING .NET ASSEMBLY CONNECTORS

A .NET Assembly Connector associates a custom assembly with an external content type
(ECT) so that you can precisely control how information is accessed, processed, and returned
from external systems. You create a .NET Assembly Connector in Visual Studio 2012 by
adding the Business Data Connectivity Model (BDCM) item. The Visual Studio BDCM item
is a complete working sample. After it is created, you can press F5 and make external lists in
SharePoint. This is a good start because the tooling can be somewhat confusing when you first
use it; a complete working sample helps guide you to success. The detailed examination of the
project item in the next section can help you understand.

Understanding the Project Tooling

When you work with the Business Data Connectivity Model item, there are three explorers/ designers available: the BDC Model Explorer, the Entity Design Surface, and the Method Details pane. The BDC Model Explorer is used to navigate the nodes of the BDC Metadata Model. The Entity Design Surface is used to design the ECT that will be associated with the .NET Assembly Connector. The Method Details pane is used to create the function signatures for ECT operations. Along with these three elements, the Business Data Connectivity Model project template also gives you the standard windows such as the Solution Explorer and the Properties pane. Figure 14-1 shows the tooling in Visual Studio 2012.

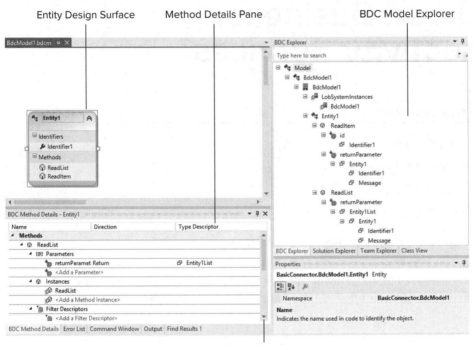

FIGURE 14-1

Although the Visual Studio tooling is helpful, there are times when you must access the underlying BDC Metadata Model as XML either for direct editing or simply to verify the work you have done using the tools. The BDC Metadata Model can be found in the Solution Explorer as the file with the .bdcm extension. You can open this file as XML by right-clicking it and selecting Open With from the context menu. From the Open With dialog box, open the file with the XML Editor.

To be successful with the tooling, you must understand how the various explorers and designers relate to the underlying model XML. Furthermore, you must understand which elements of the project are affected as you make changes. In particular the BDC Model Explorer and the Method Details pane can be confusing if their relationships to the underlying XML are not well understood.

Not all of the underlying BDC Metadata Model can be represented in the BDC Model Explorer. In particular, the BDC Model Explorer shows methods, but not method instances. Methods are used in the BDC Metadata model as prototypes, which are subsequently implemented by method instances. The Method Details pane provides the interface necessary to define the method instances.

The Entity Design Surface is also used to edit the underlying BDC Metadata Model. However, it is focused on the creation of entities. Using this tool you can create new entities, assign the Identifier, and create new methods.

Regardless of which tool you use, you can use the Properties pane to edit the selected node. The Properties pane lists the type of node and its attributes. Although the nodes have many attributes, most of them are not required. It is not always clear, however, which attributes are required to implement any given node. The better you understand the model, the more likely you are to create the one you need.

For the most part, the tooling is designed to edit the underlying BDC Metadata Model, with one exception. A class module is used to implement the method instances that you define in the model. This class module is created automatically and is always given the name of the entity followed by the word Service. This class is known as the *service class*. If you change the name of the entity in your model, the service class name is updated automatically. If you delete the service class from the project, it is re-created the next time you make any changes to the method definitions.

The methods implemented in the service class have types defined by the input and return parameters in the BDC Metadata Model. These types can be simple types or classes. Typically, however, the Finder and SpecificFinder methods return classes that represent the ECT associated with the .NET Assembly Connector. In the Business Connectivity Model item, a class named Entity1.cs is created by default and is returned from the Finder and SpecificFinder methods. These methods are also created by default when you create a project with the Business Connectivity Model item.

Even though the item template includes a class that has the same name as the entity, there is actually no connection between the entity definition and the entity class as far as the tooling is concerned. Changing the name of the entity in the model does not change the name of the class, and the class is never automatically generated. The class is actually just a payload returned from the .NET Assembly Connector. Its name is meaningless, but it is a best practice to keep the name of the class synchronized with the name of the entity it represents. The methods in the service class return instances of the entity class that are passed on to external lists for display. In more advanced scenarios, you may choose to implement the entity classes in a separate project so that they can be easily referenced by custom web parts that display the data.

The tooling is largely focused on defining and implementing methods as opposed to defining the data returned by the entity class. In the default project template, the entity has a data field named Message, which is defined as a TypeDescriptor with a TypeName of System.String. The entity class has a corresponding property whose value is set during the execution of the Finder or SpecificFinder methods. To add or modify data fields for the ECT, you must make changes to the model in the BDC Model Explorer and add new properties to the entity class. This is a manual process — the tooling never automatically generates members for the entity class.

Walking Through the Development Process

The easiest way to become familiar with the Visual Studio Business Data Connectivity Model project is to create a solution. This example walks you through the complete development process for building a .NET Assembly Connector. It makes use of a subset of product and category data from the AdventureWorks database to create a connector that allows full CRUD operations. As a starting point, an object relational model (ORM) was created over the database using the Entity Framework so that the .NET Assembly Connector can simply access the database through LINQ. To learn more about the Entity Framework, you can find complete coverage on MSDN at `http://msdn.microsoft.com/en-US/data/jj590134`.

Creating a New Project

The first step in developing the connector is to create a new empty SharePoint 2013 solutions project and add a new Business Data Connectivity Model item. For this walkthrough, you use a model named `ProductModel` that makes use of data from the AdventureWorks database. Although the default model created by the project template is valuable for learning about the tooling, it provides little help in developing a connector. For this reason, it is best simply to delete the default `Entity1` entity from the Entity Design Surface. Along with the entity, you should also delete the entity service class and the entity class from the Solution Explorer. This leaves you with a simple BDC Metadata Model that looks like the following XML, which you can view as text directly in Visual Studio:

```xml
<?xml version="1.0" encoding= "utf-8 "?>
<Model xmlns:xsi="http://www.w3.org/2001/XMLSchema-instance"
       xmlns:xsd="http://www.w3.org/2001/XMLSchema"
       xmlns= "http://schemas.microsoft.com/windows/2007/BusinessDataCatalog"
       Name= "ProductModel ">
  <LobSystems>
    <LobSystem Name= "ProductSystem" Type= "DotNetAssembly ">
      <LobSystemInstances>
        <LobSystemInstance Name= "ProductSystemInstance" />
      </LobSystemInstances>
    </LobSystem>
  </LobSystems>
</Model>
```

The `LobSystem` element is a critical part of the model. Note how the element indicates that the system will be implemented through an assembly. This syntax differs significantly from that of the examples in previous chapters, which used databases and web services. This element is also used by both SPD and Visual Studio 2012 to determine whether to provide tooling support for a model. SPD does not provide tooling support for .NET Assembly Connectors, and Visual Studio provides tooling support only for .NET Assembly Connectors.

Also notice in the preceding XML that careful attention has been paid to naming the elements. The `Model`, `LobSystem`, and `LobSystemInstance` nodes have all been named appropriately. When you create connectors, naming is critical for maintaining clarity as the BDC Metadata Model becomes more complex. Remember to name elements correctly early in the development process. Renaming elements later can cause problems, as described in the section "Packaging Considerations".

Creating a New Entity

Because the default entity was deleted, the next step is to add a new entity to the project. You can add entities to the project from the toolbox in Visual Studio, which has an `Entity` object that can be dragged onto the Entity Design Surface. When you add a new entity, you'll notice that a new service class is automatically created. In addition, the Properties pane presents several properties that you can set. Here you will at least set the `Name` property for the entity. In this case, the entity is named `Product`.

The next step is to add the `Identifier` for the entity. The `Identifier` is the primary key by which a unique entity instance can be identified. You can create a new `Identifier` by right-clicking the entity and selecting Add, Identifier. Using the Properties pane you can set the name and data type for the `Identifier`. For the walkthrough, an `Identifier` named `ProductID` was created, with a data type of `System.Int32`. The following code shows the BDC Metadata Model for the entity:

```xml
<Entities>
  <Entity Name="Product" Namespace="ProductConnector.ProductModel"
   Version="1.0.0.133">
    <Properties>
      <Property Name="Class" Type="System.String">
       ProductConnector.ProductModel.ProductService,
       ProductSystem</Property>
    </Properties>
    <Identifiers>
      <Identifier Name="ProductID" TypeName="System.Int32"/>
    </Identifiers>
  </Entity>
</Entities>
```

The next step is to create the entity class that contains the data from the external system. Remember that Visual Studio does not automatically create an entity class, so you must add a new class manually. Within the class you must add properties for each of the data fields you want to return. The following code shows the entity class created for the walkthrough:

```csharp
namespace ProductConnector.ProductModel
{
    public class Product
    {
        public int ProductID { get; set; }
        public string Name { get; set; }
        public string Number { get; set; }
        public string Color { get; set; }
        public string Description { get; set; }
    }
}
```

Although the preceding entity class is fairly simple, there are a couple of things to point out. First, each of the properties in the class corresponds to a column in an external list. Second, the data is strongly typed; the types defined in the class are returned from the connector.

Creating a Finder Method

The next step is to create the methods for the entity. Returning to the Entity Design Surface, you can create new methods by right-clicking the entity and selecting Add Method. You can also create a new method in the Method Details pane, which is a better idea because Visual Studio defines the model for the stereotype when you start here. Remember that a method is just a stereotype and that you must create a method instance to implement the method. You can create a new method instance by clicking the Add Method Instance link in the Method Details pane. After you create the method instance, you can specify the `Type` of the method instance in the Properties pane. Typically, your first method will be a `Finder` method. For the walkthrough, a `Finder` method named `ReadProducts` was created.

After the method instance is defined, you must define its parameters. In the case of the default `Finder` method, you typically define a return parameter only. Other method instances may require input parameters as well as filters. You can create a new parameter by clicking Add a Parameter in the Method Details pane. Using the Properties pane you can then change the parameter name and direction. For the walkthrough, a return parameter named `ProductList` was created.

When a parameter is defined, Visual Studio automatically creates a `TypeDescriptor` for the parameter. The `TypeDescriptor` acts as a mapping between the data types found in the external system and the data types returned by the .NET Assembly Connector. Clicking the `TypeDescriptor` in the Method Details pane enables you to define the `TypeName` for the `TypeDescriptor`. In the case of a `Finder` method, the `TypeDescriptor` is typically a collection of entity instances. Therefore, the `IsCollection` property should be set to `True` before you select the `TypeName`. After the `TypeDescriptor` is designated as a collection, you can open the `TypeName` picker, click the Current Project tab, and select the `Product` class. Visual Studio automatically sets the return type to be a collection. Figure 14-2 shows the Type Name picker in Visual Studio.

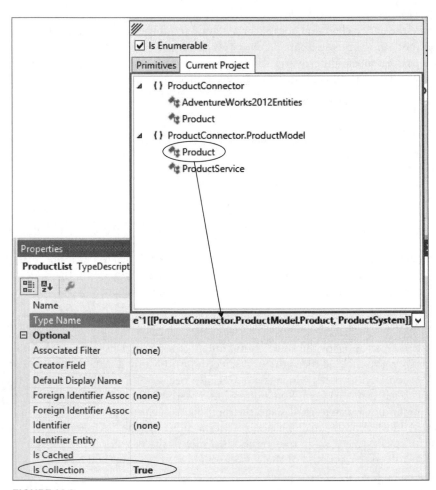

FIGURE 14-2

At this point, you can open the code for the service class and see that Visual Studio has created a method whose signature is based on the method, parameter, and TypeDescriptor settings. However, your work is not yet done because the return TypeDescriptor was designated as a collection. Therefore a new TypeDescriptor must be added to represent the member of the collection. In addition, each field in the collection member must be defined.

To create the additional TypeDescriptors, you work in the BDC Model Explorer. In the Explorer, you can see the TypeDescriptor defining the collection. You may define a collection member by right-clicking the collection TypeDescriptor and selecting Add Type Descriptor from the context menu. This TypeDescriptor has a TypeName of Product but will not be a collection. Finally, you must add a TypeDescriptor for every property of the entity you want to return. Take care to set the Identifier property for the TypeDescriptor that represents the Identifier of the entity (in this case, ProductID) to designate this property as the one containing the Identifier value.

Finally, return to the Method Details pane and select the method instance for the Finder. In the Properties pane, set Return Parameter Name and Return TypeDescriptor to reference the items already created. This completes the definition of the Finder. The following code shows the completed Finder method definition in the BDC Metadata Model.

```xml
<Method Name="ReadProducts">
  <Parameters>
    <Parameter Name="productList" Direction="Return">
      <TypeDescriptor Name="ProductList"
       TypeName="System.Collections.Generic.IEnumerable`1[
       [ProductConnector.ProductModel.Product, ProductSystem]]"
       IsCollection="true">
        <TypeDescriptors>
          <TypeDescriptor Name="Product"
           TypeName="ProductConnector.ProductModel.Product, ProductSystem"
           IsCollection="false">
            <TypeDescriptors>
              <TypeDescriptor Name="ProductID" TypeName="System.Int32"
                IsCollection="false" IdentifierName="ProductID" ReadOnly="true" />
              <TypeDescriptor Name="Name" TypeName="System.String" />
              <TypeDescriptor Name="Description" TypeName="System.String" />
              <TypeDescriptor Name="Color" TypeName="System.String" />
              <TypeDescriptor Name="Number" TypeName="System.String" />
            </TypeDescriptors>
          </TypeDescriptor>
        </TypeDescriptors>
      </TypeDescriptor>
    </Parameter>
  </Parameters>
  <MethodInstances>
    <MethodInstance Name="ReadProducts" Type="Finder"
     ReturnParameterName="productList" ReturnTypeDescriptorPath="ProductList" />
  </MethodInstances>
</Method>
```

Creating a SpecificFinder Method

Because the minimum requirements for an external list include a Finder and SpecificFinder method, the next step is to create the SpecificFinder method. You do this using the same procedure as for the `Finder` method, with two exceptions. First, the return type is a single entity instance as opposed to a collection. Second, `SpecificFinder` requires an input parameter that contains the `Identifier` of the entity instance to return. You must explicitly designate this input parameter as accepting an identifier by setting the `Identifier` property.

As with the `Finder` method, you must also add a `TypeDescriptor` for every property of the entity you want to return and set the `Identifier` property for the `TypeDescriptor` that contains the `Identifier` value. In this case, however, you can simply copy the `TypeDescriptors` from the `Finder` method in the BDC Model Explorer and paste it under the `SpecificFinder` method.

One last thing you must do is set the `Read-Only` property to `True` for the `TypeDescriptor` that represents the identifier. You must do this because the `ProductID` is handled as an identity column in the database. Users cannot update the value of this field. Setting the `Read-Only` property ensures that the auto-generated forms in SharePoint reflect that the field cannot be changed. The following code shows the completed `SpecificFinder` method definition in the model.

```
<Method Name="ReadProduct">
 <Parameters>
  <Parameter Name="product" Direction="Return">
   <TypeDescriptor Name="Product"
    TypeName="ProductConnector.ProductModel.Product, ProductSystem"
    IsCollection="false">
    <TypeDescriptors>
     <TypeDescriptor Name="ProductID" IdentifierName="ProductID" IsCollection=
     "false" TypeName="System.Int32" ReadOnly="true" />
     <TypeDescriptor Name="Name" TypeName="System.String" />
     <TypeDescriptor Name="Description" TypeName="System.String" />
     <TypeDescriptor Name="Color" TypeName="System.String" />
     <TypeDescriptor Name="Number" TypeName="System.String" />
    </TypeDescriptors>
   </TypeDescriptor>
  </Parameter>
  <Parameter Name="productID" Direction="In">
   <TypeDescriptor Name="ProductID" TypeName="System.Int32"
    IdentifierEntityName="Product"
    IdentifierEntityNamespace="ProductConnector.ProductModel"
    IdentifierName="ProductID" />
  </Parameter>
 </Parameters>
 <MethodInstances>
  <MethodInstance Name="ReadProduct" Type="SpecificFinder"
   ReturnParameterName="product" ReturnTypeDescriptorPath="Product" />
 </MethodInstances>
</Method>
```

Handling Connection Information

At this point the minimum required methods are defined, and you can turn your attention to implementing them in code. As a first order of business, you must consider how to handle connection information for the external system. The simplest way to store connection information is as a property in the BDC Metadata Model. You can add custom properties to any node in the BDC Metadata Model, and connection information is typically attached to the `LobSystemInstance` node.

In the BDC Explorer you can select the `LobSystemInstance` node and then click the Custom Properties ellipsis in the Properties pane. This opens the Property Editor dialog box, where you can add a new custom property to hold the connection string. Figure 14-3 shows the custom property for the walkthrough and the BDC Metadata Model follows.

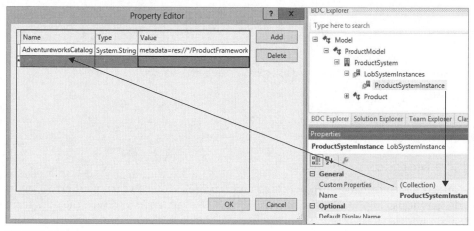

FIGURE 14-3

```
<LobSystemInstance Name="ProductSystemInstance">
 <Properties>
  <Property Name="AdventureworksCatalog" Type="System.String">
   Connection string goes here
  </Property>
 </Properties>
</LobSystemInstance>
```

After the custom property is created, the service class can be modified to support reading the connection information. You start this process by setting a reference to the `Microsoft` `.BusinessData.dll` assembly located in the `ISAPI` folder beneath the SharePoint system directory. After the reference is made, the service class must be updated to implement the `Microsoft` `.BusinessData.SystemSpecific.IContextProperty` interface.

You don't need to write any code to implement the interface because the BDC Server run time takes care of managing the properties that must be set. You can, however, now use the interface to retrieve the property previously stored in the model. The following is the interface and connection information retrieval code.

```
internal string GetConnectionInfo()
{
    INamedPropertyDictionary props =
      this.LobSystemInstance.GetProperties();
    if (props.ContainsKey("AdventureworksCatalog"))
        return props["AdventureworksCatalog"].ToString();
    else
        return string.Empty;
}
public Microsoft.BusinessData.Runtime.IExecutionContext
```

```
        ExecutionContext
{
    get;
    set;
}
public Microsoft.BusinessData.MetadataModel.ILobSystemInstance
        LobSystemInstance
{
    get;
    set;
}
public Microsoft.BusinessData.MetadataModel.IMethodInstance
        MethodInstance
{
    get;
    set;
}
```

Implementing the Methods

Now that the connection information can be stored and retrieved, you can turn your attention to implementing the methods. This is a matter of writing the necessary code to return the data from the external system, but there are two changes that must be made to the service class first.

If you examine the code that Visual Studio generates in the project, you may notice that all the methods are static. This is because the .NET Assembly Connector performs slightly better with `static` methods. However, after the `IContextProperty` interface is implemented, the class can no longer use the `static` methods. Therefore, the `static` keyword must be removed. In addition, the code generated by Visual Studio also uses `IEnumerable<T>` as the return type for the `Finder` method. If you want to open the ECT in the SharePoint Designer, however, this must be changed to `IList<T>`.

When the changes are made, the code for the methods can finally be added to the connector. After you finish and compile the code, the .NET Assembly Connector can be deployed. At this point, you can create a new external list. The following code shows the complete implementation for the methods, which uses LINQ queries against the Entity Framework layer discussed previously.

```
namespace ProductConnector.ProductModel
{
    public partial class ProductService : IContextProperty
    {
        public IList<Product> ReadProducts()
        {
            AdventureworksCatalog catalog =
              new AdventureworksCatalog(GetConnectionInfo());
            var q = from p in catalog.Products
                    orderby p.Name
                    select p;
            List<Product> products = new List<Product>();
            foreach (var i in q)
            {
                products.Add(
                    new Product()
                    {
```

```
                          ProductID = i.ProductID,
                          Name = i.Name,
                          Number = i. Number,
                          Color = i. Color,
                          Description = i.Description
                      });
            }
            return products;
        }
        public Product ReadProduct(int ProductID)
        {
            AdventureworksCatalog catalog =
              new AdventureworksCatalog(GetConnectionInfo());
            var q = from p in catalog.Products
                      where p.ProductID == ProductID
                      select p;
            if (q.Count() == 1)
            {
                return new Product()
                {
                    ProductID = q.First().ProductID,
                    Name = q.First().Name,
                    Number = q.First().Number,
                    Color = q.First().Color,
                    Description = q.First().Description
                };
            }
            else
                return null;
        }
    }
}
```

Adding Creator, Updater, and Deleter Methods

For the .NET Assembly Connector to be fully functional, it must have methods to create, update, and delete items. You can create new methods by clicking the Add a Method link in the Method Details pane. As stated previously, when you start from the Method Details pane, Visual Studio generates model elements appropriate for the method.

The Creator method takes an entity instance as input and returns a new entity instance. The input entity instance is simply a container for the new values, with the exception of Identifier, because that value is created in the external system. Each field that contains information necessary for the creation of the new item has a CreatorField property set to True. The following code shows the Creator method model definition.

```
<Method Name="CreateProduct">
 <Parameters>
  <Parameter Name="returnProduct" Direction="Return ">
   <TypeDescriptor Name="ReturnProduct"
    IsCollection="false"
    TypeName="ProductConnector.ProductModel.Product, ProductSystem">
    <TypeDescriptors>
     <TypeDescriptor Name="Color" TypeName="System.String" />
```

```
        <TypeDescriptor Name="Description" TypeName= "System.String" />
        <TypeDescriptor Name="Name" TypeName="System.String" />
        <TypeDescriptor Name="Number" TypeName="System.String" />
        <TypeDescriptor Name="ProductID" IdentifierName="ProductID"
         IsCollection="false" TypeName="System.Int32" />
      </TypeDescriptors>
     </TypeDescriptor>
    </Parameter>
    <Parameter Name="newProduct" Direction="In">
     <TypeDescriptor Name="NewProduct"
      IsCollection="false"
      TypeName="ProductConnector.Product, ProductSystem ">
      <TypeDescriptors>
       <TypeDescriptor Name="Color" TypeName="System.String"
        CreatorField= "true" />
       <TypeDescriptor Name="Description" TypeName="System.String"
        CreatorField="true" />
       <TypeDescriptor Name="Name" TypeName="System.String"
        CreatorField="true" />
       <TypeDescriptor Name="Number" TypeName="System.String"
        CreatorField="true " />
      </TypeDescriptors>
     </TypeDescriptor>
    </Parameter>
   </Parameters>
   <MethodInstances>
    <MethodInstance Name="CreateProduct" Type="Creator"
     ReturnParameterName="returnProduct "
     ReturnTypeDescriptorPath="ReturnProduct" />
   </MethodInstances>
  </Method>
```

The Updater method takes an entity instance as an input. The input entity instance is the entity
to update. Each field that contains information necessary to update the item in the external system
has an UpdaterField property set to True. The following code shows the Updater method model
definition.

```
<Method Name="UpdateProduct">
 <Parameters>
  <Parameter Name="product" Direction="In ">
   <TypeDescriptor Name="Product" IsCollection="false"
    TypeName="ProductConnector.ProductModel.Product, ProductSystem">
    <TypeDescriptors>
     <TypeDescriptor Name="Color" TypeName="System.String"
      UpdaterField="true" />
     <TypeDescriptor Name="Description" TypeName="System.String"
      UpdaterField="true" />
     <TypeDescriptor Name="Name" TypeName="System.String"
      UpdaterField="true" />
     <TypeDescriptor Name="Number" TypeName="System.String"
      UpdaterField="true" />
     <TypeDescriptor Name="ProductID" TypeName="System.Int32"
      IsCollection="false" ReadOnly="false" UpdaterField="true" />
    </TypeDescriptors>
   </TypeDescriptor>
```

```
      </Parameter>
    </Parameters>
    <MethodInstances>
     <MethodInstance Name="UpdateProduct" Type="Updater" />
    </MethodInstances>
  </Method>
```

Although it is less likely that you will want to allow end users to edit the `identifier` of an entity instance, you can provide this capability in the `Updater` method. For the `identifier` to be updated, the `Updater` method must accept a separate parameter containing the new value for the `identifier`. This parameter must have the `PreUpdaterField` property set to `True`. The following code shows the BDC Metadata Model for the parameter and the resulting function signature.

```
<Parameter Name="NewProductID" Direction="In">
 <TypeDescriptor Name="ProductID" TypeName="System.Int32"
  IsCollection="false" PreUpdaterField="true"
  IdentifierName="ProductID" />
</Parameter>

public void UpdateProduct(Product ProductIn, int NewProductID) {}
```

The `Deleter` method takes an `Identifier` as an input. The `Identifier` is the entity to delete. The following code shows the `Deleter` method model definition.

```
<Method Name="DeleteProduct ">
 <Parameters>
  <Parameter Name="productID" Direction="In">
   <TypeDescriptor Name="ProductID" TypeName="System.Int32"
    IdentifierEntityName="Product"
    IdentifierEntityNamespace="ProductConnector.ProductModel"
    IdentifierName="ProductID" />
  </Parameter>
 </Parameters>
 <MethodInstances>
  <MethodInstance Name="DeleteProduct" Type="Deleter" />
 </MethodInstances>
</Method>
```

Visual Studio offers you a list of several methods to create and even builds the correct function signature for you. The only modification you must make is to remove the `static` keyword from the signatures. Then the methods can be implemented with the following code.

```
public Product CreateProduct(Product ProductIn)
{
    AdventureworksCatalog catalog =
     new AdventureworksCatalog(GetConnectionInfo());
    AdventureworksData.Product newProduct = new AdventureworksData.Product()
    {
        Name = ProductIn.Name,
        Number = ProductIn.Number,
        Color = ProductIn.Color,
        Description = ProductIn.Description
    };
    catalog.AddToProducts(newProduct);
    catalog.SaveChanges();
    ProductIn.ProductID = newProduct.ProductID;
```

```
        return ProductIn;
    }
    public void UpdateProduct(Product ProductIn)
    {
        AdventureworksCatalog catalog =
         new AdventureworksCatalog(GetConnectionInfo());
        AdventureworksData.Product product =
         catalog.Products.First(p => p.ProductID == ProductIn.ProductID);
        product.Name = ProductIn.Name;
        product.Number = ProductIn.Number;
        product.Color = ProductIn.Color;
        product.Description = ProductIn.Description;
        catalog.SaveChanges();
    }
    public void DeleteProduct(int ProductID)
    {
        AdventureworksCatalog catalog =
         new AdventureworksCatalog(GetConnectionInfo());
        AdventureworksData.Product product =
         catalog.Products.First(p => p.ProductID == ProductID);
        catalog.DeleteObject(product);
        catalog.SaveChanges();
    }
```

Adding a StreamAccessor Method

The .NET Assembly Connector supports far more method stereotypes than SPD. Because of this support, .NET Assembly Connectors are often written solely to implement stereotypes not available in SPD. A good example of one of these additional methods is the StreamAccessor. The StreamAccessor method is used to return a stream from the .NET Assembly Connector typically associated with a file. In the walkthrough, the external system contained a photo for each product. You can use StreamAccessor to return the photo. The input parameter is the identifier and the output parameter is the stream. The following code shows the BDC Metadata Model for the StreamAccessor method definition.

```
<Method Name="ReadPhoto">
 <Parameters>
  <Parameter Name="ProductID" Direction="In">
   <TypeDescriptor Name="ProductID" TypeName="System.Int32"
    IdentifierName="ProductID" IsCollection="false" />
  </Parameter>
  <Parameter Name="Photo" Direction="Return">
   <TypeDescriptor Name="PhotoTypeDescriptor" TypeName="System.Stream" />
  </Parameter>
 </Parameters>
 <MethodInstances>
  <MethodInstance Name="ReadPhotoInstance" Type="StreamAccessor"
   ReturnParameterName="Photo"
   ReturnTypeDescriptorPath="PhotoTypeDescriptor" />
 </MethodInstances>
</Method>
```

Implementing StreamAccessor is a matter of reading the file contents and returning them as a stream. In this case, the file is kept as a BLOB in the database. The following code shows how the method is implemented in the walkthrough.

```
public Stream ReadPhoto(int ProductID)
{
    AdventureworksCatalog catalog =
     new AdventureworksCatalog(GetConnectionInfo());
    var q = from p in catalog.Products
            where p.ProductID == ProductID
            select p;
    if (q.Count() == 1)
    {
        byte[] buffer = q.First().ProductPhoto;
        return new MemoryStream(buffer);
    }
    else
        return null;
}
```

StreamAccessor methods are not supported in external lists, but they are supported in the External Data Web Parts. Of course, you can also use the BDC runtime API to call the method in your own custom code as well. Entities that expose StreamAccessor show a hyperlink in the External Data Web Part that will allow a download of the file. This hyperlink opens the DownloadExternalData .aspx page, sending a set of query string parameters to invoke the StreamAccessor method for the correct entity instance. The MIMETypeField and MIMEType properties of the MethodInstance element can be used to specify the MIME type of the ECT, which determines which application is used to open the document.

Creating Associations Among Entities

In production systems you will undoubtedly define multiple ECTs, and these ECTs will have relationships among themselves. In the walkthrough, each product was assigned to a category, so it makes sense that there should be a new ECT to represent the category, and that it should be related to the Product. To start, a new entity named Category was created, along with the Finder and SpecificFinder methods. The process of creating the new ECT is identical to the process of creating the Product entity.

In addition to the new Category entity being created, the Product entity must be updated to contain the CategoryID of the associated category. The model, entity class, and service class will all require changes to support the new CategoryID field. The changes, however, are straightforward and similar to those required by the other fields defined in the entity.

After the entities are defined, you can define an association using the Association item in the toolbox. This item works a little differently than most toolbox items. Instead of dragging and dropping the shape, you must click the shape in the toolbox. Then you can click the one (parent) entity and drag an association to the many (child) entity.

When you create the association, Visual Studio presents the Association Editor dialog box. In this dialog box, you must map each TypeDescriptor that represents the foreign key from the many (child) entity to the one (parent) entity. In the walkthrough, each of the TypeDescriptors representing the CategoryID in the Product entity was mapped to the CategoryID Identifier in the Category entity.

The Association Editor creates a one-to-many association and a reverse association by default. The one-to-many association returns all child entity instances for a given parent, and the reverse association returns the parent entity instance for a given child. In the case of the walkthrough, only the one-to-many association was retained; the reverse association was deleted.

When the Association Editor dialog box is closed, the underlying model is updated with `AssociationNavigator` methods. These methods pass in an identifier and return associated entities. In the walkthrough, `Category Identifier` was passed in, and multiple `Product` entity instances were returned. Function stubs are created in the service class for each `AssociationNavigator` method. Implementing these methods requires executing the necessary code to return the required entities. The following code shows the implementation for the walkthrough.

```
public IList<Product> CategoryToProduct(int categoryID)
{
    AdventureworksCatalog catalog =
     new AdventureworksCatalog(GetConnectionInfo());
    var q = from p in catalog.Products
            where p.CategoryID == categoryID
            orderby p.Name
            select p;
    List<Product> products = new List<Product>();
    foreach (var i in q)
    {
        products.Add(
            new Product()
            {
                ProductID = i.ProductID,
                Name = i.Name,
                Number = i.Number,
                Description = i.Description,
                Color = i.Color,
                CategoryID = i.CategoryID
            });
    }
    return products;
}
```

Understanding Nonforeign Key Relationships

Although it is common to have associations between entities through foreign keys, that is not always the case. The situation in which you're most likely to find a nonforeign key relationship is that of a many-to-many relationship. A database may be designed, for example, to keep the relationships in a separate table so that they are not directly available through a foreign key.

In addition to the `AssociationNavigator` methods, you might need to include `Associator` and `Disassociator` methods. These are intended to modify the data in the external system that manages the relationship. You can use the methods to modify the table that contains a many-to-many relationship in the database.

As a quick sidebar example, consider an external system that relates people to action items. A table named `Resources` maintains information about the people, whereas a table named `ActionItems` maintains tasks. In the system design, many tasks can be assigned to a single resource, and many resources can be assigned to a single task. Your application should show the tasks assigned to a given resource and show the resources assigned to a given task. In this case you use the Association Editor, but uncheck the Is Foreign Key Association check box. In addition, add `Associator` and `Disassociator` methods.

The `Associator` and `Disassociator` methods have two input parameters. These are the `identifiers` of the entity instances to associate or disassociate. In code you can use these values to modify the table defining the many-to-many relationship. The following code shows the BDC Metadata Model for the `Associator` method.

```
<Method Name="AssociateResourceToTask">
 <Parameters>
  <Parameter Name="resourceID" Direction="In">
   <TypeDescriptor Name="ResourceID" TypeName="System.Int32"
    IdentifierEntityName="Resource"
    IdentifierEntityNamespace="ActionItems.ActionItemsModel"
    IdentifierName="ResourceID"
    ForeignIdentifierAssociationEntityName="Resource"
    ForeignIdentifierAssociationEntityNamespace="ActionItemsModel"
    ForeignIdentifierAssociationName="AssociateResourceToTaskAssociator" />
  </Parameter>
  <Parameter Name="taskID" Direction="In">
   <TypeDescriptor Name="TaskID" TypeName="System.Int32"
    IdentifierEntityName="Task"
    IdentifierEntityNamespace="ActionItemsModel"
    IdentifierName="TaskID" />
  </Parameter>
 </Parameters>
 <MethodInstances>
  <Association Name="AssociateResourceToTaskAssociator" Type="Associator">
   <SourceEntity Name="Resource" Namespace="ActionItemsModel" />
   <DestinationEntity Name="Task" Namespace="ActionItemsModel" />
  </Association>
 </MethodInstances>
</Method>
```

Testing the Connector

When the .NET Assembly Connector is complete, you can deploy and test it. Using the connector developed in the walkthrough, you should be able to create external lists and use the External Data Web Parts. The associations between the entities should result in appropriate pickers appearing when entity instances are created or edited. As with all features created in Visual Studio 2012, you can easily debug the .NET Assembly Connector by setting breakpoints in the code and pressing F5.

Handling Runtime and Validation Errors

Handling runtime and validation errors in connectors is straightforward because unhandled errors are simply bubbled back up to the browser and displayed in the external list. The general approach is to handle any errors within the connector code when it makes sense to do so, but if the error needs to be returned to the user, a `Microsoft.BusinessData.Runtime.RuntimeException` should be thrown instead. The `RuntimeException` class has several derivations that are useful for connectors, but it is easiest to just throw a `LobBusinessErrorException`, which is the most generic derivation.

PACKAGING CONSIDERATIONS

As with all SharePoint projects, Business Data Connectivity Model projects are packaged for deployment as cabinet files with a `.wsp` extension. When projects containing BDC Metadata Models are packaged in WSP files, special attention must be given to the values set for the *feature properties*. Feature properties are set within Visual Studio 2012 and appear as `Property` elements within the `Feature.xml` file of the project. Business Data Connectivity Model projects have four key feature properties, as shown in the following code.

```xml
<?xml version="1.0" encoding="utf-8"?>
<Feature xmlns="http://schemas.microsoft.com/sharepoint/"
 Description="A .NET Assembly Connector"
 Id="bc975901-3142-4fbf-9e3c-1f124b6c890d"
 ReceiverAssembly="..."
 ReceiverClass="..."
 Scope="Farm"
 Title="My Connector">
  <Properties>
    <Property Key="MyModel"
     Value="BdcAssemblies\MyConnector.dll" />
    <Property Key="IncrementalUpdate" Value="true" />
    <Property Key="ModelFileName" Value="MyModel\MyModel.bdcm" />
    <Property Key="SiteUrl" Value="http://awserver/bcs/" />
  </Properties>
  <ElementManifests>
    <ElementFile Location="MyModel\MyModel.bdcm" />
    <ElementFile Location="BdcAssemblies\MyConnector.dll" />
  </ElementManifests>
</Feature>
```

Most of the properties in the file are set by Visual Studio and do not require any editing. However, these properties should always be verified before packaging. Renaming elements during development and the particulars of the target SharePoint environment may necessitate changes to the values.

The first property uses the name of the `LobSystem` as the Key. The `Value` references the assembly that implements the operations defined in the model. This property is set by Visual Studio and generally does not need to be changed. In some scenarios, this property may be set incorrectly if you rename `LobSystem` after creating operations in the BDC Metadata Model.

The second property is the `IncrementalUpdate` property, and it supports modifying parts of the BDC Metadata Model. This property is set by Visual Studio and also does not need to be changed.

The third property is `ModelFileName`. This property references the BDCM file that contains the model. This property is set by Visual Studio and generally does not need to be changed. In some scenarios, this property may be set incorrectly if you rename the model during development.

The fourth property is `SiteUrl`. This property is used to identify the BDC Service Application where the BDC Metadata Model should be deployed. The `SiteUrl` property is not present by default in the Business Data Connectivity Model project. When the property is not present, the deployment assumes a value for the property of `http://localhost:80`. This means that the BDC Metadata Model will be deployed to the BDC Service Application associated with the site located at `http://localhost:80`. If, however, no site exists at `http://localhost:80`, the deployment fails. In this case, you must explicitly set the `SiteUrl` value to reference a site associated with the correct BDC Service Application.

You can review and modify the Feature properties directly in Visual Studio 2012. First, select the BDC Metadata Model project item in the Solution Explorer. Second, select Feature Properties from the Properties window, which opens a dialog box. Finally, set the property values in the dialog box.

ENABLING SEARCH SUPPORT

When creating BCS solutions, you are required to define at least `Finder` and `SpecificFinder` methods to support the creation of external lists. In addition, these methods are used to support indexing and search. To enable SharePoint to search an external system through the BDC Metadata Model, you must include a `RootFinder` property in a `Finder` method instance. The following code shows how the property is used.

```
<MethodInstances>
 <MethodInstance Type="Finder" ReturnParameterName="Read List"
  Default="true" Name="Read List" DefaultDisplayName="Product Read List">
  <Properties>
   <Property Name="RootFinder" Type="System.String"></Property>
  </Properties>
 </MethodInstance>
</MethodInstances>
```

Notice that the `RootFinder` property has no value. If you include a value for this property, it is simply ignored. Sometimes you may see a value of x in the property, but this is simply a style choice. The presence of the property is enough to designate the `Finder` method as the `RootFinder`.

Although the `RootFinder` property is the only one necessary to support indexing the external system, an additional property is required to allow the ECT to be selected as a content source in the search service application (SSA). The `ShowInSearchUI` property must be present on the `LobSystemInstance` for the ECT to be selectable as a content source. The following code shows the property.

```
<LobSystemInstances>
 <LobSystemInstance Name="AWProducts">
  <Properties>
   <Property Name="AuthenticationMode" Type="System.String">
    PassThrough
   </Property>
   <Property Name="DatabaseAccessProvider" Type="System.String">
    SqlServer
   </Property>
   <Property Name="RdbConnection Data Source" Type="System.String">
    AWSERVER
   </Property>
   <Property Name="RdbConnection Initial Catalog" Type="System.String">
    AdventureworksProducts
   </Property>
   <Property Name="RdbConnection Integrated Security" Type="System.String">
    SSPI
   </Property>
   <Property Name="RdbConnection Pooling" Type="System.String">
    True
   </Property>
```

```
       <Property Name="ShowInSearchUI" Type="System.String"></Property>
      </Properties>
    </LobSystemInstance>
  </LobSystemInstances>
```

Just like the `RootFinder` property, the `ShowInSearchUI` property does not require a value. Its presence is enough to allow the ECT to appear as a content source in the Search Service Application (SSA). Again, as with the `RootFinder` property, you may occasionally see examples in which this property has a value of x.

When the `RootFinder` and `ShowInSearchUI` properties are added to the model, you can configure the ECT as a content source. Simply create a new content source in the SSA and select Line of Business Data as the type. All the ECTs with the `ShowInSearchUI` property appear next to check boxes. Check the ECT and you can immediately begin a full crawl of the external system, provided the account performing the crawl has permission to use the BDC Metadata Model and can access the external system. Figure 14-4 shows the Add Content Source page with some ECTs visible.

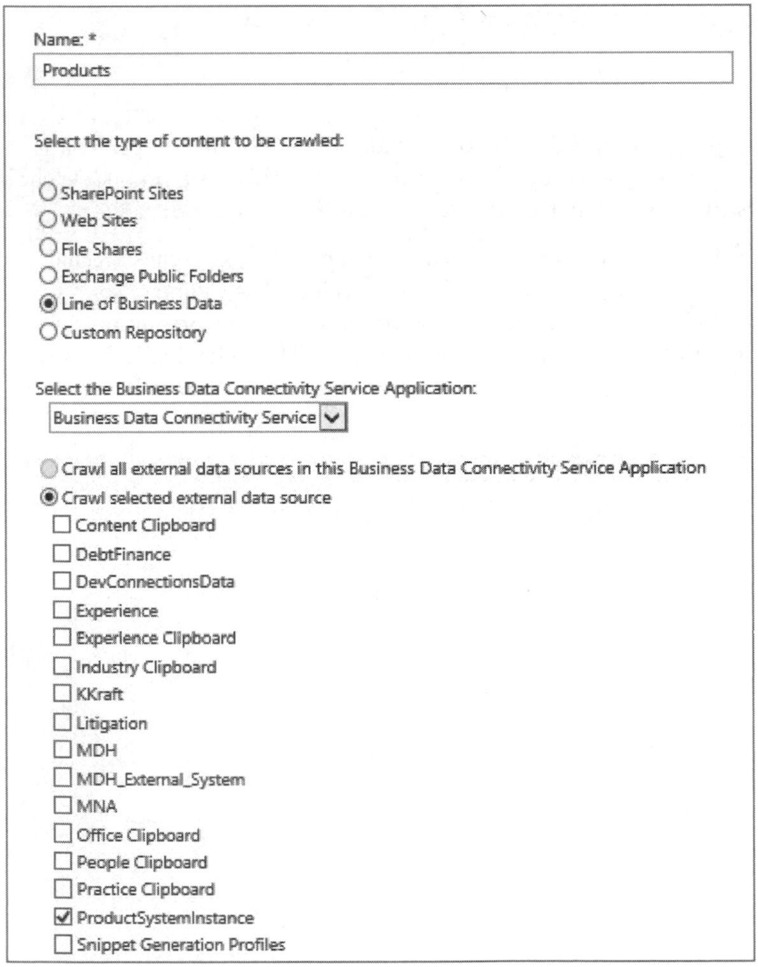

FIGURE 14-4

In addition to full crawls, BCS solutions can also support incremental crawls with the LastModifiedTimeStampField property. This property has a value that refers to a DateTime field, which indicates the last time the item was modified. If the item has not been modified since the last incremental crawl, it isn't included in the current incremental crawl. The following code shows an example of the property mapping to a field in the ECT named ChangedDateTime. This mapping specifies that the ChangedDateTime field in the external system will be used to determine whether the row of data has changed since the last crawl.

```
<MethodInstances>
 <MethodInstance Type="Finder" ReturnParameterName="Read List"
  Default="true" Name="Read List" DefaultDisplayName="Product Read List">
  <Properties>
   <Property Name="RootFinder" Type="System.String"></Property>
   <Property Name="LastModifiedTimeStampField" Type="System.String">
    ChangedDateTime
   <Property Name="UseClientCachingForSearch"
            Type="System.String"></Property>
  </Properties>
  </Property>
  </Properties>
 </MethodInstance>
</MethodInstances>
```

Along with the LastModifiedTimeStampField property, note the use of the UseClientCachingForSearch property in the Metadata Model. The presence of this property indicates that the RootFinder is capable of returning all content for an entity instance within a 30 KB data block. This tells the crawler that it does not need to make a subsequent call to the SpecificFinder method because all required data was returned from the RootFinder. Note that the cache size is fixed and works on a per-item basis, so only those items that cannot return all required data result in an additional call. If the UseClientCachingForSearch property is not present, the LastModifiedTimeStampField property must also be included under the SpecificFinder method instance because it will be called for each item crawled. It is generally a good idea to use the UseClientCachingForSearch property whenever possible because it makes crawling more efficient.

You can map the Title field in the search results by using the Title property under the Entity element in the Metadata Model. The value of the Title property refers to the name of the ECT field that should be used for the Title field. The Title field will then be used as the header for each entity instance in the search results. The following code maps the Name field of the Entity to the Title field of the search results.

```
<Entity Namespace="http://aw/bcs" Version="1.0.0.0"
 EstimatedInstanceCount="10000" Name="AWProduct"
 DefaultDisplayName="AWProduct">
 <Properties>
  <Property Name="Title" Type="System.String">Name</Property>
 </Properties>
</Entity>
```

The Author, Description, and Link fields in the search results are mapped through the AuthorField, DescriptionField, and DisplayUriField properties, respectively. The values of these properties map to fields in the ECT. The following code shows a sample.

```xml
<MethodInstances>
 <MethodInstance Name="ReadAllItems" Type="Finder"
  ReturnParameterName="documentList"
  ReturnTypeDescriptorPath="DocumentList"
  DefaultDisplayName="Read All Items" Default="true">
  <Properties>
   <Property Name="RootFinder" Type="System.String"></Property>
   <Property Name="LastModifiedTimeStampField" Type="System.String">
    Modified
   </Property>
   <Property Name="DisplayUriField" Type="System.String">
    Url
   </Property>
   <Property Name="DescriptionField" Type="System.String">
    Description
   </Property>
   <Property Name="AuthorField" Type="System.String">
    Author
   </Property>
   <Property Name="UseClientCachingForSearch"
            Type="System.String"></Property>  </Properties>
 </MethodInstance>
</MethodInstances>
```

If the `UseClientCachingForSearch` property is present, the `AuthorField`, `DescriptionField`, and `DisplayUriField` properties need be defined only beneath the `RootFinder`. If the `UseClientCachingForSearch` property is not present, these properties must also be defined under the `SpecificFinder` method instance.

WORKING WITH THE BDC SERVER RUNTIME OBJECT MODEL

The BDC Server Runtime object model is the API used to write custom solutions that run on the SharePoint 2013 server and utilize BCS artifacts. Using the object model is fairly straightforward, but it gives you significant control over how and when operations are performed. In addition, using the object model allows you to create custom user interface elements such as console applications and web parts.

The BDC Server Runtime object model is contained in the `Microsoft.SharePoint.dll` and `Microsoft.BusinessData.dll` assemblies. Both of these assemblies are located in the ISAPI directory. Any solution you create needs a reference to both of these assemblies, which contain many namespaces. The following code shows the typical `using` statements.

```
//Reference to Microsoft.SharePoint.dll
using Microsoft.SharePoint;
using Microsoft.SharePoint.Administration;
using Microsoft.SharePoint.BusinessData;
using Microsoft.SharePoint.BusinessData.Runtime;
using Microsoft.SharePoint.BusinessData.SharedService;
using Microsoft.SharePoint.BusinessData.MetadataModel;
//Reference to Microsoft.BusinessData.dll
```

```
using Microsoft.BusinessData;
using Microsoft.BusinessData.MetadataModel;
using Microsoft.BusinessData.Runtime;
using Microsoft.BusinessData.MetadataModel.Collections;
```

Connecting to the Metadata Catalog

To execute code against BCS solutions using the BDC Server Runtime, you must establish a connection to the metadata catalog where the ECTs are stored. The first step in this process is to make a connection to the BDC Service Application. You establish this connection in different ways, depending upon whether your code is running within a SharePoint context or is simply on the SharePoint server. In either case, however, you'll use the `Microsoft.SharePoint.SPServiceContext` class.

The `SPServiceContext` class enables your code to communicate with SharePoint service applications. When your code runs inside of a SharePoint context (for example, a custom web part), you can use the `Current` property to retrieve the current service context. The `GetDefaultProxy()` method may then subsequently be used to get the service proxy for any service. If your code runs outside of a SharePoint context (for example, a console application), the context must be explicitly set using a `SPSite` object. In either case, you then use the `Microsoft.SharePoint.BusinessData.SharedService.BdcServiceApplicationProxy` class to get a reference to the BDC Service Application proxy. The `GetDefaultProxy()` method of the `SPServiceContext` class returns the default service application proxy for the type specified. The `GetProxies()` method returns all available service application proxies for the type specified. The following code shows first how to get the default `BdcServiceApplicationProxy` object from within a SharePoint context and then from outside of a SharePoint context.

```
//Within SharePoint Context
BdcServiceApplicationProxy proxy =
  (BdcServiceApplicationProxy)SPServiceContext.Current.
  GetDefaultProxy(typeof(BdcServiceApplicationProxy));
//Outside SharePoint Context
using (SPSite site = new SPSite(siteCollectionUrl))
{
    BdcServiceApplicationProxy proxy =
      (BdcServiceApplicationProxy)SPServiceContext.GetContext(site).
      GetDefaultProxy(typeof(BdcServiceApplicationProxy));
}
```

In addition to using the `BdcServiceApplicationProxy` object to establish context, you can also use the `Microsoft.SharePoint.BusinessData.SharedService.BdcService` class. The `BdcService` class is an abstraction of the BDC Service Application, which is useful for determining whether a BDC Service Application is available in the farm. The following code shows how to check the availability of the BDC Service Application in a farm.

```
BdcService service = SPFarm.Local.Services.GetValue<BdcService>();
    if (service == null)
        throw new Exception("No BDC Service Application found.");
```

After you establish a context, you can connect to the metadata catalog in the BDC Service Application. The metadata catalog on the server is represented by the `Microsoft` `.SharePoint.BusinessData.MetadataModel.DatabaseBackedMetadataCatalog` class. Both the `BdcServiceApplicationProxy` object and the `BdcService` object can return a `DatabaseBackedMetadataCatalog` object. The following code shows both approaches.

```
//Using BdcServiceApplicationProxy
DatabaseBackedMetadataCatalog catalog =
   proxy.GetDatabaseBackedMetadataCatalog();
//Using BdcService
DatabaseBackedMetadataCatalog catalog =
   service.GetDatabaseBackedMetadataCatalog(
   SPServiceContext.GetContext(site));
```

Retrieving Model Elements

When you establish a connection to the metadata catalog, you can retrieve elements of the BDC Metadata Models. This includes ECTs, systems, and operations. The purpose of retrieving these items is to execute the defined method instances against the defined external system. The `DatabaseBackedMetadataCatalog` class has five methods for retrieving model elements: `GetEntity()`, `GetEntities()`, `GetLobSystem()`, `GetLobSystems()`, and `GetById()`.

Typically, your solution will start by retrieving a reference to the ECTs that represent the data you want to use. The simplest way to retrieve an ECT is to use the `GetEntity()` method passing in the name and namespace for the desired entity. The method returns a `Microsoft.BusinessData` `.MetadataModel.IEntity` interface representing the ECT, as shown in the following code.

```
IEntity ect = catalog.GetEntity("MyNamespace", "MyEntity");
```

Although the code for retrieving an ECT is simple, it is not the most efficient. Although the BDC Server Runtime object model generally interacts with cached metadata models, the `GetEntity()`, `GetEntities()`, `GetLobSystem()`, and `GetLobSystems()` methods do not. Instead, they call directly to the Metadata Catalog database, which is less efficient. The solution to this problem is to use the `GetById()` method to retrieve the ECTs and LobSystems. The `GetById()` method takes the `ID` and `type` of the element to return and executes against the cached model. The challenge in using the `GetById()` method is determining the `ID` of the wanted element. The best approach is to use the `GetEntity()` method on the first call and save the `ID` of the element for future use. The following code shows the relationship between the `GetEntity()` method and the `GetById()` method.

```
//Get Entity the easy way on first call
IEntity ect = catalog.GetEntity(entityNamespace, entityName);
//Save Entity data
uint ectId = Convert.ToUInt32(ect.Id);
Type ectType = ect.GetType();
//Get Entity the fast way on subsequent calls
ect = (IEntity)catalog.GetById(ectId, ectType);
```

Along with retrieving ECTs and LobSystems from the `DatabaseBackedMetadataCatalog` object, many objects have methods for retrieving related objects. For example, the `GetLobSystem()` method of the `IEntity` interface returns the related LobSystem for the ECT. In this way, you can retrieve whatever model elements are required for your application.

Executing Operations

The whole point of connecting to the metadata catalog and retrieving the ECT is to allow for the execution of the operations defined as method instances within the BDC Metadata Model. With full access to the operations, you can create complete custom applications. These applications can use any of the available method stereotypes, thus leaving behind any of the limitations found in the SharePoint Designer and the Business Data web parts.

The approach used to execute an operation varies slightly from stereotype to stereotype. In the case of the `Finder` methods, for example, you must first retrieve the method instance before executing. This is because a BDC Metadata Model may define multiple `Finder` methods. In the case of the `Creator`, `Updater`, and `Deleter` methods, the object model provides a more direct approach because only a single method instance of these stereotypes can exist in the model for any entity.

Along with specific support for various stereotypes, the object model also provides generic support to execute any method instance. The following code shows a console application that uses the `Execute()` method of the `IEntity` to execute a `Finder` method and display the results. This code works for any model and any `Finder` method based on the arguments passed to it.

```
static void Main(string[] args)
{
    try
    {
        if (args.Count() != 5)
            throw new Exception("Usage: ExecuteFinder.exe
                                SiteCollectionUrl,
                                LobSystemInstance,
                                EntityName,
                                EntityNamespace,
                                FinderMethodInstance");
        string siteCollectionUrl = args[0];
        string lobSystemInstance = args[1];
        string entityName = args[2];
        string entityNamespace = args[3];
        string finderMethodInstance = args[4];
        using (SPSite site = new SPSite(siteCollectionUrl))
        {
            //Connect to the BDC Service Application proxy
            BdcService service =
              SPFarm.Local.Services.GetValue<BdcService>();
            if (service == null)
                throw new Exception("No BDC Service Application found.");
            //Connect to metadata catalog
            DatabaseBackedMetadataCatalog catalog =
              service.GetDatabaseBackedMetadataCatalog(
              SPServiceContext.GetContext(site));
            //Get Entity
            IEntity ect = catalog.GetEntity(entityNamespace, entityName);
            //Get LobSystem
            ILobSystem lob = ect.GetLobSystem();
            //Get LobSystemInstance
            ILobSystemInstance lobi =
              lob.GetLobSystemInstances()[lobSystemInstance];
```

```
                    //Get Method Instance
                    IMethodInstance mi =
                        ect.GetMethodInstance(finderMethodInstance,
                                         MethodInstanceType.Finder);
                    //Execute
                    IEnumerable items = (IEnumerable)ect.Execute(mi, lobi);
                    //Display
                    foreach (Object item in items)
                    {
                        PropertyInfo[] props = item.GetType().GetProperties();
                        foreach (PropertyInfo prop in props)
                        {
                            Console.WriteLine(prop.GetValue(item, null));
                        }
                    }
                }
            }
        catch (Exception x)
        {
            Console.WriteLine(x.Message);
        }
    }
}
```

When executing methods using the generic approach provided by the `Execute()` method, you often need to pass in parameters such as when you execute a `SpecificFinder` method. In these cases, you must retrieve the required parameters from the method and set them. The following code snippet shows how to do this for a `SpecificFinder` method associated with a BDC Metadata Model that uses the SQL connector.

```
//Get Method Instance
IMethodInstance mi = ect.GetMethodInstance(specificFinderMethodInstance,
  MethodInstanceType.SpecificFinder);
//Get Parameters
IParameterCollection parameters = mi.GetMethod().GetParameters();
//Set Parameters
object[] arguments = new object[parameters.Count];
arguments[0] = entityInstanceIdentifier;
//Execute
ect.Execute(mi, lobi, ref arguments);
//Display
PropertyInfo[] props = arguments[1].GetType().GetProperties();
PropertyInfo prop = props[0];
SqlDataReader reader = (SqlDataReader)(prop.GetValue(arguments[1], null));
if (reader.HasRows)
{
    while (reader.Read())
    {
        Console.WriteLine(reader.GetString(3) + " " + reader.GetString(5));
    }
}
```

In the code, note how the arguments are passed by reference to the `Execute()` method. This is required because the `Return` parameter is placed in the array during execution. You can then read the `Return` parameter and cast it to an appropriate type for display. In the code sample, the `Return` parameter is cast to a `SqlDataReader`, which is the type returned from methods that use the SQL connector.

Although CRUD operations are certainly the most common in BCS solutions, accessing documents through streams is often a critical part of any SharePoint solution. Therefore, the `StreamAccessor` stereotype stands out as important. The `Execute()` method can be used to invoke a `StreamAccessor` method and return a stream for downloading. The following code shows a typical `StreamAccessor` method defined in a BDC Metadata Model.

```
<Method Name="ReadContents" DefaultDisplayName="Read Contents">
 <Parameters>
  <Parameter Name="id" Direction="In">
   <TypeDescriptor Name="ID" IdentifierName="ID"
    TypeName="System.Int32" IsCollection="false" />
  </Parameter>
  <Parameter Name="contents" Direction="Return">
   <TypeDescriptor Name="Contents" TypeName="System.IO.Stream" />
  </Parameter>
 </Parameters>
 <MethodInstances>
  <MethodInstance Name="ReadContents" Type="StreamAccessor"
   ReturnParameterName="contents" ReturnTypeDescriptorPath="Contents"
   DefaultDisplayName="ReadContents">
  </MethodInstance>
 </MethodInstances>
</Method>
```

The method instance returns a `System.IO.Stream` object based on a `System.Int32` value. You can use the `Execute()` method to invoke the `StreamAccessor`. The following code shows how the method instance can be invoked and the stream downloaded to the client based on query string parameters passed into an ASPX page.

```
//Connect to server-side BCS
BdcServiceApplicationProxy proxy =
  (BdcServiceApplicationProxy)SPServiceContext.
  Current.GetDefaultProxy(typeof(BdcServiceApplicationProxy));
DatabaseBackedMetadataCatalog catalog =
  proxy.GetDatabaseBackedMetadataCatalog();
IEntity ect = catalog.GetEntity("MyNamespace", "DocumentECT");
ILobSystem lob = ect.GetLobSystem();
ILobSystemInstance lobi = lob.GetLobSystemInstances()["MyDMSInstance"];
IMethodInstance mi =
  ect.GetMethodInstance("ReadContents",
                        MethodInstanceType.StreamAccessor);
//Call BCS to get stream
object[] args = { int.Parse(Request.QueryString["DocumentId"]), null };
ect.Execute(mi, lobi, ref args);
byte[] buffer = ((MemoryStream)args[1]).ToArray();
//Download
this.Page.Response.Clear();
this.Page.Response.ClearHeaders();
this.Page.Response.AddHeader("Content-Disposition",
  "attachment; filename=\"" + Request.QueryString["fileName"] + "\"");
```

```
this.Page.Response.AddHeader("Content-Length", buffer.Length.ToString());
this.Page.Response.BinaryWrite(buffer);
this.Page.Response.Flush();
this.Page.Response.End();
```

Although the `Execute()` method provides good functionality for executing any method instance, most often the application code is tailored for the specific stereotype being invoked. The following sections detail the support provided by the BDC Server Runtime object model for invoking specific method stereotypes.

Executing Finder Methods

`Finder` methods are the backbone of any custom BCS application. To invoke a `Finder` method instance, you use the `FindFiltered()` method of the `IEntity`. The `FindFiltered()` method returns entity instances from a `Finder` method using filter criteria.

If the method is the default `Finder` method, its name does not need to be provided. If the `Finder` method to execute is not the default, its name is provided as a `String` value to the `FindFiltered()` method. Be careful to use the name of the method instance as defined in the BDC Metadata Model and not the name of the method.

If the `Finder` method defines filters (such as a limit, wildcard, or page filter), these values must be provided in the call to the `FindFiltered()` method. An `IFilterCollection` can be returned by calling the `GetFilters()` method of the `IMethodInstance`. The values for the filters can then be set. The following code shows how to get the filter collection and set values.

```
IMethodInstance mi = ect.GetMethodInstance(FinderMethodInstanceName,
                                           MethodInstanceType.Finder);
IFilterCollection filters = mi.GetFilters();
(filters[0] as LimitFilter).Value = 10;
(filters[1] as PageNumberFilter).Value = 2;
(filters[3] as WildcardFilter).Value = "Bike";
(filters[4] as ComparisonFilter).Value = "CN123720";
```

In most applications, you already know which filters the method instance is expecting. In these cases, you can set the filters directly, as shown in the preceding code. If, however, you do not know which filters are expected, you can determine this dynamically by iterating through the collection of filters, as shown in the following code.

```
foreach (IFilter filter in filters)
{
    Console.WriteLine("Filter Type:        " +
      filter.FilterDescriptor.FilterType.ToString());
    Console.WriteLine("Filter Field:      " +
      filter.FilterDescriptor.FilterField);
}
```

When executing the `FindFiltered()` method, you may optionally specify an `OperationMode` for the call that allows data to be read from a cache. However, the `OperationMode` has no effect on server-side operations. The presence of the `OperationMode` is solely to maintain complementary signatures between the BDC Client and BDC Server APIs. Remember that the server never caches data — only model elements. The `OperationMode` has meaning only on the client.

The FindFiltered() method returns a Microsoft.BusinessData.Runtime
.IEntityInstanceEnumerator. The IEntityInstanceEnumerator object provides a forward-
only collection of entity instances that you can read. After reading the entity instances from the
collection, the Close() method must be called to release the resources used to access the external
system. The following code shows the basic approach.

```
//Connect to BDC Service Application
BdcService service = SPFarm.Local.Services.GetValue<BdcService>();
if (service != null)
{
//Get Metadata elements
  DatabaseBackedMetadataCatalog catalog =
    service.GetDatabaseBackedMetadataCatalog(SPServiceContext.Current);
  IEntity ect = catalog.GetEntity(EntityNamespace, EntityName);
  ILobSystem lob = ect.GetLobSystem();
  ILobSystemInstance lobi =
    lob.GetLobSystemInstances()[LobSystemInstanceName];
}
IMethodInstance mi = ect.GetMethodInstance(FinderMethodInstanceName,
                                           MethodInstanceType.Finder);
IFilterCollection filters = mi.GetFilters();
IEntityInstanceEnumerator items =
  ect.FindFiltered(filters, FinderMethodInstanceName);
while (items.MoveNext())
{
  Console.WriteLine(items.Current[FieldName].ToString());
}
items.Close();
```

In addition to enumerating entity instances, you can also return entity instances in a System.Data
.DataTable. You can use a DataTable to return entity instances by calling the CreateDataTable()
method of the Microsoft.BusinessData.Runtime.IRuntimeHelper interface. You can obtain
this interface through the Helper property of the DatabaseBackedMetadataCatalog object. The
CreateDataTable() method takes an IEntityInstanceEnumerator object and builds a DataTable
from it. The CreateDataTable() method can make it easier to work with entity instances because
the DataTable is a familiar and flexible object. In addition, the CreateDataTable() method
supports options that allow for paging through entity instances. The following code shows an
example of the CreateDataTable() method.

```
//Connect to BDC Service Application
BdcService service = SPFarm.Local.Services.GetValue<BdcService>();
if (service != null)
{
//Get Metadata elements
  DatabaseBackedMetadataCatalog catalog =
    service.GetDatabaseBackedMetadataCatalog(SPServiceContext.Current);
  IEntity ect = catalog.GetEntity(EntityNamespace, EntityName);
  ILobSystem lob = ect.GetLobSystem();
  ILobSystemInstance lobi =
    lob.GetLobSystemInstances()[LobSystemInstanceName];
}
IMethodInstance mi = ect.GetMethodInstance(FinderMethodInstanceName,
```

```
                                                    MethodInstanceType.Finder);
IFilterCollection filters = mi.GetFilters();
IEntityInstanceEnumerator items =
  ect.FindFiltered(filters, FinderMethodInstanceName);
DataTable dt = ect.Catalog.Helper.CreateDataTable(items);
```

Executing SpecificFinder Methods

To invoke a `SpecificFinder` method, you use the `FindSpecific()` method of the `IEntity` interface. The `FindSpecific()` method returns an entity `IEntityInstance` from a `SpecificFinder` method given an `Identifier`.

If the method is the default `SpecificFinder` method, its name does not need to be provided. If the `SpecificFinder` method to execute is not the default, its name is provided as a `String` value to the `FindSpecific()` method. Be careful to use the name of the method instance as defined in the BDC Metadata Model and not the name of the method.

When calling the `FindSpecific()` method, you will always provide an `Identity` object, which represents the `Identifier` for the wanted entity instance. Simply create a new `Identity` object using the appropriate value and pass the object as an argument. `Identity` objects can be created with any data type, but be aware that `string` values are case-sensitive when used as `identifiers`. The following code shows how to call the `FindSpecific()` method.

```
//Connect to BDC Service Application
BdcService service = SPFarm.Local.Services.GetValue<BdcService>();
if (service != null)
{
//Get Metadata elements
  DatabaseBackedMetadataCatalog catalog =
    service.GetDatabaseBackedMetadataCatalog(SPServiceContext.Current);
  IEntity ect = catalog.GetEntity(EntityNamespace, EntityName);
  ILobSystem lob = ect.GetLobSystem();
  ILobSystemInstance lobi =
    lob.GetLobSystemInstances()[LobSystemInstanceName];
}
//Execute SpecificFinder
int id = 5;
IMethodInstance mi =
  ect.GetMethodInstance(SpecificFinderMethodInstanceName,
                        MethodInstanceType.SpecificFinder);
IEntityInstance item =
  ect.FindSpecific(new Identity(id),
                   SpecificFinderMethodInstanceName,
                   lobi, true);
```

Executing Updater Methods

To invoke an `Updater` method, you first use the `FindSpecific()` method to return the entity to update. The value of the fields associated with the return entity may then be modified, and those modifications are committed through the `Update()` method of the `IEntityInstance` interface. The following code shows how to use the `Update()` method.

```
//Connect to BDC Service Application
BdcService service = SPFarm.Local.Services.GetValue<BdcService>();
if (service != null)
{
//Get Metadata elements
  DatabaseBackedMetadataCatalog catalog =
    service.GetDatabaseBackedMetadataCatalog(SPServiceContext.Current);
  IEntity ect = catalog.GetEntity(EntityNamespace, EntityName);
  ILobSystem lob = ect.GetLobSystem();
  ILobSystemInstance lobi =
    lob.GetLobSystemInstances()[LobSystemInstanceName];
}
//Execute SpecificFinder
int id = 5;
IMethodInstance mi =
  ect.GetMethodInstance(SpecificFinderMethodInstanceName,
                        MethodInstanceType.SpecificFinder);
IEntityInstance item =
  ect.FindSpecific(new Identity(id),
                   SpecificFinderMethodInstanceName,
                   lobi, true);
//Update entity instance
item["Title"] = "My Item";
item["Description"] = "An updated item";
item.Update();
```

Executing Creator Methods

To invoke a `Creator` method, you use the `Create()` method of the `IEntity` interface. The `Create()` method returns an `Identity` for the new entity instance.

When calling the `Create()` method, you pass the values for the new entity instance in a `Microsoft.BusinessData.Runtime.IFieldValueDictionary`. The `IFieldValueDictionary` can be created from a `Microsoft.BusinessData.MetadataModel.IView` interface. This interface represents all of the fields that are associated with a given method instance. After obtaining the `IFieldValueDictionary` object, you can either set values for the new entity instance or use the default values, as shown in the following code.

```
//Connect to BDC Service Application
BdcService service = SPFarm.Local.Services.GetValue<BdcService>();
if (service != null)
{
//Get Metadata elements
  DatabaseBackedMetadataCatalog catalog =
    service.GetDatabaseBackedMetadataCatalog(SPServiceContext.Current);
  IEntity ect = catalog.GetEntity(EntityNamespace, EntityName);
  ILobSystem lob = ect.GetLobSystem();
  ILobSystemInstance lobi =
    lob.GetLobSystemInstances()[LobSystemInstanceName];
}
//Create new entity instance with default values
IView createView = ect.GetCreatorView(CreatorMethodInstanceName);
IFieldValueDictionary fieldValueDictionary = createView.GetDefaultValues();
ect.Create(fieldValueDictionary, lobi);
```

Executing Deleter Methods

To invoke a `Deleter` method, you first use the `FindSpecific()` method to return the entity instance to delete. You can then delete the entity instance using the `Delete()` method of the `IEntityInstance` interface. The following code shows how to use the `Delete()` method.

```
//Connect to BDC Service Application
BdcService service = SPFarm.Local.Services.GetValue<BdcService>();
if (service != null)
{
//Get Metadata elements
  DatabaseBackedMetadataCatalog catalog =
    service.GetDatabaseBackedMetadataCatalog(SPServiceContext.Current);
  IEntity ect = catalog.GetEntity(EntityNamespace, EntityName);
  ILobSystem lob = ect.GetLobSystem();
  ILobSystemInstance lobi =
    lob.GetLobSystemInstances()[LobSystemInstanceName];
}
//Execute SpecificFinder
int id = 5;
IMethodInstance mi =
  ect.GetMethodInstance(SpecificFinderMethodInstanceName,
                        MethodInstanceType.SpecificFinder);
IEntityInstance item =
  ect.FindSpecific(new Identity(id),
                   SpecificFinderMethodInstanceName,
                   lobi, true);
//Delete entity instance
item.Delete();
```

USING ECTS IN SHAREPOINT APPS

Along with most of the SharePoint 2013 workloads, Business Connectivity Services has been updated to work with the app model. App support enhancements in SharePoint 2013 include support for OData sources, app-level External Content Types (ECTs), and a new client-side object model. Together, these enable you to create apps for either on-premises installation or SharePoint online.

Understanding App-Level ECTs

With SharePoint 2013, BCS supports the use of OData sources as the basis for defining an ECT. Because OData is emerging as an accepted standard for exposing data sources in the cloud, these services are an ideal source for developing BCS-based apps. When creating a SharePoint app, you can easily add an ECT based on an OData source by selecting Add ⇨ Content Types for an External Data Source from the project context menu. This action starts a wizard that will prompt you for the endpoint of the OData source. Figure 14-5 shows the wizard referring to the publicly available Northwind data source.

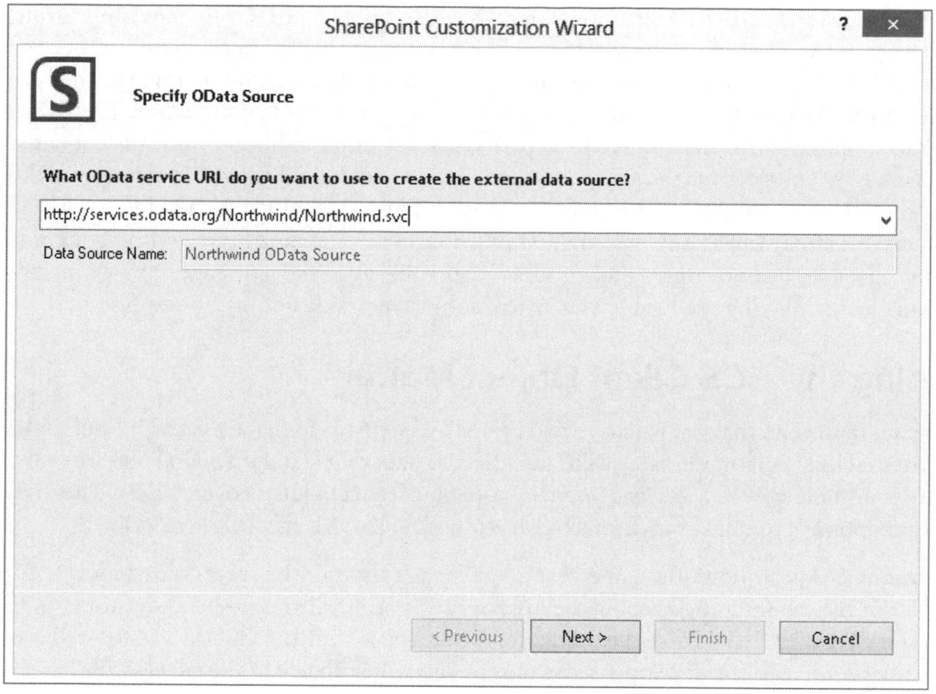

SharePoint Customization Wizard

S **Specify OData Source**

What OData service URL do you want to use to create the external data source?

http://services.odata.org/Northwind/Northwind.svc

Data Source Name: Northwind OData Source

< Previous   Next >   Finish   Cancel

FIGURE 14-5

After connecting to the source, the wizard prompts you to select from the available entities exposed by the service. All you have to do is select one or more entities and click Finish. Visual Studio then generates a BDC Metadata Model and an associated external list within your app project. The BDC Metadata Model and the external list definition are packaged and deployed with the app, which uses the model at run time to connect to the source and fill the external list. Figure 14-6 shows the basic app architecture for rendering accessing the OData source.

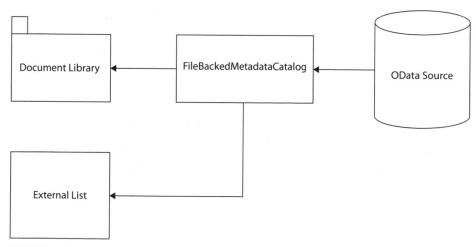

FIGURE 14-6

Under normal circumstances, BDC Metadata Models are stored in the BDC Service Application associated with the farm. Such an architecture would be unacceptable for apps, however, because apps are supposed to be isolated from the other farm elements. In the case of an app, the model is loaded in an in-memory BDC catalog known as the `FileBackedMetadataCatalog`. The BDC Metadata Model deployed with the app is stored in a special document library and subsequently loaded into the `FileBackedMetadataCatalog`. When loaded, the model is used to determine the connection to the OData source and what data to retrieve. The external list is then filled with the data in much the same way as any external list in a SharePoint farm. The only drawback is that the external list will not be immediately visible. This is because the app pages do not include a web part or code for displaying the list. This is where some client-side coding comes into play.

Understanding the BCS Client Object Model

To display the data in the external list, you have two options. The first is to make a RESTful call to the external list. External lists support the same RESTful access to data that standard SharePoint lists support. Therefore, there is nothing new to learn, and you may use standard techniques covered elsewhere in this book. The second option is to utilize the client-side object model (CSOM) through JavaScript.

CSOM access to BCS data follows the same general approach used in the server-side model discussed earlier in this chapter. By keeping the approaches similar, it should be easier for developers to learn the CSOM version. The only big difference is that the CSOM version relies on asynchronous operations, so the developer must handle several callbacks to be successful.

All of the objects necessary to work with BCS in an app are contained in the `sp.js` library found in the LAYOUTS directory. Development begins by retrieving the standard `ClientContext` object in JavaScript. When the `ClientContext` is retrieved, it may be used to access the `Web` associated with the app and then the in-memory `SP.BusinessData.AppBdcCatalog` object. When the catalog is accessed, the target `SP.BusinessData.Entity` object can be retrieved using the entity name and entity namespace, as shown in the following code.

```
var ctx = SP.ClientContext.get_current();

var ect = ctx.get_web().getAppBdcCatalog().getEntity(entityNamespace, entityName);
ctx.load(ect);
```

When the entity is retrieved, it can be used to execute the basic stereotypes associated with it. The JavaScript methods all have names that are similar to the ones found in the server-side object model, and you can see the complete definition for the methods by examining the `sp.debug.js` library found in the LAYOUTS directory. As an example, you can walk through executing the `Finder` method using the `findFiltered` method.

The `findFiltered` method requires that you provide the name of the method instance, values for any filters associated with the method instance, and the associated `SP.BusinessData`. `LobSystemInstance` object. Retrieving the associated `SP.BusinessData.LobSystemInstance` object requires a round trip, so that should be done first using the following code, which returns a `SP.BusinessData.Collections.LobSystemInstanceCollection` object.

```
var ctx = SP.ClientContext.get_current();

var ect = ctx.get_web().getAppBdcCatalog().getEntity(entityNamespace, entityName);
```

```
ctx.load(ect);

var lob = ect.getLobSystem();
ctx.load(lob);

var collection = lob.getLobSystemInstances();
ctx.load(collection);
ctx.executeQueryAsync(onLobSystemInstancesSuccess, onLobSystemInstancesError);
```

After the collection is returned, you can look through it for the associated `SP.BusinessData`
`.LobSystemInstance` object by name. Then you can retrieve and set any required filters. Finally,
you can call the `findFiltered` method, as shown in the following code.

```
var ctx = SP.ClientContext.get_current();

for (var i = 0; i < collection.get_count(); i++) {
    if (collection.get_item(i).get_name() === lobSystemInstanceName) {
        lobi = collection.get_item(i);
        break;
    }
}

var filters = ect.getFilters(methodInstanceName);
ctx.load(filters);

var results = ect.findFiltered(filters, methodInstanceName, lobi);
ctx.load(results);

ctx.executeQueryAsync(onExecuteFinderSuccess, onExecuteFinderError);
```

When the results of the operation are returned, then you can loop through them and read the
property values. Typically, you will take these values and save them into an object array for use when
displaying them in a web page. The following code shows how the resulting records can be read.

```
for (var i = 0; i < results.get_count() ; i++) {
    var entityInstance = results.get_item(i);
    var fields = entityInstance.get_fieldValues();
    var v1 = fields.ProductID;
    var v2 = fields.ProductName;
    var v3 = fields.CategoryName;
    var v4 = fields.UnitsInStock;
    var v5 = fields.ReorderLevel;
}
```

SUMMARY

Although many BCS solutions can be created with no code, there are many limitations associated
with data presentation and functionality that require custom coding to overcome. The .NET
Assembly Connector enables significant control over how external systems are accessed by
SharePoint and supports indexing of nearly any external system. As your solutions become more
complex, custom coding through the BDC Server object model can help to create professional and
efficient solutions that can scale along with your SharePoint farm. Finally, the new SharePoint 2013
app model enables the creating of apps with ECTs that utilize OData sources.

15

Workflow Development in SharePoint 2013

WHAT'S IN THIS CHAPTER?

➤ Learning about the core workflow concepts

➤ Understanding the workflow platform architecture

➤ Reviewing the key workflow development tools

➤ Modeling workflows using Visio 2013

➤ Developing workflows using SharePoint Designer 2013

➤ Developing custom declarative activity and actions using Visual Studio 2012

➤ Developing custom code activity using Visual Studio 2012

➤ Developing workflows using Visual Studio 2012

➤ Considering key development issues

Workflow systems are extremely valuable to organizations as they provide improved measurability of human performance, increased productivity, and ensure consistent execution by the individuals and groups employed and participating in the business process.

SharePoint 2013 provides in-depth support to directly host or incorporate external hosted workflows in your SharePoint environment in both cloud and on-premise scenarios. As in SharePoint 2010, SharePoint 2013 continues to provide the ability to host workflows, based on the .NET 3.5 Windows workflow run time within SharePoint 2013. In SharePoint 2013, this workflow is commonly referred to as a *SharePoint 2010 workflow*. SharePoint 2013 provides a new capability to host workflow outside of your SharePoint farm, either on-premise or using a cloud-hosted service. This is based on the .NET 4.5 Windows Azure Workflow (WAW) platform. In SharePoint 2013, this workflow is commonly referred to as a *SharePoint 2013 workflow*.

This chapter focuses on introducing the key workflow concepts to uninitiated and aspiring workflow developers and an in-depth overview of the workflow platform architecture. Next, you look at the key development tools and how they have been improved to support the WAW platform. Next, you briefly review the requirements to configure your development environment to begin developing SharePoint 2013 workflows. You look at some development scenarios that highlight the new workflow features of SharePoint 2013. You finish with a discussion on key development considerations to help you make good technical decisions to save you time and money.

INTRODUCING CORE WORKFLOW CONCEPTS

The workflow support provided by SharePoint 2013 is extensive. This support has evolved over successive releases of SharePoint technologies. As a result, it is vital to understand key workflow concepts and how they are interpreted from a SharePoint perspective.

What Is a Workflow?

Workflows, at the heart of it, model, automate, and orchestrate managed business processes by managing the series of activities and actions required to achieve the wanted final outcome or outcomes. Key categories of workflow include:

➤ *Human workflows* — Human workflows automate common processes in your organization. Common examples include document and page approval workflows. Usage of these workflows is totally dependent on human needs.

➤ *Business execution workflows* — Business execution workflows involve automating, monitoring, and improving a key business process of your organization. For example, your customer or supplier call center may receive 10,000 calls per day. Each call, after being logged and categorized, needs to follow the correct process (workflow) to completion. Bottlenecks and issues must be resolved; speed-of-ticket resolution must be monitored on a daily basis; and demand for call center staffing needs to be calculated to ensure efficient customer response times are maintained. Usage of these workflows is intrinsic and directly contributes to the success of your business.

➤ *Long-running processes* — Long-running workflows need to manage a process over a long or indeterminate period of time. A good example is a legal document that needs a quarterly or yearly review.

➤ *Connecting to external systems* — Large organizations often have a number of systems internally and a number of external organizations that they interact with. As a result workflows may need to call into these systems to send or receive information. For example, an invoice or credit note may need to be submitted to an external supplier's system, or time entry information may need to be submitted to an internal HR and billing system.

SharePoint 2013 workflows are modeled using a collection of workflow activities and actions, with defined starting and endpoints.

A key difference between workflow and other types of software is the support for long-running processes. These processes can last from seconds to months and even years. For example, a short-running process may involve a leave request or document approval, whereas a longer workflow may be responsible for managing the yearly employee review process.

Workflow Activities

Activities are the building blocks used to compose SharePoint 2013 workflows. SharePoint 2013 workflow activities, based on .NET 4.5 Windows Workflow Foundation, represent the underlying managed objects and code used to compose and drive your workflow. Each activity represents a functional component of the business process modeled by the workflow.

> **NOTE** *This section discusses* workflow activities. *These are not to be confused with* workflow actions *made available by SharePoint Designer 2013. Workflow actions are discussed in the next section.*

Figure 15-1 categorizes the key types of activities in Windows Azure Workflow.

From a SharePoint perspective, these categories can be grouped into core Windows Workflow Foundation functionality, SharePoint 2013 workflow functionality, and custom activities. The core Windows workflow categories are shown in Table 15-1. Table 15-2 lists the SharePoint workflow activity categories. Custom activities will be determined by the needs of your organization, and will provide tailored functionality to your workflow. Custom activities are discussed later in this chapter in the "Developing Custom Workflow Activities and Actions Using Visual Studio 2012" section.

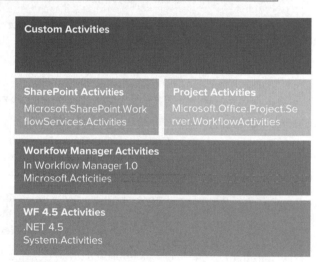

FIGURE 15-1

TABLE 15-1: Core Windows Workflow Foundation Activities in Visual Studio 2012

CATEGORY	DESCRIPTION
Control Workflow	Control Workflow designers provide activities to control the flow within your workflow. Examples include DoWhile, ForEach, If, and Parallel activities. For more information, see `http://msdn.microsoft.com/en-us/library/ee829560.aspx`.
Flowchart	Flowchart designers provide the ability to model processes. SharePoint 2013 Workflows make use of this activity to support both sequence and state machine paradigms. For more information, see `http://msdn.microsoft.com/en-us/library/ee829544.aspx`.

continues

TABLE 15-1 *(continued)*

CATEGORY	DESCRIPTION
State Machine	State machine designers are used to construct state machine activities. For more information, see `http://msdn.microsoft.com/en-us/library/hh180857.aspx`.
Messaging	Messaging activity designers provide the ability to create and configure messaging activities that send and receive Windows Communication Foundation (WCF) messages within your workflow. For more information, see `http://msdn.microsoft.com/en-us/library/ee829543.aspx`.
Runtime	Runtime activity designers are used to persist and terminate workflow activities. For more information, see `http://msdn.microsoft.com/en-us/library/ee829561.aspx`.
Primitives	Primitive activity designers are used to create and configure various activities. For more information, see `http://msdn.microsoft.com/en-us/library/ee829521.aspx`.
Transaction	Transaction activity designers are used to create and configure transactional activities such as compensate and confirm. For more information, see `http://msdn.microsoft.com/en-us/library/ee829546.aspx`.
Collection	Collection activity designers are used to create and configure activities used to manage collections. For more information, see `http://msdn.microsoft.com/en-us/library/ee829539.aspx`.
Error Handling	Error Handling activity designers are used to manage error handling in Windows Workflow Designer. For more information, see `http://msdn.microsoft.com/en-us/library/ee829550.aspx`.
Migration	The Migration activity designers are used to call workflow 3.0/3.5 activities from a workflow targeting the .NET Framework version 4. For more information, see `http://msdn.microsoft.com/en-us/library/ee839373.aspx`.
DynamicValue	Dynamic Values are a new data type. They are extremely useful because they enable you to create, store, and consume structured data in a declarative or non-programmatic way. For more information, see `http://msdn.microsoft.com/en-us/library/windowsazure/jj193505(v=azure.10).aspx`.

> **NOTE** *Visual Studio 2012 provides the core Windows Workflow Foundation activities. To get access to the SharePoint workflow activities listed, ensure you have installed the Microsoft Office Developer Tools for Visual Studio 2012. These are available via the Web Platform Installer.*

SharePoint provides a number of specific activities. Table 15-2 lists the SharePoint workflow activity categories.

TABLE 15-2: SharePoint 2013 Activities in Visual Studio 2012

CATEGORY	DESCRIPTION
Coordination Actions	Coordination actions are used to invoke workflows based on the SharePoint 2010 workflow platform.
Events	Events enable workflows to wait for an event to occur. Three events are provided as part of the SharePoint 2013 Workflow Designer including `WaitForCustomEvent`, `WaitForFieldChange`, and `WaitForItemEvent`.
List Actions	List actions group actions related to manipulation of a list and list items.
SharePoint Conditions	SharePoint Condition activities provide the ability to test for various conditions. Examples include testing whether the current item was created by a specified user, or whether the current item was created within the specified date range.
Task Actions	Task actions provide the ability to run a simple task process (`SingleTask`) or run an entire task process (`CompositeTask`). The `SingleTask` activity assigns a single task to a single person or group, and waits for the task to complete. The `CompositeTask` activity assigns multiple tasks to multiple people in series or parallel, waits for the task to complete, and calculates the aggregate outcome.
User Actions	User actions provide the ability to perform common utility-type actions relating to users and groups in SharePoint. These include validating user accounts, performing lookups to SharePoint groups and group membership, and retrieving user properties.
Utility Actions	Utility actions provide helper activities to perform common methods required by workflows. These include sending e-mail, getting the current item/list/list id/history list/ task list, and a number of other utility activities.

For more information on Workflow activity classes, see `http://msdn.microsoft.com/en-us/library/jj163790(v=office.15).aspx`.

Workflow Actions

Workflow actions wrap a set of workflow activities into a user-friendly action available to authors of workflows in SharePoint Designer 2013.

SharePoint Designer 2013 makes available a different set of workflow actions, depending on whether you opt to create a SharePoint 2010 workflow or SharePoint 2013 workflow. In addition, different actions are made available to site and list workflows.

SharePoint Designer 2013 groups these actions into the following buckets:

➤ *Core actions* — Core actions are those most commonly performed; Microsoft groups these together for easy access. Examples include Add a Comment, Log to History List, Send an Email, and Go to Stage.

➤ *Document Set actions* — SharePoint 2010 workflow provide the ability to perform actions on Document Sets. Examples include Capture a Version of the Document Set and Send Document Set to Repository.

➤ *List actions* — List actions group actions related to manipulation of list and list items. Examples include Check in Item, Copy Document, and Delete Item.

➤ *Relational actions* — SharePoint 2010 workflow provides the workflow action to Look Up Manager of a User.

➤ *Task actions* — Task actions provide the ability to invoke a workflow based on the SharePoint 2010 workflow platform from within a workflow based on SharePoint 2013 workflow platform. Examples include Assign a Task and Start a Task Process.

➤ *Utility actions* — Utility actions provide the ability to work with and manipulate strings or find the interval between dates. Examples include Trim String, Extract Substring from End of String, and Find Interval between Dates.

➤ *Coordination actions* — Coordination actions are used to invoke workflows based on the SharePoint 2010 workflow platform. Examples of these include Start a List Workflow and Start a Site Workflow.

➤ *Project actions* — Project actions support the integration of Microsoft Project. These actions are used to build workflow based on Microsoft Project.

To view a detailed list on workflow actions available in SharePoint Designer 2013, see `http://msdn.microsoft.com/en-us/library/jj164026(v=office.15).aspx`.

There are a number of scenarios in which a SharePoint 2013 workflow may need to interact with an existing (SharePoint 2010) workflow or action, or vice versa and interact with a SharePoint 2013 workflow or action from a SharePoint 2010 workflow.

To cater for interaction between the 2010 and 2013 workflows, the product teams have provided a feature called the *workflow interop bridge*. This features workflows, managed under different hosts, to communicate and leverage features from each of the hosts.

Microsoft documented the complete list of workflow actions that can be used via the workflow interop bridge. See `http://msdn.microsoft.com/en-us/library/jj163929(v=office.15).aspx`.

Workflow Forms

Forms are a key part of any SharePoint workflow because they commonly provide the main interface with which the user has to interact. As a result, forms are a pivotal aspect of any workflow development project.

Workflows use four different types of forms for associating, initiating, modifying, and providing data to a workflow. These form types apply regardless of whether the forms are the default .ASPX or InfoPath forms. The following list presents the key types of workflow forms:

➤ *Association* — Association forms enable users to associate the workflow to a site, list, library, or content type.

➤ *Initiation* — Initiation forms enable users to enter data before kicking off the workflow.

➤ *Modification* — Modification forms enable your users to alter the workflow at certain points while it is running.

➤ *Task Forms* — Task forms enable you to present custom forms to the user when they click a task.

A key difference between SharePoint 2010-based and 2013-based workflows is the support for InfoPath as the forms designer. In SharePoint 2013, Microsoft has departed from using InfoPath as the main designer of forms for SharePoint workflows. SharePoint 2013 now creates .ASPX forms instead of InfoPath forms.

You can see the forms used by a workflow by opening a workflow in SharePoint Designer and looking at the Forms section, as shown in the lower right of Figure 15-2.

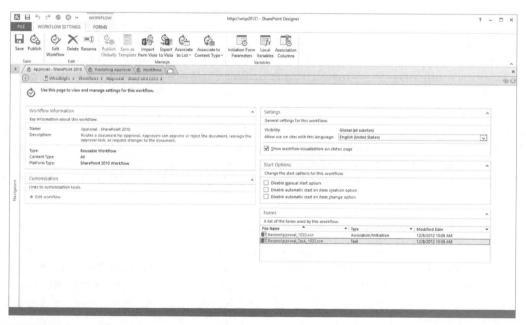

FIGURE 15-2

For SharePoint 2010-based workflows, SharePoint continues to support both .ASPX forms and InfoPath forms. When a user accesses an InfoPath form associated with a workflow, the form is rendered in an InfoPath Form web part that is hosted within an .ASPX page.

We will use the `Mandated Employee Training` scenario to explain each of these forms. The scenario relates to the common requirement to ensure employees have completed training mandated by the business. The training is web-based but is housed on various internal sites and websites, and the manager wants an automated process track and ensures his team has completed the training. The workflow will be set up against a training list. As training items are added to the list, the manager will kick off the workflow to notify the team.

Now have a look at the four different types of forms in more detail.

Workflow Association Form

The *association form* is used for initially configuring a workflow instance on a particular list, site, or content type. Association forms often capture key configuration data about the workflow behavior and its participants. Association forms are generally used only by administrators.

Using the `Mandated Employee Training` example, the workflow will require default information. In this case, the association form will be set up by administrators and may not include a lot of default data.

One key piece of information you want to capture during the setup of the workflow (against the training list) is the e-mail alias of the manager and the Human Resources team that must be notified when employees have completed the mandated training. Another key piece of information you want to capture is the name of the list containing the list of employees.

Workflow Initiation Form

The *initiation form* is used by users when they start (or initiate) a workflow. Initiation forms can be used to provide additional information on top of the default parameters defined by administrators in the association form. The association and initiation forms are often the same form but could be different in scenarios in which unique data is required to initiate the workflow, and the use of default values (from an association form) is not suitable.

Using the `Mandated Employee Training` example, the manager would add a new training item to the list. When the manager is ready, he would kick off the workflow. At this point, it is possible to display a workflow initiation form. In this case, the initiation form would typically be the form that the manager uses to provide the workflow with specific settings for this workflow. This may be the reminder date, completion date, and how many times to notify the user.

Workflow Modification Form

The *modification form* is used to alter workflows that are already running and executing. For example, an administrator may need to manually reassign tasks from one user to another user. Another example is where initiation and association variables, entered early on, need to be updated. For example, an e-mail address of the `Mandated Employee Training` example may need to be updated for existing workflows.

Workflow Task Form

The *task form* is used to collect data from users by assigning workflow tasks to the user. When the user opens the task, he will be shown the task form, which may have any number of fields, conditional formatting, and all the other features of your workflow task form.

> **NOTE** *Workflow tasks are a core part of SharePoint workflow and are explained in detail in the "Workflow Tasks" section.*

In the `Mandated Employee Training` example, the workflow task form would be used to assign a task for each employee. When employees open the task, it would show them the relevant training material, such as the link to the training and when the training must be completed.

Workflow Tasks

Tasks are a core part of SharePoint workflow. They are commonly used to progress the workflow, receive input, and collect information during steps requiring input from participants of the workflow. Tasks, by default, are stored in a list called Workflow Tasks.

By default, SharePoint 2013 workflow tasks lists implement the content type called *workflow tasks* (SharePoint 2013). The Workflow Tasks (SharePoint 2013) Content Type inherits the Task Content Type. The key difference between these is a new SharePoint 2013 column called Task Outcome, based on a new field data type called Outcome Choice.

If the defaults are accepted when associating (setting up) workflows, all workflows in a site collection use the same workflow tasks list to store tasks. For high-volume sites, this list could get large quickly.

> **NOTE** *For SharePoint workflows, the default workflow tasks list template ID is 171.*

Although the support for large lists has been improved in SharePoint 2010 and 2013, it is still a best practice to minimize list sizes where possible. On this basis, it is recommended that high-volume workflows are configured with their own dedicated Workflow Tasks list.

The next section looks at the Workflow History list. The Workflow History list is the primary audit trail for workflow activity.

Workflow History

When associating (setting up) a workflow, the administrator will be asked for a *Workflow History list*. This is a special type of SharePoint list that is used to store data about the workflow and the route that a workflow has taken. By default, the Workflow History list is hidden to users of the site.

It is part of the workflow design process to establish when and how the Workflow History list is used. The Workflow History list is intended as a human-readable audit of what has occurred during the workflow and is important if data collected in the workflow is needed for compliance or record management.

Typically, workflows will log to the history list at each activity point at the start and end of the workflow. However, remember that the workflow is intended to be read by humans, so it is important to ensure that any history list submissions are readable and relevant to any users who might be looking at the history.

The act of writing to the workflow history list is a built-in SharePoint activity that is available in both SharePoint Designer and Visual Studio workflows. The activity allows you to pull in data from the workflow and gives you a good level of control on how the history list entry is displayed and laid out.

> **WARNING** *Workflow histories automatically get removed from the SharePoint user interface 60 days after the workflow ends. If you need easy access to the history of a closed workflow, you should store the data elsewhere as part of the workflow.*

The next section delves into the various workflow flow control options and best practices for deciding which one to use.

Workflow Flow Control Templates

SharePoint 2013 supports three flow control templates, namely flowchart, sequence, and state machine. When using the SharePoint 2010 .NET 3.5 workflow host in SharePoint 2013, the sequential and state machine templates are available to develop workflows.

When using the Windows Azure Workflow host (based on .NET 4.5) in SharePoint 2013, Microsoft no longer provides a dedicated SharePoint workflow template for sequence and state machine workflows. The reason is that you can use all three flow control templates by selecting the required workflow activity from the Visual Studio 2012 toolbox. As a result, SharePoint 2013 workflows support the following flow control templates:

> ➤ *Flowchart workflow* — Flowchart workflows, based on the `FlowChart` activity, is an activity in Windows Workflow 4. Flowcharts provide the simplicity of sequence plus the ability of looping back to a previous point of execution (state machine).

> ➤ *Sequential workflow* — Sequential workflows, based on the `sequence` activity, executes a set of contained activities in a sequential order. Procedural constructs such as `ForEach`, `If`, `Switch`, `DoWhile`, and `While`; or parallel constructs such as `Parallel` and `ParallelForEach` to model parallel execution logic; any activities provided in Windows Workflow activity palette; or any third-party or custom activity can be included.

> ➤ *State machine workflow* — State Machine workflows, based on the `StateMachine` activity, enable workflows to be developed based on state transitions, as opposed to predictable, predefined paths followed by sequential workflows.

Workflow development *still* requires a good understanding of the sequential and state machine *paradigm*. It is one of the important early design decisions that will affect your workflow and development process. The flowchart workflow template caters to both the state machine and sequential workflow paradigms. Now you will look at the sequential and state machine paradigms in more detail.

Sequential Workflow Paradigm

Sequential workflows are perhaps the easiest to understand because they are what someone may intuitively understand workflows to be. Sequential workflows have a starting point and an ending point, with various defined sequential paths between the two. Each path through the workflow is constituted from a series of workflow activities (things such as "send an e-mail," "collect data from user," "update list item," "run some code," and so on). The outcome of an activity will determine the next path the workflow takes toward the endpoint. Figure 15-3 shows an example of the sequential workflow paradigm.

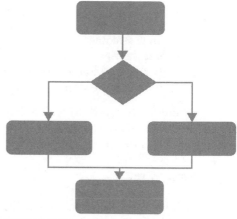

FIGURE 15-3

The main point to remember with sequential workflows are that the paths are predefined and sequential — that is, the workflow follows a defined set of activities until it reaches an endpoint. Sequential workflow does not necessarily mean linear. The use of conditional logic, branching, and so on, means that there can be multiple paths through a sequential workflow, and the outcome of activities can change the path. However, the key point is that the paths are always predefined by the workflow designer.

A good example of a sequential workflow is the `Approve Expenses` example. The starting point is that a user submits his expense report, and the ending point is that the expenses are approved or rejected by his manager and logged in the system. There may be several predefined paths and sets of activities between the start and endpoints.

State Machine Workflow Paradigm

A *state machine workflow* does not follow a predefined path but simply moves between a set of states. These workflows are event-driven in that the outcome of a given event may change the state of the workflow. Although state machine workflows do have a starting and ending state, the path between these two cannot be predetermined and is driven by the workflow. State machine workflows are generally well-suited to long-running workflows where the process may stay in a particular state for a long period of time. Figure 15-4 shows an example of the state-machine workflow paradigm.

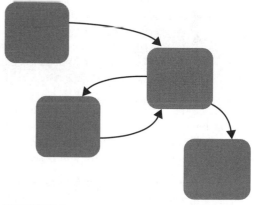

FIGURE 15-4

A state machine workflow is ideal if the process must go backward and forward between states, rather than following a sequential path. A great example of a state machine workflow is a support call that may get logged with your IT support organization. The call may have several states and may transition between them several times before the call reaches the closed state.

For example, the end user may log the call, whereby at this point it may be in the "unassigned" state. A support engineer may pick up the call from the queue and assign it to himself, at which point the state becomes "with support worker." The support worker may contact the end user and request some data, where the state may change again to "awaiting data from end user." The end user may supply this data and the state would change back to "with support worker." The process may go on and on with the states constantly changing until the call is closed off.

This kind of process is difficult to implement as a sequential workflow because the path between the start and end of the workflow is undetermined and, therefore, cannot be predefined as part of a sequential set of activities.

Workflow Scopes

SharePoint 2013, as in SharePoint 2010, enables you to bind your workflow to specific SharePoint scopes. SharePoint 2013 provides two workflow execution hosts, and the choice of host affects the out-of-the-box options available to "scope" your workflow.

When using the SharePoint 2010-based workflows engine in SharePoint 2013, you can associate and bind your workflow to sites, lists, and content types.

When using the SharePoint 2013 workflow engine in SharePoint 2013, site (`SPSite`) and list (`SPList`) scoped workflows are supported. It is worth noting that the scopes are essentially a set of subscription rules stored in the Windows Azure publication/subscription service responsible for processing incoming messages to ensure they are consumed by the associated workflow instances.

> **NOTE** *SharePoint 2013 Azure-based workflows do not support workflows associated to content types* (`SPContentType`). *As described in MSDN documentation, the messaging infrastructure makes it extensible and can be configured to support other scopes. See the "Workflow associations and association scope" section at* `http://msdn.microsoft.com/en-us/library/jj163181.aspx`.

The beauty of both workflow engines in SharePoint 2013 is that they both support site-based and list-based workflows. Site workflows are extremely valuable tools because they cater to so many scenarios that cannot be accomplished using list-based and item-based workflows. The following list describes key use cases for site-based workflows:

➤ *Site reporting workflows* — A report, summarizing key information, can be e-mailed on a regular basis for a site.

➤ *Site governance workflows* — Site preparation workflows could be used to guide users through a set of steps to automate the configuration of their site. Site disposition workflows could be created to guide site owners through common administrative tasks to manage the disposal of their site in accordance with the governance principles of your organization's SharePoint 2013 platform. Other examples include requesting additional storage, by increasing the site collection quota through a managed workflow rather than having to rely on a manual change request to your SharePoint support team.

➤ *Working on multiple items in one or more lists* — A workflow can be created to perform actions on one or more lists and one or more items in each of those lists.

➤ *Performing actions on a periodic basis* — The new support for stages, transitions, and "pause/delay until" functionality makes it possible to perform a set of actions on your site on a timer. For example, you can create a site workflow that fetches the latest stock information on a daily basis and update a list containing stock prices.

List-based workflows are the most common type of workflow used in SharePoint, and a number of workflows are provided out of the box. This type of workflow scope is fantastic for managing processes relating to individual list items. The most common example is using workflow to manage approval or a document or page.

Workflow Associations and Subscriptions

SharePoint 2013 provides a number of methods to associate workflows to libraries, lists, content types, and sites. Workflows can be associated and started either manually or automatically. This is achieved using the SharePoint website interface, using SharePoint Designer, or programmatically using Visual Studio 2012. This applies to both workflows hosted in either the SharePoint 2010 workflow engine or the SharePoint 2013 Azure-based workflow engine.

From a programmatic and object model perspective, workflows can be associated (and subscribed to) using the `Microsoft.SharePoint.Workflow` namespace.

The `SPWorkflowAssociation` class enables developers to add, configure, and remove workflow associations.

> **NOTE** *A number of methods for associating workflows were deprecated in SharePoint 2010. In SharePoint 2013 they are now marked as obsolete. These include* `SPList.AddWorkflowAssociation` *and* `SPContentType.AddWorkflowAssociation`. *Use the* `WorkflowAssociations.Add()` *methods instead.*

The `SPWorkflowManager` provides functionality to centrally control the running instances of workflows across your site collection through the object model. It provides methods to start, run, or cancel workflows; return all the workflows running on a specific item; and perform other workflow administration operations.

SharePoint 2013 workflows differ in that workflows are hosted outside of the SharePoint platform using the Azure Workflow Host. Table 15-3 describes how workflows are associated to SharePoint 2013 workflows.

TABLE 15-3: Workflow Associations for SharePoint 2013 Workflows

Manual workflows	Manual workflows are started when the PubSub service receives a `StartWorkflow` message containing the following information: ➤ Association identifier ➤ ID of the originating item context and Event Source property received during a `PublishEvent` method call ➤ Event Type for a manual start (`WorkflowStart`) ➤ Additional workflow initiation parameters, either from the subscription or initiation form, using the `CorrelationID` for the subscription and the `WFInstanceID` for the Initiation form
Auto-start workflows	Automatically started workflows are initiated using the Add message to the PubSub service. The message contains the following information: ➤ ID of the originating item context ➤ The event itself is a normal SharePoint `Add` event ➤ The workflow initiation parameters

The "other side" to workflow execution is how workflows execute based on events that are being broadcasted to the Windows Azure Workflow engine, and how specific running workflows can selectively receive and act on these events.

This "side" of the workflow puzzle defines how running workflows subscribe to and listen for specific events. In Windows workflow terminology, these are known as workflow subscriptions. SharePoint 2013 workflows must create subscriptions on the Windows Azure Service Bus using `create` and `delete` methods.

The `create` method, which is used to create the subscription, provides the ability to pass in a number of initialization and subscription parameters, including:

➤ Optional and required parameters that are defined by the workflow author

➤ Initialization parameters of the workflow definition

➤ Specific SharePoint options, either an `SPWeb` or `SPList` object, as part of one of the required parameters.

Luckily, this is simplified for SharePoint developers, as the SharePoint object model takes care of the "plumbing" between SharePoint 2013 and the Azure Workflow engine.

Workflow Event Listeners

SharePoint 2013, as in previous versions, makes it possible for your workflow to listen for events occurring in SharePoint and use these events to perform activities or actions. Table 15-4 describes the out-of-the-box workflow activities and actions provided by SharePoint.

TABLE 15-4: Out-of-the-Box Workflow Event Listeners

SHAREPOINT DESIGNER ACTION	WORKFLOW ACTIVITY	DESCRIPTION
Wait for an event in the list item	`WaitForItemEvent`	Waits for a new item to be created, or alternatively a change to be made to an existing item
Wait for a field change in the current item	`WaitForFieldChange`	Waits for a specified field to change to a specified value on the specified list item
(No corresponding event)	`WaitForCustomEvent`	Waits for a custom event to be sent in to the workflow
Wait for a project event		Waits for a project to be checked-in, committed, or submitted
Assign a task	`SingleTask`	Assigns a single task to a single person or a group and waits for the task to complete
Start a task process	`CompositeTask`	Assigns multiple tasks to multiple people in a series or parallel; waits for the task to complete and aggregates the outcome

SharePoint provides extensive support for initiating and triggering workflows using the extensive event receiver support baked into the SharePoint 2013 platform. This includes support for handling events received from the new apps for a SharePoint model as well as handling and responding to events in the classic on-premise model. Finally, SharePoint 2013 provides new functionality to support remote event receivers. These can be used to trigger workflow in one SharePoint environment based on events occurring in another environment.

Workflow Visualization

Visio 2013 and SharePoint Designer 2013 can be used to model and visualize workflows. These can then be exported to SharePoint Designer for implementation. SharePoint Designer 2013 now integrates the Visio design surface as an additional view to the text-based view.

SharePoint 2013 provides support for visualizing the stage and progress of workflows developed using the SharePoint 2010 workflow engine. This is made possible by the Visio Service Application within SharePoint 2013.

> **NOTE** *At this point in time, only workflows built using the SharePoint 2010 engine can be visualized directly in the site. The sheer number of updates required to support .NET 4.0 means that 2013 workflow visualization doesn't exist. It is hoped that support for visualizing SharePoint 2013 workflows will be released in a future upgrade.*

The Visio Service Application enables Visio diagrams to be rendered and viewed in a web browser. By default, the diagram is shown in the workflow properties screen.

> **NOTE** *All of the workflows that ship with SharePoint have Visio diagrams associated with them, so look at a default workflow to see this feature in action.*

Workflow Authorization

SharePoint workflows need to run in the context of an identity.

For SharePoint 2010-based workflows, they can run either in the context of the workflow initiator or as the publisher of the workflow. SharePoint Designer 2013 continues to provide the impersonation step action. This enables the workflow to run under the publisher of the workflow (as opposed to the user using the workflow). Using Visual Studio 2012, custom-developed SharePoint 2010 workflows can elevate privileges to run under the application pool account of the web application hosting the site collection.

For SharePoint 2013-based workflows, SharePoint 2013 workflows now support server-to-server authentication and app authentication through the implementation and extension of Open Authorization 2.0 (OAuth 2.0) web authorization protocol.

What this essentially gives you is the ability to run the SharePoint 2013 workflow under an identity, more commonly referred to as the App Principal or App Identity. As shown in Figure 15-5, this requires the site collection feature to be activated to support workflows running under an application identity.

FIGURE 15-5

Figure 15-6 shows how you can view the permissions that have been granted to apps in your site collection.

FIGURE 15-6

The next section provides an overview of the workflow platform architecture in SharePoint 2013.

UNDERSTANDING THE WORKFLOW PLATFORM ARCHITECTURE IN SHAREPOINT 2013

One of the biggest areas to evolve in SharePoint 2013 is the workflow platform architecture in SharePoint 2013, and a number of challenges were overcome successfully to provide support for both SharePoint 2010-based and 2013-based workflows in the same farm.

As a result, the SharePoint 2010 workflow host (based on the .NET 3.5 Windows Workflow Foundation) is continued in SharePoint 2013. SharePoint 2013 workflows, powered by Windows Workflow Foundation 4, provide the ability to host Windows Azure-based workflows external to the SharePoint farm and either on-premise or in a cloud-hosted environment.

As shown in Figure 15-7, look at the key components of the workflow platform in SharePoint 2013.

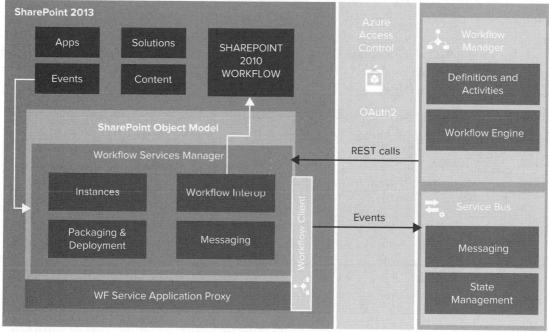

FIGURE 15-7

As you can see, SharePoint 2013 integrates the Workflow Services Manager into the heart of SharePoint 2013. Following is a list of the key components of the SharePoint 2013 workflow platform:

➤ *SharePoint 2010 workflow host* — The SharePoint 2010 workflow host is provided in SharePoint 2013 to support workflows developed using the SharePoint 2010 workflow model. The workflow host is based on the .NET 3.5 Windows Workflow run time.

➤ *Workflow Services Manager* — The Workflow Services Manager is a collective name given to the collection of additions to the SharePoint workflow object model. These additions provide support for SharePoint 2013 workflows. For example, it includes features to manage workflow instances, packaging, and deployment of workflow definitions of workflows hosted in Windows Azure Workflow. One of the key features provided is interoperability and messaging between workflows developed using the SharePoint 2010 and 2013 model.

Workflow Manager — The Workflow Manager, provided by Windows Azure, is a multitenant host for running and managing Windows Workflow Foundation workflows, supporting high-scale and high-density execution. The client essentially provides the ability to manage workflow definitions and host execution processes for workflow instances. The Workflow Manager can either be consumed from a cloud-hosted service (such as Windows Azure) or installed and used on-premise. For more information on the Workflow Manager, see `http://msdn.microsoft.com/en-us/library/jj193471(v=azure.10).aspx`.

➤ *Service bus* — The service bus, a key component of the Windows Azure platform, is the messaging infrastructure that manages the exchange messages between applications.

➤ *Azure Access Control* — Azure Access Control is a service that provides support for authenticating and authorizing users and system accounts via various protocols. From a workflow perspective, Azure Access Control mediates server-to-server authentication using Open Authorization (OAuth2).

> **NOTE** *As in SharePoint 2010, the SharePoint 2010 workflow engine is installed automatically with SharePoint 2013. The SharePoint 2013 workflow platform becomes available to you, and your tools, only after you have downloaded and installed the Workflow Manager Service and have configured it to communicate with your SharePoint 2013 farm.*

Another key challenge that was solved was how to ensure legacy SharePoint 2010 workflows (and activities) would interoperate and play nicely with workflows (and activities) based on the new Azure workflow model. This challenge was solved with the introduction of SharePoint workflow interop. TechNet provides an in-depth article explaining workflow interop. See `http://msdn.microsoft.com/en-us/library/jj670125(v=office.15).aspx`.

The next section provides an overview of the key development tools that will be used to model, author, and develop workflows, activities, and actions.

UNDERSTANDING KEY WORKFLOW DEVELOPMENT TOOLS

SharePoint offers a variety of tools that you can use to model and develop workflows. Microsoft provides three key tools to cover workflow modeling, configuration, and development.

➤ *Visio Professional 2013* — As with Visio 2010, you can create and model SharePoint workflows in Visio 2013. Visio 2013 supports both SharePoint 2010 and 2013 workflows. The

Visio file can then be exported to SharePoint Designer 2010 to be fully implemented and deployed. Visio is a fantastic tool that enables business analysts to create the workflow and hand the modeled process to the designer/developer to complete and implement in SharePoint.

➤ *SharePoint Designer 2013* — You can use SharePoint Designer 2013 to create simple, site collection-scoped, declarative (no-code) workflows. You can also build custom actions that can be used in SharePoint Designer.

➤ *Visual Studio 2012* — You can use Visual Studio 2012 to write more advanced workflows, using either the SharePoint 2010 or 2013 workflow templates. These workflows can be made available to multiple site collections and are widely accessible throughout the farm.

Now look at each of these tools in more detail.

Visio Professional 2013

Start the discussion with Visio because this tool is the most common starting point for business analysts and end users.

Visio 2013 is the go-to tool for drawing professional diagrams and is especially suitable for drawing business processes. As with the Visio 2010 application, the Visio 2013 application provides in-depth support for modeling SharePoint workflows. Additionally, these models can be used as a starting point for creating fully operational workflows in SharePoint Designer and Visual Studio 2012.

The user experience is almost the same as any other Visio diagram; the only difference is that the user must start the drawing from the Microsoft SharePoint workflow template (New ➪ Flowchart) and use either the SharePoint 2010 workflow or SharePoint 2013 workflow stencils when drawing the process. See Figure 15-8.

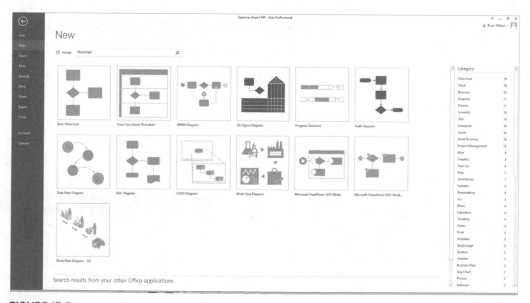

FIGURE 15-8

> **NOTE** *Visio 2010 used to export workflows to a file with the* .VWI *file extension. Visio 2013 now supports a new file format and shiny new* .VSDX *extension. These files can be opened in either Visio or SharePoint Designer 2013. It is still possible to import your legacy* .VWI *SharePoint 2010 workflows.*

What is great about the integration between Visio 2013 and SharePoint Designer is that it is two-way. This means that designers can export workflows back to Visio for the analysts to make changes to the process, and then "round-trip" back to SharePoint Designer for further updates.

Visio 2013 provides fantastic new support for SharePoint 2013 workflows. After you create a SharePoint 2013 workflow, it now starts with an empty container, called a *stage*, instead of a blank canvas. As shown in Figure 15-9, each stage contains all of the actions for each section of the workflow. Although simple workflows may have only one stage, more complex workflows may contain multiple stages.

FIGURE 15-9

SharePoint Designer 2013

SharePoint Designer 2013 is the tool of choice to undertake no-code customization across the whole range of SharePoint capabilities, including designing, deploying, and configuring workflows targeting the SharePoint 2010 and 2013 workflow engines. SharePoint Designer 2013 includes new functionality designed specifically for Windows Azure Workflow Manager and SharePoint 2013 workflows.

Both SharePoint 2010 and 2013 workflows created in SharePoint Designer are known as declarative workflows. *Declarative workflows* is the term used to describe no-code workflows in SharePoint and are essentially a set of rules that declare to SharePoint (and the underlying workflow host) how the workflow will function.

As shown in Figure 15-10, when you create a new workflow in SharePoint Designer 2013, you have the option to select the workflow platform (using the Platform Type choices) in the new workflow creation dialog. This has the effect of selecting what workflow hosting platform will be used and the type of workflow functionality available to build the workflow.

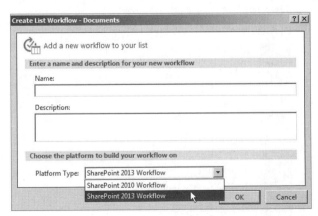

FIGURE 15-10

Designers can design workflows using all of the actions that are installed on the SharePoint server to which they are attached (including custom actions). When complete, the workflow can be published to your SharePoint site.

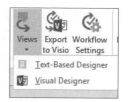

As shown in Figure 15-11, a new Visual Designer view is available within SharePoint Designer.

This view provides an alternative experience to the text-based view and enables the same modeling experience of Visio directly within SharePoint Designer.

Views
Export to Visio
Workflow Settings
Text-Based Designer
Visual Designer

FIGURE 15-11

> **NOTE** *Visio 2013 must be installed for the Visual Designer in SharePoint Designer 2013 view to be available.*

SharePoint provides a number of new actions that can be used in your workflows. Examples of these include the ability to call out to web services within your workflows, new actions for creating simple and complex task processes, and new coordination actions that provide interoperability between the SharePoint 2010 and SharePoint 2013 workflow platforms.

One of the biggest new additions in SharePoint Designer is new support for stages, loops, steps, and parallel blocks. To help understand these four new shapes, Figure 15-12 shows how these can be used to configure your workflow.

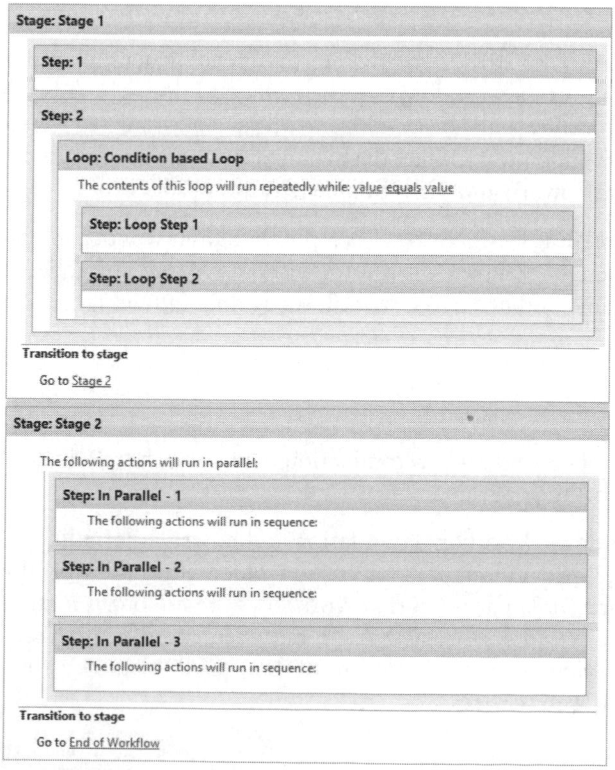

Stage: Stage 1
Step: 1
Step: 2
Loop: Condition based Loop
The contents of this loop will run repeatedly while: value equals value
Step: Loop Step 1
Step: Loop Step 2
Transition to stage
Go to Stage 2
Stage: Stage 2
The following actions will run in parallel:
Step: In Parallel - 1
The following actions will run in sequence:
Step: In Parallel - 2
The following actions will run in sequence:
Step: In Parallel - 3
The following actions will run in sequence:
Transition to stage
Go to End of Workflow

FIGURE 15-12

Following is an overview of each of these shapes:

➤ *Stage* shapes can contain any number of shapes. Stages support one path in and one path out. Most important about stages is that they support transitions to other stage shapes, or alternatively to the end of the workflow.

➤ *Steps* are different from stages in that they occur sequentially. Steps must be contained by a stage. As with a stage shape, a step shape must also define the paths in and out of the shape.

➤ *Loops* are a series of connected shapes that execute in a loop for a defined number of times or until a condition is met. Loop shapes can contain step shapes but cannot contain stage shapes.

➤ *Parallel blocks* support the execution of multiple actions at the workflow at the same time. Furthermore, parallel blocks support parallel executions of containers that host actions, including step and loop shapes. Parallel block shapes must be hosted by a stage container.

Another key enhancement is the new dictionary variable type supported by SharePoint 2013 workflows. This data type acts as a container to hold collections of variables. Working with dictionaries is supported by three new SharePoint Designer actions called Build Dictionary, Count Items in a Dictionary, and Get an Item from a Dictionary. For more information, see `http://msdn.micro soft.com/en-us/library/jj554504.aspx`.

As mentioned earlier, SharePoint Designer makes it possible to import 2010 and 2013 workflows modeled in Visio 2013. Updates can be made to the workflow, and if required, can be re-exported into Visio for further modeling.

It must be noted that although SharePoint Designer 2013 is greatly improved, deployment limitations still exist. Key examples include where an important workflow must be configured for hundreds of site collections, sites, and libraries, or when a workflow must be available to all site collections in a farm. In these cases Visual Studio is a much better option to facilitate the deployment and configuration using the solution packaging, and feature framework and activation/deactivation processes.

Despite these deployment limitations, SharePoint Designer 2013 is a powerful and wonderful tool that enables the development and deployment of complex workflows without writing any code, and hits the sweet spot when modeling, authoring, and deploying workflows against individual sites, libraries, and lists.

Visual Studio 2012

Visual Studio 2012 offers the highest level of control and customization over your SharePoint workflows and supports both 2010 and 2013 workflow development.

SharePoint 2013 workflows, based on Windows Workflow Foundation and hosted externally in the Windows Azure workflow engine, no longer provide support for custom code within the workflow. SharePoint 2013 workflows are now declarative in nature in that workflows are no longer made up of code compiled as assemblies. Instead they are described as XAML and then executed interpretively at run time. This has the effect of moving all custom code out of the workflow into custom activities (and custom actions) and external web services.

There are a number of scenarios that can be achieved only using Visual Studio 2012. These include automating the deployment of workflows and related lists required for sites in your SharePoint environment through the use of the SharePoint Feature framework.

Another key scenario is the support for workflow in SharePoint apps. Workflow can be used in all types of SharePoint apps to host middle-tier logic for managing long-running business logic.

Another key consideration for developing workflows using Visual Studio is when your workflow requires custom initiation, association, modification, or task forms. In these cases, form generation no longer uses InfoPath forms but instead relies on ASP.NET forms.

The workflow and SharePoint tooling in Visual Studio 2012 treats SharePoint 2010 and 2013 workflows as normal SharePoint project items that can be easily added to a solution, packaged, and deployed as part of a .wsp file, just like every other item in a SharePoint Visual Studio solution.

Reusable workflows that have been built in SharePoint Designer 2013 can be exported as a .wsp file and imported into Visual Studio 2012 for further customization.

> **WARNING** *When a workflow has been imported from SharePoint Designer to Visual Studio, it then must remain as a Visual Studio workflow. The integration is not two-way in the same way that it is between Visio and SharePoint Designer.*

Now that you looked at the various tools for creating workflow, look at getting your development environment set up to develop Azure workflows.

SETTING UP THE DEVELOPMENT PREREQUISITES

There are a number of prerequisite steps to complete before you can start creating SharePoint 2013-based workflows using SharePoint Designer and Visual Studio 2012. This section covers the high-level steps required to configure your environment.

Creating Your Workflow and SharePoint Development Environment

If you have not already done so, you must install and configure SharePoint 2013 on your development machine. For detailed instructions, see http://technet.microsoft.com/en-us/sharepoint/fp142376.aspx.

> **WARNING** *Your installation of the Workflow Manager will fail if you attempt to install it on a development environment that has been configured to act as a Domain Controller. It is recommended to use an alternative development virtual machine to act as your Domain Controller.*

Installing the Workflow Manager

The following steps highlight the key steps to installing the Azure Workflow engine in your development environment:

1. Install the Workflow Manager. The Workflow Manager is installed through Web Platform Installer 4.0. To install the workflow manager, follow the step-by-step MSDN guidance at `http://msdn.microsoft.com/en-us/library/jj193525(v=azure.10).aspx`.

2. Follow the Workflow Configuration Wizard. The Azure Workflow Configuration Wizard will take you through the steps to configure the workflow farm.

3. Configure the SharePoint host site collection to use the workflow service. SharePoint provides the `Register-SPWorkflowService` PowerShell command to associate a site collection to a workflow host.

To verify the Azure workflow service has been installed correctly, browse to the list of service applications in central administration, select the workflow service application, and view the service status message.

Following are some tips that may be of assistance to you:

➤ Use the correct notation/format when specifying accounts in the Azure platform configuration wizard.

➤ Understand permissions between your Azure workflow host and SharePoint.

➤ Ensure that the local policies on your development have the correct rights.

➤ Check that your database access permissions are consistent and accurate.

There is a great step-by-step walkthrough at `http://www.sharepointassist.com/2012/08/22/sharepoint-2013-lab-build-part-8-windows-azure-workflow-installation-and-configuration/`.

Installing Your Development Tools

Ensure you have installed SharePoint Designer 2013, Visual Studio 2012, and Visio 2013 (Visio is required to enable the Visual Designer view in SharePoint Designer) and the Visual Studio 2012 Tools for SharePoint 2013.

The latest Visual Studio 2012 Tools for SharePoint 2013 are available via the web platform installer. The Visual Studio tools provide the SharePoint project items and templates, including the new Azure workflow template.

This section provided a brief summary of the development prerequisites needed to develop workflows for SharePoint 2013. The next section looks at developing a sample scenario.

MODELING A WORKFLOW USING VISIO 2013

Visio has always been a wonderful tool for diagramming business processes and has grown in leaps and bounds in its usefulness to organizations needing a great diagramming tool.

One of the great features, first introduced in the Office 2010 wave, was the ability to model workflows and draw business processes in Visio before sending the diagram to designers and developers in the implementation phase. Visio 2013 improves the workflow modeling features in a number of ways, including implementation of a new file format (.VSDX); increased integration between the SharePoint Designer and Visio; and by providing a number of new SharePoint workflow stencil actions that can be dragged onto the canvas. For more information on Visio 2013 improvements, see the "Understanding the Key Development Tools" section.

In this section, you model the Request Holiday Workflow in Visio 2013 and use the file so that it can be imported into SharePoint Designer in the next section.

1. Launch Visio 2013, and either search for FlowChart or switch to the categories view and select the FlowChart category. Within the FlowChart template category, create a new file using the Microsoft SharePoint 2013 workflow drawing template, a new template just for SharePoint 2013 workflows.

   After the new drawing has been created, notice that all workflow activities are divided into three separate stencils, as follows:

   ➤ SharePoint 2013 Workflow Actions

   ➤ SharePoint 2013 Workflow Conditions

   ➤ SharePoint 2013 Workflow Components

   Notice the default stencil no longer provides a blank canvas but starts with an empty container called a *stage* and start and stop shapes. Other shapes, especially SharePoint 2013 Workflow Action shapes will be added inside the stage.

2. Generate a stage-level diagram of your workflow. Stage outlines are useful as they assist with easy visualization and modeling of your workflow. On the Ribbon, select the Process tab and click Stage Outline. This creates a new tab in your workflow diagram. Use the stage-outline diagram to sketch our workflow quickly.

3. Drag the following stages onto the stage-level diagram, as per Figure 15-13, and label them as follows.

   a. Request Holiday

   b. Approved

   c. Get Weather

   d. Send Happy Holiday Email

FIGURE 15-13

4. As shown in Figure 15-14, drag the If Any Value Equals Value condition onto the stage-level diagram between the Request Holiday and Approved Stage. Conditions can be found by selecting the condition's group of shapes. Label the condition **Holiday Approved?**

5. Connect the shapes by opening the Home tab of the Ribbon and selecting the Connector button. Connect the shapes by dragging from one shape to the next shape (refer to Figure 15-14). Notice that the shape you drag to will control the direction arrow (and flow of your workflow).

6. Switch back to the pointer tool by opening the Home tab of the Ribbon and selecting the pointer tool. Select and right-click the connection between the condition and the Approved stage (refer to Figure 15-14). This opens the properties of the connection. Select Yes.

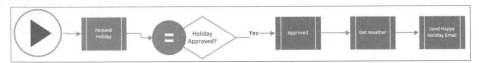

FIGURE 15-14

7. One of the great features provided by Visio is that you can use other shapes in the modeling of your workflow. The caveat is that some of these shapes may be replaced by your SharePoint Designer author when developing the workflow. As shown in Figure 15-15, add the rejected stage to the stage-outline diagram. Use a non-workflow enabled shape to demonstrate this.

On the left Shapes section, open More Shapes. In the FlowChart section, open the Workflow Steps – 3D shapes. Drag a Rejected shape below Holiday Approved? (refer to Figure 15-15). Add a down connector, but do not connect the shape because you use this issue in the next section to demonstrate and discuss the validation features of SharePoint Designer.

> **NOTE** *When designing workflows it is a good idea to ensure that Yes decisions go to the right and No decisions go down. This aids Visio's routing engine to do a better job whenever automatic layout occurs.*

8. Add the following notes to the stage outline diagram (refer to Figure 15-15). From the Insert tab of the Ribbon, add two callouts. Add the following notes:

a. Request Holiday Stage - Assign task to manager.

b. Send Happy Holiday Email Stage - Only send this email 5 days before the holiday.

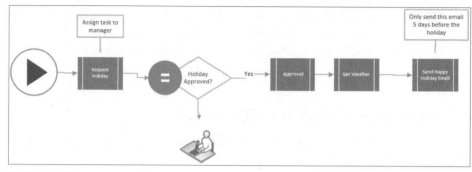

FIGURE 15-15

You have now finished modeling your workflow, and you may want to use the validation feature in Visio 2013 before passing it on to the designer to implement.

In SharePoint Designer 2010 you had to export the file to an intermediary file format. Although this feature is still supported for legacy diagrams and SharePoint 2010 workflows, it is not required for SharePoint 2013 workflows.

The next step is to save and send the diagram to your designer to use this as the basis of the workflow.

DEVELOPING WORKFLOWS USING SHAREPOINT DESIGNER 2013

After your workflow has been modeled in Visio, it can be handed off to IT professionals who are more technical to implement and extend the workflow using SharePoint Designer.

Setting Up the Site and List Prerequisites

Before starting this activity, you need to set up the development site and supporting lists.

1. Create a team site in SharePoint 2013 called **Employee Management**.

2. In the team site, browse to Site Settings, and open the Site Permissions. Create a new group called **Vacation Managers**. For the purposes of the scenario, provide it Full Control access. In production scenarios, you may want to further refine the permissions of this group.

3. Create a Vacation Request content type. To create the content type, use the out-of-the-box Item content type as the parent, and add the following columns to the Content Type:

   ➤ Title — Single Line of Text

   ➤ Description — Multiple Lines of Text

   ➤ Nearest City — Single Line of Text

   ➤ Start Date — Date Time

   ➤ Return Date — Date Time

   ➤ Number of leave days required — Number

4. With the Vacation Request content type, you should now create a new custom list called **Vacation Requests**, enable content type management in the list, and add the Vacation Request content type as the default content type to the list.

You will use this site and the list to manage vacation requests.

Importing the Visio Workflow Diagram

The first step to implement the workflow starts with importing the Visio workflow into SharePoint Designer. To start, follow these steps:

1. Open SharePoint Designer, and enter the URL for the Employee Management Team Site you created in the previous section.

2. Select the Workflows option on the Navigation bar. This has the effect of bringing up the workflow-related options on the Ribbon.

3. Under the Import from Visio drop down, select the Import Visio 2013 Diagram. Select the file containing the Visio diagram, and select Open.

4. Enter the details, as shown in Figure 15-16. Make sure you select the List Workflow type, and ensure you select the Vacation Requests list. Select OK.

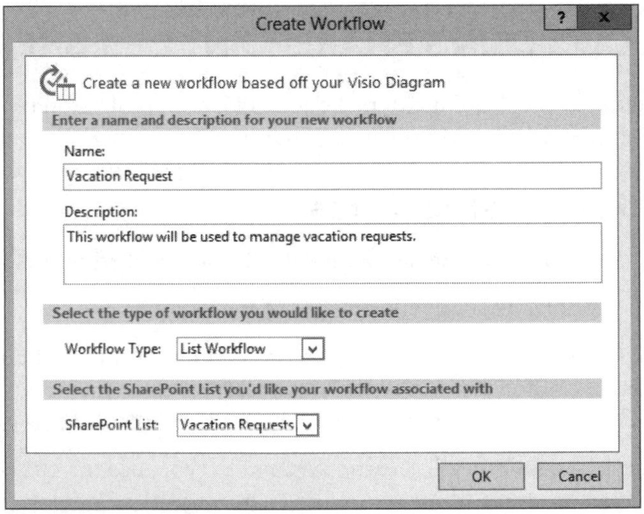

FIGURE 15-16

After the Visio 2013 diagram has been imported, the first thing you will pick up is a new Visual Designer view provided directly within SharePoint Designer.

> **WARNING** *For the Visual Designer view to be available, Visio 2013 must be installed in the same environment as SharePoint Designer.*

5. A final step is required to begin implementing and extending the workflow, which is to generate the workflow outline from the imported Visio diagram. Select Generate Workflow Outline. Did you get an error? As shown in Figure 15-17, did the Issues list pop up? Remember that during the modeling stage you "forgot" to set up one connector correctly, and you used a non-workflow-enabled shape. These issues have thankfully been picked up by the validation functionality in SharePoint Designer.

	Rule	Category	Page
Issues	The condition shape does not have connections labeled with Yes or No.	SharePoint Workflow	Default Stage Outline
	The connector must be connected to two workflow shapes.	SharePoint Workflow	Default Stage Outline

FIGURE 15-17

The validation functionality conducts two types of validation:

➤ *Shape level* — Checks that shapes, connectors, and connections are valid

➤ *XAML level* — Occurs when you select Check for Errors or Publish and validates the underlying XAML generated by SharePoint Designer

Now go ahead and fix the issues in the issue list.

a. Select the first issue. This has the effect of selecting the offending connector or shape in the diagram.

b. Delete the rejected non-workflow-enabled shape, and drag a "simple stage" to replace it. Label it **Rejected**.

c. Select the second issue, and ensure the connector is properly connected from the decision shape to the rejected shape. Right-click the connection, and select No.

d. Select Generate Workflow Outline. This will now be successful, and SharePoint Designer will transition to the new page containing the workflow outline.

On the left, stencil shapes are provided to use in implementing your workflow. Although this may look similar to the Visio modeling experience, the stencils provided are filtered based on the type of workflow created. In your case, only list-based workflow stencils will display.

You are now ready to begin fleshing out the workflow.

Creating the Vacation Request List Workflow

Creating the Vacation Request list workflow involves implementing each of the stages of workflow as described in the "Modeling a Workflow Using Visio 2013" section:

1. Request Holiday

2. Approved

3. Get Weather

4. Send Happy Holiday Email

5. Rejected

Now you'll proceed with each of the stages.

Stage: Request Holiday

The first stage of the workflow starts when an employee creates a new item in the vacation request list. When this happens, you want the vacation managers' group to be notified of the new workflow task. They either approve or reject the request. Lastly, you will progress the workflow based on their action. To do this, follow these steps:

1. Under Action stencils, drag the Start a Task Process to the Request Holiday stage, and hover over the line in the stage. Notice how two green boxes appear on either side. These boxes demonstrate the connections between your action and the workflow stage. This occurs when multiple actions exist inside a single stage. Now drop the action onto the line.

2. Hover over the Start a Task Process action, and you can see a new action menu for the action. This menu is part of the updated user interface and makes it easy to configure actions in SharePoint Designer. As shown in Figure 15-18, select the Process Settings menu item to bring up the associated action configuration dialog.

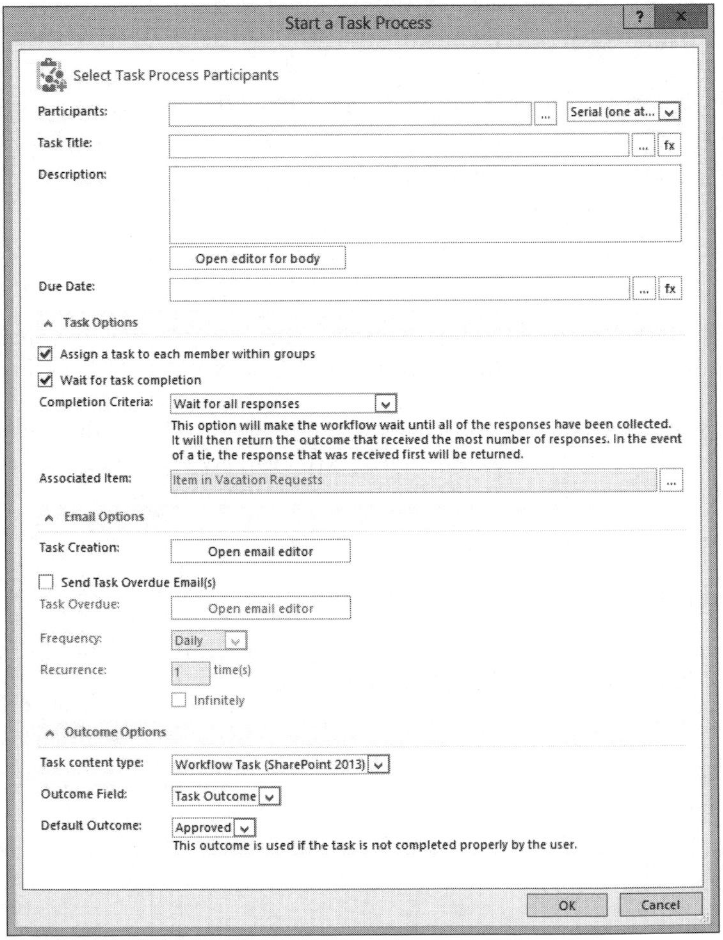

FIGURE 15-18

As you can see, the Start a Task Process dialog in SharePoint 2013 has been vastly improved from the previous version in SharePoint 2010. This includes an improved participant picker dialog and the ability to select whether each user will participate in a serial (one at a time) or parallel (all at once) mode. This feature works with Task Options ➪ Completion Criteria. Completion Criteria provides a number of options to specify under what conditions the task is deemed to be complete, including:

➤ *Wait for all responses* — This option makes the workflow wait until all of the responses have been collected. It then returns the outcome that returned the most responses.

➤ *Wait for first response* — This option makes the workflow wait until the first response is received. It then returns the outcome of the first response.

➤ *Wait for a specific response* — This option makes the workflow wait until the required outcome is received. If the required outcome is not received, it returns the default outcome.

➤ *Wait for percentage of response* — This option makes the workflow wait until a specified percentage of a particular outcome is received. If the required percentage is not achieved, it returns the default outcome.

The Email Options section provides greater control over the e-mail options, including an e-mail editor that enables you to format the e-mail as you require.

The Outcome Options section provides the ability to select the Task Content type, outcome field, and default outcome.

> **NOTE** *You are not limited to the default and out-of-the-box Approved/ Rejected task outcomes. You can provide more outcomes to meet the requirements of your workflow. To provide other options, create a custom Content Type inheriting from the parent Workflow Task (SharePoint 2013). Use the new Task Outcome data type to create Task Outcome columns (with your custom outcomes) and associate this column to your new custom workflow task Content Type.*

3. Fill in the dialog with the values described in Table 15-5.

TABLE 15-5: Start a Task Process Values

ITEM	VALUE
Participants	Vacation Managers (Use the picker to select this group)
Task Title	A new vacation request is ready for review
Description	Please review the new vacation request
Due Date	Today's date
Completion Criteria	Wait for first response

4. Switch to the text-based designer. On the Ribbon, under Views, select Text-Based Designer. You should now see the designer from SharePoint 2010.

The first thing you notice is the new top-level stage container. Stage containers consist of two key parts:

➤ *Business logic* — This part is able to host conditional logic, actions, steps, and the loops of your stage. For more information on these activities, see the "Introducing Core Workflow Concepts" section.

➤ *Transition to Stage* — This part tells your workflow what to do when the stage business logic completes. This may be to move to another stage or to finish the workflow.

5. In the text-based designer, you can see the Start a Task Process action you recently configured. The outcome of this task is saved to a local variable of your workflow.

6. The last thing you need to complete is the transition to the next stage. As shown in Figure 15-19, select Transition to Stage. On the Ribbon, use the Condition drop down to select the If Any Value Equals Value condition.

7. Update the first value to Variable: Outcome and the second to Approved.

8. For approved vacations, add a Go to a Stage action, and set this to the Approved stage.

9. For rejected vacation requests, add a Go to a Stage action, and set this to the Rejected stage.

FIGURE 15-19

Stage: Approved

Now continue with the Approved stage of the workflow. This stage executes when a vacation manager has approved a vacation request. In this stage, you want to do three key things:

➤ Log the approval to the workflow history list.

➤ Send an e-mail to the employee notifying him that the leave request was approved.

➤ Transition to the next stage.

Here are the steps:

1. Add Log to the Workflow History List action. Update the message to Leave Approved. This has the effect of creating an audit trail of all approved vacation requests, and if you want, you can include information about the approver.

2. Add a Send an Email action. Select These Users. This pops up the Email Editor dialog.

   a. In the To section, select the lookup icon, and add the User Who Created the Current Item. This should now appear on the right side. Double-click the item, and update the Return Field from Login Name to Email Address.

   b. Update the subject to Vacation Request.

   c. Update the body to Your Leave Was Approved.

3. Update Transition to Stage to Go to Get the Weather.

The stage will now be configured, as shown in Figure 15-20.

FIGURE 15-20

Stage: Get Weather

This goal of this step in the workflow is to pause the workflow until five days before the start of the employee vacation. SharePoint Designer provides two actions to accomplish this type of action:

➤ *Pause for duration* — Provides the ability to specify the number of days, hours, and minutes to pause the workflow. This action is useful in scenarios in which you need to execute business logic on a regular basis in your site. Furthermore, combining it with a looping container or the Go to a Stage action enables you to repeatedly call your business logic. For example, you can create a site workflow that retrieves the latest stock quotes on a daily basis and caches them in a list. These values can then be consumed by other functionality in your site.

➤ *Pause until date* — Provides the ability to pause execution of the workflow until a specific date and time. This action is great for scenarios in which you need to perform an action based on date information provided by users during the workflow or based on date data provided in a list.

To configure this stage to pause the workflow execution five days before the vacation, follow these steps:

1. As shown in Figure 15-21, add the Add Time to Date action to this stage.

FIGURE 15-21

2. Configure the action by adding –5 days to the vacation start date, and output this to Local Workflow Date variable. You will use this local variable in the next action.

3. Add the Pause Until Date action, and select the local date variable created in the previous step.

4. In the Transition to Stage section, Add a Go to Stage action, and configure it to transition to the Send Happy Holidays Email stage.

You have now configured this stage to pause (and resume) workflow execution 5 days before the vacation.

Stage: Send Happy Holidays E-mail

The goal of this workflow stage is to call out to an external web service to retrieve information, loop through the results, prepare a five-day weather forecast, prepare the e-mail, and send it to the employee about to take vacation.

Before you start with the steps required to set up this stage, take a step back and consider some of the new features SharePoint 2013 provides to achieve this.

The first is a powerful new action called Call HTTP Web Service that provides the ability to call out to on-premise or external web services and return data back to the workflow. The web service data is returned in JSON format. Other key features of this action include:

➤ *Web service address* — The uniform resource identifier (URI) or URL to call.

➤ *Type of HTTP Request* — HTTP defines methods, often referred to as verbs, to indicate the desired action to be performed in the identified resource. HTTP DELETE, HTTP GET, HTTP POST, and HTTP PUT verbs are supported.

➤ *Request Headers* — Attach additional headers to the HTTP request.

➤ *Request Content* — Provide content to a HTTP request that is stored in a local workflow variable based on the new dictionary variable.

➤ *Response Content* — Store the returned JSON-formatted response content into a local workflow variable.

➤ *Response Headers* — Store the HTTP response headers returned from the HTTP request into a local workflow variable.

➤ *Response Status Code* — Store the response status code of the HTTP request into a local workflow variable.

> **NOTE** *JSON is a lightweight text-based data format that is easy to read and write, and easy to generate and parse. JSON is built on two structures. The first is a collection of name/value pairs and the second is an ordered list of values.*

To cater for JSON data responses and to make it easier to work with collections of variables, SharePoint Designer provides a new variable type called the Dictionary variable. The Dictionary variable is a container designer to hold a collection of variables. Three actions are provided to assist working with dictionary data:

➤ Build Dictionary

➤ Count Items in a Dictionary

➤ Get an Item from a Dictionary

For more information, see `http://msdn.microsoft.com/en-us/library/jj554504.aspx`.

Bringing it back to HTTP web service, a dictionary variable is used to store and work with data returned from the web service.

Another key feature you use in this stage is the new looping functionality. SharePoint 2013 provides two looping constructs:

➤ *Loop n Times* — Run the loop repeatedly for the n number of times you specify. For example, you may call out to a web service that, depending on your query, returns an unknown number of items. The Count Items in a Dictionary action can return the count, and this can be specified to set up the number of items to execute the loop to process the items.

➤ *Loop with condition* — Run the loop until a condition is met. For example, you may decide to loop until you find a single item in your dictionary of items.

Now that you have examined these key constructs, you can implement the Send Happy Holidays Email stage, as shown in Figure 15-22.

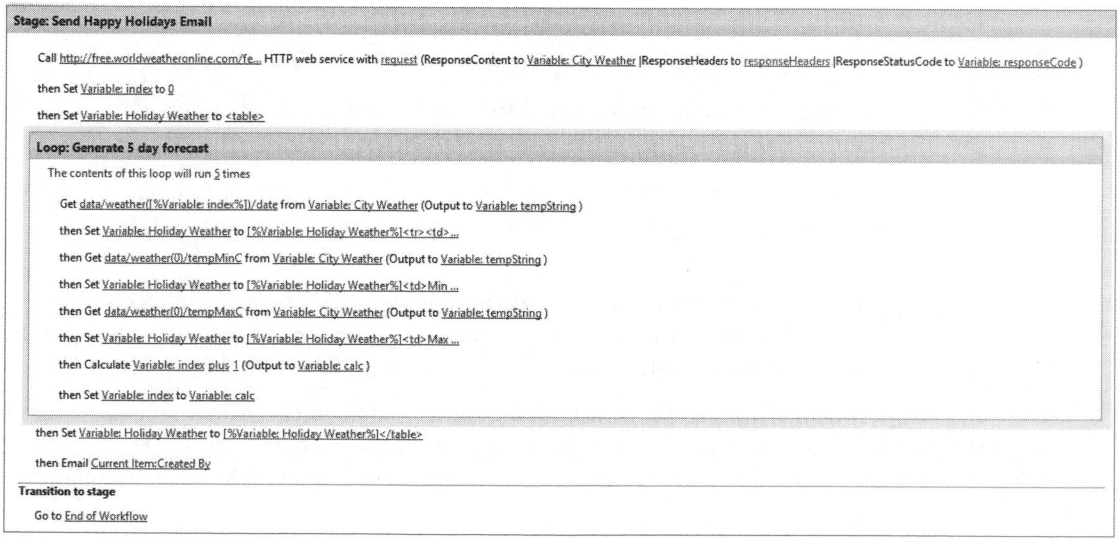

Stage: Send Happy Holidays Email

Call http://free.worldweatheronline.com/fe... HTTP web service with request (ResponseContent to Variable: City Weather |ResponseHeaders to responseHeaders |ResponseStatusCode to Variable: responseCode)

then Set Variable: index to 0

then Set Variable: Holiday Weather to <table>

Loop: Generate 5 day forecast

The contents of this loop will run 5 times

Get data/weather([%Variable: index%])/date from Variable: City Weather (Output to Variable: tempString)

then Set Variable: Holiday Weather to [%Variable: Holiday Weather%]<tr><td> ...

then Get data/weather(0)/tempMinC from Variable: City Weather (Output to Variable: tempString)

then Set Variable: Holiday Weather to [%Variable: Holiday Weather%]<td>Min ...

then Get data/weather(0)/tempMaxC from Variable: City Weather (Output to Variable: tempString)

then Set Variable: Holiday Weather to [%Variable: Holiday Weather%]<td>Max ...

then Calculate Variable: index plus 1 (Output to Variable: calc)

then Set Variable: index to Variable: calc

then Set Variable: Holiday Weather to [%Variable: Holiday Weather%]</table>

then Email Current Item:Created By

Transition to stage

Go to End of Workflow

FIGURE 15-22

1. Add the Call HTTP Web Service action. In your scenario, you can call a free weather service to return a five-day forecast for the nearest city entered at the time the employee created the vacation request.

2. Update the URL with `http://free.worldweatheronline.com/feed/weather.ashx?q=[%Current Item:NearestCity%]&format=json&num_of_days=5&Key=[key]`.

    Taking a closer look at the URL, you can see that you provide a number of `querystring` parameters to the web service including

    ➤ `q` — Provide the city name from the list item.

    ➤ `num_of_days` — Five days of weather.

    ➤ `format` — Data to be returned in JSON format.

    ➤ `Key` — A unique key that grants access to the web service. To get the key, you need to sign up for a free account at `www.worldweatheronline.com`.

3. Next you need to create a new dictionary variable to store the JSON-formatted response content. Select Response, select Create a New Variable, and label the variable **City Weather**.

4. Add a new workflow Set Workflow Variable action, select Workflow Variable, select Create a New Variable of type Integer, and label the variable **Index**.

5. Set the value of Index to 0. Add a new workflow Set Workflow Variable action, select Workflow Variable, select Create a New Variable of type String, and label the variable **Holiday Weather**.

6. Set the value of Holiday Weather to <table>.

7. Using the Ribbon, under the Loop drop down, select Loop n Times and label it **Generate 5 Day Forecast**.

8. You are retrieving a five-day forecast; therefore, set the loop to run five times.

9. At this point, before continuing, you need to understand the data structure behind the JSON-formatted data. To do this, use your web browser to retrieve the sample data.

    a. For example, using your web browser, open the following URL: `http://free.worldweatheronline.com/feed/weather.ashx?q=london&format=json&num_of_days=5&Key=replacethiswithyourkey`.

    b. Copy the resulting content into either an online JSON parser or alternatively download a free viewer at `http://jsonviewer.codeplex.com/`. Examine and understand the data structure.

10. For the purposes of this demonstration, pull out the date and the minimum and maximum temperature from the City Weather dictionary. Use the Get an Item from a Dictionary action to get each of these values, output to a temporary string, and build up a simple HTML

table of these values. Use the index variable to access the required item, and at the end of each loop, increment the index value to access the next day's forecast.

Use Table 15-6 to add and configure the required actions (refer to Figure 15-22).

TABLE 15-6: Configure the Following Actions

ACTION	VALUES
Get Item from a Dictionary	Replace Item by Name or path to data/weather/([%Variable:index%])/date. From Variable: City Weather and output to Variable: tempString.
Set Workflow Variable	Set Variable: Holiday Weather to [%Variable: Holiday Weather%]<tr><td> Date: [%Varlable: tempString%] </td>
Get Item from a Dictionary	Replace Item by Name or path to data/weather/([%Variable:index%])/ tempMinC. From Variable: City Weather and output to Variable: tempString.
Set Workflow Variable	Set Variable: Holiday Weather to [%Variable: Holiday Weather%]<td> Min Temp: [%Variable: tempString%] </td>.
Get Item from a Dictionary	Replace Item by Name or Path to data/weather/([%Variable:index%])/ tempMaxC. From Variable: City Weather and output to Variable: tempString.
Set Workflow Variable	Set Variable: Holiday Weather to [%Variable: Holiday Weather%]<td> Max Temp: [%Varlable: tempString%] </td></tr>.

11. To finish construction of the loop, you need to increment the index.

    a. Add the Do Calculation action and add 1 to the index variable. The value will be output to the Variable: calc.

    b. Add the Set Workflow variable action and set the Variable: Index to the value of Variable: calc.

You have now finished constructing the loop and are almost there! You have to finish only the HTML for the holiday weather and send the e-mail.

12. Below (and outside the loop), add the Set Workflow variable action and set the Variable: Holiday Weather to value of [%Variable: Holiday Weather%]</table>.

13. As shown in Figure 15-23, add the Send Email action and configure it to include the Holiday Weather information.

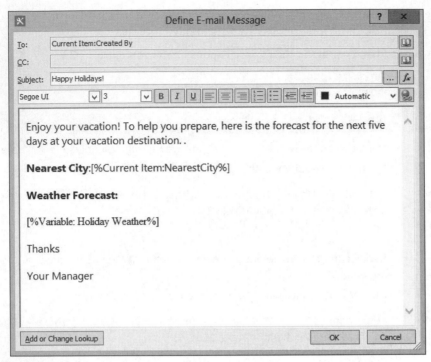

FIGURE 15-23

Stage: Rejected

As shown in Figure 15-24, the final Reject stage is similar to the Approved stage, except that Log to History and Email describe that the vacation request has been rejected.

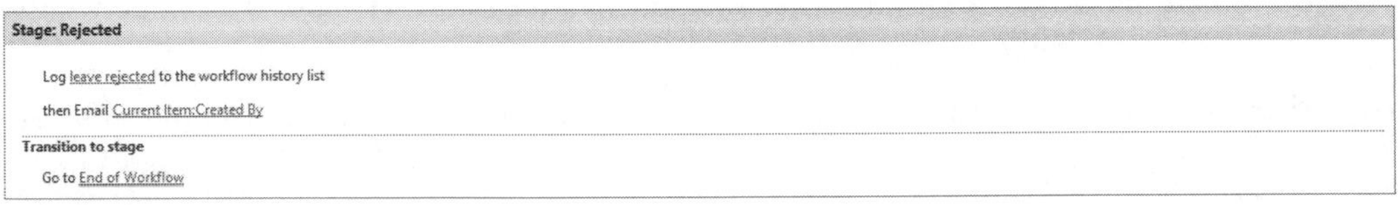

FIGURE 15-24

Publishing the Workflow

You have now finished implementing the workflow. To test the workflow, you need to check for and fix any errors, and publish the workflow to the SharePoint site. To do this, on the Ribbon, select Publish. This deploys the workflow definition to your site. Well done!

DEVELOPING CUSTOM WORKFLOW ACTIVITIES AND ACTIONS USING VISUAL STUDIO 2012

Custom workflow activities and actions can be defined as the development and composition of new workflow activities to cater for specialized requirements and new behaviors.

There are many scenarios in which it makes sense to invest time up front in the creation of useful activities and actions that can be reused over and over again. This results in further extending the rich workflow authoring experience in SharePoint Designer 2013 and Visual Studio 2012, enhancing development and authoring productivity, reducing the number of defects, and improving the maintainability and reliability of tailor-made workflow solutions.

You must understand the key building blocks that make up activities and action, as follows:

➤ A *workflow activity* is a building block of a workflow and a unit of workflow execution.

➤ A *workflow action* is a wrapper of a workflow activity with a human readable statement that makes it easy to implement via the SharePoint Designer user interface.

➤ Apart from a few exceptions, there is typically a 1:1 correlation between workflow activities and SharePoint Designer actions.

Microsoft has worked hard to move all custom code out of workflows. Consequently, SharePoint 2013 workflows are now completely declarative in nature and no longer compile as .NET assemblies. To further enhance workflows with specific business logic, Microsoft recommends the following set of options:

➤ *Leverage the out-of-the-box web services* — Microsoft has greatly improved the web services provided with SharePoint 2013. Use out-of-the-box activities and actions to interact with the out-of-the-box web services.

➤ *Develop a custom web service* — When interacting with other internal business solutions or cloud-based services, move custom code and business logic to a web service. Use out-of-the-box activities and actions to interact with the web service. Host the web service on its own machine, or alternatively host it on one of your web front ends in your farm.

➤ *Develop a custom declarative activity and action* — This is the most common option many developers use to create new activities and actions declaratively. Use out-of-the-box and custom activities to create new behaviors required by your workflow.

➤ *Develop a custom code activity and action* — Custom code activities are more advanced and require an increased knowledge to develop and deploy successfully. This option is only available in on-premise workflow environments.

Custom *declarative activities and actions* require Visual Studio 2012 to develop and package as a Windows Solution Package (WSP) to deploy to the SharePoint farm. Custom *code activity* and actions must be deployed, both to the SharePoint environment and the on-premise Windows Azure Workflow (WAW) environment. Cloud-based deployment of custom code activities is not supported by Microsoft. After the actions file has been deployed to SharePoint, they are available to workflow authors in SharePoint Designer.

Under the hood, activities are made up of a set of workflow definition files that define various parts of the activity or action. For SharePoint 2010-hosted workflows, based on Workflow Foundation 3.x, they are made up of a .RULES and .XOML file. For SharePoint 2013 workflows, based on Windows Foundation 4.x, these files have been consolidated to a single .XAML file.

To make custom code or declarative activities available as actions in SharePoint 2013, a custom .ACTIONS4 file is required. The .ACTIONS4 file is the successor of the SharePoint 2010 .ACTIONS file extension and provides key information required by SharePoint Designer, including the name, underlying class and assembly, rule designer, and input and result parameters. This file must be deployed to the following location in your SharePoint farm: `C:\Program Files\Common Files\Microsoft shared\Web Server Extensions\15\TEMPLATE\1033\Workflow`.

Creating a Custom Declarative Activity and Action

In the previous section "Developing Workflows Using SharePoint Designer," you created workflow to approve holiday vacation requests. As part of this workflow, you called out to a free weather service that returned a five-day forecast that you used to send out a happy holidays e-mail to the employee.

For the purposes of this development scenario, you create a custom declarative activity that can provide better control of the parameters supported by the free weather service to further enhance the authoring experience of the designer.

Before You Continue

Ensure you have set up the site and lists described in the previous section "Developing Workflows Using SharePoint Designer."

In addition, you shared information about free weather service that you continue to use in this section. To use this service, you need to sign up for a free account at `www.worldweatheronline.com`. You can find more information about this weather service API at `http://www.worldweatheronline.com/weather-api.aspx`. The URL and querystring you used in the Call HTTP Web Service action follows: `http://free.worldweatheronline.com/feed/weather.ashx?q=london&format=json&num_of_days=5&Key=replacewithyourkeyfromworldweatheronline`.

Furthermore, it is assumed that you now have an understanding of the JSON weather data structure and have downloaded the JSON Viewer to parse and view JSON data.

Finally, ensure you have followed the steps in the "Setting Up the Development Prerequisites" section.

Goals for Your Custom Declarative Activity

You need to develop a custom declarative activity that achieves the following goals:

➤ Wrap the inner workings and protect your key to the weather service from the author in SharePoint Designer.

➤ Make it easy to specify the city location in the SharePoint Designer action and human-readable statement.

➤ Return a dictionary containing only the date and minimum and maximum temperatures for the five-day forecast.

Implement the Custom Declarative Activity in Visual Studio

Start implementing the custom declarative activity.

1. As shown in Figure 15-25, open Visual Studio 2012 in your development environment, and create a new SharePoint Solution project by selecting New Project ➪ SharePoint Solutions ➪ SharePoint 2013 – Empty Project. Update the name of the project to **WorldWeather**.

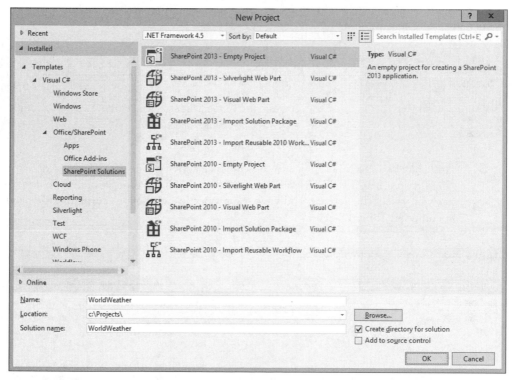

FIGURE 15-25

2. In the next dialog, select Deploy as a Sandboxed Solution, and select OK.

3. Right-click the newly created project, select Add a New Item, and select Workflow Custom Activity. Label it **WeatherActivity**, and select OK.

Before continuing, look at what has been set up by Visual Studio 2012 SharePoint templates.

➤ The project has a default feature and is responsible for setting up the custom workflow activity.

➤ The WeatherActivity folder consists of an `elements.XML` file, `WeatherActivity .ACTIONS4` file, and `WeatherActivity.XAML` definition file.

➤ The toolbox has been updated to show the various workflow categories and associated activities.

➤ A default sequence activity to begin defining your custom activity.

➤ At the bottom of the screen, there are three tabs called Variables, Arguments, and Imports. Variables enable your store and interact with content; Arguments specify input and output parameters; and Imports specify the various namespaces that have been imported to this project.

4. Select the Arguments tab and click Create Argument. (Grayed-out text indicates that you have not selected the sequence activity.) As per Table 15-7, create the following arguments:

TABLE 15-7: Argument Values

NAME	DIRECTION	ARGUMENT
location	In	String
responseContent	Out	Browse for Types... (search for DynamicValue to select Microsoft. Activities.DynamicValue)

5. Add the HTTPSEND activity to the sequence activity. This activity provides similar functionality as the Call HTTP Web Service action in SharePoint Designer. To configure this activity, select the activity, and view the properties window to configure the properties specified in Table 15-8.

TABLE 15-8: Start a Task Process Values

GROUP	PROPERTY	VALUE
Request		
	Method	GET
	Uri	http://free.worldweatheronline.com/feed/weather. ashx?q= + location + "&format=json&num_of_days=5&Key= replacewithyourkeyhere"
Response		
	responseContent	responseContent

6. Update the .ACTIONS4 file. This file tells SharePoint Designer how to display the action to the user, as well as how the user can interact with it.

Unfortunately, the designer in Visual Studio 2012 doesn't provide much of a starting point, but there is a great set of out-of-the-box examples that you can learn from at the following location: C:\Program Files\Common Files\Microsoft shared\Web Server Extensions\15\TEMPLATE\1033\Workflow.

7. Examine the following code before continuing to the observations.

```
<Action
Name="Get Weather Forecast for Location"
ClassName="WorldWeather.WeatherActivity"
Category="Custom"
AppliesTo="all">

<RuleDesigner
Sentence="Get 5 day weather forecast for %1 location (Output to %2) ">

<FieldBind
Field="Location"
DesignerType="TextArea"
Text="specify location"
Id="1"
DisplayName="Location" />

<FieldBind Field="responseContent"
DesignerType="ParameterNames"
Text="responseContent"
Id="2"
DisplayName="responseContent" />
</RuleDesigner>


<Parameters>
<Parameter
DesignerType="StringBuilder"
Name="Location"
Type="System.String, mscorlib"
Description="Name or path of the item (key)
to get from the dictionary."
Direction="In"/>

<Parameter
DesignerType="ParameterNames"
Name="responseContent"
Type="Microsoft.Activities.DynamicValue, Microsoft.Activities,
Version=1.0.0.0, Culture=neutral, PublicKeyToken=null"
Description="Output variable to store the response content"
Direction="Out"/>
</Parameters>
</Action>
```

As you can see, there are four key areas that make up the .ACTIONS4 file as follows:

➤ *Action* — Action is the top-level element that contains all elements that make up the .ACTIONS4 file. It describes the action, including the name, class name, category, and who the action applies to. The name is used in an action drop down in SharePoint Designer.

➤ *RuleDesigner* — RuleDesigner is a child of the Action top-level element. It provides the human readable sentence that will be displayed when the action is added to the SharePoint Designer user interface. The %1 tags correspond numerically to FieldBind entries within this section.

➤ *FieldBind* — The FieldBind element is a child of the RuleDesigner element. It describes each of the fields in a human-readable sentence, is associated by the ID, and lets SharePoint Designer know what type of field designer to display to the user.

➤ *Parameters and Parameter* — Parameters describe each of the underlying Visual Studio parameters that have been defined and the direction the parameter will be used.

8. Update the .ACTIONS4 file in your code project with the preceding content.

9. Build and deploy your solution to the SharePoint solution gallery. After it has been deployed to SharePoint, close SharePoint Designer.

10. Clear the SharePoint Designer client-side cache to ensure SharePoint Designer re-caches all the .ACTIONS4 files on the next "open" of SharePoint Designer. This can be accessed from your file system at `User\Username\Local\Microsoft\WebsiteCache`.

11. As shown in Figure 15-26, create a test SharePoint 2013 workflow, select the Actions drop-down, and select the Get Weather Forecast for Location action.

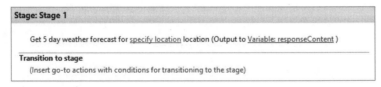

Stage: Stage 1

Get 5 day weather forecast for <u>specify location</u> location (Output to <u>Variable: responseContent</u>)

Transition to stage
(Insert go-to actions with conditions for transitioning to the stage)

FIGURE 15-26

To summarize, using custom declarative activities and Visual Studio, there is so much more we can do to further extend the features of this activity. For example, we could provide the option to only return Celsius or Fahrenheit temperature data.

Developing a Custom Code Activity and Action

Developing custom code activities requires additional development and deployment steps that are not required when developing custom declarative activities. Custom code activities can only be developed for on-premise deployments of Windows Azure. Unfortunately, due to space constraints of this chapter, only the high-level steps are provided.

1. Create a new project in Visual Studio 2012. Create a new project by selecting New Project ➩ Visual C# ➩ Workflow, and select Activity Library Project. Update the name of the project to the desired name.

2. Right-click your project to add a new item to your project, and select Code Activity. This is your initial starting point.

3. Specify the `InArguments` and whether the argument is required. `InArgument` specifies the binding terminal that supports the flow of data into an activity. For more information, see `http://msdn.microsoft.com/en-us/library/system.activities.inargument.aspx`.

4. Specify the `OutArgument` and whether the argument is required. `OutArgument` specifies the binding terminal that supports the flow of data into an activity. For more information, see `http://msdn.microsoft.com/en-us/library/system.activities.outargument.aspx`.

5. Add your business logic within the Execute method.

6. Add your .ACTIONS4 manually. Ensure you enclose your .ACTIONS4 in a complete top-level WorkflowInfo element wrapper node.

7. Create the AllowedTypes.XML file. This file contains the class information for the activity and will be deployed to the Workflow Manager machines along with the fully trusted .NET assembly containing the activity.

8. Unfortunately, the deployment process does not use the standard SharePoint solution package because these files will be deployed to the on-premise Azure workflow-hosting environment. To deploy, use the following steps:

    a. Copy the .NET Assembly and AllowedTypes.XML to `%Program Files%\Workflow Manager\1.0\Workflow\Artifacts`.

    b. Copy the .NET Assembly and AllowedTypes.XML to `%Program Files%\Workflow Manager\1.0\Workflow\WFWebRoot\bin`.

    c. Add the .NET assembly to the Global Assembly Cache on each of the machines hosting the Workflow Manager.

    d. Restart the Workflow Manager service.

    e. In your SharePoint environment, copy the .ACTIONS4 file to `C:\Program Files\Common Files\Microsoft shared\Web Server Extensions\15\TEMPLATE\1033\Workflow`.

    f. Reset Internet Information Services, and clear the client-side SharePoint Designer cache (as in the previous section) before accessing and interacting with your new custom code activity.

To summarize, the Azure Workflow engine is a powerful and extensible beast. There may be valid cases when your organization has already developed and deployed custom code activities to your on-premise workflow environment that it would like to leverage in SharePoint 2013 workflows. The previous steps provide a summary of the key steps to incorporate these into your SharePoint 2013 environment.

DEVELOPING WORKFLOWS USING VISUAL STUDIO 2012

Visual Studio 2012 fully supports developing either SharePoint 2010-based or SharePoint 2013-based workflows for SharePoint 2013. Visual Studio includes a number of SharePoint workflow project item templates to support both workflow hosts. For SharePoint 2010, the legacy state machine and sequence project item templates are available, and for SharePoint 2013, a single workflow template is available.

As in SharePoint 2010, you can import workflows created in SharePoint Designer and convert them into a Visual Studio 2012 project. SharePoint Designer supports saving a workflow as a solution package, and this solution package can be used with the following Visual Studio New Project templates:

➤ SharePoint 2013 – Import Solution Package

➤ SharePoint 2013 – Import Reusable 2010 Workflow

➤ SharePoint 2010 – Import Solution Package

➤ SharePoint 2010 – Import Reusable Workflow

Another great enhancement is that SharePoint 2013 workflows are entirely declarative in nature. This means sandboxed solutions can be used to deploy Visual Studio developed workflows to individual site collections. If the workflow is deployed as part of a SharePoint app, then only the app can access it. As in SharePoint 2010, farm-level solutions can still be used to make workflows available to all site collections in the farm.

From a SharePoint app perspective, Visual Studio must be used to incorporate, package, and deploy workflow as a SharePoint app. This is not supported by SharePoint Designer.

Earlier you learned about the new Dictionary variable data type. The underlying activity class associated to this is `DynamicValue`. `DynamicValue` enables you to create, store, and consume complex data structures and is a perfect companion for working with JSON formatted data. The following activities are available in Visual Studio to manipulate DynamicValues:

➤ `BuildDynamicValue`

➤ `ContainsDynamicValueProperty`

➤ `CopyDynamicValue`

➤ `CreateDynamicValue`

➤ `CreateUrlFromDynamicValue`

➤ `GetDynamicValueProperties`

➤ `GetDynamicValueProperty<T>`

➤ `ParseDynamicValue`

From an activity perspective, using Visual Studio gives you access to the full range of workflow activities. You are not limited to the list of actions available in SharePoint Designer. This provides a great opportunity to build new, powerful behaviors that are not possible simply using SharePoint Designer.

One final thing to note is the ability to develop custom task forms, association and initiation forms, and modification forms as .ASPX pages for your workflow.

To summarize, Visual Studio 2012 picks up where SharePoint Designer leaves off and caters for scenarios that require greater technical ability. As a result, it provides a powerful declarative workflow development model, access to the full spectrum of .NET 4.5 and SharePoint activities, extreme control of how the workflow will be packaged and deployed, and full control over the appearance of the user interface elements of your workflow. Happy coding!

KEY DEVELOPMENT CONSIDERATIONS

Beyond what has already been discussed in this chapter, there are a number of design and development factors that you should consider. These key considerations are included in this section.

SharePoint 2010 Versus SharePoint 2013 Workflow

Determining whether to develop a SharePoint 2010 or SharePoint 2013 workflow is important.

By default, where it makes sense, you should always aim to use the SharePoint 2013 workflow engine over the 2010 workflow engine. When you do this, you accomplish the following:

➤ Future-proof any new development investment in the SharePoint platform.

➤ Increase the portability, scalability, and performance of workflow-based solutions in your organization.

➤ Leverage the latest workflow software from Microsoft.

➤ Decrease the amount of custom code required by your workflows.

➤ Leverage the expressiveness SharePoint 2013-based workflows provide.

➤ Develop workflows for SharePoint 2013 cloud-hosted environments.

Specific cases may require the use of the SharePoint 2010 workflow engine, including the following:

➤ The SharePoint 2013 workflow engine is not available or configured in your SharePoint 2013 environment.

➤ Extensive SharePoint 2010 workflow development has already occurred, and your team is not ready or has not been able to move custom-coded activities and business logic into web services.

Declarative Versus Programmatic Workflows

SharePoint 2013 workflows are declarative in nature; no custom code is required to create a SharePoint 2013 workflow. The benefit is that no .NET assembly is required to run the workflow.

Programmatic workflows, available only via SharePoint 2010 workflows, can be developed using Visual Studio 2012 using custom code. These workflows are compiled and deployed as .NET Framework assemblies and must be deployed to the Global Assembly Cache (GAC).

Always prefer SharePoint 2013 workflows to SharePoint 2010 workflows.

Considering Where Workflows Execute

SharePoint 2013 supports two workflow hosts. The first workflow host, based on the SharePoint 2010 workflow host, resides within the SharePoint 2013 farm. SharePoint 2010 workflow instances execute either on the web front ends or in the background timer job of the SharePoint 2013 farm. The location it executes depends on the last action. If the last action was caused by a user, it can execute on the web front end. If the last action was caused by a delay timer or from an event occurring elsewhere, it can execute in the timer job.

SharePoint 2013 workflows execute outside of the SharePoint farm in Azure Workflow Service either on-premise or in the cloud. Execution and interaction with the SharePoint farm occurs through events occurring in SharePoint or when the Azure workflow engine processing occurs and submits information to SharePoint.

Determining Whether to Convert SharePoint 2010 Workflows to SharePoint 2013 Workflows

It depends on what your goals are for converting the workflow. The biggest benefit to investing resources in converting workflows is the scalability, performance, flexibility, and integration of the new SharePoint app model you get from the Azure Workflow engine.

Other factors to consider include

➤ *How much customization is there?* The lower the amount of customization and custom code required, the more it makes sense to move the workflow to the new Azure Workflow engine.

➤ *Is this a sensible budget investment?* Converting the workflow to SharePoint 2013 will not necessarily provide any more functionality than the previous version. It may be that this budget could be used to provide additional value in other areas of your portal deployment.

➤ *What level or privileges does your existing workflow require to execute in your on-premise or cloud-hosted farm?* Your workflow might require high-level permissions to perform actions that are not possible in SharePoint 2013. In these cases, custom logic could be moved into web services that execute under custom elevated permission sets.

SharePoint Designer Versus Visual Studio 2012

Whenever a developer cracks open Visual Studio 2012, an experienced SharePoint portal governance manager somewhere in the world unfortunately sheds a tear. The reason is that custom developed solutions tend to require a greater deal of support, assurance testing, and maintenance effort than third-party supported and out-of-the-box (supported by Microsoft) solutions.

SharePoint Designer was developed by Microsoft for a reason, and the reasons to use it include:

➤ Supports rapid development of rich and powerful workflows for the SharePoint platform

➤ Supports modeling of workflows using Visio 2013 and moving workflows back and forth between Visio 2013 and SharePoint Designer 2012

➤ Provides great authoring support for authoring workflows targeting the Azure workflow engine, without requiring developer knowledge

There is a case to be made for developing workflows using Visual Studio 2012. The benefits to developing solutions in Visual Studio over SharePoint Designer are the following:

➤ More control and options to deploy workflows, and supporting artifacts to SharePoint sites using the Feature framework

➤ Better control, packaging, and deployment options in Visual studio 2012

➤ Greater control and support for using the full range of the activities provided by Microsoft

➤ Requires advanced debugging

➤ Requires reuse of workflow definitions across multiple site collections

➤ Creating workflow apps for SharePoint

➤ Greater degree of customization and more expressive workflow development options.

➤ The ability to develop custom activities and actions, and web services required by your workflow

Consider the full life cycle of development, testing, and deployment cost associated with Visual Studio 2012 solution versus a SharePoint Designer solution. Consider the cost of hiring a SharePoint Designer author versus a SharePoint developer to maintain and enhance the workflow.

To summarize, unless there is a specific requirement that can be met using Visual Studio, always prefer SharePoint Designer.

Deciding Between Sequential Versus State Machine Workflow

In SharePoint 2010, this was a big decision because SharePoint Designer 2010 supported only sequential workflows, and Visual Studio 2010 made you choose between two templates, which locked you into a choice early on. SharePoint Designer 2013 provides stages and transitions, and Visual Studio 2012 provides one template to support both Sequential and State Machine workflows.

SUMMARY

SharePoint 2013 workflow has fully embraced the latest features of Windows Workflow Foundation 4.5 and Windows Azure to provide a great platform for hosting and scaling workflow either on-premise or in the cloud. At the same time it hasn't forgotten its roots and continues to fully support customer investments by maintaining the capability to host SharePoint 2010-based workflows.

With the introduction of SharePoint 2013-based workflow, a number of enhancements to the underlying WF 4.5 Windows Azure platform can now be leveraged. These include richer flow control paradigms, modular building blocks, stages and transitions, and the move to a fully declarative model.

SharePoint Designer 2013 and Visual Studio 2012 have been vastly improved to make it easier for authors and developers to build, connect, consume, and use complex data in workflows from external services provided on-premise or in the cloud through new features such as the capability to call REST web services, the new dictionary data type in SharePoint Designer, and the DynamicValue support in Visual Studio.

SharePoint 2013 workflow capability is a first-class citizen in the new app model and provides a fantastic opportunity for developers, independent software vendors, and Microsoft partners.

16

Integrating Reporting Services

WHAT'S IN THIS CHAPTER?

➤ Working with new and improved features in SQL Server Reporting Services 2012

➤ Caching and snapshots in SQL Server Reporting Services

➤ Reporting on SharePoint lists

➤ Creating reports

Business intelligence (BI) is an umbrella term that refers to several technologies, applications, and a number of exercises an organization may undertake to deploy shared business processes across multiple business units. BI empowers users with the right insights and enables them to make better, faster, and more relevant decisions when the users come together and collaborate in getting there.

The focus of this chapter is on the reporting part of BI and in particular a product called SQL Server Reporting Services (SSRS). Perhaps the most glaring advantage of using SSRS is its integration with Office and SharePoint products and technologies. This chapter starts you on your journey by explaining how SSRS and SharePoint can be integrated as well as showcasing some of the new features in the current wave of products with Office 2013, SharePoint 2013, and SQL Server Reporting Services 2012.

THE HISTORY

Reporting is the blood and heart of many organizations. If you have ever done a BI project, chances are that your first assignment was to turn a paper-based form into an electronic report. Regardless of the technology you used to deliver your first project, the joy of eliminating an inefficient manual process stayed with you for a long time — if not forever.

As you may recall, creating complicated or even simple electronic reports was not an easy task. Reporting was a complex process involving a report developer with a fairly good understanding of the back-end data source and a lot of hours of coding the report. Maybe you have worked with technologies such as Crystal Reports or Cognos, or maybe you are still doing custom development to create your reports. The truth is, in the last few years, however, things have changed quite rapidly in the BI world, and many reporting platforms have found their ways into the IT industry.

Microsoft's first attempt to allow developers to create branded reports was in Visual Basic 6.0 and through integration with stand-alone products such as Crystal Reports. In 2004, Microsoft introduced its reporting platform named SQL Server Reporting Services (SSRS). This product provided a variety of functionalities to help you develop your reports much easier than before, and perhaps continue carrying on the satisfaction of the good old days!

In a nutshell, SSRS was a server-side reporting platform on which you could build sophisticated reports and have them render right within the browser with maximum parity when displayed in client applications such as Windows forms. Since the initial release of Reporting Services in 2004, there have been many improvements and changes to the core architecture of SSRS.

INTRODUCING SSRS 2012

Today, the latest version of the product is named SSRS 2012, which is now part of SQL Server 2012. SSRS 2012 can be installed and configured in both SharePoint 2010 and SharePoint 2013.

> **NOTE** *Installing and configuring Reporting Services with SharePoint 2013 is beyond the scope of this chapter. For more information, see the product documentation at* `http://msdn.microsoft.com/en-us/library/jj219068.aspx.`

Until SSRS 2012, Reporting Services was never a native SharePoint service application. That means an out-of-the-box SharePoint installation had no understanding of Reporting Services, and both SharePoint and SSRS (as two separate products) had to be integrated with each other. The problem of SSRS being a separate product in the integration and installed on a separate server can be discussed from three angles.

First, you needed to deal with a minimum of two separate products and repository frameworks to implement a single reporting solution, which meant more administrative efforts and costs.

Second, users needed to go through more than a hop to get to the back-end data source. For the environments without Kerberos delegation in place, this model could cause authentication issues — also known as double hops. The double-hop (one hop from the client browser to the SharePoint server and another hop to the Report server) problem was not a bug. It was an intentional security design to restrict identities from acting on behalf of other identities.

The third issue was scalability. As you know, one of the primary drivers to change the architecture of shared services in SharePoint 2010 to follow the service application model was to support scalability. When you integrated SharePoint with a single-instance of another product, although SharePoint could scale itself, the dependent, single instance service, Reporting Services, could not scale and support multitenant installations or even single tenant, but big installations. For example, you couldn't have multiple reports in your farm that point to different instances of Reporting Services. This was due to the fact that Reporting Services integration with SharePoint was implemented and configured at the farm level, and the Report Viewer Web Part or other integration operations simply followed the same model.

Probably the most important improvement in SSRS 2012, compared to its predecessors, is that Reporting Services is now a true service application in SharePoint. That means to integrate Reporting Services with SharePoint, all you need to do is to add a new instance of a SQL Server Reporting Services service application to the farm, and you are all set.

Being a service application means Reporting Services databases are now part of SharePoint default databases. In addition, as a service application SSRS, is now installed and managed exactly like other service applications. Administrators use PowerShell to configure it, and the service can scale or be made highly available like databases in SharePoint. Add to all this that Reporting Services is the only BI service application that works cross-farm, meaning you can publish the service from farm A and consume it from farm B. Figure 16-1 shows the SQL Server Reporting Services service application in SharePoint 2013.

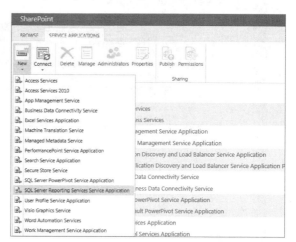

FIGURE 16-1

The next section discusses report authoring and deployment tools.

Authoring Tools

Unlike Excel and PerformancePoint, Reporting Services offers several tools for authoring and deploying SSRS reports to SharePoint.

SSDT is short for *SQL Server Data Tools*. It's a development environment that is installed as part of SQL Server 2012 installation and enables you to build reports and deploy them to SharePoint. SSDT supports four operations on Report Definition Language (RDL) files: Opening RDL files, building the RDL files, previewing the RDL files, and deploying them to a SharePoint site.

SSDT builds on the Visual Studio integrated shell. If you install SSDT on the same computer as a full version of Visual Studio, SSDT will be integrated directly into Visual Studio. SSDT adds several BI project templates (including Reporting Services, as shown in Figure 16-2) to Visual Studio.

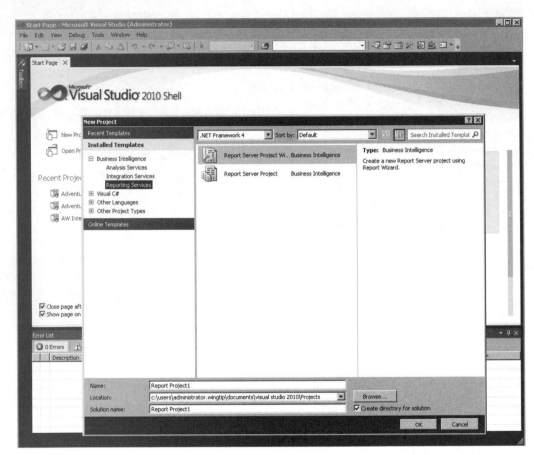

FIGURE 16-2

Another option for authoring and deploying reports to SharePoint is the Report Builder. Report Builder is a click-once application that is similar to PerformancePoint Dashboard Designer and has most of the features of SSDT.

Report Builder is installed when you configure Reporting Services in SharePoint and can be configured directly within an SSRS service application, as shown in Figure 16-3. Alternatively, you can download and install the stand-alone MSI of Report Builder 3.0 from the following shortened reference: http://www.microsoft.com/en-ca/download/details.aspx?id=29072.

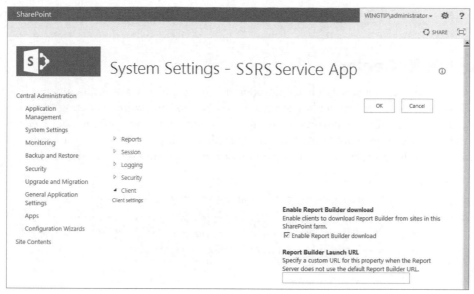

FIGURE 16-3

Both SSDT and Report Builder work with report definition files. A report definition is typically an XML file in RDL format.

Power View (it is two words) is yet another authoring and deployment tool for reports. Power View is a feature of SQL Server 2012 Reporting Services for interactive data exploration, visualization, and presentation. When you create a report using Power View, the report gets the new file format (*.rdlx). An .rdlx file is a package that is compatible with a compressed (.zip) file, and its structure follows the rules that are outlined in the Open Packaging Conventions (OPC).

Figure 16-4 shows different authoring and packaging tools for reports in SharePoint and SSRS 2012.

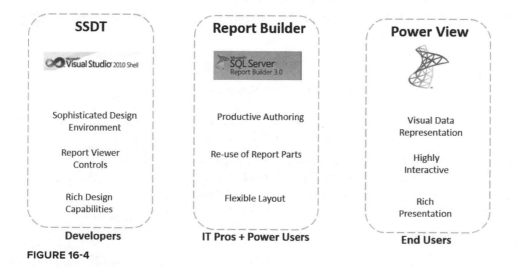

FIGURE 16-4

Because the audience of this book is mostly SharePoint developers, Reporting Builder 3.0 and Power View will be less focused.

Configuring the BI Center

Although Reporting Services reports can be deployed and managed in any site or document library, it's much easier to use the BI Center template to create a site for housing your Reporting Services reports. Think of the BI Center as a starting point, like the Document Center and Record Center templates you may have seen in SharePoint. They are specialized templates to get you up and running quickly, but nothing prevents you from building everything from scratch using a blank team site.

> **NOTE** *If you are not familiar with the BI Center template in SharePoint or require additional information to enable this template in a SharePoint site, see the product documentation at* `http://technet.microsoft.com/en-us/library/jj219656.aspx.`

To make the BI Center understand Reporting Services reports, model, and data sources, you need to add the required content types to the Data Connections and Documents libraries because they are not added by default.

And, with that, follow these steps:

1. Browse to the Data Connections library.

2. From the Ribbon, click Library Tools ⇨ Library Settings.

3. Under Content Types, click Add from existing site content types.

4. In the Select Content Types section, in Select Site Content Types From, select SQL Server Reporting Services Content Types from the drop-down list.

5. In the Available Site Content Types list, click Report Data Source, and then click Add to move the selected content type to the Content Types to Add List.

6. With the Data Connections document library properly configured, the Documents document library is next. Follow the same steps you took for the Data Connections library.

If you have followed all the steps, when you go to the Files tab ⇨ New Document, you should see what is shown in Figure 16-5.

The configuration steps you took in this section enable you to view and manage Reporting Services reports directly from the BI Center. Now, you can publish Reporting Services content to both document libraries and then view and manage those documents directly within the SharePoint context.

FIGURE 16-5

BUILDING AND DEPLOYING REPORTS

The report that you build in this section shows the AdventureWorks sales by quarter and product category. This report illustrates some of the visualization features shipped with SSRS 2008 R2 and SSRS 2012. This report also illustrates the use of a Tablix data region with nested row groups and column groups.

After you build the report, you can preview the report in SSDT and make the final adjustment before publishing it. Finally, you can deploy this report to the BI Center site and make it available for everyone to see and work with. Users can quickly get a sense of the report by looking at the visuals embedded in the report or drill down from the summary data into detailed data for more information by showing and hiding rows.

Authoring Reports

With the BI Center properly configured, now it's time to walk through the development process of a report in SSDT.

> **NOTE** *You use the AdventureWorks database throughout this chapter. To download this database, see Microsoft SQL Server Database Product Samples at* `http://msftdbprodsamples.codeplex.com/.`

There are two ways you can build your reports in SSDT: manually, or you can use the Report Wizard. In this section, you use the manual process.

1. Open SSDT.

2. Click on New Project to create a new project.

3. From the available templates, select Business Intelligence Projects ⇨ Reporting Services. Then click Report Server Project.

4. Name the project something descriptive, and click OK.

5. In the Solution Explorer, right-click the Shared Data Source, and select Add New Data Source.

6. Point the new data source to the AdventureWorks2012 database. Your Connection String should be something like *Data Source=.;Initial Catalog=AdventureWorks2012.*

7. In the Solution Explorer, right-click the Reports folder, and select Add ⇨ New Item. Then select Report template. Name the new report **SalesByQtrAndProductCat.rdl.**

8. In the Report Data tab, right-click the Datasets folder; select Add Dataset to open the Dataset Properties dialog.

9. Change the name of the data set to **DSSales,** and then select the Use a Dataset Embedded in My Report option.

> **NOTE** *Ever since Reporting Services 2008 R2, data sets that you create in your reports can be stored externally from the report and shared between multiple reports. Like shared data sources, shared data sets can be created by IT or senior developers and shared with information workers or other developers. Shared data sets can be created in two ways. Either right-click the Shared Datasets folder in the Solution Explorer and add a new data set, or simply right-click a nonshared data source, and select Convert to Shared Dataset.*

10. Click the New button to open Data Source Properties.

11. Select the Use a Shared Data Source Reference option. From the drop-down list choose the data source you created in step 5. Click OK to return to the Dataset Properties dialog.

12. Click the Query Designer button to open the Query Designer. Then click the Edit as Text button to switch to Query Mode.

13. Paste the following query in the query text box. The query is a join between ProductSubcategory, SalesOrderHeader, SalesOrderDetail, Product, and ProductCategory tables, and it's grouped by the following columns:

    a. Order date (only year)

    b. Category name

    c. Subcategory name

    d. The letter "Q" concatenated with **ProductCategoryID** (that is, Q1, Q2, …)

The query also takes two parameters named @StartDate and @EndDate to limit the calculation of the sales amount to a period of time specified by the parameters:

```
SELECT
    PC.Name AS Category, PS.Name AS Subcategory,
    DATEPART(yy, SOH.OrderDate) AS Year,
    'Q' + DATENAME(qq, SOH.OrderDate) AS Qtr,
    SUM(DET.UnitPrice * DET.OrderQty) AS Sales
FROM Production.ProductSubcategory PS INNER JOIN
    Sales.SalesOrderHeader SOH INNER JOIN
        Sales.SalesOrderDetail DET ON SOH.SalesOrderID = DET.SalesOrderID INNER JOIN
        Production.Product P ON DET.ProductID - P.ProductID
        ON PS.ProductSubcategoryID = P.ProductSubcategoryID INNER JOIN
    Production.ProductCategory PC ON PS.ProductCategoryID = PC.ProductCategoryID
WHERE (SOH.OrderDate BETWEEN (@StartDate) AND (@EndDate))
GROUP BY DATEPART(yy, SOH.OrderDate), PC.Name, PS.Name,
    'Q' + DATENAME(qq, SOH.OrderDate), PS.ProductSubcategoryID
```

14. You can examine the query result by clicking the button that has the exclamation mark on it, and then entering a sample start data and end date such as **2005-07-01** and **2005-09-01**. The returned result will be shown in the grid below the query section, as shown in Figure 16-6. When you finish, click OK to close the Query Designer.

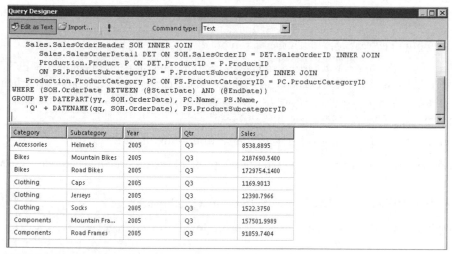

```
Query Designer                                                              _□×
⟳ Edit as Text  ✐ Import...  !        Command type: Text                ▼

     Sales.SalesOrderHeader SOH INNER JOIN
         Sales.SalesOrderDetail DET ON SOH.SalesOrderID = DET.SalesOrderID INNER JOIN
         Production.Product P ON DET.ProductID = P.ProductID
         ON PS.ProductSubcategoryID = P.ProductSubcategoryID INNER JOIN
     Production.ProductCategory PC ON PS.ProductCategoryID = PC.ProductCategoryID
WHERE (SOH.OrderDate BETWEEN (@StartDate) AND (@EndDate))
GROUP BY DATEPART(yy, SOH.OrderDate), PC.Name, PS.Name,
     'Q' + DATENAME(qq, SOH.OrderDate), PS.ProductSubcategoryID
```

Category	Subcategory	Year	Qtr	Sales
Accessories	Helmets	2005	Q3	8538.8895
Bikes	Mountain Bikes	2005	Q3	2187690.5400
Bikes	Road Bikes	2005	Q3	1729754.1400
Clothing	Caps	2005	Q3	1169.9013
Clothing	Jerseys	2005	Q3	12390.7966
Clothing	Socks	2005	Q3	1522.3750
Components	Mountain Fra...	2005	Q3	157501.9989
Components	Road Frames	2005	Q3	91059.7404

FIGURE 16-6

15. Click OK again to close the Dataset Properties dialog.

Laying Out Your Report

At this point, you should have a data set with the following fields: Category, Subcategory, Year, Qtr, and Sales. The next logical step is to actually build the report display as outlined here:

1. Start by dragging a Matrix from the Toolbox onto the Body section of the report.

2. From the Report Data tab, drag the following fields to the specified places on the design canvas:

  a. The Category field to the matrix cell where it says Rows

  b. The Year field to the matrix cell where it says Columns

  c. The Sales field to the matrix cell where it says Data

  d. The Subcategory field to below the Category field in the grouping pane where it says Row Groups (left-bottom corner)

  e. The Qtr field to below the Year field in the grouping pane where it says Column Groups (right-bottom corner)

3. Delete the column titles for Category and Subcategory fields that appear on the left side of the Year field.

4. Hold the Ctrl key, and select all the cells in the matrix except the one that says Sum (Sales). From the properties window, change the following properties:

  ➤ *BackgroundColor* — LightSteelBlue

  ➤ *Color* — White

  ➤ FontWeight — Bold

5. Select the text box that has [Sum(Sales)] in it. From the Properties windows, set **'$'#,0;('$'#,0)** as the value of the Format property. This string is used to apply the currency format to each sales amount cell that appears in the final report.

You are almost done with the initial formatting and clean up, but you still need to enable the drill down so the report takes minimum real estate. The goal is to show categories and years only when the report is first run and then allow users to see the subcategories and quarters by using the tree-style +/– controls that appear next to each category or year.

1. Click the subcategory group in the Row Groups section to highlight it.

2. Click the down arrow that appears, just to the right side of the group, and then select Group Properties.

3. When the Group Properties window opens, go to the visibility section.

4. Select the Hide option, and set the toggle item drop-down list to Category.

This makes the subcategory collapsed and hidden when the report is first run. By setting the toggle item property to Category, when the report is run, a little + sign appears next to each category, which enables users to drill down into each subcategory exactly like a tree view. You can repeat the exact same steps to toggle the Qtr field by Year.

That's everything you need to build a basic report that shows the AdventureWorks sales by quarter and product category. Finally, preview the report by clicking the Preview tab next to the Design tab.

After you provide the 2005-07-01 and 2007-09-01 as the start and end dates for the report parameters, the report look similar to what is shown in Figure 16-7.

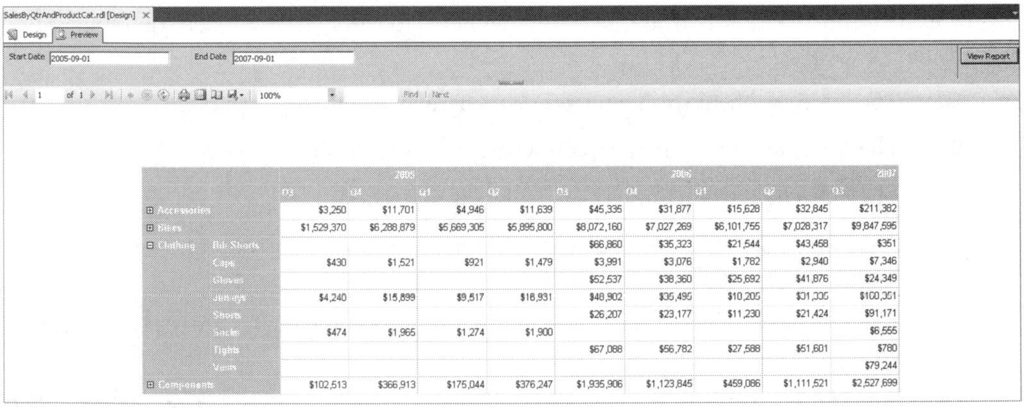

FIGURE 16-7

Data Visualizations

If you have been developing or designing reports for any amount of time, you probably know that no report is complete without some kind of visualization. Essentially, reports are there to enable end users to make fast business decisions, so if you can represent your report in such a way that end users can access its data immediately and get the key points, your report would of great value to them.

SQL Server Reporting Services 2012 includes several useful data visualizations, including the Gauge, Sparklines, Data bars, and Indicators. The Gauge enables report developers to visually display aggregated data, and it's commonly used in digital dashboards. Sparklines, Data bars, and Indicators represent the same basic chart characteristics of values, categories, and series, but without any extraneous content such as axis lines, labels, or legends.

➤ *Data Bar* — A Data bar is like a regular bar chart in which each bar can be scaled based on a given value to display one data point or more.

➤ *Sparkline* — Similar to Sparklines in Excel, a Sparkline in Reporting Services is just a mini-chart that trends over time. They are commonly used to display multiple data points.

➤ *Indicator* — An Indicator is a small icon that is often used to display the status or trend over time for a specific value.

In the example you encounter in this section, you work with Sparkline, while you continue working where you left off with the Sales by Quarter and Product Category report you created in the previous section. For a Sparkline chart you need a value field such as Sales and a group such as Quarter in which to trend it. To add this to your report, follow these steps:

1. Add a new column on the matrix by right-clicking the column that has [Year], [Quarter], and [Sum(Sales)] fields, and select Inset Column ➪ Right option. This creates a column to the right of the selected column, which you can use to place your Sparkline.

2. Add a new Sparkline to the new column by dragging and dropping it from the toolbox to the cell that appears to the right of the cell that has [Sum(Sales)]. Note that because Sparklines display aggregated data, they must be placed in a cell associated with a group.

3. From the Select Sparkline Type dialog, select Area and click OK. You should now have a Sparkline ready to be configured in the new column.

4. Click the Sparkline image. This opens the Chart Data dialog on the right. Click the green plus symbol to the right of the Values area, and select the Sales field from the DSSales data set.

5. Click the plus symbol to the right of the Category Groups area, and select SubCategory field.

Your report is now ready to preview. Switch to the preview window, and your report should look like Figure 16-8.

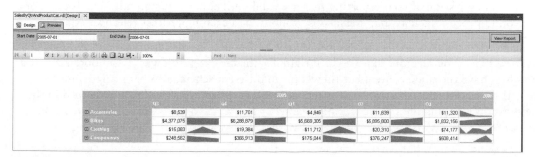

FIGURE 16-8

Tablix

Although, you used a matrix in your report, you are actually using a Tablix data region under the covers. The Tablix (table + matrix) data region offers the flexibility of the table combined with the crosstab reporting features of the matrix, all together.

As you can see in your report, Product Category and Product Subcategory share two different columns, and there is a considerable amount of horizontal spacing wasted in the first column. Well, you can save this spacing and make both groups share the same column by using a feature in Tablix called *stepped columns*. If you have been using crosstab reports, you probably know that this wasn't an easy thing to implement with the old matrix. For more information on stepped columns, refer to the official documentation at `http://msdn.microsoft.com/en-us/library/cc281376.aspx`.

Another feature in Tablix that can help you improve your crosstab reports is *side-by-side crosstab sections*. Your report is currently broken down by year at the top, but what if you want the same grouping (Product Category, and Product subcategory) by a territory section that exists side by side next to the year section? What if you want to allow users to drill down into categories and subcategories and see the year breakdown and territory breakdown at the same time?

You can use Tablix and its native support for side-by-side crosstab sections. All you need to do is to include the territory data in your return result set and add it as a parent column grouping in the same matrix you just used in your report. You can have an unlimited number of side-by-side crosstab groups (correlated or uncorrelated) on rows and columns of a Tablix data region.

The Tablix feature of Reporting Services makes asymmetric layouts in your report super easy.

Publishing Your Report to SharePoint

Now that you have prepared your report, you are ready to deploy it to SharePoint. In SSDT, the terms "publish" and "deploy" are interchangeable. They both refer to a process that makes the report available in SharePoint for online viewing. Although the publishing process may seem simple at first glance, there is more to it than just moving the content from your local drive to a SharePoint side.

But what happens during the publishing that makes it a special process?

First, SSDT validates report items before they are added to the destination libraries in SharePoint. As you may know, you can always go to a document library and upload documents yourself, but in this particular case, you should avoid direct uploads because the validation check never occurs. This means you never know if your reporting files are valid until either you manually access them or a background process such as snapshots, subscriptions, or a caching process references them.

Second, during the publishing process any shared data source in the report project will be converted to a `.rsds` filename extension. (Originally, the file extension was `.rds`.) Both `.rds` and `.rsds` files have the same content but they come in different schemas. What's important to note is that it's only the `.rsds` file that is recognizable by SharePoint, and this is defined in the file extension mapping file (Docicon.xml) located at `Drive:\Program Files\Common Files\ Microsoft Shared\Web Server Extensions\15\Template\XML` using the following:

```
<Mapping Key="rsds" Value="datasource.gif" OpenControl="SharePoint.OpenRsdsFiles"/>
```

The process of converting the .rds file extension to .rsds involves a web service call to the CreateDataSource() web method located at the ReportService2006.asmx endpoint, which makes the actual conversion.

Finally, there is one more thing that the publishing process does for you. If you publish a report that already exists in the destination document library, the report will be checked out, updated as a new version, and then checked back in for you.

Publishing your report to SharePoint is relatively simple. Right-click the solution name, and click Properties to open the Property window, as shown in Figure 16-9.

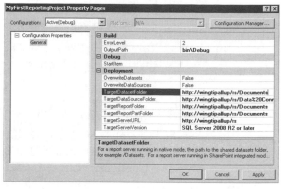

FIGURE 16-9

> **NOTE** *As you can tell, the deployment properties dialog supports deployment settings related to shared data sets and the fact that SSDT can open report definition files for SSRS 2008, SSRS 2008 R2, and later versions.*

Following are all the properties, a brief explanation of what they are for, and what you need to type in them to deploy your report to SharePoint.

➤ Boolean Properties — True or False

➤ *OverwiteDatasets* — This setting specifies whether the shared data set definitions will be overwritten if they already exist in the TargetDatasetFolder in the target SharePoint site.

➤ *OverwriteDataSources* — This setting specifies whether the shared data source definitions will be overwritten if they already exist in the TargetDataSourceFolder in the target SharePoint site.

➤ URL Properties

➤ *TargetDatasetFolder* — A folder relative to the URL you specify in the TargetServerURL property. This folder keeps all the shared data set definition files.

➤ *TargetDataSourceFolder* — A folder relative to the URL you specify in the TargetServerURL property. This folder keeps all the shared data sources' definition files (*.rsds*).

➤ *TargetReportFolder* — A folder relative to the URL you specify in the TargetServerURL property. This folder keeps all the report definition files (.rdl).

➤ *TargetReportPartFolder* — A folder relative to the URL you specify in the TargetServerURL property. This folder keeps all the report part definition files (.rcs). Report parts will be covered in more detail later in this chapter in the "Publishing Report Parts" section.

➤ *TargetServerURL* — The URL of the target SharePoint site where you want to deploy your report.

➤ *TargetServerVersion* — The expected version of SQL Server Reporting Services that is integrated with the target SharePoint site specified in the TargetServerURL property.

To configure the deployment properties, do the following:

1. Set the value of TargetDatasetFolder, TargetReportFolder, and TargetReportPartFolder properties to the fully qualified URL of the Documents document library in the BI Center (see the "Configuring the BI Center" section).

2. Next, Set TargetDataSourceFolder to the fully qualified URL of the Data Connections document library in the BI center (see the "Configuring the BI Center" section).

3. Finally, set the TargetServerURL property to the fully qualified URL of the BI Center and the TargetServerVersion property to SQL Server 2008 R2 or later.

With the deployment properties completely configured, you are ready to deploy the report with all its items to SharePoint. You need Full Control or Contribute permission in the site where you are deploying you reports; otherwise, you will get the Reporting Services login when you attempt to build and deploy the reports. To deploy this report, all you have to do is right-click the solution and click Deploy.

At this point, you can browse to the document library and click the name of the report to render it in the browser (via RSViewerPage.aspx), as shown in Figure 16-10.

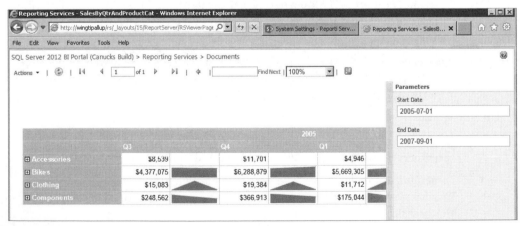

FIGURE 16-10

In case you didn't notice, there is a Cancel link on the page every time your report is run. This means that report processing is completely asynchronous and you have the option to cancel it while it's in progress.

Publishing Report Parts

By definition, report parts are individual items that make up an SSRS report. They can be anything in a report from a parameter to a data region-like matrix. The idea is like splitting an ASPX page into smaller user controls so that they can be shared across multiple pages.

The good news is that these components can be saved individually — without the rest of the report page. More precisely, however, report developers from either SSDT or Report Builder 3.0 publish report parts to a destination folder, and then other report developers or information workers can reuse the published parts and put together their own reports without needing to build everything from the ground up.

Creating report parts in SSDT is for more experienced report developers. Report Builder, on the other hand, is for less experienced users who can use report parts to build their own mashup scenarios or ad-hoc reporting.

The report that you built in this section has only three items that can be published as report parts. To make these parts available on the SharePoint site, follow these steps:

1. From the Report menu, click Publish Report Parts, as shown in Figure 16-11.

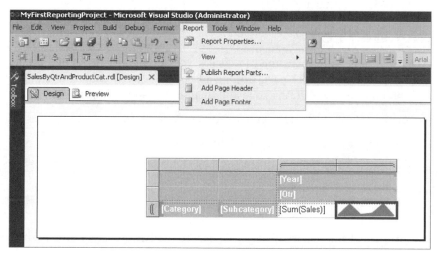

FIGURE 16-11

2. This opens the Publish Report Items dialog, where you can select which items should be published as report parts when the report is deployed. Select all the items and select OK.

3. Redeploy your report by right-clicking the solution and clicking Deploy.

4. Browse to the Documents library in SharePoint and verify that the EndDate and StartDate parameters and Tablix1 object are successfully published to SharePoint as report parts, as shown in Figure 16-12.

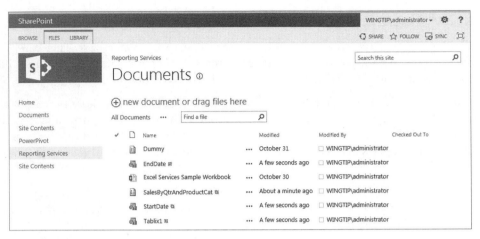

FIGURE 16-12

After the report parts are published to a site, they can be found and reused by information workers using Report Builder. To see a list of available report parts in Report Builder, browse to the View tab, and select Report Part Gallery. You can search for a specific part by typing its name in the search box provided on the top of the pane.

Report Viewer Web Part

In addition to the RSViewerPage.aspx, you can display your reports in SharePoint through the use of the stand-alone Report Viewer web part. Adding a Report Viewer web part to a page is as easy as dragging and dropping it into a Web Part zone and then setting some simple properties.

To host your report in a Report Viewer web part, follow these steps:

1. Click the Settings gear icon on the top-right corner of the page.

2. In the drop-down menu, click Add a Page.

3. In the Name text box, enter **SSRS Demo**.

4. Click the Create button.

5. Add an instance of the Report Viewer web part to the Rich Content area of the page.

6. Click the Web Part menu, and select Edit Web Part to open the tool pane. Notice the extra tabs in the tool pane, which provide custom properties specific to the Report Viewer web part.

7. In the Report text box, specify the relative path and filename of your report. In this example, it is /rs/Documents/SalesByQtrAndProductCat.rdl.

> **NOTE** *Because current integration between Reporting Services and SharePoint supports multiples zones, Report Path is relative. Report Path does not have to be a fully qualified URL.*

8. Leave the default View settings.

9. In the Parameters tab click the Load Parameters button. You can leave the report to use its current default values, or you can override the report to render with another default value of your choice.

10. Click Apply, and then click OK to close the pane.

Figure 16-13 shows a rendered report on a web part page.

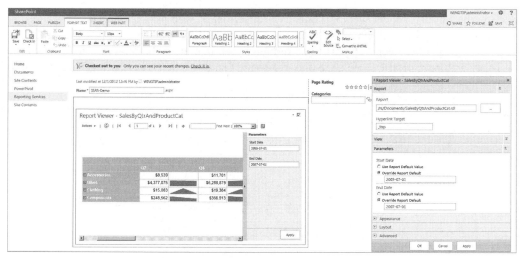

FIGURE 16-13

Limitations

Now that you have a good understanding of what the Report Viewer web part's capabilities are, you must look at a few limitations with this web part.

First, you cannot group multiple reports into a single instance of a Report Viewer web part.

Second, you cannot open a saved report as an attachment to a list item. The Report Viewer web part can respond only to reports that are stored in a document library or are passed in via a connectable web part.

Finally, the Report Viewer web part code is not made available to the public. If you need your own custom Report Viewer web part, you need to code it from scratch or put a wrapper around the Microsoft Report Viewer Control.

Connectable Report Viewer Web Part

One of the great features of SharePoint is the web part connection framework, which enables web parts to accept connections from other web parts. Basically, a connection is an association between two web parts that enables them to share data.

As demonstrated throughout this book, building dashboard pages where different types of web parts exist on the same page, each showing different content and data, is an important part of BI capabilities. In real-world scenarios, these web parts often communicate to each other and are interactive.

In the previous section, it was mentioned that one of the limitations of a Report Viewer web part is its one-to-one association with a report definition file. A stand-alone Report Viewer web part is useful when page visitors are likely to be interested in a particular report. However, in more dashboard-style scenarios, a stand-alone web part is less likely to be what you actually want. You need a web part that's more interactive.

Thankfully, the Report Viewer web part acts as a subscriber in web part connections by implementing the required interfaces. For example, Figure 16-14 shows that you can make an instance of the Report Viewer web part to communicate and get its parameters (or its definition) from another web part on the same page or across pages, such as the Query String Filter web part.

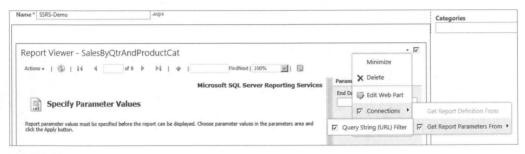

FIGURE 16-14

ATOM Data Feeds

One of the key factors to support Microsoft's BI-for-everyone vision is to enable users to access the most up-to-date data for their day-to-day analysis. The problem in many organizations is having direct access to the back-end data sources, which is something that is historically limited to a number of administrators and a few service accounts. That's mainly because directly accessing raw data without going through the business logic and security layers is not a best practice and can put organizational assets at much higher risks.

Ever since SQL Server 2008 R2, every SSRS report can render as an ATOM feed that follows a WCF data services convention. This means that you can get high-quality and refreshable data sourced from almost everywhere a report can get data from; whether data is represented in Tablix, Chart, and so on doesn't matter.

> **NOTE** *To use your SSRS reports as data feeds, you need to install and config-ure Reporting Services and PowerPivot for SharePoint in the same farm. Also, PowerPivot for Excel client must be installed on the client machine.*

After you find a report with back-end data you want to analyze, you can pull it into your PowerPivot workbook by clicking the Export to Data Feed button on the report toolbar, as shown in Figure 16-15.

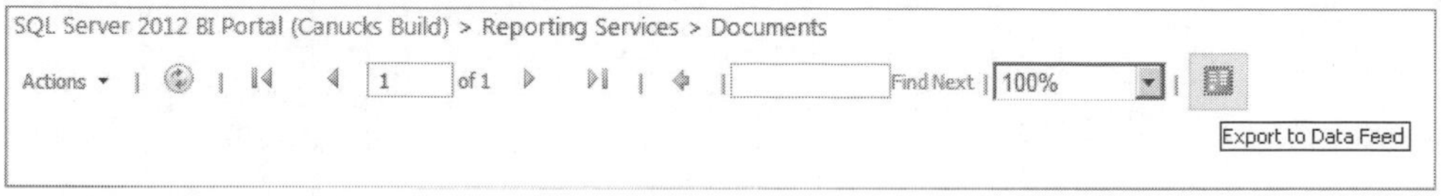

```
SQL Server 2012 BI Portal (Canucks Build) > Reporting Services > Documents

Actions ▼ | ⊕ | I◀  ◀  [ 1 ] of 1  ▷  ▷I | ◈ | [              ] Find Next | [100%    ▼] | [⊡]

                                                                    [Export to Data Feed]
```

FIGURE 16-15

This generates a `.atomsvc` output and asks you if you want to open it locally. If you already have an Excel workbook open, you will be prompted to either select an open workbook to add the data feed to, or create a new workbook for the feed. Next, the Excel client is launched and goes straight into the PowerPivot tab where the Table Import Wizard pops up.

If you click the Next button, the Table Import Wizard shows you a list of data regions in the report, which you can import into your Gemini model and specify table names. Optionally, you can preview data and select which columns from the data feed to add to your model.

Now you should be able to consume the data feed and use the Tablix1 data region as a data source in your PowerPivot workbook.

Reporting Services Data Alert

Starting in SSRS 2012, a user can access reports to set up alert rules and be alerted when report data changes occur that match the defined set of rules. This new feature is called data alert.

> **NOTE** *Data alerts require SQL Server Agent service, and the data source requires hardcoded credentials.*

Data alerts for a report can be accessed from the Actions menu, as shown in Figure 16-16.

Just like ordinary alerts in SharePoint, data alert messages are sent by e-mail. Depending on how important the changes are, users can choose to receive alert messages more or less frequently and only when results change. When setting up the data alerts, you can specify multiple recipients for the alert messages, and this way you can keep others informed. Figure 16-17 shows an example of a data alert that can be set up for the report you created earlier in this chapter:

FIGURE 16-16

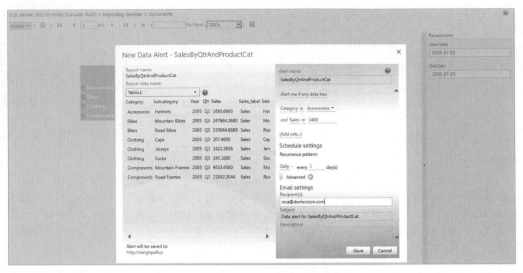

FIGURE 16-17

This data alert indicates that when a sales amount drops below $1,400 for the Accessories category, an alert e-mail needs to be sent out.

Open with Report Builder 3.0

Another option in the Actions menu of a report is Open with Report Builder. If you click the Actions menu and choose Open with Report Builder, Report Builder 3.0 launches by default if it's installed on the server. This action points to the following URL to tell Report Builder which report to open: `http://wingtipallup/_vti_bin/ReportBuilder/ReportBuilder_3_0_0_0` `.application?ReportPath=http://` `wingtipallup/rs/Documents/SalesByQtrAndProductCat.rdl`.

Also, when published, drill-through reports are opened in Report Builder 3.0, forwarded to SharePoint for further processing, and no action is taken locally.

CACHING AND SNAPSHOTS

When a user clicks your report or it's viewed in a Report Viewer web part, the data set defined in that report executes and returns data to the Reporting Services from the underlying data source. Next, the report execution engine uses the report definition file stored in the SharePoint content database to determine how to create the report from the retrieved data, transform it into HTML, and finally push it down through the HTTP pipeline to the user's browser. This process is known as *on-demand report execution*.

Although the on-demand report execution process always results in the most up-to-date data returned to users, each time the report is requested, a new instance of the report is created, which in turn results in a new query issued against the underlying data source. This can exponentially add up to the overall resource utilization in your SharePoint farm.

When users don't need on-demand report execution, and when you need fast report performance, there are some other processing options available to help you manage your report delivery needs in more efficient ways. For example, wouldn't it be nice if users could run your report from cache or snapshots instead? What are your options to prevent the report from being run at arbitrary times during peak hours?

Thankfully, SSRS offer functionality that can help you deliver your reports faster and efficiently. These options are all available from the hover panel of the report definition file, as shown in Figure 16-18.

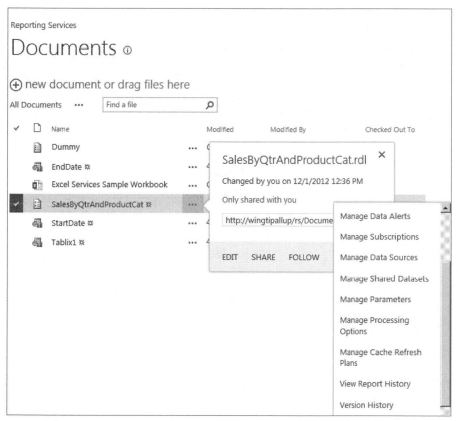

FIGURE 16-18

The goal of this section is to introduce techniques used to improve the performance of your reports, which altogether results in a better user experience.

Several operations discussed in this section require that you hard code the credentials in you report's data source. That's because such operations do not represent a valid Windows security context, and they can't access the back-end data sources by themselves.

And, with that, first start with storing credentials.

Stored Credentials

Many operations in SSRS (such as data alerts) require storing credentials in the data source of a report. To store credentials in your data source, browse to the Data Connections library where you published the data source, and click it. You will be taken directly to a page, as shown in Figure 16-19. On this page, there are multiple options, but the one you want to configure is the third one from the top where it says Stored Credentials.

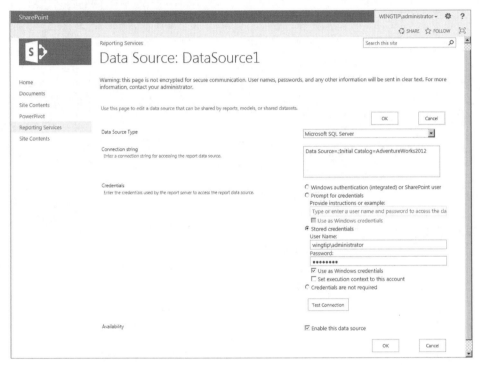

FIGURE 16-19

When you specify the stored credentials, there are two options to select that determine how the stored credentials are authenticated:

➤ *Use as Windows Credentials* — If you select Use as Windows Credentials, the stored credentials should be a Windows user account because it is passed to Windows for subsequent authentication. So you can specify this option and then use a SQL login. Obviously, the account you use here must be granted read permission at a minimum to access the resource.

There are two important tips to remember with regard to this option. First, do not check this box if your data source uses database authentication only (for example, SQL Server authentication). Second, the Windows domain user account must also have permission to log on locally. This permission allows Reporting Services to impersonate the user on the Reporting Services box and send the connection request to the external data source as that impersonated user.

➤ *Set Execution Context to This Account* — You should select this option only if you want to set the execution context on the database server by impersonating the account that represents the stored credentials. Think of this option as a Transact-SQL SETUSER function in SQL Server. There are two important tips to remember when selecting this check box. First, if your data source is going after SQL Server databases, this option is not supported with Windows users; use SQL Server users instead. Second, do not use this option for reports initialized by subscriptions, report history, or snapshots because these processes need a valid Windows user context (not a SQL login) to function.

Managing Parameters

In the real world, most of the reports you develop have one or more parameters, so before you dive into evaluating other processing options, it makes sense to first look at managing report parameters.

But why do you want to manage parameters?

Unlike when you run parameterized reports in an on-demand way, end users won't get a chance to specify parameter values for reports delivered to them behind the scenes. As you saw earlier in this chapter, you can manage the default values configured for the report parameters when authoring reports in SSDT or Report Builder. You can also manage report parameters after they are published to SharePoint without going through the publishing process again.

To manage the parameters of your report, follow these steps:

1. Browse to the Documents document library.

2. Click the hover panel, which appears to the right of the report title, and select Manage Parameters. If the report contains any parameters, they will be listed in the prompt order.

3. Click one of the available parameters, and you should be looking at a page similar to the one shown in Figure 16-20.

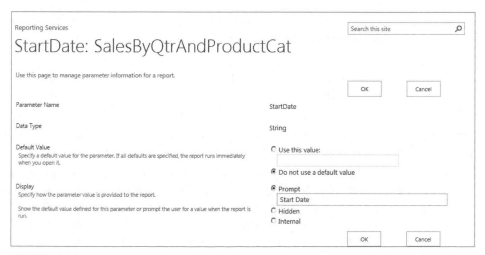

FIGURE 16-20

In this page, you can override the default value for the selected parameter as well as specify how the parameter value should be provided to the report. Available options follow:

➤ *Prompt* — The parameter appears as a text box (for single-valued parameters) or combo box (for multivalued parameters) in the parameter input pane next to the rendered report. Users can specify a new value or select from the available options.

➤ *Hidden* — By selecting this option, the parameter will be hidden in the parameter input pane, but its value can be set in background processes such as subscriptions, caching, and so on. You learn about these processes a bit later.

➤ *Internal* — An internal parameter is not exposed to end users or background processes but is still available in the report definition file.

Planning

Reporting Services provides a powerful and easy-to-use caching mechanism that helps you keep a balance between having up-to-date data in your reports and having faster access to the reports.

> **NOTE** *Like many other heavy-duty operations, caching a report is managed by Reporting Services service applications. A cached report does not utilize page output caching in SharePoint.*

Of course, caching comes at a cost and can be destructive if used in inappropriate ways. So, before you jump right into setting up your report for caching, you need to have a plan. The most important step is to figure out how your design may best utilize caching and what risks you need to be aware of.

When you configure a report for caching, the first time it is requested everything is identical to the on-demand report execution. In fact, the first user who hits the report turns the report into a cached instance and pays the price for everyone else who requests the same instance later. A cached instance is tied with the combination of parameter values. For example, if you have a parameterized report that has two parameters, A and B, then a cached instance of this report with parameter values of A1 and B1 is different than another cached instance that has A2 and B2 as parameter values.

After the report turns into a cached instance, it is stored in the Reporting Services temporary database as an intermediate format image until the cache is invalidated. At this point, if any user requests that report with the same combination of parameter values, the Reporting Services retrieves the image from the Reporting Services temporary database and translates it into a rendering format.

As you may notice, for a report that uses several parameters, there can be multiple cache instances in memory. So, this is something that you may want to consider up front.

Another thing to consider in your cache planning is the cache refresh plan. The key question you should ask yourself in this step is, "How frequently must the cache be invalidated?" The answer to this surprisingly simple question reveals a lot about the schedule you need to associate to your cache refresh plan (see the "Managing Cache Refresh Plans" section later). Remember in a transactional database that underlying data may change often; keeping an in-memory representation of data for a long time can lead to inaccurate results and obviously wrong decisions.

You don't want to get demoted for just caching a report, right?

Caching Your Report

Now that you have a plan in place, the final piece of puzzle is the most obvious one: caching the report by following these steps:

1. Browse to the Documents library.

2. Click the hover panel, which appears to the right of the report title, and select Manage Processing Options.

3. From the Data Refresh Option section, select the Use Cached Data option.

4. From Cache Options section, select Elapsed Time in Minutes and leave at 30 minutes until the cache is invalidated, as shown in Figure 16-21.

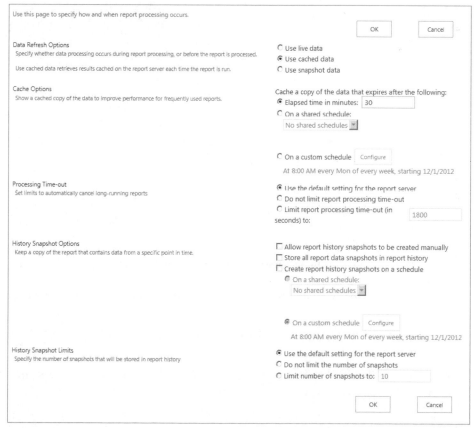

FIGURE 16-21

5. Click OK to enable caching for your report.

Managing Cache Refresh Plans

The way that you cached your report in the previous section is good, but it lacks some control over how the report should be cached. You can use Cache Refresh Plans to address this issue.

To create a cache refresh plan, follow these steps:

1. Browse to the Documents document library.

2. Click the hover panel, which appears to the right of the report title, and select Manage Cache Refresh Plans.

3. Click New Cache Refresh Plan. If you haven't enabled caching as described in the previous section, you will get the error.

4. Create a cache plan for default parameter values (2005-07-01 and 2007-07-01) and a custom schedule that caches this instance once only at 8 AM of 12/01/2012, as shown in Figure 16-22.

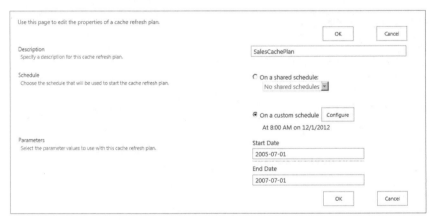

FIGURE 16-22

5. Click OK to go back to the Manage Cache Refresh Plans page.

With your cache plan properly configured, now you have your report with the following caching policy:

➤ Your report with Start Date = 2005-07-01 and End Data = 2007-07-01 will be cached once at 8 AM of 12/01/2012 only.

➤ Any other combinations of parameter values follow the default caching schedule you set up in the previous section, which is 30 minutes.

Snapshots

As mentioned previously, caching your report is a great way to give end users a reasonable balance between having current data in the report and having them access reports faster than typical on-demand report execution.

Reporting Services also offers report snapshots that can be used as an alternative approach to caching. Report snapshots can be used for the following two purposes:

➤ Creating report histories

➤ Controlling report processing

Imagine that the Finance Department of AdventureWorks requests you to maintain a copy of your report (sales by quarter and product category) every quarter and then send them to a number of stakeholders four times during the current year:

1. Browse to the Documents document library.

2. Click the hover panel, which appears to the right of the report title, and select Manage Parameters.

3. Override the default dates for the Start Date and End Date to be 2005-07-01 and 2007-07-01. Then Click OK.

4. Again, click the hover panel, and this time, select Manage Processing Options.

5. From the Data Refresh Option section, select the Use Snapshot Data option.

6. From the Data Snapshot Options section, select Schedule Data Processing, and then select the On a Custom Schedule option.

7. Define a monthly schedule that snapshots the report at 8:00 AM on day(s) 30 of Mar, Jun, Sep, Dec, starting 12/1/2012 and ending 12/31/2012.

8. Select Allow Report History Snapshots to be Created Manually and Store All Report Data Snapshots in Report History, as shown in Figure 16-23.

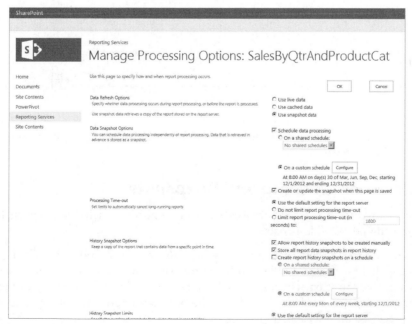

FIGURE 16-23

9.   Click OK return to the Manage Processing Options page.

10. Click OK to enable snapshot for your report.

With the snapshot properly configured, on the specified dates an image of the report with the specified parameters is created and stored in the report history. You can see the snapshots by selecting View Report History from the report hover panel, as shown in Figure 16-24.

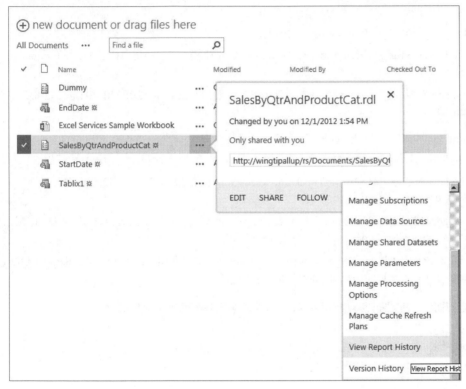

FIGURE 16-24

After you are in the snapshot gallery for a report, you can manually create snapshots, too, by clicking the New Snapshot button.

Differences Between Caching and Snapshots

In concept, report snapshots and caching are used for a single purpose: delivering reports faster while lowering on-demand execution costs.

Functionality-wise, report snapshots differ from a cached instance in several ways. The first obvious difference is that in caching you have full control over how often a cached instance must be invalidated (using an expiration schedule or cache refresh plan), but you certainly cannot control when the new cached instance should kick in. This is because cache refreshment depends on when the first request is received after a cached instance expires.

The report caching process lacks the capability to produce a persistent copy of the report from a specific point in time. However, report snapshots can be placed into the history without overwriting previous snapshots. Remember that when a report execution is persisted, end users will have the ability to compare it at various points in time as well. This is an important feature and often a common business requirement.

The schedule you defined in step 7 of the previous section was different than the schedule you defined for cache refresh plans (see "Managing Cache Refresh Plans"). This schedule is for data processing and it's independent of the report processing. So, the second difference between snapshot and caching is that in report caching you cache data and report layouts together. However, in snapshots, it's the data that can be retrieved in advance and stored as a snapshot, and when the report is actually viewed, everything is put together and returned to the end user. This makes snapshots a more lightweight report processing option compared to caching.

The third difference is that rendering information is not tied and stored with the snapshot. Instead, the final viewing format is adjusted based on what is appropriate for a user or an application requesting it. This functionality makes snapshots a much portable solution.

The fourth difference is that report snapshots offer less flexibility when compared to report caching. Snapshots are like pictures and lack interactivity to an extent. However, a cached report enables users to interact with the reports at the same level that on-demand report execution offers. For example, snapshots are always taken using default parameter values (if applicable), and there is no way to change them afterward. This limitation forces you to create a different snapshot if you need to change the report parameters. Recall that by using cache refresh plans, you can target multiple cached instances of the same report to a different set of parameters.

Figure 16-25 demonstrates a snapshot report. Notice how the parameter input pane is disabled.

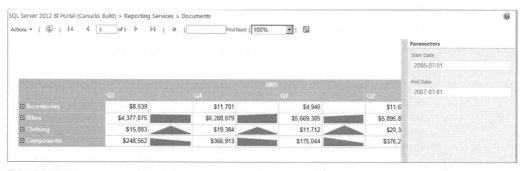

FIGURE 16-25

REPORTING ON SHAREPOINT DATA

SharePoint lists provide lots of functionalities that are already baked into the core SharePoint platform, such as UI elements for managing data, versioning, workflows, and so on. The increasing adoption of SharePoint, along with the great out-of-the-box functionalities that SharePoint lists offer, makes using SharePoint lists a popular choice for storing data.

Whether it makes sense to store your data in SharePoint lists is a discussion for another time and place. (No one solution fits every circumstance.) In reality, however, organizations often have their data stored in various structured and nonstructured data stores, including SharePoint lists.

With the prominence of Business Connectivity Services and external content types in SharePoint 2013, the data in SharePoint lists comes from various places, and no longer does all that data come in via users manually entering it. Instead you are accessing live business data through SharePoint.

No matter how that data is pumped into a SharePoint list, the raw data doesn't have any special meaning by itself. It has to be sorted, filtered, aggregated, and ultimately formatted to make a point. In general, this is referred to as reporting. In SharePoint, you can create a relationship between lists using a lookup field, but there is not an easy way to enforce relationship behavior. Moreover, joining lists, aggregating, sorting, and formatting can quickly become serious bottlenecks. Without the ability to perform such basic operations, reporting on SharePoint data could be challenging.

In the following sections, you create a report using Reporting Services against a sample SharePoint list.

Creating a Sample List

Before going any further on reporting against SharePoint list data, it makes sense to switch gears here and create a SharePoint list called Sales Order Numbers that stores some sales numbers. This is the sample list that will be used in the rest of this chapter.

To create this list in the BI Center, follow these steps:

1. Browse to Site Contents.

2. Click Add an App.

3. Click Custom List App.

4. Enter **SalesOrderNumbers** in the Name text box, and press the Create button.

5. Open the SQL Server Management Studio, and execute the following query to get some sample sales numbers:

```
SELECT TOP 10
     [SalesOrderNumber]
FROM [Sales].[SalesOrderHeader]
```

6. Browse to the SalesOrderNumbers list, and click Quick Edit on the Ribbon.

7. Add the list of top sales order numbers in the SalesOrderNumbers list.

With the list created, now it is time to build the report.

Building the Report

The SharePoint list data extension enables querying against a SharePoint list in both SSDT and Report Builder. The process of creating an SSRS report that goes against a SharePoint list is similar to the process explained in the "Authoring Reports" section earlier in this chapter, and it won't be covered in this section. However, there are a few things that need to be highlighted here.

When creating your data source, make sure you specify the Type as Microsoft SharePoint List and set a fully qualified URL reference to the BI Center site that contains the SalesOrderNumbers list, as shown in Figure 16-26.

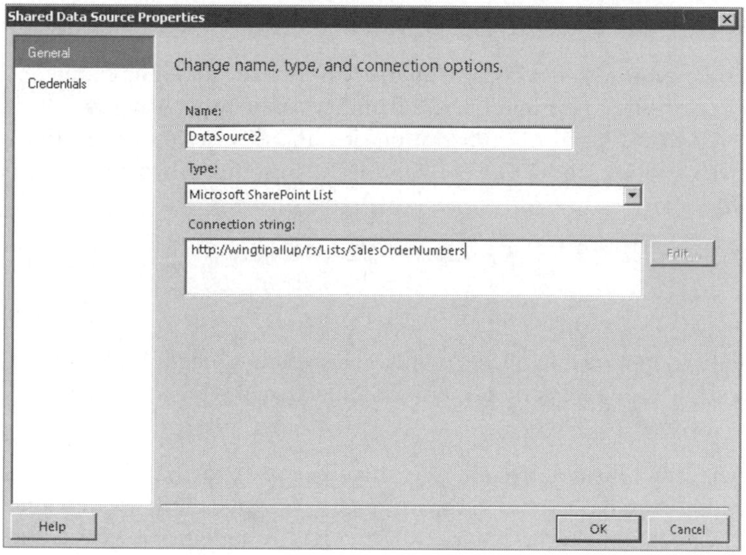

FIGURE 16-26

> **NOTE** *In SSRS 2008, you needed to specify the Type as XML, set a web reference to the* GetListItems *method of the* lists.asmx *web service, and pass in the name of the list as parameter. That is no longer the case in SSRS 2008 R2 and 2012.*

Another point to consider here is to specify a valid authentication type in the Credentials tab of the Shared Data Source properties. By default, the authentication is set to use the Do Not Use Credentials option, which causes an error when you create your data set later if it's changed here.

After the report is developed in SSDT, it can be deployed and displayed on a SharePoint page using the Report Viewer web part.

The list you set up in this section contains only 10 rows. In real-life scenarios in which the list contains more records than the list view threshold, you can snapshot the report during slow business hours and render its snapshot in the Report Viewer web part during regular business hours. For more information, see the "Caching and Snapshots" section earlier in this chapter.

Querying Large Lists

Although SQL Server 2012 has received many core platform-level improvements to support large lists, limitations of queries against large SharePoint lists still exist in SharePoint 2013.

> **NOTE** Resource throttling *is an important topic in SharePoint for report developers. For more information on this topic, see the official product documentation at* `http://technet.microsoft.com/en-us/library/cc303422.aspx`.

Farm administrators have control over how and when the queries can be executed. For example, administrators can set up query throttling to prevent queries from returning too many rows during peak business hours. If you browse to a Central Administration site, and then select Application Management ⇨ Management Web Applications ⇨ General Settings ⇨ Resource Throttling, you can see that the default is set to 5,000.

MULTIPLE ZONES

Although a claims-based authentication model in SharePoint enables you to plug multiple authentication providers into a single web application, there are still cases in which you need to extend the web application and use multiple zones.

For example, suppose that AdventureWorks requires all users to authenticate to SharePoint by using smart cards. To do so, an IT Department has extended the intranet web application, created a new zone, and set up the certificate mapping for that web application in IIS. You might be worried that you need to set up reports to be published to the same zone configured for the smart card in order to display SSRS reports to users who authenticate by using their smart cards.

Fortunately, that isn't a concern because SSRS 2008 R2 and 2012 include multizone support. The support for multiple zones continues to be applicable in SharePoint 2013 and SSRS 2012. You can use the alternative access mapping functionality in SharePoint and set up access to Reporting Services items from any of the five SharePoint zones (default, Internet, intranet, extranet, or custom).

ANONYMOUS ACCESS TO REPORTS

Suppose that AdventureWorks would like to allow access to the Catalog of Products report without forcing its Internet users to log in. With the increasing popularity of SharePoint and its growth in delivering public-facing websites, one frequently asked question has been if SSRS supports anonymous users. As you saw in the previous section, multizone support is included in SSRS 2008 R2 and SSRS 2012.

Even though SharePoint supports anonymous access to a site and maps it to the Limited Access permission level, there is an issue in displaying SSRS reports to anonymous users in Connected mode. Unfortunately, Reporting Services still requires a valid security context and doesn't support anonymous access to reports out of the box. The issue is that anonymous users do not represent a true security context in SharePoint; therefore, when they try to access reports, SSRS won't authorize their access to the Reporting Services.

> **NOTE** *Obviously, you can always use custom development and wrap anonymous users in a valid security context (that is, Guest) and solve the issue. You can find a proof-of-concept implementation of this technique in the blog at* http://www.devhorizon.com/go/6.

REPORTING SERVICES EXECUTION ACCOUNT

Reporting Services never enables its service account (configured in the Reporting Service Configuration Manager) with all its administrative privileges to be delegated when connecting to a resource on the network.

So, if you are reporting against a data source that does not require authentication or when you use a SQL account in your data source, the question is, "How is the connection between Reporting Services and the data source established? Under what security context?" Remember, Reporting Services must use a valid Windows security context to access resources such as an XML file or a SQL instance that supports SQL authentication.

In the Reporting Services world, this liaison account is referred to as an execution account, and it's mainly used in the following two scenarios:

➤ *Scenario 1: Security context for network connection* — In this scenario SSRS sends the connection requests over the network to connect to external data sources such as an XML file or SQL Server when the report uses a SQL account to login to a SQL Server instance. If the execution account is not specified, Reporting Services impersonates its service account but removes all administrator permissions when sending the connection request.

➤ *Scenario 2: Access to external resource* — In this scenario SSRS sends the connection requests to retrieve external resources used in a report that doesn't store credentials in its data source.

For example, when you create a report that has a link to an external image stored in a remote server, in the preview mode your credentials will be used to display the image. However, when the report is deployed and viewed on a SharePoint site, Reporting Services uses its execution account to retrieve the image. If the execution account is not specified, the image is retrieved using no credentials (that is, anonymous access). Obviously, if neither of these two accounts has sufficient rights to access the image, it won't show up in the report. This is important to remember for deploying reports to SharePoint because images used in your report may or may not be in the same site collection that the current report viewer has permission to access.

> **NOTE** *The Reporting Services execution account is totally different than an unattended account in Excel services or PerformancePoint. An SSRS execution account must be used only for specific functions as described in this section. Microsoft has made it crystal clear that the execution account must not be used as a login account or for retrieving data from back-end data sources.*

The simplest way to set up an execution account is to specify it on the Execution Account page in the Reporting Services service application, as shown in Figure 16-27.

FIGURE 16-27

SUMMARY

When you put together all the pieces you learned in this chapter, you have a powerful array of options for displaying and interacting with reports deployed to your SharePoint sites.

This chapter began with an overview of the out-of-the-box ways of displaying reports onto SharePoint pages. Next, it covered some caching techniques in Reporting Services and some unique must-know techniques to help speed up your report deliveries.

To ensure a successful enterprise implementation of your business intelligence solutions, you need to have an efficient mechanism of delivering information through reports to end users. Therefore, reporting performance must be consistent and balanced. In this chapter, you learned how to use these functionalities rather than having users access the reports in an on-demand manner. Most of the techniques discussed in this chapter have the advantage of being scheduled and run in the background, thus giving you greater control over when and where the execution occurs.

17

Developing Excel Applications in SharePoint 2013

Excel is one of the most-used application platforms for constructing business applications. Excel provides the ability to have complex business logic along with displaying data and rich chart support. It is no surprise that Microsoft wanted to take those experiences a step further and enable these Excel applications for all users to consume and interact with. To accomplish this Microsoft introduced Excel Services with SharePoint 2007 and has been improving the experience with each version. Now in SharePoint 2013 the new features are more focused on the web-based technologies and enabling developers to take advantage of the rich set of APIs.

Excel Services can be thought of as the engine that drives Excel on the web. It is responsible for displaying workbook data, tables, and charts or content, making web-based calls to data, and running large calculations on an application server in your SharePoint Farm. Excel Services is much more than just Excel on the web. You can use it to build the same complex applications on the desk as you can on the web. Simply put, Excel

Services lets you upload E spreadsheets and then access the data or display them on your SharePoint site or any other web page.

The introduction of Excel Services and having the ability to interact with Excel workbooks on the web was an amazing step forward, but Microsoft also wanted to make it easier to view, edit, and update Excel workbooks directly on the web. Excel Services did not provide all this functionality, but luckily Microsoft introduced Microsoft Office Web Apps. SharePoint 2010 introduced the Microsoft Office Web Applications, but they have become developer platforms with SharePoint 2013 and the new Office apps that can be built either in the client or within SharePoint. As you see in this chapter, you now have the ability to work with Excel workbooks using Excel Web Apps, but also have amazing options for programming solutions with the Excel Services API.

Some of the key features of Excel applications are

➤ The ability to upload workbooks and view them in the browser

➤ Web-based endpoints with REST, OData, and SOAP

➤ Scripting APIs for rich web-based apps

➤ Apps for Office for full enterprise experiences in the client and web

As you can see in Figure 17-1, the goal of displaying rich Excel data is still one of the primary scenarios of all the tools of Excel. Depending on your requirements, you might use only a few aspects of Excel applications or all the components together.

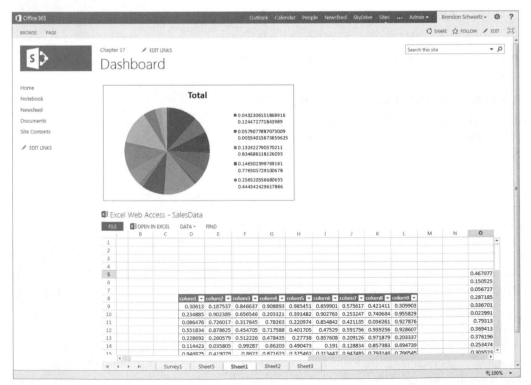

FIGURE 17-1

WHAT'S NEW

Excel applications related to SharePoint have become more than just Excel Services applications. The whole suite of tools now used to build these applications includes the rich client application with Apps for Office, Excel Web Apps, and Excel Services. There have been improvements in each area with a focus on allowing developers to create applications quickly that can be reused no matter what the viewing surface.

Updates to the Client

Many of the changes to the client are based on the general user and the user interaction of the client application of Excel. There are updates to the user interface of Excel as well as many of the wizards that you notice as soon as you start using the rich client.

Some of the new features include:

➤ Flash Fill

➤ Web service functions

Customization Enhancements

Excel and Excel Web Apps now enable a new type of development called Apps for Office that enables you to develop applications that can be rendered inside of the client application. These apps can be hosted either in the client or within SharePoint providing endless customization options.

New Enhancements to Excel Service APIs

Excel Services has added some exciting technologies in addition to the features that were already available in SharePoint 2010. These new features focus on the web scripting and interface APIs to get data.

The new features are:

➤ JavaScript UDFs

➤ Excel Interactive View

➤ OData in Excel Services

These new features will be covered in depth, so let's take a look at the how to build these dynamic Excel business applications.

DASHBOARDS AND EXCEL MASHUPS

Creating powerful applications with Excel data starts with the Excel workbook and then ends by displaying that data in a meaningful way to end users. The visualizations have been known as Dashboards and are now introduced as *Excel Mashups*. To build a Dashboard you could use the

REST services and Excel Web Access web part. These components are now further enhanced by the ability to bring in HTML table data directly from a web page. After the data is in Excel Services, you can generate the tables and charts, connect the components to work with each, and build business applications with Excel Mashups.

> **NOTE** *The Excel team is building a site with code and documentation at* `http://www.excelmashup.com`.

To build Excel Mashups you can use a number of APIs that are readily available. These APIs are used in both the web-based versions of Office Web Apps and within SharePoint. The REST and SOAP APIs built into Excel Services are only available within SharePoint, whereas the JavaScript API and Interactive view are both available using Excel Services on the web.

Microsoft has introduced these features on the web through its online tools such as SkyDrive using Office Web Apps with the Excel Services JavaScript API exposed to the client browser. There is even an online API browser tool located at `http://www.excelmashup.com/APIBrowser` that you can use to try out code before you deploy it, as shown in Figure 17-2.

FIGURE 17-2

Excel Interactive View (Excel Everywhere)

With the amount of data that has moved to the web, there is a need to use the data quickly in Excel, but also display it as a standard HTML table on the web. Many times users would copy and paste web pages with HTML data directly into Excel, but this was difficult with formatting issues and web page content being copied into the Excel workbook. To help build full dashboards on the web, Microsoft has introduced technology that can convert the HTML tables into an Excel work-book in either the Office Web Apps or full client. The idea that you could consume these standard HTML tables in Excel is called Excel Everywhere and is enabled by a new technology called Excel Interactive View. After you open the HTML data in Office Web Apps, you also have the ability to open it in the full Excel client application.

Users can now add a button to their website that opens the data in the Office Web App version of Excel without any software required for installation. This requires having an Internet connection to the service providing the application for rendering, but this should not be an issue because the web pages are hosted on the web. Also the HTML tables created need to have proper W3C formatting and not have broken formatting with the data. A header value is important for determining what the names of the columns are, but you can simply add the `<thead>` value in your HTML table. To gen-erate a button for your page, Microsoft has provided a page located at `http://www.excelmashup.com/eiv/addbutton` where you can fill out the details and automatically generate the code needed for your HTML page, as shown in Figure 17-3.

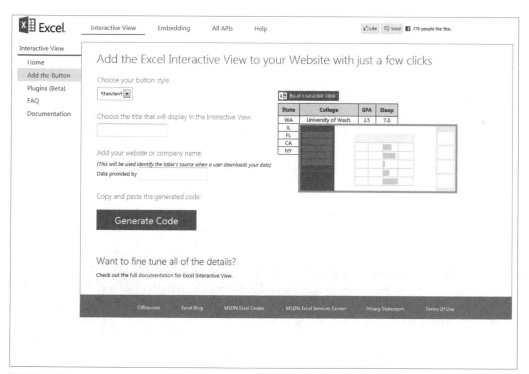

FIGURE 17-3

After you generate the code to put on your page, you can edit the values if needed and add the HTML to the correct location. There are two HTML tags that you need to add to the HTML page: one for the button to open Excel Interactive View and the other as the script tag for the required JavaScript libraries that are needed. The following code shows the required anchor tag with the attributes and the script tag. Make sure that the script tag references the correct protocol, or you get an error about displaying the button. This means if you use HTTPS, use `https` in the script tag reference such as `https://r.office.microsoft.com/r/rlidExcelButton?v=1&kip=1`. The reason the script tag is at the bottom of the code reference is because you don't want the script to slow down the page from rendering. You should always put external references such as this one at the bottom of your HTML page if possible:

```html
<a href="#" name="MicrosoftExcelButton" data-xl-tableTitle="First Table"
     data-xl-buttonStyle="Standard" data-xl-fileName="Book1"
     data-xl-attribution="Data provided by Brendon Schwartz" ></a>

<table>
     <thead>
<tr>
<td>Rank</td>
<td>Name</td>
<td>Number of Games</td>
<td>First Game</td>
<td>Last Game</td>
</tr>
</thead>
<tr>
<td>1</td>
<td>Cal Ripken, Jr.</td>
<td>2,632</td>
<td>05-30-1982</td>
<td>09-19-1998</td>
</tr>
<td>2</td>
<tr>Lou Gehrig</td>
<td>2,130</td>
<td>06-01-1925</td>
<td>04-30-1939</td>
</tr>
</table>
<script type="text/javascript"
     src="http://r.office.microsoft.com/r/rlidExcelButton?v=1&kip=1">
</script>
```

There are a few optional attributes that you could add to the embedded HTML. These attributes help Excel determine initial information and meta data about the data it displays. They are not required to make the functionality work, but it is highly recommended to use them when using the Interactive view. These attributes are listed in Table 17-1.

TABLE 17-1: Optional Attributes Used with Excel Interactive View

ATTRIBUTE	DEFAULT VALUE	DESCRIPTION
data-xl-dataTableID	N/A	Enables each table on a web page to have a unique identifier.
data-xl-buttonStyle	Standard	There are two types of buttons that can be used: the Standard and Small options.
data-xl-fileName	Book1	Enables you to set the name of the workbook when it is opened in Excel.
data-xl-tableTitle	Same as the web page title	Provides a name for the table that can be up to 255 characters long.
data-xl-attribution	Data provided by \<web site domain>	Enables you to define who is providing the data that shows up in Excel and Excel Web Apps. This data can also be only up to 255 characters.

EXCEL

Excel applications are built with the same concept of providing data, functions, and visualizations to the user. Excel still provides the one-stop shop for creating these workbooks to contain as many Worksheets as needed. The data is not as structured as some applications, which enable you to build robust applications, but you must understand some of the basics.

When understanding how to build an Excel application, there are a few concepts that can help you know how to navigate the landscape. As previously mentioned, the first is the application container called a workbook. This single file contains all the elements needed to store data and display charts, as well as complex business logic using a number of programming techniques. Each Excel workbook has at least a single worksheet, which is the canvas for adding the formulas and data. This data is organized into cells or a number of cells called a range. The importance of knowing each of the components is that you programmatically access this information and must know how to get to the data you want to display or work with.

Flash Fill

This new feature builds on the AutoComplete feature already used when typing in the same column. To get the Flash Fill to occur, Excel uses columns adjacent to the current column to create patterns that could provide useful information. For example, if you have the first name in a column and the last name in the next column, the flash fill would be able to create the Last Name, First Name pattern if it were used in the first cell of the next column.

Web Service Functions

The use of data on the web has become important for understanding real-time data. To assist with this, Microsoft Excel now has a set of functions built directly into the application that enable you to call anonymous web services. This is done directly from within Excel cells and formulas, and you are even provided functions to parse the data to display in the Excel sheet. This is a great way to consume REST and RSS services that do not require any authentication, but you are required to find other alternatives if you require authenticated sources. If you want to consume authenticated data sources, consider the data connections or user-defined functions (UDF) discussed in the chapter. Table 17-2 shows the new Web category functions added to Excel 2013.

TABLE 17-2: Excel Web Service Functions

FUNCTION	DESCRIPTION
=WEBSERVICE(url)	Enables the call of anonymous web services.
=ENCODEURL()	Used to encode the values passed through a URL, usually used with the call to WEBSERVICE.
=FILTERXML()	Based on the XML source and XPath, this function returns the parsed XML from the requested path.

> **NOTE** *For a list of data sources on the web, look in the Programmable Web at* `http://www.programmableweb.com/` *or* `Data.Gov` @ `http://data.gov.`

WEBSERVICE Function

The WEBSERVICE function is designed to pull data into an Excel workbook from any REST endpoint. This works well for most RSS types of feeds and single post reads. If you want a more robust and customized solution, you can still build that out, but you now have the option of using a quick read to a web service without writing any code:

```
=WEBSERVICE(
    "http://rss.weather.com/weather/rss/local/30068?cm_ven=LWO&
    cm_cat=rss&par=LWO_rss")
```

ENCODEURL Function

Using the ENCODEURL function takes any values that are not safe for passing on the URL menu and automatically encodes them for the request. This helps prevent the accidental use of special characters or unknown values when using the WEBSERVICE requests. Always use this function if you pull data from somewhere on your Excel workbook. You can see the results provided when you use a set of special characters returned in the following example with %24pecial%20%26Charact%2Ars:

```
=ENCODEURL("$pecial &Charact*rs")
```

FILTERXML Function

The FILTERXML function enables you to take any XML in your workbook and return the XPath values that you have requested. The value is going to be returned as text and not HTML, so make sure the returned results are what you expect before parsing them. Although this function is not dependent on any of the other web category functions, you will most likely use it any time you use the WEBSERVICES function calls.

```
=FILTERXML(D11,"rss/channel/item[1]/title")
```

EXCEL WEB APPS

Excel Web Apps is an extension of the Excel rich client that enables users to view and edit workbooks in the browser. They provide the rich online experience for working with Excel workbooks. These tools are designed to extend the rich Excel client to the browser and create a seamless experience in working with the Excel workbooks, either on the desktop or online. Excel Web App has evolved into an application available in your Enterprise, hosted online with Office 365 and for personal use in Windows Live SkyDrive. The online experience provides the same look and feel as Excel and many of the same feature sets used in the client.

The advantages of using your Excel workbook in Excel Web Apps are that you can read and edit your data without installing a full client. This allows you to make quick changes to an Excel workbook or even create a new one. In addition to the working with the data, Excel Web App also provides a rich set of collaboration tools for working with other team members. You can see the team members working with the Excel workbook and reach out to them if you have an instant messaging application such as Lync installed. If you need to use the Excel client, the tool enables you to open the Excel workbook in the client with a single-click button.

EXCEL APPS FOR OFFICE

Apps for Office enables you to build rich web-based solutions inside the Office platform. For Excel this applies to building apps for Office that run both in the client and in SharePoint using Excel Web Apps. This topic is covered only briefly as it relates to Excel and SharePoint.

Apps for Office uses standard web-based technologies like HTML, CSS, JavaScript, REST, OData, and OAuth. This enables a developer to design a solution that can be deployed to the rich Excel client and used in the web browser. Excel provides two types of extension projects; these are the Excel Content apps and the Excel Task Pane apps. For a full understanding of apps, read Chapter 6. The app chapter has details on the anatomy of apps and architecture.

Excel 2013 has a new section on the Insert tab that enables end users to insert the Apps for Office that they would like to use. This also enables users to review items in the Office Store if they have a valid user they are logged into Excel with. To build these apps you need to make sure you have set up your development environment using the Microsoft Office Developer Tools for Visual Studio 2012 for more details, see Chapter 3, "Developer Tools for SharePoint 2013," on tooling. In addition to the developer tools, you need to have Excel 2013 installed on the development machine for testing.

Apps for Office are just web-based components, which mean they can be easily reused in other Office applications. For example, you could create a Task Pane app for Excel but leave the option to also install it in Word and Project. You do not need to worry about selecting the right type of app ahead of time because you can change between the Task Pane app and the Content app easily. The full list of supported office applications and the type of apps for Office they support are listed at `http://msdn.microsoft.com/en-us/library/office/apps/jj220082(v=office.15)#StartBu ildingApps_TypesofApps`.

The core difference between the two Excel apps for Office is an XML element in the package that specifies where the app will be hosted. The `OfficeApp` element has an attribute that will be defined as either `TaskPaneApp` or `ContentApp`. This type of attribute is the directive for Excel on where to load the app on the workbook surface. The same interaction using the API is available with the workbook using either type, but the Content app will not work in other Office applications like the Task Pane app.

Excel Task Pane Apps

The ability to build a Task Pane add-in to Excel is not a new experience, but the way that you can now create the task pane and also have it displayed in SharePoint is different. The task panes built with the managed code in the past had some areas that were difficult to manage such as deployment and portability. Excel 2013 has incorporated all the components of Excel, such as the rich client, Office Web Apps, Excel Services, and SharePoint 2013 together to create a powerful framework that eliminates some of these issues.

The Task Pane apps are designed to be hosted in their own container in Excel and provide contextual information or functionality to the worksheet. The task pane can respond to events, update the workbook, or even just provide relevant information. This type of app does not overlap or interfere with the workbook content that is on the page. To build a basic sample Task Pane app, use the following steps.

1. Open Visual Studio 2012.

2. Start a new project, and select Visual C# ➪ Office/SharePoint ➪ Apps. Then select the App for Office 2013 project.

3. Provide a name for the project such as **ExcelTaskPane**.

4. Leave the radio box on the Task Pane app and leave the check boxes checked for Excel, Word, and Project. This enables you to run your task pane in another Office app.

5. Click Finish, and you will have the project structure of the app.

6. To try out the sample code on the default HTML page, press F5, and you should see the task pane in Excel, as shown in Figure 17-4.

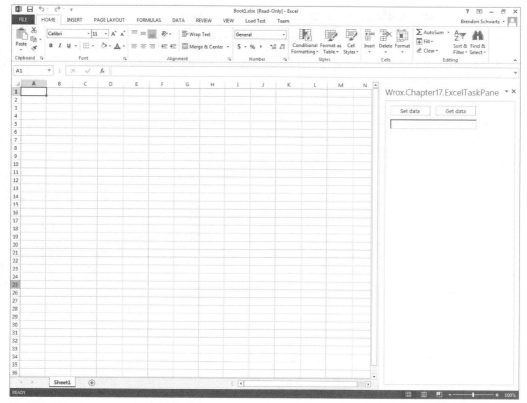

FIGURE 17-4

You must have script debugging turned on in Internet Explorer to debug directly from Visual Studio in the Office applications because they are web apps. If you do not have it turned on, you see an error, as shown in Figure 17-5.

Excel Content Apps

The Excel Content apps are web-based elements that can be embedded into the content of the Excel workbook. These apps can perform the same interaction

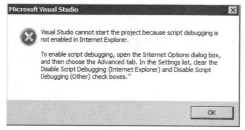

FIGURE 17-5

with the workbook that Task Pane apps can and are built in the same way using the JavaScript API for Office. These apps for Office can provide rich content in your Excel workbooks and even media such as videos or pictures. Excel is the only Office application that provides that ability to have the Content app with this release. Now look at the difference between the two when creating the project with Visual Studio.

1. Open Visual Studio 2012.

2. Start a new project and select Visual C# ➪ Office/SharePoint ➪ Apps, and then select the App for Office 2013 project.

3. Provide a name for the project such as **ExcelContentApp**.

4. Select the radio button for Content app in Excel; then click Finish.

5. To see what this app looks like, press F5 and see that the app shows up in the workbook this time. See Figure 17-6.

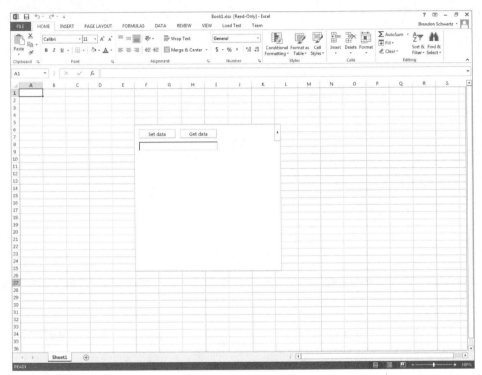

FIGURE 17-6

The Content app can be sized based on the needs of what you are building using the RequestedWidth and RequestedHeight XML elements located in the manifest.xml. You can see these attributes in the Properties window of the Manifest and can easily update them. The Content app can also be moved around inside of the Excel workbook by the end user to place it where it fits best for them.

> **NOTE** *If you want more details on the JavaScript API for Office, use the link on MSDN at* http://msdn.microsoft.com/en-us/library/office/apps/fp160953(v=office.15).

EXCEL SERVICES

Excel Services was designed for scalability and is composed of three distinct components. The Excel Calculation Services component gathers data, performs calculations, and handles user sessions. The Excel Web Access (EWA) web part renders a server-based spreadsheet using only HTML and JavaScript, which enables users to access the spreadsheet from just about any browser and platform. The final piece of Excel Services is the Excel Web Services (EWS) service layer that enables developers to build custom applications that take advantage of Excel workbooks.

Excel Services Architecture

The Excel Services architecture is built using the SharePoint Service Application framework and can be scaled for load-balancing scenarios such as supporting a large number of Excel workbooks or concurrent requests. All the settings can be configured from Central Administration using the Excel Services service application settings. Excel Services uses the workbooks built in either the Excel client or Excel Web Apps and then deployed to Excel Services, which are stored and secured in the SharePoint content database.

The architecture enables multiple web applications to use the service, but many of the settings are based on specific locations that are considered trusted. On each web application the Excel workbooks can be rendered with the EWA web part. This web part provides the ability to have interactive code using the JavaScript Object Model (JSOM) that can automate tasks.

There is also a set of rich web service APIs provided to enable application access to the workbooks through the REST API, now including OData and the existing SOAP interface. These web services provide the ability to render and modify the Excel workbook data without have to use server-side code or JavaScript located on a page. Using all of the components together provides the ability to access the Excel workbook with any of the APIs depending on the application architecture and the business requirements.

Excel Services Data Access

Data access in Excel and specifically in Excel Services is a key component of building critical business applications. Usually, the data in the spreadsheet is only part of the business data and must be combined or measured against other values in the organization's application set. There are two types of data connections you want to work with in SharePoint 2013. The first is making connections to external data sources such as SQL Server or web services. The second is the ability to have a data connection to the sources that are external to the Excel workbook. Both of these options are available using the data connections' REST API and UDF functions with Excel Services.

Trusted Locations

Making Excel workbooks available requires having a trusted location to publish to. There are many configuration settings that can be applied to the Excel Services application and the site that hosts the published workbooks. Determine where you want to allow trusted Excel file locations and trusted connection document libraries in your SharePoint farm. Then use the settings in the Excel Services service application to configure those locations. The following steps walk you through defining these locations:

1. Browse to the Central Administration site.

2. From the Application Management Category, choose Manage Service Applications.

3. From the list of existing service applications, click Excel Services.

4. From the Manage Excel Services Application page, select Trusted File Locations.

5. If the location where you plan to publish your workbook is not in the list of trusted locations, click Add Trusted File Location and define that location.

6. Make sure you enable the workbook to make external connections available by setting the Allow External Data setting to either Trusted Data Connection Libraries Only or Trusted Data Connection Libraries and Embedded.

7. Click OK to return to the Excel Services Trusted File Locations page. At this point, the list of trusted file locations should look like Figure 17-7.

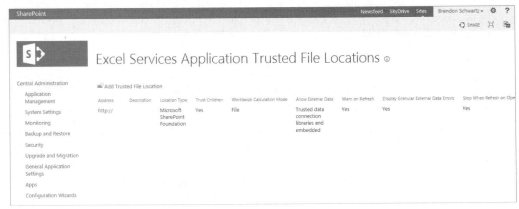

FIGURE 17-7

8. Browse back to the Manage Excel Services page, and this time, select Trusted Data Connection Libraries.

9. From the Excel Services Trusted Data Connection Libraries page, specify the Data Connection Library from which Excel workbooks opened in Excel Services are allowed to access the Office Data Connection files.

> **NOTE** *The service applications can be associated with multiple web application, so you should define the trusted locations for each web application that hosts your Excel workbooks based on your sites. The same thing is true if you have assigned multiple Excel Services service applications to one web application. You need to define the trusted locations for each service application.*

Office Data Connection

Excel and SharePoint 2013 provide the ability to connect to external data sources using predefined settings. These predefined settings are stored in an Office Data Connection (.odc) file and stored in a Data Connections Library. The Data Connections Library can be added to your sites but must be a trusted location to run the data connections designed for the Excel workbooks. You can see in Figure 17-8 that there are number of new data connections that Excel now allows directly from the Get External Data menu.

FIGURE 17-8

The following steps guide you through connecting to the new OData Data Feed connection, but any of the connection types such as SQL Server or Analysis Services could be used:

1. Open Microsoft Excel 2013, and open a new blank workbook.

2. Click the Data tab on the Ribbon; then click the From Other Sources drop down.

3. Select the From OData Data Feed with the small, orange square icon.

4. Select the feed to use; this could be an Excel Services OData feed as you will see later, but for this example you can use the test service from odata.org at `http://services.odata .org/Northwind/Northwind.svc/`.

5. The tables in the model are shown to you; select the Customers table from the list, and Click Next again.

6. Click Next again and change the filename and friendly name to something familiar, such as ODataTestSite- Customers.odc or Customer OData Test Site from OData.org.

7. Make sure to check Always Attempt to Use This File to Refresh Data.

8. Click Authentication Settings to view the method of authentication for Excel Services. This should be set to Use the Authenticated User's Account, but you can see the other options available.

9. Click Finish. Then when Excel displays the Import Data dialog box, click OK to see the data and the new Quick Analysis feature in Excel.

10. Browse to `C:\Users\[Current User]\Documents\My Data Sources` and upload the `ODataTestSite- Customers.odc` file to a Data Connection Library on your site.

11. When you upload the file, make sure to select New ⇨ Office Data Connection when uploading to set the Content Type to the correct type.

12. Now anyone who clicks the Office Data Connection can open Excel to see the data in the workbook.

Creating the `.odc` files ensures that all users can view data to connections that are already defined, and they do not need to locate where the data is every time. The Office Data Connection files automatically have the security defined and define with credentials to send to the server. This also gives the site administrators the ability to manage the connections for their site and adjust them as needed when anything changes. After settings changes are made, they are immediately available for future connection requests.

Unattended Service Account

The Unattended Service Account is used as a way to provide a single account for all users when accessing back-end data sources. The Unattended Service account is used in the Excel Services Application but is not the same account as the application pool identity. Actually, the unattended service account is stored in the service application database and is not used with IIS. The unattended service account can be used in many service applications such as Excel Services, Visio Services, Business Connectivity Services, and PerformancePoint Services.

In Excel Services, each workbook can have its own unattended service account, or they can all share a global unattended service account. If the workbook connection's authentication type is set to Secure Store Service (SSS), you need to reference a target application ID that stores the unattended service account credentials required for authenticating to the data source. This makes the service account reusable across applications and connections.

> **NOTE** *Each account created requires administrative effort so you should plan accordingly.*

If the authentication type is set to None in the workbook connection settings, the global unattended service account is used. This account, along with many other Excel Services settings are configured in the Excel Services service application. If you use the global account but do not configure it, you get an error when trying to open a data source connection.

The process to create the unattended service account is straightforward. Before you start creating this account, you need to ensure that you are either the farm administrator or the service application administrator for the instance of the Secure Store Service.

To create this account, perform the following steps:

1. Browse to the Central Administration site.

2. From the Application Management category, click Manage Service Applications.

3. From the list of existing service applications, click Secure Store Service application.

4. From the Ribbon, click the New button.

5. Figure 17-9 shows the settings for the new target application. In the Target Application ID box, type a name to identify this target application. In the Display Name box, type a friendly name that is shown in the user interface. In the Contact Email box, type the e-mail address of the primary contact for this target application. Change the Target Application Type to Group for mapping all the members of one or more groups to a single set of credentials that can be authenticated to the data source, and then click Next.

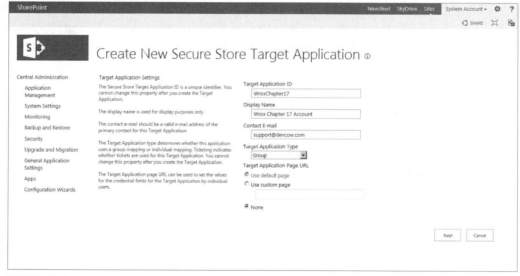

FIGURE 17-9

6. Because the Target Application Type is Group, you can leave the default values in the Create New Secure Store Target Application and move to the next step by clicking Next.

7. In the Specify the Membership Settings page, in the Target Application Administrator field, specify all users who have access to manage the target application settings. Specify the groups or users that are mapped to the credentials for this Target Application in the Members field.

8. Click OK.

At this point you should see the new target application along with other target applications in the Manage Target Applications page, as shown in Figure 17-10.

FIGURE 17-10

After creating the target application, you should set credentials for it. To set credentials for the target application you have just created, follow these steps:

1. Select the target application you just created, and then in the menu, click Set Credentials.

2. Fill out the fields for setting credentials (see Figure 17-11) and click OK. This is the account that is used to authenticate to the data source, so you need to ensure this account has the correct permission.

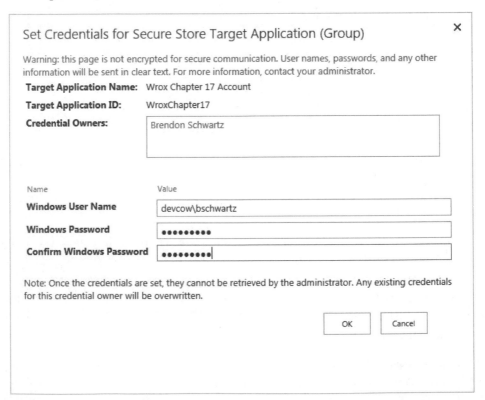

FIGURE 17-11

Finally, the last action is to introduce the new target application to Excel Services. You can accomplish this by following these steps:

1. Browse to the Central Administration site.

2. From the Application Management category, choose Manage Service Applications.

3. From the list of existing service applications, click Excel Services.

4. From the Manage Excel Services page, click Global Settings.

5. Browse all the way down to the External Data section, and specify the new target application ID (string text) in the Target Application ID text box, as shown in Figure 17-12.

6. Click OK when you are done.

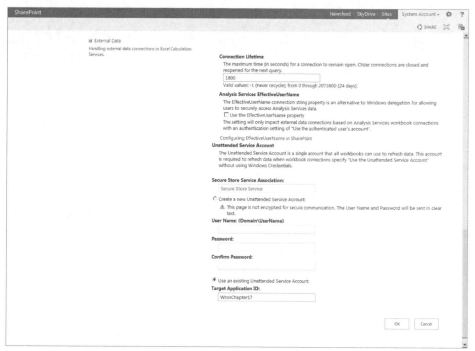

FIGURE 17-12

REST API

Providing access to data is important especially from web-based technologies such as JavaScript. Microsoft introduced a REST-based framework providing data from Excel Services in SharePoint 2010 to allow any client to make calls using REST calls. These REST calls were used to pull back HTML, Images, and ATOM results for Excel workbooks hosted with Excel Services. This functionality has now been extended to also include the use of OData as an option when using the REST endpoints.

The REST API now is allowed for use on SharePoint Online, which provides a new set of applications that can be built using the SharePoint Online platform. Also, there has been the introduction of the OData protocol into the REST API to all Excel Services calls, for a more structured format of data access of the tables in Excel workbooks.

> **NOTE** *The first step to understand how to develop with the REST API is to understand what REST is. REST web services are based on the underlying web technologies and specifically on the Hypertext Transfer Protocol (HTTP) that web browsers like Internet Explorer use for showing web pages.*
>
> *REST web services use a Uniform Resource Identifier (URI) as a base location or starting point for calling the REST service. This URI looks just like a URL you would use for web browsing in most cases. Using the URI and a language such as JavaScript or C#, you create requests using standard HTTP web requests and provide the verb that defines what type of request you are making. The standard methods for REST web services are GET, PUT, POST, and DELETE. Each one of the commands issues the request you are making just like calling a method in a standard ASP.NET web service. The expectation from a REST web service is that the results returned from the service are one of the supported Internet media types, usually XML or JSON.*
>
> *Although this section doesn't go into depth about REST endpoints, you can find more online about consuming and creating REST-based endpoints and OData because this is an ever-evolving area on data access.*

The REST API is designed to allow easy discovery and access to the Excel Services workbook. To make calls to the Excel Services REST API, you need to know what the URI format will be. In Excel Services, the URI, as shown in Table 17-3, includes the SharePoint site, location of the document, and the element or object you would like to return. If you don't know what the values are or the URI of the specific object, you can use Internet Explorer to provide the results of XML from a call to the service.

TABLE 17-3: REST API URI Format

URI SEGMENT	VALUE/EXAMPLE	DESCRIPTION
SharePoint site URL	`http://devcow.sharepoint.com` or `http://devcow.sharepoint.com/sites/projectsite`	This is the full path to the SharePoint site that where the Excel workbook is located.
Excel Services REST API page	`_vti_bin/ExcelRest.aspx`	This is the same location on every site within SharePoint.
Relative location to workbook	`Shared Documents/SalesData.xlsx`	This is the location of the workbook, including the library where the workbook is stored.

Type of Request	`Model` or `OData`	This defines what type of request the request is performing to pull back data. Model using the SharePoint 2010 implementation of REST while OData returns the new OData implementation.
REST Elements	`Charts('SalesByYear')` or `SalesDataTable`	These are the elements that define in the URI what part of the workbook you want to pull back.

```
http://devcow.sharepoint.com/_vti_bin/ExcelRest.aspx/
        Shared%20Documents/SalesData.xlsx/Model/Charts('SalesByYear')?format=image
```

```
https://devcow.sharepoint.com/_vti_bin/ExcelRest.aspx/
        Shared%20Documents/SalesData.xlsx/OData/
        YearlySalesTable?$filter=RegionSales gt 5000
```

You will look at both the Model and OData implementation in detail, but if you want to see how the service works, you can open Internet Explorer and type in the URI into the address bar, as shown in Figure 17-13. Internet Explorer or any web browser makes a GET request using the URI and displays the results. The results will be formatted if you use Internet Explorer in the Feed Reading options. If you would like to see the raw output, you can right-click and use View Source or turn off the Feed Reading option to see the raw output. You can do this by clicking Tools ⇨ Internet Options ⇨ Content Tab ⇨ Settings in the Feeds and Web Slices section ⇨ Uncheck Turn on Feed Reading view.

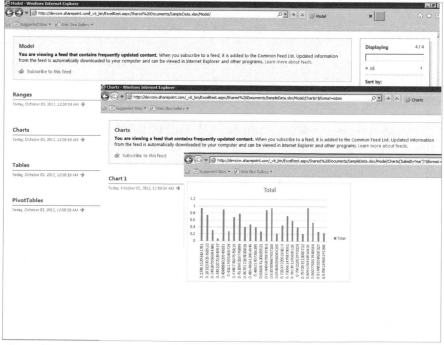

FIGURE 17-13

Model REST Implementation

This implementation was introduced with SharePoint 2010 and provides live and up-to-date Excel data based on a call to the request location of /Model. The REST API provides the ability to make calls, update values, recalculate the workbook, and view the data as needed.

Many different types of output can be generated from the Model REST API calls. These are images, HTML, ATOM Feeds, and the actual Excel Workbook in binary format. Not all the formats are supported on each resource, and the default format for each element depends on the resource called. Table 17-4 lists the resources and formats supported. To select the wanted format option, add `?$format=<type>` to the end of the URI.

TABLE 17-4: REST End Points for Excel Services

RESOURCE	ATOM	WORKBOOK	IMAGE	HTML
/Model	Yes	Yes		
/Charts	Yes			
/Charts('<Chart Name>')	Yes		Yes	
/Ranges	Yes			
/Ranges('<Range Name>')	Yes			Yes
/Tables	Yes			
/Tables('Table Name')	Yes			Yes
/PivotTables	Yes			
/PivotTables('PivotTable Name')	Yes			Yes

The REST service has many scenarios in which it can be used. This includes creating a dashboard that contains the images of charts and table HTML. Also, you can directly link Microsoft Word or PowerPoint to contain an image of the chart with a live link to data as it updates, so all users would see the most up-to-date data. To put this all together, follow these steps to insert a chart into PowerPoint:

1. Upload the sample workbook called `SalesData.xlsx` to the Shared Documents library on your root site.

2. Create the URI to the /Model location; for example, `http://intranet.devcow.com/_vti_bin/ExcelRest.aspx/Shared%20Documents/SalesData.xlsx/Model/`.

3. Type the URI into Internet Explorer and press Enter.

4. In the ATOM feed, click the Charts link.

5. In the ATOM feed, click the Sales by Year Chart link.

6. This shows the chart in Internet Explorer; copy the URI from the Address Bar.

7. Open PowerPoint to the slide where you want to add the chart; click the Insert tab and select Pictures.

8. Paste the URI into the File Name and click Insert. Then click OK, and you should have a slide that looks like Figure 17-14.

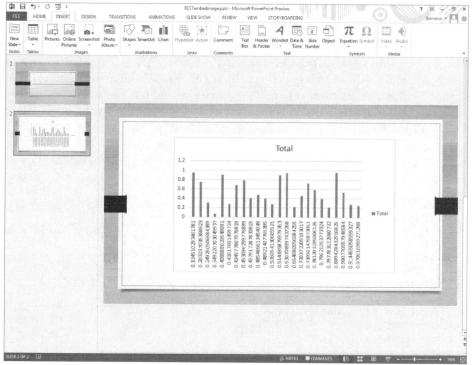

FIGURE 17-14

OData Implementation

New to SharePoint 2013 is an implementation of an Open Data Protocol (OData) built on the foundation of the existing Excel Services REST API. This service adds another way to request data from Excel Services and also allows for a number of filters. To better understand how to make an OData call and what filters are provided, you must first know what OData is. The OData service enables you to query tables in the workbook because it is designed to work with data. This means you would still use the REST API for other elements such as charts.

> **NOTE** *For full documentation on OData, read the documentation at* http://www.odata.org/.

OData is similar to the REST API and is built on web technologies used in REST such as HTTP, URIs, and ATOM. The primary goal for OData is to standardize these API calls and provide a way to have a uniform set of URIs. All the data, including the type of system, relationship, and structure of data, has guidance on how it is designed to allow multiple applications to work with the data. To help understand what OData is, look at an example of a call to the server. Notice that it is almost identical in structure to the REST API and that the major difference is the way to address each element.

Making a simple call to the root of the OData URI workbook displays the tables in the workbook as shown in the following code:

```
https://devcow.sharepoint.com/_vti_bin/ExcelRest.aspx/
       Shared%20Documents/SalesData.xlsx/odata/
```

The data returned from the calls to the OData service are in ATOM format. The following code shows the results of the root OData element being requested. There are only elements for the tables in a workbook, and the links to supporting calls are not provided like the REST API. Also when using a tool like Internet Explorer, the results from OData do not display like an RSS feed but display in the XML format. This call is the same as adding the query string in the URI with $metadata at the end:

```
<?xml version="1.0" encoding="utf-8" standalone="yes"?>
<service xml:base="https://devcow.sharepoint.com/_vti_bin/ExcelRest.aspx/
    Shared%20Documents/SalesData.xlsx/OData"
    xmlns:atom="http://www.w3.org/2005/Atom"
    xmlns:app="http://www.w3.org/2007/app"
    xmlns="http://www.w3.org/2007/app">
  <workspace>
    <atom:title>Default</atom:title>
    <collection href="SurveyData">
      <atom:title>SurveyData</atom:title>
    </collection>
    <collection href="SalesByYearTable">
      <atom:title>SalesByYearTable</atom:title>
    </collection>
  </workspace>
</service>
```

The advantage to use OData for rich applications is that the service treats the table data just as it would any other structured data, such as SQL Server or a CSV file. This means that you can use built-in data queries to refine what you are pulling back from the data and not just display the entire table. The query options available are listed in Table 17-5 and Table 17-6. The query options provided on the table can be combined together using the & URL element to make complex query statements.

TABLE 17-5: Query Options on the /OData Element

QUERY OPTION	EXAMPLE	DESCRIPTION
$metadata	/OData/$metadata	Provides the list of tables in the workbook

TABLE 17-6: Query Options on the /OData/<tablename> Element

QUERY OPTION	EXAMPLE	DESCRIPTION
/<tablename>	/OData/SalesByYearTable	Returns the data in the requested table without any filters. The maximum amount of data returned is 500 rows at a time.
$orderby	/OData/SalesByYearTable$orderby=Year	Allows the data to be returned in a specified order either ascending or descending using the column name provided.
$top	/OData/SalesByYearTable$top=2	Returns the top number of elements requested in the query option based on how the current data source is sorted unless more sort options are provided.
$skip	/OData/SalesByYearTable$skip=2	Returns the data in the table starting after the number of rows specified in the skip query have been satisfied.
$skiptoken	/OData/SalesByYearTable$skiptoken=499	The skip a token is similar to the skip query option except that it is zero-based, so the value specified will be that value plus one (skip amount = $skiptoken + 1). You should use this value to get the next page of data if you have more than 500 records.
$filter	/OData/SalesByYearTable?$filter=RegionSales LE 5000	The filter command provides a complex set of operations that can be used to work with the data, including logical operators, arithmetic operators, string operators and grouping operators. This enables you to create almost any query you would do on a full data source to work with the correct data.
$format	/OData/SalesByYearTable?$format=atom	Provides the ability to specify different format options, but the only supported type stated by Microsoft is the ATOM format. All calls to the format option return ATOM.
$inlinecount	/OData/SalesByYearTable?$inlinecount=allpages	Uses two token values to determine if the page count should be provided in the ATOM returned. The two options are: * allpages, which displays the count * none, which does not display the count

> **NOTE** *For a full listing of query options, review the OData site for URI conventions at* `http://www.odata.org/documentation/uri-conventions`.

Using REST API in SharePoint Online

All these REST APIs are now available with SharePoint online. This means that you can quickly build dashboards and Excel Mashups using this Excel Services data directly from SharePoint Online. To use the service on SharePoint Online, upload an Excel Services workbook to your SharePoint Online site. When the Excel workbook is on the site, you can test the functionality by using the REST commands with either the Model API or the OData API from Internet Explorer. If you pull the data remotely, you must provide the authentication to the URI before it displays correctly.

Excel Services Web Access

Excel Web Access provides the ability to view Excel workbooks using an Excel Services web part, also known as EWA. This is the component that generates the HTML for the workbook data and adds the JavaScript files to the page. Using the web part, you can also manipulate the published Excel workbook using the JavaScript library.

The EWA has no dependency on client-side scripts or Active X control to function properly. You can navigate through the sheets within the published workbook just as you do when using the Excel client. Not only can the entire workbook be hosted and rendered in a EWA web part, a section of the workbook can be as well. This is done based on named parameters within the workbook, which should be created when authoring it.

Interactivity in the EWA web parts is not the same as editing the Excel workbook in Excel Web Apps. In the Excel Web App, the changes users make to the workbook are written back to the original workbook. When interacting with EWA, users can see changes in calculations and visualization objects, but the original workbook remains the same.

The Excel Services Web Access web part is also available from the namespace `Microsoft.Office.Excel.Server.WebUI` that you can include in your application. This allows you to create the web part and render the wanted workbook dynamically. The class that is exposed for use is the `ExcelWebRenderer` class that inherits from the `WebPart` class. The following code shows how you can create the web part dynamically and set how the user interact with it:

```
ExcelWebRenderer ewa1 = new ExcelWebRenderer();
ewa1.WorkbookUri = "Shared%20Documents/SalesData.xlsx";
ewa1.AllowFiltering = true;
ewa1.ShowWorkbookParameters = true;
ewa1.TypingAndFormulaEntry = true;
```

JavaScript Object Model (JSOM)

The JavaScript Object Model (JSOM) provides the libraries needed to interact with the Excel Services Web Access web parts. The JSOM was added in SharePoint 2010 but has been improved with SharePoint 2013 by adding new events and methods. The JSOM library allows scripting to build rich Excel applications using spreadsheets in the Excel Services web part and requires having the Excel Web App web part on page with Excel workbook loaded before making any JavaScript calls. There are even additions to the JSOM to allow User-Defined functions (see the "User-Defined Functions (UDF)" section later in the chapter).

The JavaScript file is located in the Layouts directory and must be included on the page. When you add an Excel Web Access web part to the page, the script link to the JavaScript file is automatically added to the page. The file has been minified and provides only readability of variables exposed for public use. This is done to help make the file smaller so that it can be downloaded quickly. The file is located on the SharePoint server at the following location:

```
%ProgramFiles%\Common Files\Microsoft Shared\
    web server extensions\15\TEMPLATE\LAYOUTS\EwaMoss.js
```

All the code is JavaScript and must be placed on a SharePoint page to run. SharePoint 2013 adds a new web part called the Script Editor web part that makes it easy to add JavaScript to the page. The Content Editor web part was traditionally used for this purpose but would not always add the code to the page without modifying it. Now you can add the Script Editor web part to the web page when the JavaScript is ready and know that it will remain the same set of code that you have built.

The JavaScript language and browsers, like Internet Explorer, load files in a top-down manner. This means that variables and methods written in JavaScript are not accessible until they are processed by the DOM that is displaying them. To prevent issues with calling JavaScript that is not yet loaded, but that you know will be available, SharePoint provides a method called `ExecuteOrDelayUntilScript Loaded()` that waits to use critical functions in script libraries such as sp.js and other foundational scripts.

Accessing the EWA Objects

The root class for all interaction with Excel Web Access web parts is the JavaScript class `Ewa`. This is a global class that can be called from your functions and allows access to the controls, workbooks, and elements of the workbook such as Sheets and Ranges. The most common use of the `Ewa` control is the use of the `EwaControl` class that provides methods to get the web part control. To create a variable and set it to the EWA control, use the following code:

```
ewa = Ewa.EwaControl.getInstances().getItem(0);
```

As it might appear from the code, this returns an object of type `EwaControl` using the static function on the class called `getInstances()`. As you can see the `getInstances()` returns all the EWA web parts on the page as a collection and requires using the `getItem` method to specify which one you want. In the previous example it returns the first EWA web part.

The web part instance will be returned only if the web part is fully loaded. This means that you must make the call to the `Ewa` control after the page and web part are loaded. With the ability to get an instance of the web part, you now need to create some standard JavaScript code that allows you to set up the calls at the correct time. As mentioned, this requires having the page load and EWA controls loaded. You can use the following format as a starting point for a standard framework for you to use in the calls to the `EWAControls`.

```
<script type="text/javascript">
if (window.attachEvent)
{
    window.attachEvent("onload", Wrox_PageLoad);
}

//Runs when the page is loaded and the EWA control should be set.
//Then adds a function to be called when the EWAControl is ready.
function Wrox_PageLoad()
{

        if (typeof (Ewa) != "undefined")

        {
            Ewa.EwaControl.add_applicationReady(Wrox_EwaControlsReady);
        }

        else

        {
            alert("The Ewa Control is not set or ready to be used yet.");
        }
}

//attach to the individual Excel Web Access (EWA) web parts
function Wrox_EwaControlsReady()
{
    ewa = Ewa.EwaControl.getInstances().getItem(0);

    //Perform code calls to the EWA Control

}
</script>
```

This code uses a call to the Window OnLoad event, which usually has other controls using the same event handler. Although it makes it clear to read what the intent of the code is, it would be better to use the _spBodyOnLoadFunctionNames function that allows multiple load events and allows SharePoint to process the event when it is ready. This also helps ensure that the required supporting libraries have been called from the page. The new code would replace the window.attachEvent block. This is also a better option than using the $(document).ready function if you use JQuery because the order of the calls to the JQuery function may not be in the expected order:

```
<script type="text/javascript">
_spBodyOnLoadFunctionNames.push("Wrox_PageLoad");

//Runs when the page is loaded and the EWA control should be set.
//Then adds a function to be called when the EWAControl is ready.
function Wrox_PageLoad()
{

        if (typeof (Ewa) != "undefined")

        {
```

```
            Ewa.EwaControl.add_applicationReady(Wrox_EwaControlsReady);
        }

        else

        {
            alert("The Ewa Control is not set or ready to be used yet.");
        }
    }

    //attach to the individual Excel Web Access (EWA) web parts
    function Wrox_EwaControlsReady()
    {
        ewa = Ewa.EwaControl.getInstances().getItem(0);

        //Perform code calls to the EWA Control
    }
</script>
```

Now that you have access to the `EWAControl`, you can create code that uses the objects and events to work with the Excel workbook. There are some global functions that enable you to access objects from the global `Ewa` control, but most of the objects and events are accessible directly from the instance you have created.

EWA Objects

The primary objects provided by the EWA classes are the Workbook, Sheets, Ranges, and Charts. In SharePoint 2013 there is new support for Hidden Sheets as well as Chart Objects and embedded XML data called XmlParts. The classes built in with JSOM have the instance of the class and collection objects associated with each one. Table 17-7 shows the `Ewa` classes that can be used in your JavaScript. Keep in mind these references are to the `Ewa` object, but they are only the definitions of the class structure. The instance of these classes must be called from supporting methods like the `getInstances()` function on the `EWAControl` class.

TABLE 17-7: Ewa JavaScript Classes

NAME	DESCRIPTION
Ewa.Workbook	Provides the methods and properties of the requested Excel workbook
Ewa.Sheet	Defines the Excel sheet and the data on the sheet
Ewa.Range	Provides a range of cells in the Excel Workbook and is returned from many of the functions using Workbook Cells
Ewa.NamedItem	Represents one of the NamedItems supported in Excel Services, such as NamedRange, Parameter, Table, PivotTable, and Chart

To use these classes and get the instantiated objects, use the `getActive` methods for the object you work with. The following example shows how to get the active Excel workbook and then also in the same statement get the active sheet from that workbook. The same principals can be used with the other classes and `getActive` methods for those classes. Remember the code snippets are just examples of the code that would be run, and you should have the full set of code with the proper events to make calls to the `Ewa` objects.

```
ewa = Ewa.EwaControl.getInstances().getItem(0);
var EwaSheet = ewa.getActiveWorkbook().getActiveSheet();
```

Having a firm understanding of the `Ewa` objects is important for modifying or working with an Excel workbook, but you need a way to trigger the actions. Most of the code you write will rely on the ability to know what the end user is doing to make the necessary changes.

EWA JavaScript Events

The EWA events enable you to write code that can run when the user clicks or changes the active Excel workbook. The most common events are when something occurs to the Cell, Sheet, or workbook. When these events occur they provide information to the function with objects like the `RangeEventArgs` and `WorkbookEventArgs`. The events can be subscribed to through the `Ewa.EwaControl`, as shown in the following code:

```
<script type="text/javascript">
_spBodyOnLoadFunctionNames.push("Wrox_PageLoad");

//Runs when the page is loaded and the EWA control should be set.
//Then adds a function to be called when the EWAControl is ready.
function Wrox_PageLoad()
{

        if (typeof (Ewa) != "undefined")

        {
            Ewa.EwaControl.add_applicationReady(Wrox_EwaControlsReady);
        }

        else

        {
            alert("The Ewa Control is not set or ready to be used yet.");
        }

}

//attach to the individual Excel Web Access (EWA) web parts
function Wrox_EwaControlsReady()
{
    ewa = Ewa.EwaControl.getInstances().getItem(0);
    ewa.add_activeCellChanged(Wrox_UpdateCellChanged);
}

function Wrox_UpdateCellChanged(rangeArgs)
{
```

```
    var column = rangeArgs.getRange().getColumn();
    var row = rangeArgs.getRange().getRow();
    var value = rangeArgs.getFormattedValues();
    alert("Value Changed In Cell (" + row + "," column + ") to " + value);
}

</script>
```

Support for SharePoint Online

One of the most powerful enhancements to the JSOM API is not within the script itself, but it is now supported in SharePoint online. This means that you can use the JSOM and REST APIs within SharePoint Online to work with the data inside the Excel workbooks being uploaded.

User Defined Functions (UDF)

User Defined Functions (UDFs) are developer-created custom functionality that extends the capabilities of Excel. UDFs are created in code, both managed .NET code and JavaScript code, and are used in workbooks just like the built-in Excel formulas, in a cell using the "MyUDF(A1:B2)" syntax.

The concept of UDF actions is incorporated into many applications as extension points for customizing. SQL Server has UDF actions added to also allow the running of managed code as inline functions. Even Excel has had UDF actions for years. Excel originally provided this capability using the Visual Basic Editor that allowed code to be attached to an Excel workbook. The server-side version of Excel Services UDFs allows users to reuse the business logic and functions as well as connect to resources in a secure and managed way.

A UDF function allows developers to create their own Excel functions to complement the existing functions that can be called in cells within Excel. This is a great way to extend Excel for combining data or calculations that cannot be done easily within Excel. Be careful not to overuse UDF functions when built-in functions with Excel can be used due to performance concerns.

One of the primary reasons UDFs have been built has been to retrieve data from data sources not supported in Excel. Even though Excel has added the web service functions, UDFs provide the ability to make connections to data sources that need authentication. UDFs also provide a great way to import data from sources that are not provided natively.

You could use an example such as finding geo-location information directly in Excel by building a Location UDF, as shown in the following example. This example shows what value you enter into the Excel cell to get the location back from a string value:

```
=Location("1 Microsoft Way");
```

To use UDFs you must enabled the UDF assemblies or registered JavaScript by setting the Allow UDFs flag per Excel Services' trusted location. These settings can be set per location and need to be managed by the administrators of the SharePoint farm. These trusted locations can be set up at a granular level or more global depending on your needs.

In previous versions of Excel Services, there was a detailed process for creating managed code and deploying to the server to get the UDF features installed. Many users just wanted a way to pull back data quickly but didn't want to have to build .NET assemblies for web-based calls. As the web has progressed and frameworks have made it easier to make calls in JavaScript, it now make sense to also have the UDF functionality in JavaScript that can be used on a specific page. With SharePoint 2013, Microsoft extended the UDF framework and created the JavaScript methods needed to register and call UDFs directly from JavaScript.

Managed Code UDF Development

Building managed .NET UDFs has been around since SharePoint 2007 and have provided this plug-in ability server-side for all applications. User Defined Function classes must be marked with the `Microsoft.Office.Excel.Server.Udf.UdfClass` attribute, and UDF methods must be marked with the `Microsoft.Office.Excel.Server.Udf.UdfMethod` attribute, or they will be ignored by Excel Calculation Services.

To build a UDF in managed code, you must create the Visual Studio project and add a reference to the following SharePoint DLL reference `Microsoft.Office.Excel.Server.Udf.dll`. This reference is located in the following path listed in the ISAPI folder with most of the common DLLs. After the DLL is added, you must add the attributes to the correct locations to make the UDF registered in Excel Services:

```
[drive:]\Program Files\Common Files\Microsoft Shared\
    web server extensions\15\ISAPI
```

Creating a UDF

Creating a Managed UDF can be quick and provide you powerful functions with a small amount of code. This example takes a bar code number and provides the price of the item:

1. Open Visual Studio 2012.

2. Create a new SharePoint 2013 project, and name your project Wrox.Chapter17 .UDFExamples.

3. Select Deploy as a Farm Solution.

4. Click Add ⇨ New Item from the project, and select Code ⇨ Class.

5. Name the new class file UDFItemLookup.cs.

6. Make the class public by adding the required token.

7. After the class has been created, in the Solution Explorer, right-click the References folder and click Add Reference.

8. Click the Extensions filter, and then select the Excel Services Application UDF Framework DLL. Be sure to click the check box next to the name and not just select the item.

9. In the `UPDItemLookup.cs` class add the using statement : using `Microsoft.Office.Excel. Server.Udf;`.

10. Decorate your class with the `UdfClass` attribute.

11. Create a method to accept the string value and return the Item Look Up information with the `UdfMethod` attribute, as shown in the following example:

```
[UdfClass]
public class UDFItemLookup
{
    [UdfMethod]
    public string ItemLookup(string UPCcode)
    {
        //Calls mocked web service to find the price
        SalesEngineWS request = new SalesEngineWS();
        SalesEngineWS.SalesProduct product = request.GetProduct(UPCcode);
        return product.Price.ToString();

    }
}
```

> **NOTE** *The code example makes use of built-in classes to make the example easy to compile and use, but you can easily change the class to point to live web services.*

Deploying a UDF

The UDF you just built will not be loaded until you deploy it to a server with Excel Services. The following steps walk you through creating a trusted location on the server and deploying the managed assembly. Using the previous sample you can easily deploy the UDF class to the server because it is already packaged in a SharePoint solution.

1. In Visual Studio click the Build menu; then click Deploy `Wrox.Chapter17.UDFExamples`.

2. Navigate to the Solution Management settings page, and verify that the wrox.chapter17. udfexamples.wsp has been deployed globally under System Settings ➪ Manage Farm Solutions.

3. Now navigate to the Managed Service Applications page for Excel Services under Application Management ➪ Manage service applications ➪ Excel Services Application.

4. In the Excel Services Settings section, click the Trusted File Locations link. Add a trusted file location if one does not already exist.

5. In the trusted file location, identify the URL of the SharePoint site or library on which you will be allowing Excel Services to run UDF functions.

6. Set the maximum workbook size to a high enough value for the size of your workbooks. You need to increase the size of the searched workbooks or you will get File Not Found errors when you try to view the workbook in the web browser.

7. Under Trust Children, select Children Trusted to Trust All Items below the selected URL.

8. Under the Allow User-Defined Functions section, select User-Defined Functions Allowed.

9. Click OK.

10. Return to the Manage Excel Services Application and select the User Defined Function Assemblies.

11. Add the new User Defined Function.

12. In the Assembly box, type in the strong name of the UDF class just created, such as **Wrox.Chapter17.UDFExamples, Version=1.0.0.0, Culture=neutral, PublicKey Token=875b61f81a9d3d29.**

13. Leave the assembly location as Global assembly cache because that is where the project deployed it. Make sure the check box is set to True for Assembly Enabled, then click OK.

14. After the UDF has been loaded, you need to run IISReset on all the servers to close existing Excel Services connections and reload them with the new UDF.

> **NOTE** *An easy way to get the strong name of the assembly is to use the* `gacutil-l` *command from a Visual Studio command window.*

Using the UDF in Excel

With the Managed .NET UDF function built, deployed, and configured on the server, you can start using it within Excel workbooks. There is nothing special that needs to be done to take advantage of the UDF, but you must make sure all the steps have been followed so that the UDF loads correctly. To make use of the new UDF you have just created, enter the formula into a cell, and upload the Excel document as detailed here:

1. On Sheet1 of your workbook or the sheet you want to display the information on, type **=ItemLookup("12345678")** into cell B2. Don't be alarmed when the cell evaluates to #Name? in Excel. User Defined Functions work only when the workbook is displayed by Excel Services.

2. Save the file and publish the Excel workbook to the SharePoint Server.

After the function has been entered into the Excel workbook and the file has been published to the server, you can view the file in Excel Services to see the results of the UDF. If there are any issues with the UDF in Excel Services, the value of the cell will remain #NAME?. Make sure to check the ULS logs and that you did recycle the app pools after you installed the UDF into the configuration settings.

JavaScript UDF Development (ECMAScript)

The managed .NET assemblies have been the extension point for adding code-based solutions to Excel workbooks running inside of Excel Services. This allows for power server-side calculation and a load-balancing scenario, but there are times when you just want to make a quick call to a web service or pull back data already on the page. The addition of JavaScript UDF functions enables developers to quickly create or reuse JavaScript functions that can be reused in an Excel cell. This makes the extensions limitless on what can be done.

Creating a UDF

Creating a UDF with JavaScript is a great way to make client-side web requests or run code that can be done within the web browser. Any function defined on the page in JavaScript can be registered as a JavaScript UDF function using the Excel Web Access (EWA) JavaScript library. When creating a JavaScript UDF, if you use Visual Studio 2012, you can also have IntelliSense to help you build the necessary JavaScript functions.

The next steps show how to create a simple function to return the UPC value from a JavaScript UDF function:

1. Open Visual Studio and open a SharePoint Project.

2. Add the Mapped SharePoint folder of Layouts using Add ➪ SharePoint "Layouts" Mapped Folder.

3. Rename the default folder in the Layouts folder to Wrox or your company name.

4. Now add a JavaScript code file to the same directly called `Chapter17UDFExamples.js`. Click Add ➪ New Item; then select the Web category and JavaScript file.

5. Add the JavaScript UDF function to your new JavaScript page and the code required to register a JavaScript UDF function, as shown in the following code:

```
//JavaScript UDF
function Wrox_UDF_UPCLength(upc)
{
    return upc.length;
}

                Ewa.BrowserUdfs().add(
                        "UPCLength",
                        Wrox_UDF_UPCLength,
                        "Returns the length of the UPC",
                        false,
                        false
                    );
```

Deploying a UDF

There are many ways that you can deploy a set of JavaScript UDF functions. The easiest way is to manually deploy it using the built-in Script Editor web part. You can copy the JavaScript required for the function and the registration code into the web part. This can be a good way to test your code while you are building it. The method used in the sample code is to create a JavaScript file that can be reused and deploy it to the Layouts folder. After you deploy the solution, either edit the web page and put a link directly to the JavaScript file, or add a content editor web part that calls the JavaScript file.

SOAP Web Services

The SOAP web services have been around since SharePoint 2007 and are still available for use especially if you use managed .NET code or build .NET custom applications. There is both an object model accessible on the server and a set of web services accessible from anywhere on the network. No major changes have been made to this API for SharePoint 2013.

This SOAP web service enables access to the components just as you have seen in the REST and JSOM object models but provides a true SOAP-based interface. The primary namespace that will be used for these objects is `Microsoft.Office.Excel.Server.WebServices`. This namespace has an object called ExcelService that provides the Get and Set methods for the workbooks as well as the ability to start calculations in the workbook. The following URL is the site-relative URL for creating a web reference to the service on your server:

```
http://<sharepointsite>/_vti_bin/ExcelService.asmx
```

> **NOTE** *The entire ExcelService class and supporting objects are listed at* `http://msdn.microsoft.com/en-us/library/ms545810.aspx`.

SUMMARY

This chapter provides an overview to growing a number of tools and technologies that can be used to build Excel applications. You were introduced to Excel, Excel Web Apps, and Excel Services that now enable building rich online apps that can be hosted in SharePoint. You saw some of the changes in Excel and the new functions added to help with data access. One of the major changes to the Excel Applications is that you can now build your Apps for Office that allow Content and Task Pane apps for Excel. These new apps are built using standard web technologies and are designed to be portable now. Even the deployment from SharePoint 2013 makes them easier for Enterprises to use. Finally, the new additions to the JavaScript Object Model and JavaScript UDFs provide the ability to build dashboard and Excel Mashups creating powerful end-user experiences.

18

PerformancePoint Dashboards

WHAT'S IN THIS CHAPTER?

➤ Exploring Microsoft's approach to business intelligence

➤ Configuring PerformancePoint Services

➤ Building a dashboard

➤ Extending PerformancePoint with custom data sources

WROX.COM CODE DOWNLOADS FOR THIS CHAPTER

The wrox.com code downloads for this chapter are found at www.wrox.com/remtitle .cgi?isbn=1118495829 on the Download Code tab. The code is in the chapter 18 download and individually named according to the names throughout the chapter.

BUSINESS INTELLIGENCE

Data is the blood and heart of any organization. Businesses need data to help determine where to spend the next dollar, which customer to chase first, and which server is out of disk space. Business Intelligence (BI) is the organization's capability to convert its data outputs into knowledge that can be used to identify new opportunities and competitive strategies.

BI technologies provide historical, current, and predictive views of business operations. Common functions of BI technologies include reporting, analytics and data mining, performance management, and more. These technologies come together to support better decision making.

Given the relative importance of data to an organization, how can Microsoft and SharePoint assist in the delivery of data to assist people in making effective business decisions? Microsoft approaches the BI conversation with a stack of tools aimed at enabling end users and enterprises. These tools range in complexity of configuration and execution from the familiar and simple Microsoft Excel to the complex and specialized Microsoft SQL Server Analysis Services.

The business intelligence stack from Microsoft is one of the world's most popular and widely deployed suites of BI tools. Both Forrester and Gartner recognize Microsoft as a leader in the space, with Microsoft coming in at #3 in Gartner's Feb 6, 2012 BI Platform Magic Quadrant (`http://www.gartner.com/technology/reprints.do?id=1-196VVFJ&ct=120207&st=sb`) and #2 in Forrester's 2012 BI Wave (`http://download.microsoft.com/download/8/F/F/8FFFD378-159C-4107-898C-B60835D85384/The_Forrester_Wave_Self-Service_BI_Platforms_Q2_2012.pdf`). This strong showing across the two most recognizable technology industry analyst firms is a result of Microsoft's investment in Office (especially Excel), SQL Server, and SharePoint, and the power of these tools, combined with the undeniable value proposition and lowest in class total cost of ownership (TCO). The next section looks at the history of Microsoft BI, the integration of BI into SharePoint products and technologies, and how Microsoft addresses the major complexities of building quality BI solutions with a do-it-yourself toolkit, which doesn't force every problem to require an enormous solution.

History

Until recently, the greatest challenge in many organizations was that accessing data for the purpose of analysis was restricted to certain groups of people using specialized tools. With only a handful of staff members using the BI solutions, business users would come with ad hoc inquiries for information resulting in highly qualified BI experts focusing on tactical report generation rather than delivering value for an organization's long-term business intelligence strategy.

Furthermore, it was difficult to give the company leaders the ability to gauge the state of their business at a glance, so they could make agile decisions to keep the business moving forward. In many cases, delivering timely and accurate reports to key decision makers that summarized strategic and operational data has been done in unbelievably inefficient ways, such as manually assembled PowerPoint and Excel files delivered via e-mail and file shares, which contribute to report proliferation and an inability to understand which version of a report is the accurate version.

This combination of scarce skillsets and inefficient reporting processes left the door open for developers and third-party vendors to build custom applications that delivered reports to key decision makers efficiently, which in turn translated into more upfront and maintenance costs as well as brittle data dependencies.

From the hardware perspective, building a decent BI solution in the not too distant past required assembling the right hardware, compression algorithms, and networking components that constitute the solution. The challenge for many organizations extending the reach of their BI solutions to broader sets of users was the storage and the computing power that was required to host decent BI solutions and make them available to the masses.

BI is not only for answering the questions that users may have in mind. The more important part of BI is to help users ask the right questions, and also to guide them through an often resource-intensive process to get the insights they need. The types of questions may not necessarily be anticipated or pre-aggregated into the BI solutions, so the hardware, software, and bandwidth specifications for hosting those solutions must be powerful enough to respond to such on-demand queries in a reasonably fast manner.

Like many other BI vendors at the time, Microsoft started its significant BI investment with the same limitations in adoption, lacking must-have functionalities and requirements for strong computing power. The problem was that most Microsoft BI solutions were strongly tied to SQL Server technology, and SQL Enterprise Manager was the primary interface to interact with those solutions. Again, unless you knew how to work with SQL Server and its set of BI-related specialized domain-specific languages, the chances that you were just a bystander in the whole BI world were high.

Soon, Microsoft realized that the value of its BI platform would not become apparent until a paradigm shift occurred in its approach to doing traditional BI. Looking for a way to excel, Microsoft developed a new vision in the year 2000, which looked at things differently than before.

The new vision was based on taking BI to the masses, using it to connect people to each other and to connect people to data more easily than ever before. The key area of focus was to take the BI out of the realm of specialty and niche tools and turn it into something mainstream. There were two primary justifications for the new vision. First, it would hide the difficulties of the underlying platform from the general public. Second, it would make the adoption of the platform much easier because when more people use a platform, the more valuable it becomes and the more quickly it is adopted by others.

Following the overall vision of "BI for everyone" and starting with SharePoint Portal Server 2003, Microsoft fostered this notion of integrating some aspects of its BI offering into its Information Portal technology. Theoretically, because SharePoint brings people together to work and make decisions collaboratively, it could have been the right starting point. However, this integration never extended beyond a couple of web parts natively rendering BI artifacts that are stored outside SharePoint content databases, in products such as Microsoft SQL Server Reporting Services 2000 and Microsoft Business Scorecard Manager 2005.

Fortunately, Microsoft learned three lessons as a result of this approach. First, separation of data objects and the point of user experience mean that IT is required to deal with a minimum of two separate products and repository frameworks to implement a single BI solution, which means more administrative effort. Second, due to the distributed environment, users have to go through at least two server authentications or hops to get to the back-end data source. For the environments without Kerberos delegation in place, this double-hop model causes authentication issues. The double-hop (one hop from the client browser to the SharePoint server and another hop to the BI server) problem is not a bug; rather it is an intentional security design to restrict identities from acting on behalf of other identities. Third, because the SQL Server-based BI products and SharePoint Portal Server 2003 were using different security models, it was difficult to map SharePoint roles and permission levels directly to the roles and permissions understandable by the BI product. In other words, it was difficult to apply a unified authorization model across the products.

In 2006, Microsoft acquired analytics vendor ProClarity, and soon Business Scorecard Manager 2005 and ProClarityAnalytics products were merged and formed a new product named Microsoft PerformancePoint Server 2007, offered as a separate SKU that could operate on top of SharePoint 2007.

Later, with the release of Microsoft Office SharePoint Server 2007, Microsoft's BI offering turned into something that was more than just a couple of integration hooks, as is the case with SharePoint

Portal Server 2003. In Microsoft Office SharePoint Server 2007 (MOSS 2007), Microsoft made major improvements in four different areas: the Report Center template, full integration with SQL Server Reporting Services (SQL Server 2005 SP2), new Excel Services, and a Business Data Catalog for integration with line-of-business (LOB) applications.

Fortunately, Microsoft didn't stop there; it released more features that could change the way people build dashboard-style applications. Customers could use PerformancePoint Scorecard Builder 2007 and put together their own dashboards and publish them to the PerformancePoint monitoring server. After the dashboards are published, customers could then use the Dashboard Viewer web part to integrate the dashboard into SharePoint pages. Again, the integration is just a web part that calls into PerformancePoint Server 2007 functioning as a standalone server. Both products were sold separately and they had different management environments and operations.

Even though the attempts Microsoft made to bring the best of both the SharePoint and BI worlds together in MOSS 2007 were great, it was still not enough to call it a full-fledged integration. The separate pricing structure, on top of the enterprise client access license required by SharePoint 2007, turned a number of customers off from the product. In addition, PerformancePoint 2007 did not eliminate many of the dual maintenance tasks previously identified. The team that was building SharePoint Server 2010 made significant changes based on the customer feedback and the lessons learned in MOSS 2007. Starting with SharePoint Server 2010 Server, PerformancePoint is designed as a service application on top of the SharePoint 2010 Server platform. What is important about the new design is that PerformancePoint and SharePoint are no longer two separate products. Instead, both are finally offered as an integrated product on the Enterprise CAL. The biggest advantage of this move is that PerformancePoint contents are all stored and secured within SharePoint libraries, and they can benefit from the new features and enhancements made to the core SharePoint platform. PerformancePoint got many new features and enhancements.

In addition to the enhancements made in SharePoint 2010 and its newly native PerformancePoint Services Application, Microsoft enhanced the self-service BI capabilities of Excel 2010 with PowerPivot and Access 2010 with the introduction of Access Services. With the addition of IT-centric SQL Server Reporting Services enhancements such as the SSRS integration local mode, Microsoft rounded out its investment in SharePoint as the front end for business intelligence interactions.

Microsoft has not stopped the investment in BI technologies since moving from SharePoint 2010 to SharePoint 2013. The rest of this chapter reviews those enhancements and improvements.

SharePoint 2013 Business Intelligence Components

Microsoft has invested in several areas of the SharePoint 2013 BI toolkit including Microsoft Access 2013, Access Services, Microsoft Excel 2013, Excel Services, PerformancePoint Services, SharePoint Server 2013, Visio Services, SQL Server 2012, and more. The three-pronged sets of technologies that make up the BI components are represented in Figure 18-1.

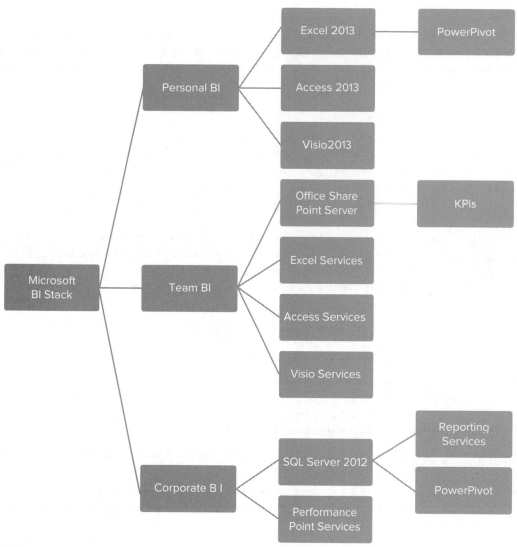

FIGURE 18-1

Consider the target use cases for Microsoft's suite of business intelligence tools. Some users are focused on understanding data that they will used for individual decisions, and no sharing of reports is necessary. These users are concerned with themselves and need a personal business intelligence solution. Other users are participants in a team or department's BI-related decision-making as part of a larger organization. These users need to be able to share queries and results in a flexible manner as the nature of these team reports is frequently quite fluid. Team business intelligence solutions are aimed at solving data-related problems for "we, the team." Finally, a level of consistency is required for corporate-level reporting, which necessitates a strong centralized presentation platform. In this sense, personal BI can be considered "BI for Me," team BI can be considered "BI for We," and corporate reporting can be considered "BI for the World."

Personal BI

Microsoft uses the term Personal BI to describe technologies that deliver information to people when they need it, and in the formats they are comfortable with. The majority of Personal BI solutions are independent of a connected data source such as a self-contained spreadsheet. Personal BI is usually completely independent from IT services and support.

Access 2013

Access 2013 is a powerful tool that enables business users and subject matter experts to independently build database-backed applications accessible to numerous concurrent users. Access 2013 delivers applications capable of adhering to code-free embedded business logic, report on embedded data, and which can be shared on the desktop or on the web.

Excel 2013

Microsoft Excel is the world's most widely utilized BI tool for a reason: It provides users the ability to analyze and explore data of any size, to visualize that data, and to integrate disparate data sources through live connections to data stores as well as fully self-contained operational capabilities. Excel 2013 offers the following new features, which support Personal BI solutions.

➤ *In-Memory Analytics* — Excel 2013 builds in the local Analysis Services xVelocity in-memory analytics engine (VertiPaq), which manages the compression and DAX querying of millions of rows of data. Excel 2010 offered VertiPaq as an optional download included in the PowerPivot add-in.

➤ *Power View for Excel* — Power View enables users to see and interact with data through interactive graphics and animations. Users can present and share insights with others through rich storyboard presentation capabilities. Power View is powered by the BI Semantic Model and the VertiPaq engine.

➤ *Decoupled PivotChart and PivotTable reports* — Users can now create PivotChart reports without including a PivotTable report on the same page.

➤ *JavaScript user-defined functions* — Whether sharing a workbook via SharePoint and Excel Services or via SkyDrive, JavaScript UDFs enable the creation of custom functions that can be called from inside formulas in the Excel web app.

Team BI

Considering the hierarchical self-identification of Me, We, and World, people don't work just as individuals but in teams to accomplish tasks. Microsoft uses the term Team BI to represent the BI solutions that deliver information that focuses on accountability to promote collaboration, and rapid sharing of information to drive to a common decision.

Access Services

Access 2013 desktop databases have not significantly changed, but Access Services has gone through a significant evolution in functionality. Access Services provides a new web interface for Access applications that enable rapid development of scalable applications without IT. New features in Access Services include:

➤ *New application model* — On-premise Access 2013 web applications are now backed by SQL Server and hosted by SharePoint. Office 365 cloud-based Access web applications are backed by SQL Azure for global scalability. Being backed by SQL Server not only improves scalability, but also improves IT manageability of Access applications due to centralization of data into SQL Server.

➤ *Views* — Web applications developed in Access automatically generate high-quality HTML5 user interfaces that focus application developers on business problems.

Excel Services

Excel Services enables users to view and work with Excel spreadsheets and workbooks that have been published to SharePoint sites. Users can explore data and conduct analysis in a browser window just as they would by using the Excel client because of the new Excel Interactive View. Building on the successes of Excel Services in SharePoint 2010, Excel Services 2013 offers the following new capabilities:

➤ *Data exploration improvements* — It is now easier to explore and analyze data in Excel Services reports because of SQL Server Analysis Services and PowerPivot data models. PivotCharts and PivotTables now suggest ways users can view individual values as hover tips. Analysis commands such as Drill Down are now available with a single mouse-click.

➤ *Calculated measures and members* — Excel Services supports calculated measures and calculated members that are created in Excel.

➤ *Analysis Services support* — Administrators can specify SQL Server Analysis Services servers to support more advanced analytic capabilities in Excel Services.

➤ *Trend analysis* — Excel Services supports the ability to conduct trend analysis from cells in PivotTable reports that use OLAP data, such as Analysis Services cubes or PowerPivot data models.

➤ *Updated APIs* — The JavaScript Object Model (JSOM) API and Excel Services REST API have been updated to enable more control and better access at more granular levels.

➤ *Power View for SharePoint* — Similar to the technology embedded in Excel 2013, Power View for SharePoint is available as part of the SQL Server 2012 Service Pack 1 Reporting Services Add-In for SharePoint 2013 Enterprise Edition.

Visio Services

Visio Services is a service application that enables users to share and view Microsoft Visio Drawing and Visio 2010 web drawing files. 2013 ushers in the ability to refresh data-connected Visio drawings which support automated data refreshes in addition to the following new features:

➤ *Maximum Cache Size* — A new service parameter designed to enable administrators to improve Visio web access experiences. Configuration settings to update the default value from 5120 MB are found in Central Administration or via a new PowerShell cmdlet, Set_SPVisioPerformance.

➤ *Health Analyzer rules* — New corresponding Health Analyzer rules have been added to reflect the new Maximum Cache Size parameter.

➤ *Commenting on drawings* — Users can add meaningful comments to a Visio Drawing (*.vsdx) collaboratively on the web via Visio Services in full-page rendering mode.

Corporate BI

Considering once again the Me, We, World personal relationship hierarchy, people work as part of an enterprise to meet strategic objectives. Microsoft refers to Corporate BI as a set of tools that help people align their objectives and activities with overall company goals, objectives, and metrics. This is BI that helps synchronize individual efforts by using scorecards, strategy maps, and other tools that connect to corporate data.

PerformancePoint Services

PerformancePoint Services enables users to create interactive dashboards that display key performance indicators (KPIs) and data visualizations in the form of scorecards, reports, and filters. In SharePoint Server 2013, PerformancePoint Services have been updated with the following new capabilities and features:

➤ *Dashboard migration* — Users can copy entire dashboards and dependencies, including the `.aspx` file, to other users, servers, or site collections. This feature also enables the ability to migrate single items to other environments and migrate content by using Windows PowerShell commands.

➤ *Filter enhancements and filter search* — The UI has been enhanced to enable users to easily view and manage filters including giving users the ability to search for items within filters without navigating through the tree.

➤ *BI Center update* — The new BI Center is cleaner and easier to use with folders and libraries configured for easy use.

➤ *Support for Analysis Services Effective User* — This new feature eliminates the need for Kerberos delegation when per-user authentication is used for Analysis Services data sources. By supporting the Analysis Services Effective User feature, authorization checks can based on the user specified by the `EffectiveUserName` property instead of using the currently authenticated user.

➤ *PerformancePoint support on iPad* — PerformancePoint dashboards can now be viewed and interacted with on iPad devices using the Safari web browser.

Important BI Terms and Concepts

Because BI developers may be confused when they first hear commonly used terms in SharePoint, such as *site* and *site collection*, there are some BI terms that may sound a bit vague to SharePoint developers with no BI background. Many BI techniques share terminology, and some terms are used interchangeably. In the interest of clarity, some of these terms are defined in this section and then referenced later.

If you are a SharePoint developer, you are most likely familiar with flat, table-style data structures because lists in SharePoint mimic the same data storage format. Relational database management systems (RDBMSs), such as the SQL Server database engine, also use tables for storing data. Although storing data in tables has its own advantages, browsing through rows and columns rarely leads to useful analysis, especially when someone is looking for patterns and relationships that lie hidden in huge piles of data and information.

For instance, if you were analyzing Internet sales information of Microsoft's fictional AdventureWorks company over the past few years, you would be more interested in the sums of sales per product, per country, and per quarter than in an analysis of the individual sales. Aggregating data at this level, although possible with most RDBMS engines, isn't the most optimized process.

Online Analytical Processing (OLAP) is a technology that tends to remove any granularity in the underlying data and focuses on enhanced data storage, faster data retrieval, and more intuitive navigational capabilities in large databases. Typically, OLAP's information comes from a database, referred to as a *data warehouse*. Compared to a relational database, a data warehouse requires much tighter design work upfront for supporting analyses and data aggregation, such as summed totals and counts.

Because the storage unit used in OLAP is multidimensional, it's called a *cube* instead of a table. The interesting aspect of OLAP is its capability to store aggregated data hierarchically and give users the ability to drill down or up aggregates by dimensional traits. *Dimensions* are a set of attributes representing an area of interest. For example, if you are looking at sales figures generally, you would be interested in geography, time, and product sales, as shown in Figure 18-2.

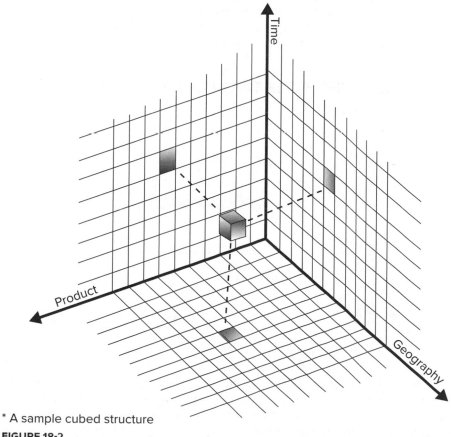

* A sample cubed structure

FIGURE 18-2

Dimensions give contextual information to the numerical figures, or *measures*, that you are aggregating on; for example, Internet sales amount, Internet gross profit, and Internet gross profit margin. OLAP calls each of these a measure. Because the measures are always pre-aggregated and anticipated by the cube, OLAP makes navigation through the data almost instantaneous.

If you want to look at a particular region that had a good quarter of sales, OLAP's navigational feature enables you to expand the quarterly view to see each month or day of the quarter. At the same time, you can also drill down into the region to find the cities with major increases in sales.

There are two more terms that need to be mentioned:

➤ *Multidimensional Expressions* (MDX) — MDX is the query language that enables you to query cubes and return data.

➤ *Data source* — A data source is a stored set of information, such as a tabular database, OLAP cube, Excel spreadsheet, SharePoint list, or any other data object that contains the actual data.

The Business Intelligence Center

Business Intelligence as a core capability of SharePoint has evolved since its introduction in SharePoint 2007. Beginning with the Report Center, SharePoint 2010 introduced the Business Intelligence Center. SharePoint 2013 updates the Business Intelligence site template with streamlined language and emphasis on the visual language conveyed through images, as shown in Figure 18-3.

FIGURE 18-3

The SharePoint 2010 Business Intelligence Center is a site template designed to provide a central location for teams and departments within your organization to store, retrieve, and modify shared reports. The focus of the 2010 update over 2007 was the inclusion of samples and guidance intended to accelerate users with links to articles and preconfigured special-purpose libraries:

> *Dashboards Document Library* — A library that contains exported PerformancePoint dashboards organized in folders

> *Data Connections Document Library* (DCL) — A library that contains ODC Office Data Connection (ODC) files, UDC Universal Data Connection (UDC) files, and PerformancePoint data connections

> *PerformancePoint Content List* — A list that contains PerformancePoint content and OOB views for organizing content

The Microsoft SharePoint Server 2013 Enterprise Edition BI Center site has again evolved. The focus of this new version is to make the site template easier to use and to explicitly highlight capabilities using action verbs such as:

> **Explore and Analyze Data** with PowerPivot.

> **Design Interactive Reports** with Excel and Power View.

> **Share Dashboards** with Excel Services.

The emphasis on separated graphics and action words helps to reduce the complexity of the page, and lead users through the process of SharePoint-hosted BI.

Creating a Business Intelligence Center

To begin creating and using the Business Intelligence Center, you must first enable a few site collection scoped features. To enable these features, perform the following steps:

1. Click Settings ⇨ Site Settings.

2. In the Site Collection Administration list, click the Site collection features link.

3. Activate the SharePoint Server Publishing Infrastructure feature because it is required for the publishing of dashboards.

4. Activate the SharePoint Server Enterprise Site Collection Features feature. This feature enables Excel Services, Visio Services, and Access Services, included in the SharePoint Server Enterprise License.

5. Activate the PerformancePoint Services Site Collection Features feature. This feature adds PerformancePoint content types and a Business Intelligence Center site template.

To properly examine the capabilities of the Business Intelligence Center in SharePoint Server 2013, create a new site with this template by clicking Site Contents ⇨ New Sub site and then choosing the Business Intelligence Center template from the Enterprise templates tab, as shown in Figure 18-4. View an example page by navigating to /Pages/ppssample.aspx.

Just like any other site template, the customizable Business Intelligence Center includes several features that can help you organize dashboards, reports, and the connections to external data sources in one centralized and standardized place.

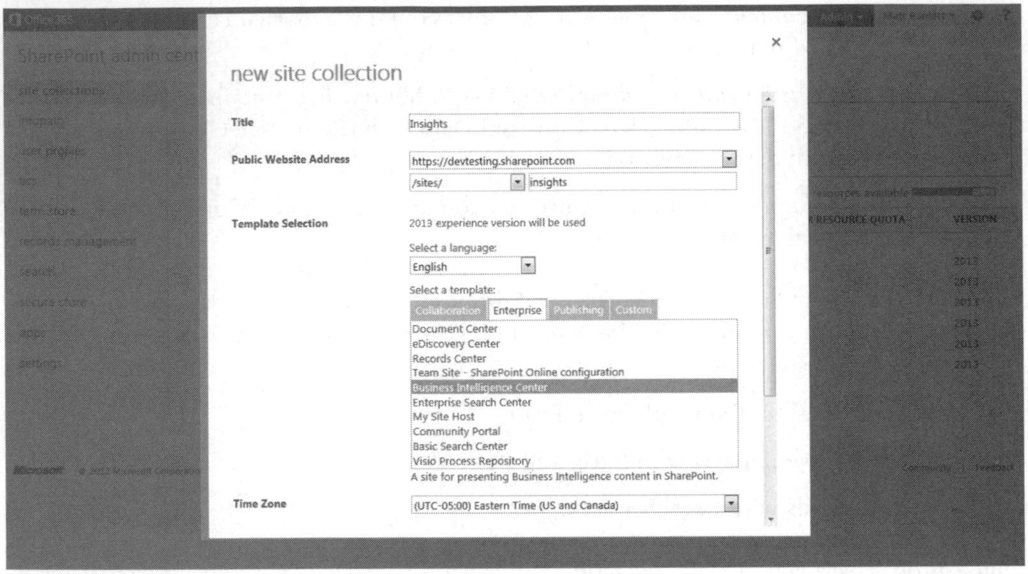

FIGURE 18-4

INTRODUCING PERFORMANCEPOINT 2013

As previously discussed, PerformancePoint Services are the technologies that enable IT departments to design compelling and interactive dashboards that consolidate data from numerous data sources into charts, graphs, and tables. The intent of PerformancePoint Services is to grant businesses the capability to see how their enterprise is performing and to react quickly. The visibility to monitored performance imparted by PerformancePoint Services helps to increase accountability. The interactive components enable aggregation of data into elegant charts that enable deep levels of drill-down and root cause analysis.

PerformancePoint Services leverages its unique SharePoint web parts and tools including Key Performance Indicators (KPIs), Analytic Charts and Grids, Reports, and Filters. These components are configured and combined into Scorecards and Dashboards with the WYSIWYG Dashboard Designer. The Dashboard Designer, combined with PowerPivot's capability to create data models enables rapid development of BI solutions.

PerformancePoint Services Architecture

The fundamental architecture of PerformancePoint Services has not changed between 2010 and 2013. A front-end web server is used to serve content to the browsing user and to the Dashboard Designer. An application server runs the PerformancePoint Services service application, which makes use of the Secure Store service. A database server is required to host the SharePoint databases, including the PerformancePoint Services service database. PerformancePoint Services connects to data sources (OLAP, OLTP, Excel, and so on) through the unattended service account. Although a single server installation is supported, it is not recommended. The traditional multitier server farm configuration is generally represented, as shown in Figure 18-5.

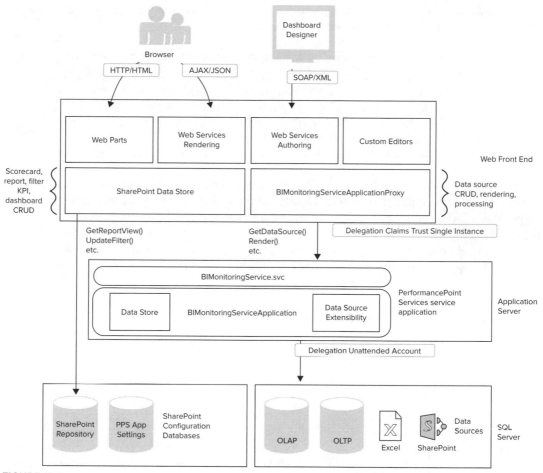

FIGURE 18-5

The functionalities that PerformancePoint Services offer are handled in three tiers of a SharePoint Server farm topology: SQL Server, Application Server, and Web Front End (refer to Figure 18-5).

The Web Front End server hosts the Dashboard Designer application, PerformancePoint web parts, PerformancePoint web services, and the service application proxy that is required to communicate with the PerformancePoint Services application installed on the application server. Like all other service application proxies, the PerformancePoint proxy talks to the PerformancePoint Services application using claims, so even the environments without a Kerberos implementation are not affected by the double-hop security issue.

In the middle tier, two service applications make the integration happen:

➤ *Secure Store Service* — This service application stores the password for the PerformancePoint Services unattended account. The unattended service account is covered in the next section.

➤ *PerformancePoint Services* — This service application stores the settings needed for the instance.

In the database layer, most of the configurations required for PerformancePoint service applications are stored in the PerformancePoint service database.

> **NOTE** *At the time of writing this book, PerformancePoint still doesn't support web applications with multiple authentication stores as part of a claims configuration. This is because of the way the click-once Dashboard Designer is structured. To overcome this limitation, the web application must be extended and must leverage Windows Integrated Authentication.*

Refer to Figure 18-5, which not only depicts the various server roles and component placements, but also denotes the types of custom extensions that take place on either the web server or app server. Customizations that run on the front-end web server include custom editors, which are typically .aspx pages installed in the Layouts directory of the 15 Hive. Customizations that run on the application server include custom transforms and providers/renders that provide custom business logic. Additional detail concerning customizing PerformancePoint Services follows in the "Extending PerformancePoint" section later in this chapter.

Changes in PerformancePoint 2013

PerformancePoint Services, built on the same architecture as the 2010 edition, offers the following new enhancements over the previous version.

EffectiveUsername

A pain point of both PerformancePoint and Excel Services 2010 was the requirement that SharePoint administrators must set up Kerberos-constrained delegation to leverage per-user authentication with SQL Server Analysis Services. Turning to a service account and launching without per-user authentication means that content couldn't be secured at a cell level and BI solutions ran the risk of exposing data to unauthorized users.

The EffectiveUsername feature reduces complexity by eliminating the need for Kerberos constrained delegation and works with both Excel Services and PerformancePoint Services in SharePoint 2013. The EffectiveUsername is essentially a query parameter passed to Analysis Services. When the query with this parameter is executed, Analysis Services will security trim the result set before returning the query results. Enabling EffectiveUsername is as simple as checking a box in the PerformancePoint Service's service application configuration screen in Central Administration.

Custom Target Applications from Secure Store

Another security enhancement, PerformancePoint Services 2013 now supports targeting applications with secure store credentials like Excel Services 2010 did. The secure store defines the set of credentials used to access a back-end data source. Before this change, PerformancePoint did not have the same level of administrative manageability because users were effectively required to use the same set of credentials for all target applications. Now users can be provided with a number of different target applications, each with different credential sets that map correctly to the authorization allowed by the back-end data source. This secure store credential can be configured when defining a data source in the dashboard designer or for an entire service in Central Administration.

Filters

Filters are leveraged by PerformancePoint to create a link between web parts to synchronize the data. SharePoint 2013 leverages six different filter types, including the Custom Table, MDX Query, Member Selection, Named Set, Time Intelligence, and Time Intelligence Connection Formula. Although none of these filter types are new since the 2010 version, SharePoint 2013 improves the user experience with better performance and more intuitive filter actions.

The most significant enhancement made to filters is the capability to do a filter search, as shown in Figure 18-6. A filter search enables users to:

➤   Search within single-select and multiselect tree filters

➤   Search Analysis Services/PowerPivot data sources

➤   Search Member Selection, MDX Query, and Named Set filters

Server Side Migration

PerformancePoint 2010 was a big change from the 2007 version in that all of the components were finally stored inside of SharePoint, leveraging versioning, consistent backups, and so on. Unfortunately, the content types that drove PerformancePoint Services 2010 were not supported by the content deployment functionality or publishing infrastructure. This has now changed in 2013. Appropriately permissioned end users can now leverage the Ribbon to migrate PerformancePoint components anywhere inside of a farm. This capability has been added to support the enterprise IT and regulatory controls that dictate split development ⇨ test ⇨ production environments.

FIGURE 18-6

Themes

The PerformancePoint user experience team worked overtime during the development of SharePoint 2013 to enable support of SharePoint 2013's new Change the Look theming capability. Figure 18-7 shows how effectively this change punches up a dashboard. It is important to note that the only two PerformancePoint components that do not support themes are the Analytic Charts and Decomposition trees (which always pop up a new window with a white background).

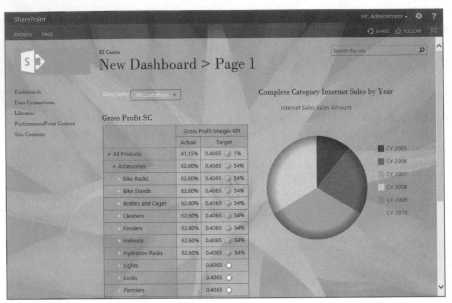

FIGURE 18-7

USING PERFORMANCEPOINT 2013

The following sections walk you through the steps required to correctly configure PerformancePoint Services, create a sample dashboard based on the freely downloadable AdventureWorks database, and finally to extend PerformancePoint Services.

Configuring PerformancePoint Services

The following sections cover how to ensure PerformancePoint Services has been installed and configured for the purposes of creating a simple dashboard based on the AdventureWorksDW Analysis Services sample downloaded and installed in the previous steps.

> **NOTE** *PerformancePoint leverages the SQL2008R2 version of ADOMD.NET, version 10. If SQL Server 2012 is installed, ADOMD.NET 11 will be installed, which will cause the PerformancePoint Dashboard Designer to be unable to connect to Analysis Services databases or cubes. To resolve this issue, simply download and install ADOMD.NET, part of the SQL Server 2008 R2 Feature Pack. ADOMD.NET is also available at* `http://go.microsoft.com/fwlink/` `?LinkID=188442&clcid=0x409.`

Using the AdventureWorks Sample Databases

The database source for examples provided in this chapter is the AdventureWorks data warehouse for SQL Server 2012. You can download this sample data warehouse, AdventureWorksDW2012 from CodePlex at `http://msftdbprodsamples.codeplex.com`. It's worth mentioning that a link to the installation instructions on TechNet is also available on the CodePlex download page.

If the installation goes smoothly, you should be able to start SQL Server Management Studio, connect to the Database Engine, and see the new AdventureWorks databases in your SQL Server 2012 instance.

Unfortunately, the installation package does not automatically deploy the Analysis Services database. The quickest path to deploying the Analysis Services database is to leverage the Analysis Services Tutorials available on the same CodePlcx download page as the AdventureWorksdw2012 Data File.

Before you can start the following instructions, ensure that the SSAS service account has permission to the SQL Server instance where the AdventureWorksDW2012 sample database exists. In addition, ensure that the SSAS service account has permission to access the databases and is at least a member of the `db_datareader` role for the AdventureWorksDW2012 database.

To deploy this database, you need to perform the following steps:

1. Start SQL Server Data Tools, which are based on a Visual Studio 2010 installation.

2. Choose File ➪ Open ➪ Project ➪ Solution, and navigate to the location where you have downloaded and extracted the CodePlex Analysis Services Tutorial SQL Server 2012 which are available online at `http://msftdbprodsamples.codeplex.com/releases/view/55330`. Open the Lesson Analysis Services Tutorial.sln found in the Lesson 9 Complete folder in order to deploy the pre-built sample cube.

3. Next, in the Visual Studio 2010 shell's Solution Explorer, double-click the Adventure Works. ds data source. This opens the Data Source Designer dialog box, as shown in Figure 18-8.

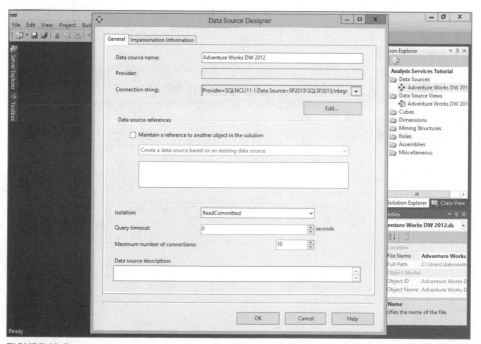

FIGURE 18-8

4. Click the Edit button, and in the Connection Manager, supply your SQL Server Database Engine connection information. Click the Test Connection button. If the test succeeds, click OK, and click OK again to save the changes.

5. In the Solution Explorer, right-click the solution, and click Deploy Solution.

At this point, you should be able to start SQL Server Management Studio, if it's not already open, connect to the Analysis Services, and see the new AdventureWorks databases, which are inside of the Data Sources folder of the new Analysis Services Tutorial database.

Unattended Service Account

PerformancePoint Services 2010 introduced per data source authentication to restrict end users from inadvertently accessing unauthorized databases such as the SharePoint content databases. As mentioned in the "Changes in PerformancePoint 2013" section, SharePoint 2013 enhances the potential of the unattended service account by allowing truly targeted security configurations from inside of the Secure Store Service.

An unattended account can be created using directly in the secure store service or directly in the PerformancePoint Service Application using the following steps:

1. Browse to the Central Administration site.

2. From the Application Management category, choose Manage Service Applications.

3. From the list of existing service applications, click PerformancePoint Service Application.

4. Click the PerformancePoint Service Application Settings link.

5. Specify the unattended service account for PerformancePoint, and click OK. As shown in Figure 18-9, unlike in SharePoint 2010, PerformancePoint Service can optionally leverage a target application ID from the Secure Store Service.

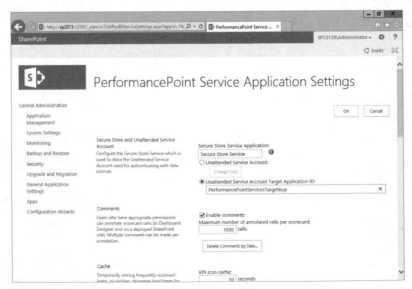

FIGURE 18-9

6. If a Secure Store Service target application did not previously exist, one will be created for PerformancePoint. Browse to the Secure Store Service application's settings page and verify that the new unattended account has been created.

Claims Authentication and BI Solutions

In SharePoint Server 2013, there are some important considerations related to authentication and authorization, which affect all of the services running on the top of the new platform. These changes are particularly important for BI solutions deployed to SharePoint and when SharePoint plays the role of middleman in accessing the back-end data. Perhaps the most important impact involves the way claims-based identity has been plugged into the SharePoint authentication and authorization semantics through a new service called Security Token Service (STS).

Introduced in SharePoint 2010, when a user authenticates to a claims-aware web application, regardless of identity system or authentication type, a claims identity is issued by STS and then it's translated into a SPUser object. This identity is issued based on the standard protocols (SAML, WS-Trust, and WS-Federation) and works with any corporate identity system, such as Active Directory, WebSSO, Live ID, LDAP, SQL, or Custom. Without any special configuration, the claims identity flows along with the request through the server tiers (service applications) in a SharePoint farm.

In terms of the authorization semantics, things haven't changed much in SharePoint 2010, with one exception. With the claims authentication infrastructure, you can now leverage claims attributes during the authorization process, reducing the need to proliferate role-based security groups for every imaginable security permutation. You can also use the claim provider APIs and augment the existing claims for handling your custom authorization scenarios. For more information, see the official documentation at http://www.devhorizon.com/go/23.

Although the service application infrastructure in SharePoint is claims-aware, many external data sources are still not claims-aware. In many scenarios, such as the following, claims cannot be used for the end-to-end solution:

➤ *Scenario 1* — In this scenario, an Excel workbook or PerformancePoint scorecard is used against an Analysis Services cube that has role-based security (that is, every role has its own view of the data). This requires Windows authentication for Analysis Services and, thus, a way to pass the identity for every user from SharePoint to Analysis Services. SQL Server Analysis Services is not claims-aware and has no idea who or what the SharePoint user is. Before the advent of the SharePoint 2013 EffectiveUsername feature, administrators were required to configure Kerberos or the unattended service account and add an authenticated username in the connection string. In this scenario, the EffectiveUsername connection to Analysis Services saves a tremendous amount of complex configuration!

➤ *Scenario 2* — Front-end web servers, the Excel Calculation Services application, and the SharePoint database servers run on different computers. In this scenario, if Excel Calculation Services is opening workbooks stored in SharePoint content databases, you should use Kerberos or the unattended account.

➤ Scenario 3 — In this scenario, Excel Calculation Services is opening a workbook from non–Microsoft SharePoint Foundation trusted file locations, such as UNC shares or HTTP websites. The authentication method used in this scenario is to use impersonation or process an account.

➤ *Scenario 4* — A common scenario in which Kerberos is needed is when there are multiple machine hops from mid-tier to the last data source, as shown in Figure 18-10. Remember, the minute an identity leaves the boundary of the service application tier; the claims identity may no longer be meaningful if a data source doesn't understand the compliant SAML protocol.

The scenario depicted in Figure 18-11 shows how the combination of claims and the unattended account can help you properly authenticate to the back-end data source. In this scenario, the claims identity flows between multiple service applications, and the Analysis Services engine impersonates the unattended account to connect to the external data source.

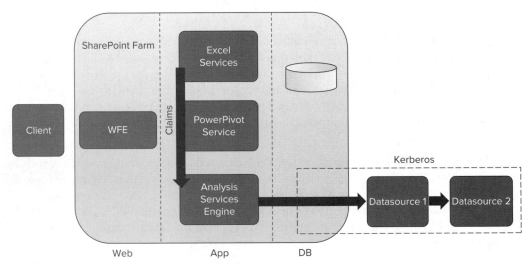

FIGURE 18-10

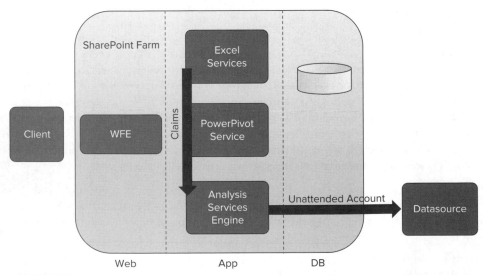

FIGURE 18-11

Creating a Dashboard

Now that PerformancePoint Services has been properly configured with secure access through the EffectiveUsername and Unattended Service Account, it is time to kick the tires and create an actual dashboard.

Launching the Dashboard Designer

In this section, you kick off PerformancePoint dashboard designer by following these steps:

1. In Internet Explorer, navigate to the Business Intelligence Center site created at the beginning of this chapter.

2. Navigate to a web part page or to the Dashboards library in the Site Contents page to see the PerformancePoint Ribbon tab.

3. In the Create and Edit group of the PerformancePoint Ribbon tab, click the Dashboard Designer button to launch the click-once application, as shown in Figure 18-12.

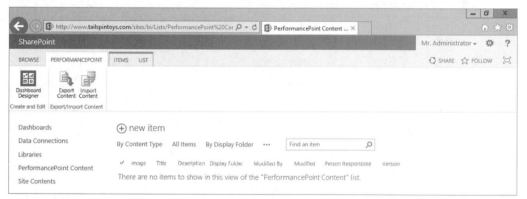

FIGURE 18-12

4. After the executable file is downloaded and installed on your computer via Click-once deployment, the PerformancePoint Dashboard Designer appears and opens an empty workspace. A workspace is a primary container for all of the elements that you can use to build your dashboard, and it keeps its content synched with the site from which it was launched.

5. Essentially, the workspace becomes an XML file (.ddwx) that encapsulates all the meta data required to describe a PerformancePoint dashboard. In the workspace, you can build new elements or you can import existing elements from a published dashboard such as scorecards, KPIs, reports, filters, indicators, and dashboards.

Assembling a Dashboard

Now that you have created a PerformancePoint workspace, you are ready to create your first dashboard, which displays historical and real-time information as an asymmetrical report and compares it to an established goal. And with that, it's time to build the actual dashboard from the ground up.

Dashboard Data Source

As with any other BI solution, the first thing that you want to do is to go after data. To create the data source used for this dashboard, follow these steps:

1. Right-click the Data Connections folder in the Workspace Browser, and then select New ⇨ Data Source.

2. From the Select a Data Source Template menu, choose the Analysis Services template to create a data source that connects to Microsoft SQL Server Analysis Services, and click OK.

3. In the Connection Settings, specify the Analysis Services instance you want to connect to. In the next field, select the database and the cube you want to connect to. For this example, you want to connect to the Analysis Services Tutorial database and the Internet Sales cube, as shown in Figure 18-13.

> **NOTE** *In the Data Source Settings, note the Cache Lifetime setting. The value of this textbox (in minutes) indicates the interval of refreshing the dashboard information from the backend data source.*

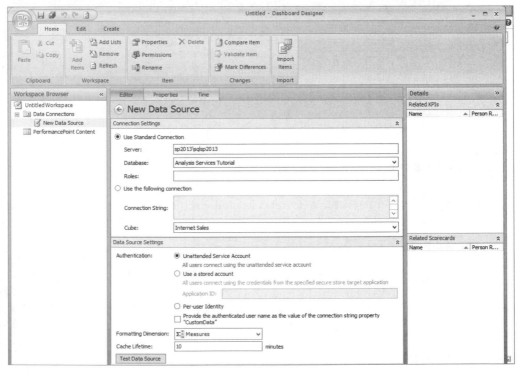

FIGURE 18-13

4. Click Test Data Source to make sure that your connection settings are correct.

5. Switch to the Properties tab and change the Name to **AdventureWorksDW_ADCube**.

6. Save the new data source by right-clicking it in the Workspace Browser and then selecting Save.

At this point, you have successfully created the dashboard's main data source and it's been uploaded to the Data Connections Document Library by the Dashboard Designer.

Data Source Authentication Types

There are three authentication types available for the data source you are building (refer to Figure 18-13).

The unattended service account option has been previously discussed, and by now you should know what it does, but the other two options and the checkbox deserve more attention:

➤ *Use a stored account* — By leveraging a pre-configured secure store target application, administrators can centrally control a service account that all end users use to connect to the database.

➤ *Per-user identity* — There are cases that may not require you to create the unattended service account. Picture this: Your back-end data source supports Windows authentication, and user identities must be delegated all the way down to the back-end data source when they access the PerformancePoint dashboards. In PerformancePoint, this authentication type is known as per-user identity, and only Kerberos enables it.

➤ *Provide the authenticated user name in as the value of the connection string property* — This checkbox is available to any authentication selection. If this option is selected, PerformancePoint supplies the SharePoint authenticated provider and username (Forms, SAML, Windows, and so on) as a string in the `CustomData` field in Analysis Services. You can then create a role (or set of roles) and write MDX queries using the `CustomData` string to dynamically restrict access to the cube data. The main challenge of this solution is that you need to modify the cube data to include the users of the system and their relationships to the data; this can be somewhat difficult to maintain.

> **NOTE** *No matter what authentication type you choose for PerformancePoint Services, always make sure that it has proper access to the back-end data source that will be required.*

Tracking Performance Using KPIs

How can you measure success? How can the measurement of success be implemented in a dashboard? Success (or the goal) in a certain area of the business is defined by someone in your organization who knows the business inside and out. In PerformancePoint, a primary metric used to implement and measure this success is a *key performance indicator* (KPI). The KPI measures progress toward a goal and as such readily lends itself to representation with the classic Red/Yellow/Green indicator as to the status of current progress towards the goal. After a KPI is defined and implemented, it can be used to monitor the organization's progress in a specific area, such as gross profit margin per product category earned from Internet sales.

To create a new KPI to track gross profit margin for Internet sales, you need to follow these steps:

1. Right-click the `PerformancePoint Content` folder, and select New ⇨ KPI, as shown in Figure 18-14.

2. In the Select a KPI Template dialog box, select Blank KPI, and then click OK.

3. Figure 18-15 shows the new KPI. Here, you can define your actual and target values. You can also continue adding new actuals or targets to the current KPI. For example, if your organization has defined a minimum goal and stretched goal, you may want to bring them into the KPI by defining two target values.

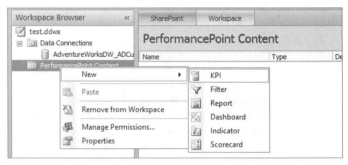

FIGURE 18-14

FIGURE 18-15

4. The current value for Actual is set to 1, which doesn't represent anything. Click the 1 (Fixed Values) link in the Data Mappings column for Actual. Then in the Fixed Values Data Source Mapping dialog box, click the Change Source button.

> **NOTE** *In Analysis Services, you can build KPIs that have four values: Actual, Target, Status, and Trend. In PerformancePoint KPIs, you have only two values: Actual and Target. One interesting aspect about Actual and Target values in PerformancePoint is that they do not need to come from the same data source. For example, you can define a KPI that gets the Actual Value from the cube and then have the Target value loaded from a SharePoint list. This makes PerformancePoint KPIs flexible.*

1. Select the AdventureWorksDW_ADCube_PerfPoint data connection, and click OK.

2. From the Select a Measure drop-down list, select Internet Gross Profit Margin.

3. Click OK to close the dialog box.

4. Select the Target row, and click the Set Scoring Pattern and Indicator button in the Thresholds area, as shown in Figure 18-16.

5. In the first step of the Edit Banding Settings dialog box (see Figure 18-17), you need to identify how the actual value compares to a target. From the Scoring Pattern list, select the Increasing Is Better option. Most of the time, you would use a normalized value where you take the actual value and divide it by the target value, so select the first option (Band by Normalized Value of Actual/Target) from the Banding Method drop-down list, and then click Next.

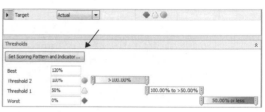

FIGURE 18-16

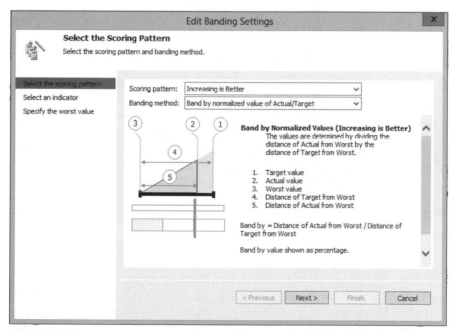

FIGURE 18-17

6. In the Select an Indicator step, select an indicator to use for the target that clearly shows whether the goal is met. You can choose from a collection of indicator templates available in PerformancePoint Dashboard Designer. When you are done, click Next.

7. In the last step of the wizard, leave the worse value intact and click Finish. Now, you can see how target values from 0% to beyond 100% are categorized by different colors. You can

type the ultimate values for each threshold, or you can use the slider of each color to adjust the size of the percentage ranges.

8. You need to change the fixed value of the target, which represents 100 percent gross profit margin. Although 100 percent is an ideal percentage, you may want to adjust this value to something that's more realistic and makes more sense in your business, for example 40.65 percent of the actual value. Click the 1 (Fixed Values) link and change the value from 1 to 0.4065.

> **NOTE** *The AdventureWorks 2008 R2 cube does not have measures that can be used for the target values of the sample KPI in this section. You need to use Fixed Values instead. Typically, Fixed Values are great when the measure doesn't change often.*

9. Click OK.

10. Change the name of the KPI to Gross Profit Margin, by right-clicking it in the Workspace Browser and clicking Rename.

11. Save the KPI by right-clicking it in the Workspace Browser and then choosing Save.

At this point, your new KPI should look like Figure 18-18. Notice on the Details pane that you have all available information about the KPI, such as related data sources.

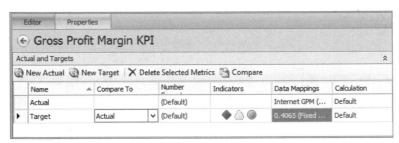

FIGURE 18-18

Building the Scorecard

With the dashboard's data source and KPI complete, you have all the elements that you need to build the scorecard. This scorecard will contain the Gross Profit Margin KPI, show all sales across all years, and is broken down by product category.

1. Right-click the `PerformancePoint Content` folder, and then click New ⇨ Scorecard. Change the name to Profit Margin SC.

2. From the Select a Scorecard Template dialog box, select Standard Category. From the Template pane, select Blank Scorecard, and click Next.

3. Drag Gross Profit Margin KPI (Details KPIs ⇨ PerformancePoint Content) and drop it onto the first row where it says Drop Items Here.

4. Click the Update button in the Edit tab.

5. From the Data Source drop-down list, select AdventureWorksDW_ADCube_PerfPoint to make all the dimensions in the cube available for the scorecard, as shown in Figure 18-19.

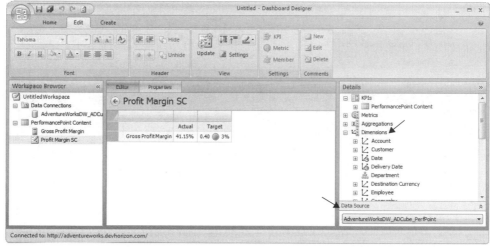

FIGURE 18-19

6. From the list of available dimensions, find and expand Product Dimension.

7. Select the Categories Member.

8. Drag Categories to the left side of the Gross Profit Margin cell. If everything has been configured correctly, the first row of the expandable KPI will be displayed as All Products, as shown in Figure 18-20.

9. From Select Members dialog box, select All Products.

10. Click the Update button in the Edit tab to view the updated data, as shown in Figure 18-21.

11. Save the scorecard by right-clicking it in the Workspace Browser and then choosing Save.

FIGURE 18-20

FIGURE 18-21

Native Reporting

In this section, you create a report that connects to the scorecard you created in the previous section and display Internet sales for all years grouped by product category.

1. Right-click the `PerformancePoint Content` folder, and then click New ⇨ Report.

2. From the Select a Report Template dialog box, select Analytic Chart (see Figure 18-22), and then click OK.

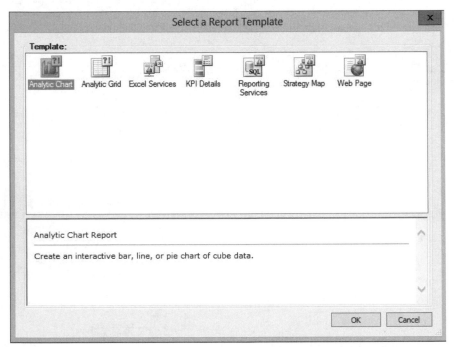

FIGURE 18-22

> **NOTE** *In addition to the native reports, PerformancePoint supports referencing the Analytic Chart and Analytic Grid, a SQL Server Reporting Services report, an Excel Services workbook, a KPI Details object, a web page, and a Microsoft Office Visio strategy map in your dashboards.*

3. From the Select a Data Connection dialog box, select the data source in the current workspace, and click Finish. Figure 18-23 shows what the workspace should look like when you build any type of report.

4. Expand the Measures node in the Details task pane on the right.

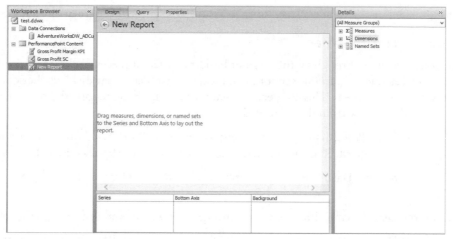

FIGURE 18-23

5.   Drag the Internet Sales Amount item into the Bottom Axis box.

6.   Expand the Dimensions and Product nodes, and drag Categories into the background. Even if you will not show the actual categories in the chart, you still need to reference Categories in the background so that when you build the dashboard, the filter that connects categories from the scorecard to the chart knows where to filter. You learn about the dashboard in the next section.

7.   Expand Date Dimension and drag the Calendar Year into the Series section.

8.   Change the name of the report to Complete Category Internet Sales by Year, by right-clicking it in the Workspace Browser and clicking Rename.

9.   In the Ribbon's Edit tab, select Report Type ➪ Pie Chart. Your workspace should look like Figure 18-24.

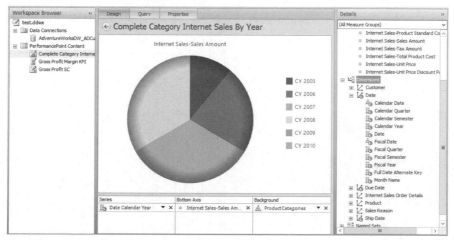

FIGURE 18-24

10. Save the report by right-clicking it in the Workspace Browser and then choosing Save.

Putting Everything Together

Now that you have gone through all the steps of building different pieces of the dashboard, it's time to put all the pieces together. In this section, you create a dashboard that displays the scorecard and the report and connects them. This connection enables filtering of the report (the pie chart) using the currently selected category from the scorecard.

1. Right-click the PerformancePoint Content folder in the Workspace Browser, and then click New ⇨ Dashboard. Rename the new dashboard **Internet Sales Dashboard**.

2. From the Select a Dashboard Page template, select the 2 Columns page template, and click OK.

3. From the Details pane, drag the Gross Profit SC scorecard, and drop it into the left column.

4. From the Details pane, drag the Complete Category Internet Sales By Year report into the right column.

5. Drag the Row Member item from the scorecard column into the report column.

6. In the Connection dialog box, change the Source value drop-down list to Member Row: Member Unique Name. Remember, the filter that connects the scorecard to the report bases this connection on the product category that exists in both elements.

7. Save the dashboard by right-clicking it in the Workspace Browser and then choosing Save. Figure 18-25 shows the finished dashboard.

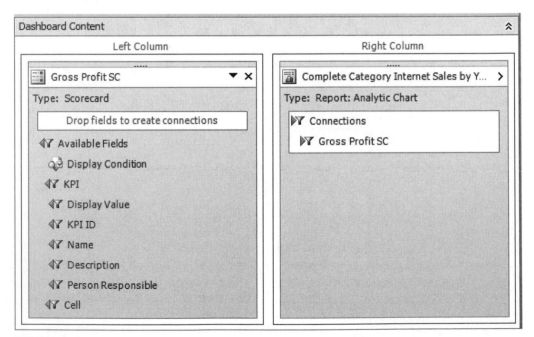

FIGURE 18-25

Publishing to SharePoint

With the dashboard layout completed, the next step is to make it available in SharePoint for online viewing. Remember, the dashboard contents are already stored in the BI Center site, so publishing here means creating an instance of the dashboard definition and dumping it as an .aspx page (an exported dashboard) in a dashboard's document library.

> **NOTE** *The distinction between a dashboard definition and the actual dashboard page still exists, as was the case in PerformancePoint 2007. If you take an exported dashboard (an .aspx file), customize it using an HTML editor, and replace the existing one with the customized version of the dashboard, the next time the same dashboard is published to SharePoint, your changes will be overwritten. That's because you modified the instance, not the definition.*

You can publish your dashboard to any document if the following two conditions are met:

➤ The page is in a document library with PerformancePoint content types.

➤ The page has access to the dashboard elements in the BI Center.

Publishing the dashboard to SharePoint is relatively straightforward:

1. Right-click the dashboard in the Workspace Browser, and then select the Deploy to SharePoint menu item.

2. Select the Dashboards folder, and click OK.

3. From the Deploy To dialog box, select the site and Dashboard Document Library, and click OK. Optionally, you can select any of the available Master Pages in the current site collection for your dashboard. For example, if you want to see your dashboards with no chrome, you can develop a custom Master Page and select it to use when publishing your dashboard.

When the deployment is completed, you are redirected to a page (see Figure 18-26) where your dashboard is rendered with 100 percent fidelity to what you experienced in the authoring environment.

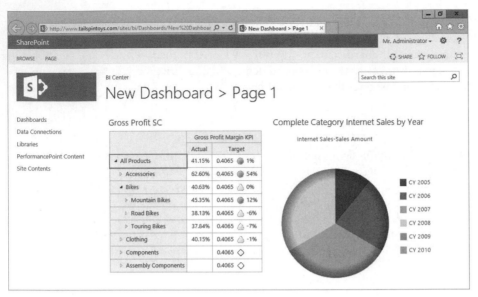

FIGURE 18-26

What Else Is in the Box?

The dashboard that you just published is nothing more than a web part page, two web parts, and a web part connection, which were all set up automatically as part of the dashboard-publishing process.

These connections are not exclusive to PerformancePoint web parts. Using the web part connection, you can take your dashboard design to the next level by adding more web parts to the page representing more complex analytical scenarios. You can examine the content of the dashboard by switching the page to edit mode, as shown in Figure 18-27.

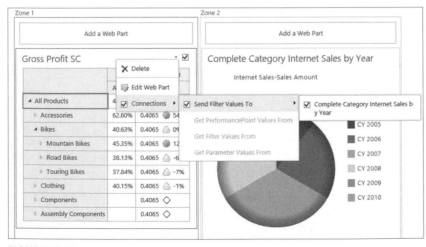

FIGURE 18-27

There are many functionalities available on the chart. Suppose that, for the purpose of trend analysis, you need to change the type of the chart. To do so, right-click underneath the chart's legend, and from the context menu, select Report Type ➪ Pie Chart, as shown in Figure 18-28.

If you right-click the analytic chart, you can see that there are plenty of helpful built-in functionalities at your fingertips, as shown in Figure 18-29.

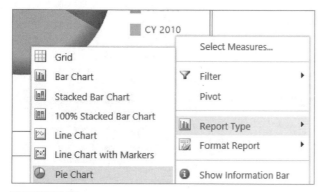

FIGURE 18-28

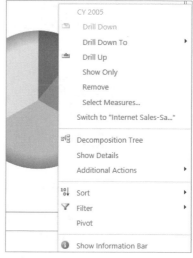

FIGURE 18-29

There are three options in this menu that need to be highlighted:

➤ *Drill Down To or Drill Up* — These options enable you to drill down or up to see different levels of detail presented by the chart element.

➤ *Select Measures* — If the measure that the report represents is not enough for your analysis, click Select Measures, and select one or more items from the list of all measures that exist in the perspective.

➤ *Decomposition Tree* — This option offers another interactive way of navigating your dashboard. An advantage of using the Decomposition Tree is that it keeps the report sorted and places insignificant contributors at the bottom of the hierarchy (see Figure 18-30). Of course, if you want to analyze negativity (that is, cities with worse sales amounts), you can always flip the default sorting style using the drop-down list on the top of each level. Decomposition Tree is a Silverlight application and requires the Microsoft Silverlight 3 framework to be installed on the client machine.

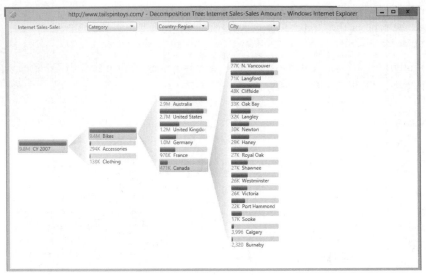

FIGURE 18-30

Finally, if you ever decide to show a dashboard element in a completely new page to have more real estate, from the web part that hosts the element, modify the properties, and select Open in New Window, as shown in Figure 18-31. You can also reset the view to the element's original state.

FIGURE 18-31

Time Intelligence Filtering

In your analysis, you are often required to base your time formulas and functions on a time dimension such as your company's fiscal year. In such scenarios, if your data source is not aware of the time dimension you use, you get the error message that says the data source has an invalid time intelligence configuration, as shown in Figure 18-32.

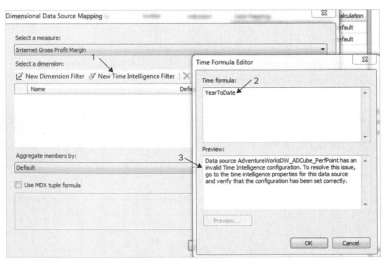

FIGURE 18-32

As suggested by the error message, setting the time intelligence configuration in your data source prepares the groundwork for time intelligence. To configure the time intelligence in your data source, follow these steps:

1. Navigate to the Time tab in your data source to select a time dimension, as shown in Figure 18-33.

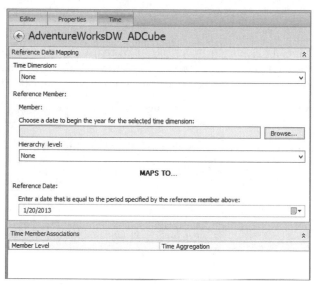

FIGURE 18-33

2. From the Time Dimension drop-down list, select Data.Date.Fiscal Date, as shown in Figure 18-34.

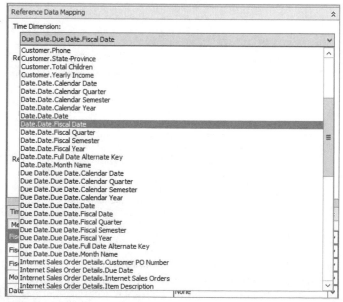

FIGURE 18-34

3. Click the Browse button in the Reference Member field and, from the Select Members dialog box, select July 1, 2005. Now suppose that your company's fiscal year starts on July 1st. By selecting a reference of July 1st, you make the data source aware that your time dimension has a starting point on the first day of July each year.

4. From the Hierarchy level drop-down list, specify the granularity of the member you just referenced in the previous step. Because July 1st represents a day, you should select Day from the drop-down menu.

5. In the Date picker control, specify a date (such as 11/1/2009) that is equal to the period specified by the reference member you chose in step 2 (see Figure 18-35). PerformancePoint Services uses this date to associate the Reference Member to the traditional calendar.

6. In the Time Member Associations, map your time dimension hierarchies (on the left) to the defined Time Aggregations (on the right).

Now you can go ahead and create any formulas or filters that are based on this intelligent time dimension, such as [Date.Fiscal].[FY 2006 to Date by Day].

FIGURE 18-35

Strategy Maps

Another requirement for understanding the performance of an organization is the ability to understand the relationship between strategic business objectives and the various KPIs that measure progress toward those strategic goals. In PerformancePoint, a strategy map is composed of a Visio services hosted diagram, which works in mobile browsers and is touch-enabled, which means that PerformancePoint dashboards and strategy maps natively support the iPad and other tablet devices. In a PerformancePoint dashboard, a scorecard monitoring performance may make more sense to users if placed on the page next to a strategy map.

PerformancePoint does not restrict the format of the shapes in the Visio diagram to a hierarchical diagram. Actually, any shape can be used because the process of adding a strategy map to the Dashboard Designer links each shape in the drawing to a KPI in the Strategy Map Editor dialog, as long as the shape is a simple shape (excluding grouped objects). This connection enables each shape in the diagram to represent a KPI by changing color to reflect the performance of that particular KPI. For instance, in the previous example, several of the shapes reflect that the KPI is on track with the green color while a few items are in trouble and are shaded red.

Although strategy maps can be anything the dashboard designer wants, there is a management science technique known as the Balanced Scorecard framework that uses four dimensions to define organizational performance

➤ *Financial* — This dimension measures the financial metrics such as revenue, cost, and profit.

➤ *Customer* — This dimension measures customer satisfaction and includes metrics such as customer counts, market share, and number of complaints.

➤ *Internal process* — This dimension measures an organization's operational metrics including time to market for new products, service error rates, and quality control measures.

➤ *Learning and growth* — This dimension focuses on the people side of an organization, watching metrics such as employee turnover rates, the number of new employees, and hiring data.

The Balanced Scorecard framework is a useful strategic performance management tool that has been adopted worldwide to keep track of organizational effectiveness and to monitor the results of employee actions. The strategy map component of the Balanced Scorecard framework, introduced in the mid-1990s, enables a great deal of contextual justification when determining which measures and metrics to monitor because the strategy map enable business leaders to understand the relationships between metrics.

EXTENDING PERFORMANCEPOINT

PerformancePoint Services does support customization through a number of different vectors. Enterprising developers can take advantage of the available APIs to hook custom reports, filters, tabular data sources, and scorecard transforms into the application. The following sections discuss the three required components to create custom reports, filters, and tabular data sources: a renderer/provider, an editor, and the extension meta data.

Extensibility Targets in PerformancePoint 2013

Earlier in this chapter, the "PerformancePoint Services Architecture" section introduced you to the numerous approaches to customizing PerformancePoint Services in SharePoint 2013. See Figure 18-36 for a refresher of the PerformancePoint Services architecture.

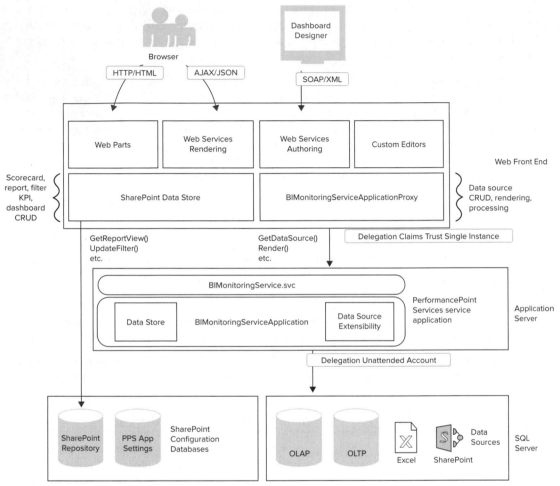

FIGURE 18-36

As previously noted, customizations that run on the front-end web server include custom editors. Custom editors enable end users to define property settings on custom reports, filters, and tabular data sources. Custom editors are essentially .aspx pages installed in the Layouts directory of the 15 Hive. As you can see, custom editors are built on top of the BIMonitoringServiceApplicationProxy class, which handles data source CRUD, rendering, and processing.

Customizations that run on the middle-tier application server include custom scorecard transforms and renders/providers that provide custom business logic. Custom scorecard transforms are used to change the appearance and content of scorecards before rendering.

> **NOTE** *PerformancePoint clearly supports a number of custom extension points for developers; it is worth reiterating that SharePoint 2013 supports a number of new Design Manager capabilities that enable deep levels of HTML, CSS, and JavaScript control on Publishing Pages. PerformancePoint publishes dashboards on Publishing Pages. You may achieve your customization goals through the use of CSS and JavaScript without turning to the more expensive option of maintaining custom code. You can find more information on the Design Manager features in Chapter 10, "Web Content Management."*

Custom Data Sources

Consider the following scenario: A SharePoint development team has been asked by the TailSpin Toys business leadership to create an integrated dashboard reflecting the performance of the marketing team's investments in various campaigns. To successfully accomplish this task, the SharePoint developer must first understand which metrics are important and then work backward to discover the data integration requirements.

In the example scenario, business owners want to understand at what rate a direct marketing campaign, and the sales and marketing team's marketing platform convert into sales. When a campaign is launched from the marketing platform, a special offer is delivered via e-mail to the prospective customer. This offer is a call to action, a call for the customer to click a link to view the deal and receive the discount. This offer link contains a special code, called a response attribution code, which enables the sales team to track the sale back to the originating campaign. Considering that the TailSpin Toys sales and marketing teams are aggressive overachievers who launch hundreds of targeted campaigns a year, this measurement must take the following shape:

> ➤ *Understand for all campaigns the rate of views of offers.* This can measure whether or not the e-mail containing the offer was viewed or deleted without being opened.

> ➤ *Understand for all campaigns the rate of clicks on offers.* This can measure whether or not the recipient of the e-mail clicked the link to open the TailSpin Toys' e-commerce site.

> ➤ *Understand for all campaigns the rate of conversion of offers.* This can measure whether or not the recipient of the e-mail actually purchased a product using the campaign's suggested offer (normally a discount or an offer of free shipping).

> ➤ *Drill down in each of the preceding aggregate measures.* This can help to understand the rates for each individual campaign.

The intent here is to enable PerformancePoint's decomposition tree component to highlight especially effective and ineffective campaigns for more intelligent marketing investments. This scenario is a fairly common set of metrics with which the performance of sales and marketing organizations can be measured.

If TailSpin Toys leveraged Microsoft Dynamics CRM, the easy approach would be to connect the Dashboard Designer to the CRM database directly. Unfortunately for the SharePoint developer, TailSpin Toys leverages Salesforce.com as a marketing platform, so all CRM details such as direct marketing campaign metrics are contained there. Fortunately, the e-commerce website is based on a custom ASP.NET Web Forms application, which leverages a SQL Server back end.

The solution approach in this scenario would weigh the following options:

➤ Should the data from Salesforce.com be downloaded to a SQL Server OLTP database for easy reporting purposes?

➤ Should the data from Salesforce.com be downloaded to an enterprise Data Warehouse (EDW) hosted by SQL Server Analysis Services for deep analytical understanding and coincidentally easy reporting via PerformancePoint?

➤ Does the business require a near real-time view of the data, which requires direct read access of the Salesforce.com data?

For the purposes of this example, the near real-time requirements are going to require that the SharePoint developer connect directly to the Salesforce.com platform via web services to retrieve the data.

PerformancePoint Services can use the following as tabular data sources for reporting purposes: Excel and Excel Services worksheets, SharePoint lists, and SQL Server tables. Leveraging data from web services is not available out-of-the-box, so what is the fictitious SharePoint developer to do? Why, create a custom tabular data source, of course! The other custom back-end options, creating custom reports and filters, don't apply to this specific example.

Salesforce.com offers a *SOAP API Developers Guide*, available at `http://www.salesforce.com/us/developer/docs/api/index.htm`. The full exploration of interconnecting .NET and Salesforce.com data is beyond the scope of this chapter, but the code snippet that appears later in this section reveals an approach to creating a custom tabular data source. The specific Salesforce.com objects worth investigating in the dashboard are the Campaign, CampaignMember, Lead, and Opportunity objects. The Lead object tracks inside of Salesforce.com whether or not that lead has been converted into an Account, Contact, or Opportunity. The `query()` method of the `connection` object enables the retrieval of data from an object and works with a SQL-like syntax and can be paged if multiple results occur. Figure 18-37 reflects this subset of the Salesforce.com Sales objects data model.

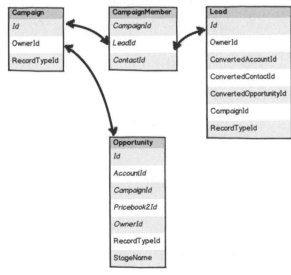

The code snippet that appears later in this section can retrieve Opportunities and turn that data into a tabular data source. Before this code can be created, a WSDL must be generated inside of Salesforce.com. To generate a WSDL, click Account Name ➪ Set Up ➪ Develop ➪ API ➪ Generate enterprise WSDL ➪ Generate. After the WSDL has

FIGURE 18-37

been created and saved to the developer's hard drive, add a service reference to that WSDL in Visual Studio.

> **NOTE** *The code snippet that appears later in this section ignores the login requirements for Salesforce.com. The SFDC Developer Quick Start Guide is available at* `http://www.salesforce.com/us/developer/docs/api/Content/ sforce_api_quickstart_steps.htm` *and describes the following steps:*
>
> **1.** *Obtain a Salesforce Developer Edition Organization.*
> **2.** *Generate or obtain the web service WSDL.*
> **3.** *Import the WSDL file into your development platform.*
> **4.** *Walk through sample code.*
> **5.** *Prompt the user for SFDC username and password.*
> **6.** *Call* `login()` *to log into the server.*
> **7.** *Call* `describeGlobal()` *to list all objects available to the logged in user.*
> **8.** *Call* `describeSObjects()` *to list meta data for a specific object.*
> **9.** *Call* `query()` *to pass a simple query string.*
> **10.** *Call* `logout()` *to log the user out.*
>
> *The code snippet that appears later in this section is intended to be an example only and is not a fully functional application.*

To create a custom tabular data source, you must first create the properly configured solution in Visual Studio.

1. In a development environment with access to the PerformancePoint DLLs, create a C# class library project.

2. Add the following PerformancePoint Services DLLs:

➤ `Microsoft.PerformancePoint.Scorecards.Client.dll`

➤ `Microsoft.PerformancePoint.Scorecards.DataSourceProviders.Standard.dll`

The code snippet that appears later in this section represents an extremely simplified approach to creating a tabular data source from Salesforce.com data. This code does the following things when executed:

➤ Defines a Salesforce Object array to store results from the Salesforce.com web service query.

➤ Validates that the data source object is correctly configured with dimension and fact tables. This step effectively ensures that PerformancePoint Services can use the output of the custom code as it would an Analysis Services cube. The pertinent functions are the overridden `SetDataSource()` and the internal `CreateDataColumnMappings()` functions.

➤ Fills the tabular data source with data retrieved from Salesforce.com. This step (abbreviated to serve as an example) queries the Salesforce.com Opportunities object with the following chain of functions:

➤ The overridden `GetDataSet()` defines the data table to be mapped to the tabular data source and then calls `FillResultTable()`.

➤ `FillResultTable()` is an internal function that first checks the cache for archived results and then calls `queryRecords()` to get actual data from the Salesforce.com web service.

```
using System;
using System.Data;
using System.IO;
using System.Linq;
using System.Xml.Linq;
using Microsoft.PerformancePoint.Scorecards;
using Microsoft.PerformancePoint.SDK.Samples.SampleDataSource;

namespace TailSpinToys.Wrox.Samples.ExampleTabularDataSource
{

  // Represents the class that defines the sample data source provider.
  // It inherits from the BasicTabularDataSourceProvider class, which
  // contains overridden abstract methods that are not implemented.  The
  // BasicTabularDataSourceProvider class and the SampleDSCacheHandler class
  // are provided in the Microsoft PerformancePoint Services SDK Reference
  // Sample (available http://archive.msdn.microsoft.com/ppsSdkRefSample)

  // Code also requires access to SalesForce.com WSDL and generated proxy classes
  // before this code will compile
  public class SFDCTabularDataSourceProvider : BasicTabularDataSourceProvider
  {

    #region Properties

    // This property stores the array of results from
    // the queried SFDC Web service.
    private Object[] OpportunitiesArray
    {
      get;
      set;
    }

    #endregion

    #region Overridden methods

    // The source name for your data source. This value must match the key
    // attribute that is registered in the web.config file.  Modifying the
    // web.config file is discussed in the deployment section of this chapter
    public override string GetId()
    {
      return "SFDCTabularDataSource";
    }
```

```csharp
// Add column mappings for the sample columns if they do not exist.
// Column mappings may be missing if the custom data source has never
// been edited or if the workspace was not refreshed, which saves
// changes to the server.
public override void SetDataSource(DataSource dataSource)
{

  base.SetDataSource(dataSource);

  // Check whether column mappings exist. Do not overwrite them.
  if (dataSource.DataTableMapping.ColumnMappings.Count == 0)
  {
    dataSource.DataTableMapping = CreateDataColumnMappings();
  }
}

// Get the data from the data source.
// GetDataSet contains the core logic for the provider.
public override DataSet GetDataSet()
{

  // Create a dataset and a data table to store the data.
  DataSet resultSet = new DataSet();
  DataTable resultTable = resultSet.Tables.Add();

  // Define column names and the type of data that they contain.
  resultTable.Columns.Add("OpportunityId", typeof(string));
  resultTable.Columns.Add("StageName", typeof(string));
  resultTable.Columns.Add("CampaignId", typeof(string));

  FillResultTable(ref resultTable);

  return resultSet;
}
#endregion

#region Internal methods

// Fill the data table with the retrieved values from
// the Salesforce.com Web service
protected void FillResultTable(ref DataTable resultsTable)
{

  // Check the sematic validity of symbols (out of scope for this sample).
  if (null != OpportunitiesArray &&
    OpportunitiesArray.Length > 0 &&
    !string.IsNullOrEmpty(SampleDSCacheHandler.CacheFileLocation))
  {
    try
    {
      if (!File.Exists(SampleDSCacheHandler.CacheFileLocation))
      {

        // Create the cache file.
        XDocument doc = SampleDSCacheHandler.DefaultCacheFileContent;
        doc.Save(@SampleDSCacheHandler.CacheFileLocation);
      }
```

```
             // Get values and update cache file.
             queryRecords();

             SampleDSCacheHandler.UpdateXMLCacheFile(wsResult);

             // Check if a valid cache file location exists, which SHOULD exist
             // given that it was just filled from a query of the web service.
             if (SampleDSCacheHandler.CacheFileContent != null)
             {
               var query = from c in SampleDSCacheHandler.CacheFileContent
    .Elements("Opportunities").Elements("Opportunity")
                   select c;

               foreach (var opportunityInstance in query)
               {
                 DataRow row = resultsTable.NewRow();
                 row["OpportunityId"] = opportunityInstance.Attribute
    ("OpportunityId ").Value;
                 row["StageName"] = opportunityInstance.Element("StageName").Value;
                 row["CampaignId"] = opportunityInstance.Element("CampaignId")
    .Value;

                 resultsTable.Rows.Add(row);
               }
             }
           }
           catch (Exception ex)
           {
             // Insert proper exception handling
           }
         }
       }

       // Get real-time data from the Salesforce.com Web service.
       // requires access to Partner WSDL files to work
       public void queryRecords()
       {
         QueryResult qResult = null;
         try
         {
           // this sample code deliberately ignores the
           // code required to connect to SFDC
           String soqlQuery = "SELECT Id, StageName, CampaignId FROM Opportunity";
           qResult = connection.query(soqlQuery);
           Boolean done = false;
           if (qResult.size > 0)
           {
             while (!done)
             {
               // grab the results and store them in the
               // OpportunitiesArray property
               OpportunitiesArray = qResult.records;
```

```csharp
          // check to see if this set of results contains the final result
          if (qResult.done)
          {
            done = true;
          }
          else
          {
            // SFDC uses paging to prevent timeouts
            qResult = connection.queryMore(qResult.queryLocator);
          }
        }
      }
      else
      {
        Console.WriteLine("No records found.");
      }
      Console.WriteLine("Query succesfully executed.");
    }
    catch (Exception e)
    {
      Console.WriteLine("An unexpected error has occurred: " +
                  e.Message + "\n" + e.StackTrace);
    }
}

// Create the column mappings.
// Notice that the table below contains only dimension fields and no
// fact data.  This will obviously limit the practical application but
// suffices for this demonstration
internal static DataTableMapping CreateDataColumnMappings()
{
  DataTableMapping dtTableMapping = new DataTableMapping();

  // Define the data in the ID column as dimension data.
  dtTableMapping.ColumnMappings.Add(new DataColumnMapping
  {
    SourceColumnName = "Id",
    FriendlyColumnName = "OpportunityId",
    UniqueName = "OpportunityId",
    ColumnType = MappedColumnTypes.Dimension,
    FactAggregation = FactAggregations.None,
    ColumnDataType = MappedColumnDataTypes.String
  });

  // Define the data in the StageName column as dimension data.
  dtTableMapping.ColumnMappings.Add(new DataColumnMapping
  {
    SourceColumnName = "StageName",
    FriendlyColumnName = "StageName",
    UniqueName = "StageName",
    ColumnType = MappedColumnTypes.Dimension,
    FactAggregation = FactAggregations.None,
    ColumnDataType = MappedColumnDataTypes.String
  });
```

```
        // Define the data in the CampaignId column as dimension data.
        dtTableMapping.ColumnMappings.Add(new DataColumnMapping
        {
          SourceColumnName = " CampaignId ",
          FriendlyColumnName = " CampaignId ",
          UniqueName = " CampaignId ",
          ColumnType = MappedColumnTypes.Dimension,
          FactAggregation = FactAggregations.None,
          ColumnDataType = MappedColumnDataTypes.String
        });


        return dtTableMapping;
      }
      #endregion
    }
  }
```

Notable in the code are the following items:

➤ Add using directives for the following PerformancePoint Services namespaces:

  ➤ `Microsoft.PerformancePoint.Scorecards`

  ➤ `Microsoft.PerformancePoint.Scorecards.ServerCommon`

➤ Add the `BasicTabularDataSourceProvider` and `SampleDSCacheHandler` classes from Microsoft's PerformancePoint Services SDK Reference Sample available at `http://archive.msdn.microsoft.com/ppsSdkRefSample`.

➤ Override the `GetId()` method with the key attribute registered in the `web.config`.

➤ Override the `SetDataSource()` method to define column mappings.

➤ Override the `GetDataSet()` method to create the DataSet object, which acts as the tabular data source.

The preceding code fulfills part of the requirements in the scenario. Now that the SharePoint developer can see data from Salesforce.com, the next tasks are to integrate this data with data from the e-commerce platform to match conversions (orders) to campaigns. Finishing up the scenario is an exercise for you.

Custom Reports, Filters, and Transformations

Given the ability to create custom data sources, it becomes easy to see how flexible PerformancePoint is with the integration of disparate data. But what happens if the data elements don't converge naturally into a single set of numbers? In this case a custom report experience may be required. Imagine creating specialized reports for specific vertical industries. Perhaps a custom report could be presented to end users in the form of an infographic with numerous data points dynamically updating images, maps, and data bars. The possibilities are endless because custom reports are nothing more than web server controls that write HTML based on incoming report parameters.

Should an entirely custom report be more than is necessary, a custom scorecard transformation offers developers the ability to inject code into the PerformancePoint Services page rendering pipeline to impact a change to rendered data. An example scenario is to apply a heat-map–style color coding to cells in a grid in the event of high or low values.

To handle a user's need to slice and dice the data, PerformancePoint offers the SharePoint developer a custom filter development target. A filter data provider understands the underlying data source and leverages DataTable objects to organize data for consumer objects.

Of course, any self-respecting SharePoint component requires an in-browser editor experience. Custom reports, filters, and tabular data sources are no exception. Custom PerformancePoint editors inherit from the Page, UserControl, or WebPart class and are thoroughly documented in MSDN (http://msdn.microsoft.com/en-us/library/ee559635(v=office.15).aspx) with fully functional sample editors that Microsoft recommends using as templates.

Deploying Customizations

The deployment process for custom functionality is no different than any other farm deployment of custom DLLs to the environment except that a web.config modification is necessary. Naturally, the requirement of server-side code deployment and modification of core files means that Office 365 will probably never enable PerformancePoint Services extensions. web.config files can be modified via PowerShell scripts, timer jobs, or feature receivers, which identify and modify every instance of PerformancePoint Services in the farm.

You can find the PerformancePoint Services web.config in the 15 Hive at C:\Program Files\ Microsoft Office Servers\15.0\WebServices\PpsMonitoringServer.

The first customization must add a <CustomFCOGroup></CustomFCOGroup> element inside of the Bpm element to register the following new section group:

```
<section name="CustomFCOGroup"
  type="Microsoft.PerformancePoint.Scorecards.Common.Extensions.CustomFCOSection,
  Microsoft.PerformancePoint.Scorecards.Common, Version=15.0.0.0,
  Culture=neutral, PublicKeyToken=71e9bce111e9429c" allowLocation="true"
  allowDefinition="Everywhere" />
```

After the section group has been added, update the previously added CustomFCOGroup element (inside of Bpm) with the following code snippet:

```
<CustomFCO type="[The object type: ReportView, Filter, or DataSource.]"
  subType="[The unique identifier for your custom ReportView, Filter, or
  DataSource object.]" >
  <Resources assemblyName="[The fully qualified name of the resources assembly.]"
    resourcesName="[The fully qualified name of the resources file.]"
    FCOName="[The display name for the custom object.]"
    FCODescription="[The description for the custom object.]"
    FCOTemplateIcon="[The image resource to use as the icon for the custom
    object.]"/>
  <RendererClass name="[The fully qualified name of the renderer class in the
    format:
    Namespace.Class name, DLL name, DLL version number, DLL culture, DLL public
    key token.
    Applies to ReportView and Filter objects only.]" />
  <EditorURI uri="[The URI of the custom editor.]" />
</CustomFCO>
```

You can find detailed schema explanations on MSDN at `http://msdn.microsoft.com/en-us/library/ee556434(v=office.15).aspx`.

SUMMARY

PerformancePoint Services in SharePoint Server Enterprise 2013 is a minor evolution in functionality, improving slightly over previous versions. As an element in the suite of portal-based BI technologies including Excel Services, Visio Services, and Access Services, the native components that make up PerformancePoint Services round out Microsoft's vision of Business Intelligence for Me, We, and the World. In the Me category of personal BI, Microsoft Office products such as Excel and Access enable individualized tracking and reporting capabilities. In the We category of team BI, SharePoint 2013 hosts Office applications such as Excel Services and Visio Services to distribute self-service BI capabilities to wider audiences. In the World category of corporate BI, PerformancePoint scorecards and dashboards monitor an organization's progress toward its goals via highly graphical representations of numbers.

This chapter delved deep into the architecture and application of one of the most important BI service applications in SharePoint Server 2010: PerformancePoint Services. In this chapter, you were introduced to key concepts, the components of the service application, common usage patterns such as Time Intelligence Filtering, and to creating custom extensions for PerformancePoint Services. With this introduction and in spite of the deployment complexities, it is not unreasonable to expect a host of customized data solutions incorporating disparate data into understandable and actionable dashboards.

The next chapter expands on this chapter's introduction to Access Services in SharePoint 2013. In the next chapter you learn how Access Services was rewritten from the ground up to create compelling and scalable data-backed web applications with zero intervention from IT.

19

Developing Applications with Access

WHAT'S IN THIS CHAPTER?

➤ Learning about Access Services 2013's new approach to web applications

➤ Automating business logic with macros

➤ Building a fully functional Access Services 2013 web application

➤ Delivering familiar Access reporting capabilities on top of new web application Interfaces

WROX.COM CODE DOWNLOADS FOR THIS CHAPTER

The wrox.com code downloads for this chapter are found at www.wrox.com/remtitle .cgi?isbn=1118495829 on the Download Code tab. The code is in the chapter 19 download and individually named according to the names throughout the chapter.

Microsoft Access is the premier integrated desktop developer tool, currently in its tenth release as Microsoft Access 2013. Access 2013 is ready to speed business users through complex data management and reporting tasks with a number of packaged database templates and a wide array of organizational and data access capabilities. Databases and data access concepts are certainly not new concepts, especially considering that this chapter immediately follows the PerformancePoint chapter, at the end of a book focused on Microsoft SharePoint 2013. Nevertheless, Microsoft Access 2013 brings a lot of problem-solving potential to the intermediate and advanced business user. This potential is worth understanding to help the SharePoint architect and developer know when to use an out-of-the-box approach such as the use of Microsoft Access instead of a customization or extension of SharePoint.

The new version of Access rebuilds the entire approach to database and application development by leveraging an extensive library of table templates; a vastly improved application experience that natively leverages HTML5, CSS, and JavaScript; and instant deployment of developed database applications to SharePoint for rapid collaboration. Microsoft made this investment in re-creating Access for a singular purpose: to enable business users to create data-centric web applications. Previous versions of Access enabled business users to rapidly create line-of-business (LOB) desktop applications. With the new 2013 version of Access, Microsoft acknowledges that the need for enablement of subject matter experts (SMEs) persists, while at the same time recognizing the need for broad access and greater IT control.

Before diving into the updated client application, it makes sense to pause and review some fundamental vocabulary and concepts related to databases and how they pertain to Microsoft Access 2013.

A *database* consists of one or more database tables, the relationships between the tables, and the functional and business logic enforced by the tables and relationships. A *table* is a logical representation of the database structure that groups a set of attributes together for the purpose of describing data. Conceptually, a table can be thought of as having rows and columns. All data in the table shares the same set of attributes, also known as *columns* or *fields*. A *record,* also called a *row* or a *tuple*, is a single entry or data item in a table. Because of this row-and-column concept, data in a table is thought of as being *structured data*. Structured data is easy to discover and understand in a table because of the rigid table concept. This is distinct from the unstructured data contained in Word documents and PowerPoint slide decks, which may be rich in detail but difficult for a computer to discover and interpret.

Because a database can contain a large number of tables, systematically understanding the relationship between the tables becomes important. Consider the following example: A small sporting equipment storefront wants to track sales of its products in a database for easy monthly and quarterly reporting. When considering the database tables in a simplistic data modeling exercise, the following entities are identified as requiring five independent database tables due to the unique set of attributes: customers, employees, orders, order details, and products. The relationships between these tables can be leveraged to keep the attributes of each table concise, as shown in Figure 19-1, which illustrates these various tables and their relationships. For example, an order may consist of a dozen or more items, but there is no need to track the order date for each item in the order. However, it is important to be able to relate the sale of an item back to the customer making the purchase. This separation of the order's header details and the order's line item details in the respective order and OrderDetails tables can be overcome through table relationships leveraging primary key and foreign key fields.

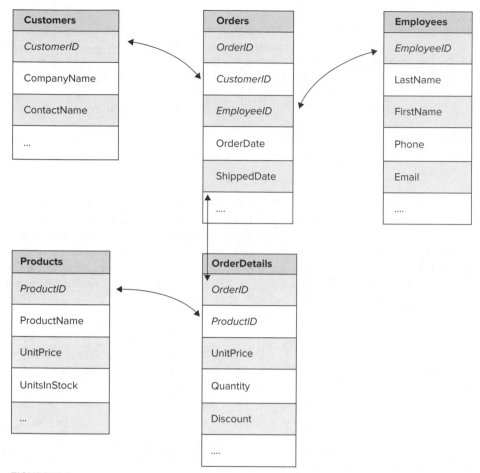

FIGURE 19-1

The practice of leveraging field values from other tables as foreign keys contributes to the easy retrieval of records from the database through a standard query language known as Structured Query Language (SQL). SQL enables operators to read, insert, delete, and update records in existing tables, as well as the ability to create, alter, and delete database structural elements such as tables and relationships.

A deep discussion of SQL and relational databases is beyond the scope of this book. Indeed, Microsoft's relational database, SQL Server, is a foundational component of SharePoint and is the subject of hundreds of technical books. Although SQL Server is beyond the scope of this chapter, you must understand that SQL Server is the back-end database system to which Access connects. The significance of this change is that Access is now faster and more stable than ever before! Even better, with SQL Server as the back end to your Microsoft Access applications, other SQL Server tools such as Excel, SQL Server Reporting Services, and even Crystal Reports can easily connect and report on application data.

ACCESS 2013

Access 2013 offers a significant level of empowerment to business users and SMEs without requiring the services of a developer. With Access 2013 an end user can:

➤ Create new web applications using predeveloped templates.

➤ Download existing web applications from the public or corporate app store.

➤ Develop custom web applications from scratch.

➤ Rely on desktop database applications that require all other users to have Microsoft Access installed as well.

To add an app to any SharePoint 2013 site from the public app store or the private corporate store, simply click the settings icon in the top-right corner of the screen, and click Add an App from the drop-down menu, as shown in Figure 19-2. The list of available apps includes a number of prebuilt apps, built-in customizable templates, and customizable templates available on Microsoft.com, such as the Customer Billing and Time Tracking app shown in Figure 19-3. After an app has been installed to a SharePoint site, that particular instance of the template web app can be easily customized and extended with the Access 2013 client.

> **NOTE** *Among the list of available apps is the Add Access App, which enables site owners to provision placeholders for Access web applications that can be created at a later time.*

Creating Access web apps requires either Office 365 (Small Business Premium or Enterprise editions) or SharePoint 2013. If neither is available to act as a web app host, the desktop database application is the only option available. One benefit unique to desktop database applications is that these are the only Access applications that leverage Visual Basic for Applications (VBA) to extend functionality. Web applications instead leverage a pair of macro types to extend functionality, which is discussed more in the "Database Components" section later in this chapter.

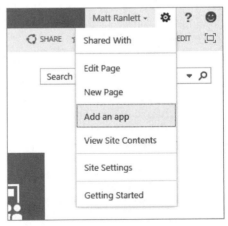

FIGURE 19-2

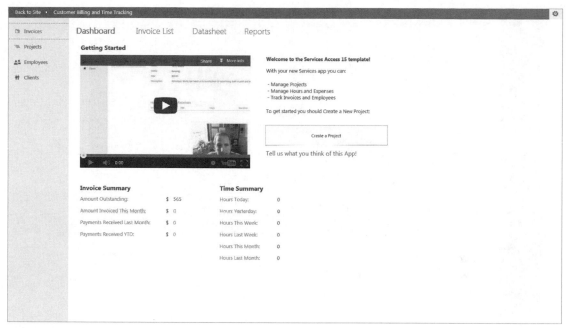

FIGURE 19-3

Exploring Access 2013

Opening Access 2013 is your first exposure to the revolutionary new approach to web and desktop databases. Fully three-quarters of the opening page, the Backstage view, is dedicated to easily discoverable application templates in an eye-catching, tiled screenshot interface. This instant application template discovery engine is a big improvement over Access 2010, which offered similar choices in a small, horizontally scrolling strip of categorized templates. Where Access 2010 required numerous clicks to find an application template, Access 2013 focuses on speeding the user to the task.

This task focus extends to the integrated application template search experience. The top of the screen sports a search box and a handful of suggested searches that queries installed templates and Microsoft Online. Search results can be filtered by category to instantly enhance relevance.

Searching for a template in any new Office 2013 application is instantly a cross-application experience. When a search returns, the bottom of the search results includes instant access to valid templates for other Office applications. For example, a search in Access for Employee yields 10 results for Access and 46 results for Word. Expanding the options for Word reveals a tiled list of Word template screenshots, each of which offers the opportunity to instantly jump to the more task-relevant Office application. Figure 19-4 shows the initial template selection screen, with easy access to other Office applications based on search results.

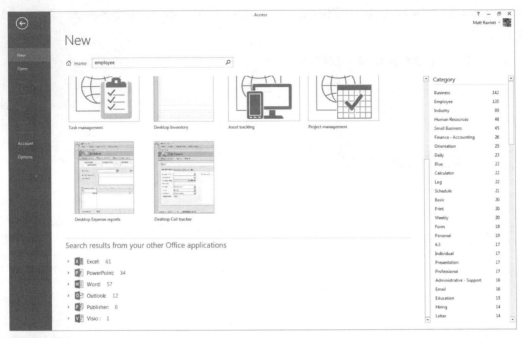

FIGURE 19-4

Immediately worth pointing out is the new emphasis on Access web applications. Default templates such as the Issue Tracker, Task Management, and Contacts default to web interfaces and offer desktop experiences as an explicitly alternative option. This is not a huge change from the previous version; Access 2010 did offer a web database option but that option was offered *after* the desktop experience, which implies a selection preference. The explicit reversal of that implied selection preference is just one indication as to the continuing significance of Microsoft Access to the business application developer.

Microsoft uses the vocabulary word *noun* to represent the template entities available from the search box. For example, should a user want to track Issues, the search experience represents Issues as a noun, but the web application has tables for Issues, Customers, Employees, and Comments. The noun is actually one of hundreds of publicly available database schema templates hosted by Microsoft.

Clicking any of the application templates provides a functional business application in 60 seconds or less. For example, the Issue Tracker application instantly creates data storage tables and data management forms for contacts and issues. The web application and desktop application offer near-feature parity, with the only major difference being the user interface for the web app is inside the browser. Otherwise, access to forms, views, tables, and automated functionality are all available in online applications and desktop applications. The most important difference between Access and other Office applications is that when a new Access application is created, a unique intermediate step requires the user to define the web application's deployment destination as a local server or an Office 365 environment. Business and consumer users without access to SharePoint or Office 365 can leverage SkyDrive for desktop database applications but cannot create web applications.

The Access 2013 Client Application

The Access client application sports the new touch-friendly interface with design inspirations taken from Windows 8 and the Windows Phone. The Ribbon interface, the backstage view of database information and application options, trusted documents and the associated security warnings, navigation panes, and the tabbed single-document interface (SDI) for form and table manipulation were all carried forward from the 2010 application version with little more than cosmetic changes. Another change carried forward from the 2010 version is the use of the ACCDB file format for desktop applications.

One change from previous versions is that there is now a concept of a user profile in Office applications, including Access. The user profile allows Access to persist credentials for services such as SkyDrive and Office 365. The profile either pulls from the corporate Active Directory, from Office 365's user profile system, or from the user's Windows Live account. Office applications, including Access, offer the ability to manage multiple accounts, although only one can be active at a time. The active user account is identified by name and photo in the top-right corner of the Office application.

When starting with a preconfigured application template such as the desktop task management application, the navigation pane is one of the most important user interaction points for Access application developers. This filterable pane organizes all the application elements for easy access. Although this chapter dives deeper into the contained elements in the "Database Components" section later in this chapter, you must understand that the navigation pane supports instant access to tables, queries, forms, reports, macros, and code modules, as seen in Figure 19-5.

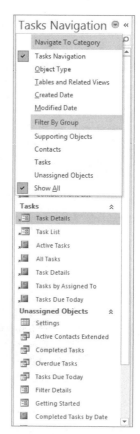

Two of the most useful navigation pane configurations, holdovers from Access 2010, are to set the Navigate To option to the Object Type and [Custom] Navigation. The Object Type view groups Access objects together by type, whereas the [Custom] Navigation view groups Access objects together by related user activities. [Custom] Navigation in a Tasks application is called Tasks Navigation, and in an Issues application, the navigation option is called Issues Navigation. You can rename the [Custom] Navigation group inside of the Navigation Options dialog and explicitly control which Access objects appear on the Navigation pane.

The Access client application experience for desktop applications has not significantly changed. Most if not all of the investment by Microsoft in Access 2013 has been focused on a new web application model, which has been explicitly designed to simplify web development. Given the focus of Microsoft's investment, it makes sense for the rest of this chapter to similarly focus on Access web apps and the development of such apps.

Access 2013 Web Applications

Microsoft Access 2013 has gone through a near ground-up rebuild for the user interface. The emphasis of the Access changes has been on the web experience, which now features a web application or web app front end

FIGURE 19-5

driven by HTML, CSS, and JavaScript. This new front end enables the same rich cross-platform accessibility experience in the core SharePoint 2013 application.

In addition to the new front end, the back end for Access web apps has been replaced entirely by SQL Server. Where the previous version of Access leveraged SharePoint lists as the actual data storage mechanism for Access 2010 tables, Access 2013 automatically creates a full-blown SQL Server database housed either on SQL Server or on SQL Azure. SQL Server enables dramatic improvements in scalability and eliminates many of the problems of user contention and locked tables. Because of the SQL back end, Access can now store and rapidly calculate across millions of records. Furthermore, the move to leverage SQL Server as the back end enables IT to inventory and manage enterprise Access applications because all the data is stored in SQL Server.

> **WARNING** *What does the backing of Access applications by SQL Server imply for financial and IT controls à la SOX and PCI compliance? Business application developers are now required to have read/write access to SQL Server databases, which may drive financial reports and may open material holes in otherwise restricted systems. This is an important consideration when setting up Access Services because the default experience is to connect to SQL via Windows Integrated Authentication.*

The Access 2013 client application can also be considered the designer of web applications. Creating a web application using Access leverages a built-in forms generation engine, which applies a default layout and CSS-based formatting to the on-screen elements. This form-template engine ensures that business and IT users can rapidly create eye-pleasing interfaces that offer a consistent user experience across apps, regardless of the actual application author. This web form generation engine automatically creates a consistent interface from Microsoft's schema templates, existing data imports, and custom schemas created in Access. Access can read the data schema, and generate direct table editing interfaces, which perform like Excel grids, individual record views, record search interfaces, and navigation buttons. Should the schema enforce a relationship between tables, Access automatically creates linked and drill-down enabled views of this relationship. Should the out-of-the-box interface not correctly prioritize data elements or navigation experiences, it is a simple matter to use the Access form designer to reposition or reformat elements. It is worth noting that the Access form designer does *not* offer an HTML or code-editing experience.

> **WARNING** *The HTML5 functionality generated by the Access forms engine is extremely complex and should not be modified. This includes attempts to modify the look and function of Access web apps via custom CSS or JavaScript.*

Similar to end-user experiences with new SharePoint sites, the approach Microsoft took with Access was to create a call to action when a new blank application is created. Access 2010 starts users with a blank screen, which frequently causes confusion in novice users. Access 2013 immediately asks users to add tables to the application and supports that call to action with both a search interface and a selection of existing data source connection options.

Power users of Access 2010 and earlier may have invested energy into automating repetitive tasks and business processes with VBA. Although VBA does continue to function in the Access desktop client, web forms cannot leverage VBA. Instead, Access web forms support a pair of macro designers that can react to user interface and data changes. These macro designers are explored in more depth later in the "Database Components" section.

Exploring a Sample Access Web Application

Figure 19-3 (shown earlier in this chapter) illustrates the basic makeup of an Access web app with Microsoft's freely available Customer Billing and Time Tracking application. This application shares a number of characteristics with all Access web apps:

➤ Trimmed down hierarchical breadcrumb navigation bar across the top of the screen.

➤ Tables representing business entities organized vertically along the left side of the screen. This list of tables is called the Tile Pane. When designing applications with Access, every table is added to the Tile Pane, but each table can be independently hidden.

➤ Task-oriented views organized horizontally along the top of the screen. Selecting different nouns changes the available views across the top of the screen.

The Microsoft application serves as a model of an Access web app's capabilities with the inclusion of several YouTube videos through the clever use of web browser controls on the various views. Beyond the eye-catching video, this business application does an excellent job of showcasing the four different view types and macros. The section "Creating an Access Web App" later in this chapter is an exercise that walks you through the creation of a similar Access web app where you can explore all these possible building blocks in detail.

Navigating to the Site Contents page reveals that the Customer Billing and Time Tracking app is treated by SharePoint like any other SharePoint app. It can be secured and removed. The app can also be opened in Access 2013 from the browser where it can be modified and republished. Should the app be treated as a template and get published to a number of different sites, the data in each instance of the app is private to that single site.

ACCESS SERVICES

As mentioned previously, Microsoft heavily invested in the new Microsoft Access 2013 application model to reduce barriers that may otherwise prevent SMEs from creating business applications. By leveraging the on-premise model of SharePoint 2013 and SQL Server for respective front- and back-end hosting, Access 2013 dramatically increases application manageability and scalability for Access-based business applications. By leveraging the hosted app model and relying on Office 365 to host the front end of the app and SQL Azure to store the data, the reach and scalability of Access applications increases significantly.

On-Premise Architecture

When leveraging a local SharePoint 2013 installation for publication and sharing of Access web apps, SQL Server 2012 provides the back-end functionality, whereas SharePoint and its Access Services service application provide the user interface and security. Figure 19-6 describes the Access Services architecture.

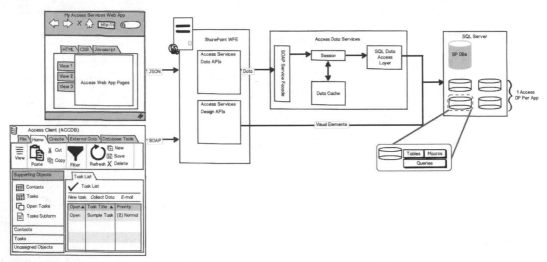

FIGURE 19-6

Although the Microsoft Access Office 2013 client communicates via SOAP protocols, the web front end relies entirely on RESTful services. Both web and desktop clients communicate to the load balanced SharePoint web front ends that host the Access Services data and design APIs.

> **NOTE** *Unlike most of the rest of SharePoint 2013 service applications, the Access Services data and design APIs are private and are not development targets outside of the use of the Microsoft Access 2013 client.*

Access Data Services (ADS) contains the session, cache, and data access layer responsible for extracting data from the SQL Server back end. The Access Services design APIs, responsible for retrieving only visual elements, bypass the ADS and directly connect to the SQL Server back end.

For each Access Services application, a new application database is created on the Access Services Application Database Server. This new database contains the new app's data, views (forms), queries, and macros. By default, the Access Services Application Database Server is the same SQL Server that is used by SharePoint, but a new database server can easily be configured on Central Administration's Manage Service Applications page to enforce a distinct separation of concerns. Only one Access Services Application Database Server is available per Access Services service application at a time.

> **NOTE** *An important consideration when activating Access Services in an on-premise environment is an organization's disaster recovery and data retention policies. An environment with open access to Access 2013 web apps can produce a large number of new databases quite rapidly!*

Hosted Architecture

The hosted architecture for Access Services leverages Office 365 Small Business Premium or Enterprise editions and SQL Azure to scale upward to a theoretically infinite number of users and to contain a theoretically infinite amount of data. Beyond the changes to an Access web app's reach, there are no functional differences in the architecture (refer to Figure 19-6 in the previous section) and that of an Office 365 hosted app beyond the potential difficulty in connecting reporting tools to the hosted database.

Upgrade Considerations

As mentioned previously, Access 2013 desktop applications have not changed — existing ACCDB database applications continue to function. However, Access Data Projects (ADPs) are no longer supported due to incompatibilities with SQL Azure. ADPs have been replaced with the new web-based Access app. Microsoft's guidance for ADP developers is as follows:

➤ Convert the ADP to an Access app by importing existing tables into a new Access app. This causes new forms to be automatically generated.

➤ Convert to a linked desktop database by converting the ADP application to an .accdb format.

➤ Create a hybrid application by importing data into an Access app (hosted on SQL Server/SQL Azure) and link to the newly stored back-end data via a .accdb client application.

➤ Upgrade to a .NET application and leave Microsoft Access as a platform behind.

Database Components

Databases can contain several types of components, including tables, queries, views, reports, and macros. This section will examine all of them in more detail.

Tables and Queries

As previously mentioned several times in this chapter, Access 2013 web apps leverage the entirely new back end of SQL Server or SQL Azure. This is new compared to the Access 2010 model for Access Services, where all data was stored in SharePoint lists. Now pause for a moment to consider a few of the implications of this change, as shown in Table 19-1.

TABLE 19-1: Access 2013 Versus Access 2010

ACCESS 2013 WEB APP BENEFITS	ACCESS 2010 WEB APP BENEFITS
SQL Server and SQL Azure are both *much* faster and more scalable than SharePoint lists.	All data is stored in a SharePoint site's lists (provisioned by Access 2010 automatically when the application is created).
Data in dedicated SQL databases is accessible by a wide array of self-service BI tools, such as Excel and Crystal Reports.	Data hosted by a single site reduces the total number of databases created/required.

Although the management overhead for the number of databases definitely increases with the new model, Access 2013, complete with its dedicated web app databases, is more flexible than the previous version.

A level of translation is required to understand how Access objects are stored in SQL Server. Table 19-2 identifies a number of key vocabulary terms in each database environment.

TABLE 19-2: Access 2013/SQL Server 2012 Vocabulary Map

ACCESS OBJECT	SQL SERVER OBJECT
Table	Table
Query	View
Parameter Query	Table-Valued Function
Standalone Data Macro	Stored Procedure
Table Event Data Macro	Trigger
Validation Rule	Check Constraint

Any table created in Access will be stored in the SQL Server database with the same name as in Access. Similarly, a table's fields will be identically named in Access and SQL Server. The data types leveraged by Access do not match those of SQL Server exactly, so Table 19-3 has been provided as a reference.

TABLE 19-3: Access/SQL Data Type Map

ACCESS DATA TYPE	SQL SERVER DATA TYPE
Single line of text	nvarchar(1—4000, MAX)
Multiple lines of text	nvarchar(1—4000, MAX)
Number	Float
Number	Int

Currency	Float
Date	Date
Date/Time	datetime2(6)
Time	Time
True/False	Bit
Image	varbinary(MAX)

Each table created in an Access web app is available in the Tile Pane on the left side of the browsing user's page (refer to Figure 19-3 in the beginning of the "Access 2013" section at the beginning of this chapter). Figure 19-3 displays Invoices, Projects, Employees, and Clients as navigation options representing the source tables and the views associated with each. However, opening the application with the Access desktop client reveals that several tables are not displayed in the web browser. Tables in the Tile Pane can be hidden or moved up and down, but if a tile in the Tile Pane is deleted, the table and all associated views are also deleted. If a tile is hidden, the backing table schema and associated views can still be modified. This is typically done to enable macro-based access to views which would otherwise be hidden.

Access leverages queries to join multiple tables together for purposes of targeted data discovery or data aggregation. Access leverages a SME-friendly visual query builder to develop a persisted mechanism to access the wanted data. This query is stored in SQL Server as a view or a table-valued function, depending on whether the query requires any parameters. The name of the SQL Server object matches the names in Access. Figure 19-7 shows an Access query from the Microsoft sample Customer Billing and Time Tracking application.

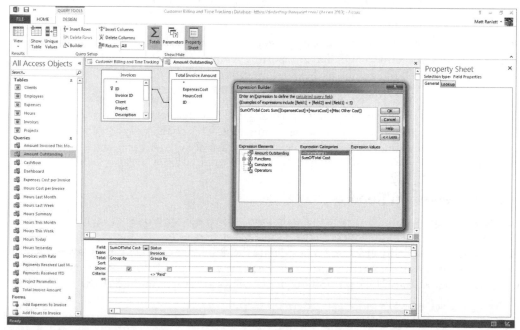

FIGURE 19-7

To access the SQL Server instance behind an Access web app, navigate to the Access client's Backstage, and click the Info option to view the server name and database name associated with the published web app. In the event of an Office 365 published Access web app, the database will be hosted on a SQL Azure instance. To connect to this instance, use the management tools available in the Azure management portal. Be sure to follow Microsoft's How To article titled "Guidelines for Connecting to Windows Azure SQL Database" available online at http://msdn.microsoft.com/en-us/library/ee336282.aspx. The SQL Server view for the previously referenced Access Query is:

```
CREATE VIEW [Access].[AmountOutstanding]
AS
SELECT
        SUM[Total Invoice Amount].[ExpenseCost],
        [Total Invoice Amount].[HoursCost],
        [Invoices].[Misc Other Cost]
FROM
        [Access].[Invoices]
LEFT JOIN
        [Access].[Total Invoice Amount]
ON
        [Invoices].[ID] = [Total Invoice Amount].[ID]
WHERE
        [Invoices].[Status] <>"Paid"
```

SQL Server Schemas

Within the dedicated SQL Server database, Access leverages three separate SQL Server schemas: Access, AccessSystem, and AccessRuntime. The *AccessSystem* and *AccessRuntime* schemas store the system information used by Access Services and the ADS to allow the web app to function properly. These schemas are used both by the Access web app at run time and the Access client during design-time activities.

The *Access* schema contains all the application's end user-created tables, queries, and macros. This is where advanced users connect SQL Server reporting services or other external self-service BI applications for advanced integration and extension scenarios.

As mentioned previously, SQL Server login details are available in the application's Backstage Info section. In addition to the server and database details, the Manage connections button enables the creation of new logins with read or read/write permissions. This enables explicit control of who can access back-end data without requiring advanced knowledge of SQL Server permissions management techniques.

Applications: Views and Reports

In an Access web application, a view is the main interactive page for browsing users to use the app. The Access 2013 client app refers to these same constructs as *forms*. Views in an Access 2013 application are automatically generated to accelerate the developer through the UI layout tasks and to ensure a level of consistency across interfaces. Each view is available for customization inside of the Access design surface. Like tables and queries, views are stored in the SQL Server database.

However, because they are HTML and JavaScript rather than native SQL objects, such as tables or table-value functions, views are stored as text in the Access system tables.

Access web apps offer four distinct types of views for data-centric business application developers:

➤ *List Details* — A single scrolling column of records with an editable details interface for each record on the right of the records list. The list of records is searchable and filterable.

➤ *Datasheet* — An editable Excel-like grid. Each column in the datasheet grid is sortable and filterable.

➤ *Summary* — A view used to group records.

➤ *Blank* — Entirely customizable views capable of hosting any of the twelve available Access controls.

A view must be based on a table. The act of creating a new table automatically generates the List Details and Datasheet views. The views are organized by the tables they're associated with. The views for each table can be moved. In addition, views can be edited, duplicated, renamed, and deleted.

Customizing Views

Access 2013 shipped with a built-in design surface, but the designer for web apps is less precise than the designer for desktop database applications. The view designer and the 12 controls available to Access developers are intended to keep web applications designed by business-savvy Access developers from requiring web design skills.

The view designer works on a grid system that automatically ensures components line up and are spaced properly. After a control has been added to a view, selecting the control allows access to the relevant properties in a pop-up, as shown in Figure 19-8. Note that the available properties are divided into Data, Formatting, and Actions categories, and each is accessed by distinct buttons in the view designer.

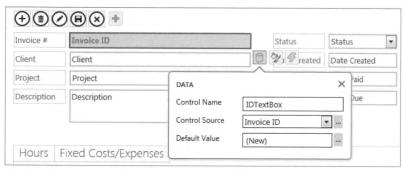

FIGURE 19-8

Also visible in Figure 19-8 is the Action Bar, which contains icons for actions such as New, Delete, Edit, Save, and Cancel. The green plus sign allows the addition of custom actions. Access offers web app developers 20 different custom actions to choose from. These actions will be explored in the

"Applications: Macros section." In addition to the ability to add custom actions, web app developers can opt to delete buttons or even hide the Action Bar as the business process dictates.

Applications: Macros

Where previous versions of Access leverage VBA to add automation and business logic to an application, Access 2013 web apps rely on data macros. Users familiar with SharePoint Designer's If-Then-Else workflow designer will be at home with Access 2013's data macro designer, as shown in Figure 19-9.

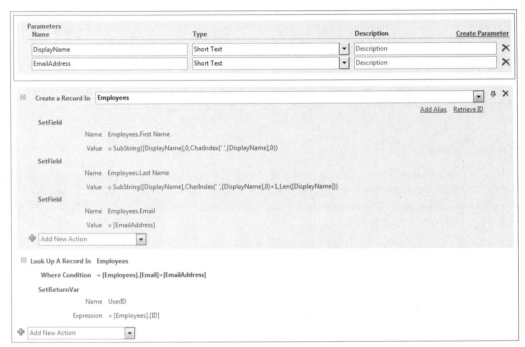

FIGURE 19-9

Macros come in three main varieties, as described by the Access 2013 user interface:

➤ Data macros

➤ User Interface macros

➤ On-Start macros

Data Macros

Data macros are the business logic workhorses of Access web apps, capable of adding, editing, or deleting data records. Data macros come in two flavors, embedded or stand alone. Embedded macros are stored in SQL Server as AFTER triggers on the tables that they are attached to, where they react to the types of data events shown in Table 19-4.

TABLE 19-4: Data Macro Events

EVENT TYPE	TRIGGER
On Insert	Fires when a new record is added to the table
On Update	Fires when an existing record is modified
On Delete	Fires when an existing record is deleted

To add or edit a table-bound data macro, open the relevant table in Access, and click one of the Events on the Design tab on the Ribbon. Events that are highlighted already have a macro applied. Figure 19-10 shows an embedded Data macro used by the Invoices table to display the internal ID of a record on the Invoice view's read-only ID field.

FIGURE 19-10

Data macros also support a stand-alone version of a macro that is designed to promote code reuse. A stand-alone macro is visible in the Access navigation pane but is not directly executable by an Access web app's end users. Stand-alone data macros are stored in SQL Server as stored procedures and can be invoked by other UI or data macros using the RunDataMacro action. To create a stand-alone macro, click the Advanced button in the Create section of the Home tab on the Ribbon, and select Data Macro. Notice that this type of macro can accept parameters.

User Interface Macros

A User Interface macro is embedded in UI elements such as buttons and other web controls and is used to react to application events like On Click. Figure 19-8 in the "Customizing Views" section shows the control Actions button as a pop-up lightning bolt. Table 19-5 lists the available UI events.

TABLE 19-5: User Interface Macro Events

EVENT TYPE	TRIGGER
After Update	Fires after data has been entered or selected by the control
On Click	Fires when the control is selected
On Current	Fires when the user changes records in the view
On Load	Fires when a view is opened

Not all UI controls expose all the supported events. For example, a Button exposes an On Click event, but a Combo Box exposes only the After Update event.

UI macros also support a stand-alone type of macro that is stored in the SQL Server database as a stored procedure to define reusable logic. Similar to stand-alone data macros, stand-alone UI macros are visible in the Navigation pane in the Access client but are not directly executable. Stand-alone UI macros can be executed only by calling them from an embedded UI macro with the RunMacro command.

On Start Macros

On Start macros are used to set up an application, including the setting of default values for variables, navigating to default views, or creating targeted messages. To create a stand-alone macro, click the Advanced button in the Create section of the Home tab on the Ribbon, and select On Start Macro.

BUILDING AN APPLICATION WITH ACCESS SERVICES

Microsoft Access 2013 is a rapid application development platform for business-focused web applications. However, although it may take only a minute to start, Access works well with SharePoint to enable iterative app development. This iterative development process enables continual testing and refinement of apps.

Prerequisites

Working with Access 2013 web apps requires one of the two following combinations:

➤ Microsoft Office Access 2013 desktop client and an Office 365 account

➤ Microsoft Office Access 2013 desktop client and a SharePoint 2013 development environment.

Regardless of whether an on-premise or hosted development environment is chosen, a download and installation of Office 2013 is required to gain access to Microsoft Access 2013.

Configuring for Hosted Access Web Application Development

If you are interested in building applications for Office 365 environments, applications that do not require full trust solutions, or just want to get started with Access web apps as quickly as possible, sign up for a free trial of Office 365 Small Business Premium or Enterprise. Other license levels of Office 365 such as Pro Plus and Home Premium do not include SharePoint online and do not work with Access 2013 web apps.

After a copy of Access 2013 has been installed and an account with Office 365 has been created, test the connection by opening Access and creating your first web app based on a template. Give your test application a name and place the URL for your SharePoint Online site in the Web Location text box. Your Office 365 URL will be something like this:

```
http://[company].onmicrosoft.com/sites/[myteamsite]
```

Click the Create button, and Access will create your application on the server and take you directly into the application designer in the Access Client. Click the Launch App button to experience your basic application in the browser. Access web apps work in every major browser, including IE, Firefox, Chrome, and Safari.

Configuring an On-premise Development Environment

Although an Office 365 account will certainly speed up the process of building Access web apps, there are certain capabilities that have not yet been implemented in Office 365 that may force you to turn to an on-premise development environment. Configuring an on-premise environment for Access Services requires a few steps beyond the default installation of SharePoint 2013 itself. These steps include:

1. Configure an isolated application domain.
2. Configure SQL Server 2012.
    1. Add the required SQL Server features.
    2. Enable the contained databases.
    3. Enable the mixed authentication security mode.
    4. Ensure the appropriate service account permissions.
    5. Enable the required networking protocols.
3. Configure the Windows development environment.
4. Configure SharePoint 2013.
    1. Start the required services.
    2. Create a Secure Store service application.
    3. Create the Access Services 2013 service application.

Configuring an Isolated Application Domain

SharePoint 2013 requires a general wildcard host header domain to provision SharePoint-hosted apps. This domain will likely derive from your corporate domain such that if your company domain is www.mycompany.com then an ideal SharePoint app domain is app.mycompany.com. If this domain is reserved via the isolated app domain process described next, SharePoint can automatically manage the URL.

The first step in a stand-alone development environment that does not have access to an actual DNS reserved URL is to modify the hosts file to fool your computer into thinking that the URL is valid.

Microsoft has created a detailed seven-step guide for creating an isolated app domain on MSDN at http://msdn.microsoft.com/en-us/library/fp179923(v=office.15) .aspx#SP15appdevonprem_bk_configure, but a premier field engineer at Microsoft, Tom Van Gaever, has created a comprehensive PowerShell script that is easier to execute. Tom Van Gaever posted the original script online at his blog: http://tomvangaever.be/blogv2/2012/08/ prepare-sharepoint-2013-server-for-app-development-create-an-isolated-app-domain/ . The PowerShell script, which must be run as an administrator, has been reproduced here for completeness:

```
# Check if the execution policy is set to Unrestricted
$policy = Get-ExecutionPolicy
if($policy -ne "Unrestricted"){
    Set-ExecutionPolicy "Unrestricted"
}

# Check if current script is running under administrator credentials
$currentPrincipal = New-Object Security.Principal.WindowsPrincipal
    ( [Security.Principal.WindowsIdentity]::GetCurrent() )
if ($currentPrincipal.IsInRole( [Security.Principal.WindowsBuiltInRole]::
    Administrator ) -eq $false) {
    (get-host).UI.RawUI.Backgroundcolor="DarkRed"
    clear-host
    write-host "Warning: PowerShell is not running as an Administrator.'n"
    exit
}

# Load SharePoint powershell commands
Add-PSSnapin "microsoft.sharepoint.powershell" -ErrorAction SilentlyContinue

cls

# Ensure that the spadmin and sptimer services are running
Write-Host
Write-Host "Ensure that the spadmin and sptimer services are running"
    -ForegroundColor Yellow
net start spadminv4
net start sptimerv4

# Create your isolated app domain by running the SharePoint Management Shell as
    an administrator and typing the following command.
Write-Host
Write-Host "Create your isolated app domain by running the SharePoint Management
    Shell as an administrator and typing the following command."
    -ForegroundColor Yellow
$appdomain = Read-Host "Your App Domain Name"
```

```
Set-SPAppDomain $appdomain

# Ensure that the SPSubscriptionSettingsService and AppManagementServiceInstance
    services are running
Write-Host
Write-Host "Ensure that the SPSubscriptionSettingsService and
    AppManagementServiceInstance services are running." -ForegroundColor Yellow
Get-SPServiceInstance | where{$_.GetType().Name -eq "AppManagementServiceInstance"
    -or $_.GetType().Name -eq "SPSubscriptionSettingsServiceInstance"} |
    Start-SPServiceInstance

# Verify that the SPSubscriptionSettingsService and AppManagementServiceInstance
    services are running
Write-Host
Write-Host "Verify that the SPSubscriptionSettingsService and
    AppManagementServiceInstance services are running." -ForegroundColor Yellow
Get-SPServiceInstance | where{$_.GetType().Name -eq "AppManagementServiceInstance"
    -or $_.GetType().Name -eq "SPSubscriptionSettingsServiceInstance"}

# Specify an account, application pool, and database settings for the
    SPSubscriptionService and AppManagementServiceInstance services
Write-Host
Write-Host "Specify an account, application pool, and database settings for the
    SPSubscriptionService and AppManagementServiceInstance services."
    -ForegroundColor Yellow
$login = Read-Host "The login of a managed account"
$account = Get-SPManagedAccount $login
$appPoolSubSvc = New-SPServiceApplicationPool -Name SettingsServiceAppPool
    -Account $account
Write-Host "SettingsServiceAppPool created (1/6)" -ForegroundColor Green
$appPoolAppSvc = New-SPServiceApplicationPool -Name AppServiceAppPool -Account
    $account
Write-Host "AppServiceAppPool created  (2/6)" -ForegroundColor Green
$appSubSvc = New-SPSubscriptionSettingsServiceApplication –ApplicationPool
    $appPoolSubSvc –Name SettingsServiceApp –DatabaseName SettingsServiceDB
Write-Host "SubscriptionSettingsServiceApplication created  (3/6)"
    -ForegroundColor Green
$proxySubSvc = New-SPSubscriptionSettingsServiceApplicationProxy
    -ServiceApplication $appSubSvc
Write-Host "SubscriptionSettingsServiceApplicationProxy created  (4/6)"
    -ForegroundColor Green
$appAppSvc = New-SPAppManagementServiceApplication -ApplicationPool
    $appPoolAppSvc -Name AppServiceApp -DatabaseName AppServiceDB
Write-Host "AppManagementServiceApplication created  (5/6)" -ForegroundColor Green
$proxyAppSvc = New-SPAppManagementServiceApplicationProxy -ServiceApplication
    $appAppSvc
Write-Host "AppManagementServiceApplicationProxy created  (6/6)" -ForegroundColor
    Green

# Specify your tenant name
write-host
Write-Host "Set AppSiteSubscriptionName to 'app'" -ForegroundColor Yellow
Set-SPAppSiteSubscriptionName -Name "app" -Confirm:$false
Write-Host "AppSiteSubscriptionName set" -ForegroundColor Green
```

```
# Disable the loopbackcheck in the registry
Write-Host "Disable the loopbackcheck in the registry" -ForegroundColor Yellow
New-ItemProperty -Path "HKLM:\SYSTEM\CurrentControlSet\Control\Lsa\" -Name
    "DisableLoopbackCheck" -PropertyType DWord -Value 1

Write-Host "Completed"
```

The modification of the development computer's hosts file (if necessary) and the successful execution of this PowerShell script completes all necessary networking configuration for Access Services 2013.

Configuring SQL Server 2012

SQL Server must be correctly configured to support the demands of Access Services 2013. The first of the following required steps requires the installation media to be available.

Adding Required SQL Server Features

Run the setup (or rerun the setup to adjust an existing installation), and ensure that the following features are enabled in the development environment:

- ➤ Database Engine Services
- ➤ Full-Test and Semantic Extractions for Search
- ➤ SQL Management Tools (Basic and Advanced)
- ➤ Client Tools Connectivity

This step requires the original installation media and may require the reinstallation of service packs. Follow proper protocols when updating production machines!

Enabling Contained Databases

SQL Server 2012 helps to isolate databases from other databases via the concept of contained databases. The containment of databases in SQL Server 2012 is required by Access Services to not only protect each database but also the SQL Server instance. SQL Server implements database isolation from the instance in four ways:

- ➤ Meta data describing the database is maintained in the database rather than in the master database.
- ➤ All meta data is stored with the same collation.
- ➤ User authentication is performed by the database rather than by SQL Server.
- ➤ SQL Server support reporting on containment information.

Activating containment is as simple as setting the Enable Contained Databases flag to True in the SQL Server's Advanced Properties dialog. Open SQL Server Management Studio, right-click the server, and choose Properties. On the Advanced page is the option to Enable Contained Databases. Set this to True.

Enabling the Mixed Authentication Security Mode

Access Services 2013 supports both Windows and SQL Server authentication, so SQL Server must be configured to support both as well. In SQL Server Management Studio, right-click the server and choose Properties. On the Security page is the option to allow SQL Server and Windows Authentication Mode.

Ensuring Appropriate Service Account Permissions

SharePoint 2013 continues the long tradition of service accounts available previously in SharePoint 2010 and 2007. When an Access Services 2013 service application is created, a service account must be either assigned or created. This service account must be a pre-existing Active Directory account and must have been granted the **dbcreator, public,** and **securityadmin** roles for the server. Open SQL Server Management Studio and locate the service account in the Security ➪ Logins section. Right-click the account, and select the Server Roles page to ensure the required server roles have been granted.

Enabling Required Networking Protocols

Open the SQL Server Configuration Manager tool, and expand the SQL Server Network Configuration group to select Protocols for MSSQLSERVER. By default, only Shared Memory is enabled. Right-click Named Pipes and select Enabled. Right-click TCP/IP and select Enabled. At this point, all available network protocols should be enabled.

Configuring the Windows Development Environment Firewall

Now that SQL Server has been properly configured, the Windows environment hosting SQL Server must be prepared to receive HTTP traffic on ports 1433 and 1434 for TCP and UDP.

1. Open the Windows Firewall with the Advanced Security utility.

2. Right-click the Inbound Rules option and select New Rule.

3. The New Inbound Rule Wizard pops up and asks which type of rule should be created.

4. Select Port and click Next.

5. The wizard advances to the Protocols and Ports screen. Select TCP and type **1433, 1434** into the Specific Ports field; then click Next.

6. The wizard advances to the Action screen. Select Allow the Connection and click Next.

7. The wizard advances to the Profile screen. Leave Domain and Private, clearing the check-mark from Public, and click Next.

8. The wizard advances to the Name screen. Type **SQL TCP** into the Name field, and click Finish.

Repeat the previous steps with the following changes for the UDP incoming rule:

➤ On the Protocols and Ports screen, select UDP and type **1433, 1434** into the Specific Ports field; then click **Next**.

➤ On the Name screen, type **SQL UDP** into the Name field, and click Finish.

Configuring SharePoint 2013

At this point, SQL Server is fully configured, the firewall is ready to accept inbound traffic on the SQL Server environment, and an isolated app domain has been created. The final prerequisite step is to create and configure the Access Services 2013 service application.

Starting Required Services

In Central Administration, go to Manage Services on Server to ensure the following services are started. Start them if they are not already running:

➤ Access Services 2013

➤ Access Services (Access Database Service 2010 for viewing and modifying existing 2010 Access web databases)

➤ App Management Service

➤ Microsoft SharePoint Foundation Subscription Settings Service

➤ Secure Store Service

Creating a Secure Store Service Application

Open Central Administration and go to Manage Services on Server. In the Service Applications Ribbon tab, click the New drop down, and select to create a new Secure Store Service Application. The default settings are all valid, so click OK to create the new service application. After the new application has been created, run an IISRESET to ensure enough memory is available for the next step. Click the Generate New Key button on the Ribbon to fully activate the Secure Store Service. This last step takes a while; don't be alarmed if nothing happens for a few minutes.

Creating the Access Services 2013 Service Application

The final step is to create the actual Access Services 2013 service application. Open Central Administration, and go to Manage Services on Server. On the Service Applications Ribbon tab, click the New drop-down, and select the Access Services option (not the Access Services 2010 option, which is used to support legacy Access Services 2010 instances).

The Create New Access Services Application dialog opens and asks for the Application Database Server. This server is used to create new application databases and is expected not to be the same SQL Server instance that SharePoint is using; although that configuration is supported. If a new SQL Server is brought online for Access Services databases in the future, opening the Access Services Application configuration offers an opportunity to change the database server.

Creating an Access Web App

Creating Access web applications should now be possible given the properly configured Office 365 or on-premise environment. Consider the following scenario for the first Access web app: The consulting arm of the TailSpin Toy company needs to track its various employees for their physical locations and client consulting engagements. Naturally this application should be available via the company's intranet, which is hosted by Office 365. To create an application that meets the TailSpin Toys requirements, follow the following steps:

Creating the Basic Application

The first thing to do is to create the initial shell of the application and test it to make sure that the application can be deployed successfully and that it possesses the expected user experience. The following six steps walk you through the creation of an app up to the point of data entry and should take approximately 60 seconds to complete.

1. Open Access and choose Custom web app.

2. Enter a name such as **TailSpin Toys Consultant Tracker** and the web location for your app such as `http://tailspintoys.com/sites/staffing` and choose Create.

3. Now that the application has been created, add some initial tables by searching for relevant templates by typing **Employee** into the What Would You Like to Track? search box. Then press Enter.

4. Select the Employees table template.

5. Search for and add the Clients table and the Projects table.

6. Before continuing to add any additional tables, take the time to explore the newly added tables and associated views in the browser by clicking the Launch App button on the Ribbon:

    1. Notice that the Tile Pane contains entries for the Employees, Clients, Projects, and Tasks tables, as shown in Figure 19-11. The Tasks table was added with the Projects table as part of the default schema associated with the Projects noun.

    2. Notice that each table has three default views: List, Datasheet, and a By Group or By Status view.

    3. Perform a bit of data entry on the Projects table and notice the built-in relationship between the Projects, Employees, and Clients table. As a name is typed into the Owner or Customer field, an auto-complete functionality attempts to find the relevant record or offers the user the ability to create a new record if a matching record can't be found. Create a project, an employee, and a client. Each table except Tasks now contains data in each view.

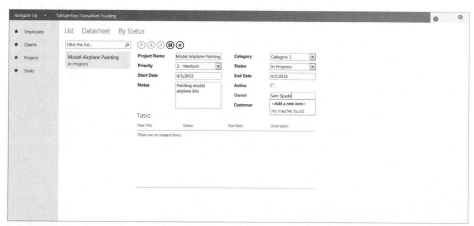

FIGURE 19-11

Adding, Removing, and Editing Tables

The basic tables added by the Employees, Clients, and Projects nouns are close to the application's requirements, but the current configuration offers no mechanism to track a consultant's location. The Tasks table is extraneous and should be removed to prevent end user confusion. The following steps walk you through the process to remove the Tasks table and to add two completely custom tables. After the database contains the tables necessary to meet the requirements to track consultants on projects and consultants at locations, you need to configure the relationships between tables. Figure 19-12 demonstrates the relationships necessary for the application to function properly.

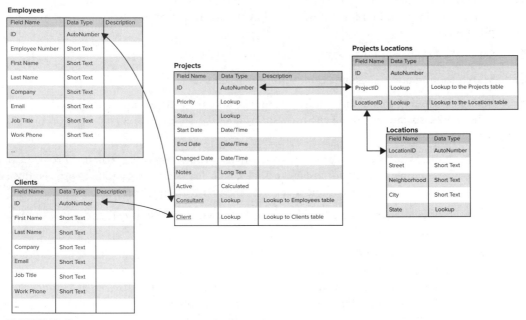

FIGURE 19-12

Defining a relation between tables in an Access web app is managed through the Lookup data type. A Lookup can work either as a choice column or as a link to data from a table or query. In addition to the linking of tables, some of the column names in the Projects table need to change to keep a consistent application vocabulary for the end users. The necessary column changes are reflected as underlined columns (refer to Figure 19-12). Follow these steps to create the new lookup and edit the existing column names:

1. Return to the Access 2013 client, and right-click Tasks in the Tile Pane. Notice that the Settings/Actions dialog pops up offering choices such as View Data, Edit Table, Delete, and Hide. Hide removes Tasks from the Tile Pane but does not delete the back-end table or associated views.

2. Select Delete and proceed through the confirmation dialog.

3. Open the Projects table.

4. Change the Owner field name to **Consultant**.

5. Change the Customer field name to **Client**.

6. To add a table, click the Table button in the Create section of the Ribbon. Click the Add a New Blank Table link on the right to create the following table:

LOCATIONS

FIELD NAME	DATA TYPE
LocationID	AutoNumber
Street	Short Text
Neighborhood	Short Text
City	Short Text
State	Lookup

The LocationID functions as the primary key. When you enter Lookup as the Data Type for State, a Lookup Wizard automatically pops up. Select I Will Type in the Values that I Want, and type in several codes, as shown in Figure 19-13.

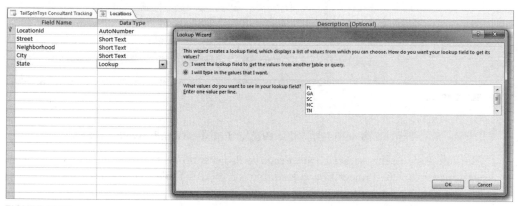

FIGURE 19-13

7. Click the Save button to name the table **Locations** and save it to the server.

8. Create another new table, the Project Locations table. This table serves as the Many-to-Many Lookup table between the Projects and Locations tables. The following table describes the necessary columns:

PROJECT LOCATIONS

FIELD NAME	DATA TYPE	NOTES
ID	AutoNumber	Functions as the primary key.
LocationID	Lookup	As shown in Figure 19-13, a Lookup Wizard automatically pops up. Set this field to retrieve data from the Locations table, neighborhood column. Figure 19-14 demonstrates the proper wizard settings.
ProjectID	Lookup	Create a lookup to the Projects table.

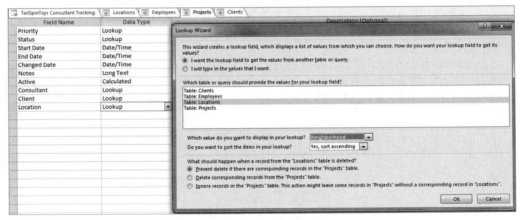

FIGURE 19-14

9. Click the Save button to name the table **Project Locations** and save it to the server.

10. In the Tile Pane in the Access client, drag the Projects tab to the top and hide the Project Locations table. The Project Locations table is a linking table that should not be directly edited by end users.

Modifying Application Views

The next steps involve creating a mechanism for end users to interact with the new relationship between Projects and Locations. Both the List view and the Datasheet view must be edited. The following steps detail the process required to edit the automatically generated List and Datasheet views:

1. In the Tile Pane click the Projects tab; then select the Datasheet view from the list of available views.

2. Click the Edit button over the main content area to enter the view editor.

3. Click the Add Existing Fields button in the Tools section of the Ribbon's View Design tab to display the Field List pane in Access.

4. Drag the Location field from the Field List pane onto the right end of the Datasheet's list of fields, as shown in Figure 19-15.

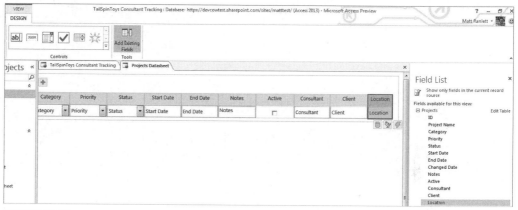

FIGURE 19-15

5. Click the Save button to send the view changes to the server.

6. Close the Projects Datasheet tab, and open the List view for editing by clicking the view name and then clicking the Edit button over the main content area.

7. Click the Tasks related items field, and press Delete on the keyboard. With the Tasks table having been deleted, the interface on the List view is unnecessary.

8. The Project Locations related field should have been automatically added to the view, but if it hasn't been added, simply double-click the Related Items control to add one to the page.

Creating a Query

Referring to Figure 19-12 in the "Adding, Removing, and Editing Tables" section, Employees are related to Locations through the Projects and Project Locations tables. Users of the consultant tracking application may want to understand which consultants work in which locations. Building a query to link these data elements more closely together allows the app to use the query as a data source in later tasks. Follow these steps to create a new query, which will be stored in SQL Server as a table-value function:

1. On the Home tab on the Ribbon, click the Advanced drop down in the Create section, and select Query.

2. In the Show Table pop-up, select the Employees, Projects, Project Location, and Locations tables, and click OK.

3. In the Builder grid, set the first field to Neighborhood from the Locations table and the second field to Display Name First Last from the Employees table, as shown in Figure 19-16.

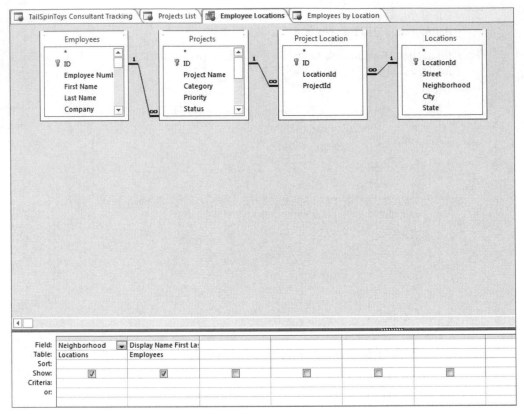

FIGURE 19-16

4. Save the query as Employee Locations.

Creating a New View

Now that you can identify which locations an employee has visited, it is time to expose that information to end users. Follow these steps to create an Employees by Location view on the Locations tab in the Tile Pane:

1. Click Locations in the Tile Pane.

2. Click the Add New View button. Set the View Name to Employees by Location, the View Type to Summary, and the Record Source to Employee Locations. Click the Add New View button.

3. Edit the Employees by Location view, and ensure that the left column displays the list of neighborhoods and the right column displays the Employee's Display Name. This should happen by default.

4. Launch the application and view the results in the browser. Now end users can track projects, assign employees to those projects, and track employees by location.

Adding a Macro

Recall from the previous macros discussion that there are two distinct types of macros that can be added to an Access web application: Data macros, which impact the data in an app as an automatic reaction to data changes, and UI macros, which add user experience options as a result of user behavior in the application. For example, you could use a Data macro to automatically copy contact details from the Consultant record to the Project table after a Consultant has been assigned to the Project. User Interface macros add interactivity elements to the application. Follow these steps to add a pop-up to the app that enables an end user to see the employee details of an employee assigned to a Project in the Datasheet view.

1. In Access, click the Projects tile in the Tile Pane, and select the Datasheet View for editing.

2. Click the Consultant field; then select the Actions pop-up menu by clicking the lightning bolt button.

3. Click the On Click action button, and select OpenPopup from the list of available actions.

4. In the View field, select Employees List, and click OK.

5. Save changes to send the updates to the server; then launch the app to see the UI macro in action.

Coding for Access Web Applications

Unfortunately, there is simply no way to write code to extend or change an Access web app. There are no APIs published by Microsoft for Access Services or the ADS, and Microsoft strongly recommends against attempting to modify the HTML, CSS, or JavaScript emitted on the page of an Access web app.

Reporting and External Data

Data managed via an Access web app is actually stored in a dedicated SQL Server database. The connection details for the Access database are available in Backstage. In addition to identifying the database's connection path, the Access Backstage view enables the creation of read-only and read/write user accounts. In addition, the Info tab of the Backstage view allows for the creation of client-side reporting databases. The Access reporting database cannot currently exist as a cloud-based web application, so Access will automatically create the required connections for reporting, as seen in Figure 19-17.

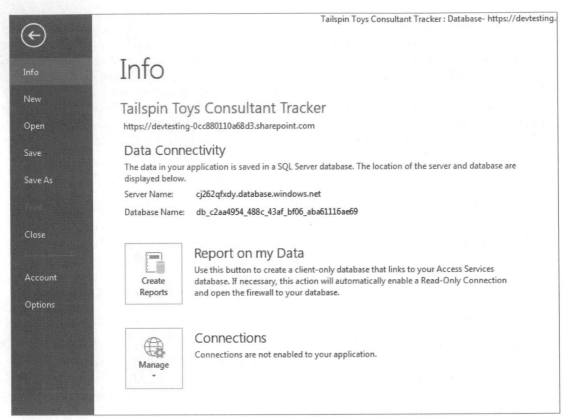

FIGURE 19-17

In addition to Access web apps allowing for external applications to access data, Access can leverage the data in other data stores such as SharePoint and SQL Server to create linked tables. In this manner, Access web apps can be leveraged to provide complex business logic, whereas SharePoint offers easy data access and management. When a SharePoint list is connected inside of Access apps as linked tables, the connection is a read-only connection. Data changes to the source list must be done inside of SharePoint.

Deploying Access Applications

Access 2013 has no deployment story because an Access web app is online from the moment the application designer supplies a location during the creation of the app. When the app has been created and uploaded to the site, it becomes available for other appropriately permitted users. Access apps can also be deployed to the private corporate store and the Microsoft online Office.com public store. Deploying an Access application online requires a code submission to Microsoft Online where the code is packaged, reviewed, and accepted to or rejected from the Office Store.

SUMMARY

Access 2013 is a powerful new tool in the arsenal of a savvy business user. Freed from the traditional web development requirements of managing the user experience and data access layer, a subject matter expert can quickly produce a business-focused application that leverages the scalability and power of SQL Server. Access web apps support cascading delete restrictions, queries, triggers, and stored procedures in the form of macros. Although Access does not offer the developer an opportunity for code-based customization, that is not the intent for this tool. Instead Access provides the opportunity to continue SharePoint's mission of empowering the end user to create important business-focused applications without dependencies on software developers and expensive-to-maintain customizations.

Additional Help and Resources

WHAT'S IN THIS APPENDIX?

➤ Discovering help and additional resources

Developing for SharePoint involves bringing together a number of technologies, including SharePoint, developer tools, and web development technologies. To be effective in developing for SharePoint, you need to understand the resources available to help you, both from Microsoft and from the community. There are high-quality tools and documentation available from both resources.

DOWNLOADABLE HELP FILES FROM MICROSOFT

The key resource from Microsoft that every SharePoint developer should download is the SharePoint SDK. The SDK comes in two versions, one for SharePoint Foundation and another for SharePoint Server. You should download both sets of SDKs onto your development machine.

ONLINE HELP FROM MICROSOFT

You can find one of the key resources available online for learning what's new in SharePoint 2013 for developers at http://msdn.microsoft.com/en-us/library/jj163091.aspx.

In addition to the What's New site, you can look at a number of other resources, including the SharePoint 2013 training for developers at http://msdn.microsoft.com/en-us/sharepoint/fp123633.aspx.

Another key resource to keep track of is the SharePoint team blog. On this blog, the SharePoint team posts relevant information about SharePoint that customers and partners would be interested in. The blog is located at `http://sharepoint.microsoft.com/blog/Pages/default.aspx`.

The last resource is the SharePoint Developer Documentation team blog. This blog is the location where the developer documentation team posts important information that may not be in the SDK, or best practices for developing with SharePoint. You can find the blog at `http://blogs.msdn.com/b/sharepointdev/`.

HELP FROM THE COMMUNITY

SharePoint has a rich community that develops community-driven tools. For example, `http://apps.codeplex.com/` is a CodePlex project where developers can contribute and share their apps for SharePoint with others in the community. In addition, there are a number of other online resources that you should review as you develop your SharePoint solutions. The following list shows some of the sites that might help you with your SharePoint development.

➤ **Reza Alirezaei's blog:** `http://blogs.devhorizon.com/reza`

➤ **Scot Hillier's blog:** `http://www.shillier.com/default.aspx`

➤ **Amit Vasu's blog:** `http://www.amitvasu.com/Blog/default.aspx`

➤ **Andrew Connell's blog:** `www.andrewconnell.com/blog/`

➤ **Joel Oleson's SharePoint blog:** `www.sharepointjoel.com/default.aspx`

➤ **Eli Robillard's blog:** `http://weblogs.asp.net/erobillard/`

➤ **Noorez Khamis's blog:** `http://www.khamis.net/blog/default.aspx`

➤ **CodePlex:** `www.codeplex.com/`

➤ **Steve Peschka's blog:** `http://blogs.technet.com/b/speschka/`

INDEX

F

Q